PORNOGRAPHY AND SEXUAL REPRESENTATION

VOLUME I

**Recent Titles in
American Popular Culture**

PORNOGRAPHY AND SEXUAL REPRESENTATION

A Reference Guide

VOLUME I

Joseph W. Slade

American Popular Culture
M. Thomas Inge, Series Editor

GREENWOOD PRESS
Westport, Connecticut • London

Library of Congress Cataloging-in-Publication Data

Slade, Joseph W.
  Pornography and sexual representation : a reference guide / by Joseph W. Slade.
    p. cm.—(American popular culture, ISSN 0193–6859)
  Includes bibliographical references and index.
    ISBN 0–313–27568–8 (set : alk. paper)—ISBN 0–313–31519–1 (vol. I : alk. paper)—
  ISBN 0–313–31520–5 (vol. II : alk. paper)—ISBN 0–313–31521–3 (vol. III : alk. paper)
    1. Pornography—United States—Bibliography. 2. Pornography—United States. I. Title.
  II. Series.
  Z7164.P84S56 2001
  [HQ472.U6]
  016.3634'7—dc21   99–085695

British Library Cataloguing in Publication Data is available.

An on-line version of *Pornography and Sexual Representation:
A Reference Guide* is available from Greenwood Press,
an imprint of Greenwood Publishing Group, Inc.
(ISBN 0–313–31536–1)

Library of Congress Catalog Card Number: 99–085695
ISBN: 0–313–27568–8 (set)
         0–313–31519–1 (Volume I)
         0–313–31520–5 (Volume II)
         0–313–31521–3 (Volume III)
ISSN: 0193–6859

First published in 2001

Greenwood Press, 88 Post Road West, Westport, CT 06881
An imprint of Greenwood Publishing Group, Inc.
www.greenwood.com

Printed in the United States of America

The paper used in this book complies with the
Permanent Paper Standard issued by the National
Information Standards Organization (Z39.48–1984).

10 9 8 7 6 5 4 3 2 1

Copyright Acknowledgments

The author and the publisher gratefully acknowledge permission for use of the following material:

Excerpts from David Aaron Clark, "Madonna Exposed," *Gauntlet*, 5 (1993): 18–23. Reprinted with permission from *Gauntlet*.

Excerpts from David Aaron Clark, "Interview with Annie Sprinkle," *Gauntlet*, 1:5 (1993): 123–130. Reprinted with permission from *Gauntlet*.

Excerpts from Nina Hartley, "Pornography at the Millennium," *Gauntlet*, 14 (1997): 20–24. Reprinted with permission from *Gauntlet*.

Excerpts from Nina Hartley, "Reflections of a Feminist Porn Star," *Gauntlet*, 5 (1993): 62–68. Reprinted with permission from *Gauntlet*.

Excerpts from Rhonda Nettles, "Let Me Tell Ya 'bout Suffering," *Gauntlet*, 5 (1993): 69–70.

Every reasonable effort has been made to trace the owners of copyright materials in this book, but in some instances this has proven impossible. The author and publisher will be glad to receive information leading to more complete acknowledgments in subsequent printings of the book and in the meantime extend their apologies for any omissions.

For

Judith, Joey, and Marya

Contents

Preface

This *Reference Guide* is structured around two premises. The first is that regardless of how one may feel about pornography, sexual expression, and representation, it has profoundly enriched American culture. Rather than try to "prove" this assertion, I allow the sources cited to speak for themselves. At the very least, gathering materials together indicates the degree to which pornography has permeated the social, economic, and political life of America, and I am confident that readers of this *Guide* will be just as astonished as I am by the evidence from so many quarters. As members of a culture, we think about pornography in many different ways. The diversity of opinion is a reminder that far from encapsulating dominant or hegemonic ideas and attitudes—as some critics hold—pornography does not compel assent to a particular agenda. Rather, it invites a constant reevaluation that has so far not tapped the secret of its marginality. Sexual expression somehow continuously refreshes itself, so that it *remains* taboo and thus, in a version of cultural thermodynamics, continuously energizes mainstream social and political expression. *How* pornography remains forever at the edge is not always clear; that it does so is manifest in the debate that it engenders.

The second premise is that pornography and what we say about pornography constitute our principal ways of speaking about sex, one reason that many researchers prefer the neutral term *sexual materials* to the more charged word *pornography*. Traced far enough, all such materials, all such forms of speaking, are rooted in the oral genres of folklore. "All folklore is erotic," said the late folklorist Gershon Legman, who had in mind the speech of the unwashed. But, in a larger sense, pornography and the comment that it generates, some of it sophisticated, much of it carried by advanced communication conduits, are contemporary versions of the same ancient narratives, jokes, and legends that Legman studied. Calling pornography sexual folklore helps to explain its pervasiveness and also its humanity. Pornography can demystify and secularize sexuality and thus weaken the barriers that divide genders and classes of people; it can also betray and shame our erotic longing and thus reinforce those barriers. The sexual discourse of "others" can seem demeaning, dehumanizing, cheap, tawdry, inauthentic, dangerous, commercial, pathetic, or political, while our own seems inspirational, natural, objective, "real," dignified, safe, and spiritual. Agreeing to disagree about sexual expression will probably bring no more permanent peace than agreeing to disagree about religion, politics, or other things we think important, and this *Guide* does not argue that we should.

Comment on pornography—and eroticism—is, without exception, biased along gender, class, racial, religious, aesthetic, and/or ideological lines. My own biases, easily visible, are of the type traditionally called liberal. Moreover, to pretend that my interest is solely academic would be dishonest. Few academics choose to study materials they abhor. The sheer volume of materials I have canvassed has left me largely unaroused, though I do believe that seeking arousal is a perfectly legitimate goal. Every now and then, fortunately, I run across some passage or image that I do find erotic—or, if you will, pornographic—and hope of stimulation can always spring anew. And yes, I am just as often repulsed by what I see and hear and read.

One final observation. When the South African photojournalist Kevin Carter won the Pulitzer Prize in 1993 for his shot of a vulture patiently waiting near a tiny Sudanese child only seconds away from death by starvation, one of my students asked me how a human being who had taken such a photograph could go on living. She received her answer in mid-1994, when Carter committed suicide. Over the years, I have seen in excess of 5,000 pornographic films or videos, and I have looked at perhaps 150,000 pornographic photos in which bodies have been frozen in states of false passion by entirely unrepentant photographers. Not even the most extreme of these have come remotely close to the inhumanity of the scene captured by Carter. The point, made before, though not often enough, is that as Americans we lack a sense of proportion. We are affronted by a picture of an erect penis or a bare breast, but we glance thoughtlessly every day at obscenities that by rights should stop our hearts.

ACKNOWLEDGMENTS

Many people who assisted me in finding material wish to remain anonymous, but I want to thank them anyway. They include writers and fellow academics, casual and professional correspondents, theater owners, bookshop staffs, photographers and publishers, producers and directors, performers and sex workers, and especially collectors; the latter have given me information about, and often access to, some remarkable archives. Of those friends and correspondents I can name, Joe Amato, Bob and Jean Ashton, Bob Barr, Kenneth Bernard, Ruth Bradley, Joan Brewer, Bill Brigman, Joani Blank, Ray Browne, Vern Bullough,

James Card, Greg Crosbie, Bill Dellenback, Paul Gebhard, Jay Gertzman, Larry Gross, Martha Harsanyi, Christie Hefner, Gary Hunt, Tom Inge, Cathy Janes, Walter Kendrick, George Korn, Raoul Kulberg, Gershon Legman, Terence Malley, Ted McIlvenna, J. B. Rund, C. J. Scheiner, Ivan Stormgart, Joan Templeton, and Joseph Vasta all gave generous amounts of encouragement, information, criticism, or time. Graduate assistants Anthony Bush, Usha Zacharias, and Sharon Zechowski have meticulously traced sources and copied articles. Librarians at many institutions here and abroad have been gracious and patient, especially those at the Kinsey Institute for Research in Sex, Gender, and Reproduction; British Film Archives; Long Island University; New York Public Library; George Eastman House; New York University; Ohio University; and University of Texas. I am grateful to three editors at Greenwood Press, Alicia Merritt, Pamela St. Clair, and M. Thomas Inge, the latter the editor for the series of which this *Guide* is a part, for their help and forbearance. Any mistakes in this *Guide* are mine, of course, not theirs.

The influence of two mentors, perhaps visible only to me, has strongly shaped this project. A quarter century ago, long before writing about pornography was commonplace among academics, my first published article on the subject was reprinted in one of those office magazines compiled for doctors by a drug company. In its pages, next to mine, was an article by Margaret Mead (1901–1978), who, to my enormous surprise and pleasure, invited me to tea. A compilation of comment on pornography, she suggested, would be an anthropological treasure. About the same time, my dean at Long Island University, Felice Flanery Lewis, author of *Literature, Obscenity, and the Law* (still one of the best books on literary censorship), shielded me from attacks on my research into sexual expression. That I was granted tenure was due, in large measure, to her principled defenses of faculty. To these two, then, the first an intrepid voyager of cultures, the second a steadfast guardian of intellectual freedom, I owe major debts.

Because immersing one's self in pornography for so long stimulates a sense of the transgressive, I am conscious of having finished this *Guide* with time stolen from my wife and children. I cannot give that time back, but I hope I can repay the affection with which they allowed me to take it.

How to Use This Guide

Organizing the vast comment on pornography and ancillary, but related, representations of sexuality and gender is difficult. The best scheme begins with historical, bibliographic, and broad theoretical approaches, moves to comment on specific genres arranged by communication media, and concludes with overviews of research and policy. Though I hope the merits of this structure will be evident, some redundancy has been inevitable, in part because historians and commentators often make forays into different genres and periods. To assist the reader I have placed "See Also" notations to other chapters where I think they might help.

The *Guide* has been divided into twenty-one chapters arranged in three volumes, with complete table of contents reproduced in each volume. The sequence is roughly from general to specific, with the first volume offering the broadest view. Chapter 1 is a chronology of significant dates in the history of American pornography. Leaving aside a brief introduction and a reflection on the nature of pornography, the first volume begins with a history of American pornography that discusses pornographic media as they become popular: books, art, and magazines precede photography, film, dance, and the Internet. Should you not find what you are looking for at first glance, look further in Chapter 3, **A Brief History of American Pornography**. Bibliographies, indexes, and encyclopedias (Chapter 4) are broken down into categories for convenience, on the assumption that the reader may wish to locate a starting point for research. As Chapter 5 makes clear, context is important; here are other starting points, located in historical commentaries on various issues and sectors of culture. Chapter 6 outlines major theoretical positions (e.g., aesthetic, technological) on the subject of sexual representation.

The remaining sections in volume I are intended as fairly quick references.

Chapter 7 provides information on famous collectors and collections of porno-graphic materials, on major research libraries, and on important subcollections and archives broken down, when possible, by genres or media. Chapter 8 covers child pornography, a category that our culture has legally and conceptually sep-arated from other forms of erotic expression, even though conservatives try to conflate them. Despite the dangers that Michel Foucault thought inherent in classifications of sexuality and gender, categorizing types of erotic expression counters the American tendency to lump all such expression together and makes exploration possible.

The other two volumes treat specific categories. The first chapter of volume II addresses scholarship on beauty, bodies, clothing, fetishes, genitalia, mastur-bation, and appliances. The remaining chapters of the volume explore comment on pornographic expression in dramatic, visual, and electronic media. Here are to be found citations to works dealing with performance, art, photography, mo-tion pictures and videotapes, and electronic media such as the Internet. Volume III outlines criticism on oral, print, and journalistic media by treating folklore, books, newspapers, magazines, advertising, and comic books. Also in the final volume are chapters on research into the nature and effects of pornography, law and censorship, and, finally, economics.

If your subject is exploitation films, for instance, you might begin in volume I with chapter 3 **A Brief History of American Pornography**, look next in film bibliographies in Chapter 4, check Chapter 1 (**Chronology**) for useful dates, and then move to Chapter 13 in volume II for the section on **Exploitation Films**, and go from there to Chapter 19 (**Research on Pornography in the Medical and Social Sciences**) of volume III for studies of effects or to Chapter 20 on **Censorship of Film and Video**. Conversely, you might begin with discussion of the films themselves (Chapter 13) and then backtrack to the broader chapters. The table of contents is detailed enough to suggest links. Almost always, finding material on topics requires looking at several chapters. Comment on *Playboy* magazine, for example, appears in chapters on magazines (17, **Playboy and Its Imitators**), on photography (12, **Female Pinups, Centerfolds, and Magazine Pictorials** and **Models and Techniques**), on research, and on economics, as well as in **A Brief History of American Pornography** (volume I, Chapter 3). As another example, a book of photographic studies of striptease dancers is more likely to be covered in the section on photography (12, **Documentary Photographs**) unless it contains significant textual comment, in which case it would appear in the chapter on performance (10, **Erotic Dance**).

Because this *Guide* deals only with American pornography, I have omitted many excellent works (e.g., Graham Greene's *Lord Rochester's Monkey*, a study of John Wilmot, one of the great British pornographers) that deal with artifacts of other nationalities. It hardly needs saying, I hope, that most of the citations here are to materials designed to shed light on pornography, not to titillate in themselves. Referring to a particular artifact in the larger context of the continuing discussion of sexual representation does not imply that the example is itself pornographic, let alone obscene. Even so, the desire to be as comprehensive as possible has led me to include citations to works that someone, somewhere, has called pornographic. It is silly to speak about pornography without providing examples.

The cutoff point for sources gathered here is late 1998, when the *Guide* started on its way to editors and printers, though as it moved along I added a few in the early part of 1999. Those disappointed not to find up-to-date sources must forgive the lengthy time necessary to make ready so large a work.

Introduction: Tracking Pornography Through History and Theory

Ick.

Overheard in the Premiere Video Store in Athens, Ohio, from a college student whose girlfriend had eagerly pulled him into the adult section

Given the premises announced in the Preface to this *Guide* that pornography enriches culture and that it constitutes our principal means of speaking about sex and gender, a couple of caveats are in order.

First, even charitable assessments of pornography conclude that much of it is garbage. To be sure, we often say the same about mainstream movies, books, recordings, television, and so on. Gresham's law operates in most markets; cheap products drive out better products. One difference, perhaps, is that pornography has traditionally made a place for, even a fetish of, representations of low quality. Pornographers can hardly be faulted for employing words and images that will arouse, and if the tawdrier varieties do the job more efficiently, then such products will naturally be prized by producers and consumers. Moreover, the need to outrage morality and to affront taste and, beyond those goals, the desire to mock the order and structure of society itself are also perverse, but legitimate, missions of pornography. The impulse that leads the pornographer to encroach upon taboo and obscenity is part of a recognizable social dynamic, but neither that impulse nor the pornographer's equally understandable contempt for "standards" fully explains the romanticizing of "dirty" perspectives. Rightly or wrongly, many consumers apparently assume that the sleazier the example, the more authentic it is, as if ugliness depicted as unskillfully as possible will free audiences from lies told by older generations—a view that characterizes pornography as a species of cultural adolescence. Since later generations routinely indulge in nostalgia for pictures and passages once called pornographic, the view would seem to have merit.

Second, plowing through the stuff can be a distasteful chore. Knowing that time rehabilitates the once-anathematized makes the historian's task a little easier. Even so, studying pornography requires persistence, not to say courage, especially if one wishes to sample a wide range of ephemeral representations and the sometimes dopey criticism lavished on them. The scholar must treat seriously materials that others condemn not simply as nasty but also as beneath notice. It is necessary to make the point because some of the reference works—the encyclopedias, indexes, and bibliographies—included in the chapter called **Bibliographies and Reference Tools** will strike some readers of this *Guide* as hopelessly unrigorous, if not downright silly. With all their faults, they are simply what is available, a sort of baseline (pun optional) for further study. A sense of humor helps.

Scholars encounter many other problems, most of them outlined in **A Brief History of American Pornography** in this first volume. One worth reiterating is that, a few common examples aside, few Americans agree on what pornography is, a point also stressed in the chapter called **Thinking about Pornography**. Cherished folklore to the contrary, there is no Pornography with a capital "P," no unified system of images or discourse. There are simply lots of examples, not always identifiable by medium or genre; the inability to pigeonhole adds zest and perhaps meaning to otherwise unremarkable representations. More basic still is our ignorance about sexuality. We understand the crucial role of sexuality in the survival of the species, as a mechanism for eliminating mutations that would prove lethal. But we do not understand much else. Some scholars have grown accustomed to thinking of gender as mutable, but in a technological era sexuality itself may turn out to be more fragile. The utility of pornography may transcend our fondness for telling sexy stories and may connect at some essential biological level. We simply do not know. Rather than celebrate the mystery, however, the chapter on **Histories of Sexuality and Its Representations** attempts to locate what we know about the history of pornography in a context of sexual historiography. It is impossible to discuss the "invention" of pornography without reference to the larger issues of gender and sexuality.

Not that everyone agrees. The chapter called **Theoretical Works on Erotica and Pornography** includes both reasoned and ranting approaches to sexual representation, arranged in loose categories outlined in the Contents. So general a *Guide* must ignore nuance in the hope of capturing the force of arguments. Because the summaries in Chapter 6 treat theories as if they had equal weight, the reader will want to look at the originals for their respective literary and philosophical merits. Reading Angela Carter and Andrea Dworkin on sexual expression, for example, reveals vastly different minds, the first inspired by gender inequity, the second shriveled by it. A similar unevenness is everywhere visible in the works cited in this chapter. Where possible I have indicated those essays and monographs that I think most valuable and enduring, but readers must ultimately follow their own instincts.

Theories also strain against each other. Years ago, the great pornography scholar Gershon Legman argued that violence became a surrogate for sex when sexual expression was suppressed. His is a Freudian reading of sublimation and thwarted love. Sex is one thing, he said, and violence quite another. Condemning the first and not the second was for Legman the hallmark of an American culture besotted with power structures that denied the legitimacy of sexuality. By contrast, Michel Foucault's position, perhaps the consequence of his practice of sadomasochism, that most Christian dynamic of exaltation and degradation, secularizes a traditionally puritanical universe. In Foucault's world, God—or some version of authority—is always monitoring a sexuality that is, at base, power. It follows that any kind of sexual expression manifests—does not simply mask—aggression. Radical feminists have adopted this view because it seems so clearly an expression of original sin, wedding the story of the Garden to poststructuralist theory and thus finessing the ancient question as to whether humans offended God by acquiring rationality or by discovering sex. For Legman and for Freud, violence is a perversion of sexuality. For Foucault and the radical feminists, sadomasochism is the rule rather than the exception: it *is* human sexuality. Readers who believe that sexual expression can speak of and to affection, passion, and respect will find Legman and many other theorists more congenial.

Finding collections of pornographic and erotic materials can be difficult. Relatively few academics have brought to the collecting of pornographic drawings or videotapes the degree of obsession that animates collectors of Barbie dolls or Zippo lighters, but librarians are slowly building archives of erotic ephemera and are fortunate when they receive bequests from the truly knowledgeable. Archives are covered in chapter 7, which also contains information about housing and permitting access to such materials in a profession still of two minds about the wisdom of doing either. Less sober in tone, the chronology in Chapter 1 should be useful and amusing and is intended to help the reader get a quick feel not simply for personalities, events, and court cases but also for momentum, continuity, and narrative. Assembling such a chronology is fun because of the color it imparts to the past, but I hope that it also furnishes armatures that will shape neglected areas of covert culture.

Finally, this volume's last chapter, **Child Pornography**, offers citations to the most reliable information to be found on this most problematic of genres.

1

Chronology of Important Dates in the History of American Pornography

1656   In Boston, a Captain Kemble, home from a long voyage, is sentenced to the stocks for publicly kissing his wife on a Sunday.

1690   The very first issue of the very first colonial newspaper, *Publick Occurrences*, published by Benjamin Harris in Boston, is immediately suppressed by the Massachusetts Bay Colony because of a story about the scandalous behavior of the French king, accused of sleeping with his son's wife.

1712   Massachusetts passes law against obscene writing and pictures.

1724   Tenth edition of the European journal *Onania* is reprinted on a domestic press in Boston.

1744   Jonathan Edwards in Northampton, Massachusetts, reprimands young men for reading "Aristotle's" sex guides (*Masterpiece, Compleat Midwife, Problems*), popular quasi-medical texts reprinted by various American presses.

1745   Benjamin Franklin writes *Advice to a Young Man*.

1780s   Advertisements for imported erotic novels appear in New York and Massachusetts newspapers.

1791   Adoption of the Bill of Rights, whose ten amendments to the Constitution begin with the right of free speech.

1806	Pennsylvania Academy of Fine Arts drapes statues of human figures on loan from Louvre on Mondays, the only day women are permitted to view them.
1810	Isaiah Thomas prints first American edition of John Cleland's *Fanny Hill* in Worcester, Massachusetts.
1815	In Philadelphia, a man named Sharples and five others are prosecuted for selling obscene prints; John Vanderlyn's painting of a nude, *Ariadne*, is condemned in New York City as an "example of European depravity."
1818	Thomas Bowdler publishes an expurgated edition of Shakespeare and gives his name to a form of censorship.
1821	In Boston, two booksellers are prosecuted for selling *Fanny Hill*.
1830s	Manhattan "sporting papers" such as the *Whip*, the *Flash*, the *Weekly Rake*, and the *Libertine* and New Orleans tabloids such as *The Mascot* create a domestic pornography out of Jacksonian political invective and prurient interest in prostitutes and nightlife.
1833	Rev. John McDowall of New York details pornographic traffic in his *McDowall's Journal*.
1839	Charles Goodyear vulcanizes rubber and makes possible not only modern condoms but a wide variety of fetish items.
1840s	Women in loose drapes and thick tights begin to appear on New York stage as *tableaux vivants*.
1842	Tariff Act, the first federal obscenity law, bans the importation of obscene contraband into the United States.
1843	Nine snuffboxes, their tops decorated with painted nudes, are confiscated in the first prosecution under the Tariff Act.
1845	*National Police Gazette* founded.
1846	According to Clowes and Ashbee, a surgeon turned bookseller, William Haynes of New York, begins to issue pornographic novels, at first reprints of Continental works, then, later, commissioned domestic fiction; titles number 320 by 1871, when according to legend Haynes kills himself to escape Anthony Comstock.
c.1848	First truly graphic daguerreotype, of a stiffly posed couple engaged in intercourse.

1849	Publisher James Ramerio in New York brings out *Venus in Boston*, by George Thompson, the first indigenous erotic novel to be published in the United States.
1850	The word *pornographer* makes its first appearance in a translation from a German work; Boston art school refuses to allow the American sculptor Harriet Hosner to study anatomy.
1852	Hawthorne's *The Scarlet Letter* attacked as obscene.
1857	Tariff Act of 1842 amended to prohibit erotic daguerreotypes; the noun *pornography* appears for the first time in English, according to the *Oxford English Dictionary*, in a medical dictionary.
1862	Calvin Blanchard publishes a translation of Ovid's *Art of Love*.
1863	Spurred by demand from soldiers in the field, a New Orleans publisher turns out "native erotic novels," suitably illustrated with drawings, sporting titles such as *The Libertine Enchantress, or the Adventures of Lucinda Hartley; Confessions of a Washington Belle; Beautiful Creole of Havana; Adventures of Anna P., or the Belle of New York; Child of Passion, or the Amorous Foundling*.
1865	Tariff Act of 1842 amended to prohibit military traffic in pornographic novels by a Congress fearful that Union troops might be masturbating instead of killing.
1866	*The Black Crook*, a stage spectacular, opens in New York, featuring a dance by performers in opaque, full-body tights that caused audiences to gasp at "nudity"; Library of the British Museum accepts George Witt's bequest of a collection of erotica.
1868	The Hicklin decision in England, which was for years to provide the basis for American prosecution of obscenity, is the judicial response to Lord Campbell's Act of 1857 forbidding the sale and distribution of "obscene libel."
1873	Congress passes Comstock Act, named after Anthony.
1876	Congress amends Comstock Act to give Post Office power to censor; Mark Twain writes *1601*.
1879	Twain writes *Some Thoughts on the Science of Onanism*.
1882	Boston bans Whitman's *Leaves of Grass*.

1885	According to Clowes and Ashbee, 100,000 pornographic books are sold in New York City this year.
1887	Charles Dana Gibson begins drawing "Gibson Girl" for *Life*.
1890s	Dr. Clelia Duel Mosher conducts sexual survey of 45 married women (not published until 1980) to discover that many enjoy sex.
1890	Attorney General Miller and Postmaster General Wanamaker ban Tolstoy's *Kreutzer Sonata* from the mails under the Comstock Act.
1893	"Little Egypt" performs her belly dance on the midway at the Chicago Columbian Exposition.
1895	Edison films Fatima's fully clothed "serpentine dance," also first performed at Chicago Exposition, in his studio; authorities later censor it by drawing black bars across her undulating bosom and buttocks.
1896	The first commercial exhibition of Edison's projector takes place in a former bawdy house, the Koster and Bial Music Hall on 34th Street in New York City; Edison's film *The Kiss* features osculation lasting sixty seconds between John C. Rice and May Irwin, a scene audiences find titillating; Supreme Court upholds obscenity conviction of Lew Rosen, publisher of *Broadway* magazine, the first federal prosecution under the Comstock Act; Eugene Field writes *Only a Boy*.
1897	In *People v. Doris* (153 NY 678), a New York court rules that a motion picture (*Orange Blossoms*) depicting a wedding night is indecent.
1900	Library of the British Museum accepts erotica collection of Henry Spencer Ashbee, greatest of all erotic bibliographers; U.S. Congress defines the sending of contraceptive information through the mails as a criminal act of obscenity; publisher withdraws Dreiser's *Sister Carrie* after attacks on it.
1901	Claude Hartland writes *The Story of a Life*, the first published autobiography of an admitted American homosexual.
1902	American publication of *My Secret Life*, British classic; publication of *The Story of Mary MacLane*, the autobiography of an admitted American lesbian.
1903	Charles Dana Gibson begins drawing "Gibson Girl" for *Collier's* magazine.

1904	First American pinup calendar, St. Paul, Minnesota.

1906   Edward Bok, editor of *The Ladies Home Journal*, begins a crusade against venereal disease, and the editorials and articles cause 75,000 subscribers to cancel.

1907   Florenz Ziegfeld stages the first of his *Follies*, featuring scantily-clad women.

1908   On Christmas Day the mayor of New York closes all cinemas on grounds of immorality.

1909   New York Board of Censorship established to oversee films, later to become an industry-supported, self-policing agency, the National Board of Censorship, aka (1915) National Board of Review; Chicago establishes a film censorship committee; the "serpentine dance" (see 1895) is censored.

1910–1911   Eugene O'Neill works as ticket-seller to pornographic movies in Barracas, the port of Buenos Aires; versions of a nude "The Dance of All Veils" and topless hula dances performed by various women in marginal nightclubs in New York City; Pennsylvania establishes a board of censors (1911).

1912   First recorded police raid on an exhibit of pornographic films as they are being shown at a storefront in Manhattan; first issue of *Snappy Stories*.

1913   Judge Learned Hand, though upholding the Hicklin principle in the prosecution of Daniel Goodman's *Hagar Revelly* (a novel of social comment), expresses doubt about the wisdom of suppressing a work of ideas; Anthony Comstock seizes copies of *September Morn*, a painting by Paul Chabas, which causes sales to soar; Ohio establishes a state film censorship board.

1914   Annette Kellerman appears nude, with tresses curled around her nipples, in *Daughter of the Gods*; Comstock indicts Margaret Sanger for writing "obscene" articles about contraception; Kansas establishes a state film censorship board.

1915   *A Grass Sandwich*, aka *A Free Ride*, the first surviving American hard-core film, is shot (according to legend) in New Jersey; Supreme Court rules in *Mutual Film Corporation v. Industrial Commission of Ohio*, 236 U.S. 230, that cinema is unprotected by First and Fourteenth Amendments; bill to establish federal film censorship authority is defeated.

1916   Cincinnati bans Dreiser's *The Genius*; Maryland establishes a
                film censorship board.

1917   Clara Bow appears nude, naughty parts shielded, in *Hula*;
                Charles Carrington issues *The Rakish Rhymer*, a collection of
                Civil War ribaldry, as *Some Yarns*.

1919   In *Schenck v. United States* (249 U.S. 47), Justice Holmes says
                that the First Amendment cannot shield those who shout "Fire"
                in a crowded theater and thus establishes the "clear and present
                danger" test; Joseph Patterson begins publishing the *Daily
                News*, filled with sensationalism so intense that it is dubbed
                the "servant girl's Bible"; *True Story*, first of the "confession"
                magazines, launched.

1920s   Eight-page pornographic comic books, called "Tijuana Bi-
                bles," a term applied also to typed pages of fiction stapled
                together, multiply in urban areas.

1920   Judge in *Halsey v. New York Society for the Suppression of
                Vice*, 180 N.Y.S. 836 rules that a book should be evaluated as
                a whole, not just in terms of isolated passages, by qualified
                critics rather than professional smut-hunters.

1922   *The Way of a Virgin*, by L. and C. Brovan; creation of the
                Motion Picture Producers and Distributors of America
                (MPPDA), with Will H. Hays as the Hollywood censorship
                czar; New York state establishes a film censorship board.

1923   Senator Jimmy Walker of New York speaks against a pro-
                posed "Clean Books" amendment to the New York State Penal
                Code: "I have never yet heard of a girl being ruined by a
                book"; National Association of Broadcasters is established.

1924   Virginia establishes a state film censorship board; Bernarr
                Macfadden begins the *New York Evening Graphic*, and Wil-
                liam Randolph Hearst founds the *Daily Mirror*.

1925   Prodded by John Sumner of the New York Society for the
                Suppression of Vice, police raid Minsky's burlesque show in
                New York; Manhattan police also seize copies of volume II
                of Frank Harris' *My Life and Loves* as it is being printed, and
                Esar Levine, the publisher, is sentenced to three months; ani-
                mators honor pioneer cartoonist Winsor McCay by creating
                Everready, most famous of all animated pornographic films.

1926   Boston bans the sale of the April issue of H. L. Mencken's *American Mercury* because of a story called "Hatrack," which is denounced by the Watch and Ward Society as "salacious"; the arrested Mencken spends $20,000 on a successful defense.

1927   *Anecdota Americana*, by "Joseph Fleisler"; Mae West in New York sentenced to ten days in jail for doing an "obscene" dance as part of the play *Sex*, which she had written.

1928   *The Well of Loneliness*, by Radclyffe Hall; Samuel Roth convicted of dealing in obscene materials, but paroled.

1929   *The Well of Loneliness* declared obscene in New York City under Hicklin principle; *Factors in the Sex Life of Twenty-Two Hundred Women*, by Katherine Bement Davis; first American nudist camp founded.

1930s   Offset lithographic processes make publication of erotic materials easier, while the depression lowers prices of sexually oriented materials.

1930   Theodore Dreiser's *An American Tragedy* declared obscene in Boston under Hicklin principle; Massachusetts also condemns D. H. Lawrence's *Lady Chatterley's Lover*; federal judge Augustus Hand, cousin of Learned, reverses conviction of an educational pamphlet, *The Sex Side of Life*, by Mary Ware Dennett; *MPPDA* adopts the Production Code for Hollywood movies as a way of heading off federal censorship; National Organization for Decent Literature founded by Catholic bishop, John Noll; Congress passes another Tariff Act, which forbids importation of obscenity but transfers authority for determining whether an article is obscene from Customs Department and Post Office to the courts; Samuel Roth, parole revoked, sent to prison.

1931   Georgia Southern, greatest of American strippers, still in her teens, takes off her clothes for the first time to the beat of *Hold That Tiger!* and literally stops the show at the Bijou Theatre in Buffalo, New York; Supreme Court rules in *Near v. Minnesota*, 283 U.S. 697, that government may not engage in "prior restraint" of scandalous material.

1933   Judge John M. Woolsey overturns Hicklin principle in *United States v. One Book Called "Ulysses"* by declaring that book must be considered as a whole; Sally Rand, the celebrated fan dancer, grosses $6,000 a week at the Chicago World's Fair; Payne Fund supports studies of moral effects of movies; Mae

West's sly performance in film *She Done Him Wrong* triggers formation of Catholic Legion of Decency; first "Petty Girl" pinup by artist George Petty appears in *Esquire; Wild Cherries*, a "spicy magazine," first published.

1934   Augustus Hand upholds Woolsey decision on *Ulysses*; Legion of Decency pressures Hollywood into accepting a stringent revision of the Production Code written by Catholics Martin Quigley and Father Daniel Lord; Joseph I. Breen takes over as head of MPPDA and enforcer of code to tighten censorship of Hollywood movies; Congress passes Communications Act, with section 233B dealing with speech, later amended to prohibit indecency.

1935   The Treasury Department burns a seized copy of *Ecstasy*, the Czech film starring Hedy Lamarr, who swims nude in a brief sequence; Ilsley Boone, dean of American nudists, publishes first issue of *Sunshine and Health*; Samuel Roth jailed again for distributing obscene books.

1937   LaGuardia shuts down burlesque in New York City; American Medical Association grudgingly endorses birth control; congressional furor develops over Mae West's appearance on NBC's *Chase and Sanborn Hour*.

1938   National Office for Decent Literature prosecutes *Life* magazine for publishing an illustrated article, "The Birth of a Baby," because the mother's labia are visible.

1940s   Anaïs Nin and Henry Miller write pornography for an American collector; when Miller tires of the project, Nin assigns duties to Caresse Crosby and Virginia Admiral; Irving Klaw and his sister Paula open Movie Star News, a store for movie stills and fetish photos; John Willie arrives from Australia to work for Klaw.

1940   Supreme Court upholds conviction of Ben Rebhuhn of Falstaff Press for selling obscene books; first "Varga Girl" appears in *Esquire*; City College of New York refuses to hire Bertrand Russell because of his "salacious" *Marriage and Morals*.

1942   Betty Grable poses for the most famous pinup of World War II and gets her legs insured for $1 million.

1943   Postmaster General Frank Walker denies second-class mailing
              privileges to *Esquire*, a magazine he thinks obscene; Howard
              Hughes invents a cleavage-emphasizing bra for Jane Russell,
              star of *The Outlaw*, then launches an advertising campaign
              featuring a suggestive portrait of Russell rendered by the lead-
              ing female pinup artist Zöe Mozert, with the result that the
              Legion of Decency forces withdrawal of the film.

1944   *The Devil's Advocate*, aka *The Sign of the Scorpion*, by Robert
              Sewall, one of the most important American erotic novels;
              Kroger Babb exploits movie *Birth of a Baby*.

1945   Justice Elijah Adlow of Boston rejects as a species of idiocy
              the Watch and Ward Society's contention that readers of Er-
              skine Caldwell's *Tragic Ground* will be harmed by passages
              in which a young woman sees a bare male chest; Eric Johnson
              becomes head of Motion Picture Producers' Association
              (MPPA), the new name for Motion Picture Producers and Dis-
              tributors of America.

1946   Court rules in *Hannegan v. Esquire* that postmaster general
              does not have authority to deny mailing privileges without a
              prior judicial hearing; John Willie begins publication of *Bi-
              zarre* (1946–1959) in Canada; Federal Communications Com-
              mission (FCC) issues "Blue Book" codifying "responsibilities"
              of broadcasters, who fear censorship.

1947   Short-lived publication of *Vice Versa*, first American lesbian
              magazine.

1948   *Sexual Behavior in the Human Male*, by Alfred C. Kinsey,
              Wardell B. Pomeroy, and Clyde E. Martin; Frederick's of Hol-
              lywood markets the first crotchless panty; Bettie Page arrives
              in New York from Pennsylvania to work for Irving Klaw;
              publishers form the Association of Comics Magazine Publish-
              ers, aka Comics Magazine Association of America (1954), and
              adopt code of ethics.

1949   John Kelly shoots pinup of a nude Marilyn Monroe.

1950   Mattachine Society (gays) founded in Los Angeles.

1951   *Confidential* magazine begins publication; sixteen-year-old
              Juanita Slusher, who will adopt the stage name Candy Barr,
              is forced against her will to appear in the stag film *Smart Alec*;
              soap opera *Search for Tomorrow* begins its multidecade run
              on CBS; Senator Estes Kefauver cancels Chicago hearings

on organized crime when Mafia threatens to release a photograph of Kefauver in bed with a young woman—rumor has it that other photos feature different women; the Post Office attempts to ban Gershon Legman's scholarly *Love and Death* because of four-letter words.

1952   Supreme Court decides that cinema is protected by First and Fourteenth Amendments in the case of *The Miracle*, a motion picture prosecuted for sacrilege in *Joseph Burstyn, Inc. v. Wilson*, 343 U.S. 495; Will Hays' wife, seeking divorce, testifies that her husband could not tell the difference between her navel and her clitoris; National Association of Broadcasters adopts Television Code (declared unconstitutional in 1982).

1953   *Sexual Behavior in the Human Female*, by Alfred C. Kinsey, Wardell B. Pomeroy, Clyde E. Martin, and Paul H. Gebhard; first edition (December) of *Playboy* magazine; John Baumgarth Company issues the "Golden Dreams" calendar featuring the 1949 John Kelly photo of Marilyn Monroe; Otto Preminger releases *The Moon Is Blue* and destroys the Production Code.

1954   Senator Estes Kefauver holds hearings on television; Comics Magazine Association publishes the Comics Code, to which publishers must subscribe to get seal of approval.

1955   Formation of Daughters of Bilitis, lesbian group, in San Francisco; Senator Kefauver's subcommittee holds hearings on the relationship of pornography and juvenile delinquency and calls Irving Klaw as a witness; Maurice Girodias publishes Nabokov's *Lolita* in Paris.

1956   Allen Ginsberg publishes *Howl*; cameramen on the *Ed Sullivan Show* focus on Elvis Presley's torso to avoid showing his gyrating hips.

1957   In *Roth v. United States*, 354 U.S. 476, the Warren Supreme Court upholds Samuel Roth's conviction 5–4 on grounds that the material appeals to prurient interest; in *Butler v. Michigan*, however, the Court rejects argument that distribution of adult material must be restricted because it might harm minors; *Garden of Eden* (1955), first of the nudist colony films, cleared for exhibition by New York State Court of Appeals (*Excelsior Pictures Corporation v. Regents of the University of the State of New York*) on grounds that nudity is not obscenity; in *U.S. v. Thirty-One Photographs*, in Federal District Court in New

York, the Kinsey Institute wins battle against U.S. Customs, which seized a shipment of erotica consigned to the archives.

1958   Nabokov's *Lolita* (Paris, 1955) published in United States; Paul Krassner begins publishing *The Realist*; Supreme Court reverses lower-court decision condemning a gay magazine as obscene in *One, Inc v. Olesen*, 355 U.S. 371; FCC says it does not have authority to regulate cable television.

1959   Lawrence's *Lady Chatterley's Lover* ruled not obscene; in *Kingsley Int'l Picture Corp v. Regents (NY)*, 360 U.S. 684, Supreme Court reverses conviction of a distributor of a French movie based on *Lady Chatterley's Lover* on grounds that "ideological obscenity," in this case adultery, is an "idea" and therefore protected speech; in *Smith v. California*, 361 U.S. 147, the Supreme Court ruled that to be found guilty of selling an obscene book, the seller must know ahead of time that the book *is* obscene, a burden that would cause the public to suffer from a limited stock of information; *The Naked Lunch*, by William Burroughs; *The Immoral Mr. Teas*, directed by filmmaker Russ Meyer; Ed Sanders of the musical group the Fugs publishes *Fuck You! A Magazine of the Arts* (later [1965] known as *Intercourse*); Billy Wilder's *Some Like It Hot* makes transvestism a cult subject.

1961   Henry Miller's *Tropic of Cancer* (Paris, 1934) published in United States; Francis Ford Coppola makes first film, the "nudie" *Tonight for Sure*; Supreme Court in *Times Film Corporation v. Chicago*, 365 U.S. 43, upholds Chicago's right to license films; the birth control pill introduced in America; National Council of Churches endorses birth control.

1962   Publication of *The Housewife's Handbook on Selective Promiscuity*, by Rey Anthony, one of the books for which Ralph Ginzburg will be prosecuted; Ginzburg publishes first issue of *Eros*; Supreme Court rules in *Manual Enterprises v. Day*, 370 U.S. 478, that the Post Office cannot ban homosexual magazines from the mails.

1963   Jack Smith's *Flaming Creatures* and Andy Warhol's *Blow Job* screened; John Rechy's *City of Night*; Ralph Ginzburg is found guilty in Philadelphia of criminal use of the mails for selling *Eros*, a magazine, *The Housewife's Handbook on Selective Promiscuity*, an explicit memoir, and *Liaison*, a newsletter of mildly erotic items; magazine *Male Models* begins publication; in *Bantam Books v. Sullivan*, 37 U.S. 58, the Supreme Court condemns as prior restraint a case in which a Rhode Island youth commission made a list of books it found objectionable (including the usual classics) and threatened publishers with prosecution, a precedent later used against the Meese Commission, which will employ the same illegal tactics.

1964   Lenny Bruce tried for obscenity, but Illinois federal court voids his conviction; topless dancer Carol Doda enlarges her breasts; Library of British Museum accepts erotica bequests of Charles Reginald Dawes and Beecher Moore; the Supreme Court rules in *Jacobellis v. Ohio*, 378 U.S. 184, that the test of obscenity requires national standards; Justice Potter Stewart observes of obscenity, "I know it when I see it," a statement often taken ironically because of Stewart's failing eyesight; Federal Bureau of Investigation (FBI) launches investigation of "obscenity" in the lyrics of "Louie Louie," the popular song by the Kingsmen, but eventually gives up, after hundreds of pages of analysis, when no one can agree on the meaning of *anything* in the song; San Francisco tries to prohibit exhibit of Ron Boise's sexualized auto sculptures; Kenneth Anger's *Scorpio Rising*; Sex Information and Education Council of the United States (SIECUS) founded, immediately attacked as operated by pornographers; in *Grove Press v. Gerstein*, 378 U.S. 577, the Supreme Court finally brings to an end the prosecution of *Tropic of Cancer*, "the most litigated book in the history of literature;" Carolee Schneemann makes *Fuses*, an explicit, avant-garde film featuring Schneemann and James Tenney.

1965   David Friedman produces *The Notorious Daughter of Fanny Hill*, a successful soft-core film shot by Laszlo Kovacs, one of Hollywood's greatest cinematographers; Thelma Oliver bares breasts in Sidney Lumet's *The Pawnbroker*; New York abolishes its censorship laws on grounds of unconstitutionality; in *Freedman v. Maryland*, 380 U.S. 51, the Supreme Court says that the burden of proof that a film is obscene is on the state censorship board, which must act promptly and have its decision to censor approved by a court; first issue of *Berkeley Barb*.

1966   *Human Sexual Response*, by William H. Masters and Virginia E. Johnson; Supreme Court upholds conviction of Ralph Ginzburg in *Ginzburg v. U.S.*, 383 U.S. 463, on grounds that while the works in question were not obscene, he did pander through the mails; Court also reverses Massachusetts finding that

Fanny Hill is obscene in *Memoirs v. Massachusetts*, 383 U.S. 413, but affirms conviction of Edward Mishkin of New York for publishing "sadistic and masochistic" books; National Organization for Women founded; Lenny Bruce dies of overdose; Motion Picture Producers' Association (MPPA) amends production code to permit references to abortion and the use of occasional mild profanity.

1967   Performance artist Charlotte Moorman arrested at Cinemathéque, New York City, for playing cello in the nude; Congress creates Commission on Obscenity and Pornography; James Broughton's film *The Bed*; first issue of R. Crumb's *Zap*; Wallace Wood draws cartoon "The Disneyland Memorial Orgy" for *The Realist*; Supreme Court in *Redrup v. New York*, 386 U.S. 767, reverses three state obscenity convictions but offers categories of aggressive distribution that might be grounds for prosecution; Hippie Summer of Love; Maurice Girodias moves Olympia Press to New York from Paris; Anne Halprin's troupe performs "Parades and Changes" at Hunter College, New York City; according to one report, 7,000 women work as stripteasers in America.

1968   First issue of *Screw*, the sex and politics tabloid; first heterosexual hard-core film (untitled) in theatrical release in the United States shown at the Hudson Theater (later called the Avon), on Sixth Avenue and 44th Street in New York City, in February; first homosexual hard-core feature shown publicly at the Park Theater in Los Angeles in June; Stan Brakhage finishes *Lovemaking*, an exquisite underground film; National Sex Forum begun in San Francisco, under auspices of Methodist Church, later to become the Institute for the Advanced Study of Sexuality; Richard Amory publishes first of his *Song of the Loon* series of explicit homosexual novels, which have sold more than 2 million copies in the United States; Pandering Advertisement Act of 1968 (39 U.S.C. 3008) permits addressee to determine what is objectionable in his or her mail; *Dionysius in 69*, Richard Schechner's version of Euripedes' *The Bacchae*, presented by the sometimes-nude members of the Performance Group, New York City; MPPA adopts PG, R, and X rating system for movies; first performance of *The Boys in the Band*; Swedish film *I Am Curious—Yellow* plays in America; Russ Meyer's *Vixen* depicts simulated nude sexual acts; John Lennon and Yoko Ono appear nude on the album cover of *Two Virgins*; feminists picket the Miss America Pageant but, contrary to legend, do not burn bras; *Hair* staged on Broadway; courts uphold FCC's authority over cable television.

1969   *Oh! Calcutta!* opens in New York for a run of many years; Lyle Stuart publishes *Naked Came the Stranger*, by "Penelope Ashe," the pseudonym for a group of writers spoofing porn genres; Marilyn Chambers makes a nudist film called *Together* (Hallmark Distributors); homosexuals revolt against police discrimination at the Stonewall Bar in Manhattan; pornographers begin shooting hard-core movies in San Francisco; first American edition of *Penthouse*; Supreme Court in *Stanley v. Georgia*, 394 U.S. 557, overturns conviction of a man accused of possessing pornographic films for his private use, after police raided his home on a bookkeeping charge; Jim Morrison arrested at a Doors concert for exposing himself; police raid offices of *Screw* when it runs a composite photo of Mayor John Lindsay with a huge penis alleged to be more effective than his political skills; Alex de Renzy's *A History of the Blue Movie* and Bill Osco's *Hollywood Blue*, both compilations of stag films; playwright and performers of *Che!* arrested for obscenity in New York.

1970   *Mona, the Virgin Queen*, by Bill Osco, is the first hard-core feature film to be distributed nationally, followed by *Censorship in Denmark*; David Reuben publishes *Everything You Always Wanted to Know about Sex But Were Afraid to Ask*, a runaway best-seller; President's Commission on Obscenity and Pornography publishes report recommending abolishing restrictions on distributing sexual expression to consenting adults, a conclusion rejected by President Nixon; in its April centerfold, *Penthouse* reveals the pubic hair of the monthly Pet, which causes a sensation; Kate Millet publishes *Sexual Politics*; Post Office receives its highest number of complaints about obscenity in the mails (284,000).

1971   Ralph Bakshi releases *Fritz the Cat*, based on R. Crumb's character, first mainstream erotic cartoon; *Boys in the Sand* and *Pink Narcissus*, gay porn films; Supreme Court affirms in *U.S. v. Reidel*, 402 U.S. 351, that the federal law forbidding obscenity through the mails is constitutional; in *U.S. v. Thirty-Seven Photographs*, 402 U.S. 363, the Court affirms the right of Customs to seize obscene materials in baggage of a citizen returning from abroad.

1972   *Deep Throat*, directed by Gerard Damiano for $25,000, bank-
                rolled by Lou Perry and Phil Parisi, the latter a Mafia con-
                nection; Damiano's *The Devil in Miss Jones* is almost as
                popular, and it and *Behind the Green Door* (a film loosely
                based on Hesse's *Steppenwolf*, made by the Mitchell Brothers
                for $18,000) make hard-core chic; Fred Halstead makes *L.A.
                Plays Itself*, classic gay porn; in legitimate cinema, Bertolucci
                releases *Last Tango in Paris*, with Marlon Brando and Maria
                Schneider; Burt Reynolds poses nude for *Cosmopolitan* mag-
                azine; Chin Lyvely and Joyce Farmer found all-women un-
                derground comic book *Tits and Clits*.

1973   The Kronhausens open the Museum of Erotic Art in San Fran-
                cisco; Charlene Webb shoots *Goldenrod*, the first hard-core
                feature film made by a female director; *Screw* runs photos of
                a totally nude Jackie Kennedy as she was caught sunbathing
                by paparazzi on the island of Skorpios; Boston establishes
                Adult Entertainment District, or "Combat Zone," to contain
                sex-oriented businesses; "streaking" popular on college cam-
                puses; *Resurrection of Eve* shot for $35,000; WBAI (Pacifica)
                broadcasts a monologue by George Carlin in which the co-
                median reflects on the meaning of "filthy words," for which
                the FCC imposes sanctions; in *Miller v. California*, Supreme
                Court pays no attention to recommendations of the President's
                Commission on Obscenity and Pornography and tries to for-
                mulate criteria by which works can be suppressed, ruling that
                community standards can be determined by states; in *Paris
                Adult Theatre I v. Slaton*, 413 U.S. 49, the Court holds that
                states (in this case, Georgia) can close adult theaters; American
                Psychiatric Association drops homosexuality from its list of
                mental disorders; Supreme Court rules in *Roe v. Wade* that
                women have a constitutional right to choose abortion.

1974   Barbara Hammer makes *Dyketactics*, first explicit film shot by
                a lesbian; *Screw* launches *Midnight Blue*, its sex show on Man-
                hattan Cable Television; *Emmanuelle*, a French soft-core film,
                draws huge American audiences; Roberta Findlay shoots *An-
                gel Number 9* (aka *Angel on Fire*), her first hard-core film; the
                publisher of Greenleaf Classics, William Hamling, is sen-
                tenced to prison for publishing *The Illustrated Presidential
                Report of the Commission on Obscenity and Pornography*
                (1970); in *Jenkins v. Georgia*, 413 U.S. 496 (1973), Supreme
                Court reverses Georgia's conviction of mainstream film *Car-
                nal Knowledge*, a seizure inspired by the *Miller* decision;

Larry Flynt launches *Hustler* magazine first as a newsletter; Phil Gramm, later senator and presidential hopeful, becomes involved in the making of an R-rated film; first issue of *Playgirl*.

1975   Independent producers appropriate the film rating systems to assign (the uncopyrighted) "X" to pornographic films; *Exhibition*, a French hard-core porn film by Davy, appears at the Lincoln Center Film Festival; Sony introduces the Betamax but refuses to license format to pornographers; Time Inc. initiates Home Box Office, which distributes R-rated movies by satellite.

1976   Supreme Court rules that Detroit may limit establishment of sex-related businesses by zoning in *Young v. American Mini-Theatres*, 427 U.S. 50; Al Goldstein, publisher of *Screw*, convicted of obscenity in Wichita in a verdict that will be overturned; Radley Metzger shoots *The Opening of Misty Beethoven*, a top porn feature; Women against Violence against Women, a group in California, successfully protests a Warner Brothers' billboard image of a woman in chains, captioned "I'm black and blue from the Rolling Stones and I love it," a move that leads to formation of Women against Violence in Pornography and Media; publication of *The Hite Report*, which debunked the vaginal orgasm in favor of clitoral stimulation; *The Slaughter* (1970), a low-budget film shot in Argentina by Michael and Roberta Findlay, is altered and retitled as *Snuff*, then marketed in a sensational campaign that *Variety* immediately denounces as a hoax, though feminist groups dutifully picket theaters, and receipts soar; Carolee Schneemann's *Meat Joy*; in the encyclical *Declaration on Certain Questions concerning Sexual Ethics*, the Vatican reaffirms its condemnation of masturbation as a source of physical ills; JVC introduces the VHS video recorder/player and allows pornographers freely to adopt format, a decision that ensures supremacy of VHS.

1977   Anita Bryant begins antigay crusade; First Annual New York City Hookers' Ball; Paul Krassner briefly publisher of *Hustler*; House holds hearings on sex and violence on television.

1978   Larry Flynt, publisher of *Hustler*, crippled by gunshot; in appeal of the *Pacifica* case (George Carlin's "Seven Dirty Words"), the Supreme Court affirms FCC's power to regulate indecency in broadcasting; "Feminist Perspectives on Pornography" conference held in San Francisco in November.

1979   Tara Alexandar has public, filmed intercourse with eighty-three men at highly promoted "Spermathon" held at Plato's Retreat in New York City; Women against Pornography founded in New York City; Bob Guccione releases *Caligula*; the Mitchell Brothers film Marilyn Chambers' sadomasochistic (S/M) performance in *Never a Tender Moment*; Andrea Dworkin publishes *Pornography: Men Possessing Women*.

1980   *Gay Comix* founded; Andrea Dworkin publishes *The New Woman's Broken Heart*, a collection of erotic stories; Great American Lesbian Art Show, Los Angeles; Supreme Court limits use of nuisance laws by municipalities seeking to control sex-related businesses in *Vance v. Universal Amusement*, 445 U.S. 308, by requiring constitutional procedures as to expressive content; Rita Jenrette, wife of bribery-convicted South Carolina congressman, poses nude for April *Playboy*; Women against Violence in Pornography and the Media holds Berkeley conference attacking S/M, and is itself picketed by angry lesbian S/M enthusiasts.

1981   Maryland is the last state to abolish its movie censorship board; AIDS recognized as killer disease, a factor that enhances pornography as a "safe sex" alternative; televangelist Jerry Falwell sues *Penthouse* to block publication of an interview; Supreme Court places limits on zoning of sex-related businesses in *Schad v. Mt. Ephraim*, 452 U.S. 61, by forbidding a municipality to eliminate such businesses entirely; Wendy O. Williams of the Plasmatics is arrested for simulating copulation onstage; publication of special issue on sexuality by *Heresies* undercuts ideological solidarity of antiporn feminist groups by insisting on human dimension to sexuality; Jerry Falwell attacks libraries holding copies of *Our Bodies, Ourselves*, a feminist self-help text published by feminist collective; Warner Cable starts Music Television.

1982   Larry Weiz begins drawing *Cherry Poptart* for Last Gasp Comix; Barnard College devotes its annual conference to "Women and Sexuality," which attracts factions whose accusations against each other swirl for months afterward; obscenity complaints to the Post Office plummet to 5,000.

1983   In *Bolger v. Young Drug Products*, 463 U.S. 60, the Supreme
             Court at last ends the ban on advertising contraceptive devices
             through the mail; dial-a-porn industry begins, with recorded
             messages; Catharine MacKinnon and Andrea Dworkin write
             the Minneapolis ordinance banning pornography.

1984   Franklin Furnace, the Manhattan gallery/performance space,
             holds "Tattoo," an event featuring Spider Webb tattooing var-
             ious porn stars, and Annie Sprinkle in the first upscale per-
             formance of her "Boob Ballet"; Minneapolis City Council
             passes MacKinnon/Dworkin ordinance, which is immediately
             vetoed by Mayor Fraser; other radical feminists write an In-
             dianapolis version; Feminist Anti-Censorship Taskforce
             founded to counter Indianapolis and other censorship laws;
             first issues of *Bad Attitude* and *On Our Backs*, both lesbian
             journals endorsing sexual freedom; MPPA adds PG-13 (Pa-
             rental Guidance) rating; new law applies Racketeer Influenced
             and Corrupt Organizations (Act) (RICO) provisions to ob-
             scenity cases.

1985   Federal judge Sarah Evans Barker of Seventh District Court
             rules that Indianapolis ordinance violates First Amendment;
             Virginia passes law prohibiting display of magazines such as
             Playboy and *Penthouse* on newsstands, to be struck down the
             following year by Supreme Court as unconstitutional; San
             Francisco police arrest Marilyn Chambers for lewd acts in the
             O'Farrell Theater; two lesbian porn film companies begin pro-
             duction: Tigress Productions (*Erotic in Nature*), begun by
             Chris Cassidy, a former star of heterosexual porn, and Blush
             Productions (*Fun with a Sausage, L'Ingénue, Private Pleas-
             ures, Shadows*); First New York Women's Erotic Film Festival
             produced by Steffani Martin at Eighth Street Playhouse (15–
             21 May); after congressional hearings on disturbing lyrics, Re-
             cording Industry Association of America agrees to a rating
             system.

1986   Attorney General Meese impanels commission to overturn
             findings of the 1970 Presidential Commission on Obscenity
             and Pornography; Meese creates National Obscenity Enforce-
             ment Unit; Attorney General's Commission recommends Proj-
             ect Post Porn to harass sex businesses and encourages the
             Justice Department to entrap consumers of pornography in
             what the American Civil Liberties Union (ACLU) calls "a con-
             stitutionally renegade operation"; Playboy Enterprises, Amer-

ican Booksellers Association, and other groups sue Meese and the members of the commission to stop harassment and "blacklisting"; Supreme Court upholds right of a municipality to zone sex-related businesses to remote areas in *Renton v. Playtime Theatres*, 475 U.S. 41; Library of Congress (LC) successfully sued by Playboy Enterprises, the American Council of the Blind, the Blinded Veterans Association, and the American Library Association when Congress cuts LC appropriation to prevent the brailling of *Playboy*; Andrea Dworkin publishes *Ice and Fire*, a work of pornographic fiction; Mike Saenz creates *Virtual Valerie*, an interactive porn floppy disk; Supreme Court refuses to hear *Hudnut v. American Booksellers*, 475 U.S. 1001, and thus affirms lower court's ruling that the Indianapolis (antiporn feminist) law censoring material that allegedly violates the civil rights of women itself violates First Amendment; intimidated by Justice Department and badgered by fundamentalist groups, Southland Corporation removes *Playboy* and *Penthouse* from the newsstands in Seven-Eleven stores, which leads U.S. District Judge John Penn to order the Justice Department to end its assaults on the First Amendment; characterizing rock music as "degenerate filth" and a threat to family values, evangelist Jimmy Swaggart persuades the Wal-Mart chain of stores to purge its shelves of offensive records and music magazines; John Holmes, star of more than 2,000 porn loops and films, tests positive for HIV; Supreme Court upholds right of Georgia to prohibit homosexual acts even in privacy of the home and upholds Texas, which also criminalized homosexual and lesbian acts.

1988   Congress passes Telephone Indecency Act; passes legislation requiring FCC to ban indecency in broadcasting at any time of day; actor Rob Lowe gets in trouble over an amateur videotape of himself and a teenaged girl; Congress passes Child Protection and Obscenity Enforcement Act, which leads coalition of organizations, including the American Library Association and various artists' groups, to challenge it in *American Library Association v. Thornburgh*, 713 F. Supp. 469 (1989), forcing Congress to alter its most draconian record-keeping provisions.

1989   Pat Robertson founds Christian Coalition to campaign against liberal thought; conservatives launch attacks on the National Endowment for the Arts for funding museums displaying the photos of Robert Mapplethorpe.

1990   Motion Picture Association of America (MPAA), the renamed
              Motion Picture Producers' Association (MPPA), discards X
              category of films, which it had never copyrighted, and replaces
              it with NC-17; FCC announces twenty-four-hour ban on in-
              decent broadcasting; Home Dish Satellite Corporation, oper-
              ator of the national American Exxxstacy Channel, forced out
              of business by successful prosecution in Montgomery County,
              Alabama, an example of a local prosecution determining what
              the rest of the nation can see; Cincinnati arrests Dennis Barrie,
              the director of the Contemporary Arts Center, for exhibiting a
              show of the photographs of Robert Mapplethorpe; a federal
              judge in Florida finds a record album by rap group 2 Live
              Crew obscene; MTV refuses to air Madonna's *Justify My
              Love*, a candid video; artist David Wojnarowicz successfully
              sues Donald Wildmon and the American Family Association
              for misrepresenting his work as obscene; Charles H. Keating
              Jr., a major crusader against pornography, is convicted of
              swindling hundreds in a savings and loan scam; Father Bruce
              Ritter, another vocal opponent of pornography, resigns from
              Covenant House because of accusations of sexually abusing
              minors in his care; National Endowment for the Arts (NEA)
              director John Frohnmayer overturns panel's recommendations
              and denies grants to performance artists Karen Finley, John
              Fleck, Tim Miller, and Holly Hughes in an attempt to defuse
              congressional threats to dismantle agency; House cuts budget
              of District of Columbia by exact amount required to install in
              a museum Judy Chicago's *The Dinner Party*, described by one
              congressman as "ceramic 3-D pornography."

1991   Supreme Court overturns FCC's twenty-four-hour ban on in-
              decent broadcasting; Reuben Sturman, the "world's leading
              purveyor of X-rated materials," is acquitted of obscenity
              charge when a Las Vegas jury decides that bestiality is not
              obscene; Anita Hill accuses Clarence Thomas, Supreme Court
              nominee, of boasting that his penis is as impressive as that of
              Long Dong Silver (minor porn star of the late 1970s, which
              leads to revival of the latter's films) and of sexually harassing
              her; in *Barnes v. Glen Theatre, Inc.*, 115 L Ed 2nd 504, Su-
              preme Court rules that it is permissible for Indiana to restrict
              "expressive performance," to force strippers to wear pasties on
              their nipples, on the grounds that "traditional moral belief" in
              the demoralizing effects of nudity on public order provides a
              "rational basis" for doing so; porn impresario Jim Mitchell

kills his brother Artie; federal judge overturns NEA's requirement that artists receiving grants sign an antiobscenity pledge as violating the First Amendment; the National Obscenity Enforcement Unit conducts massive sting operations and extensive "forum shopping" so as to convict pornographers by prosecuting them in the most conservative communities.

1992   Canada adopts a stringent, new antiporn law at urging of MacKinnon and Dworkin, and Canadian Customs promptly seizes *Bad Attitude*, published by a Boston lesbian collective, then confiscates books by Dworkin but returns them as a professional courtesy; Reuben Sturman, largest porn entrepreneur, sentenced to ten years in prison and fined $2.46 million for tax evasion; Paul Ruebens, stage name Pee Wee Herman, is arrested for masturbating in a porn theater by Miami police permanently assigned to watch for throbbing penises; Madonna publishes photo-book *Sex*; federal judge overturns Florida court's ruling that *As Nasty as They Wanna Be*, an album by 2 Live Crew, is obscene; federal court overturns restrictions on AIDS information prohibited as obscene; female singer with the Insaints arrested in Berkeley, California, for inserting banana in her vagina during concert; Speech, Equality, and Harm Conference held by the MacKinnon/Dworkin group at the University of Chicago Law School to excoriate opponents of censorship; Congress passes over Bush's presidential veto the Cable Television Consumer Protection and Competition Act, which contains provisions banning indecency; *United States v. Knox*, 977 F.2d 815 (3d Cir.), raises issues of child pornography, though no genitals are visible in images; Supreme Court rules in *Jacobson v. United States*, 503 U.S. 540, that the government had illegally entrapped a purchaser of child pornography through a deception that lasted for years.

1993   In *Alexander v. U.S.*, 113 S. Ct. 2766, Supreme Court holds that federal agents may seize assets of adult businesses under RICO after some items are declared obscene but in *Austin v. U.S.*, 113 S. Ct. 2801, appears to place limits on how many assets may be seized; Lorena Bobbitt slices off husband, John's, penis, and networks cover every aspect of his trial for wife abuse and hers for assault, both of which end in acquittal; conference on "Women, Censorship and Pornography" held by Libertarian feminists opposed to MacKinnon/Dworkin formulations at Graduate Center of City University in New York

City; the German company Cyber SM clothes a man and a woman in data suits so that they can engage in virtual reality intercourse.

1994   After John Bobbitt appears in hard-core porn film to prove that reattached penis still works, he is arrested for abusing women; Patti Reagan Davis, daughter of former president, poses nude for *Playboy*; Savannah, star of porn movies, kills herself; Memphis, Tennessee, convicts on obscenity charges the California operators of the Amateur Action Bulletin Board accessed by the Internet; *Penthouse* releases *Tonya's Wedding Night*, an amateur videotape of ice skater Tonya Harding and ex-husband Jeff Gillooly.

1995   Amendment to U.S. Code Title 18 (Sexual Exploitation and Other Abuse of Children, Section 2257, "Record Keeping Provisions") requires that producers of porn films keep precise records of the ages of performers, even if they are clearly elderly, in films made after 3 July; Congress begins a campaign against smut on the Internet; the Senate passes the Communications Decency Act (CDA), aimed at porn on the Internet; *Playboy*'s videotape of Pamela Anderson (star of television's *Baywatch*) outstrips in popularity the video version of mainstream blockbuster *Forrest Gump*; Catholic Communications Campaign, a reincarnation of the Legion of Decency, publishes its own movie rating system; final *Knox* decision criminalizes even digitally constructed images of fully clothed children if they can be said to sexually appeal to someone; FCC fines Howard Stern $2 million for indecency.

1996   Court of Appeals declares CDA's ban on Internet indecency unconstitutional; President Clinton signs new telecommunications act with provision requiring all future television sets to incorporate a "V-chip" for blocking objectionable programming; Internet providers develop filters (e.g., Surf Watch) for parents to use in screening sites for children; networks adopt a rating system for television shows that is immediately disputed as not being precise enough.

1997   Supreme Court upholds Court of Appeals decision that the CDA is unconstitutional; House votes to end the National Endowment for the Arts on grounds that it promotes obscenity; networks agree to more detailed ratings designating nudity, sex, and violence, with NBC the only holdout; Women's Studies Program at SUNY-New Paltz sponsors "Revolting Behavior" conference featuring porn in a positive light; on basis of *Knox*, Oklahoma City police seize as child pornography the film *The Tin Drum*, winner of 1979 Academy Award for Best Foreign Picture, and take names of those who rented the videotape; number of Internet sex sites reaches 10,000.

1998   World Pornography Conference brings academics and sex industry workers together at Universal City, California; Kenneth Starr releases pornographic report on Bill Clinton's trysts with Monica Lewinsky that leads to Republican impeachment of president; Larry Flynt retaliates by exposing sexual secrets of some of Clinton's enemies; nation is divided on question of whether fellatio is real sex or just friendship between executive and intern; FCC cannot stop journalists from repeating the word *penis* on the air; revenues of women's romance novels reach $1 billion per year, as do revenues from Web sex sites; 2,500 clubs employ 250,000 strippers per year; *The Economist* predicts that pornography will become a legitimate component of the global entertainment industry within a few years.

1999   Adult video industry produces 10,000 new cassettes.

2

Thinking about Pornography

One half of the world cannot understand the pleasures of the other.
—Jane Austen

Much of the comment expended on the subject of pornography in America is suffused with the kind of passion lavished, say, on the issue of abortion, which may seem a social good to one group and a social crime to another. To some, pornography brings light to repressed areas of the psyche, overcomes irrational guilt, and teaches people how to give and get more physical pleasure; to others, it robs humans of their spirituality, objectifies bodies, and fosters gender discrimination. Such polarization not only constantly reshapes the arena of debate but also ensures that no single definition of pornography will satisfy everyone.

The word "pornography" derives from the Greek word *pornographos*, "writing about prostitutes," or a "tale told by prostitutes" (prostitutes to the Greeks being either male or female), and has been used more or less consistently to designate material specifically *intended* to arouse a person sexually. (An old joke holds that something is pornographic if it gives seven out of twelve men on a jury an erection.) Although sexual arousal would appear to be a laudable goal, few Americans endorse it, and even defenders of pornography usually find such intent an insufficient justification. An exception is Lionel Trilling, who confides that he can find no reason "why literature should not have as one of its intentions the arousing of thoughts of lust."[1] Nor will most critics comment on how successfully a particular pornographic example actually arouses. *Screw*, the sex tabloid that has achieved a kind of permanence through longevity, made its reputation, in part, by rating movies on a "Peter Meter," according to how sexually stimulating the reviewer found them. Even this innovation begs the question, of course, for what excites one person will bore or repel another. Attempts to draw distinctions between the "erotic" and the "pornographic," like trying to distinguish between "nude" and "naked," founder on psychological, class, gender, and aesthetic prejudices. Where Gloria Steinem will insist that the differences between the two types are clear,[2] Al Goldstein, publisher of *Screw*, deflates such pretensions with his often-quoted remark, "Pornography is what turns *you* on. Eroticism is what turns *me* on."

The ineluctable subjectivity of such definitions has never prevented people from trying to separate candor that is acceptable from that which is not. Indeed, making such distinctions, specious or otherwise, is almost obligatory; the critic who wishes to be taken seriously almost always condemns "pornographic" depictions (i.e., those in bad taste) in order to win tolerance for those he or she considers erotic. That is the strategy even of D. H. Lawrence in *Sex, Literature, and Censorship* or of Vladimir Nabokov in his remarks "On a Book Entitled *Lolita*."[3] Among American authors, Henry Miller seems unique when he suggests in *Remember to Remember* that obscenity should not be an issue; to be obscene, he says, is simply "to spy on the secret processes of the universe."[4] Perhaps the best-known, and in some ways the most successful, division is that sketched by Phyllis Kronhausen and Eberhard Kronhausen in *Pornography and the Law*. Some works, like Edmund Wilson's *Memoirs of Hecate County*, they assert, should be classed as "erotic realism" because they offer graphic accounts of intercourse within a larger intellectual and emotional context. By contrast, the label "hard-core pornographic" applies to works operating almost entirely as fantasy, although the Kronhausens do not think this category is contemptible; implied in their argument is a belief that fantasy is valuable in itself because it fuels life. Perhaps nothing ages faster than criticism of pornography, however, and even the remarks of the Kronhausens seem dated now. Only one thing seems clear: culture changes over time, and so do standards of sexuality. What appeared outrageous to earlier generations strikes modern audiences as quaint. Taboos erode, to be replaced by others: that is the dynamic of pornography, which continuously assaults limits, and that function is precisely its value to a culture in transition. At a minimum, pornography historically redefines taste.

Tastes are not democratic and often diverge along class and economic lines. Traditionally, there have been at least two kinds of pornography, the lower-class crude drawing or smutty story that made up the stuff of folklore, and the more expensive type, available to wealthy collectors and those who could pay for elegant entertainment. In America, this separation is sometimes called the Las Vegas syndrome. The test is expense: it is socially acceptable for those who can afford it to journey to casinos to watch bare-breasted showgirls but reprehensible for beer-drinkers to see topless dancers in their corner bars. The most comprehensive Supreme Court decision (*Miller v. California*, 1973) enshrines this kind of thinking. In that decision, the Court left the question of expression's acceptability to local communities (provided that local laws are constitutional). Another casualty of this kind of division is that criticism of the pornographic tends to be somber and solemn, the consequence of cultural biases of middle-class critics; they lose sight of an essential aspect of much pornography—its raucous, comic, leveling role, inherent in folklore and dirty jokes. The most extreme pornography seems impervious to condemnation, at base untouchable—it is an irrepressible spirit of denial, impelled to blaspheme not only against religious dogma but, what is more important, against human pretense, specifically, the notion that humans are elevated above other species. Despite the discomfort it can occasion, despite the downright ugliness and stupidity of some examples, pornography may ultimately be benign because it forces us to reexamine what it means to be human.

The law has traditionally taken a less sanguine view. Legal definitions usually complicate matters further since they typically conflate pornography with obscenity, a much broader term even more difficult to define and one that weighs pornography with a taint that individual examples may not carry. Jurists are primarily concerned with sexual expression in public, and their definitions tend to address the question of who is reading, watching, or listening to such expression. Authorities rarely apply the term "pornography" to performance (although recently critics have so characterized rock music), as in ballet, theater, or even striptease; if candor or exposure oversteps local ordinances, such activities are usually designated obscene.

In other words, pornography commonly connotes a representation, not the sexual act itself, although here, too, complications occur. An explicit painting or drawing may be accorded the status of art when it is an individual, unique work but anathematized as pornographic when it is mass-produced, that is, available to anyone. The history of mass media in America is one of such discrimination. When the first motion pictures were exhibited in this country, they were attacked as pornographic precisely because they were assumed to titillate vast numbers, just as books have often been condemned because anyone can read them. In fact, most modern definitions of pornography focus on reproducible technologies that cater to the "wrong" people. The technologies are numerous, of course: pornography can include not just books and magazines, cartoons and photographs, motion pictures and videotapes but computer programs and dial-a-porn telephone messages—even written or filmed commentaries on pornography designed to stimulate under the guise of analysis or condemnation. Some of these forms are actually genres, their outlines delineated by sexual tastes, degrees of explicitness, and mutations with other genres. I. C. Jarvie, the Canadian political scientist, suggests that "anti-pornography"—attacks on pornography—is itself a genre of political commentary that defines itself in terms of what it deplores; the more explicit the condemnation, the more indistinguishable from its target it becomes.[5]

Such profusion should disprove the notion that pornography is monolithic, a fallacy similar to the cold warrior's cherished belief that communism is the same everywhere. Just as we have learned that communism varied in Yugoslavia and Romania, Cuba or Poland, so we are gradually realizing that pornography mutates across a range as wide as human sexuality itself, if only because the psyche is plastic enough to wrap itself around almost anything. Some pornography contains violence, and some contains none whatever. A "slasher" film, for example, is invariably soft-core and portrays a universe radically at variance with the cinematic world in which two lovers engage, say, in literal oral-genital activity. With films in particular, the more a given example concentrates on sexual intercourse, the less violent it will be.[6] Pornography appears in different media and offers different styles and content for different constituencies, the most basic of which are, for obvious reasons, gender-determined. The mass production of sexually explicit materials in some ways is less significant than the rise of specialized audiences to which producers can cater. Pornography can be shaped not only for males and females, for males *or* females, and for homosexuals of either gender but also for specific sexual fetishes—long hair, say, or lingerie, high-heeled shoes, or small buttocks—or behaviors—coprophagia, urolagnia, sadomasochism, or incest. Like all observations about pornography, however, the fragmentation of the market, though easily documented, is by no means accepted by everyone.

Beliefs about pornography, perhaps because they are part of religious, social, or political agendas, are often impervious to statistics. Some of these beliefs fall into the category of folklore. Recently, for instance, using an interesting variation on gender stereotyping, radical feminists tried to define pornography in law as an exclusively male phenomenon, an attempt struck down by the courts as inherently unconstitutional. Other groups commonly link pornography with aggression, as in the phrase "sex and violence," lampooned by Art Buchwald as emotionally charged, but inappropriate, buzzwords.[7] Even sociologists seem to take little interest in the manifest differences among types of pornography—some of which contain violence, many of which do not—primarily, one suspects, because funding is more readily available for research on violence and its effects. In his study of the history of violence research on television, for example, Willard Rowland points out that no one really expects to "prove" effects; the research is a form of national theater and an excuse for academic funding.[8]

Its theatricality is the most charitable interpretation to be put on the most recent federal study, the Attorney General's Commission on Pornography of 1986 (sometimes called the Meese Commission), a highly publicized and entertaining attempt to reverse the findings of the first such study, the President's Commission on Obscenity and Pornography of 1970, itself an entertaining, if more decorous, proceeding. Each commission was radically different in the proportion of researchers, laypeople, lawyers, ministers, and politicians that made up their memberships. Each drew on different assumptions and conducted different studies. The first study found that pornography had few antisocial effects; the second, that the effects were evil in the extreme. While the contradictory conclusions do not cancel each other out, they do indicate that sexual politics play a cathartic role for various constituencies. Among the ironies, considering the liberal makeup of the first group, was that when a pornographic publisher brought out an *illustrated* edition of the 1970 report, he went to prison. The Meese Commission brought out its *own* explicit text, published by the Government Printing Office, for which no one has been prosecuted.

That each commission could find from the materials it examined such divergent conclusions is hardly surprising. Such ambiguity goes far beyond semantics, however, and is matched in the material itself. Nearly all sexually explicit material contains contradictory messages, sometimes overt, sometimes subtle. According to Carole S. Vance, pornography for males, like hard-core films, may oppress women yet at the same time urge upon them a sexual autonomy.[9] Pornography for females, such as Regency romances, may prize sensitivity in men but also delight in depicting males as aggressive. Similarly, though few people seem to applaud masturbation despite the pleasure it brings to millions, many studies suggest that such activity is the most common result of exposure to the sexual fantasies inherent in pornography and that it can harmlessly discharge sexual tension and aggression. In the absence of unchallengeable studies asserting the opposite, though data purporting to establish clear links between pornography and criminal activity constantly proliferate,[10] it seems likely that exposure to pornography might foster sexual transgressions in one person but prevent them in another. Some scholars believe that all mass media have long-term, indirect, and cumulative effects on audiences, and some forms of pornography may have some undesirable effects on at least some categories of people. Where basic types of behavior—like sex and language—are concerned, however, it is wise to remember that seven decades of general American speech patterns broadcast on radio and television have not significantly altered regional speech or substandard English around the country.

Pornography is a commodity, like every other cultural artifact; in a capitalist economy in an information age, every idea and every image are bought and sold. To condemn pornography on the grounds that its sexual expression is somehow tainted by commerce is to adopt the most obvious of double standards, particularly when that notion is advanced, say, over a multimillion-dollar religious broadcasting network. While pornography may or may not have been brought into being by capitalism or industrialization, as suggested by Steven Marcus in *The Other Victorians* and by Walter Kendrick in *The Secret Museum*, it certainly has grown along with them and, like virtually every other form of communication, has increased its audience steadily through the growth of information channels.

Technology is intimately connected with pornography. Pornography is often accused of turning humans into machines, reifying them. Nonetheless, even here its contradictory messages are apparent. Pornography may also be a human response to technology, an attempt to find essence in the objectification that is a prerequisite and a consequence of an industrialized society. To function in an industrialized society requires that humans adopt interchangeable roles: in the workplace, most obviously, but also in social relationships with others who can be known, in the final analysis, chiefly by the roles they also play in both small and huge populations. Pornography does not merely cast all humans as objects; it insists on that reification as the real world, by recognizing that we can never get inside the minds of other individuals. We are all objects to one another, now and forever. What is so disquieting about extreme forms of pornography is that they remind us of the immutability of that fact.

But not all pornography enshrines so tragic a sense of life. Pornography has been called, somewhat patronizingly, "other people's fantasies." What justifies these fantasies, however, is that they are common to so many of us; if we cannot share fantasies, we can never communicate sexually. One type of pornography, that associated with males, romanticizes a landscape of flesh and insists that the ways of knowing that flesh are legion. Another type, that associated with females, romanticizes social or verbal fantasies and insists that those ways of sexual knowing are just as real as flesh. Such types constantly fertilize each other. Demystifying bodies, it can even be argued, has made pornography one of the parents of feminism. If a body is only a body, then its ownership is vested in the person who inhabits it; ownership of a female's body cannot be automatically transferred by marriage or custom to husband or male lover—it is hers, to do with as *she* wishes. Soap operas, a traditionally feminine form of pornography, full of endlessly discussed sexual relationships and formulaic emotional anguish, have emerged as powerful influences on hard-core pornographic films, which have become more verbal and more psychological, more conscious of social realities and responsibilities. In any case, pornographic genres speak to popular needs and concerns. From the pornographic imagination flow some of the most important tributaries of American culture.

NOTES

1. Lionel Trilling quoted by Kenneth Tynan, "In Praise of Hard Core," *The Sound of Two Hands Clapping* (New York: Holt, Rinehart, and Winston, 1975), p. 184.

2. Gloria Steinem, "Erotica and Pornography: A Clear and Present Difference," *Take Back the Night: Women on Pornography* (New York: William Morrow, 1980), pp. 35–39.

3. Vladimir Nabokov, "On a Book Entitled *Lolita*," appended to his *Lolita* (New York: Berkeley Medallion, 1966).

4. Henry Miller, "Obscenity and the Law of Reflection," *The Intimate Henry Miller* (New York: New American Library, 1959), p. 153.

5. I. C. Jarvie, "Methodological and Conceptual Problems in the Study of Pornography and Violence," *Thinking about Society: Theory and Practice* (Dordrecht, Netherlands: Reidel, 1985), pp. 453ff.

6. See Joseph W. Slade, "Violence in the Hard-Core Pornographic Film: A Historical Survey," *Journal of Communication*, 34 (Summer 1984):148–163.

7. Art Buchwald, "Mixing Sex and Frozen Yogurt," *New York Post*, 20 August 1981, p. 28.

8. Willard D. Rowland Jr., *The Politics of TV Violence: Policy Uses of Communication Research* (Beverly Hills, CA: Sage, 1983).

9. Alison Hume, "Fear of Porn: What's Really Behind It? An Interview with Carole S. Vance," *Vogue*, 175 (September 1985):679.

10. Debate over conclusions is equally constant. Disputes are usually over methodologies and assumptions. As just one example among hundreds, see Larry Gross' critique of Dolf Zillmann and Jennings Bryant, "Pornography and Social Science Research: Serious Questions," *Journal of Communication*, 33:4 (Autumn 1983):107–111.

3

A Brief History of American Pornography

The title of an essay[1] by Joan Hoff asks, "Why Is There No History of Pornography?" The question is familiar, having been asked by lots of Americans, including members of the Meese Commission. There are also lots of answers, the most obvious of which is that pornography is not a monolithic category but is instead a number of different genres and/or discourses and that there *are* histories of various periods and genres, inadequate as they individually may be. A better answer is that pornography, virtually by definition, has operated for most of its history at the margins of culture, in varying degrees of secrecy, and that its artifacts routinely suffered destruction. That fact limits accurate information and works against smoothly constructed chronologies. Moreover, pornography has always functioned as a carrier of sexual folklore, a realm notoriously difficult to map. Nowadays, thanks to voracious media that fetch and carry material from margins, cultural edges become centers far more quickly than in centuries past, and tracking ephemeral ideas and artifacts as they move from fringe to fad is a good deal easier.

By far the best answer, however, is that the history of pornography is really many histories, not only of specific genres and their gender and ethnic variations but also of specific sectors of different cultures. An incomplete listing of American sectors, for example, would include a history of:

American morality, as shaped by religious and secular sensibilities;

ideologies, since American schools of thought from Puritanism to feminism have traditionally institutionalized attitudes and opinions toward sexual representations;

the First Amendment, since free speech is an important category of American law;

capitalism, since a secularized America still clings to the notion of sex as the last refuge of spirituality and bemoans the commodification of sexuality even as it cheerfully accepts the commodification of everything else, including religion itself;

American popular culture, since porn is one stimulus of a popular imagination stratified by class;

traditional folklore, since porn is an important vernacular that over time moves from sub-rosa status to quasi respectability;

prostitution, since one enduring definition of pornography is "writing about prostitutes";

birth control, since information about that subject was, until recently, anathematized by many American states as a species of pornography and proscribed under obscenity statutes;

homosexuality, since the sexual expression of "deviants" was proscribed as "pornographic" by law and custom;

communication, since all media carry sexual messages;

technology, since successive technologies not only can represent sexuality in forms each more sophisticated than its predecessors but may also create an "artificial" eroticism that is either horribly inhuman or wonderfully exciting, depending on one's point of view;

sexology, or the "science of sexuality," a discipline still in formation because of the uneven contributions of medicine, physiology, psychology, and less obvious disciplines, which have yet to arrive at a consensus on what constitutes "normal" human sexuality;

archives, since librarians and collectors have always fought to preserve forbidden artifacts.

One factor in particular complicates discussion. In the essay cited earlier, Joan Hoff assumes that pornography has traditionally been an aristocratic pursuit (she has in mind lavishly printed and bound classic texts and museum-grade painting and sculpture) and that it has descended from these upper reaches of cultural hegemony to corrupt a middle-class sensibility. As Alice Goldfarb Marquis has demonstrated in *Hopes and Ashes: The Birth of Modern Times*,[2] revolutionary movements typically characterize the art and literature of the bourgeoisie as having been infected by the decadence of the upper classes or a ruling elite, who have thereby rendered it pornographic. The argument is common to national socialist, communist, and feminist movements in this century, though the politics of each group, of course, markedly differ. But pornography enriches culture through a far more complex dynamic, one that involves a potentially much more subversive upwelling of language and images from much more anonymous, much more demotic lower strata. Sexual folklore has long energized black subcultures, to cite one such example, but has only recently surfaced in the form of rap music, a voice still redolent of rage and authentic nastiness, though well on its way to legitimacy through commercialization.

Defenders of porn also focus on *high* porn, such as books, works of art, or films hallowed by time: Lawrence's *Lady Chatterley's Lover*, say, or Rembrandt's sketches of fornicating couples or Bertolucci's *Last Tango in Paris*. In the past, such works were often justified on aesthetic grounds, before cultural critics reduced moral and aesthetic questions to issues of political or social power. In any case, high porn has a rich history, fairly easily discerned. Opponents, on the other hand, often think of *low* porn, the alleged obscenity of the unwashed masses, the stuff that defies both aesthetic authority and individual authorship and thus was never called "beautiful": dirty jokes, crude drawings, Tijuana bibles, stag films, "trashy" photographs, or the vulgar chat that appears on computer bulletin boards. The signature of low porn, the sign of its authenticity, is its crudity and its anonymity or, at most, its pseudonymity. Tracing its history is much more difficult. Few museums have collected it, and few critics have written about it, though the entries in this *Guide* list those who have.

Ideally, this chapter would marshal information on the categories listed earlier, but many of them are still being invented, all of them would require chapters to themselves, and we have room merely to outline some of them in the chapters to follow. Following, however, is a rapid historical survey of significant genres of *American* pornography, with no pretense to global significance.

EARLY DOMESTIC EXPRESSION

European settlers took a dim view of the sexual expression of the native peoples they displaced and regarded Indian fondness for obscenity as evidence of their savagery. Given Eurocentric prudishness, it is just as well that immigrants could not understand the raucous sexuality that seems natural to a tribal life in which private and public mores are so intermixed. So far as historians can tell, Native Americans enjoyed a richly sexualized discourse, carved or painted suggestive artifacts, and evolved their own protocols for dealing with gender issues and sexual deviance.[3] The written constitutions adopted in the nineteenth century by the Cherokee, Choctaw, Chickasaw, and Muskogee tribes made no provision for obscenity, apparently because it was never a matter of dispute.[4] Because the sexual traditions and representations of Native Americans were oral, however, much has been lost and will probably never be fully recovered.

The history of pornography in America among European immigrants generally resembles that of other cultural artifacts: most of it was imported until native industries developed. That is not to say that early colonial Americans had no appetite for eroticism. The single issue of the very first newspaper in the colonies, *Publick Occurrences* (25 September 1690), printed in Boston by Benjamin Harris, was instantly suppressed because of a story—lifted from foreign papers—that the French king was sleeping with his son's wife. Until the Zenger trial of 1734 sorted out what constituted libel (the term "pornography" was not yet invented), newspapers had to be circumspect, and the few domestic book publishers stuck to psalms or speeches. If books were expensive in the colonies, talk was cheap, and lexicographers and folklorists are just now beginning to understand how rich our early oral pornographic heritage is; smutty jokes and songs, sexually explicit slang, and suggestive tales were normal reactions to

Puritan authority. Among the first domestic printed materials, only Indian captivity narratives, some of which dwelled on the plight of female settlers abducted by savages, might have qualified as pornographic. In the colonies, traffic in pornographic playing cards, carved objects, music boxes, prints, and books of European origin was large enough to attract attention, but only Massachusetts passed a law against it. This act of 1711 was aimed principally at antireligious expression, or blasphemy, especially when couched in bawdy songs; no prosecutions under the act were recorded until 1821, when the state convicted two men for selling *Fanny Hill.*

In 1744 Jonathan Edwards reprimanded young men in Northampton, Massachusetts, for reading "Aristotle's" *Masterpiece,* an often imported and extremely popular sex guide, which was reprinted in many American editions.[5] Edwards seems to have been afraid that reading this quasi-pornographic text would lead to masturbation, a practice whose ubiquity has tormented American sexual reformers from Cotton Mather to Catharine MacKinnon as much as it has delighted writers like Mark Twain and Benjamin Franklin. Franklin wrote his "Advice to a Young Man on Choosing a Mistress," a manuscript regarded as pornographic in 1745, and "A Letter to the Royal Academy at Brussels," an amusing essay on flatulence, sometime later, both for friends. Americans began to circulate pornographic stories in manuscript, an underground practice—similar to samizdat distribution of forbidden texts in the Soviet Union a few years ago—that would continue until the mid-twentieth century.

Most of the first American states passed obscenity legislation only as their citizens became literate, a syndrome that attests to cultural anxieties over new media. The pattern remains similar as communication technologies succeed one another: cheap printing processes, photography, telephones, motion pictures, television, and computers have all undermined the status quo by reconfiguring the power structures that rest on the control of communication, and all have enshrined novel genres of pornography as essential elements in that destabilization. Such novelties frighten older generations and the politicians they elect. The first actual trial for "obscenity" in the United States, held in 1815 in Pennsylvania, involved images. The defendants were several men who had exhibited (for profit) a painting of a man and a woman in an embrace held to be salacious. Ironically, considering the repression associated with the Victorian period, few states bothered to prosecute pornography before the middle of the nineteenth century, probably because artifacts were expensive and therefore limited in circulation. Rough frontiers tolerated and even celebrated raucous speech, while polite communities simply ostracized the offenders. The first federal obscenity restrictions (as opposed to state regulation) did not become law until 1842, when Congress included in the new Customs (or Tariff) Act language intended to curtail the foreign contagion of "French postcards" and obscene books. (With the possible exception of France, most countries have clung as long as possible to the belief that pornography originates outside their own borders.)

In banning the importation of obscenity, the Tariff Act of 1842 in effect made the Customs Bureau the nation's chief censor, with wide powers. The bureau could interdict or destroy materials without first seeking a judicial determination of obscenity. Predictably, the Tariff Act spurred domestic production, there being no greater incentive to pornographers than interdicting the originals they routinely pirated. Domestic production of "pornography" had actually begun in the 1830s and 1840s when Jacksonian democrats in Manhattan began attacking Whig opponents in scurrilous words and pictures. "Sporting papers," the precursors of the *Police Gazette* later in the century and of *Screw* in the next, blended calls for social and political reform with smutty stories, guides to masculine amusements, and condemnations of hypocritical politicians. A few examples, like *The Mascot*, cropped up in other cities to function as a guide to the nightlife and bordellos of New Orleans and the backrooms of the city's political machine. The New York versions, with names such as the *Whip*, the *Flash*, the *Weekly Rake*, and the *Libertine*, were just as likely to detail the charms of local prostitutes as to rehearse the malfeasances of a corrupt official. When they began to cut into the audiences of the New York penny press, however, they were suppressed. Benjamin Day's *New York Sun* (1833) and James Gordon Bennett's *New York Herald* (1835), though almost as scandalous as their upstart rivals, had much stronger political patrons.

The Tariff Act also "protected" the production of pornographic novels against competition from foreign authors. One George Lippard, author of the salacious *The Quaker City; or, The Monks of Monk Hall, a Romance of Philadelphia Life, Mystery and Crime* (1844), watched his novel sell 300,000 copies over the next decade.[6] Most of the publishers operated out of major cities. The New Yorker William Haynes, an Irish ex-surgeon, in 1846 reprinted *Fanny Hill*, which sold so well that he published over 300 additional volumes, many written by himself under pseudonyms. The first unequivocally pornographic domestic novel, George Thompson's *Venus in Boston*, appeared in 1849 from the press of James Ramerio, and thus for both men launched careers in erotica. Thompson's blend of reformist zeal and prurient interest surfaced again and again, most notably in *The G'hals of Boston* (1850) and *The Delights of Love* (1850); Ramerio became a target of Anthony Comstock and other censors.

Publishers in Philadelphia, Boston, New Orleans, and other population centers brought out sex manuals such as James Teller's *Doctor's Pocket Companion and Marriage Guide* (Albany, NY, 1864) and examples of a favorite American genre, the sexual exploits of celebrities, such as the anonymously written *The Amorous Intrigues of Aaron Burr* (1848?). (Wayland Young also mentions obscene drawings of Burr.[7]) In a democracy, celebrities are the closest thing to royalty that Americans have, and the impulse to debunk them through pornography is irresistible. Newspapers and pamphlets detailed spicy stories of Jefferson's alleged liaison with his slave Sally Hemings, and folklore has continued to enshrine the sexual peccadilloes, real and imagined, of Alexander Hamilton, Jim Fisk, Henry Ward Beecher, Grover Cleveland, Russell Sage, Warren G. Harding, Franklin Roosevelt, Dwight D. Eisenhower, John F. Kennedy, Gary

Hart, Clarence Thomas, and innumerable others. More recently, fundamentalist critics of President Clinton produced salacious videotapes of his alleged affairs, thus joining the ranks of the pornographers they inveigh against.

In terms of content, however, American pornographers have always demonstrated not so much antipolitical bias—though obscene jokes about politicians are a staple of our folklore—as anticultural prejudice, a somewhat different subversion of established order. In 1833 the lexicographer Noah Webster began his bowdlerization of the Bible, altering or obliterating passages he thought obscene, and thus set the tone for a presumptuous and insecure middle class. It seemed to Europeans, who thought Webster and other American prudes hilarious, that America had institutionalized false modesty. The folklorist Allen Walker Read points out that under such circumstances parodying sexual reticence was irresistible and notes examples like *Lie-ary in America! with Yarns on Its Institutions* (1840), an anonymously written British parody of American modesty that was followed by domestic versions.[8] A revisionist Peter Gay has demonstrated that Americans were not so absurd as legend would have it; he can find no evidence that American women put pantaloons on their piano legs, for example.[9]

Rather than cast their stories in classical settings, like English pornographers, Americans learned to parody topical matters of the day, as in *Flora Montgomery, the Factory Girl* (published by James Ramerio in 1856), which was a response to the social changes wrought by the new factory system at Lowell, Massachusetts, or Thompson's *Fanny Greely; Or, the Confessions of a Free-Love Sister Written by Herself* (c. 1850), which exploited scandals surrounding communitarian movements of the time, or *A Plea for Polygamy* (1870), which capitalized on the titillating reputation of the Mormons, or, for that matter, a modern film like *Rears* (1987), which sends up the popular television series *Cheers*. Behind this kind of exuberance the folkways of sexuality itself were expanding, as chronicled by John D'Emilio and Estelle Freedman in *Intimate Matters: A History of Sexuality in America*. Prostitution and vulgar entertainment flourished, but these were less important than subtle increments of sexual sophistication, as people of various sexual persuasions began to discover others with whom to share sex and fantasies. Docks and harbors gave shelter to homosexuals, and the growth of urban centers encouraged sexual contacts of all sorts, including occasional public displays.

Indecent performance has been part of American culture for a long time, though nobody is sure just how long. For most of the republic's history such performance has been secret, the clandestine underside of a society that both disdains and embraces exhibitionism. In 1656, for example, a Captain Kemble, arriving home in Boston after a long sea voyage, bussed his wife out of doors, despite its being a Sunday, and was promptly clapped in the stocks. Americans quickly learned to be circumspect. Probably Ben Franklin during his tenure as ambassador to France attended "secret," that is, pornographic, theatricals in Paris, but whether there were counterparts in the American underground at the time is unclear. In any case, the notoriety of some "actresses" quickly made that occupation a stereotype of Victorian pornography.[10] In rural areas, suggestive shows became staples of fairs and carnivals; these could include women dancing in the nude, followed by audience participation in the form of public masturbation and the rare act of intercourse. More common were raconteurs of dirty jokes and drunken males acting out blue skits, "mooning" the crowd, cavorting with exposed genitals, and cross-dressing at farm festivals. Bawdy performance was sufficiently established as a tradition in river towns for Mark Twain to use it as a plot device in *Huckleberry Finn* (1885), when he has the Duke and the Dauphin perform "the Royal Nonesuch." The descendants of those performers satirized by Twain are modern equivalents such as Chris Lynam, whose March 1991 show at the West Bank Cafe in New York City climaxed with his lighting a Roman candle gripped between his exposed buttocks.

According to Timothy J. Gilfoyle, museums in New York mounted anatomical exhibits that pushed the envelope of respectability as early as 1850.[11] "Freak shows" on midways, as Robert Bogdan has pointed out, frequently featured women so hirsute that the barkers could then ask them to strip to "prove" their gender or presented human oddities in revealing costumes and postures to capitalize on the erotic aspects of deformity.[12] Lewd performance was common to "the Sporting Life," as magazines such as the *Police Gazette* called the commerce in whorehouses, bars, cockfights, and other masculine amusements in major cities. Scantily clad women pirouetted nightly in tawdry dives and cheesy "music halls" in New York, Philadelphia, and Chicago. Men in smaller cities and towns across the country hired local prostitutes to dance and to have intercourse with bridegrooms as part of the "stag" celebrations that would later give blue movies their name. Brothels in many states occasionally staged shows of prostitutes either posing nude in tableaux or servicing a male performer. At some distance from respectable scrutiny—but not unknown to police—was the specifically homosexual performance, fairly common in waterfront cities like New Orleans, much more private elsewhere.

By contrast, transvestite revues freely toured the United States from the 1930s onward. So long as homosexuals were presented as freaks or could be rationalized as comic travesties of femininity, they seemed unthreatening. Otherwise, to the official culture, gays and lesbians were simply invisible *except* as pornographic presences. As John Preston has observed, "Erotica was never written about gay men. We were, by definition, obscene; therefore, anything written about us had to be declared pornography."[13] Even if pornography had no other merit, it would deserve commendation for one of its classic functions, that of providing identity and cohesion for sexual minorities and outsiders. It is easy to forget that pornography is created by humans for humans and that the longing to share fantasies is one source of its appeal. Pornography not only bolsters what have been called "imagined communities"[14] but also dreams them into existence.

LEGISLATION, TECHNOLOGY, AND WAR AS SPURS TO EXPRESSION

In 1865 the first mail obscenity statute gave postmasters legal authority to interdict sexual materials shipped across state lines. The statute may have been a response to the discovery by military censors that soldiers clung to sexual fantasies as they faced death during the Civil War; as Thomas P. Lowry has pointed out, "so many soldiers wrote letters that it contributed to a nationwide paper shortage,"[15] and desire suffused their pages. In any case, war, urbanization, and rapid industrialization combined to boost traffic in the salacious. Modern wars have traditionally fostered male-oriented pornography, as soldiers separated from women cling to affirmations of life. Demand among the troops of the Civil War led to reprints of pamphlets such as *The Rakish Rhymer* (1840?) and a line of cheap books called *Cupid's Own Library*. Congress belatedly amended the Customs Act in 1865 to prohibit traffic in obscenity among troops to counter rumors that Union soldiers had been reading trashy novels when they should have been killing Confederates. Almost as available were photographs of nudes that could be handed around in the trenches or displayed in peep-show cabinets in bivouacs.

Perhaps more clearly than any other medium, photography illustrates what we might call Slade's law: whenever one person invents a new communication technology, another person will invent a sexual use for it. In previous ages, cave painting led to obscene pictures, clay tablets to erotic cuneiform narratives, printing to typographical erotica; more recently, erotic applications have fueled the evolution of videocassette recorders (VCRs) and computers.[16] The lag time for photography was brief. Louis Daguerre unveiled his daguerreotype in 1839. By 1846, give or take a couple of years, a daguerreotypist produced a beautiful plate depicting a solemn, middle-aged man inserting his penis into the vagina of an equally solemn, middle-aged woman, nationalities unknown; a collector left this unique artifact to the Kinsey Institute. That early photographers seized on sexual subjects is hardly odd, because, as Robert Taft has pointed out, by the 1850s Americans both professional and amateur were producing 3 million daguerreotypes *each year.*[17] Daguerreotypes, however, could be copied only with difficulty and could not be mass-produced. Even so, thanks to the foresight of an alarmed Congress, the Customs Act of 1842 was amended in 1857 to add explicit daguerreotypes to the list of prohibited articles.[18] The following year, one of the very first American photography magazines began its premier issue with an editorial deploring the circulation of smutty stereographs.[19] Across the Atlantic, Charles Baudelaire in an 1859 *Revue Française* article denounced the burgeoning traffic in erotic photographs as an affront to art.[20]

Civil War veterans formed an enduring audience for sexually explicit messages. More significant than the spur of war was the advent of new techniques of photographic mass reproduction (calotypes, ambrotypes, tintypes, and the *carte de visite* camera, which took eight identical prints) and high-speed presses, which made it possible to turn out pictures, newspapers, and books in large quantities. The latter inventions fostered lurid magazines like *Day's Doings, Last Sensation, Stetson's Dime Illustrated* (all 1868), *Fox's Illustrated Week's Doings* (1883), and *Illustrated Day's Doings and Sporting World* (1885). In their pages were spicy gravures of burlesque queens clad in tights and corsets. Similar images appeared on playing cards and cigarette cards. Periodicals still found it safer to print drawings or paintings of lightly clad humans, since taboos against photographic nudity were powerful. One exception was the photograph of the nude child, though Americans seem to have shot few of these. An ocean away, the Reverend Charles Dodgson, better known as Lewis Carroll, began to invent the modern concept of childhood as a place of sensual innocence by writing about a character named Alice and by shooting hundreds of nude photographs of prepubescent girls.[21] America was still decades away from child labor laws and a long way from recognizing children as anything but adults in miniature. During the next century, however, child pornography, a new, socially constructed realm, would become the ultimate taboo.

At the most clandestine level pornographic photographs, shot in both Europe and America, circulated by the hundreds. Distribution channels included docks, bars, fairs, barbershops, train stations, theaters, shipping companies, and pushcarts. Photographs circulated underground as (1) single prints, sold as novelties on the street, less often by mail, sometimes in postcard format because of the more durable paper stock; as (2) sets of prints, sometimes stapled together, sometimes loose, featuring specific figures—a woman in various states of undress, a couple in multiple positions, or several couples illustrating various sexual practices; as (3) albums (bound collections on seductive themes); as (4) books, a rarer format because of the difficulty of keeping heavy press runs secret; as (5) illustrations for some erotic classic volume; and as (6) magazines, almost exclusively (until the 1960s) of a soft-core nature, chiefly pictures of scantily clad women. During the century stretching from the dawn of photography until the 1950s, most unmistakably pornographic photos, those depicting direct sexual contact, were sold as single prints or in small sets, anonymously produced, anonymously distributed, difficult to trace to their sources.

The more stylish brothels began to keep albums of their employees; each page presented a revealing photograph atop a paragraph on the lady's expertise. The New Orleans "Blue Books," published from around 1880 to roughly 1910, ran ads, sometimes illustrated, by local madams. George Eastman's cheap box camera tapped a hidden, but powerful, vein in the American popular consciousness: the urge to photograph each other in nude or "indecent" poses. Amateurs have continued to employ this most democratic of technologies, whether one calls the fantasies that photographs depict socially constructed or merely perverse. The appeal of such artifacts was measurably enhanced by the threat of prosecution. By 1877 arrests in New York were commonplace.[22] None of the New York entrepreneurs matched the scale of a man named Hayler, one of the few producer-dealers to be identified, whose London studio shipped from an inventory of more than a quarter of a million photographs of himself, his wife, and their children engaged in various sexual acts.[23] Hayler's contraband had been spotted in the United States by American officials, who were increasingly assisted by professional smut-hunters. The smut-hounds spent most of their energies in sting operations, pretending to be customers of bookstore clerks, hotel concierges, and cigar store owners who sold spicy pictures as a sideline. Major cities soon institutionalized the pursuit of the salacious: Boston's New England Watch and Ward Society, New York's Society for the Suppression of Vice, Chicago's Illinois Vigilance League, and Washington's International Reform Federation were the largest; all employed undercover agents.

The first celebrated crusader had appeared in 1833, when the Reverend John McDowall of New York began to haunt the canals and brothels of the city, publishing exposés in *McDowall's Journal*. In 1834 he held an exhibit of obscene articles—books, prints, playing cards, music and snuffboxes, and so on— to the repugnance of other ministers, who detected in McDowall the prurience he sought to suppress. The transformation of pornography into a species of cultural subversion, however, was largely the work of Anthony Comstock, a grocery store clerk who parlayed his Young Men's Christian Association (YMCA) connections into political clout. Comstock formed the New York Society for the Suppression of Vice, then in 1868 persuaded the New York state legislature to pass a law to punish local retailers of material Comstock thought pernicious. Section 1141 of the New York State Penal Code endowed the New York Society for the Suppression of Vice with authority to investigate complaints concerning blasphemy, gambling, theatrical performance, lewd writings and pictures (including some by Americans now regarded as masterpieces), scientific treatises on hygiene and anthropological customs, tracts on birth control and family planning, and other offenses against public decency. In return, the society received *half* of all fines levied against convicted offenders,[24] a provision that understandably led Comstock to redouble his zeal. Comstock and his successor, John Sumner, routinely engaged in entrapment, docket-fixing—in order to find a hanging judge—harassment, and downright persecution; Comstock boasted of having driven publishers and abortionists to suicide.[25] More important, Comstock lobbied successfully in Washington to expand the 1865 postal law to include penalties against publishers as well as distributors of offensive material. Following this new legislation (commonly called the Comstock Act) of 1873, some thirty states adopted more stringent obscenity laws, and local watch and ward societies sprang up to ferret out smut. Comstock himself, as a special agent of the Post Office, conducted seizures and prosecutions over several decades.

The Comstock Act of 1873 revised Title 18 of the U.S. Code. The so-called Comstock Codes are Section 1461, which prohibited materials dealing not simply with lewd expression or articles and devices used for immoral purposes but also with birth control articles "advertised or described in a manner calculated to lead another to use or apply it for preventing conception or producing abortion, or for any indecent or immoral use"; Section 1462, which prohibited the importation of obscene matter and its interstate transportation; and Section 1463, which was aimed at advertising, especially obscene language on "wrappers deposited for mailing." Later, Section 1464 would be added to cover indecent radio communication. It is difficult to overstate Comstock's influence. Pressured by him, Congress amended the Comstock Act in 1876 to strengthen the 1865 prohibitions against sending obscene publications through the mails and thus gave to the Post Office broad censorship powers that the agency would wield vigorously and, later, illegally. To a degree, as in most matters governmental, the right to censor has pitted one agency against another, and Congress, following the doctrine of checks and balances, has periodically tried to reapportion authority in order to prevent individual departments from gaining too much power.

Federal and state courts determined obscenity through a body of case law based on the *Regina v. Hicklin* decision (1868) in England. That decision was a judicial response to Lord Campbell's Act of 1857, which criminalized the sale and distribution of "obscene libel." The Hicklin test for obscene libel was: Did the material in question, even in isolated passages, tend to "deprave and corrupt" those whose minds might be open to immoral influences? Everybody who counted in society knew who *those* corruptible people were, of course: women and minors, to be sure, but also the socially inferior, the poor, and the ethnically different. (At first, for all practical purposes, only books were at issue.) Because American justice was founded on principles of English common law, the English precedents were considered binding. Pornography was only gradually beginning to emerge as a legal, moral, and aesthethic category as distinct from obscenity, which was still stretched to cover libel, on one hand, and blasphemy, on the other. According to historian Peter Wagner, the word *pornographer* made its first appearance in 1850 in a translation from a German work; seven years later, the noun *pornography* appeared for the first time in English (says the *Oxford English Dictionary*) in a medical dictionary. Its etymology is usually given as "writing about prostitutes." Both instances referred to salacious expression of a sexually prurient nature, definitions promoted in part by smut-hunters, who are essential to the concept of tabooed or forbidden sexuality.

PORNOGRAPHY AS A FUNCTION OF CLASS AND POLITICS

Historians such as Wagner, Walter Kendrick, Jean Marie Goulemot, and Lynn Hunt say that while sexual representation in words or pictures is as old as civilization itself, the concept of pornography as a distinct category is tied to the rise of modernism. "Early modern pornography," says Lynn Hunt, "reveals some of the most important nascent characteristics of modern culture. It was linked to free-thinking and heresy, to science and natural philosophy, and to attacks on absolutist political authority. It was especially revealing about the gender differentiations being developed within the culture of modernity."[26] By the end of the eighteenth century, the formally subversive properties of pornography had dissipated, though they survived in tales of political scandal and in vulgar folklore. In another sense, however, the political implications become more obvious. For one thing, pornography unconsciously embodied the gender taxonomies that Michel Foucault believes arise out of configurations of economic and social power.

By the same token, the concept of pornography became a consciously charged political term as democracy began to gain ground. Because printing presses could reach large masses, the upper classes wanted to proscribe representations that could fall into "the wrong hands," a belief made possible by upper-class ignorance of lower-class, largely oral expression. So long as books and pictures were the prerogatives of a moneyed class, there was no real need to separate sexual content from any other kind; it is culturally desirable only when materials become available to everyone. An emerging middle class shared with the aristocracy the nightmare of proletarians with hyperactive genitals and thus gradually embraced the idea of proscription also. Condemning the desires and representations of others thus served, and still serves, as a safety valve for the pressures of democracy. An otherwise democratic society can employ censors to control speech by reminding the unwashed where the real power lies.

Shielded by custom and hypocrisy, the powerful could still enjoy sexual representation legitimated by elegance; the poor were left with dirty jokes, smutty stories, and outrageous images—a domain more sympathetic to gender inversions and more skeptical of official morality, taste, and custom, a realm raucous, even corrosive with the sort of obscenity that escapes historians. Caution seems justified, however, lest theory skew history. We need to look further than the elegant artifacts in museums and collections, and we need to be aware as well of the naïveté of believing that pornography is a trigger for sexual rapaciousness. Prior to the modern era, pornography was just folklore, and in a sense, given the sexual myths and legends clearly visible in all forms of porn, folklore it remains. Only Roman aristocrats had access to the explicit murals in the villas of Pompeii, and only they could read the amusing sexual stories of Ovid, but Ovid himself picked those stories from an older oral storehouse, put there by common people who enjoyed sexuality as much as their social betters. Plebians told stories, too, and drew obscene images on walls and streets and caves.

Scholars study *folklore* as a realm more powerful and fertile than the high culture with which it often conflicts and as the authentic, unquenchable fountainhead of pornography. The dean of sexual folklorists, Gershon Legman, suggests that "folklore" is also the most accurate term that we can apply to the understanding of sexuality at any given time, if only because its mysteries are so compounded of myth and ignorance. Perhaps the most significant aspects of traditional folklore, that is, low porn, are (1) that it is eternal, (2) that it is endlessly generative, and (3) that it is invisible to most Americans, despite its impact on their sexual consciousnesses. Ever more precise technologies of representation continuously suck up images from this pool of inchoate desire and nasty impulse. Newer and faster communication technologies reach wider and wider audiences and thus layer myth on fantasy on folklore. Thus far, scholars have focused on the etymologies, morphologies, and genre narratives of sexual expression, the surfacings of archetypes, the recurrence of motifs, and their ethnic and national variations. The field still awaits the Noam Chomsky who can find the deep structure beneath the welter of erotic data.

The absence of theoretical norms of sexuality also contributes to confusion over pornography. Trying to fix the "invention" of American pornography is further complicated by factors too numerous for a brief history to mention: the politics of race and eugenics, the waves of immigration, the reaction against industrialization, the rise of middle-class domesticity, the pull of romanticism, the gradual emergence of folkways, and so on. Suffice it to say that "pornography" in common parlance comes to mean the sexual folklore of *others*; in Tony Duvert's formulation, pornography is "other people's fantasies." By contrast, *erotica* comes to mean fantasies that appeal to elites. Cultural and legal battles over pornography result from attempts by some groups to replace the sexual folklore of other groups with their own.

Another problem may be that pornography has been "invented" too many times. Pornographic works inspired and buttressed political upheaval in France. Because their revolutions were largely bloodless, however, pornography in England and, by proxy, America first took the form of obscene libel. The Hicklin principle treated obscenity as a trespass against religion[27] and thus helped soothe the lingering resentment that Jefferson and Madison had fought to avoid establishment of a national church. At the turn of the nineteenth century accusations of obscenity became in the hands of crusaders such as Comstock a weapon to use against immigrants, especially Jews and East Europeans. That view of pornography as the filthy expression of lower, alien classes retained its currency through the 1950s.[28] During the 1960s, flower children employed explicit expression as a political tool to destabilize society, but by the end of the 1970s social constructionists and feminists elevated pornography to middle- and upper-class status in order to indict white male elites with charges of hegemony and patriarchy. In the 1990s, various ethnic and gender groups embraced pornography to forge communities of identity. Andrea Dworkin, a vocal crusader against sexual expression, finds that critics call her "revolutionary" fiction clearly pornographic.[29]

Sexuality itself was continually "reinvented" as well. Ministers, doctors, scientists, politicians, judges, and other authorities constructed versions of sexuality and gender in the nineteenth century. By most accounts, sexology begins just before the turn of the century with pioneers such as Havelock Ellis, whose multivolume *Studies in the Psychology of Sex*, published between 1898 and 1910, ventured into every corner of human sexuality, and, of course, Freud, whose enormous reach can be appreciated in the standard edition of the works he produced over his lifetime. As John Gagnon has put it in "Sex Research and

Social Change," the individual discoveries of Ellis and Freud (their approaches were vastly different) have less value than the panoramic sweep of their investigations. As a result, for the first time, sexuality emerged as an element of "the normal social order" (116), as a discourse no longer limited to the extremes of pathology or spirituality. Moreover, said Gagnon, aside from setting inquiry in motion, they defined research techniques for those who followed them.[30]

But Comstock remained the most vocal arbiter in the American public arena. He became so predictable that entrepreneurs learned to profit by using the man's tactics against him, a publicity ploy still cherished today. The ur-story involved Harry Reichenbach, a press agent hired in 1912 by a Brooklyn art dealer who was trying to sell calendar copies of *September Morn*, a mediocre painting by Paul Chabus of a nude young woman washing herself in a lake. Reichenbach paid thirty or forty children to stand in front of the gallery and stare at the picture in the window. As soon as they were in place, Reichenbach called Anthony Comstock, who came huffing up, declared that minors were being corrupted, and forced police to arrest the dealer. The newspapers whooped; the dealer deducted the modest court fine and Reichenbach's fee from the proceeds of the sale of hundreds of thousands of copies of the picture. As a side note, the U.S. Army in 1923 rejected a recruit who had a tattoo of "September Morn" on his biceps on the grounds that it was obscene.[31] Comstock attacked marginal enterprises rather than carriage-trade publishers, though he certainly pressured the latter (his successor as head of the New York Society for the Suppression of Vice, John Sumner, may well have accepted bribes to leave upscale publishers alone). According to his enemies, Comstock in 1881 paid three prostitutes $14.50 to strip and fondle each other privately for an hour and twenty minutes *before* arresting them.[32]

PORNOGRAPHY, BIRTH CONTROL, AND RACISM

Hal D. Sears has chronicled Post Office prosecution and persecution of early feminists, free-love advocates, champions of birth control, and abortionists as disseminators of obscenity under the Comstock Act of 1873. The culture seemed bent on curtailing information that could lead to individual control of bodies and reproduction, though the legal rationale was that contraception encouraged "irresponsible" sex. In 1890 Attorney General Miller and Postmaster General Wanamaker banned Tolstoy's *Kreutzer Sonata* from the mails under the Comstock Act but reserved their heaviest weapons for feminists like Victoria Woodhull and free-thought crusaders like Moses Harmon. The latter published *Lucifer, the Light Bearer* (1883–1907) in Missouri as a midwestern voice of radical sexuality.

From the standpoint of the censors, the beauty of the act was that it could be wielded against anarchists Ezra and Angela Heywood, who edited the Massachusetts publication *The Word*, a political journal that sometimes dealt with free love and contraception; the Post Office suppressed it as obscene.[33] As James

Reed demonstrates in *From Private Vice to Public Virtue: The Birth Control Movement and American Society since 1830*, from the nineteenth century until quite recently, the American legal system treated birth control information as pornography, especially in states like Massachusetts. As late as the 1970s, Harvard's Widener Library classified Norman Himes' *Medical History of Contraception* (1936) as a dirty book and shelved it in a locked cabinet. A sociologist, Himes had originally labeled his book a medical history in order to avoid being prosecuted under the Comstock Act. In 1900, just to make sure that Americans understood that recreational sex was out of the question, Congress once again "defined the mailing of birth control information as an obscene act and a felony."[34] Only in *1983*, in *Bolger v. Young Drug Products* (463 U.S. 60) did the Supreme Court finally end the ban on sending advertisements for contraceptive devices through the mail. (The contemporary variation is the anathema with which many Americans view dissemination of information on AIDS.) It is well to remember that in 1932, in the depths of the depression, the quasi-legal contraceptive industry in the United States *netted* a quarter-billion preinflationary dollars a year.[35]

Comstock, his colleagues in other cities, and his successors did not distinguish between prizefighting, billiards, cardplaying, and sex and hardly bothered to sort out erotica from racing sheets, contraceptive advice, feminist brochures, and sex education pamphlets. The annual reports of the New York Society for the Suppression of Vice listed contraband by number of items or weight, as so much trash, always with a reference to the nationality of those arrested. This practice illustrated the society's belief in America's vulnerability to infection by "inferior" races alleged to be more "sexually active" than *real* Americans. Comstock sought to protect his fellow Americans by preventing their "mongrelization." The tactic would be repeated more successfully by a similarly marginal social group in another country a few decades later. The Nazi platform in Germany condemned the liberality of the Weimar Republic's constitution, which forbade censorship, and one of the planks specifically targeted was pornography. Censors almost always define pornography as the expression of those they do not like; for the Nazis, pornography was a Jewish expression, whose prevalence, they said, had made German art and letters decadent and anti-German. One of the first fascist book burnings, held (6 May 1933) on the lawn of the Institute for Sexual Advancement in Berlin, destroyed the institute's entire library, including copies of the works of the major German sexologists (virtually all the pre-1933 German titles listed in bibliographies elsewhere in this volume).[36] In America, Comstock would eventually become a stereotype, the crusader who ensured the success of that which he strove against, and ultimately an object of ridicule because he was reacting to a culture being reshaped by industrialization, immigration, and education. (His censorship society would eventually metamorphose into the New York Police Athletic League.[37])

It hardly needs saying, but not even Comstock's contemporaries necessarily subscribed to the man's sexual pathologies, let alone his mean-spirited racism.

In 1929 the Boston public prosecutor, Robert T. Bushnell, condemned the New England Watch and Ward Society for its nasty campaign against D. H. Lawrence's *Lady Chatterley's Lover* by threatening to charge the group with criminal conspiracy for impugning the integrity of booksellers.[38] Comstock prevailed as long as he did because of a sexual ignorance so widespread in America that it sometimes seems profound. It is important to realize, however, that the ignorance was "official," the product of superficial and supercilious folklore, a circumstance that permitted, even encouraged a rich subterranean sexuality for those who knew how to claim it and that fostered contempt for smug, hypocritical virtues on the part of the sophisticated and the rebellious. Victorian physicians and medical "authorities" published marriage manuals and guides ludicrous in their misinformation about masturbation, intercourse, and "perversities," but that they were published at all indicates that Americans were becoming aware of the need for talk.

The arrival of other sexual technologies destabilized morality. The vulcanization of rubber in 1839, a discovery that led immediately to an improved condom, is another illustration of Slade's law, but that law can be extended to many historically significant sexual appliances. In one of the most brilliant articles ever written on the subject, "Socially Camouflaged Technologies: The Case of the Electromechanical Vibrator," Rachel Maines has written of the subterfuges by which the nineteenth-century American medical establishment masked women's sexual excitement with the term *hysteria*. Female "hysteria," the code term for sexual frustration, was a commonly diagnosed complaint in the nineteenth century. Maines discovered that doctors routinely treated female patients so diagnosed by manually manipulating the clitoris to orgasm, which provided relief. According to the mores of the time, such treatment could be regarded as therapeutic rather than sexual because no penetration of the vagina was involved. Because some doctors specialized in female complaints, up to *70 percent* of their practices might be devoted to treating hysteria through masturbation; Maines thus views the evolution of vibrators as a technological and economic response to need. With so many women requiring masturbation, physicians needed a technology to reduce their medical labor and increase their income.

At first, the electromechanical vibrator, disguised as a therapeutic massager, replaced the doctor's fingers and substantially shortened the time to orgasm. Advances in technology led in the twentieth century to miniaturization of vibrators, eventually producing the battery-operated device that can be used independently of a power source. By then, however, it was clear from the shape of the vibrator that it could be employed for penetration. The overt phallicism (in short, the pornographic representation) made it difficult to pretend that such tools were nonsexual, although many Americans apparently still do try to delude themselves. At first, then, vibrators—Maines even identifies a steam-powered model—made it possible for doctors to treat, that is, masturbate, more women, but the technology eventually hurt their practices by permitting patients to stimulate themselves—and thus, to an extent, to regain control of their bodies. In fact, less obviously sexual technologies have often inspired fear that females might use them to reclaim eroticism and thus escape male control. The automobile, sometimes decried as a bedroom on wheels, was one such, but so was its precursor, the bicycle, which gave women a degree of mobility and freedom. Worse, said conservatives, women who straddled bicycle seats could not help but be stimulated by the pressure on their clitorides. Indeed, to the paranoid, bicycles seemed to have been designed to help women masturbate.[39] In any case, a war of countertechnologies broke out. For every madman who designed a device to prevent youngsters from masturbating—and as Vern Bullough has noted, there were quite a lot of these[40]—other inventors built instruments of pleasure, though all were distributed covertly. Eventually, sexual aids would surface in the mainstream: by 1993 the Doc Johnson Company, located in California's San Fernando Valley, manufactured 2,200 different sexual aids: dildos, inflatable dolls, cock rings, butt plugs, nipple extenders, lubricants, and novelties of all sorts. Nothing if not au courant, Doc Johnson would be sued by gay porn star Jeff Stryker (actor Charles Peyton) for selling neoprene replicas of his penis without permission.[41]

Appropriately enough, the steam engine, symbol of industrialization, furnished Sigmund Freud with a metaphor for the psyche that would account for such phenomena as sexual hysteria. It is not uncommon for technologies to serve as explanatory models for the human self. Deists like Jefferson and Madison who wrote the new republic into being preferred the metaphor of the timepiece; they construed the elements of the universe and the self as parts of a watch set in motion by a Supreme Being, just as the Greeks had borrowed the notion of the Fates spinning threads as warp and woof of the personality. Freud reconstructed the self as a steam engine whose ego is fueled by the sexual energies bubbling in the boiler of the id, its pace controlled by the superego, a psychological analogue of James Watts' flywheel governor. While Freudianism advanced an understanding of sexuality that lasted well into the next century, it would begin to falter when new communication technologies offered more compelling metaphors. From that point on, though psychologists clung to the notion that humans were driven by forces they could not always control, increasingly, they characterized those forces as programming by cultural institutions. Communication and codes now dominate discussion of the social construction of sexuality; the programming and feedback of computers are the metaphors of choice.

In the meantime, Freud had a lot to say about sexual fetishes, which were widespread. In fact, as scholars have noted, recognition of the power of sexual fetishes is as old as a folkloristic witchcraft that touted the efficacy of erotic objects and symbols. Moreover, any number of historians maintain that Victorian Americans were not nearly so stuffy about sex as the pronouncements of the official culture suggest; they just kept their behavior private. Most of the modern lingerie fetishes had already demonstrated their power to arouse. The corset that slimmed the waist and pushed up and exposed the breasts, the garter belt that framed the pubic mound, the stockings that accentuated, colored, and patterned the legs—all have evolved according to the dictates of fashion from these earlier templates. Items of stage lingerie, such as the pasties that covered nipples and the *couche-sexe* that hid the labia (ingeniously adapted from the bicycle spring clip that prevented the cyclist's trousers from being caught in the chain), the G-string that replaced it, and the breakaway panel brassiere, would eventually find their way into milady's boudoir as well. Leather, rubber, and neoprene garments had to wait on technologies to fabricate them into fetishistic apparel, but nipple, navel, and labia rings and tattoos for various genders, so often characterized as "primitive" devices, actually appeared among Americans during the last century. In private revolt against public opposition to excessive ornamentation, for example, American women of the Victorian and Edwardian eras pierced their nipples in order to be able to wear jewels *beneath* their bombazine.[42] (The increased sensitivity of the breasts may well have aggravated "hysteria.") The fetish for large breasts was also well advanced, and women of the period were advised to rub their bosoms with various salves, bathe in crushed strawberries, or drink special teas to enhance their busts.

Genuine pornography, as distinct from the increasingly irrelevant borderline material, that is, what we sometimes call *high* porn or erotica—the sort easily seized by censors—simply went further underground. American folklorists did their best to track it, but the most notable successes were registered by German scholars associated with various sexual institutes. From this period dates the pioneering work that led to the great *Bilderlexicon*, for example. Gathering stories, tales, and jokes, folklorists gradually began to realize the vastness of this hidden ocean, into which pour the erotic oral storehouses of every language, a tide invisible to Foucault and his school. It antedates America, of course, and Western Europe, too, though it has flowed into the United States with every group that migrates here: low, obscene, irrepressible folklore, forever rebellious, endlessly renewed, the fountainhead of all sexual expression.

As Comstockery became an embarrassment, ersatz erotica surfaced again, where it formed a kind of boundary, beyond which, outlawed and therefore largely untouched, hard-core pornography could prosper as an authentic subculture. The borderline gradually widened. During the 1890s, *Munsey's* (1889–1929) ran "nude art," chiefly reproductions of paintings but occasionally photos of decorously posed models, as did *Nickell Magazine* (1894–1905), *Metropolitan Magazine* (1895–1911), *Broadway* (1898–1911), and *Peterson's* (1842–1898). In its early incarnation (1883–1936), *Life* helped create the pinup by opening its pages to the breezy debutantes drawn by Charles Dana Gibson.

After the turn of the century, changing attitudes toward art and social issues permitted slightly greater explicitness in painting and sculpture. During the Progressive Era, the urban realist John Sloan, editor of the radical *The Masses*, printed his drawings of prostitutes in the magazine's pages, the photographer Lewis Hine shot pictures of streetwalkers, and the sculptor Abastenia St. Leger

Eberle carved statues of women being abducted. The images offended because they acknowledged the sex worker as a figure of the urban landscape. Robert Hughes has spoken of "the crisis of the ideal nude" as the hallmark of a twentieth-century period "beginning with Degas's pastels and continued by the unconsoling candor of Lucian Freud, Sigmund's grandson."[43] During the 1920s and the 1930s, American artists such as Marsden Hartley and Charles Demuth ventured into depictions of homosexuality, but these they kept secret. American artists who wished training in figure painting or sculpture had to go to Europe to find it; classes in life studies were risky here.

Where once Hawthorne and Twain had condemned paintings by Titian as obscene, modern viewers were less shocked by nudity in galleries, though every now and then some zealot would complain to local police. Cities such as Cincinnati and Boston did become celebrated for puritanical pathologies manifest in campaigns against nude statues and avant-garde paintings, but they were exceptions. Not even Comstock targeted books of art reproductions (provided that they were not sold by immigrants), partly because they were books rather than magazines and therefore beyond the pocketbooks of the unwashed and partly because their compilers did not include scenes of copulation even by acknowledged masters like Rembrandt. Americans had heard rumors about the erotica uncovered at Pompeii and other archaeological digs, but publishers did not test public tolerance by reproducing it. On the other hand, in one of the few such stories of egregious outrage to be true, an American customs inspector seized imported reproductions of the ceiling of the Sistine Chapel on the grounds that so many nude figures must be obscene. Prosecutions occurred often enough to make artists aware of limits. More significantly, educated Americans learned to dismiss such events as barbaric, a response occasioned by wide gaps in knowledge among classes.

Marriage manuals could sometimes slip by the law, but quasi-medical texts ran into trouble. *Light on Dark Corners* (1894), a guide to purity in the American Midwest, by B. G. Jefferies and J. L. Nichols, was a little too explicit for the police, as was John G. Bourke's *Scatalogic Rites of All Nations* (1891). Private editions of Boccaccio, Aretino, Petronius, Poggio, Casanova, Robert Burns, Frank Harris, George Herbert, and Sir Richard Burton's translations of *The Arabian Nights*, the *Ananga Ranga*, the *Kama Sutra*, and the *Perfumed Garden*, often richly printed by dealers on their own presses, sold in limited, beautifully bound editions to the wealthy. The *Memoirs of Dolly Morton* (1904), the reminiscences of a madam, began a less elegant genre that still flourishes today in works like Nell Kimball's *Her Life as an American Madam, by Herself* (written in 1922, published in 1970) or Pauline Tabor's *Pauline's* (1972).

LOOSENING OF RESTRAINTS

World War I acquainted many servicemen with the candor of sexual expression in Europe, and the rhythms of the jazz age lent exuberance and good humor to depictions of intercourse. Jazz, the word itself a synonym for intercourse, seemed to inflame the nation's youth; the censorious became alarmed at music's ability to stimulate unhealthy passions. "A wave of vulgar, filthy and suggestive music has inundated the land," intoned a music trade journal in 1899, recapping an attack on ragtime for "its obscene posturings, its lewd gestures."[44] In 1911 officials investigated the licentious pronoun in Irving Berlin's "Everybody's Doing It Now" and thus set in motion the scrutiny of song lyrics that would peak in the congressional hearings on rock music in the 1980s and rap music in the 1990s.

Books by many hands appeared, such as *The Horn Book: A Girl's Guide to the Knowledge of Good and Evil* (1899, rpt. 1923), the work Gershon Legman calls the "principal work in English on sex technique" until that time, together with endless pamphlets of dirty jokes. Pseudoscientific texts such as the reprint of the 1750 *Padlocks and Girdles of Chastity* (1928) emerged, but so did authentic studies of eroticism, such as Bronislaw Malinowski's *The Sexual Life of Savages* (1929). Samuel Roth, most indefatigable of pornographic publishers, began a career of publishing borderline texts, including—according to rumor—a volume he wrote himself, *The Strange Confessions of Monsieur Mountcairn* (1928), erroneously billed as one of the earliest authentic homosexual novels in America. Pornography for women, in the form of "confession" magazines such as *True Story* (1919), *True Confessions* (1922), and *Modern Romance* (1930), all combining sentiment and transgression, grew explosively. Markets for more explicit erotica aimed at heterosexual females would not develop for another three decades, when demands for candor helped foster the feminist movement. By the turn of the century explicit photographs of male homosexual activity were available through the same underground channels that distributed the heterosexual type, but the lesbian market had little commerce, largely for lack of an identifiable audience. Male-oriented countercultures seized on lesbianism for their own titillation; couplings between ersatz-lesbians were staples of porn aimed at men. When Radclyffe Hall's lesbian novel, *The Well of Loneliness*, created a scandal on its publication in 1928, a New York publisher in 1930 reprinted a French parody of pornography, *The Imitation of Sappho*, under the name "Sumner J. Radclyffe" (a conflation of the names of Hall and John S. Sumner, Comstock's successor as head of the New York Society for the Suppression of Vice).[45]

Women began appearing seminude or clad in body stockings on public stages in Europe in the mid-nineteenth century, though usually standing stock-still in tableaux groupings; the daring protagonist of Zola's *Nana* (1880) not only performed solo but also moved. One of the attractions of the Chicago Exposition of 1893 was "Little Egypt," first of a series of generically named belly dancers to gyrate at subsequent international expositions.[46] Semirespectable American cabarets and nightclubs in major cities presented occasionally topless hula and "cooch" dancers in abbreviated costumes around the turn of the century, but nudity did not appear in legitimate theaters until the teens. In 1914 a reporter for the *New York American* ventured the hope that La Milo, an opulent blond star of nude tableaux on the Continent, would display her charms in New York's Palace Theater.[47] The musical revue, a mixture of satire and spectacle, had already been imported from abroad in 1907 by Florenz Ziegfeld, who annually staged ever more elaborate *Follies*, sandwiching comic routines and dance numbers between parades of lavishly decorated showgirls. By 1916 he was mounting "Ben Ali Haggin Tableaux" of total, but discreetly "frozen," nudity, although, given the theater lighting of the time, a spectator in the twentieth row could barely make out the nipples under the powder caked on breasts.

Soon Ziegfeld had competitors like the Shuberts, George White, Earl Carroll, and, most important, the Minsky brothers, who invented the runway stretching into the audience to enhance visibility. The nude models in J. J. Shubert's *Artists and Models of 1923* actually moved; Earl Carroll personally supervised the removal of the showgirls' pubic hair so that their nakedness became more "acceptable" for the stage spectacles he called *Vanities*.[48] Tradition credits the Minskys with originating the slow, sinuous disrobing to music that became known as the striptease. While that is unlikely, American dancers do seem to have been the first to structure the form into distinct phases and to use net bras, flash panels, and rhinestoned G-strings as costumes. In any case, American burlesque (the name that steadily set shows featuring comics and strippers apart from the older vaudeville routines) adopted nudity the better to compete with movies. Just as movies themselves in the 1950s would deepen their candor to counter the economic menace of television, so burlesque impresarios in the 1920s headlined stripteasers to lure back the crowds siphoned off by the cinema. When Mayor LaGuardia forced burlesque off the stage in New York City in 1937, it was at the behest of property owners concerned about declining property values in neighborhoods where strippers attracted riffraff, just as similar arguments would be made in the 1970s and 1980s against adult bookstores and arcades. By the mid-1940s burlesque moved off the Main-Street stages into small cabarets and clubs. Men's magazines such as *Flirt, Beauty, Eyeful*, and, above all, *Cabaret* (1955–1959) regularly featured the strippers, who also starred in mildly revealing movies (Ann Corio, e.g., made *Call of the Jungle* [1944]) when opportunities presented themselves.

Bare breasts began to appear in newsstand "art" magazines like *Art Inspirations* and *Artists and Models* in the 1920s, though airbrushing removed still-taboo pubic hair. By contrast, "girlie" magazines like *Breezy, Titter*, and *The Flapper* stuck mostly to drawings or photographs of women in bathing suits between pages of jokes, cartoons, and arch fiction. The most ribald of these, *Captain Billy's Whiz Bang*, actually began as mimeographed sheets of jokes (an early zine) circulated to American troops during World War I by William Fawcett, who stretched the enterprise into the Fawcett publishing house. In perhaps the most famous sociological survey of the midcentury, the pioneering *Middletown: A Study in Contemporary American Culture*, Robert and Helen Lynd reported in 1929 that 20 to 40 percent of American homes subscribed to *Captain*

Billy's Whiz Bang, True Story, or *True Romance,* and lots of other citizens purchased periodicals like *Hot Dog, Art Lovers, Breezy Stories,* and *La Vie Parisienne.*[49] Much more common were tabloid newspapers and scandal magazines specializing in the prurient, such as Bernarr Macfadden's *New York Daily Graphic, True Experiences* (1922), *Love and Romance* (1923), and *Intimate Stories* (1948), precursors of both steamy romances directed at women and the tabloids found in supermarkets today. In 1927 *Time* twitted Macfadden for threatening to sue the Broadway producers of a skit entitled "Bernarr Hires a Stenographer" for depicting the publisher and his staff parading around the office in skimpy bathing suits. Said the magazine: Macfadden "publishes composite faked pictures of old lechers, young miscegenators, alleged murderers, undressed girls. But Publisher Macfadden rises in dudgeon when similar liberties are taken with his own, more robust physique."[50]

Photographs of full-frontal nudes of both sexes could be ordered by mail, sometimes through ads in these magazines. The sale of photographs of actual intercourse was a furtive transaction between customers who met sellers face-to-face. Girlie magazines became slightly bolder during the 1930s and 1940s but remained essentially innocuous. Some of these, or periodicals very like them—*Wild Cherries, Love's Revels*—lasted well into the 1950s, but Mayor LaGuardia enjoyed the drama of publicly burning them in New York City.[51] Modestly fetishistic fare like *High Heels, Beauty Parade, Eyeful,* and *Wink* (mostly lingerie poses) could be found at newsstands near train stations and bus terminals, in secondhand bookstores and backdate magazine shops, in barbershops, dance halls, and bars, and in drugstores that rented erotic novels—rather like video stores several decades later. The principal fetish journal, however, was *Bizarre* (1946–1959), largely the work of the talented Australian-American illustrator John Willie (J.A.S. Coutts); it emphasized sadomasochism and bondage in fiction, reader correspondence, and comic book–style drawings. It paved the way for successors such as *Spanking Digest,* popular in the 1960s. *Vice Versa,* the first American lesbian magazine (1947), did not survive the year, although the circumspection of *One: The Homosexual Viewpoint,* a gay magazine published in New York, lengthened its life from 1956 to 1965.

Censors were confused by erotica of serious intent. No artists of the whimsical erotic stature of Aubrey Beardsly or Felicien Rops appeared in the United States. During the 1930s and 1940s Reginald Marsh drew voluptuous images of Times Square strippers, but painters and sculptors generally crafted conventional nudes, idealized and nonprovocative. Mahlon Blaine, Keene Wallis, David Plotkin, Alexander King, and Clara Tice illustrated editions of European erotica for publishers such as the Panurge Press and for Samuel Roth's prodigious output of books and periodicals. The 1940s and 1950s were, however, the golden age of the painted or drawn pinup. Major artists included Alberto Vargas, Rolf Armstrong, Billy DeVorss, Gil Elvgren, Zöe Mozert, Harry Aikman, Earl MacPherson, Peter Driben, Fritz Willis, and Bill Randall. Their hyperbolic cheesecake parodied, rather than set standards of, feminine pulchritude and sensuality and was reproduced for calendars, cigarette lighters, playing cards, aircraft fuselages, and so on. Photographs were more problematic. Albert Arthur Allen shot gamboling nudes and declined to retouch their pubic hair, and Arnold Genthe photographed dancers in drapery that hid nothing. Edward Weston explored landscapes of flesh imposed on desert settings just as evocative—or mute. Police seized their prints along with the anonymous frames of far less talented photographers.

Much later, during the 1950s, fashion photographers such as John Rawlings after hours photographed their mannequins without clothes, a practice that continues today. Fashion and pornographic photography share visual elements, not least the focus on bodies posed at voyeuristic angles in improbable venues. The two genres have vectored together often. A recent apotheosis is fashion photographer Peter Lindbergh's 1990 shot of a richly paneled corporate boardroom, against whose conference table languishes celebrated runway model Helena Christensen, clad only in an intricate bead necklace, her glorious breasts an evocation of the nation's conflation of flesh and money. The sepia tones, stilted angles, and lush eroticism make Lindbergh's image virtually identical to pornographic photographs from the 1940s that have been preserved in the Kinsey Institute.[52]

TIJUANA BIBLES AND SLEAZY FICTION

Although sexually oriented comic books and cartoons appeared as early as the late nineteenth century, they are a twentieth-century form. Those produced in the United States cluster in four major periods. The first is the era of the "Tijuana bibles," a term applied initially to stapled pages of fiction and then, more commonly, to little booklets of comic strip panels. The latter type, also called "eight-pagers" because of their size, blossomed in the 1920s and 1930s as a kind of depression literature. More than any other pornographic genre, the drawings and dialogue were demotic expressions of lower-class sensibility. A typical sequence would poke fun at cultural celebrities or parody characters from the legitimate funny papers. An artist might draw a lascivious Clara Bow in intercourse with a series of football players (yet another version of the tabloid rumors that Bow had participated in orgies with the University of Southern California team) or pencil a familiar, wide-eyed adolescent fellating Daddy Warbucks and Punjab in panels imitating "Little Orphan Annie." So far as is known, only one woman artist (Susan Aguerra?), under the name "Rhangild," drew Tijuana bibles.[53] The comics were crudely drawn, deliberately so, and distributed widely by truck drivers and novelty salesmen to rural areas beyond the reach of stag films, which were confined largely to cities and towns.

Tijuana bibles also crossed over into erotic animated movies, whose history has yet to be written. We do know it began with *Buried Treasure* (aka *Everready*, 1922?), an animated film of a disembodied penis running amok. It was beautifully drawn, as well it should have been, since every major cartoonist of the 1920s worked on it as a birthday present to the dean of American animators, Windsor McKay, creator of "Gertie the Dinosaur." Closer to the mainstream were Max and Dave Fleischer, creators of the short-lived, highly suggestive "Betty Boop" series, and the animators of the Van Beuren Studio, which turned out risqué comedies such as *Nursery Scandal, Hot Tamale*, and *Red Riding Hood* in the 1920s and 1930s. Pornographic send-ups of important mainstream cartoon features began with the hard-core Czechoslovakian parody (1939) of Disney's *Snow White* (1938), in which the saccharine heroine enjoys vivid fellatio, cunnilingus, and intercourse with all seven dwarfs. The parodic tradition continues down to the present.

During the second period of the print form, roughly the decade of the 1950s, comics emphasizing bondage and fetish themes—as opposed to depictions of nudity or graphic sex—appeared as a response to postwar normalcy and Eisenhower blandness. Commissioned by entrepreneurs such as Irving Klaw, such exotica circulated on the margins of the comic book world, though it soon came under the scrutiny of the national crusade against mainstream comic books, a social movement that seems quintessentially American. The Kefauver Hearings highlighted comic books among materials alleged to promote delinquency. Within the same period, much closer to a cultural center yet often heavily influenced by the fetish artists, were the cartoons drawn by George Petty, Alberto Vargas, and their talented rivals, usually published in magazines like *Esquire* and *Playboy*; these featured skimpily clad women with torpedo-breasts in risquély captioned panels.

A third period began in the following decade, when the alternative press of the 1960s, the outgrowth of both anti–Vietnam War sentiment and flower child rebellion, spawned underground comics—sometimes spelled *comix*—whose panels combined political comment with sexually outrageous images. Cartoonists trained at the *Berkeley Tribe* or the *East Village Other*, but also at *Mad* and *Help* (which nurtured Gilbert Shelton, Robert Crumb, and Jay Lynch) under the supervision of Harvey Kurtzman, himself the creator of *Little Annie Fanny* for *Playboy*. Robert Crumb defined the field in comics like *Zap* and *Snatch*, with S. Clay Wilson bringing almost as much talent to bear on social issues in *Radical Amerika Komiks* and *Bent*. Shelton's *The Fabulous Furry Freak Brothers*, Larry Welz's lighthearted, but explicit, *Cherry* (aka *Cherry Poptart*), the saga of a nubile teenager memorably represented as a bimbo Statue of Liberty holding aloft a vibrator, and Howard Chaykin's S/M-oriented *Black Kiss* drew cult readers, as did magazines like *Bizarre Sex, Weird Smut*, and *Young Lust*. Gilbert Hernandez used science fiction to fill the panels of *Love and Rockets* and *Birdland*. Other artists drawing in the 1960s include Ed "Big Daddy" Roth, Jim Steranko, Robert Williams, Roberta Gregory, Mary Fleener, Julie Doucet, Shary Flenniken, and the late Dori Seda (*Lonely Nights Comics*). Popular during the 1970s were Dave Sheridan, Gilbert Shelton, Richard Corben, and the members of the Women's Cartoonist's Collective: Trina Robbins, Lee Mars, Patricia Moodian, and others.

A final category, a direct outgrowth and overlapping of the third, represents a mature sensibility that has benefited from the increasingly high regard accorded comic illustration in the present. Comix publishers Fantagraphics and Drawn and Quarterly now compete with pioneers such as Rip Off Press and Kitchen Sink Press. Recent ventures, sometimes called "alternative comics," sometimes "pomo" (postmodern) strips, are more sophisticated and more straightforward treatments of sexual power and dominance, shifting gender roles, and topical scandal. Beginning in the late 1970s, gay and lesbian artists drew strips featuring themes and characters aimed at different genders, a diversification that continues today. Here are to be found gay comics by Craig Maynard (*Up from Bondage*), Gerald Conelan, and Alison Bechdel and unusual sex strips drawn around real-life porn stars like Annie Sprinkle (Rip Off Press) and Sarah Jane Hamilton (Renegade Press). More obviously didactic are strips and panels dealing with AIDS.

Adult comic books now appeal to sophisticates, but in the early part of the century they were cheap, plentiful, and aimed at the uneducated, though just as culturally parodistic as more conventional pornographic fiction pitched at wealthier pocketbooks. In the latter category were *A Sea-Side Venus at Fifteen* (1933), by George Byrnes, a tale of adolescent sexuality at Asbury Park, New Jersey; *Nelly, or The Confessions of a Doctor* (1930), a familiar story of a lascivious doctor who seduces patients; *The Masquerader or the Affairs of Sissie* (c. 1940), a fantasy of a boy who dresses like a girl in order to spy on women; *Grushenka* (1933), by Val Luten (?), an extended scenario involving a Russian peasant girl; *The Prodigal Virgin* (1936?), by Homer Thomas, an account of a young lady seduced into a life of debauchery; *Crimson Hairs* (1938), by Whidden Graham, an erotic parody of detective novels; and *Lust Is a Cripple* (1940), author unknown, a tale of, well, lust. During this period, it was common to mimeograph typescripts for limited circulation. Stories like "Jane of the Bouncing Bottom" and "Liza the Lesbian," written, says Legman, by Robert Sewall, were hand-sewn together to form *An Oxford Thesis on Love* (1938). Sewall and Legman together wrote a sequel, *The Oxford Professor* (c.1948), and also *The Devil's Advocate* (1942), one of the better pornographic novels. During the 1930s a U.S. printer began to copy *My Secret Life*, the most famous of all sexual memoirs (sometimes attributed to Ashbee), but police raided the press before the fourth and fifth volumes could be run off. A bit later, someone surreptitiously printed 100 copies of Mark Twain's *1601* on the press at the U.S. Military Academy at West Point. Marginal publishers such as Panurge Press and Falstaff Press slowly widened a market for quasi-scholarly erotica.

Books by reputable publishers usually escaped massive attack, although there were exceptions: Cabell's *Jurgen* (1919) or Dreiser's *Sister Carrie* (1900) and *An American Tragedy* (1925), the latter held to be obscene by a Massachusetts court in 1930. One strain of paranoia or another roiled ad hoc censorship groups all over the country; these rise and fall according to constantly shifting social, political, and religious agendas today. They may threaten, boycott, or persecute publishers, librarians, educators, broadcasters, newsdealers, and—rarely—real pornographers, in what is a peculiarly American version of intolerance—the Comstock syndrome—directed at novel ideas or tastes. Given this climate, it is pointless to identify every monument of American literature taxed at one time or another with licentiousness. Suffice it to say that American authors from William Hill Brown (*The Power of Sympathy* [1789]) and Charles Brockton Brown (*Arthur Mervyn* [1799–1800], through Edgar Allan Poe ("The Mystery of Marie Roget," based on an abortion scandal of 1841), Whitman, Crane, and Chopin, and on up to Henry Miller, William Burroughs, Hubert Selby, Erica Jong, and Kathy Acker in the present have pushed at the limits of modesty and that these threats to decorum have often frightened those who rarely read them. It took editor Maxwell Perkins several weeks to persuade Charles Scribner to accept Hemingway's *The Sun also Rises* (1926) because the publisher was convinced that it was just another dirty book.[54]

Comparatively few well-known American writers have composed manuscripts for deliberately clandestine circulation, although scholars may discover others in the future. Among those who did, in addition to Franklin, are Mark Twain (*1601: Conversation as It Was by the Social Fireside in the Time of the Tudors* [1876], *Some Thoughts on the Science of Onanism* [1879], *The Mammoth Cod* [1890s?]); Eugene Field (*When Willie Wet the Bed* [1901], *Only a Boy* [1886]); James Gibbons Huneker (*Painted Veils* [1920]); Clement Wood (*The Private Life of Frank Harris* [1931]); Ben Hecht and Max Bodenheim (*Cutie: A Warm Mama* [1924]); and Anaïs Nin (*Delta of Venus* [1940–1941]). Desperate for cash, Nin and Henry Miller wrote smutty stories on commission for a brief period in the 1940s. Scholars are still arguing over just what Edith Wharton intended to do with the "Beatrice Palmato Fragment" (c. 1917), her three-page manuscript on incest between a father and daughter caught up in oral-genital excess. In any case, no American author seems to have produced "forbidden" work on the scale of, say, de Sade. Like the legends of famous directors and actresses making smutty films to support themselves, the notion that major writers routinely wrote erotic potboilers has only modest substance. From time to time gay novels written by mainstream authors, usually penned out of deep psychic need and suppressed by themselves, come to light; an example is *Forbidden Fires*, by Margaret Anderson, cofounder of *The Little Review*.

BATTLES AMONG THE CENSORS

The Hicklin principle remained the touchstone of obscenity until 1913, when Judge Learned Hand, though upholding conviction in a case involving a sociological novel, *Hagar Revelly*, by Daniel Goodman, expressed doubts about Hicklin's applicability (*United States v. Kennerly* [209 F. 119, 1913]). Another chink appeared in 1920, when the judge in *Halsey v. New York Society for the Suppression of Vice* (180 N.Y.S. 836) ruled that a book should be evaluated as a whole, not just in terms of isolated passages, and that qualified critics rather than smut-hunters should be asked for their opinions. This did not sit well with many judges, one of whom, John Ford of the New York Supreme Court, found his daughter reading a copy of D. H. Lawrence's *Women in Love*. The furious Ford founded the Clean Books League to lobby against liberalization of the law.[55] The Hicklin precedent remained in force long enough for a New York City court to ban *The Well of Loneliness* in 1929 and for a Boston court similarly to suppress *An American Tragedy* in 1930. In that same year, however, Judge Augustus Hand, cousin of Learned, reversed the conviction of Mary Ware Dennett's sex education pamphlet, *The Sex Side of Life*, and thus set in motion the final assault on Hicklin. Judge John M. Woolsey was the instrument. In *United States v. One Book Called "Ulysses"* (5F. Supp. 182, 1933), Woolsey decreed that a book must be judged as a whole, not on the basis of offensive passages. In the majority as appellate justices, Learned and Augustus Hand upheld this interpretation on the government's 1934 appeal. Two years later, in still another case, Learned Hand applied the Woolsey decision and specifically rejected Hicklin as too narrow a test.

The *Ulysses* decision was articulated not just to protect works of merit from unwarranted prosecution by distinguishing them from baser examples but also to protect society from the pathologies of those who would censor the most innocent forms of sexual expression. There were still gray areas. Learned Hand refused to overturn the 1939 conviction of Ben Rebhuhn, publisher of Falstaff Press (and of Rebhuhn's wife and nephew), for publishing and selling several texts that Hand admitted were not obscene but that had been advertised in a prurient manner, by "pandering" (*U.S. v. Rebhuhn et al.* [109 F2d 512 (2nd Circuit, 1940)]). Some government agencies continued to exploit the uncertainty in public book burnings; these lasted until World War II, when they were discontinued because of the fascist associations of the sport.[56]

In a historically important shift of power, both the Customs Department and the Post Office lost the authority to determine what was obscene with passage of the Tariff Act of 1930. The act prevented the importation of obscene pictures, drawings, prints, and figures "made from paper and other materials." A companion act listed books, pamphlets, pictures, motion pictures, film, paper, letters, writing, print, or other "matter of indecent character" that could be fined for explicitness short of legally established obscenity. Under the act, customs officers could destroy any suspicious items "if they were not of great financial value" *with the consent of the receiver*. That is, a customs officer could inform the addressee that the contents of a package appeared to be in violation of the act and ask for permission to destroy them. If the addressee refused, the official could not destroy them without a judicial ruling.

In short, the Tariff Act specifically vested authority in the courts, which had to rule that an item was, in fact, obscene before customs or the post office could prosecute item or person. Despite the clarity of this revision, the post office not only clung to its former prerogatives but tried to augment them, which put it in conflict with other agencies and with the First Amendment. In 1935, in a partisan attempt to bolster the Post Office's role as the nation's chief censor, the House Subcommittee on the Post Office and Post Roads encouraged a procession of postal workers to testify on the "river of filth" flowing through the postal conduits, especially birth control materials. Still mired in the depression, Americans had other things to worry about, and the hearings attracted little notice. In 1943, when Postmaster General Frank Walker denied second-class mailing privileges to *Esquire* and other publications he thought obscene, the courts declined to ignore the Post Office's abuses of power. *Hannegan v. Esquire. Inc.* (1946) ruled that the postmaster general had exceeded his authority by denying mailing privileges before the magazine had received its day in court. Implied in the decision was a recognition that few Americans would have considered the magazine obscene. Thereafter, in theory at least, no material could be banned from the mails without prior hearings. Even so, more than a decade later, in 1959, both houses of Congress held hearings to renew concern about the use of the mails to disseminate obscenity—which is always characterized as a flood, never a trickle. The politicians were perhaps envious of Senator Kefauver's success in using hearings on juvenile delinquency to further his presidential ambitions, and officials of the Post Office seized the chance to reconvince Congress and the public that the agency should remain the nation's first line of defense against the evil tide.

The Post Office's prurience, however, was corrupting, said John F. Kennedy's postmaster general, J. Edward Day, in an astonishing article called "Mailing Lists and Pornography" (1966). Day boasted that he had angered antismut groups by refusing to provide them with free samples of confiscated materials. By contrast, said Day, his predecessor as postmaster general had employed three full-time "smut" consultants and speechwriters and had established a museum of smut "divided among various perversions," through which guides escorted visitors, a tour climaxed by an exhibit of the "worst" examples, suddenly revealed when the guide dramatically pulled a drawstring to open black velvet curtains. The previous postmaster general, in short, had employed what might be called the J. Edgar Hoover method of agency promotion. Hoover himself routinely condemned pornography as a wellspring of the nation's crime but loved to show seized stag movies to his cronies.[57]

The pressures that had led to the *Ulysses* decision in the 1930s were aggravated by economics in the 1940s and 1950s, as American publishers began to chafe at moral restrictions that cost them money. By the 1950s, as John D'Emilio and Estelle Freedman have noted, the United States had become a thoroughly "sexualized society"[58] whose credo was that men and women were entitled to sexual happiness. Americans wanted to purchase information on that newly discovered birthright, and the law was slow to recognize the shift in expectations. Massachusetts suppressed Smith's *Strange Fruit* and New York state Wilson's *Memoirs of Hecate County* in the 1940s, at the same time that American soldiers returning from World War II brought back works like Miller's *Tropic of Cancer* (1934), printed by Jack Kahane's Obelisk Press in Paris. Kahane's son, Maurice

Girodias, in 1953 founded the Olympia Press, also in Paris, to continue publishing erotica such as the first English translations of de Sade. In that year, too, Hugh Hefner founded *Playboy* magazine in Chicago. The success of the magazine, which monthly offered photos of brightly nippled Playmates, coupled with early intimations of the sexual revolution to follow in the next decade, made American publishers bolder, especially since many women approved.[59] High-speed magazine presses were beginning to spin out paperback titles by Erskine Caldwell and other steamy novelists, and these borderline works needed legal protection that would stabilize a booming market. The vertical files at the Kinsey Institute contain dozens of brochures for sensational books published during the 1950s and 1960s. These ranged from the hundreds of spicy novels turned out by Peggy Gaddis for Phoenix, William Godwin, and Arcadia House, to the potboiling detective and mystery fiction written by Mickey Spillane and his imitators.

Respectable publishers did not defend Samuel Roth, who was convicted in 1954 for publishing obscenity, but argued instead for the right to publish "classic" works, winning that right in a series of famous cases: *Lady Chatterley's Lover* (Grove Press, 1960), *Tropic of Cancer* (Grove Press, 1964), and *Fanny Hill* (Putnam, 1966). The Supreme Court affirmed the Roth conviction in 1957 (in a 5–4 decision written by Brennan) and also the conviction of David Alberts in *Alberts v. California* for violating a state law against possession of obscene materials but introduced a new obscenity test: "whether to the average person, applying contemporary community standards, the dominant theme of the material taken as a whole appeals to prurient interest" (*Roth v. United States* [354 U.S. 476 (1957)]). Justice Brennan, writing the opinion, added that prosecutors must demonstrate that the work in question was "utterly without redeeming social value." That same year the Court issued another opinion in *Butler v. Michigan* (written by Frankfurter), throwing out the argument that books could be banned because of possible effects on minors. To do so, said the Court, would reduce the level of public information to that appropriate only for children. In 1958 and 1959 the Court ruled in favor of nudist, art, and homosexual publications and declared unconstitutional state laws prohibiting themes like adultery and others holding bookstore owners liable for the content of books they sold. The 1966 decision in favor of *Fanny Hill* (*Memoirs v. Massachusetts* [383 U.S. 413] spelled out the test more clearly: the Roth criteria applied, but in addition the work in question must exhibit "patent offensiveness" and be "utterly without redeeming social value." Wayne Overbeck observes that the *Roth* case led to a series of powerful dissents by Justices Black and Douglas, who held that the First Amendment shielded even obscenity from prosecution. This absolutist position, says Overbeck, "enabled the high court to reverse obscenity convictions, but made it impossible for a majority of the court to agree on the reason for the reversal. The result was a series of plurality decisions that left the nation unsure what the law really was."[60] Between 1957 and 1965, says William Brigman, the Court's thirteen major obscenity decisions involved fifty-five different concurring and dissenting opinions.[61] The issue was more than academic: in 1965 the legal atmosphere was heated by more than 300 smut-hunting organizations.[62]

Underground publishers had continued all along to supply pornographic works such as Jack Borge's *Primrose* (1950). West Coast printers turned out beefcake magazines such as *Grecian Guild Pictorial* and *Vim: America's Best Built Physiques*, aimed principally at homosexuals. Robert Mizer, the founder of the (Los Angeles) Athletic Model Guild (AMG), produced more than 1 million gay nude photos during a career that began in the 1940s. AMG printed *Physique Pictorial*, featuring males clad in jockstraps and mineral oil, from 1951 to about 1968, then sporadically until it was displaced as a gay favorite by more explicit magazines like *Male Man* in the 1960s and *Yearling* in the 1980s. The AMG earned a place in history by persuading a court (*Manual Enterprises v. Day* [370 U.S. 478]) that a representation of homosexuality, involving nudity or not, in and of itself was not obscene. Mizer's chief rivals were Bruce Bellas of Bruce of Los Angeles, Constantine of Spartan, and Don Whitman of the Western Photography Guild.

Fetish magazines (some, like *Exotique*, modeled on *Bizarre*), were permitted because their illustrations never showed penises or female nipples no matter how graphically the models were posed. Iconographies of cruelty had become acceptable forms of sexual expression before the law. The largest single producer of fetish material was Irving Klaw, the owner of Movie Star News in New York. During the 1940s and 1950s, Klaw sold various photos and magazines like *Movie Star News* and *Model Parade*, featuring bondage and discipline, lingerie, high heels, and leather costumes worn by models such as Bettie Page, Donna Brown, and Joann Rydell. Klaw boosted the careers of strippers Blaze Starr, Tempest Storm, and Lili St. Cyr; Page became an American cult figure. Investigated by the Kefauver Commission, Klaw bowed out of the business. He had actually begun to lose sales when courts upheld the right of nudist magazines such as *Sunshine and Health* to feature frontal nudity in photographs of both sexes. The rise of soft-core "men's" magazines, cheaper imitations of *Playboy*, also eroded the market for aggressive fetishes. *Dazzle, Frolic, Caper, Escapade, Dude, Scamp, Monsieur*, and a couple of dozen others revealed breasts instead. Burlesque magazines such as *Cabaret* and *Cavalcade of Burlesque* (the latter an incomparable historical record) competed with domestic scandal magazines such as *Hollywood Confidential* and imports such as *Paris Cocktail*. As a sideline, Samuel Roth dealt in limit-testing soft-core photographs (see *Roth v. Albert Goldman 62–397 U.S. District Court, Southern District of New York [1951]*), as did other marginal publishers, who sometimes got into trouble as a result.

The Kefauver Commission, drawing on Post Office reports, concluded that the mail-order business in soft-core porn (pulp novels, photographs, and motion pictures) was large, particularly that portion devoted to homosexuality, but that traffic in hard-core material was small. What hard-core material there was tended to be ancient: investigators for the President's Commission on Obscenity and Pornography of 1970 found that old porn photos seemed never to die; they cited the longevity of sixteen photos of a woman coupling with a horse shot in Peru, Indiana, in 1933 that were still being sold in the 1960s.[63] The same held true for stag films. In fact, photos and stag films were usually shot simultaneously: audiences watching vintage stags can sometimes see the flashes from the tripod just outside the frame of the cinema camera. The men who made the stag film *Smart Alec* (1951–1952), starring Candy Barr, took dozens of black-and-white stills at the same time; the large number of prints pulled from the originals was one source of the legend that Barr made several stag films. A half dozen or so of these poses are in the photo archives of the Kinsey Institute, which holds more than 100,000 individual prints, but at least twenty others of Barr and her partners have circulated throughout the United States (and abroad), can be found in major private photo collections, and still turn up in attics from time to time.

THE "SEXUAL REVOLUTION" OF THE 1960s

During the 1960s the market for porn novels changed radically. The Supreme Court upheld the conviction of Ralph Ginzburg for pandering (the precedent was the Rebhuhn decision of 1940), rather than for the content of any of the publications he sold, in 1966 (*Ginzburg v. U.S.* [383 U.S. 463]). The next year, in *Redrup v. New York* (386 U.S. 767), the Court said that material might be prosecuted if vendors aimed it at minors, infringed on an individual's right to privacy by marketing it so aggressively that the citizen could not escape exposure to it, or clearly pandered. The reasoning offered publishers an amber light. Driven out of Paris by French censorship and encouraged by the American Court decisions in favor of publishers, Maurice Girodias reestablished Olympia Press in New York in 1967 but found that his books were already being openly pirated by the California publishers Brandon House and Essex House, which were commissioning new erotic works as well. Angelo d'Arcangelo (*The Homosexual Handbook* [1969]), Harriet Daimler (*Darling* [1973]), Alexander Trocchi (*White Thighs* [1967]), Marco Vassi (*Pro Ball Groupie* [1974]), and Charles Bukowski (*Notes of a Dirty Old Man* [1969]), along with dozens of lesser novelists, could now publish their works legally in the United States. In 1968 Greenleaf Classics brought out the first megaseller gay porn novel, Richard Amory's *Song of the Loon*; by 1982, sales exceeded 2 million copies.[64] Attracted by such numbers, mainline publishers followed with Gael Greene (*Blue Skies, No Candy*, Morrow [1976]) and John Colleton (*Between Cloris and Amy*, Signet [1976]). In 1969, with the first issue of *Screw*, Al Goldstein and Jim Buckley created what was virtually a new American genre, the tabloid of political pornography, different from historical predecessors such as the *Police Gazette* and from contemporary competitors such as the *Berkeley Barb* not just in its partisanship but also in its constituency and its content.

Painters, sculptors, and photographers from schools ranging from pop to realism steadily appropriated materials and drew inspiration from themes and images previously thought pornographic. The same rebelliousness that drove antiwar protestors inflamed the brushes, chisels, and lenses of artists tired of older forms, anxious to exhaust storehouses of images, galvanized by the deviant and perverse. The roster of experimenters would eventually include the most famous names in modern American art: Alice Neel, Louise Bourgeois, Henriette Francis, Morton Kaish, Mel Ramos, Robert Andrew Parker, William de Kooning, Robert Broderson, Martha Edelhart, Andy Warhol, George Segal, Jim Dine, Claes Oldenberg, Larry Clark, Roy Lichtenstein, Duane Michaels, Philip Pearlstein, Lucas Samaras, Eric Fischl, Ronald Kitaj, Robert Mapplethorpe, Jeff Koons, Eleanor Antin, Lynda Benglis, Joan Semmel, Hannah Wilke, Cindy Sherman, Nan Goldin, and hundreds of the lesser-known. Some works became causes célèbres: the sodomitical posture of Larry Rivers' "Lampman Loves It" (1966), the ceramic vaginas of Judy Chicago's "The Dinner Party" (1979), the glowing fellatio of Tom Wesselman's "Great American Nude #87" (1966), the large penises of black males captured in photos by Robert Mapplethorpe (1980s), the candy-colored renditions of Jeff Koons in oral and anal intercourse with his wife, Ilona Staller (1991–1992)—all transgressed moral and aesthetic norms. Others dramatically altered American conceptions of what art should be and do: the witty penis constructions of Louise Bourgeois, the voluptuous sculptures of Mary Frank, and the gaudy porn-magazine collages of David Salle reeducated audiences. Artists reenvisioned human forms, exposed their frailties and powers, deconstructed their most intimate behavior—sometimes innocently, often shockingly—and hung these graphic explorations in galleries both expensive and tawdry. Boundaries of the permissible were the new starting lines for racing sensibilities. Ravished by boldness, Americans paid high prices; Wall Street took notice of the investment opportunities.[65] Phyllis and Eberhard Kronhausen, the Scandinavian sexologists, opened a museum of erotic art in San Francisco.

Candor in the 1960s led Congress in 1967 to impanel another subcommittee to investigate pornography, but President Johnson preempted it by appointing the Presidential Commission on Obscenity and Pornography. The Post Office, alarmed at poaching on territory it considered its own, persuaded Congress to hold pornography hearings in 1969 anyway. But the Post Office's hold on porn was loosening. That same year, the Supreme Court ruled in *Stanley v. Georgia* (394 U.S. 557) that Americans could legally possess obscenity for personal use. In part because Denmark decriminalized pornography in 1967, with few adverse effects (a finding challenged but never refuted), the President's Commission on Obscenity and Pornography in 1970 concluded that the United States could safely follow suit. Simply put, the commission recommended the decriminalization of sexual materials for adults (minors could and should remain protected). Even so, when the publisher of Greenleaf Classics, William Hamling, issued *The Illustrated Presidential Report of the Commission on Obscenity and Pornography* (San Diego: Greenleaf Classics, 1970), he was promptly sentenced to two years in prison.[66] The commission gathered the largest corpus of research ever assembled on pornography (available in the nine volumes of *Technical Reports*), but its real function, as with all such public spectacles, was to dramatize the sexual "revolution" that had swept across the United States.

Soon that revolution would stall; it would wane as the war in Vietnam came to an indecisive and unseemly close, lose its energy as flower children aged, and flutter out with the advent of AIDS. Well before then, feminists began to chafe at a male dominance visible, in part, in the sexual explicitness that had seemed to promise personal and social freedom. The 1960s had elevated sexual discourse to new levels of explicitness without fundamentally altering patterns of behavior, in particular, the discrimination against gays and lesbians or the subordination of women. Revisionist historians, taking their cue from Michel Foucault, who characterized seemingly immutable sexuality and gender categories as expressions of social power structures, trashed the theories of Wilhelm Reich, Paul Goodman, and Herbert Marcuse, all apostles of liberation through sexuality. After Kate Millett charged Henry Miller with sexism, other liberal icons began to topple. When Robin Morgan coined the phrase "pornography is the theory, rape the practice" in 1974, sex—and its representations—became ideological. Ten years later, Catharine MacKinnon, a law professor, and Andrea Dworkin, herself the writer of brutal sexual fiction, defined sex *as* violence, argued that pornography was the origin of male aggression against women, and crafted censorship legislation premised on the theory that pornography violated the civil rights of women and was therefore actionable. Cynics viewed these moves as efforts to reinvigorate a feminism already starting to rest on its laurels, but the culture seemed ready for renewed debate.

Feminist opposition coincided with conservative backlash, which took the form of condemnations of sex education in schools, efforts to remove candid books from libraries, fulminations against sex in television programming, and protests against sex-related businesses in neighborhoods. In a suitably theatrical gesture, President Nixon rejected the Johnson Commission's Report, though a majority of Americans, while disturbed by public displays of vulgarity, declined to share his hope for restricting what Americans saw, watched, or did in private. The conservative offense nonetheless chipped away at public indulgence. As legal scholar William Brigman has pointed out, *Stanley v. Georgia* was "the last outpost for liberal obscenity jurisprudence."[67] *Miller v. California* (413 U.S. 15 [1973]), however, written by Nixon-appointed chief justice Burger, redefined the prurient interest test for obscenity established in *Roth* as "whether the work depicts or describes, in a patently offensive way, sexual conduct specifically defined by state law," thus inviting states to prohibit certain conduct, which many did. Burger rejected the "utterly without redeeming social interest" test, thus further weakening the shield of protection. Georgia promptly suppressed the mainstream film *Carnal Knowledge*. Reversing the conviction in *Jenkins v. Georgia* (413 U.S. 496 [1973]), the flustered Court said that it had only "real" obscenity in mind. Burger's opinion in a companion case, *Paris Adult Theatre*

I v. Slaton (413 U.S. 49 [1973]), nevertheless asserted that the government might proscribe certain works "to protect the weak, the uninformed, the unsuspecting, and the gullible," thus reinvoking the principle of *Hicklin*. The rulings led armies of social scientists to compute local community standards. In *United States v. 12–1200 Foot Reels of Super 8mm Film* (413 U.S. 123 [1973]), the Burger Court mocked *Stanley* by ruling that a citizen did not have a First Amendment right to purchase obscenity (though he or she could own it). More significantly, the Supreme Court refused to overturn a conviction obtained in *Novick, Haim and Unique Specialities, Inc. v. U.S. District Court* (423 U.S. 911 [1975]), in which Louisiana prosecutors seized materials being shipped from California to New York. The decision opened the door to "forum shopping," the practice of prosecuting material that would be acceptable in a liberal community by holding the trial in a conservative community that would call the same material obscene. Federal prosecutors now need only go to, say, Alabama, order a magazine or movie from an urban center such as San Francisco, and secure a virtually predetermined conviction from a rural jury. National standards of morality, thanks to *Miller*, did not apply. Censors took heart.

THEATRICAL FORMS OF SEX

For many communities, the thorniest issue involved performance. As Robert Allen has noted, class differences drove a wedge between vaudeville revues and the vulgar shows that routinely and raucously poked fun at everything; from about 1870 on, he says, American culture "marginalized" working-class amusements like burlesque.[68] Gradually, the strip show separated itself from its burlesque origins, though in some venues it retained classic comic routines and durable performers. Gypsy Rose Lee, Tempest Storm, and Ann Corio held their prominence well into the 1950s. Unlike entertainers who would come after them, these headliners *teased*; that is, they removed their clothing to music slowly and did not remove it all; some, like Gypsy Rose Lee, never actually revealed their breasts, and still others wore pasties over nipples. By contrast, Sally Rand took pride in performing completely nude, never depilated her labia, and refused to use "stage white" (a heavy cosmetic) to mask her pubis.[69] At the Chicago World's Fair of 1933, Rand grossed $6,000 a week dancing behind two huge fans that never revealed the "naughty parts."[70] During the 1950s, less talented strippers moved into small bars and seedy storefronts in urban areas, where the owners accommodated themselves to local ordinances by paying fines for the occasional spasm of political morality. Jack Ruby's Theater Lounge in Dallas was a typical example.

While many Americans consider nude dancing an acceptable art form, others hold that it is, in the words of Marilyn Salutin, "hard-core pornography set to music."[71] During the 1960s and 1970s that characterization seemed apt. The casual nudity of the hippie movement led to nude beaches on both coasts, to seminude fashions, and to topless bars. In San Francisco, performers mingled with crowds dancing to rock 'n' roll, then gradually lowered the tops of their dresses. Soon the performers moved to cages hung above the dance floor and from there to stages or, like the silicon-enhanced Carol Doda, descended to the Condor Club's stage from an opening in the ceiling. Soon topless bars in major cities became bottomless as well. These, in turn, metamorphosed in the late 1970s into "stroke bars" or, when establishments were unable to secure a liquor license, "juice bars," where touching was permitted. In Times Square, Chinatown, the Lower East Side, and the West Side meatpacking district of New York City, for example, customers sat at bars on which nude performers gyrated, or, increasingly, the performers engaged in "lap dancing," that is, wriggling lasciviously while sitting in the customer's lap. At the Anvil on West 12th Street, under the old West Side Highway, women danced until midnight for heterosexual customers; at the Cinderella hour of twelve, homosexuals replaced the earlier patrons to watch nude male dancers. For a dollar the women permitted audience members to suck breasts and digitally penetrate vaginas; gay performers allowed incomplete fellatio.

During the same decades, "adult" arcades presented low-rent displays of flesh using walls of booths clustered around a central arena. Once the customer entered the booth, he dropped a quarter into a slot to raise a panel through which he could watch nude or copulating performers. In some arcades, he could, for additional money, touch the performer, obtain oral sex, or over a telephone in the booth ask for a particular scenario. Storefront theaters in Times Square presented intercourse on raised platforms. Veronica Hart, perhaps the most talented of porn actresses, began her career on a mattress in one of these rooms on 42d Street. Honeysuckle Divine could "smoke" a cigarette with her vagina or explosively expel Ping-Pong balls while she prattled about alleged affairs with Pierre Salinger, Everett Dirksen, and LBJ.[72] Monica Kennedy stripped while an assistant served champagne to the audience; she then chose several customers for intercourse with her onstage. Porn stars toured as strippers in major cities, a practice that continues today; the real money comes from dancing, and starring in the movies attracts customers along the dance circuit. On both coasts during the 1980s stars headlined live sex shows. The O'Farrell Theater in San Francisco, run by the filmmaking Mitchell Brothers (*Behind the Green Door* [1972]) showcased performers such as Marilyn Chambers, whose act climaxed with her being anally fisted by another woman, a performance recorded in the film *Never a Tender Moment* (1979). In an on-camera interview during the film, Chambers, after Linda Lovelace the best-known of American sexual stars, said that each performance was a personal milestone because it tested her physical and emotional limits.

Partly because it is so theatrical, sadomasochism flourished in scenarios conducted nightly at New York City's Chateau at 133 West 19th Street and in events sponsored by the Eulenspiegel Society, which floated from location to location; here members of the audience detailed fantasies for the performers to enact, sometimes joining in. Swing clubs, like Plato's Retreat at 230 West 74th

Street in the Ansonia Hotel, and Night Moves, which shared quarters with the Chateau, provided space for people of various orientations to enjoy orgiastic sex. Some rooms were set aside for private couplings, while the less inhibited could opt for sex in swimming pools or join daisy chains on mattresses in larger halls, but voyeurism was the main ingredient. In 1979 Club Hedonism rented Roseland, the fabled dance ballroom on 52d, for "the World's Biggest Toga Party." The Ansonia 73 Baths, also located in the Ansonia Hotel, catered to homosexuals; it became chic when the rising Bette Midler began singing there between the sex sessions. Andy Warhol and Robert Mapplethorpe frequented gay establishments like the Toilet, where tastes ran to S/M, coprophilia, and urolagnia. Similarly, gay movie houses in Times Square and along the Hudson River waterfront and, to a lesser extent, in other large cities featured nude dancers who would engage in oral-genital sex with patrons between and during the film showings. Patrons of lesbian bars in New York and California cities engaged in less explicit displays.[73] The onset of AIDS diminished open performances considerably in the 1990s, although "safe sex" still takes place in swing clubs in major cities.[74] The most notorious performance club at this writing is the Vault in Manhattan.[75]

Nude dancing—without the explicit excesses of the 1970s and 1980s—is still a significant form of entertainment in America, despite its being a largely unsung profession. Venues range from biker conventions, which almost always include "bikerchick" strip shows (photos of which fill biker magazines); carnivals, where nude dancing animates sideshows; elegant cabarets in New York, Houston, and Atlanta, which attract couples; lesbian bars like Baybrick's in San Francisco, which cater to gender-specific audiences; and the Chippendale franchises in metropolitan areas that offer male strippers for female audiences. Those who attend the latter shows notice that the female patrons respond most enthusiastically when the male strippers imitate female ecdysiasts.

In 1991, according to D. Keith Mano, 62,000 women were dancing topless in the United States, and some 750,000 had been dancers at one time or another. The estimated annual income, including tips given to performers, approached $2 billion.[76] By 1998 the number had risen to 250,000 dancers employed in some 2,500 clubs.[77] Comparable figures for male dancers, either those working in Chippendale-style clubs or in gay bars, or for women appearing in lesbian hangouts are unavailable. Fashion magazines like *Allure* point out that stripping is once again respectable for all genders. Writers, Wall Streeters, Soho artists, and television personalities jostle the construction workers in the audiences in Billy's Topless (Sixth Avenue and 24th Street in New York City), the most venerable bar in the United States, whose owner, Milton Anthony, has probably nurtured the careers of more female strippers than Billy Rose. Since Tina Brown became editor of the staid *New Yorker* in 1992, that magazine has occasionally reviewed performances by male and female strippers in Manhattan clubs for yuppies. In an age of heavy ideological Puritanism and AIDS-generated fear of actual sex, Americans apparently feel an urgent need to study each other's bodies unadorned, despite the fulminations of feminists and fundamentalists. Perhaps the best indicator of nude dancing's cultural importance is the spectacle—an antiporn performance—of the justices of the Supreme Court writing learned opinions on the pasties that the state of Indiana might place upon the nipples of topless dancers (*Barnes v. Glen Theatre* [111 S. Ct. 2456 (1991)]).

In recent decades, moreover, American *performance artists*—drawing on older European examples—have established serious theatrical forms based on explicit revelation. According to RoseLee Goldberg, performance art is "a permissive, open-ended medium with endless variables, executed by artists impatient with the limitations of more established artforms, and determined to take their art directly to the public."[78] To a degree, performance art is a reaction against traditional proscenium drama. From the 1920s to the 1950s, the legitimate theater, especially in New York, experimented with sexual themes, usually with scandalous results. In the late 1920s, for example, Comstockers raided Mae West's *The Drag*, a show devoted to female impersonators, her productions of *Sex* and *The Virgin Man*, both witty commentaries on mores, and Edouard Bourdet's *The Captive*, a drama with a lesbian theme.[79] The publisher Horace Liveright bought the rights to the latter in order to fight efforts at censorship. Prosecutions of plays that outraged timid sensibilities continued sporadically for decades.

Considered against that background, performance art was not so much an underground theater as an alternative medium. Artists fleeing the conflicts in Europe during the 1930s and 1940s took refuge in Black Mountain College in North Carolina and the New School in New York City, where they introduced Americans to strains of futurism, surrealism, and dadaism, all of which had theatrical components. Jim Dine, Allan Kaprow, John Cage, and Merce Cunningham began to generate the sort of inchoate stagings (like the European Fluxus events) that would become known as *happenings*, a form that suited the tastes of an emerging counterculture. In New York, Yoko Ono, Robert Morris, and Nam June Paik wove sexual scenes and images into their presentations. These involved swirls of music, scenes of body sculpture juxtaposed with artifacts, action painting, multimedia images, and live nude dance. Nakedness served to disorient audiences, to undercut convention. The Judson Memorial Church on Washington Square became a center for artistic experimentation. There Carolee Schneemann staged her "flesh celebration," *Meat Joy* (1964), a work featuring writhing, naked human bodies covered with blood from animal carcasses. Members of the Judson Dance Troupe occasionally used nudity as a means of locating bodies in cultural space; Yvonne Rainer appeared nude with Robert Morris in one of his compositions (1965). In 1967 Ann Halprin's dance troupe performed naked at Hunter College in "Parades and Changes," one of the monuments of modern dance. Since then, serious dancers have frequently performed nude or seminude: Molissa Fenley's bare-breasted rendition of Ravel's *Bolero* delighted Lincoln Center audiences, for example, and the athletic nudity of the Pilobolus dance troupe continues to awe.

Also in 1967 Charles Ludlam founded the Theater of the Ridiculous, while Tom O'Horgan staged *Hair, Futz,* and *Tom Paine,* all of which featured nudity. Performance artist Yayoi Kusama staged nude-ins at the Statue of Liberty, Central Park, and Wall Street; Charlotte Moorman played a cello topless at Town Hall (1968) in New York City; Kenneth Tynan opened *Oh! Calcutta!* (1969); Richard Schechner mounted *Dionysus in 69* (1968); Julian Beck and Judith Malina's Living Theatre offered *Paradise Now* (1970); audiences in other major cities attended traveling versions of similar events. Invited onstage, audiences stripped along with performers and sometimes behaved dangerously. After being raped onstage by a member of the audience during a performance of *Paradise Now,* Malina observed, "If we're going to be brave, we're going to be misunderstood."[80] Nudity and explicit dialogue energized the works of playwrights such as Robert Wilson (*The Life and Times of Sigmund Freud* [1969]) and Richard Foreman (*Birth of the Poet* [1985]).

While nudity made its way to commercial stages, for a time making naked bodies on Broadway almost commonplace, performance artists remained more comfortable in small settings and storefronts or in theaters devoted to the avant-garde. Women performers in particular found in nudity a way to reexplore the landscape of the body but also to examine topics like child abuse, the exploitation of women, homophobia, sexism, racism, abortion, and a host of other concerns. In such contexts, the images and devices assert the classic function of pornography to *subvert,* to *satirize,* to *expose*—or, as current jargon would have it, to *deconstruct*—sexual and gender assumptions of the established social and political order. When it employs sexual representations, performance art confronts, shocks, and sometimes arouses, forcing reexamination of sexual anxieties, gender roles, the place of sexuality in the state, and the nature of eroticism itself.

Significant artists in this vein were the fearless Hannah Wilke (*Super-T-Art,* 1974), Colette (*Nude Environments,* 1975), Carolee Schneemann (*Interior Scroll,* 1975, in which the performer extracted a rolled-up text from her vagina), Karen Finley (*I Like the Dwarf on the Table When I Give Him Head,* 1983, and *Yams Up My Granny's Ass,* 1986, during which Finley crammed yams between her buttocks), and Robbie McCauley, whose protest against female servitude stood her naked on an auction block. The painfulness of such words, gestures, and graphic sexual representations attested to intellectual intent. Researchers need only page through *High Performance,* the magazine that records these events, to get a sense of just how prolific they are. Once controversial artists gained a reputation for seriousness, they applied for grants; the practice triggered continuing criticism from conservatives such as Senator Jesse Helms. In the early 1990s Helms led campaigns to restrict the funding that the National Endowment for the Arts could offer artists like Finley and Holly Hughes and to force artists receiving funding to sign a pledge not to include obscenity in their work (a stipulation declared unconstitutional). Some commentators thought that the actual target of attacks on the National Endowment was "not obscenity but dread of the nameless 'Other' "[81] and that fear of sex had supplanted the waning fear of communism as a strategy for shoring up conservative identity.

The whole point of such performances is nevertheless their shock. Many Americans consider the representations obscene, too strong, or just plain vulgar, and skeptics point out that the artists are sometimes too young and attractive to be convincing in their announced intention of exploding standards of beauty, age, and gender. Some performers reject characterizations of their work as erotic, but others, persuaded that sexuality is inextricably tied to pornographic representation, deliberately draw attention to parallels. Whatever else they convey, performance artists remind us that the body is a medium, not merely a text, not merely a surface inscripted by culture, but a means of communicating, one that might escape the prison of language. Because sex is medium and message, channel and content, sex workers can aspire to artistic status.

For example, Annie Sprinkle, doyenne of pornographic movie stars turned performance artist, bounces her breasts in a "bosom ballet," invites audiences to inspect her cervix, and generally emphasizes the ambiguous messages of pornographic representation. Other porn stars have also graduated from films to performance. The *Village Voice* regularly chronicles their events, as do small papers in other cities. In the 6 August 1991 issue of the *Voice*, "La Dolce Musto," the column by Michael Musto, comments on performers at Limelight's Disco 2000 in New York City: people who drink their own urine, a dancing amputee, music groups like Barney Rubble and the Cunt Stubble, Lady Hennessy Brown, who shoots milk from her breasts, and other performers, Musto says, who make Karen Finley look "like the Carpenters" (48). In 1989 one theater dramatized Michel Foucault's *The History of Sexuality*, and another staged *Excerpts from the Attorney General's Report on Pornography* in efforts to establish a drama of contemporary sexual discourse. Foucault's work will doubtless come full circle when *The History of Sexuality* becomes a musical, which would be no more odd than basing *Evita* on Peron's political career; given Foucault's fondness for kinky sex, his life and ideas would probably stage well, especially if mounted by Andrew Lloyd Webber. The screeds of Attorney General Meese, on the other hand, would appear to offer greater theatrical possibilities. Soon after its report, one of the members of the Meese Commission, Father Bruce Ritter, was rusticated by the Catholic Church because of reports that he had molested children; another, Charles Keating, was sent to prison for defrauding investors in Lincoln National; and Meese himself left office under a cloud of accusations. Contrary to legend, there is no more evidence that public opposition to pornography masks hypocrisy than evidence that pornography itself has deleterious effects; both conclusions are entirely anecdotal. Even so, the large number of scandals attached to the Meese Commission made for humor.

The Attorney General's Commission of 1986 was convened by the conservative Meese to reinvigorate censorship. Meese was encouraged by antiporn feminist efforts to establish censorship in Minneapolis and Indianapolis. In 1984 the Minneapolis City Council passed an ordinance written by Catharine

MacKinnon and Andrea Dworkin holding that pornography (broadly defined) violated the civil rights of women; Mayor Fraser vetoed it. Radical feminists in Indianapolis then wrote a similar ordinance, which was adopted. Mainstream feminists mobilized anticensorship task forces to counter the zealots and, joined by publishers and book dealers, pushed for a quick Court decision. In 1985 federal judge Sarah Evans Barker of the Seventh District Court ruled that the Indianapolis ordinance violated the First Amendment and was upheld in 1986 when the Supreme Court refused to hear further argument (*Hudnut v. American Booksellers*, 475 U.S. 1001). Meese went ahead anyway. A parade of antiporn feminists, conservatives, and religious groups testified on the dangers of pornography. The members of the commission, realizing that it was too late to suppress written works, endorsed Meese's belief that pornography generated by newer technologies had once again put the nation's morality at risk. The commission dutifully condemned visual images in general and telephone, computer, and videotaped pornography in particular. The report would thus seem to adhere to a larger syndrome, according to which Americans find older technologies (like books) acceptable but newer ones (like computers) disquieting.

MOTION PICTURES TRANSFORM SEXUAL EXPRESSION

It is hard to think of a technology more radical than the printing press, which robbed the upper classes of power by spreading knowledge and later informed the masses of sexual matters, though these effects became apparent only after the fact. The dangers of a novel communications medium like the motion picture, however, were apparent from the start: the new medium seemed cheap and vulgar, intent on recycling folklore from lower strata, just as, for our generation, the discourse of the Internet recapitulates the folkways of the past and present. The more demotic the new medium, the more obvious is the recycling of low humor, crude stories, and titillating images, all of which are given new life by media able to reproduce them.

As Erwin Panofsky has noted, sexual folklore created the movies.[82] However one defines pornography, which depends chiefly on where one stands at the intersections of ideologies, there is no question that sex and celluloid have been linked from the beginning. The first commercial exhibition of Edison's projector in 1896 took place in a former bawdy house, the Koster and Bial Music Hall on 34th Street in New York City. Major pioneers—Edison, Méliès, Pathé—all produced filmstrips of questionable taste until about 1910—and did so, we might add, during a period when audiences cheerfully watched anything that moved on a screen and hardly needed to be attracted by suggestiveness. We sometimes assume that the many ministers, politicians, and social critics to attack peep shows, nickelodeons, and storefront theaters as dens of vice were merely Puritans afraid that audiences were having a good time. It is virtually impossible, however, to overstate the vulgar origins of the cinema. The early movie industry was often marginally criminal, from the fly-by-night production companies, shady investors, and pirates who stole and copied the reels of others, to the sleazy tactics of the first film exchanges to spring up in New York and Chicago. The American movie industry spent the first three decades of this century cleansing itself of seedy beginnings in order to elevate itself to the status of Art.

The first erotic movies in America appeared soon after the appearance of the motion picture camera. The inventor of the camera, Edison's assistant W.K.L. Dickson, shot a fetish film, *What the Bootblack Saw*, in 1896; what the bootblack saw were the pretty feet, high-laced boots, and underskirts of the women on his stand. Edison's company shot double-entendre titles like *How Bridget Served the Salad Undressed* (1898)—Bridget neglected to put mayonnaise on the lettuce—and *Love in a Hammock* (1898)—in which a man climbs into a lawn swing with a young lady, only to fall out each time. Edison also scandalized many Americans with *The Kiss* (1896), a long shot of two performers osculating, and with modestly risqué dance films. Traditional artists smiled at the crass new technology. In "Fun One Cent," a 1904 etching by Ash Can painter John Sloan, giggling women jostle one another to peer through peep-show cabinets lining the sidewalk at Fourteenth Street and Third Avenue in New York. The titles above the cabinets carry messages such as "Girls in Their Night Gowns! Spicy!"[83] Censorship boards flourished in various cities, beginning with New York in 1907. Large-scale censorship loomed in 1915, just as Hollywood was becoming the center of legitimate film production, when the Supreme Court, in a case involving D. W. Griffith's *Birth of a Nation* (the most heavily censored movie of all time), ruled that the cinema was a form of spectacle (like circuses or carnivals) and therefore was not protected by the First Amendment (*Mutual Film Corporation v. Industrial Commission of Ohio* [236 U.S. 230]).

Censoring of mainstream movies led in 1922 to the establishment of the Motion Picture Producers and Distributors of America (MPPDA), commonly called Hays Office, which regulated the industry through a mix of common sense and absurd directives (even married couples had to sleep in separate beds onscreen). Still fearful of financially ruinous prosecution or loss of audience through the efforts of censorship groups like the Legion of Decency, Hollywood adopted a stronger Production Code in 1934, an industry self-policing policy that denied to directors any degree of sexual explicitness. The Production Code did, however, forestall the enactment of federal censorship laws aimed at films and often circumvented state ordinances as well. The code remained in force until the 1950s, when the challenge of television led a motion picture industry desperate to recapture audiences to give moviegoers more sex. Courts cooperated during that decade by bestowing upon film the once-denied First Amendment protections given other media. Although there were several such decisions, involving films such as *The Moon Is Blue*, the most far-reaching was the 1957 New York State Court of Appeals ruling that the 1955 nudist "documentary" *Garden of Eden* (in which little pubic hair was visible) was not obscene because depictions of the human body in and of themselves were not obscene.

For so long as they endured, however, prohibitions against nudity and sexual candor in the legitimate industry encouraged violence as a substitute, the phenomenon documented by Gershon Legman in *Love and Death*. This tendency was pronounced in biblical epics, whose themes allowed Cecil B. DeMille and his imitators to shoot scenes of torture sanctioned by religious tradition. Violence overflowed into other melodramas, where embraces would end in the aggressively phallic image of a locomotive's penetrating a tunnel, or where scenes of death and destruction became satisfying ends in themselves. Outside Hollywood, beginning in the 1920s, striptease films featuring burlesque queens circulated freely in amusement parks, in part because the ladies always retained their G-strings, in part because the carnival setting—the source of film's disfranchisement in *Mutual v. Ohio*—actually provided a haven. By the mid-1930s, however, burlesque had been driven off the stages of America, and the strip films were similarly proscribed. As early—or late—as 1929, Wolcott Gibbs complained in the *New Yorker* that the spicy fare of the peep-show cabinets at the penny arcades along Sixth Avenue was dull in the extreme. Neither the American nor the European ladies who starred in these loops stripped further than "winter-weight underwear."[84] They were replaced by fetish films that were generally tolerated (though not in theaters), provided that no nipples, labia, or penises were visible. Irving Klaw and his sister Paula turned out a series of female boxing movies and reels in which women ankled around in rubber or leather garments or tied each other up in ropes with very large knots.

The back lots of legitimate, but minor, studios developed exploitation films, which promised, but did not deliver, sexual frankness. They began with "exposés" of the white slave traffic in 1913 and reached an apotheosis in the 1930s and 1940s, when a group of producer-distributors known as the "Forty Thieves" fed drive-in movies a stream of lurid "educational" films on the subjects of venereal disease, birth, premarital sex, interracial marriage, and contraception. The *Garden of Eden* decision triggered several dozen nudies, usually dopey scenarios in which topless women bounced their way through volleyball or sunbathed in improbable places. In 1959 appeared *The Immoral Mr. Teas*, the first film by Russ Meyer, the doyen of soft-core directors. Mr. Teas acquires a pair of glasses that enable him to see through the clothes of the women he meets; more important, the audience can see, too. Suddenly, breasts seemed to become primary sex organs in American culture, a cachet they would retain at least until 1970, when *Penthouse* magazine relocated male desire to a site farther south. The penis, however, retained its reticence. Despite Freud's many references to penis envy, the penis was not the fetish that the breast was, perhaps because, as some feminists hold, the penis could retain its authority in a patriarchal culture only by remaining invisible; it is only now, thanks to Lacanian psychology and theories of gender hegemony, that the phallus has been erected to full fetishistic status.

Meyer and other producers like David F. Friedman, as if to borrow a page from Gershon Legman's thesis, steadily moved toward the blending of nudity and violence. Friedman shot *Blood Feast* in 1963 and followed it with other "roughies," as did Meyer and a few dozen others. They did not wish to overstep lines by depicting actual intercourse, so they symbolized it with brutality, a weird and far-reaching displacement that persists. When censors accepted this stratagem, hundreds of roughies poured from sleazy studios. Roughies are now a virtual genre, having spawned "slasher" films like *The Texas Chain Saw Murders* and *Halloween* and its clones, which are to be distinguished from the still occasionally made soft-core nudie and the violence-resistant hard-core movie.

Competition from foreign studios also forced Hollywood toward greater explicitness. In the late 1950s and early 1960s, films with mature themes from abroad, such as *The Cousins* (France, 1959), *La Dolce Vita* (Italy, 1959), *The Silence* (Sweden, 1963), *Persona* (Sweden, *1966*), and *I Am Curious (Yellow)* (Sweden, 1967), were cleared for showing here. Arguments on their behalf cited artistic merit. In the majority opinion for the Supreme Court in *Jacobellis v. Ohio* (378 U.S. 184), Justice Brennan wrote in 1964 that a national, rather than a local, standard of obscenity must be applied to films like *Les Amants*, a French film prosecuted in Ohio. Chief Justice Warren, dissenting, protested that local standards must apply, and his view eventually prevailed. The decision also occasioned Justice Potter Stewart's observation about obscenity, "I know it when I see it," a statement often taken ironically because of Stewart's failing eyesight.

With the Production Code eviscerated by directors' refusal to follow it, major studios in 1945 reorganized the MPPDA into the Motion Picture Producers' Association (MPPA). In 1966, with Jack Valenti as head, the MPPA issued a new PG, R, and X rating system to ease the transition to greater candor. Over the years it adjusted these categories; in 1984, for instance, the MPPA added a PG-13 (Parental Guidance) rating. By 1990, a once-again reorganized Motion Picture Association of America (MPAA) was forced to replace the "X" rating with "NC-17" (No Children). The reason was that the MPPA had not trademarked the "X," which was then appropriated by adult moviemakers to signify strong content in their ads. The intent of the NC-17 designation was to permit serious treatment of sexuality without burdening a film with the onus of an "X," since many newspapers would not carry advertising for movies bearing the older label.

Similar in their profession of serious intent were American avant-garde filmmakers; Brakhage's *Lovemaking* (1968), Smith's *Flaming Creatures* (1963), Anger's *Scorpio Rising* (1964), and Warhol's *Blow Job* (1963), shown in storefront theaters in major cities, widened the arena of the permissible. By the 1970s, nudity was commonplace in Hollywood films, as was serious treatment of sexual themes. The presence of Marlon Brando gave legitimacy to Bertolucci's *Last Tango in Paris* (1972), as did that of Jane Fonda to *Coming Home* (1978), to mention just two films of explicit degree. Nevertheless, legitimate films (graphic or merely candid), soft-core movies (rough or otherwise), and nudies (simpleminded or just plain stupid) remain separated by an enormous distance from the hard-core pornographic film.

The hard-core or stag film developed independently of the legitimate cinema and quite consciously as an alternative to it. The producer of such films exhibited them only to closed groups without any justification of socially redeeming importance. The history of stag films for the first six decades is largely anonymous. The first short of a totally nude female probably appeared in America in 1900, slightly later than on the Continent. The first filmed act of intercourse was probably shot in France, but others appeared in Vienna (at least by 1907) and Argentina (by 1910), where the American playwright Eugene O'Neill actually worked for a German expatriate pornographer in Buenos Aires. The earliest surviving American hard-core reel is *A Free Ride* (aka *A Grass Sandwich*), involving a man, two women, and a Model-T Ford; it dates from 1915 and was probably shot in New Jersey. That such films appeared earlier, however, is evident from newspaper accounts of seizures by police in 1912.[85] Only a few hard-core reels, like *The Casting Couch* (1920), a lampoon of Mack Sennett, the inventor (according to Kenneth Anger's *Hollywood Babylon*) of the practice of requiring actresses to sleep with the producer before getting the part, were actually shot in Hollywood. By the late 1920s American amateurs were turning out more stags than those of any other nationality and continued to do so until the 1950s, when they were outpaced by the English; during the 1960s, the Scandinavians pulled ahead, only to drop behind in the 1970s as the Danes and the Swedes tired of the stuff. America now produces more hard-core videotapes than all other nations combined (its only significant competitors are Germany, France, and Hungary, in that order) and exports them all over the world.

Shot at first on 35mm film stock, then 16mm, the hard-core films circulated clandestinely; police seized them mostly by accident. It was a decidedly demotic form, drawing heavily on traditional folklore, deliberately crude and anachronistic; before 1965, only five were shot in sound, only four in color.[86] By and large, they were exhibited by their makers, who hired themselves, their projectors, and their reels out to fraternities, men's clubs, and American Legion posts. These gatherings were called "smokers" or "stag parties," and the films became known as stags. Because of their illegality and the fact that they were distributed by hand (few were exhibited more than 100 miles from where they were made), the producers made little money from them. In almost every sense, they were artifacts of popular male culture. Although some homosexual films were made in the 1920s and three or four per decade thereafter, the audience for stags was heterosexual. Because viewers responded uncomfortably to gay behavior, producers simply did not include homosexual intercourse. Nor did they include violence, sadomasochistic activity, coprophagia, or underage performers, whose presence distressed the predominantly middle-class, white, male audiences.[87] Garden-variety sex, its depiction on-screen a violation of taboo, was quite enough to shock and to satisfy. The first genuine sadomasochistic film, *Song of the Lash*, an import from Germany, did not appear in America until 1956. Very occasionally, underage girls who looked older, like the sixteen-year-old Juanita Slusher (aka Candy Barr) featured in *Smart Alec* (1951/1952), made an appearance, but the first film (*The Sexy Sexteens*) to star obvious minors *as* minors was not shot in America until the mid-1960s.

Technology altered not so much the form as the content. Low prices for the 8mm film projector meant that individuals could watch films at home rather than in the Legion Hall, and soon producers were turning out multiple copies in narrow format. Youthful rebellion and the liberalized sexual climate of the 1960s, paced by a series of tolerant Court decisions (in one of these, Justice Brennan lamented that it was silly for the Supreme Court to agonize over whether a penis was erect or semierect[88]), led to an explosion in the manufacture of 8mm hard-core films. More significantly, this new film format made it possible to produce for specialized audiences—those who *did* want to watch fellatio or anal intercourse or simply naked people with freckles and red hair. Soon films incorporated a gamut of fetishes, some of which apparently were offered just to see if anybody liked them.

The 8mm reel coexisted briefly with the feature-length theatrical film. The first hard-core feature to be shown publicly in the United States was an untitled, hour-long, 16mm reel exhibited for three days at the Avon Theater in New York City in 1968; it was not prosecuted, nor were subsequent forays into actual intercourse. The first feature to be nationally distributed was Bill Osco's *Mona* (1970). "Documentaries" like *Sexual Freedom in Denmark* (1970), under the guise of including comment of "socially redeeming importance," made theaters safe for pornography, as did Alex de Renzy's *A History of the Blue Movie* (1970). The market quickly bifurcated into heterosexual and homosexual types, the latter pioneered by Wakefield Poole's *Boys in the Sand* (1972). In 1972 two films, *Deep Throat* and *Behind the Green Door*, attracted enormous audiences. To date, *Deep Throat*, made for around $25,000, has earned through exhibition and videotape copies well over $100 million (though exact figures are impossible to ascertain), not much (even adjusting for inflation) when one considers that a mainstream blockbuster like *Men in Black* (1997) can garner that on the first *weekend*. The high point of hard-core movie production was 1973–1975, when American 35mm features numbered over 100 per year, and 8mm shorts rose to about 500 annually. By the late 1970s, videocassettes began to render 8mm films obsolete. Now virtually all pornographic scenarios are shot on videotape; theatrical exhibition is almost a thing of the past.

Annual videotape production now vastly exceeds film production in the mid-1970s though some "new" titles are merely older films transferred onto cassette. While thus far hard-core has made only modest inroads into legitimate film (e.g., Catherine Breillat's *Romance* [1999]), Bob Guccione did insert some hard-core scenes into his multimillion-dollar *Caligula* (1979), and various Hollywood features (Paul Schrader's *Hardcore* or Brian De Palma's *Dressed to Kill*) have used the pornographic scene as setting. A few ambitious hard-core directors have tried to include serious comment, as in Chuck Vincent's *Roommates* (1982), but most have been content merely to address heterosexual or homosexual fantasies in return for modest profits. The Adult Film Association holds annual ceremonies modeled on the Academy Awards to recognize directors and performers. Gerard Damiano, who made his reputation with *Deep Throat* and other features, has given way to Svetlana (*Miami Spice* [1987]) and Robert McCallum (*Doll Face* [1986]) and to former actors turned directors like John Leslie (*Fresh Meat* [1995]) and John Stagliano (the *Buttman* series [1987–]). At least two generations of stars have appeared among the more than 10,000 Americans who have appeared in hard-core formats: John Holmes is dead of AIDS, Tina Russell of drugs, and Savannah of suicide while Annette Haven, Marc Stevens, and Sharon Mitchell have retired. They have been replaced, of course, by many others; the eagerness with which newcomers join the profession seems undiminished by the threat of AIDS. Given the economic decline of the middle class since the 1970s, the medium attracts the underemployed. Stars make a lot of money and are pampered; the rest experience working conditions ranging from the squalid and dingy, to the mechanical routines of any business, and they are paid accordingly.

Large numbers of fans follow many hard-core performers, their popularity boosted by afternoon television show appearances, striptease tours (often their primary careers), trading cards carrying their images, and product endorsements—all enterprises borrowed from mainstream entertainment. Even so, no American porn stars have achieved the celebrity of Italian actresses Ilona Staller, known as Cicciolina ("Cuddles"), who was elected to Parliament and married American pop artist Jeff Koons, and Moana Pozzi, who died in 1994 of cancer at thirty-three and who has been virtually beatified by her fans. American notoriety seems more tawdry, as in the case of John Bobbitt, who appeared in a hard-core movie in 1994 to prove that his penis still worked after his abused wife cut it off. Another reason may be the culturally parodic nature of the American porn genre. The most cursory glance at the adult section of a video rental shop will find titles such as *Real Men Eat Keisha* (1988), *Hanna Does Her Sisters* (1986), *On Golden Blond* (1984), and *Teenage Ninja Sluts from Hell* (1989); *The Addams Family* (1991) had been out only a month when *The Anus Family* ripped it off. Some of the humor is disarming: it is hard to stay angry at a videotape entitled *Topless Brain Surgeons* (1996). In 1999 the adult industry churned out just over 10,000 porn videos.

Pornographic videocassettes quite literally built the VCR industry. Sales and rentals of adult tapes accounted for more than 50 percent of the market until the early 1980s, when Americans began to watch legitimate films in the new format. Porn tapes now account for less than 25 percent of the American market, though the number of women customers has risen dramatically. Because women tend to rent tapes for an evening's viewing with a mate, they choose erotic cassettes that appeal to both. That fact has made producers more sensitive to the "couples" market and has encouraged women—such as Candida Royalle, whose *Femme* series is geared to women viewers—to produce and direct. Royalle, Chris Cassidy, and other directors aim at a women-centered erotica to counter the truism that most porn films "aren't about women having a good time; they're about women working hard to give men a good time."[89] Veteran actress Veronica Hart has recently directed 50-year-old stalwarts, such as Marilyn Chambers in *Still Insatiable* (VCA, 1999) and Ginger Lynn in *Torn* (VCA, 1999).

Magazines (*Blue Movie Exposé, Adult Film Review*) featuring interviews and photos of hard-core actors and actresses allow fans to see more of them, in much the same way that magazines like *Afternoon TV* tell audiences for soap operas more about the careers and private lives of their favorites. Soap operas, routinely called pornography for women, began to attract male viewers when porn stars like Wade Nichols and Kristin De Bell moved from hard core to shows like *The Edge of Night* and *General Hospital*. The importance of these developments should not go unnoticed; males seem to want to share fantasies with women. At the very least, that should make possible movement toward less gender-specific eroticism and greater respect for each other's erotic needs. Homosexual producers capture only a fraction of the heterosexual home audience but otherwise aim at a significant gay market. Possibly because the audience for authentic (as opposed to male fantasies about lesbians) lesbian films and videocassettes is only now emerging, few lesbian examples have appeared. Among the finest, however, are those by Constance Beeson and Juliet Bashore.

Antagonism lingering from the Meese debacle infected conservative legislators angered at growing mainstream acceptance of sexual expression. The Child Protection and Obscenity Enforcement Act of 1988, which grew out of the Meese Commission's recommendations that the Justice Department harass and intimidate everyone who produced or distributed sexual materials, established record-keeping provisions for visual depictions of sexual conduct. Ostensibly aimed at protecting children, the provisions were transparently aimed at any kind of sexual expression. These were draconian: everyone who handled such visual depictions had to independently secure and maintain records on every performer, not merely those who seemed young, but even those clearly past their fifties. A coalition of organizations including the American Library Association and various artists' groups challenged the requirement (*American Library Association v. Thornburgh*, 713 F. Supp. 469 [1989]) on the grounds that such requirements would throttle visual production of any kind. A librarian, for example, would have been required to verify the age, and keep a birth certificate on file, for every performer in, say, Bertolucci's *Last Tango in Paris*, or every skimpily-clad model in *Cosmopolitan*, before those items could be checked out by anyone. A Federal District Court Judge in Washington enjoined the law in 1989, and Congress in 1990 altered the requirement while the case was on appeal to apply only to those involved in the actual hiring and supervision of performers, and to be applicable only to "lascivious" productions. In 1992, a justice questioned the record-keeping requirement (he said that if the act applied only to underage—rather than people of all ages—it would be constitutional) but left its major provisions intact.[90] Further challenges are unlikely, and producers of x-rated films carefully keep proofs of age under section 2257 (h)(1) of the law.

In 1991, Senators Dole and McConnell sponsored the Pornography Victims Compensation Act (S. 472). The bill's classifications of "sexually explicit" and "sexually explicit and violent" material were so vague as to threaten a great many films, television programs, records, books, newspapers, and magazines. Moreover, the bill would have encouraged sex crime victims to sue for damages if the attacker was provoked *after* (not necessarily as a result of) reading or viewing obscene material or child pornography. The President of the American Booksellers Association said that the bill "would produce the most pervasive censorship the U.S. has ever experienced."[91] The largest anticensorship coalition ever formed in the United States quickly assembled: the Alliance of Motion Picture & Television Producers, the Association of Independent Television Stations, the Motion Picture Association of America, the National Association of Theater Owners, the National Association of Video Distributors, the National Cable Television Association, the Writers Guild of America, and various other print and library organizations. The bill died before a vote.[92]

New and massive battle lines reformed when the bill was resurrected in the Senate in 1992 (S. 982), suggesting that sexual expression had taken on a significance never before apparent in the republic. Against conservative, fundamentalist, and antiporn feminist groups, liberals now had the economic interests of media producers and distributors on their side. The latter saw a threat to intellectual property rights of all kinds in a global media market.[93] Despite the same opposition as before, many senators sensed that support for the bill offered political benefit and insisted that, vague language notwithstanding, a plantiff could sue for damages only if he or she could *prove* that an attacker was provoked by viewing or reading material thought to be pornographic or obscene.[94] Alarmed sociologists Daniel Linz and Edward Donnerstein, whose work was cited as demonstrating a causal connection between pornography and aggression, complained that their work provided no evidence for the bill's assumption that sexual materials lead to rape and murder.[95] Novelist John Irving attacked the bill as a recrudescence of virulent, irrational, antitechnological Puritanism.[96] So did the performance artist Teller, who asserted that movies cannot be held responsible for depicting life; as he put it, "We might as well punish Agatha Christie for murder and John Le Carré for espionage."[97] The slipperiness of the language and the opposition of artists and attorneys again doomed the bill.

Opponents also pointed out that warriors against obscenity already possessed weapons in abundance. In 1984 prosecutors were given the authority to apply RICO (Racketeer Influenced and Corrupt Organizations [Act]) legislation to those indicted for obscenity, which allowed authorities to seize all the assets of the defendants and to confiscate those assets on conviction. If even one item were declared obscene, then the defendants forfeited all their property, even if those assets were not acquired through traffic in obscenity. That provision, along with forum-shopping to obtain convictions, was upheld by the Supreme Court in *Pryba v. United States* (900 F.2d 748 [1990]). Acting on the recommendation of the Meese Commission, the Justice Department created an Obscenity Task Force designed to drive pornographers into bankruptcy. The vigilantes of the task force were rebuked by a federal judge in 1990 for trampling on the First Amendment rights of defendants but continued to obtain convictions with a zeal unmatched since Comstock.

INDECENCY IN ELECTRONIC MEDIA

Congress has been more successful in cowing broadcasters. Although a Marconi shot erotic photographs that circulated for years in postcard form, his relative Guglielmo Marconi, the inventor of radio, apparently never envisioned the medium's being used to represent sensuality. In any case, questions of external censorship of sexual candor on radio in the United States rarely arose during the medium's formative years. Authorities were far more concerned with matters like fraud, libel, editorializing, political fairness, transmission power levels, and ideology. Moreover, the portfolio of the National Association of Broadcasters (NAB), founded in 1923 primarily to cheapen music-licensing fees, expanded to include broadcast standards with provisions similar to those of the Motion Picture Code. Before they were declared unconstitutional, these provisions defined acceptable program matter, the limits of dramatic license, and forbidden forms of expression. The NAB's member stations "self-policed" themselves by adhering to the standards; network censors cleared scripts before airtime. Every once in a while, someone would complain: in 1937, when Mae West appeared on the *Chase and Sanborn Hour*, congressmen objected on the grounds that she was an "immoral" person, not for anything she said on the air. Much later, in 1973, another complaint led to the George Carlin case, sometimes called the "Seven Dirty Words" decision because the comedian had speculated on the air about the strange power of words such as *fuck* and *shit*. After review, the Supreme Court ruled that the FCC did have the authority to regulate broadcast "indecency" (the courts avoided wrestling with what might constitute broadcast "obscenity") primarily on the grounds that children had access to radio.

For much of its history, television programming has illustrated Gershon Legman's thesis that repressing normal sexual content will result in greater degrees of violence. The culture cherishes the conviction that violence (and sex, which we may be prone to conflate with violence precisely because of the syndrome Legman identifies) rules television and that reengineering program content would end many social problems. It is not so much that Americans scapegoat television—though it is a convenient vessel for sins—as that they need an official folklore of cultural malaise, a conventional wisdom that no one wants to examine too closely for fear that we might actually have to deal with poverty, class, and education. That said, however, it is clear that radio and television broadcasters began in the 1980s to air more candid material to counter the threat of cable television, the classic economic gambit that calls for increasing candor in order to win back audiences.

Since then, conservative pressure groups have attacked television broadcasters for programs such as *Married with Children* and have lobbied sponsors not to advertise on them, even as soap operas, ever more steamy, have escaped condemnation. Afternoon talk show hosts invite sex workers to recall their kinkiest moments before live audiences; evening tabloid shows retail juicy tidbits about the lives of celebrities. Partial nudity—no nipples or genitals—is common on shows such as *NYPD Blue*; PBS offers programs such as *Tales of the City* in two versions, one in which nipples are optically censored for stations in less tolerant regions. Leaving aside questions of taste, the principal issue remains whether speech and images on public airwaves must be sanitized for the sake of children, or whether adults have the right to listen and watch mature material. After a brief endorsement of the concept of "safe harbors," that is, late evening hours where adults can see and hear messages inappropriate for five-year-olds,[98] a reconstituted FCC—pressured by Congress—insisted on a total ban on broadcast indecency, while the courts disagreed. A federal court ruled in 1991 that indecency could be forbidden between 6 A.M. and 10 P.M., but that a twenty-four-hour prohibition was unconstitutional. Despite continuing government challenges, the courts have been steadfast, though broadcasters are still too timid to venture far.

The advent of the V-chip (mandated under section 551 of the Communications Act of 1996), which should permit parents to block material for children, may render the dispute moot. The chip will filter out programs rated for adults, if effective ratings can be devised. The Communications Act of 1996 required the television industry to adopt a rating system for its programs or face government intervention. Initial ratings, similar to those carried by motion pictures, seemed insufficiently precise; the networks are still revising. In the interim the FCC fires warning shots: in the early 1990s the agency fined Infinity Broadcasting for producing the talk show of "shock-jock" Howard Stern, who immediately wrote two best-sellers on the strength of his notoriety, while New Jersey governor Christine Todd Whitman named a highway rest stop (Interstate 295 near Trenton) after him.[99] Some cultural commentators think that the issue is moot, that television has already robbed children of their childhood by feeding them grown-up entertainment. According to this view, television has long since ensured that children are exposed to information previously reserved for adults.[100] Moreover, say others, Americans can readily access graphic materials on alternative electronic media. In any case, the V-chip may prove a Trojan horse by providing a rationale for broadcasters to offer more sexually oriented programming on the grounds that technology can prevent minors from watching.

Less stringently regulated cable systems show uncut R-rated movies satellite-distributed by premium distributors like HBO and Showtime, some erotic specials produced by those same distributors, and soft-core channels such as *Spice* and *Playboy*. For a time, public access channels programmed raunchy shows. The longest running of these is *Screw* magazine's *Midnight Blue*, which currently occupies a leased channel in Manhattan, though California systems have carried material such as *The Barbara Dare Show*, hosted by the well-known porn actress, and *The Susan Block Show*, conducted by a saucy sociology Ph.D. Because the 1992 Cable Act holds cable companies liable for obscene material, some operators have tried to end public access, violating their charters in order to protect themselves from zealots, a familiar tale of the collision between official morality and a demotic technology. American Exxxstacy, a service carrying hard-core porn, operated on the Galaxy II satellite until it was forced into bankruptcy by a "forum-shopped" prosecution under Alabama's local obscenity laws; it has since been resurrected as Exxxstacy II on Telstar I and other satellites.

During the 1960s, urban counseling groups operated telephone "hot lines" to dispense sexual advice to troubled teenagers. By the late 1970s, entrepreneurs seized on the idea as a way of selling explicit messages to those titillated by sexual discourse. In 1983 Congress amended the Telecommunications Act of 1934 (section 223 [b]) to restrict telephone transmission of obscene or indecent messages to minors. Amendments to the 1988 Education Bill outlawed 800 ("Watts-line") number dial-a-porn services, which simply moved to 900 ("party-line") numbers instead. Additional attempts to censor dial-a-porn encountered constitutional rulings that eviscerated the constraints, though the courts have upheld federal laws requiring phone companies to block access by minors at the request of their parents. Dial-a-porn, now a large industry, demonstrates once again the erotic possibilities of advanced technologies.

The use of Ravel's *Bolero* as the sound track for Blake Edwards' movie *10* (1979) reminded Americans of just how sexual music can be, but, in fact, the same associations and objections date back to the 1920s, when the word "jazz" stood simultaneously for a musical genre and sexual intercourse. Elvis Presley, Jim Morrison and the Doors, the Rolling Stones, and dozens of other rock stars were castigated for their performances long before Porno for Pyros began singing songs such as "Bad Shit" and "Orgasm." In 1985 the Senate held hearings on explicit and violent lyrics on audio recordings; by 1990 a frightened National Association of Recording Merchandisers "voluntarily" stuck warning labels on record, disc, and cassette jackets. At first the labels increased sales, at least in urban areas,[101] but the practice has resulted in an effective form of censorship for other regions, since the largest chains—like Wal-Mart and Blockbuster (often the only stores in town)—refuse to carry products with the labels, thus blocking access for many Americans. In 1990 a Florida court ruled that *As Nasty as They Wanna Be*, an album by 2 Live Crew, was obscene, despite warning labels on the cover; sales fell when several hundred stores refused to carry it before the Eleventh Court of Appeals overturned the decision. That case represents a convergence of the concerns of two kinds of censors, since 2 Live Crew's lyrics offended fundamentalists because of their "obscene" words and offended antiporn feminists because of their perceived hostility toward women. Because such "rap" music can fall into the category of ethnic discourse, however, the issue remains complicated and politically thorny, as was apparent in Senate hearings on rap music in 1993.

The most entertaining debate, however, has swirled around pornography on the Internet. In 1995, just as Congress was debating the provisions of what became the Communication Decency Act, a sensational survey claimed that more than three-quarters of all images posted on the Internet were pornographic,[102] a figure immediately seized upon by antiporn activist Catharine MacKinnon as evidence for her thesis that pornography is the central evil in Western culture. One could hardly find a better example of folklore in the making: the media ballooned the news without checking. Although legitimate researchers swiftly concluded that the study was a fraud, most Americans still do not realize that it was bogus. Congress passed the act anyway. At the request of all parties, the Clinton administration as well as the many media industries and civil rights groups to oppose the measure, the courts (first the Court of Appeals and then the Supreme Court) acted quickly on what was really a test of cultural acceleration. Never before had the debate over the alleged evils of a new technology been so compressed into brief compass. Never before had the stakes been so high, since the act would have crippled the Internet beyond repair. The judicial declaration that the law was unconstitutional reminded Americans that pornography is inextricably connected not simply with technological advance but also with human intelligence itself.

Over the last several decades, that recognition has fueled academic investigations of pornography as an important cultural site of sexual and gender assumptions. From popular and academic presses pour works on sexual representation and sexual discourse, on the mutability of gender and the shifting loci of desire, on erotic pasts and erotic futures, all works that previous generations would have called pornographic themselves. The feminist antiporn rendition of pornography, based on an equation of sex and violence, seems to have been swamped by the gender disputations that feminism itself set in motion. Gay and lesbian discourse, once anathematized as pornographic by definition, has entered a new phase; historians are now reclaiming artifacts as their erotic heritage. The sheer weight of scholarship has sanitized genres previously under attack. Digitalization, interactivity, and information highways have expanded cyberspace communities of erotic discourse, while the prospect of a sexual "virtual reality" now looms. In the future, sexual sites will probably resemble legitimate corporate enterprises in their efforts to control the market. Steve Silberman observes that the majority of triple-X images on the Net come from only two or three vendors such as ZMaster in Florida.[103] On the other hand, Americans are experimenting with digicams that transmit images of themselves and their friends or make "bit movies" designed specifically for the Web. Over the next few years, the need for "safe" voyeurism in an age of AIDS and for a rich fantasy life in an age of corporate sterility will probably outweigh the demands of Puritanism and political correctness.

In 1980 Andrea Dworkin claimed that "in the United States, the pornography industry is larger than the record and film industries combined,"[104] a claim apparently made of whole cloth. According to Eric Schlosser's "The Business of Pornography," Americans in 1996 spent $8 billion "on hard-core videos, peep shows, live sex acts, adult cable programming, sexual devices, computer porn, and sex magazines."[105] If Schlosser's $8 billion estimate is accurate (it omits book revenues, especially the $1 billion that American women spend on steamy romances annually), then the amount Americans spend on those forms of sexual expression each year is roughly twice what they spend on hot dogs, but only a third of what they spend on gardening supplies.[106]

Even so, such numbers doubtless infuriate the National Obscenity Unit, though the activities of this agency have already attracted the attention of an FBI concerned about overzealous prosecutions.[107] It still harasses producers and dealers of sexual materials, twists the law, and even goes after people who criticize its operations.[108] The Supreme Court's rejection of the censorship provisions of the Communication Decency Act should not obscure the implications of other decisions, in particular, *United States v. Knox* (977 F.2d 815 [3d cir. 1992]), which concluded in 1995. This child pornography case led to a conviction whose effect, says one scholar, is to "let images of children, *and potentially all images*, slip from the category of 'speech' protected by the First Amendment into the unprotected category of 'action.' "[109] A defiantly conservative Congress in 1998 also attempted to circumvent the courts by adopting the Child Online Protection Act, a statute that would again undercut the rights of adults.

Continuing uncertainty reminds us that perhaps the most enduring contribution that pornography has made to American culture is its function as a heat sink for antidemocratic impulses. The endless attempts of legal scholars to exclude sexual expression from First Amendment protections have almost certainly helped to discharge the frustrations of authoritarian personalities who find free speech problematic. At the very least, prosecutions allow our political system to scapegoat pornographers, who thus carry the burden of free speech for us all. That is the message of Milos Forman's *The People versus Larry Flynt*, an otherwise unremarkable film, but it is a message Americans resist. Given the inherent instabilities of a democracy, especially in the absence of the external enemies who defined national morality so well during the Cold War, pornographers are simply too tempting as targets. Given a level playing field, it would be difficult to decide which group—the most extreme pornographers or their most vociferous opponents—has the nastier view of sex or the greater contempt for the law. We are left with a cultural environment in which, as Gayle Rubin says, "sexual acts are burdened with an excess of significance."[110]

NOTES

1. Joan Hoff, "Why Is There No History of Pornography?," *For Adult Users Only: The Dilemma of Violent Pornography*, ed. Susan Gubar and Joan Hoff (Bloomington: University of Indiana Press, 1989), pp. 17–46.

2. Alice Goldfarb Marquis, *Hopes and Ashes: The Birth of Modern Times* (New York: Collier Macmillan, 1986).

3. See James Axtell, ed., *The Indian Peoples of Eastern America: A Documentary History of the Sexes* (New York: Oxford, 1981) and Walter L. Williams, *The Spirit and the Flesh: Sexual Diversity in American Indian Culture* (Boston: Beacon Press, 1986).

4. Stephen A. Smith, "Freedom of Expression in Native American Constitutions," *Journal of Communication Inquiry*, 15:1 (Winter 1991): 23–42.

5. Peter Wagner, "Eros Goes West: European and 'Homespun' Erotica in Eighteenth-Century America," *The Transit of Civilization from Europe to America*, ed. Winfried Herget and Kan Ortseifen (Tübingen: G. Narr, 1986), p. 148.

6. Milton Rugoff, *Prudery and Passion: Sexuality in Victorian America* (New York: Putnam, 1971), pp. 305–306.

7. Wayland Young, *Eros Denied: Sex in Western Society* (New York: Grove Press, 1964), p. 324.

8. Allen Walker Read, "The Nature of Obscenity," *Neurotica*, 1:5 (Autumn 1949): 224.

9. Peter Gay, *Education of the Senses* (New York: Oxford University Press, 1984), p. 495.

10. Tracy C. Davis, "The Actress in Victorian Pornography," *Theatre Journal*, 41 (October 1989): 294–315.

11. Timothy J. Gilfoyle, *City of Eros: New York City, Prostitution, and the Commercialization of Sex, 1790–1920* (New York: Norton, 1992), p. 127.

12. Robert Bogdan, *Freak Show: Presenting Human Oddities for Amusement and Profit* (Chicago: University of Chicago Press, 1988).

13. John Preston, *Flesh and the Word: An Anthology of Erotic Writing*, 2 vols. (New York: Plume, 1992, 1993), II:2.

14. See, for example, Benedict Anderson, *Imagined Communities: Reflections on the Origin and Spread of Nationalism*, rev. ed. (New York: Verso, 1991). Anderson does not have pornographers in mind, but many of his remarks would clearly apply.

15. Thomas P. Lowry, *The Story the Soldiers Wouldn't Tell: Sex in the Civil War* (Mechanicsburg, PA: Stackpole Books, 1994), p. 27.

16. See John Tierney, "Porn, the Low-Slung Engine of Progress," *New York Times*, 9 January 1994, sec. 2, pp. 1, 18.

17. Robert Taft, *Photography and the American Scene* (New York: Macmillan, 1938), p. 76.

18. John Tebbel, in *The Media in America* (New York: NAL, 1974), p. 142, suggests that the original 1842 Customs Act was aimed at photographs, but that hardly seems likely.

19. "Questionable Subjects for Photography," *Photographic News*, 1 (26 November 1858): 135–136.

20. Charles Baudelaire, "The Modern Public and Photography," *The Mirror of Art: Critical Studies of Charles Baudelaire*, trans. and ed. by Jonathan Mayne (London: Phaidon Press, 1955); see also Thomas P. Lowry, *The Story the Soldiers Wouldn't Tell: Sex in the Civil War* (Mechanicsburg, PA: Stackpole Books, 1994), illustrations between pp. 82 and 83.

21. See Morton N. Cohen's *Lewis Carroll's Photographs of Nude Children* (Philadelphia: Rosenbach Foundation, 1978).

22. "Dealers in Obscene Pictures," *New York Tribune*, 10 July 1877, p. 2.

23. Iwan Bloch, *Anthropological Studies in the Strange Sexual Practices of All Races in All Ages*, trans. Keene Wallis (New York: Anthropological Press, 1933; rpt. Berlin, 1902), chapter 16.

24. Jay Gertzman, *Bookleggers and Smuthounds: The Trade in Erotica, 1920–1940* (Philadelphia: University of Pennsylvania Press, 1999), chapter 6.

25. Heywood Broun and Margaret Leech, *Anthony Comstock: Roundsman of the Lord* (New York: Boni, 1927), pp. 155–157, 192–193.

26. Lynn Hunt, "Introduction," *The Invention of Modernity: Obscenity and the Origins of Modernity, 1500–1800* (New York: Zone Books, 1993), p. 11.

27. Karin Dovring, "Troubles with Mass Communication and Semantic Differentials in 1744 and Today," *American Behavioral Scientist*, 8:1 (1965): 9–14.

28. See, as just one of many such sources, James J. Kilpatrick's *The Smut Peddlers: The Pornography Racket and the Law Dealing with Obscenity Censorship* (Garden City, NY: Doubleday, 1960).

29. See Naomi Morgenstern, " 'There Is Nothing Else like This': Sex and Citation in Pornogothic Feminism," *Sex Positives? The Cultural Politics of Dissident Sexualities*, ed. Thomas Foster, Carol Siegel, and Ellen E. Berry (New York: New York University Press, 1997), pp. 39–67.

30. John Gagnon, "Sex Research and Social Change," *Archives of Sexual Behavior*, 4 (1975): 116.

31. Barrington Boardman, *Flappers, Bootleggers, "Typhoid Mary," and the Bomb: An Anecdotal History of the United States* (New York: Perennial, 1988), p. 18.

32. Hal D. Sears, *The Sex Radicals: Free Love in Victorian America* (Lawrence: Regents Press of Kansas, 1977), p. 73.

33. Ibid., p. 28.

34. James Reed, *From Private Vice to Public Virtue: The Birth Control Movement and American Society since 1830* (New York: Basic Books, 1978), pp. xv, 34; chapter 3, "The Suppression of Contraceptive Information," is excellent.

35. William Manchester, *The Glory and the Dream: A Narrative History of America, 1932–1972* (Boston: Little, Brown, 1974), p. 33.

36. According to some observers, the real motive for the attacks on the institute was the destruction of the records of patients "treated" for homosexuality by Dr. Magnus Hirschfeld, who knew a great deal about the homosexuals in the Brown Shirts.

37. Charles Rembar, *The End of Obscenity* (New York: Bantam Books, 1969), p. 18.

38. Harry T. Moore, "D. H. Lawrence and the 'Censor-morons,' " D. H. Lawrence's *Sex, Literature and Censorship: Essays*, ed. Harry T. Moore (New York: Twayne, 1953), p. 25.

39. See John S. and Robin M. Haller, *The Physician and Sexuality in Victorian America* (New York: Norton, 1977), p. 185.

40. See Vern L. Bullough, "Technology for the Prevention of 'Les Maladies Produites par La Masturbation,' " *Technology and Culture*, 28 (October 1987): 828–832.

41. Chuck Shepherd and Chip Rogers, "News of the Weird," *Athens (Ohio) News*, 14 October 1993, p. 6.

42. Trish Hall, "Piercing Fad Is Turning Convention on Its Ear," *New York Times*, national ed., 19 May 1991, p. 17.

43. Robert Hughes, "Singular and Grand Britons," *Time*, 129 (6 April 1987): 46–47.

44. Quoted by Richard Harrington, "Exercising the Right to Censor the Censors,"

Messages 3: The Washington Post Media Companion, ed. Thomas Beel (Boston: Allyn and Bacon, 1996), p. 99.

45. According to Gershon Legman's "Erotic Folksongs and Ballads: An International Bibliography," *Journal of American Folklore*, 103 (October/December 1990): 482, this volume is a continuation by other hands of Pierre Louÿs' hoax, *Les Chansons de Bilitis*.

46. *The Streets of Paris* (Chicago: Paris Art, 1933), the souvenir program from the "girlie show" at the International Exposition of 1933 in Chicago, was typical.

47. "La Milo, Sensation of Europe, to Appear at the Palace Theater," *New York American*, 8 November 1914, p. M7.

48. Ken Murray, *The Body Merchant: The Story of Earl Carroll* (Pasadena, CA: Ward Ritchie Press, 1976), p. 45.

49. Robert S. Lynn and Helen M. Lynd, *Middletown: A Study in Contemporary American Culture* (New York: Harcourt Brace, 1929), pp. 239–242.

50. "Porno-Petard," *Time*, 18 April 1927, p. 23.

51. "Lewd Magazines Burn amid Cheers," *New York Times*, 28 January 1941, p. 1.

52. Lindbergh's photograph of Christensen is appropriately reproduced in the magazine *Art and Auction*, 19:6 (January 1997): 17. See also "Lindbergh's Show" in *Vogue* (February 1997): 150, for comment on the exhibit at the James Danziger Gallery in New York City (18 January–1 March 1997).

53. C. J. Scheiner, *Compendium* (Brooklyn: C. J. Scheiner Books, 1989), p. 31.

54. Jonathan Karp, "Decline? What Decline?" *Media Studies Journal*, 6:3 (Summer 1992): 45–53.

55. Harry T. Moore, "D. H. Lawrence and the 'Censor-morons,' " in D. H. Lawrence's *Sex, Literature and Censorship*, ed. Harry T. Moore (New York: Twayne, 1953), p. 17.

56. See, for example, "Police to Burn $500,000 in Obscene Books," *New York Times*, 14 March 1935, p. 1; "Police Burn Literature They Seize as Indecent," *New York Herald Tribune*, 13 November 1936, p. 1.

57. Curt Gentry, *J. Edgar Hoover: The Man behind the Secrets* (New York: W. W. Norton, 1991), p. 236.

58. John D'Emilio and Estelle B. Freedman, *Intimate Matters: A History of Sexuality in America* (New York: Harper and Row, 1988), pp. 326–343.

59. Joanne Meyerowitz, "Women, Cheesecake, and Borderline Material," *Journal of Women's History*, 8:3 (Fall 1996): 9–35.

60. Wayne Overbeck, with Rick D. Pullen, *Major Principles of Media Law* (New York: Harcourt Brace, 1994), pp. 310–311.

61. William Brigman, "Politics and the Pornography Wars," *Wide Angle*, 19:3 (July 1997): 152.

62. Dan Wakefield, "An Unhurried View of Ralph Ginzburg," *Playboy*, 12:10 (October 1965): 172.

63. *Technical Reports of the Commission on Obscenity and Pornography* (Washington, DC: Government Printing Office, 1971–72), III: 197.

64. Daniel Eisenberg, "Toward a Bibliography of Erotic Pulps," *Journal of Popular Culture*, 15:4 (Spring 1982): 184.

65. "A Passion for Collecting: Erotic Art Comes out of the Closet and into the Auction Rooms," *Economist* (10 January 1987): 78.

66. *New York Times*, 15 October 1974, p. 23.

67. Brigman, "Politics and the Pornography Wars," p. 153.

68. Robert C. Allen, *Horrible Prettiness: Burlesque and American Culture* (Chapel Hill: University of North Carolina Press, 1991).

69. She also specified the color and intensity of her spotlights, which further obscured her labia. Personal interview, State Fair Music Hall, Dallas, TX, 11 November 1959.

70. Manchester, *The Glory and the Dream*, p. 34.

71. Marilyn Salutin, "Stripper Morality," *The Sexual Scene*, ed. by John H. Gagnon and William Simon, 2d ed. (New Brunswick, NJ: Transaction/Dutton, 1973), p. 172.

72. "As Slime Goes By," *Screw*, no. 819 (12 November 1984): 6.

73. Candida Royalle's "Down the Snatch: Porn Star Candida Royalle's Straight Gal's Guide to Manhattan Muff Dives," *Screw*, no. 704 (30 August 1982): 4–7, is a tour of bars such as the Duchess, Cafe Society, and Peeches 'n' Creem.

74. "Mode Squad: The New Porn Order," *Village Voice*, 21 July 1992, p. 44, recounts a demonstration of intercourse sponsored by the Nelson Safer Sex Institute; see also Steven Chapple and David Talbot, *Burning Desires* (New York: Signet, 1990), chapter 1.

75. See, for example, Michael Musto's column (p. 46) in the *Village Voice* of 29 December 1992.

76. D. Keith Mano, "Playboy after Hours," *Playboy*, 38:12 (December 1991): 27.

77. *Strippers: The Naked Stages*, HBO America Undercover Series, produced by Anthony Radziwill (New York: HBO, 1998).

78. RoseLee Goldberg, *Performance Art: From Futurism to the Present* (New York: Harry Abrams, 1988), p. 9.

79. "Police Raid Three Shows, Sex, Captive, and Virgin Man; Hold Actors and Managers," *New York Times*, 10 February 1927, p. 1.

80. Quoted by Sarah Boxer, "Enter, the Audience," *New York Times*, 29 August 1998, p. A15.

81. David Leavitt, "Fears That Haunt a Scrubbed America," *New York Times*, 19 August 1990, pp. C1, 27.

82. Erwin Panofsky, "Style and Medium in the Motion Pictures" [1934], *Film Theory and Criticism*, ed. Gerald Mast and Marshall Cohen, 2d ed. (New York: Oxford University Press, 1979), pp. 243–263.

83. See Peter Morse, *John Sloan's Prints: A Catalogue Raisonné of the Etchings, Lithographs, and Posters* (New Haven, CT: Yale University Press, 1969), p. 54.

84. Wolcott Gibbs, "The Peepshow Season in Retrospect," *New Yorker*, 5:31 (21 September 1929): 25–26.

85. "Police to Run Down All Illegal Films," *New York Times*, 17 January 1912, p. 13.

86. Joseph Slade's forthcoming *Shades of Blue* recounts the history of stag films.

87. The information on preferences was gleaned by Eugene Slabaugh and George Huntington, who conducted interviews in the 1960s with the aging producers of vintage stags and deposited the tape recordings in the Kinsey Institute.

88. Quoted in Edward De Grazia and Roger K. Newman, *Banned Films: Movies, Censors and the First Amendment* (New York: Bowker, 1982), p. 138.

89. Jan Hoffman, "Porn in the U.S.A.," *Village Voice*, 21 May 1985, p. 63.

90. "Judge Overturns Part of Child-Pornography Law," *New York Times*, 28 May 1992, p. A7.

91. Dennis Wharton, "Vid Retailers, Booksellers Testify to Porn Bill 'Chill,' " *Variety*, 29 July 1991, p. 15.

92. Marc Berman, "Group Takes on Sex/Violence Bill," *Variety*, 10 June 1991, p. 10.

93. See Joseph W. Slade, "Pornography in the Late Nineties," *Wide Angle*, 19:3 (July 1997), pp. 1–12.

94. "Porn Bill Gains Senators' Support," *Variety*, 17 February 1992, p. 32.

95. Daniel Linz and Edward Donnerstein, "Research Can Help Us Explain Violence and Pornography," *Chronicle of Higher Education*, 30 September 1992, B3–B4.

96. John Irving, "Pornography and the New Puritans," *New York Times Book Review*, 29 March 1992, pp. 1, 24–25, 27.

97. Teller, "Movies Don't Cause Crime," *New York Times*, 17 January 1992, p. A13.

98. Irvin Molotsky, "F.C.C. Rules on Indecent Programming," *New York Times*, 25 November 1987, p. C25.

99. Jeff Gordiner, "Next Exit, Howard Stern," *Entertainment Weekly*, 270 (14 April 1995): 14.

100. See Joshua Meyrowitz, *No Sense of Place: The Impact of Electronic Mediation on Social Behavior* (New York: Oxford University Press, 1985); Neil Postman, *Amusing Ourselves to Death* (New York: Viking, 1985).

101. Steve Jones, "Ban(ned) in the U.S.A.: Popular Music and Censorship," *Journal of Communication Inquiry*, 15:1 (Winter 1991): 78.

102. Martin Rimm, "Marketing Pornography on the Information Superhighway: A Survey of 917,410 Images, Descriptions, Short Stories, and Animations Downloaded 8.5 Million Times by Consumers in Over 2000 Cities in Forty Countries, Provinces, and Territories," *Georgetown Law Review*, 83 (June 1995): 1849–1958.

103. "The Golden Age of Porn Online," an article for *Wired News*, www.wired.com/news/news/culture/story/16175.html.

104. Andrea Dworkin, *Pornography: Men Possessing Women* (New York: Putnam's, 1980), p. 201.

105. Eric Schlosser, "The Business of Pornography," *U.S. News and World Report* (10 February 1997): 44.

106. American Meat Institute, "Just the Facts," *AMI OnLine* (www.meatami.org), August 1997; Sally Johnson, "Reaping What the Boomers Sow: Getting Down and Dirty in the Garden Is Big Business," *New York Times*, 28 September 1996, pp. 21, 23; a glance at the *Statistical Abstract of the United States* will elicit information on comparable industries.

107. Stephen Rae, "X-Rated Raids," *Playboy*, 39:6 (June 1992): 44–45.

108. See American Civil Liberties Union, *Above the Law: The Justice Department's War against the First Amendment* (New York: ACLU, 1991).

109. Anne Higonnet, "Conclusions Based on Observation," *Yale Journal of Criticism*, 9:1 (1996): 1; emphasis added.

110. Gayle Rubin, "Thinking Sex," *Pleasure and Danger: Exploring Female Sexuality*, ed. by Carole S. Vance (Boston: Routledge and Kegan Paul, 1984), p. 279.

4

Bibliographies and Reference Tools

Any scholar knows to begin research with forays into standard indexes such as the *Readers' Guide to Periodical Literature, Education Index, Humanities Index, Social Sciences Index*, and *Communication Abstracts*. Those using this guide are also advised to look at chapter 7, **Major Research Collections**, which lists collections in archives and libraries. What follows are specialized sources. A word of caution: this chapter is intended not for the bibliophile fascinated by plates, bindings, typefaces, and publishing histories of often magnificent classics but for scholars trying to trace criticism. For that reason I have tried to identify the most accessible, rather than the most beautiful, editions. (Collectors may contact dealers like C. J. Scheiner, whose catalogs are listed later.) Even so, many of these works are rare and virtually unobtainable outside large research libraries. Included here are items with the most relevance to American erotica and pornography, a restriction that necessarily excludes extraordinary feats of scholarship on African, Oriental, and European subjects. Most of the classic bibliographies begin with lexicography or folklore and move on to literature, while later efforts deal with iconographic representations of more modern technologies. Many of the classic bibliographies are as much artistic as scholarly achievements and are justly prized as both.

Despite very real contributions to our understanding of sexual materials, the current debate over pornography, especially that enjoined by antiporn feminists, obscures the evolution of sexual representation. More to the point, it ignores the rich scholarship devoted to various genres. For most of its history, the production and distribution of erotica have been illegal activities, and historians and bibliographers have of necessity preferred the shadows themselves. It is probably no accident, for example, that H. Montgomery Hyde decided to write *A History of Pornography* (see chapter 16, **Histories of Erotic Books**), one of the first

English-language attempts at a chronicle, after he retired from the British Secret Service. Nowadays historians and theorists compile bibliographies of criticism; in the past, they were more anxious to identify primary material, at a time when merely to describe it was risky. To protect themselves from prosecution, the early scholars frequently published their reference works anonymously or under assumed names and, like pornographic publishers themselves, just as frequently disguised the names and locations of their presses. Because producing erotica itself is so often a pseudonymous activity, bibliographies can be erroneous, and their errors easily perpetuated. Besides, publishers, collectors, and bibliographers of erotica sometimes authored the material listed in their compilations, pirated it from other sources, disguised it as science, humor, or criticism, called it art, or otherwise covered their tracks.

It is nevertheless impossible to overstate the importance of bibliographies in the study of pornography. They have functioned as tracers for ephemeral, fugitive, marginal representations, and clustered examples so that genres could be recognized and their traditions and formulas understood. Of the many available, the classic bibliographies, which deal principally with printed works, have a special status. In the first place, they list primary or secondary works, sometimes with locations of texts or materials, that permit researchers to conduct searches, to follow the evolution of genres, and to make interpretations. Second, they enable sellers and consumers to determine the provenance, the publishing history, the cultural context, the mutation of traditional plots and themes, and the commercial value of texts. Third, they frequently constitute the best available histories of particular genres. Fourth, they serve as delights in themselves.

The compiling of bibliographies has long been part of the appeal for the serious collector, who is keenly interested in the creation and circulation of a particular work, especially those often beautifully bound editions of famous erotic artifacts or texts. As a case in point, Franklin J. Meine's bibliographic essay and the richly annotated bibliography appended to his edition of Mark Twain's *[1601] Conversation As It Was by the Social Fireside in the Time of the Tudors* provide a guide to the many editions privately printed in different American cities prior to 1938 and give some indication of the book's underground diffusion throughout the culture. Even so, Meine's bibliography omits at least one edition that has since come to light, and such inevitable flaws are incentives for other scholars to keep working. Like so many other forays into erotic bibliography, Meine's is enlivened by an appreciation of the felicities of printing, binding, format, and textual integrity. It is entertaining to compare it with Gershon Legman's "Introduction" to the Maledicta Press edition of *The Mammoth Cod*, an important bibliographic essay on Twain's manuscript in praise of large penises and on Twain's "Address to the Stomach Club of Paris," on the mores of masturbation, which is also reprinted in the same volume. Scholarship of such caliber is its own reward.

HUMAN SEXUALITY

Because pornography does not exist in a vacuum, the scholar may well need to review broad areas of sexuality if only to become aware of pertinent cultural context. Useful is Mervyn L. Mason's *Human Sexuality: A Bibliography and Critical Evaluation of Recent Texts*; it also ranges across many aspects of sexuality, some of which shed light on pornography. Dated, too, but still useful is the five-volume *Handbook of Sexology*, edited by John Money and Herman Musaph, a massive compilation of studies from anthropology to law. The heavily annotated essays in *Handbook of Human Sexuality*, edited by Benjamin B. Wolman and John Money, are also valuable in scope. More specialized is Money's *Sex Research: New Developments*, which deals with (chiefly) psychological sex research until 1965, with indexes of subjects, authors, and practitioners. Bibliographies on many aspects of human sexuality, chiefly aimed at professional counselors and therapists, but some at popular audiences, can be ordered from SIECUS (Sex Information and Education Council of the United States). Less helpful because of its age, *Sex and Sex Education: A Bibliography*, compiled by Flora C. Seruya, Susan Losher, and Albert Ellis in the early 1970s, is still good on materials available up until that time. Patricia J. Campbell's *Sex Guides: Books and Films about Sexuality for Young Adults* incorporates some of the material in her earlier *Sex Education Books for Young Adults, 1892–1979. International Bibliography of Research in Marriage and the Family*, compiled by Joan Aldous and Reuben Hill and published in the 1960s, covers some still-pertinent matters. The Coalition on Sexuality and Disability publishes *Sexuality and Disability*, a journal devoted to the psychological and medical aspects of sexuality in rehabilitation and community settings, as well as a bimonthly newsletter that reports frequently on the therapeutic use of erotica and sexual technologies. *The Sexual Politics of Disability: Untold Desires*, by Tom Shakespeare, Kath Gillespie-Sells, and Dominic Davies, insists on the sexual rights of the disabled and through firsthand accounts explores their sexual expression.

The Kinsey Institute publishes a monthly journal of sex research including scholarship on erotica, the *International Directory of Sex Research and Related Fields*, which began in 1976 as a spin-off from Ruth Beasley's volume, also called the *International Directory of Sex Research and Related Fields*. The latter categorizes scholarship under seventy-seven subject areas, including pornography. Additional information on institute-sponsored research can be found in Martin Weinberg's *Sex Research: Studies from the Kinsey Institute*, somewhat dated now but a good introduction to the early work of scholars at the institute in various endeavors involving sex and its representation, and also in the institute's *Sex Studies Index: 1980. The Frontiers of Sex Research*, edited by Vern Bullough, is also an excellent map to the many paths of research into sexuality and is only slightly dated. *Sex in Contemporary Society: A Catalog of Disser-*

tations lists dissertations across various disciplines until 1973; some bear on pornography, while others on related subjects can be extracted and updated by a database search request to University Microfilms. Excellent ongoing sources are the *Journal of Sex Research*, the *Journal of the History of Sexuality*, and the *Archives of Sexual Behavior*, all of which regularly report on pornography scholarship. In 1976, Eli A. Rubinstein, Richard Green, and Edward Brecher collected major articles from the latter journal for a volume called *New Directions in Sex Research.*

Still more pertinent to those seeking information on categories of topics are the authoritative subject bibliographies compiled by the Kinsey Institute; these are available xeroxed from the institute at modest cost. For example, "Sex Research History," a seventeen-page bibliography, includes pioneering works not easily found elsewhere. The only drawback to these otherwise fine bibliographies is that they are updated on a revolving basis, so that some of them may not be current. Scholars should inquire about cutoff dates before ordering. Those bibliographies compiled before 1978 are collected in Joan S. Brewer and Rod W. Wright's *Sex Research: Bibliographies from the Institute for Sex Research.* The 4,000 entries are not annotated but give some idea of the enormous variety of materials. *Studies in Human Sexuality: A Selected Guide*, by Susanne G. Frayser and Thomas J. Whitby, provides fine annotations of some 600 books in different categories, many of which are about erotica or touch on it. Vern L. Bullough, Bonnie Bullough, and Alice Stein have compiled *Human Sexuality: An Encyclopedia*, an extremely catholic reference tool covering law, medicine, behavior, expression, and so on. Less scholarly are popular works of broad scope. Of a field quite large, several offer reliable information. Guiseppe Lo Duca's *Dictionnaire de Sexologie* and *Supplement A–Z* alphabetize entries of sexual subjects, many of which are expanded with bibliographies. Though published in 1975 partly as a play on the wildly successful *Whole Earth Catalog*, Bernhardt Hurwood's *The Whole Sex Catalog* holds up well. In it the reader will find discussion of a wide variety of American sexual interests, including pornographic media during the 1970s, arranged for leisurely perusal. Saul Braun's *Catalog of Sexual Consciousness*, published the same year, contains entries on topics such as abortion, sex and the handicapped, masturbation, spiritual eroticism, sexual techniques, pornographic genres, and so on. The cachet of *The Visual Dictionary of Sex* derives from its illustrations of terms and concepts, from the vulgar to the medical, though the text is not so slight as might be imagined. Outdated now, but interesting as a map to the sexual folklore of the 1970s and 1980s, is *The Book of Sex Lists*, which Albert B. Gerber intends as a guide to nudist parks, gay bars, porn stores, erotic movies, and so on. Finally, users of the Internet will be familiar with the alt.sex hierarchy of newsgroups, a vast categorization of material on sexual topics, fetishes, and stories ranging from alt.sex.anal to alt.sex.zoophilia. The quality and reliability of information available from these groups range from scientific to folkloristic, and surfers should be cautious.

Finally, while any number of bibliographies of works on American history will group sources under sexuality, including a full listing here would swamp this *Guide*. One example will suffice. The section entitled Sexuality" (388–399) in *Journal of Women's History Guide to Periodical Literature*, edited by Gayle V. Fischer, contains rich veins of articles on a variety of approaches to women's sexuality over time.

SEXUAL SUBCULTURES

The American Psychiatric Association no longer regards homosexuality as a form of deviant behavior, and Americans are increasingly, if still insufficiently, tolerant of homosexuality. Until quite recently, however, *all* homosexual discourse, even in medical texts devoid of explicitness, has been regarded as pornographic *by definition*. General bibliographies of homosexuality as a subject are concerned with broad aspects and facets of experience but may be just as helpful as those that concentrate on erotic representations of homosexuality because they provide social, political, or economic contexts for the representations. Moreover, gay and lesbian bibliographies assemble and legitimate a homosexual history.

The two-volume *An Annotated Bibliography of Homosexuality*, by Vern Bullough and others, is a comprehensive survey across artistic, cultural, medical, and legal categories until the mid-1970s. Wayne R. Dynes' *Homosexuality: A Research Guide* does not deal in particular with literature or art in its 5,000 academic and popular books and articles but is a useful tool for study of many other forms of homosexual expression. So is Dynes' *Encyclopedia of Homosexuality* (which does have entries on writers and artists). Despite controversies engendered by Dyer's own scholarship, *Studies in Homosexuality*, edited by Dynes and Stephen Donaldson, is also a standard source; the thirteen volumes give weight to homosexual history through coverage of the sociology of subcultures, their customs, mores, and values, their sexual practices, their art and literature, their enduring concerns. Dee Michel lists some 1,000 descriptive headings for librarians and archivists in *Gay Studies Thesaurus*. The 1966 version of William Parker's "Homosexuality: Selected Abstracts and Bibliography," full of citations to legal, medical, religious, political, and cultural sources, appears in *A Gay Bibliography: Eight Bibliographies on Lesbian and Male Homosexuality*. Parker updated it as *Homosexuality: A Selective Bibliography of Over 3000 Items* and added yet another supplement, a very wide listing remarkable for the comprehensiveness that can be achieved through careful selectivity of comment. The essays in *Homosexuality: An Annotated Bibliography*, edited by Martin Weinberg and Alan Bell, survey psychological, psychiatric, and sociological research on the subject during the years 1940–1968. Dennis Saunders' *Gay Source: A Catalogue for Men* collects two dozen essays on organizations, clubs, legal matters, and medical information, but also gay art, periodicals, films, and literature. Entries on cinema, Tom of Finland, bodybuilding, and representations of all sorts fill *Completely Queer: The Gay and Lesbian Encyclopedia*, edited by Steve Hogan and Lee Hudson. Similarly, Dell Richards' *Lesbian Lists: A Look at Lesbian Culture, History, and Personalities* boasts an exceptionally wide range of information ranging across trivia, aphrodisiacs, entertainers, banned books, and so on. J. R. Roberts has compiled *Black Lesbians: An Annotated Bibliography*; the materials are indexed by author and subject. In addition to reprinting articles popular and scientific, Thomas Geller provides in *Bisexuality: A Reader and Sourcebook* lists of organizations, books, films, and magazines on the subject. Charles Steir's "A Bibliography on Bisexuality" subordinates material that might be considered prurient to medical and legal comment of clearly scholarly intent.

Lacking the impetus of organized advocacy, more marginal sexual groups lack the kind of documentation that scholars are using to construct a gay past and a present identity. Many general surveys of "deviant" behavior are significant chiefly because they indicate what commentators of different periods thought bizarre, and it is interesting to compare older texts with the fourth edition of the *Diagnostic and Statistical Manual of Mental Disorders* of the American Psychiatric Association, which is the official guide to predilections considered "deviant" today. Almost as authoritative is John Money's *Lovemaps: Clinical Concepts of Sexual/Erotic Health and Pathology, Paraphilia, and Gender Transposition of Childhood, Adolescence and Maturity*, a guide to the origin and nature of paraphilias, or deviations, that arise chiefly from childhood trauma, repression, or some other distortion. Money has grouped about forty common paraphilias into six categories of psychological aberration or strategy: sacrifice and expiation (sadomasochism, self-asphyxiation), marauding and predation (rape, kleptomania), mercantile and venal strategies (prostitution, sex for reward), fetishes and talismans (a token substitute for lovers, such as odors, tactile artifacts, clothing of rubber, fur, silk, etc.), stigmata (exogamous lovers, religious fixations, amputees), and solicitation and allure (exhibitionism, voyeurism). Ismond Rosen has gathered treatises by various authorities on deviations in *The Pathology and Treatment of Sexual Deviation* (e.g., Rosen himself on "Exhibitionism, Scopophilia and Voyeurism").

Still worth study are Iwan Bloch's *Strange Sexual Practices*, a reprint of a turn-of-the-century text on bizarre customs throughout the world, and John Davenport's 1875 *Curiositates Eroticae Physiologiae, or Tabooed Subjects Freely Treated*. Another venerable text, Roger Goodland's *A Bibliography of Sex Rites and Customs*, has been reprinted for its cross-cultural perspective. One hundred experts talk about different types of behaviors in *The Encyclopedia of Sexual Behavior*, a slightly dated, but still fine, reference tool compiled by Albert Ellis and Albert Abarbanel. Similar in intent and execution is *Encyclopedia Sexualis*, edited by Victor Robinson, with another 100 entries, some by the same experts as those in the Ellis and Abarbanel book, with lots of other authorities from various disciplines writing on aspects of sexuality and its representations. Modeled on the *Bilderlexicon* but written in English, Robinson's volume was novel for its time, is still a good source of information on early twentieth-century erotica, and, of course, allots more space to American behavioral categories and erotic genres than the German classic. Another standard reference work is J. E. Schmidt's *The Cyclopedic Lexicon of Sex: Erotic Practices, Expressions, Variations of the Libido*, which categorizes and identifies deviations, fetishes, and bizarre behavior. Norman Gelb also takes the larger stage of Western culture as a context for *The Irresistible Impulse: An Evocative Study of Erotic Notions and Practices through the Ages*, which runs through most of the major obsessions of hair, legs, breasts, shoes, and so on and devotes discussion to several fixations specific to local areas or subcultures, such as penis inserts and buttock and breast deformations. Recent and informative, though popular, are Brenda Love's *Encyclopedia of Unusual Sexual Practices* and Rufus C. Camphausen's *The Encyclopedia of Erotic Wisdom, a Reference Guide to the Symbolism, Techniques, Rituals, Sacred Texts, Anatomy, and History of Sexuality*. Questions such as who invented the condom, why males have nipples, and what lesbians actually do with their clitorides are all answered by Charles Panati in *Sexy Origins and Intimate Things: The Rites and Rituals of Straights, Gays, Bi's, Drags, Trans, Virgins, and Others*, an amusing and useful work.

Roland Villeneuve's *Fetischisme et Amour*, a very explicit text, combines rich illustrations with comment on historically significant fetishes, none of them specifically American but none limited by national boundaries either. A historically important essay on what sort of arousing materials Americans searched for in the 1940s, how they found them, and the networks of correspondence with others they established is John Goldston's "The World of the Borderline Fetichist." Lars Ullerstam's classic *The Erotic Minorities*, a sympathetic view of fetishes and deviations, suggests that most are harmless and that they provide a sense of identity and community for sexual outsiders. Michael Leigh's *The Velvet Underground* sensationalizes many types of group behavior in twentieth-century America; he traces the networks of communication by which Americans reach out to one another in their desire for sexual contact of all sorts. What gives substance to "The Liberation of Sexual Fantasy" by Daniel Goleman and Sherida Bush is their survey of various American sexual organizations, many organized around specific fetishes.

Valerie Steele's bibliography in her *Fetish: Fashion, Sex and Power*, though selective, is perhaps the most useful on fetishes shared by significant numbers of Americans and on the ways in which these forms of sexual expression manifest themselves in mainstream fashion, art, literature, cinema, politics, and so on. In addition to major fetish periodicals, Steele's list contains valuable research nuggets, such as the three notebooks of clippings and comment called "The Pictorial History of the Corset" to be found in the Art Library of the Brooklyn Museum. Indispensable for research in areas of clothing and sexuality is Vern L. and Bonnie Bullough's *Cross Dressing, Sex, and Gender*, a massive survey of cross-dressing as a behavior among heterosexuals and homosexuals. In the past, the Bulloughs point out, cross-dressing was more common among women, whereas in this century men are more likely to engage in it. F. Michael Moore's *Drag! Male and Female Impersonators on Stage, Screen and Television: An Illustrated World History* covers many interesting recesses of an art form and provides an excellent bibliography. Spencer R. Smith's "Voyeurism: A Review of Literature" is more concerned with behavior syndromes than with their representation, though voyeurism is obviously crucial to the appeal of some pornographic genres. *Variant Sexuality: Research and Theory*, a series of papers edited by the British psychologist Glenn Wilson, is probably the most authoritative book on the subject, though its language and orientation are, of course, medical, as is William B. Arndt's *Gender Disorders and the Paraphilias*, another excellent reference text. In *Sexual Variations: Fetishism, Sadomasochism and Transvestism*, Chris Gosselin and Glen Wilson define terms, offer statistical analyses, review and challenge leading theories, and provide useful bibliographic information. For a briefer, but still solid, survey of current professional thinking, scholars should consult Thomas N. Wise's "Fetishism—Etiology and Treatment: A Review from Multiple Perspectives."

Other deviations that provide themes and images for pornography are covered mostly in clinical literature, with occasional excursions by cultural critics. John Money, Gordon Wainwright, and David Hingsburger have produced a critical version of a patient's autobiography entitled *The Breathless Orgasm: A Lovemap Biography of Asphyxiophilia*. The erotic appeal of asphyxiation is also one of the subjects of *Bottoms Up! A Pathologist's Essays on Medicine and the Humanities*, in which William B. Ober covers representations in pornography and medicine. Midas Dekkers chronicles sexual relations with animals as manifest in various art and texts, including representations in religion, advertising, and pornography, in *Dearest Pet: On Bestiality*. Roland Villeneuve tracks themes and images of bestiality, or sex with animals, in various forms of art and literature and also makes extensive reference to legal cases of actual bestiality in *La Musée du la Bestialitié*. A classic text sold as much for its titillation as for its information is Gaston Dubois-Desaulle's *Bestiality: An Historical, Medical, Legal, and Literary Study, with Addenda*, which traces the subject in folklore and literature. Although it is not recent enough to cover the current American national moral panic over incest that has reinvigorated the theme for writers and broadcasters, *Incest: The Last Taboo: An Annotated Bibliography* by Rich Rubin and Greg Byerly lists some literary treatments of incest along with medical, sociological, psychological, legal, and other aspects of the subject. Robert J. Barry's similarly titled volume, *Incest: The Last Taboo*, is a reference tool for legal and sociological studies.

Prostitution: An Illustrated Source History, by Vern Bullough and his wife, Bonnie, contains an erudite history massively documented with contributions from sociology, anthropology, medicine, and literature, to which have been added pictures of famous courtesans. It is hard to find because its illustrations make it an instant target of library thieves. Fortunately, its content has been thoroughly updated and expanded (sans pictures) as *Prostitution: A Guide to*

Sources by Vern L. Bullough with L. U. Sentz and Dorothy Tao, whose efforts range far beyond representations of whores to anthropological, sociological, medical, legal, and cultural fields. *A Bibliography of Prostitution*, compiled by Bullough, Margaret Deacon, Barrett Elcano, and Bonnie Bullough, breaks down hundreds of entries into categories like "Biography and Autobiography," "Fiction," and "Guide and Descriptive History." A glance at either volume will persuade anyone that the number of documentary accounts, journalistic exposés, academic studies, law enforcement texts, health-related reports, and ideological tracts on prostitution in America is beyond counting; becoming familiar with prostitution as a literary theme is only slightly less daunting. Volume XIII of *Studies in Homosexuality*, edited by Dynes and Donaldson, entitled "Sociology of Homosexuality," contains material on gay prostitution and its chronicles.

GENERAL WORKS ON PORNOGRAPHY AND EROTICA

Because there is nothing monolithic about pornography's numerous genres and enormous range, researchers must quickly limit their search to particular areas. Over the years only a very few general texts have proved to be useful. (For historical, rather than encyclopedic, works, see **General Histories of Sex** in chapter 5, especially Bolen, Bremmer, Brusendorff, Fuchs, Schidrowitz.) The indispensable reference tool for investigating all forms of sexual expression is the *Bilderlexicon der Erotik*; the first four volumes were edited by Leo Schidrowitz in 1928–1931, and the last two by Armand Mergen in 1963. Because it includes the lifework of most of the great German sexologists of the Weimar Republic, bibliographers of the erotic usually list it by its title rather than the editors as homage to the greatest of all reference works on erotica, a masterpiece of collective achievement. The six volumes contain thousands of illustrations, including American examples, and extensive documentation; volumes II and IV are mostly bibliographic. If the scholar of vintage porn had to choose only one reference work, the *Bilderlexicon* would be that one. Well below this level is *The Encyclopedia of Erotica*, for which Paul Gillette and Robert Dicks managed to annotate more than 1,000 entries, many of them twentieth-century examples, with excerpts.

Available for a nominal fee are bibliographies of specialized erotic materials in the Kinsey Institute's collections. A nearly random sampling of several hundred titles bearing on pornography might include Annotated List of Audio-Visual Materials with Sexual Content; Aphrodisiacs; Censorship in Art and Literature; Condoms; Contemporary Erotic Literature—History and Criticism; Contraception; Dildos; Drugs and Sex Behavior; Effects of Zoning Laws; Erotica (Pornography); Erotica Industry: Eroticism in Cinema; Fetishism; Girlie Magazines in the Kinsey Institute; Graffiti; Homosexuality in Art and Literature; Legal Aspects of Obscenity; Masturbation; Nineteenth Century American Erotica; Nudism; Penis in Art; Penis Size; Professional Use of Erotica; Randolph Folklore Collection; Rubber Fetishism; Sex Aids; Sex Aid Dealers; Sex in Television; Sex Slang Dictionaries; Spanking; Stripteasers; Tattoos and Tattooing; Voyeurism; Women's Image in Cinema and Girlie Magazines. Those titles represent a fraction of the subject headings.

Both the 1970 *Report* and the accompanying *Technical Report* of the President's Commission on Obscenity and Pornography remain important reference tools. The commission dealt with four clumsy categories: (1) motion pictures; (2) books and magazines; (3) postal commerce, that is, mail-order sales of sexual aids and toys, fairly explicit books, magazines, home movies (8mm), photographs, lingerie and exotic wearing apparel, playing cards, novelties, and so on; and (4) hard-core materials (films and photos) at the time sold surreptitiously. It did not investigate performance such as dance or theatrical presentations, or radio, television, or journalism generally, except for the "underground press." It also specifically dismissed the romance novel as outside its purview, though it did provide some interesting content analyses, because only a few people at the time thought of romance fiction, however steamy, as pornographic. The nine-volume *Technical Report* includes articles and studies conducted by the commission's staff and outside researchers on porn artifacts, the marketplace, social issues, behavior, and other subjects, all of which are indexed by author in volume IX. The titles of individual volumes are indicative of content.

GENERAL GUIDES TO CENSORSHIP

Essential also is the *Final Report* of the Attorney General's Commission on Pornography, though it is shorter than its predecessor, more clearly ideologically motivated, and academically inferior. Parts Four and Five include lists of books, magazines, movies, and performers, sometimes with annotations, and a bibliography of sources of many types, from sociological to anecdotal. Volume II provides an overview of production, distribution, and sales of pornographic and sexually oriented materials. These include videotape, cable television, telephone, and computer markets. The focus is on the criminal aspects of pornography and its alleged antisocial effects. The commissioners lavished a great deal of attention on bizarre minority fetishes and on child pornography, and those materials are highlighted. The organization of both the 1970 and the 1986 reports illustrates the difficulty of coping with pornography in all its cultural manifestations; the chaos of human sexuality, as always, defeats schemes of classification.

As yet another reminder of the controversy that bibliographies of pornography can stimulate, scholars should look at *Sourcebook on Pornography*, in which Franklin Mark Osanka and Sara Lee Johann have compiled an enormous list of effects research to buttress their contention that pornography is dangerous. Most commentators refer to the book as a map of the dark side of porn, as does so sober a critic as Richard Posner, who says that it helps "us understand why so much contemporary pornography is violent, filthy, and grotesque."[1] According to the reviewer in *Choice*, however, the four-and-a-half-pound volume is "a frightening farrago of anecdotal 'evidence,' horror stories about child pornography, tactics for harassing bookstores, legal strategies that have been repeatedly thrown out of court, and ugly attacks on the integrity of all who would oppose censorship."[2] That is probably an overstatement, since the book is mostly a list of sociological studies whose cookie-cutter methodologies are remarkable chiefly for their inconclusiveness and for the visible sexual prejudices of the researchers. The volume is perhaps the definitive example of the genre of anti-porn, which exhibits most of the unpleasant characteristics with which pornography itself is often tasked; reductiveness, mean-spiritedness, and hostility toward sexuality. In any case, readers should be aware that Osanka and Johann make little attempt to rate the sources for accuracy or trustworthiness.

The conservative *Pornography: An Annotated Bibliography*, edited by P. Fagan, covers studies in which pornography is seen as inimical to family values; it was used by the Meese Commission. Rosalie F. Zoltano's *Erotica with Medical Aspects: Index of Modern Information* deals with psychological and medical articles on the subject. *Pornography: Research Advances and Policy Considerations*, edited by Dolf Zillman and Jennings Bryant, is a more balanced volume, though compiled by two researchers who believe that they did find some evidence of causal links between sexual representations and violence. Sometimes known as the report of the Koop Commission, it presents research findings both "asocial and prosocial" as a basis for policy considerations.

Much more reliable is the bibliographic volume published by Marcia Pally as *Sense and Censorship: The Vanity of Bonfires: Resource Materials on Sexually Explicit Material, Violent Material, and Censorship*. The annual research reviews conducted by Donald Macdonald for the Canadian government from 1984 to 1988 are available under the title *Pornography. Communication Abstracts* abstracts studies on pornography, obscenity, and indecency in various media and also content analyses of programs, texts, and other materials over several decades. Two books published by Facts on File are excellent quick reference sources of information on specific cases both major and minor. The first, *The Encyclopedia of Censorship*, by Jonathan Green, is more up-to-date than the second, *Pornography, Obscenity and the Law*, by Lester A. Sobel, but Sobel's volume is more closely focused on sexual expression. Both are organized by multiple-entry and cross-referenced to jurists, defendants, and precedents. The useful three-volume *Censorship*, edited by Lawrence Amey, Timothy Hall, Carl Jansen, Charles May, and Richard Wilson, contains biographies of individuals, brief essays, astute comments on events, and explications of cases both celebrated and small.

Published in the 1920s but still useful for occasional nuggets is *Bibliography on Censorship and Propaganda*, by Kimball Young and Raymond D. Lawrence; Young and Lawrence are more concerned with political than sexual examples, though they do deal with some classic works on sexual expression. For *Pornography: The Conflict over Sexually Explicit Material in the United States, An Annotated Bibliography*, Greg Byerly and Rick Rubin assembled secondary sources on philosophical, religious, sociological, legal, psychological, and popular aspects of pornography. Also dated somewhat, it provides a window on earlier decades less in terms of legalities than in terms of cultural dynamics. By contrast, as the title implies, *Pornography and Censorship*, edited by Joan Nordquist, is a bibliographic tool for scholars interested in court battles joined over issues of representation. Rama K. Rao began *An Annotated Bibliography on Pornography: Current Literature, 1980–1986* as the current debates began to heat up, and the large number of items, given the brevity of the period covered, is an accurate indicator of the passions unleashed by the subject. *Index on Censorship*, published since 1972, covers all forms of censorship, not merely that of sexual expression, and is invaluable. Banned Books Online, an electronic exhibit/gallery of books that censors have tried to suppress, is regularly updated on the Web.

In recent years, antiporn feminists have assembled bibliographies of materials sympathetic to their position. A good example is Mary Francesca Chervenak's "Selected Bibliography on Pornography and Violence," a legal scholar's list of sources supporting the antiporn feminist reconstruction of pornography as the literal inscription of male desire and as a physical stimulus to sexual aggression. Much larger is *Feminists, Pornography and the Law: An Annotated Bibliography of Conflict, 1970–1986*, compiled by Betty-Carol Sellen and Patricia A. Young, an excellent bibliography of materials relating to the antiporn feminist attempt to define pornography as male oppression of females and to legislate against it. The volume is obviously more concerned with antiporn feminist positions rather than a balanced view, but the chronology of newspaper notices (1976–1986) of the feminist, antiporn movement is especially valuable in its revelation of the alliance of antiporn feminists, religious fundamentalists, and political conservatives in a campaign to curtail the sometimes startling forms of expression they define as pornographic. The chronology ends with the Supreme Court's striking down of the Indianapolis ordinance and the release of the Meese Report. The entries are also helpful in sorting out byzantine disputes among feminists of various ideological positions.

Like Sellen and Young's book, Margaret Smith and Barbara Waisberg's *Pornography: A Feminist Survey* lists a few sources by feminists who deplore the philosophy and tactics of antiporn groups; it is a small, annotated list of American, Canadian, and British articles and books. Chapter 5 of Carolyn F. Wilson's *Violence against Women: An Annotated Bibliography* is predicated on the Dworkin-MacKinnon definition of pornography as exclusively a form of violence toward women (although Wilson apparently does not endorse Catharine MacKinnon's equation of sex itself with violence). The material in Nancy Ann Sahli's *Women and Sexuality in America: A Bibliography* goes well beyond critical articles and books on pornography to sexual topics of much wider interest, many of which help to put pornography in cultural and political perspective; it is highly recommended because it insists on the complexity of female sexuality. Wendy McElroy covers antiporn, feminist arguments, political correctness, and trends that would deny women rights to their sexuality in *Sexual*

Correctness: The Gender-Feminist Attack on Women. In "Censorship and Intellectual Freedom: A Bibliography, 1970–1981," Charles H. Busha lists 100 books and library science dissertations on censorship written in a single recent decade; some have particular reference to pornography and erotica. The ERIC database can generate "Libraries and the Censorship Issue: A Selected ERIC Bibliography" of on-line materials on the conflict between censors and librarians.

Scholars may wish to consult agency and government reports on pornography other than those of the national commissions, although their accuracy and pertinence vary. *Congressional Committee Hearings Index* by Congressional Information Services is an always-current guide to hearings, including the information gathered by various committees over the years, generally available at any library designated as a government documents depository. The National Archives holds Post Office records, other legal proceedings, court records at major cities, and so on.

EROTIC BOOKS

The starting point for research in print pornography is Terence J. Deakin's bibliography of bibliographies, *Catalogi Librorum Eroticorum: A Critical Bibliography of Erotic Bibliographies and Book-Catalogues*, which annotates seventy-eight bibliographies and private catalogs of erotic literature. It is especially prized because it pinpoints the shelf locations of volumes in major archives. Only 400 copies of Deakin's compilation were printed, so it is likely to be found only in large research libraries. Inferior to it but more widely available is Peter Jenner's *Erotic Bibliographies: A Brief Survey*, which is chiefly concerned with the work of Rose, Ashbee, and Deakin himself. Most of those listed by Deakin and Jenner are vintage bibliographies, of use principally to the student of print pornography published before or during the nineteenth century.

Among older bibliographies, the most celebrated and the most authoritative is that by Pisanus Fraxi, the pseudonym of Henry Spencer Ashbee, whose large (15,000+ volumes) collection of books, including a few hundred erotic volumes, was willed to the British Museum. His three volumes of bibliography—*Index Librorum Prohibitorum* (1877), *Centuria Librorum Absconditorum* (1879), and *Catena Librorum Tacendorum* (1885)—are, of course, dated but are still easily the greatest of all bibliographies of erotica, bar none. Ashbee personally knew many publishers and dealers, which accounts for the accuracy and thoroughness of his annotations. *Index Librorum Prohibitorum* is indexed by author and publisher, while *Centuria Librorum Absconditorum* and *Catena Librorum Tacendorum* are indexed by subject. Only 250 copies of each of the original volumes were printed, so first editions are scarce and expensive. The London publisher Skilton brought out in 1960 a complete facsimile edition that is available in some libraries. Two years later Jack Brussel published a New York edition called *Bibliography of Forbidden Books*, which is recommended because of Gershon Legman's superb bibliographic introduction. *The Encyclopedia of Erotic Literature*, also published in 1962, by Ralph Ginzburg's Documentary Books, is yet another facsimile of Ashbee's work. Peter Fryer edited Ashbee's original three volumes into one entitled *Forbidden Books of the Victorians: Henry Spencer Ashbee's Bibliographies of Erotica*, an abridgment to highlight those books Fryer thinks "most interesting" to modern readers. Collectors will appreciate the edition because Fryer includes the marginalia written in Ashbee's own hand (after his books were printed) and appends a solid biography of Ashbee as well.

Ashbee thought "useful" the work of William Laird Clowes, whose *Bibliotheca Arcana Seu Catalogs Librorum Penetralium: Being Brief Notices of Books That Have Been Secretly Printed, Prohibited by Law, Seized, Anathematised, Burnt or Bowdlerised, by Speculator Morum* was published the same year as Ashbee's *Catena Librorum Tacendorum*. Clowes' volume lists some 600 works and includes references to American works that Clowes saw in private libraries in the United States. This work, itself much indebted to Ashbee's first two volumes, is the source for many of Ashbee's observations about American publishers (see **Publishers and Booksellers** in chapter 16). Clowes appends a short essay on the problems and pleasures of erotic bibliography. Charles R. Dawes' *A Study of Erotic Literature in England Considered with Special Reference to Social Life*, a privately printed compendium, also known in manuscript form as *History of English Erotic Literature*, draws on his own experience as a collector. (Dawes also wrote important bibliographic studies of Restif de la Bretonne and the Marquis de Sade.) (See **Major Research Collections**, in chapter 7, especially Bodleian, Reade.)

Historians of American pornography inevitably gravitate toward vintage bibliographies compiled in other countries because classic texts and artifacts found their way to colonial America, were collected by Americans like William Byrd, and continued to circulate even when Americans began producing indigenous erotica. Ashbee, for instance, was not particularly knowledgeable about American pornography because the domestic industry was relatively immature when he completed his great reference guides, although he did note some examples and publishers. Many of the European works Ashbee cites were already here, traced by Peter Wagner, the unchallenged period authority on the traffic in early America. Wagner's "Eros Goes West: European and 'Homespun' Erotica in Eighteenth-Century America" is a superb historical and bibliographic investigation of the period. Still more impressive is the chapter in Wagner's *Eros Revived: Erotica of the Enlightenment in England and America* called "Erotica in Early America" (292–302). The volume's wonderful bibliography is mandatory for scholars of the period. For the best single recent overview, however, scholars should consult *Clandestine Erotic Fiction in English 1800–1930: A Bibliographical Study*, for which Peter Mendes has assembled information on dealers, collectors, and the narratives that occupied them.

Wagner and Mendes make frequent reference to standard British histories and bibliographies like David Foxon's *Libertine Literature in England, 1660–1745*, a very comprehensive, well-researched, historically invaluable bibliographic study of English porn as it derived from European models and thus relevant for those interested in what Americans of congruent periods were reading. Roger Thompson's *Unfit for Modest Ears* is the key work on more than fifty obscene books published in England in the seventeenth century, with information on publishers, authors, and collectors. It and Donald Thomas' *A Long Time Burning: The History of Literary Censorship in England* provide rare and essential bibliographic details in their running account of English prosecutions of books.

Collectors especially of high pornography have always traded erotica across borders, and American members of a wealthy, educated class prized books in various languages. Henri Cohen's *Guide de l'Amateur des Livres a Gravures du XVIIIe Siècle*, updated by Seymour De Ricci in 1912 and reprinted in 1951 and 1973, contains dozens of entries for eighteenth-century illustrated French books; the plates are marvelous. The most accurate bibliographies of nineteenth-century French erotica are Louis Perceau's *Bibliographie du Roman Érotique du XIX Siècle*, based on personal and private collections of novels as well as that of the Bibliotheque Nationale and on dealer catalogs of the period 1800 to 1929, which resulted in thorough annotations of different editions and imprints; and the Lemonnyer updating of Jules Gay's four-volume *Bibliographie des Ouvrages Relatifs à l'Amour, aux Femmes et au Marriage*, widely considered to be the most important bibliography of French erotica, though it contains some foreign items. Patrick J. Kearney's *A Bibliography of Jules and Jean Gay* annotates a list of mostly erotic books published by father and son during the last century, drawing from the Gays' own catalog of 1876; the volume contains an introduction to erotica "scissored" from Paul Englisch's *Irrgarten der Erotik* (1931). According to Peter Wagner, Gilbert Minazzoli's *Dictionnaire des oeuvres érotiques: Domaine Francais* is not entirely reliable, though its bibliographic reviews, essays, and annotations cover hundreds of French erotic novels and are supplemented by explicit photographs. Daniel Becourt's *Livres Condamnes, Livres Interdits* is really a history of works suppressed by French courts, with lengthy lists of materials assembled by a legal expert. Jean Marie Goulemot's *Ces livres qu'on ne lit que d'une main: lecture et lecteurs de livres pornographiques au XVIIIe siècle* offers a fresh reading of some classic pornographic texts of the eighteenth century, with a serviceable bibliography, while Annie Stora-Lamarre's *L'enfer de la IIIe Republique: censeurs et pornographes, 1881–1914* covers pornographic works attacked and suppressed during the early days of the Third Republic. Both of the latter texts investigate the "invention" of pornography as a species of political subversion on the Continent. (See also **Major Research Collections** in Chapter 7, Apollonaire, Pia.)

The most enthusiastic of all bibliographers and anthologists, however, were the German sexologists of the early twentieth century; they brought to the task the kind of passion that led British explorers to search for the source of the Nile River. (Sir Richard Burton was one of those explorers, but he was as well known for his translations of Middle Eastern erotic works, like *The Perfumed Garden* and The Kama Sutra, most of which were imported into the United States around the turn of the century; *An Annotated Bibliography of Sir Richard Burton* by Burton's friend Norman Penzer not only lists them but contains a great deal of information on their publishing and marketing.) Hugo Hayn and Alfred Gotendorf compiled their massive, eight-volume *Bibliotheca Germanorum Erotica and Curiosa* in 1912–1914. Paul Englisch added a *Supplement: 1914–1928*, in 1929, and all nine volumes were reissued in 1968. It is very good on European literature, with an obvious tilt toward German. Englisch's *Irrgarten der Erotik* contains a bibliography of erotic bibliographies, supplemented by biographies of European publishers, editors, writers, artists, and collectors. Volume II of the *Bilderlexicon* lists classic editions. Bernhard Stern's *Illustrierte Geschichte der Erotischen Literatur aller Zeiten und Völker* is mostly anthology rather than bibliography. Dr. Stern, also known as Stern-Szana, was an authority on the erotica of many countries and printed a richly detailed catalog of his personal library of more than 250 titles, complete with synopses of important works, essays on Casanova and Aretino, arcana on Turkish and Russian works, and digressions on genres of other nationalities. The catalog is called *Bibliotheca Curiosa et Erotica* and contains information to be found nowhere else. Deserving of notice but hardly large enough to constitute a national category by itself is *Om Erotisk og Galant Literatur*, by Pierre Marteau, the pseudonym of E. Sarnum, a Danish bookseller. The bibliography does list Scandinavian erotica but is more concerned with Continental examples. H. E. Wedeck lists authors and works alphabetically in *Dictionary of Erotic Literature*, a modest source on international writers, publishers, and collectors. Wedeck also organizes categories of themes and sexual behaviors, which can be especially useful.

Dealers in clandestine material have always informed their clients of the availability of specific items. Because they frequently annotated the entries and provided bibliographic details of specific editions, catalogs are often the only source of information on rare or lost books, manuscripts, and so on. Typical examples are *Bibliothèque des Curieux* and *Catalogue: Livres Rare and Curieux, Curiosities Bibliographiques: La Plus Jolie Collection D'Ouvrages Secrets*, all early twentieth-century listings of erotic warhorses, all pretending to be French. Probably the most notorious turn-of-the-century dealer catering to the American market was Charles Carrington (1877–1922), who set up shop in various venues, the most successful of which was Paris. *Chas. Carrington's List of Choice English Books* became well known to collectors in Britain and America. Carrington apparently hired the lexicographer/pornographer John S. Farmer to write *Forbidden Books: Notes and Gossip on Tabooed Literature, Bibliographies and Excerpts . . . by an Old Bibliophile* in 1902. Ostensibly an advertisement for Carrington's dealer stock, it was actually a 227-page annotated bibliography of books of erotology and sexology, some of them published by Carrington himself. Samuel Roth reissued it as a bibliography twenty years later. (For classic

American dealers and bookstore owners, see **Publishers and Booksellers** in chapter 16.)

The first public sale of vintage print erotica in America was conducted by Parke-Bernet in New York in 1971; collector and publisher J. B. Rund wrote the catalog, *Libertine Literature*, for the 256 items. Two contemporary American dealers in erotica should be singled out as experts in the field of printed erotica because their catalogs are themselves bibliographic treasures, always packed with information on the items listed. These are C. J. Scheiner, an attorney turned antiquarian book dealer, and Ivan Stormgart, a San Francisco specialist in unusual and erotic works. The catalogs of both repay study, and both will respond to scholarly inquiry. Scheiner is on the faculty of the Institute for the Advanced Study of Sexuality, which grants doctoral degrees. He has published his *Erotica-Curiosa-Sexology Catalog* since 1978 and merged the entries of the first decade's catalogs into *Compendium: Being a List of All the Books (Erotica, Curiosa, & Sexology) Listed in Our Catalogs 1–6 (1978–1988)*. Librarians rightly prize his catalogs for their accuracy; they are also far more available than the expensive collector's items that most classic bibliographies have become. A sampling of current lists published by Stormgart includes Bibliographies and Linguistic Dictionaries; Censorship, Suppression and Sexual Privacy; Erotic Art; Erotic Image in Photography; Homosexuality—Fiction and Art; Masturbation; Motion Picture and Erotic Theatre; Pornographic Paperbacks; S/M; Transsexuals, Transvestites and Hermaphrodites. The *Catalog* of Loompanics Unlimited advertises weird books, magazines, and comics. The generously annotated entries in the catalog of the Amok Bookstore, which specializes in underground, often sexual texts, has been updated most recently by Stuart Swezey and Brian King as *Amok: Fourth Dispatch—Sourcebook of the Extremes of Information in Print*. A keyword search accomplished by pointing a browser will elicit bibliographic information on fiction and nonfiction arranged by specific fetishes on the Internet. A typical site is Pink Flamingo Publications, which catalogs and sells books on "Erotic and Spanking Fiction." There are many others.

Persistent themes in literature and (less often) other media unify several important print bibliographies. These vary in quality and comprehensiveness and may be labors of love or the consequence of personal obsessions with the particular theme. One of the first bibliographers to map the field of "variant" literature was Jeannette H. Foster, a Kinsey librarian, whose *Sex Variant Women in Literature* was a meticulous listing based on the Bloomington archives spliced with discussion of writers such as Amy Lowell and Edna St. Vincent Millay. Marion Z. Bradley and Gene Damon, the pseudonym of Barbara Grier, widened the field by suggesting that several genres had at least marginalization in common in *A Complete Cumulative Checklist of Lesbian, Variant, and Homosexual Fiction in English*. *The Lesbian in Literature: A Bibliography*, compiled by Damon, Jan Watson, and Robin Jordan, originally intended as a supplement to

Foster's volume, has now gone through several editions; the latest uses Grier's real name. It quickly became a standard research tool and with Foster's became a prime entry in bibliographies of erotic bibliographies. Monika Kehoe's excellent *Historical, Literary and Erotic Aspects of Lesbianism* branches out beyond fiction and is highly recommended. Noel I. Garde annotates more than 600 literary entries in *The Homosexual in Literature: A Chronological Bibliography circa 700 B.C.–1958. A Gay Bibliography: Eight Bibliographies on Lesbian and Male Homosexuality* contains classics: the 1958 and 1959 versions of Marion Bradley's "Astra's Tower"; the 1961 and 1962 versions of Bradley and Damon's "Checklist Supplement"; the 1967 version of Damon and Stuart's "The Lesbian and Literature: A Bibliography"; and the samizdat version of Garde's "Chronological Bibliography." The volume is a valuable historical document because it reproduces dog-eared manuscripts that were passed from hand to hand; the printing is a reminder that such bibliographies themselves circulated quietly. Ian Young's more recent *The Male Homosexual in Literature: A Bibliography* is more comprehensive. Volume VIII of *Studies in Homosexuality*, edited by Wayne R. Dynes and Stephen Donaldson, entitled *Homosexual Themes in Literary Studies*, contains twenty-two articles on American and other national literatures. Two book catalogs, both put out by the Giovanni's Room bookstore of Philadelphia in the 1980s, are virtual bibliographies. They are *Lesbian Literature Catalog*, edited by Arlene Olsham, and *Gay Men's Fiction Catalog*, edited by Ed Hermance; both include explicit works. Another valuable catalog is the "Homosexuality—Fiction and Art" list available from the San Francisco dealer Ivan Stormgart, as is the equally current catalog of a Different Light, a New York City bookstore specializing in lesbian materials.

To *Bookleggers and Smuthounds: The Trade in Erotica, 1920–1940*, Jay A. Gertzman appends extensive bibliographies of works published by marginal publishers such as Panurge Press, Falstaff Press, and Samuel Roth's various imprints: Avalon Press, Big Dollar Book Company, Black Hawk Press, Book Awards, Bridgehead Books, Candide Press, Philosophical Book Club, and so on. These were more often than not reprints of European books. In this regard, Gertzman examines the provenance of American editions of a famous English import in *A Descriptive Bibliography of Lady Chatterley's Lover, with Essays toward a Publishing History of the Novel*, a superb piece of scholarship, complete with an overview of legal and cultural battles faced by publishers in the United States. The volume contains a running discussion of pulp fiction published between the 1920s and 1950s, with lots of information on publishers and prosecutors, and a bibliography of Samuel Roth's William Faro imprint. Lawrence J. Shifreen and Roger Jackson have traced the many editions, pirated and otherwise, of America's most celebrated "obscene" author in *Henry Miller: A Bibliography of Primary Sources*.

Miller aside, American erotic fiction has yet to find its bibliographers. Michael Perkins has observed somewhat inaccurately that modern American erotic writers have "almost no indigenous tradition to draw upon."[3] American pornographic novels have flourished in specific periods, though, to be sure, most were published and circulated clandestinely. Some have been lost, while others are listed in catalogs of rarities, like those of C. J. Scheiner (see later). Perkins is referring to open publication of post–World War II works. Since, before the 1960s, American fiction too candid for this side of the Atlantic was often brought out by the Olympia Press in France, scholars may wish to consult Patrick Kearney's *The Olympia Press, Paris 1953–1965: A Handlist*, which has been reprinted as *The Paris Olympia Press*. This is easily the most complete listing of the Olympia Press titles, with dates, pseudonyms of authors, lists of translators and illustrators; Girodias himself wrote the Preface. From Kearney's volume one learns that Harriet Daimler's real name is Iris Owens and that Akbar del Piombo's is Norman Rubington and that the first title in the Olympia Press Traveller's Companion series was Jock Carroll's *Bottoms Up* (1961), later reprinted as *The Shy Pornographer*. Kearney also sorts out the different imprints of Kahane-Girodias: The Atlantic Library, Othello Books, Ophelia Press. Kearney's *A Bibliography of the New York Olympia Press* picks up with the removal of the press to the United States, where it printed during the years 1967–1974. Kearney devotes a good deal of space to the piracy of Olympia works by other presses, and his indexes of titles, authors' names, and pseudonyms are detailed. Michael Perkins appends short, but accurate, bibliographies of publishers who ripped off Olympia to *The Secret Record*. Significant titles of domestic fiction from those publishers are listed in Daniel Eisenberg's "Toward a Bibliography of Erotic Pulps Published in the U.S., 1962–1972," one of the Kinsey bibliographies later expanded into an article for the *Journal of Popular Culture*. Useful in this regard is the *Vintage Paperback Catalogue* of San Francisco erotica dealer Ivan Stormgart, a regularly updated (*No. 5* is 1993) list of erotic paperbacks from the years 1955–1985, noting most of the important pornographic authors and their publishers, such as Olympia Press, Brandon House, Holloway House, Greenleaf Classics, and Collectors Publications. John Martin's *Bibliographical Catalogue of Privately Printed Books* has largely supplanted Will Ransom's *Private Presses and Their Books* as a guide to occasionally offbeat, sometimes sexually explicit works published privately in the United States.

Eileen Fallon's *Words of Love: A Complete Guide to Romance Fiction* is an extremely useful compilation of critical essays on subgenres like Regencies and historic romances, annotated lists of important authors past and present by real names and pseudonyms, indexes of novels, and information on writers' conferences, associations, and special publications. More popular is *Happily Ever After: A Guide to Reading Interests in Romance Fiction*, a guide by Kristen Ramsdell, who breaks out categories for librarians and consumers. Claiming that heavy readers can plow through eighty paperbacks per month, Rosemary Griley also offers shortcuts for the consumer in a hurry with *Lovelines: The Romance Reader's Guide to Printed Pleasures*.

FOLKLORE AND HUMOR

Most of the great German reference works on erotica cited earlier cover Continental folklore. The *Bibliotheca Germanorum Erotica and Curiosa* by Hayn, Gotendorf, and Englisch, for instance, recounts folktales and stories and reprints bawdy songs and smutty verse. The principal reference tools for the folklorists are Stith Thompson's six-volume *Motif-Index of Folk Literature: A Classification of Narrative Elements in Folktales, Ballads, Myths, Fables, Medieval Romances, Exempla, Fabliaux, Jestbooks, and Local Legends* and *The Types of the Folktale: A Classification and Bibliography*, by Antti Aarne and Stith Thompson, a classification scheme refined from Thompson's magnum opus. Both works are international in scope.

The United States can boast of only two scholars who genuinely deserve to be called great erotica bibliographers. The first is Gershon Legman (Eugene Slabaugh is the second—see chapter 7, **Major Research Collections**), the most knowledgeable of all authorities on virtually any form of erotica or pornography and the undisputed master of bawdy and/or obscene folklore and humor. He is also one of the most prolific scholars. Legman is opinionated, irascible, painstakingly accurate, and honest to a fault. His bibliographic essays contain no cant, no fudging, no unidentified guesses. He is, quite simply, the best there is. Helen Dudar interviewed the scholar for "Love and Death (and Schmutz): G. Legman's Second Thoughts," in which Legman reflects on his career as a writer and researcher in erotica and delivers himself of opinions on scholarship, Puritanism, and sexuality. John Vinocur's article, "Gershon Legman Doesn't Tell Dirty Jokes . . . But He Has the World's Largest Collection of Them Lying around His House" chronicles Legman's career, with particular attention to the collection of dirty jokes on which Legman based perhaps his best-known books. Legman died before he could bring into print *Peregrine Penis: An Autobiography of Innocence*, in which he was expected to recount his experiences as a writer, dealer, and bibliographer of erotica.

The essays on bibliography, folklore, collectors, publishers, and authors in Gershon Legman's *The Horn Book: Studies in Erotic Folklore and Bibliography*, though written some years ago, are still without peer. Legman's much more recent "Erotic Folksongs and Ballads: An International Bibliography" is without question the greatest annotated bibliography on folklore, humor, and bawdy songs. The life work of a mature scholar, it sparkles with wit and erudition (Legman planned but did not complete a discography supplement). The bibliography is full of esoterica, such as information on T. S. Eliot's bawdy poems (p. 442), but its main value is that it outlines the dimensions of the field with entries on Polish, Czech, German, Serbian, French, Turkish, and a dozen other nationalities, with most attention to American, all rendered with Legman's usual, immaculate scholarship. It contains citations to virtually every notable collection of obscene or bawdy drinking, campfire, music hall, military, cowboy, sailor, college and fraternity, and working songs, as well as sea chanties, folk songs, ballads, and verses, with occasional interpolations of stories, salty puns, and erotic miscellany, all drawn from classic and fugitive bibliographies, hand- and typewritten manuscripts, xeroxed, mimeographed, and samizdat compilations, private publications, personal contacts, and academic and student papers. The material listed in chapter 15, **Folklore and Oral Genres** of this *Reference Guide*, is a mere fraction of that to be found in Legman's magnum opus.

Less notable but still valuable is Joseph C. Hickerson's "A Bibliography of American Folksong in the English Language," which includes some bawdy examples among the more respectable. Frank Hoffmann's *Analytical Survey of Anglo-American Traditional Erotica* contains a good deal of bibliographic material. The *Directory of Humor Magazines and Humor Organizations in America (and Canada)*, edited by Glenn C. Ellenbogen, will alert scholars to periodicals and zines they never knew existed. David E. E. Sloane's magisterial *American Humor Magazines and Comic Periodicals* is still more useful. The volume provides publication data, brief content analysis, censorship problems, and archival locations for hundreds of magazines; typical entries for types featuring "gags and girls" include *Comic Cuties* (1966), *Dash* (1941), *Dolls and Gags* (1953), *Laff* (1940), *Spicy Fun* (1968?), and *Zowie* (1966). Sloane includes sections on "College Humor Magazines," "Scholarly Humor Magazines," and "Humor in American Almanacs: From the Colonial Period to the Civil War and After," each by an authority in the field. Sooner or later scholars will adopt Sloane's model for cataloging more explicit pornographic magazines.

Students of American sexual language need to know Gershon Legman's "On Sexual Speech and Slang," a bibliographic essay. Roger Goodland's justly famous *A Bibliography of Sex Rites and Customs*, a pioneering book first published in 1931, compiles almost 1,000 citations to sexual expression in various cultures, with annotations on their social, religious, and folkloristic aspects. Goodland gives plenty of space to fetishes as well, drawing on classical texts from the conventional to the bizarre in various cultures; the volume is often treated as an example of pornography itself. "Sex Similarities and Differences in Language, Speech, and Nonverbal Communication: An Annotated Bibliography," by Barrie Thorne, Cheris Kramaae, and Nancy Henley is a splendid, comprehensive list of articles on the subject and is itself an updating of the earlier "Sex Differences in Language, Speech, and Nonverbal Communication: An Annotated Bibliography," by Thorne and Henley. Both deal to some extent with erotic and/or obscene speech. Joseph J. Hayes' "Language Behavior of Lesbian Women and Gay Men: A Selected Bibliography (Part I)" is comprehensive on academic treatments until the late 1970s.

EROTIC ART

Scholars in recent years have published photographic compilations of erotic art (painting, sculpture, crafts, artifacts) from around the world, most of it ancient, European, or Oriental rather than American. While some of the classic historians of erotic expression list critical texts, they are more often concerned with identifying the painters and sculptors of questionable works of art. Cary von Karwath's *Die Erotik in der Kunst* is the definitive work on pictorial erotica before 1900; it includes illustrations, a few of them American, as does Eduard Fuchs' three-volume *Geschichte der Erotischen Kunst*, and both of them refer the reader to the smattering of comment on specific items. Volume II of *Bilderlexicon der Erotik*, entitled *Literatur und Kunst*, contains mostly bibliographic essays ranging widely over Western art, definitive only for the time. After all, scholars compiled these reference tools precisely because there were so few information sources.

For *Art Censorship*, Jane Clapp annotates hundreds of images that have offended someone in the West and cross-references critical, biographical, and historical data. A towering achievement, it is still the principal information source on works of art that have engendered controversy over the years. More important, it is easy to use, with more than 600 entries arranged chronologically and also indexed. The drawback is that Clapp's work was published in 1972 and is hard to find. Eugene C. Burt has filled in the ensuing two decades of comment admirably with *Erotic Art: An Annotated Bibliography with Essays*, an ambitious survey of criticism dealing with the subject of erotic art throughout history and in many countries. Its shortcomings are the modesty of the essays and the raggedness of the citations, but it is highly recommended nonetheless. In addition to general background categories, sections are arranged chronologically, beginning with ancient art and running through the present, and geographically, beginning with the Near East and continuing through the Mediterranean, Asia, Africa, Oceania, North and Latin America, and Europe. The Burt volume is a fine source of criticism on the eroticism of individual American artists, though nationalities are not always noted. Much shorter but useful to novices as a readily available annotated bibliography in English is that appended to Peter Webb's *The Erotic Arts*. It is divided for quick reference into chapters titled General, Art (Prehistoric and Primitive; The Oriental World; The Western World), Literature (Erotic; Pornography and Related Topics); and The Performing Arts. Extremely valuable is Lise Vogel's "Fine Arts and Feminism: The Awakening Consciousness," a bibliographic essay on eroticism in modern art in general and women's art in particular.

Of legendary exhibitions, the most famous were those mounted by Phyllis Kronhausen and Eberhard Kronhausen, whose catalogs and guides have become collectors' items. Their *Erotic Art: A Survey of Erotic Fact and Fancy in the Fine Arts* and *The 2nd International Exhibition of Erotic Art (Liljevalchs Konsthal, Stockholm, April 2–May 18, 1969)* provide extensive commentary on the *First and Second International Exhibitions of Erotic Art*, which toured Scandinavia in 1968–1969. In the two volumes (also issued as one, *The Complete Book of Erotic Art*), the Kronhausens allow contemporary artists to speak in two ways, first by reproducing their works and second by interviewing them about erotica and their intent; the most interesting are those with Larry Rivers and

Andy Warhol. The range of media is large: wood, canvas, pen-and-ink drawings, watercolors, lithographs, collages, assemblages, etchings, and so on. The two shows became the nucleus of the *Third International Exhibition*, which eventually was housed in the Kronhausens' own museum in San Francisco. The Kronhausens published selections as a catalog entitled *The International Museum of Erotic Art*. They quote Duncan F. Cameron, director of the Brooklyn Museum, to the effect that "in the collections of all major art museums there are collections of erotic art" (62). Among American artists represented are Larry Rivers, Robert Stanley, Andy Warhol, Tom Wesselman, Claes Oldenburg, George Segal, Kienholz, John Wesley, Tomi Ungerer, Charles Stark, Francis Souza, Knox Martin, Betty Dodson, Robert Grossman, Anne Sharp, Samuels, Robert Parker, and Budd Hopkins. The expense of the museum led the Kronhausens to sell the collection, which was auctioned off in several venues. *The Kronhausen Collection of Erotic Art from the International Museum of Erotic Art, Sold by Phillips* is the catalog of the New York sale, held 31 March 1979 (another took place in Paris the year before).

Other notable catalogs include *Erotic Art '66*, the Sidney Janis Gallery show, celebrated because it was the first such exhibition to be held openly by an upscale American gallery. The copy comments on contemporary works by Steinberg, Rosenquist, Segal, Rotella, Wesselman, Lindner, Dine, Marisol, Kitaj, Fahlstrom, Jones, Stevenson, Warhol, Watts, Klein, and Rivers. *Erotic Art October 30–December 19, 1973*, a landmark exhibition held at the Art Center of the New School for Social Research, while strongest on Oriental material, offered Western images by Picasso, Schiele, and Bellmer but also recent work by George Segal, Tom Wesselman, and Harriette Frances. Still more comprehensive was *Erotic Rarities, 1760–1980*, compiled by Edie Solow, held at the Erotics Gallery in New York. The catalog of 166 drawings, paintings, and objects appended historical essays and notes to photos of the items in order to attract American buyers. The various auction catalogs of erotic art published under the title *Erotische Kunst* since 1979 by D. M. Klinger, the leading European dealer in rarities, offer European and American drawings and paintings mostly produced before the nineteenth century; some are annotated, and all the entries aim at establishing provenance. The Erotic Print Society offers catalogs of contemporary illustrations by mail or Internet. Fisher's Erotic Encyclopedia, a CD-ROM, contains hundreds of examples of erotic art. C. J. Scheiner's *Compendium* and his sporadic catalogs will also repay close study; their pages list art texts on every conceivable form of erotic art.

Just as accessible to American scholars are the bibliographies on erotic painting, sculpture, drawing, woodcuts, lithographs, objets d'art, and a great many other specialized erotic art forms compiled by the Kinsey Institute of Sex, Reproduction, and Gender. These vary in balance and usefulness, depending on the date they were compiled and the strength of the collections in the institute; generally speaking, the larger the collection, the better the bibliography, if only because curators have been working in the area longer. Volume IV of *Studies in Homosexuality*, edited by Dynes and Donaldson, entitled *Homosexuality and Homosexuals in the Arts*, contains articles on artists, writers, performers, and themes. Tee Corinne's *Lesbian Images in the Fine Arts* lists and annotates materials (rather than criticism) in the Kinsey Institute, but it and gallery or exhibition catalogs of erotic paintings or objects do not take the scholar very far. Since American artists now create erotica in many media, students are probably better off consulting individual biographies or critical texts on specific individuals such as, say, Andy Warhol or Eric Fischel, at least where contemporary painters or sculptors are concerned. Finally, as if to illustrate the dynamic of pornography in its movement from margins to kitsch, the Tom of Finland Company of Los Angeles, which holds all rights to this gay artist's drawings, now offers a selection of his images on coffee cups, greeting cards, T-shirts, refrigerator magnets, and other novelties.

PHOTOGRAPHS

Erotic photographs attract collectors. Lee D. Witkin's *The Photograph Collector's Guide* and Richard Blodgett's *Photographs: A Collector's Guide* offer advice on pursuing and authenticating period photos in general rather than erotic varieties in particular. Jonathan Steele's "The Stereoscope and Collecting Stereocards: Part III: Nude Studies in Stereo-Daguerreotypes" is useful for historians as well as collectors of very early images. The several auction catalogs of the Klinger Collection, though frequently overlapping, are authoritative on individual prints and sets. Volume V, *Die Frühzeit der erotischen Fotografie und Postkarten*, describes dozens of shots, sets, and series, including daguerreotypes and collodion stocks, from 1850 to 1920; volume VI, *Die Frühzeit der erotischen Fotografie 1900–1950*, annotates a private collection of positive prints. Other catalogs are auction guides to collections from Vienna, Berlin, and Baltimore. The dealer catalog of the Michel Simon collection, *Erotisme: Dispersion d'une Collection Partielle Provenant de Michel Simon: Varia, Estampes, Livres, Dessins, Cartes Postales, Photographies*, lists some well-known photographs, including some featuring classic European stars of the screen in the nude. Simon had apparently acquired some erotic mutoscope frames, the edges of which could be flipped to simulate motion. Scholars seem to have paid little attention to these or to the arcade-style "peep-show" cabinet mutoscopes that flipped photos of naked ladies past a lens well into the 1950s. The principle is the same in the flip-book; here the photos are stapled at one side and ruffled by the thumb, with the same result; in any case, erotic versions of both types are rare today. A catalog compiled by Fabien Sabates, *1000 Cartes Postales "Tres Coquines"* listed erotic postcards for sale by a Parisian dealer in 1986.

Still the best historical guide to identify individual prints is *Die Erotik in der Photographie*, by Erich Wulffen and his colleagues at the Institute for Sexual Advancement in Vienna during the late 1920s; it contains many essays on erotic images and considers motion pictures as well. Gershon Legman made a start in the 1940s on categorizing the erotic images in the photographs in the archives of the Kinsey Institute according to subject and/or fetish with his *Toward an Historical Bibliography of Sex Technique*, a typescript, but seems to have walked away from the project. Jane Clapp's *Art Censorship*, its pages preponderantly concerned with attacks on painting and sculpture, saves some space for specific suppressed photographs, as does Moshe Carmilly-Weinberger's *Fear of Art: Censorship and Freedom of Expression in Art*, a similarly broad survey, excellent on censorship by U.S. Customs in the first decades of this century. James J. Kilpatrick's *The Smut Peddlers* is better on purveyors of sleazy paperbacks but touches on trade in photographs. Volume III of the President's Commission on Obscenity and Pornography's *Technical Reports of the Commission on Obscenity and Pornography*, deals with the traffic in photographic materials over several decades, while volume IX includes sociological and psychological studies of photos and visual erotica, though similar studies are scattered throughout the nine volumes. Ironically, Greenleaf Classics brought out an *Illustrated Presidential Report of the Commission on Obscenity and Pornography*, edited by Earl Kemp, replete with the sort of photographs the commission examined, which was promptly suppressed. It is prized by collectors today. Part Two (volume I) of the *Attorney General's Commission on Pornography: Final Report, July 1986* includes long lists and descriptions of photographic materials in its discussion of pictorial pornography.

The leading contemporary authority on erotic photographs in the United States is Joseph Vasta. The *Vasta Images/Books Catalogues*, published erratically since 1985, are crucial sources of information on books, classic photo and pinup periodicals, collections, sets, series, portfolios, and individual original prints from around the world. John Howell's " 'The Explicit Image': Ex Voto Gallery," a review for *Artforum* of a 1986 exhibit of selected prints from the Vasta Collection, says that the broad nature of the show revives the "libidinous freedom that ideally exists in erotic photography." Though primarily a dealer in classic print erotica and thus not so authoritative on photographs, C. J. Scheiner does annotate significant images in the catalogs he has published since 1978.

Although Internet surfers can find dozens of erotic image archives, two illustrate the relative merits of such sources. "The Web Museum of Public Nudity" is a huge, commercial archive of photographs and videos of Mardi Gras celebrations, river festivals, public beaches, and exhibitions, but like many Web sites its documentation is lax and nearly worthless. By contrast, John Cox, who operates archive@badpuppy.com, a historical site devoted to gay porn photos, has not only collected some 800,000 images drawn from the files of gay producers such as Spartacus during the years 1950–1980 but also included model releases, business records, and other documents that will someday make possible a genuine history of such enterprises. Himself a photographer in the 1970s and 1980s and owner of Man-Age Studios (producer of magazines like *Outcome* featuring nude males), Cox is determined to preserve the ephemera of the period.

FILMS AND VIDEOTAPES

Easily the most ambitious bibliography of erotic cinema is James L. Limbacher's *Sexuality in World Cinema*, in two volumes. In addition to brief, witty essays, it provides an annotated list of 13,000 legitimate and pornographic films divided into twenty-six categories, with a 280-page index. Traditionally, softcore movies—films that might be pornographic by minority standards—have occupied a borderline state, sometimes prohibited, sometimes ignored, depending mostly on the zealotry of censors. By contrast, until very recently in America, hard-core films flourished beyond the law; there was no question of their intent or content, and the laws governing public exhibition were not intended to apply to such examples, which were simply illegal. Edward De Grazia and Roger K. Newman provide a wealth of information on virtually every mainstream film whose public exhibition has been prohibited in the United States in *Banned Films: Movies, Censors and the First Amendment*. Since most of those movies were, at worst, guilty of displays of nudity or candor regarding birth control, and since some were proscribed for political or racial reasons, the list does not include many that were actually pornographic by modern standards, but it is a splendid resource, especially for those interested in American attitudes toward nudity on-screen.

Craig Hosoda's *The Bare Facts Video Guide* (updated annually) is a quick reference guide to nude scenes in mainstream and soft-core movies indexed by the names of actors and actresses, useful for determining which performers have taken off their clothes for the camera, with exact videotape footage markers. Marvin Jones' *Movie Buff Checklist: A History of Male Nudity in the Movies*, primarily concerned with films in which penises and masculine buttocks are visible, also covers photographs in magazines, advertisements, and album covers. The *Ultimate Directory of Lingerie and Nude Scenes from Movies and TV* adds cable television programs to the mix. The recent appearance of yet another index, Jami Bernard's *Total Exposure: The Movie Buff's Guide to Celebrity Nude Scenes* indicates that Americans suffer from a profound need to see movie royalty in the flesh. *Celebrity Skin* and its competitor, *Celebrity Sleuth*, regularly run pictures.

Reviews of older exploitation films can be found by consulting *The New Film Index: A Bibliography of Magazine Articles in English 1930–1970* by Richard D. Maccann and Edward Perry, and another standard reference tool, the four-volume *Film Study: An Analytical Bibliography*, by Frank Manchell, who categorizes entries under censorship and also under the names of individual directors. James Robert Parish provides synopses, commentary, and technical information on mainstream films dealing with sex for sale in *Prostitution in Hollywood Films: Plots, Critiques, Casts and Credits for 389 Theatrical and Made-for-Television Releases*. As Parish indicates, dealing with the subject in film and television still invokes controversy. "The Nurse as Sex-Object in Motion Pictures, 1930–1980," by Beatrice Kalisch, Philip A. Kalisch, and Mary L. McHugh, offers an amazing list of films dealing with nurses as virtual fetishes. To the genre sections of *Incredibly Strange Films*, edited by Andrea Juno and V. Vale, are appended filmographies and bibliographies available nowhere else on exploitation, "slasher," pornographic, and just plain oddball films. Gregory Waller's entries in "An Annotated Filmography of R-Rated Sexploitation Films Released during the 1970s" are amusing and accurate descriptions of the productions of a decade. The Kinsey Institute owns a copy of Sandra Holtzman's unpublished "A Russ Meyer Bibliography," which lists material on him published until 1974, but it has largely been superseded by David K. Frasier's *Russ Meyer—the Life and Films: A Biography and a Comprehensive, Illustrated, and Annotated Filmography and Bibliography*. Frasier's Introduction offers a pretty good history of erotic cinema as context for Meyer's career and a thorough biography as well but the book is mainly devoted to an astonishing bibliography of 1,144 reviews and articles, including sections on actors and actresses in Meyer's films, from Eve Meyer to Candy Samples. Vintage exploitation footage is included in Mike Varney's video series *Nudie Cuties*, thirteen compilations of nudie films (bare breasts, no visible pubic hair) shot between the 1920s and 1960s. Varney has also compiled three reels of classic exploitation films under the title *Twisted Sex*. Of the many mail-order houses dealing in soft-core exploitation, Something Weird Video, which publishes an extensive catalog, is typical. Rhino Films produces *Sleazemania, Sleazemania Strikes Back*, and *Sleazemania III*, each a three-hour-long compilation of nudies, exploitation films, and burlesque routines, with individual titles like *Scum of the Earth, Beach Blanket Blood Bath, Test Tube Babies*, and so on. *Underground Video* is a catalog of mostly sadistic films, divided into categories such as prison and horror. Though it is entirely tangential to pornography, Mikita Brottman's *Offensive Films: Toward an Anthropology of Cinéma Vomitif* studies disgusting (rather than erotic) films.

The most extensive published bibliography of classic stag films is appended to Di Lauro and Rabkin's *Dirty Movies*; it includes most of the classic films in the Kinsey archive, with interpolations from Hugh Hefner's collection. (For the Kinsey holdings, see chapter 7, **Major Research Collections**, Slabaugh.) Georg Sesslen also includes as an appendix to *Der Pornographische Film* a filmography of more than 2,000 items; given Sesslen's Continental focus, a surprising number of these are American, a statistic that reflects the loss of so many European stags from early decades. Volume III of the *Technical Reports of the President's Commission* contains historical material on stag or smoker films, much of it provided by Kinsey researchers. The Klinger auction catalog for the world's last major sale of vintage stags, *Die Frühzeit des erotischen Films von 1900–1935*, provides brief annotations for several dozen reels, virtually all of which are American. Several American dealers sell old stag films. Global Media offers hundreds of these under the series title "Historic Erotica." FilmFan Video

Labs markets others under the title "Blue Vanities: Classic Vintage Films." Advertisements for other compilations can be found in any number of men's magazines.

A growing number of vintage stags have been transferred to videotape, usually in "nostalgia" compilations. Since the late 1980s, most hard core has been shot directly onto videotape, but many feature-length films from the 1960s, 1970s, and 1980s are also available in VHS. Though hardly academic, the guides and compilations of Jim Holliday, a historian of porn films, merit close attention by researchers. The best of these is his *Only the Best: Jim Holliday's Adult Video Almanac and Trivia Treasury*, an idiosyncratic, but solid, approach to criticism, especially of what have by now become classic films from the 1970s and 1980s. It is indispensable for chronologies, pseudonyms, trivia, anecdotes, awards, checklists, memorable scenes, brief biographies, and input from a dozen other critics. Holliday's earlier *The Top 100 X-Rated Films of All Time* is much sketchier, as is his *How to Build Your X-Rated Video Library*, a book of advice to collectors, but his videotape compilation of scenes featuring leading American porn stars of the 1970s and 1980s, *Legends of Porn*, is extremely useful, as is his *Only the Best: Volumes I and II*, a video anthology of scenes from historically important American porn films. The latter have been reedited to become parts of Holliday's seven-videocassette anthology, *True Legends of Adult Cinema*. These cover the entire history of feature-length American pornographic films and videotapes.

Many quasi-porn magazines like *Adult Cinema Review, Blue Movie Exposé*, and *Cinema Blue*, all of which lasted for a few years in the 1980s, provide not always accurate information about contemporary X-rated films and videotapes and the performers in them for their periods of publication. For contemporary pornographic videotapes, the researcher should consult instead the articles and reviews of the authoritative *Adult Video News* (*AVN*), the trade journal of the industry, aimed at video store owners and consumers. Founded in 1983, *AVN* superseded both the *Bulletin of the Adult Film Association of America* and *TAB (The Adult Business) Report*, which are nonetheless informative about the industry during the late 1970s and early 1980s. *AVN* is indispensable to an understanding of the industry, its conventions, its skirmishes with legislation (often broken down state by state), and, most significantly, its economics, the latter replete with graphs, charts, and reports. Each winter *AVN* publishes an *Alternative Adult Video* supplement, which often contains historical essays on exploitation films, news and reviews of soft-core films, and related materials. Typical sidebars discuss the adult videotape box cover both as a merchandising ploy and an aesthetic achievement, or the appearance of porn star trading cards, a variation on baseball cards, featuring performers of both sexes, clothed and unclothed, as a manifestation of a fan mentality similar to that of the devotees of soap operas. An annual *AVN* rounds up the most notable and popular old and new films and videos; the 1993 *Adult Entertainment Guide* lists 1,200 "top-rated XXX features, amateur, fetish and gay tapes." Once the reader is accustomed to the discourse, a blend of *Variety*-style abbreviation and sophomoric sexual humor, the reviews are often genuinely witty, though they are aimed primarily at video-store owners. Nevertheless, the reader will pick up esoterica about the business: that among an assistant director's responsibilities is the administration of enemas to performers scheduled for scenes of anal intercourse; that property masters must maintain a wide selection of antiallergenic lubricants, condoms, and dildos, the latter lest a penis remain flaccid during a scene; that performers should be provided private showers and space so that they might prepare for scenes or privately couple for relief after scenes that did not reach orgasm.

Extremely valuable are the reports, reviews, and gossip of *Adam Film World and Adult Video Guide*, the oldest American monthly devoted to explicit cinema and generally more reliable than similar magazines, though the information on actors and actresses should be approached with caution. Best described as a fan magazine, *Adam Film World* hypes the careers of performers for a credulous audience, but partly for that reason it is unparalleled as a guide to the mores and customs of the porn subculture. Similar are *XXX Gay Video Showcase*, its monthly gay counterpart, and *Adam Black Video Illustrated*, a bimonthly that deals with Afro-American porn, both from the same publisher. The annual *Adam Film World Directory of Adult Films* and *Adam Film World Directory of Gay Adult Video* are important directories of heterosexual and gay hard-core films and videos of the previous eighteen months, with lists of notable films of the past, capsule reviews that rate eroticism from "warm" to "volcanic," addresses of distributors and retail outlets, brief biographies of actors, directors, and producers, and indexes by theme, director, and performer. Interviews with performers in *Adam Film World* follow, to a degree, the celebrity interviews of popular mainstream magazines: actors and actresses usually begin by talking about their parents, their adolescence, their own children, lovers, the importance of grooming, then move on to discussions of augmented breasts, relative penis sizes, favorite costars and directors, preferred techniques of oral, vaginal, or anal sex, striptease dancing on tour as a sideline, and—most important—their fan clubs or their 900-telephone numbers. Other periodicals of utility include *Hustler Erotic Video Guide*, which specializes in reviews of "gonzo" rather than couples genres; *Video Xcitement*, which searches for videos appealing to wide tastes; and *Gay Video Guide* (quarterly) and *Manshots* (bimonthly), both of which provide extensive coverage of many gay genres (prison, military, bisexual, etc.). The Adult Movie FAQ, a Web site, collates and updates reviews of porn videos.

Occasional reports on porn films and performers in *Playboy* and *Penthouse* are accurate and useful. Except for the *Hustler Erotic Video Guide*, the most gritty reviews and gossip about the industry are to be found in *Screw*, which always answers the question so many critiques of pornographic films neglect to ask: is the film erotic? *Screw* rates the film (or video) on its "Peter Meter," depending on how erect the reviewer thinks the average male viewer should become; the magazine has no comparable scale for female reactions but in recent years has tried to indicate whether or not a particular film would appeal to more than one gender. The *Village Voice* regularly reviewed porn films in the 1970s and early 1980s, a practice that has now dwindled to the occasional article on notable artifacts, but it still accepts ads for gay films. Finally, F.O.X.E. (Fans of X-rated Entertainment) bills itself as information clearinghouse and advocacy group, though its role seems equivocal.

For the consumer or cultural critic, the best handbooks are the seven volumes of *The X-Rated Videotape Guide*, which identifies performers and specific sexual acts, critically summarizes plots, discusses conventions and formulas, and codes sexual behaviors. The first two volumes are by erotic novelist Robert H. Rimmer, the third and fourth by Rimmer and Patrick Riley, and the fifth, sixth, and seventh by Riley alone. Volume I summarizes the plots or lists by category 2,800 films and videotapes shot from 1970 to 1985; volume II covers 1,200 films and videotapes shot between 1986 and 1991, with a listing of older films newly transferred to videotape; volume III surveys tapes released from 1990 to 1992 and indexes the first three volumes; volume IV reviews 1,200 examples shot between October 1992 and October 1993; volumes V (1993–1994), VI (1995–1996), and VII (1997–1998) carry cumulative indexes to earlier volumes. All provide current addresses for film producers and distributors. Large adult bookstores commonly stock illustrated catalogs by major distributors. The most comprehensive is *Video Index '94/95* (updated annually), which catalogs the productions of the Climax Prestige, Blue Climax, Color Climax, Danish Hard-Core, Exciting, Bestsellers, and Rodox lines. Most of these are videotapes from Scandinavia, where the video format has reanimated a porn film industry that was virtually dead, but few of them are distributed outside larger American cities. Moreover, the decline of Scandinavian pornography in the 1980s, before its resuscitation, led Swedish and Danish entrepreneurs to hire American performers to heighten product recognition. Illustrated brochures of other films and videotapes can be found at adult stores.

The *Interactive Adult Movie Almanac*, a CD-ROM, contains 1,000 photos, 750 reviews of adult movies, 250 biographies of stars, and full-motion previews. Other annotated indexes include the *Blue Guides*, which are updated twice annually. *The Blue Guide to Adult Films*, a directory of more than 6,000 hard-core heterosexual and gay films and videos, though available to consumers, is printed from a Boolean database designed to compile commercial catalogs for video retailers and renters. The publisher alphabetizes by title but will break out by performer, director or producer, sexual activity, date, and so on. This volume includes capsule reviews and information on plots and types and ranks films (on tape) on the basis of technical merit, cast, plot, and eroticism. *The Blue Guide to Adult Film Stars* is a directory of more than 3,500 performers who have appeared more than once in heterosexual or gay hard-core films and videos; *The Blue Guide to Male Films and Stars* is a guide to more than 1,000 gay films and performers. *The Best of the Superstars: The Year in Sex*, an annual roundup of performers, has been compiled by John Patrick since 1989. Patrick Riley indexes more than 17,000 porn films and 10,000 performers, including 2,000 pseudonyms or alternative names in the two-volume *The X-Rated Videotape Star Index*. Out-of-date but still useful guides are *Adult Video Index '84* by Keith L. Justice, a listing of some 2,250 cassettes, and *Adult Movies* by Kent Smith, Darrell W. Moore, and Merl Reagle, a collection of capsule plots for 200 films and cassettes shot prior to 1982; both annotate and summarize. *Adult Video News* and *Adult Film World* publish indispensable, annual updates of more than 1,000 features, amateur, fetish, and gay tapes, and even comment on rereleases of exploitation classics. Didier Saillac's *X Vidéo Guide* is a guide to porn videocassettes, many of them American, that are available in France, with biographies of performers and directors, reviews, and other information.

One film catalog worth singling out is that of Studio One, the nation's largest dealer in amateur videos; it lists over 800, with special sections on authentic lesbian films, a genre only gradually freeing itself from heterosexual inscription. Three guides assist women in finding videos to their liking: *The Couple's Guide to the Best Erotic Videos* by the Brents, *The Wise Woman's Guide to Erotic Videos* by Cohen and Fox, and *The Good Vibrations Guide to Adult Videos* by Cathy Winks. All of these list woman-centered films. *Camera Obscura*'s special issue (20/21 [May–September 1989]) on feminists and film contains an exceptionally fine bibliography of feminist work on motion pictures from various perspectives. *Women's Films in Print: An Annotated Guide to 800 16mm Films by Women*, compiled by Bonnie Dawson, includes entries on explicit films by Constance Beeson (*Holding* [1971], a lyrical evocation of lesbian passion), Linda Feferman (*Dirty Books* [1971], a comic spin on a woman who writes porn when her serious books do not sell), Christine Pihl (*Jump Cut* [n.d.], in which a woman experiments with penises, rejecting them all as too big or too little), Pearlyn Goodman (*Richard's Bath* [n.d.], a sensual film of a young man taking a bath), Rosalind Schneider (*Tulip* [1973], a fantasy of the male body as a flower). Patricia Erens' *Sexual Stratagems: The World of Women in Film*, while mostly concerned with legitimate film, has an extensive bibliography of women directors and filmmakers, some of whom, like Constance Beeson and Bonnie Friedman (*Becoming Orgasmic: A Sexual Growth Program for Women* [1975]) and Cathy Joritz (*Bond/Weld* [1982]) have pushed against boundaries. The annual catalogs published by Women Make Movies list films on the body, lesbianism, and sexuality in various degrees of explicitness. *Angry Women*, edited by Andrea Juno and V. Vale, carries filmographies of performance artists.

In compiling its *Annotated Filmography of Selected Films with Lesbian/Gay Content*, the Commission on Gay/Lesbian Issues in Social Work Education attempts to exclude films depicting homosexual stereotypes "for the sole purpose of titillating heterosexual audiences" by listing films the commission considers educational but does include explicit films, such as examples by Constance Beeson, Barbara Hammer, and Ann Hershey, with addresses of sources and distributors. Lesbians have long had the courage of their convictions and list explicit works along with conventional films; a coalition of individuals and groups—Andea Weiss, Altermedia, Women Make Movies, and Greta Schiller—has compiled "Filmography of Lesbian Works," which does exactly that. More popular is Alison Darren's *The Lesbian Film Guide*, an encyclopedia index to mainstream and marginal lesbian films of varying degrees of explicitness. *Facets Gay and Lesbian Video Guide* annotates hundreds of gay and lesbian mainstream and marginal videos, indexed by director and subject, with special sections on videos devoted to AIDS and health-related issues. Raymond Murray's *Images in the Dark: An Encyclopedia of Gay and Lesbian Film and Video* is also an important reference tool. *The Ultimate Guide to Lesbian and Gay Film and Video*, edited by Jenni Olsen, offers more than 2,000 entries on important films indexed by subject, as well as information on significant gay and lesbian film festivals. The two-volume *High Camp: A Gay Guide to Camp and Cult Films* by Paul Roe covers camp films thoroughly if somewhat lightheartedly. *Gay Video: A Guide to Erotica*, a history and directory of explicit gay videos and films on video by John W. Rowberry (*Adam Film World*'s gay editor), is a comprehensive and indispensable annotated filmography of gay and transsexual porn, male striptease films, index to directors, lists of distributors, information on gay film festivals, and a selected list of mainstream films dealing with gay and lesbian matters. Rowberry also lists several historical anthology reels that compile early stags. Richard Dyer's *Now You See It: Studies on Lesbian and Gay Film* appends a splendid bibliography of hard-to-find criticism and a filmography of landmark cinema. The most comprehensive indexing of homosexual characters in Hollywood films is James Robert Parish's *Gays and Lesbians in Mainstream Cinema: Plots, Critiques, Casts and Credits for 272 Theatrical and Made-for-Television Hollywood Releases*, which deals with the years 1914 to 1992. Parish provides technical statistics, reviews, and synopses along with a generous sampling of critical commentary. Wayne M. Bryant surveys eight decades of films from twenty countries in order to distill *Bisexual Characters in Films*, a listing replete with issues of censorship and stereotyping. Among the artifacts of a subculture covered by Leigh Rutledge in his *The Gay Book of Lists* and its more recent updating are gay porn movies and porn stars. *Old Reliable Catalogues* by Old Reliable Company lists and annotates vintage gay videos, photos, and audiotapes, with particular interest in nude boxing and wrestling movies.

The Kinsey Institute maintains an address file of producers whose films are above average, divided according to gender appeal and purpose (e.g., didacticism or entertainment); ask for "Sources of Information and Materials Relating to Human Sexuality: Audio-Visual Materials" and "Annotated List of Audio-Visual Materials with Sexual Content." Focus International distributes educational videotapes on many aspects of human sexual behavior. Many of James Broughton's films, along with media by Laird Sutton, Honey Lee Cottrell, Dick Kortz, Connie Beeson, and the National Sex Forum (the formerly Methodist-funded predecessor of the institute), are annotated in the *Multi-Focus, Incorporated Media Catalog* published by the Institute for Advanced Study of Sexuality. These video, film, and slide packages deal explicitly with sexual topics ranging from masturbation, to homosexuality, lovemaking for the disabled and the elderly, erotica, massage, AIDS, vasectomies, patterns of sexual behavior, abortion, women's health issues, and sex therapy, in addition to aiming at more traditional erotic goals. Electronic Arts Intermix publishes a filmography of vintage avant-garde films from around the world as "Videotapes by Artist/ Producer." Finally, *Artists' Video: An International Guide*, by Lori Zippay et al., is a guide to many categories of continuing serious video experimentation, some of them erotic or explicit.

SEXUAL AIDS AND EQUIPMENT

Some catalogs of sexual appliances have become legendary and have defined what is, in fact, a genre of porn. Perhaps the most famous is the *Illustrated Manual of Sexual Aids* catalog of 1973, published by the Evelyn Rainbird Company, which was harassed into bankruptcy by the Justice Department. The Rainbird catalog was especially ambitious in its brief histories of devices, some cross-referenced against erotic texts in which they are mentioned. The staff of *Screw* collaborated on *The Whole Bedroom Catalog: Everything You Always Wanted to Know about What Comes in the Mail in a Plain Brown Wrapper*, edited by Stephen Lewis; sexual aids get a whole chapter to themselves. John Milton edited *Sex Sense*, a bimonthly consumers' guide to mail-order sex products from 1975 until about 1981. This newsletter was really an extension of his regular feature for *Screw* called "Mail-Order Madness," a shopping guide; *Screw* billed itself as a consumers' tabloid with a mission to evaluate products. Other collector's items are the Spartacus Company's kinky and copiously illustrated *Male Cock Restraints* of 1986 and *The Pleasure Chest Compendium of Amourous and Prurient Paraphernalia* (1979), published by Pleasure Chest, Ltd., which opened stores in major cities. Increased sales of appliances led to books like Bernhardt J. Hurwood's *The Sensuous New Yorker*, a now-dated survey of sex-oriented businesses in New York City (storefront sex shows, porn theaters, adult bookstores, stroke bars, and gay and lesbian clubs) that includes looks at stores that sell sexual aids and toys. The most fascinating single source, however, is the catalog of Doc Johnson Enterprises, manufacturer of more than 2,000 sexual aids, technologies, and novelties.

The Kinsey Institute maintains a source file on sex aids dealers and will provide a list. Other Kinsey bibliographies offer information sources on Aphrodisiacs, Drugs and Sex Behavior, Attitudes on Masturbation, Clothing, Condoms, Contraception, Dildos, Vibrators, Various Fetishes, Humor, Penis Size, and Obscene Telephone Calls. The most reliable information on sexual aids is available from reputable dealers. The most knowledgeable are the saleswomen at San Francisco's Good Vibrations, whose founder, Joani Blank, has written or edited several books on sexual pleasure. The store publishes a quarterly newsletter called *Good Vibes Gazette*, replete with data on new products, reviews of erotic films, and reports on conferences and ideas. The store's catalog offers advice on using products, the relative merits of latex as opposed to other materials, appropriate lubricants, descriptions of sensations and experiences, and exhortations to experiment. The store caters to all genders but is especially sensitive to gay and straight women. Another store designed to be comfortable for women, Eve's Garden in New York, distributes a descriptive catalog by Dell Williams called *Celebrate the Joy*. Like the Good Vibrations catalog, it annotates entries on dildos, harnesses, lubricants, vibrators, lotions, condoms for penises or dildos, dental dams, light restraints, and many books on sexual technique for heterosexuals and lesbians. Comparable firms advertise in magazines of general distribution; one firm, *Intimate Treasures*, sells catalogs of different suppliers. Products can include erotic candies, fetishistic garments, cosmetics, novelties, games, toys, penis enlargers, nipple, labia, and scrotum jewelry, penis rings (for maintaining erections), aphrodisiacs, vitamins, and books on how to seduce or pleasure potential partners. Easily obtainable is the *Catalog of Sexual Novelties* from the mail-order company Adam and Eve. While chiefly concerned with substance abuse, *Drugs and Sex: A Bibliography*, by Ernest L. Abel, provides extensive information on the alleged aphrodisiac effects of some drugs and on bizarre practices. Finally, though it is not particularly relevant to American pornography, Lilian P. Sanderson's *Female Genital Mutilation: A Bibliography* is a comprehensive listing of such practices.

MAGAZINES, NEWSPAPERS, AND COMICS

Researchers attempting to find material on pornographic periodicals will swiftly exhaust standard research tools such as the *Union Guide*, the *Sears List to Periodicals*, the *Reader's Guide to Periodical Literature*, and various electronic databases like ERIC, though all of them may be helpful at the start. More specialized is Samia Husni's *Samia Husni's Guide to New Magazines*, an annual guide to new magazines, including sexually oriented ones (e.g., *Wet Lips, Erotic Lingerie, Sexual Secrets*). Parts 2 and 3 of the *Report* of the President's Commission on Pornography and Obscenity deal extensively with soft- and hardcore magazines sold in stores and by mail. Volumes III (*The Marketplace: The Industry*), VI (*National Survey*), and IX (*The Consumer and the Community*) of the *Technical Report* offer in-depth looks at magazine sales and consumption. Parts 4 and 5 of the two-volume *Final Report* of the Attorney General's Commission devote more space to soft- and hard-core magazines than any previous study; some critics believe that this commission's only genuine accomplishment was to *list* 2,700 fetish titles (everybody's favorite: *Anal Sweat*), a perverse labor that reflects the commissioners' own obsessions. The bibliography is so explicit that it gives credence to charges that the *Final Report* is itself pornographic.

The fastest source is alt.magazines.pornographic on the Internet, a continuously updated listing of materials. John Locke's *The Pulp Magazines Quick Reference Guide* contains a section on "Adult/Racy" types, and Leslie Friedman's *Sex Role Stereotyping in the Mass Media: An Annotated Bibliography* covers "skin magazines and pornography" and comic books. Alan Betrock's books on cult magazines of the 1950s and 1960s are authoritative, especially his *Complete Guide to Cult Magazines. Access: The Supplementary Index to Periodicals*, published since 1975, indexes magazines such as *Playboy, Penthouse, After Dark*, and *Oui* (the latter two now defunct) and, perhaps more important, regional and local magazines such as the *Village Voice, Miami Magazine, Atlanta*, and *Los Angeles Magazine*. Categories include "Exotic Dancing" (helpful on locating information on popular strippers in different areas of the country, local ordinances against nudity, etc.), "Vibrators," "Masturbation," "Voyeurism," "Aphrodisiacs," "Music, Rock—Pornography," and many others. Articles on erotic performance can be found under title and reviews, on prosecutions under subject or individual (e.g., Reuben Sturman), and on erotic miscellany under "Pornography—Denver" and many other city names. For several years during the 1960s and 1970s, Hugh Hefner wrote regular installments of what seemed an interminable "Playboy Philosophy," some of which is indexed by Mildred Miles in *Index to Playboy*, which cites other articles and features. Nancy K. Humphreys provides publication data and cultural context for an enormous variety of journals in *American Women's Magazines: An Annotated Historical Guide*, which, while very general, can help the scholar locate marginal titles. The second volume (135–139) of *Women in American History: A Bibliography*, edited by C. E. Harrison, lists entries under "The Depiction of Women in the Popular Media (Television, Film, Magazines, the Press, Advertising, and Pornography)." The twenty-three reels of women's journals, newsletters, and other material from 1956 to 1974 collected by Herstory as *Herstory, Women's History Collection, Microfilm Collection* can sometimes be useful. Susan Searing's quarterly, *Feminist Periodicals: A Current Listing of Contents*, is a comprehensive guide to topics of interest since the early 1980s. An excellent guide to three periodicals that often deal with erotica as a manifestation of popular culture is *Popular Abstracts: Journal of Popular Culture, 1967–1977; Journal of Popular Film, 1972–1977; Popular Music and Society, 1971–1975*, edited by Ray Browne and Christopher Geist.

The success of *High Weirdness by Mail: A Directory of the Fringe: Mad Prophets, Crackpots, Kooks & True Visionaries*, a guide to finding bizarre texts and journalism, led Ivan Stang to go on-line with *High Weirdness by Email. Small Press Review*, compiled yearly by the Committee on Small Magazines and Publishers, lists publication data for magazines both obscure and strange, though most entries detail the output of quite respectable, independent publishers and small presses. Gerald S. Greenberg comments on criticism of sensational print and television journalism in *Tabloid Journalism: An Annotated Bibliography of English-Language Sources*. Alan Betrock's *Sleazy Business: A Pictorial History of Exploitation Tabloids (1959–1974)* covers notorious tabloids of the 1960s and early 1970s. The *Underground Newspaper Microfilm Collection* contains 147 reels of papers published between 1965 and 1973, drawn from various archives. University Microfilm sells two collections of underground newspapers and supplies a guide for each; these are *Alternative Press Collection: A Guide to the Microfilm Collection* and *Underground Press Collection: A Guide to the Microfilm Collection.*

Published decades ago, Gillian Freeman's *The Undergrowth of Literature* remains the most ambitious investigation of sexual periodicals in English, and the strange titles can still generate interest amid the bizarre zines that seem emissaries from various fringes today. Rayozine Studios of New York holds an annual exhibition of fanzines, including the pornographic types, and publishes catalogs called *Samizines.* Penguin has published *The World of Zines: A Guide to the Independent Magazine Revolution,* by Mike Gunderloy and Cari G. Janice, who discuss some 400 zines, not all of them pornographic, though many of them are ephemeral. Richard Kadrey's two-volume *Covert Culture Sourcebook* annotates books, films, and magazines on sexual subjects and fetishes from music to mutilation. Tuppy Owens' *The (Safer) Sex Maniac's Bible* lists some of the more specialized contemporary publications by fetish (piercing, S/M, bondage and discipline, rubber and leather enthusiasts, shaved pubic areas, enemas, tickling, mud wrestling, cross-dressing, foot fetishes, swingers, spanking, lactation, mutilation, penises and foreskins, large or small breasts, tattoos, corsets, transvestites and transsexuals, and so on). Bill Brent's *The Black Book,* now in its fifth (1998) edition, covers publications even more bizarre, as do Russ Kick's *Outposts: A Catalog of Rare and Disturbing Alternative Information* and its sequel, *Psychotropia. Outposts* bills itself as designed to help citizens aim at "authority's crotch." In both volumes Kick annotates books, magazines, and comics on subjects ranging from surveillance, cyberculture, the body, political extremism, the occult, and, of course, sexual representation.

Hardly a bibliography in the accepted sense, Andrea Fleck Clardy's *Words to the Wise: A Writer's Guide to the Feminist and Lesbian Periodicals and Publishers* indicates which magazines are interested in gender-specific erotica. The *Directory of Homosexual Organizations and Publications,* edited by Ursula Enters Copley, is good on earlier journals and magazines. An author/subject index to some forty lesbian journals, the earliest of which dates to 1947, is the finding key to *Lesbian Periodicals Index,* by Clare Potter. Ginny Vida's *Our Right to Love: A Lesbian Resource Book* is an extensive guide to materials by, for, and about lesbians, including fiction and magazines. The title of Linda Garber's *Lesbian Sources: A Bibliography of Periodical Articles, 1970–1990* is self-explanatory. The zine *Queer Zine Explosion* annotates lesbian and gay zines as they appear.

The most useful bibliographies on comic book criticism are Doug Highsmith's "Comic Books: A Guide to Information Sources," Randall W. Scott's *Comic Books and Strips: An Information Sourcebook,* and the Appendix to Tom Inge's *Comics as Culture.* In *R. Crumb Checklist of Work and Criticism,* Donald M. Fiene covers work by and about the comic artist R. Crumb until 1980. Carl Richter picks up where Fiene leaves off; Richter lists book and magazine appearances, exhibitions, anthologized pieces, theatrical and film adaptations by the artist, and material on Crumb in *Crumb-ology: The Works of R. Crumb, 1981–1994*. The *Last Gasp Catalog* of underground comix is one of the most comprehensive mail-order catalogs available, as is *The Ultimate Comics Catalog*, issued by Fantagraphics. Almost as good is *Bud Plant's Incredible Catalog*, which lists many adult comic books, including contemporary fetish fare like *Big Top Bondage* and *Stiletto* (not to mention posters, books, zines, novelties, buttons, figurines, T-shirts, trading cards, and so on). Plant also publishes a newsletter called *Comic Art Update* in between its three annual catalogs. The See Hear Web Catalog offers comics (and their radical counterpart known as comix) and collections. Updated irregularly, Jay Kennedy's *The Official Underground and Newave Comix Price Guide*, aimed primarily at collectors, includes pornographic, along with mainstream, titles and thus functions as a rough bibliographic tool. For those who wish information on contemporary materials, *Indy Magazine: The Guide to Alternative Comix and Film* contains articles and reviews by cognoscenti; it is more authoritative on comics than on movies. The annotated listings in David Sloane's *American Humor Magazines and Comic Periodicals* will help scholars find magazines that have published risqué cartoons.

ELECTRONIC MEDIA

Jeanne Steele and Jane Brown provide a bibliography of bibliographies in "Sexuality and the Mass Media: An Overview." The title of Nancy Signorelli's *Role Portrayal and Stereotyping on Television: An Annotated Bibliography of Studies Relating to Women, Minorities, Aging, Sexual Behavior, Health and Handicaps* indicates its coverage; its comprehensiveness should generate relevant sources for the scholar interested in sex roles and sex behavior as depicted on the small screen. In other useful bibliographies, Leslie Friedman surveys articles on "skin magazines and pornography," humor, comic books, science fiction, rock and roll lyrics, misogynistic album covers, and programming on radio and television in *Sex Role Stereotyping in the Mass Media: An Annotated Bibliography*, while Odasuo Alali deals with criticism of images of sensuality and gender on electronic media in *Mass Media Sex and Adolescent Values: An Annotated Bibliography and Directory of Organizations*. *Violence and Terror in the Mass Media: An Annotated Bibliography*, by Nancy Signorelli and George Gerbner, folds in some criticism of sex on electronic channels. Although somewhat dated now, Catherine E. Johnson's *TV Guide 25 Year Index: By Author and Subject* can be useful in tracking down articles on sexual subjects on talk shows, tabloids, and prime-time television in *TV Guide*, the magazine with a large circulation in the United States and thus an excellent bellwether of popular tastes; articles on sex, indecency, censorship, and government and network policy on expression are among those listed. An exceptionally close, even obsessional reading of sex on television is G. Allen Marburger's "Bondage Fantasies in Popular Entertainment: An Annotated Listing of Sequences from Movies and

Television." This fifty-one-page paper deals with bondage as a theme in identified scenes and might serve as a reminder that pornography may be in the mind of the beholder. James Robert Parish offers a pretty exhaustive survey of the treatment of one of America's favorite stereotypes on television in *Prostitution in Hollywood Films: Plots, Critiques, Casts and Credits for 389 Theatrical and Made-for-Television Releases*. Parish's other guide, *Gays and Lesbians in Mainstream Cinema: Plots, Critiques, Casts and Credits for 272 Theatrical and Made-for-Television Hollywood Releases* is also valuable for its examination of the treatment of homosexuality by electronic media.

Useful are several guides to modern music published by Penguin; none have any specific orientation toward pornography or sexual expression, but all are authoritative and helpful in tracking lyrics and performers. These are *Rock: The Rough Guide* (no editor listed), *Jazz: The Rough Guide*, edited by Ian Carr, and *Punk*, edited by Adrian Boot. Richard Kadrey's *Covert Culture Sourcebook* and *Covert Culture Sourcebook 2.0* are informative on erotic and esoteric music. Shannon T. Boyer's *Misogynist Music and Its Effect on Listeners* reviews the literature on the subject. For other sources and studies, the scholar should turn to B. Lee Cooper's *A Resource Guide to Themes in Contemporary American Song Lyrics, 1950–1985*.

Numerous on-line Listserv-based Conferences, Newsletters, and Bulletin Boards in the Humanities and Social Sciences (e.g., FOLKLORE@TAMVMI) offer information on research (serious and light) in pornographic genres via BITNET. Such sites encourage inquiry and robust exchange on obscure topics. Again, nearly all of these are eminently scholarly and respectable. Bob Jackson, for example, runs "IntimAge Biblio: Comserve Database," a database on intimacy and sexuality in later life accessible on BITNET. Also reached through BITNET is Thomas L. Tedford's "CensrSex Biblio: Comserve Database," essentially an annotated list of books treating the censorship of sexual materials. A guide to underground computer networks on the Internet entitled the Computer Underground Digest can be accessed at its e-mail address. Another site, E-zines Database Menu, breaks out electronic zines by category.

Fringeware Review, available by zine or e-mail, is devoted to esoteric products for use on on-line systems. The same is true of *High Weirdness by Email*, a catalog of books and materials on esoterica. Printed maps to sites include both volumes of the *Covert Culture Sourcebook*, by Richard Kadrey, which contains electronic addresses for erotica; *The Adult BBS Guidebook*, by Billy Wildhack, who reviews the protocols of more than 500 erotic BBSs, with information on chat services, downloading capability, advertising, and so on; *Erotic Connections: Love and Lust on the Information Highway*, also by Wildhack, with a similar intent and focus; *The Internet Directory*, by Eric Braun, who offers a general guide to information sources and other features available on the Internet, with no excessive emphasis on erotica; *NET.SEX*, by Candi Rose and Dirk Thomas, who make arch and coy comments on favorite sites; and *The Penthouse*

Guide to Cybersex, by Nancy Tamosaitis, who comments on a list of erotic sites in cyberspace. Even more comprehensive is William E. Brigman's "Appendix to Sex on Internet." This is a forty-page typescript to sex-oriented services on the superhighway, divided into sections such as World Wide Webs, Gopher Sites, E-Mail Lists, IRC Chat Groups, Bulletin Board Services, and many others. Brigman, a legal scholar and an authority on erotica, has annotated many of the entries. Brigman himself defers to Philip Mason's *The Complete Internet Sex Resource Guide*, a vast appendix updated monthly. It can be accessed in *alt.magazines.pornographic* or requested by e-mail to Philip@iglou.com (message area: Send Sex Surfer Catalog). Diversified Services publishes a series of pamphlets on dominance, bondage, and other kinky addresses in *Prodigy, Genie, Delphi, AmericaOnline, Internet*, and *Compuserve*; their general guide is "Finding D & S on On-Line Services." Richard Kadrey examines the topics discussed on Usenet, where participants trade narratives, in "alt.sex.bondage" in *Wired*, one of several journals that regularly cover such subjects. In his *Gay Sex: A Manual for Men Who Love Men*, Jack Hart includes information on accessing homosexual bulletin boards.

Fringe materials on the Internet are also cited by Stephen Daly and Nathaniel Wice in *Alt. Culture: An A–Z Guide to the '90s—Underground, Online, and over the Counter*. Net surfers can access Anne Balsamo's "Bibliography of Cyberspace, Cyberpunk, Electronic Communication, and Postmodernism," a continuously updated listing of comment on the subjects listed, only a few of which deal with fantasy, gender, and the body. "Regulating the Internet," a special issue of *CQ Researcher*, carries an excellent bibliography drawn from popular, academic, and congressional sources. Still more authoritative are the videotapes offered by Sweet Pea Productions: the 1996–1997 catalog *Computers, Freedom and Privacy* lists dozens of videotaped discussions on such topics as "The Communications Decency Act," "Censorship and Content Control on the Internet," and "Ethics, Morality and Criminality Online."

PERFORMANCE

The scholar of the erotic stage should begin with Arthur Maria Rabenalt's magnum opus *Mimus Eroticus*, a five-volume, in-depth study of erotic dramatic representation from classical to modern periods; the last volume covers the American stage, and the bibliography is authoritative. Peter Webb's *The Erotic Arts* deals with erotic theater in the course of its running commentary on many genres and contains an appendix by David F. Chesire on "Eroticism in the Performing Arts" on dance, music, opera, theater, happenings, and so on. Webb himself deals with the "Theatre of Celebration," on the avant-garde of the 1960s and 1970s, in chapter 10. M. B. Wallace's *The Striptease: An Annotated Bibliography* (1973) has been updated (1981) as a standard Kinsey Institute bibliography. Even better is David Scott's *Behind the G-String: An Exploration of the Stripper's Image, Her Person, and Her Meaning*; he intersperses a source survey with interviews with strippers, some of whom regard the profession as demeaning, others as empowering. *Exotic Dancer: Directory of Gentlemen's Clubs* is an annual guide to agencies, go-go clubs, and nude, topless, and stripper bars, and *Stripper Magazine* is the trade journal of the exotic dance industry and the more than 2,500 emporiums that dot the map. Chipper Dove's "Bare Necessities" reviews the first issue (1993) of *Gentleman's Club*, a journal of topless and nude dancing, and its associated line of videotapes and trading cards of headliners. The magazine itself is valuable for its information on contemporary dancers, who travel the national circuits of major cities. Municipal magazines for many other cities (Los Angeles, Denver, Atlanta, and so on) frequently run articles on local strippers, around whom subcultures can form; perusing these is a good way to study regional styles (Texas clubs, e.g., brag that they are unique). Such articles are indexed under "Exotic Dancing" in *Access: The Supplementary Index to Periodicals.* In *The (Safer) Sex Maniac's Bible*, Tuppy Owens, herself mistress of London's annual Sex Maniacs' Ball, provides very comprehensive listings of sex clubs, descriptions of specialties, and protocols. Retailers of costumes for strippers and topless dancers advertise regularly in the back pages of the *Village Voice*, which also carries want ads for establishments in the metropolitan New York area recruiting performers. Both kinds of ads are a good index of current styles in nude and seminude choreography. The Web site Exotic Dancer Page functions as a clearinghouse for dancers seeking employment or information. *Danzine*, aimed at women in the stripping industry, offers articles on working conditions, salaries, and advice on improving routines. Dancerlink is a Web index of dancers' home pages.

John Gray's *Active Art: A Bibliography of Artists' Performance from Futurism to Fluxus and Beyond* is useful in researching performance art during the periods indicated in the title. So is Richard Kostelanetz's *On Innovative Performance(s): Three Decades of Recollections on Alternative Theater*; the critic covers an enormous number of performances and performers. Scholars following the current performance art scene should consult journals such as *High Performance*, especially for events on the West Coast, *Screw*, or the *Village Voice*. For the week of 17 September 1991, the *Voice* ran a review of what the paper called Annie Sprinkle's "Post-Post-Porn Modernist" show at the Sanford Meisner Theater and another of Penny Arcade's *State of Grace* at P.S. 122, along with such diverse items as a report that a San Francisco federal grand jury had refused to indict the photographer Jock Sturges on child porn charges, despite the government's fifteen-month effort to censor his visual studies of nude families, a bemused observation that posters featuring bare male buttocks had offended some people even on Fire Island, and many announcements of other shows and performances dealing with matters sexual. In his weekly page, "La Dolce Musto," *Voice* columnist Michael Musto reports on his visits to the Manhattan club scene. Tourists may consult specialized guides to sexual activities in larger cities. Typical are *Erotic New York: A Guide to the Red Hot Apple*, by the staff of *T & A*, and *L.A. Bizarro: The Insider's Guide to the Obscure, the Absurd, and the Perverse in Los Angeles*, by Anthony R. Lovett and Matt Maranian.

NOTES

1. Richard Posner, *Sex and Reason* (Cambridge: Harvard University Press, 1992), p. 364, n. 32.
2. R. S. Bravard, *"Sourcebook on Pornography*, by Franklin Mark Osanka and Sara Lee Johann," *Choice* (May 1990): 1488.
3. Michael Perkins, *The Secret Record: Modern Erotic Literature* (New York: William Morrow, 1977), p. 90.

REFERENCES

Aarne, Antti, and Stith Thompson. *The Types of the Folktale: A Classification and Bibliography*. Folklore Fellows Communication, 184. Helsinki: Suomalainen Tiedekatemia, 1961.

Abel, Ernest L. *Drugs and Sex: A Bibliography*. Westport, CT: Greenwood Press, 1983.

Access: The Supplementary Index to Periodicals, 1975–. Syracuse, NY: Gaylord Professional Publishers, 1975–1977; Evanston, IL: J. G. Burke Publishers, 1978–.

Adam and Eve. *Catalog of Sexual Novelties*. P.O. Box 800, Carrboro, NC 27510.

Adam Black Video Illustrated. Los Angeles: Knight Publishing, 1995–.

Adam Film World and Adult Video Guide. Los Angeles: Knight Publishing, 1968–.

Adam Film World Directory of Adult Films. Los Angeles: Knight Publishing, annual.

Adam Film World Directory of Gay Adult Video. Los Angeles: Knight Publishing, annual.

Adam Presents Amateur Porn. Los Angeles: Knight Publishing, 1993–.

Adam X-Rated Movie Handbook. Los Angeles: Knight Publishing, 1982–, annual.

Adult Cinema Review. New York, 1981–1988.

Adult Movie FAQ. faq@ramenet.

Adult Video News. Upper Darby, PA, 1983–1996; Van Nuys, CA, 1996–.

Adult Video News. Adult Entertainment Guide. Upper Darby, PA: AVN, 1983–1996; Van Nuys, CA: AVN, 1996–, annual.

Adult Video News, Alternative Adult Video. Upper Darby, PA: AVN, 1983–1996; Van Nuys, CA: AVN, 1996–, annual.

Alali, A. Odasuo. *Mass Media Sex and Adolescent Values: An Annotated Bibliography and Directory of Organizations*. Jefferson, NC: McFarland, 1991.

Aldous, Joan, and Reuben Hill, comps. *International Bibliography of Research in Marriage and the Family*. 2 vols. Minneapolis: University of Minnesota Press/Institute of Life Insurance for the Minnesota Family Study Center, 1964–1972.

Alternative Press Index. College Park, MD: Alternative Press Centre, 1969–.

alt.magazines.pornographic.

alt.sex hierarchy of newsgroups.

American Psychiatric Association (APA). *Diagnostic and Statistical Manual of Mental Disorders*. 4th ed. rev. Washington, DC: APA, 1994.

Amey, Lawrence, Timothy Hall, Carl Jansen, Charles May, and Richard Wilson, eds. *Censorship*. 3 vols. Pasadena, CA: Salem Press, 1997.

Archives of Sexual Behavior. New York, 1971–.

Arndt, William B. *Gender Disorders and the Paraphilias.* Madison, CT: International Universities Press, 1991.

Attorney General's Commission on Pornography. *Attorney General's Commission on Pornography: Final Report, July 1986.* 2 vols. Washington, DC: Government Printing Office, 1986.

Balsamo, Anne. "Bibliography of Cyberspace, Cyberpunk, Electronic Communication, and Postmodernism." anne.balsamo@lcc.gatech.edu.

Barry, Robert J. *Incest: The Last Taboo.* Washington, DC: Federal Bureau of Investigation/Department of Justice, 1984.

Beasley, Ruth. *International Directory of Sex Research and Related Fields.* Boston: G. K. Hall, 1976.

Becourt, Daniel. *Livres Condamnes, Livres Interdits.* 2d ed. Paris: Cercle Libraire, 1972.

Bernard, Jami. *Total Exposure: The Movie Buff's Guide to Celebrity Nude Scenes.* New York: Citadel, 1995.

Betrock, Alan. *Complete Guide to Cult Magazines.* Brooklyn, NY: Shake Books, 1998.

———. *Sleazy Business: A Pictorial History of Exploitation Tabloids (1959–1974).* Brooklyn, NY: Shake Books, 1996.

Bibliothèque des Curieux. Paris: Privately printed, 1923.

Bilderlexicon der Erotik. Ein bibliographisches und biographisches Nachschlagewerk, eine Kunst- und Literaturgeschichte für die Gebiete der erotischen Belletristik . . . von der Antike zur Gegenwart. 6 vols. Vienna and Hamburg: Verlag für Kulturforschung, 1928–1931, 1963. Edited by Leo Schidrowitz: I: *Kulturgeschichte*; II: *Literatur und Kunst*; III: *Sexualwissenschaft*; IV: *Ergänzungsband.* Edited by Armand Mergen: V and VI: *Sexualforschung: Stichwort und Bild.*

Bloch, Iwan (aka Eugen Dühren, aka Albert Hagen). *Anthropological Studies in the Strange Sexual Practices in All Races of the World.* New York: Falstaff Press, 1933; rpt. *Strange Sexual Practices.* North Hollywood, CA: Brandon House, 1967.

Blodgett, Richard. *Photographs: A Collector's Guide.* New York: Ballantine, 1979.

The Blue Guide to Adult Films. The Blue Guide, Box 16, Ogdensburg, NJ 07439, annual.

The Blue Guide to Adult Film Stars. The Blue Guide, Box 16, Ogdensburg, NJ 07439, annual.

The Blue Guide to Male Films and Stars. The Blue Guide, Box 16, Ogdensburg, NJ 07439, annual.

Blue Movie Exposé. New York, 1981–1985.

Boot, Adrian. *Punk.* New York: Penguin, 1996.

Boyer, Shannon T. *Misogynist Music and Its Effect on Listeners.* Ph.D. dissertation, Texas A&M University, 1995.

Bradley, Marion Z., and Gene Damon [Barbara Grier]. *A Complete Cumulative Checklist of Lesbian, Variant, and Homosexual Fiction in English.* Rochester, TX: N.p., 1960.

Braun, Eric. *The Internet Directory.* New York: Fawcett, 1993.

Braun, Saul, ed. *Catalog of Sexual Consciousness.* New York: Grove Press, 1975.

Brent, Bill, ed. *The Black Book.* Editions 1–5. Brent/Amador, P.O. Box 31155, San Francisco, 94131–0155, 1993–1998.

Brent, S., and E. Brent. *The Couple's Guide to the Best Erotic Videos.* New York: St. Martin's, 1997.

Brewer, Joan S., and Rod W. Wright. *Sex Research: Bibliographies from the Institute for Sex Research.* Phoenix, AZ: Oryx Press, 1979.

Brigman, William E. "Appendix to Sex on Internet." University of Houston–Downtown. Brigman@uhdux2.dt.uh.edu.

Brottman, Mikita. *Offensive Films: Toward an Anthropology of Cinéma Vomitif.* Westport, CT: Greenwood Press, 1997.

Browne, Ray B., and Christopher D. Geist, eds. *Popular Abstracts: Journal of Popular Culture, 1967–1977: Journal of Popular Film, 1972–1977; Popular Music and Society, 1971–1975.* Bowling Green, OH: Popular Press, 1978.

Bryant, Wayne M. *Bisexual Characters in Films: From Anaïs to Zee.* Binghamton, NY: Haworth Press, 1997.

Bud Plant's Comic Art Update. P.O. Box 1689, Grass Valley, CA 95945, current.

Bud Plant's Incredible Catalog. P.O. Box 1689, Grass Valley, CA 95945, current.

Bulletin of the Adult Film Association of America. Los Angeles, 1979–1982.

Bullough, Vern, ed. *The Frontiers of Sex Research.* Buffalo, NY: Prometheus Books, 1979.

Bullough, Vern, and Bonnie Bullough. *Cross Dressing, Sex, and Gender.* Philadelphia: University of Pennsylvania Press, 1993.

———. *Prostitution: An Illustrated Source History.* New York: Crown, 1978.

Bullough, Vern, Bonnie Bullough, and Alice Stein. *Human Sexuality: An Encyclopedia.* Hamden, CT: Garland, 1993.

Bullough, Vern, Margaret Deacon, Barrett Elcano, and Bonnie Bullough. *A Bibliography of Prostitution.* New York: Garland, 1977.

Bullough, Vern, W. Dorr Legg, Barrett W. Elcano, and James Kepner. *An Annotated Bibliography of Homosexuality.* 2 vols. Hamden, CT: Garland, 1976.

Bullough, Vern, with L. U. Sentz and Dorothy Tao. *Prostitution: A Guide to Sources.* Hamden, CT: Garland, 1992.

Burt, Eugene C. *Erotic Art: An Annotated Bibliography with Essays.* Boston: G. K. Hall, 1989.

Busha, Charles H. "Censorship and Intellectual Freedom: A Bibliography, 1970–1981." *Drexel Library Quarterly*, 18 (Winter 1982): 101–108.

Byerly, Greg, and Rick Rubin. *Pornography: The Conflict over Sexually Explicit Material in the United States. An Annotated Bibliography.* New York: Garland, 1980.

Camera Obscura. Special issue on Feminists and Film. 20/21 (May–September 1989): 336–372.

Campbell, Patricia J. *Sex Education Books for Young Adults, 1892–1979.* New York: Bowker, 1979.

———. *Sex Guides: Books and Films about Sexuality for Young Adults.* New York: Garland, 1986.

Camphausen, Rufus C. *The Encyclopedia of Erotic Wisdom, a Reference Guide to the Symbolism, Techniques, Rituals, Sacred Texts, Anatomy, and History of Sexuality.* Rochester, VT: Inner Traditions International, 1991.

Carmilly-Weinberger, Moshe. *Fear of Art: Censorship and Freedom of Expression in Art.* New York: Bowker, 1986.

Carr, Ian. *Jazz: The Rough Guide.* New York: Penguin, 1996.

Carrington, Charles. *Chas. Carrington's List of Choice English Books.* Paris: Briffaut Brothers, n.d.

Catalogue: Livres Rare and Curieux. Paris: Librairie Artistique, n.d.

Celebrity Skin. New York, 1979–.

Celebrity Sleuth. Los Angeles, 1989–.

Chervenak, Mary Francesca. "Selected Bibliography on Pornography and Violence." *University of Pittsburgh Law Review*, 40 (1979): 652–660.

Chesire, David F. "Eroticism in the Performing Arts." *The Erotic Arts*, by Peter Webb. Boston: New York Graphic Society, 1975, pp. 297–328.

Cinema Blue. New York, 1980–1985.

Clapp, Jane. *Art Censorship*. Metuchen, NJ: Scarecrow Press, 1972.

Clardy, Andrea Fleck. *Words to the Wise: A Writer's Guide to the Feminist and Lesbian Periodicals and Publishers*. Ithaca, NY: Firebrand Pubs., 1986.

[Clowes, William Laird.] *Bibliotheca Arcana Seu Catalogs Librorum Penetralium: Being Brief Notices of Books That Have Been Secretly Printed, Prohibited by Law, Seized, Anathematised, Burnt or Bowdlerised, by Speculator Morum*. London: privately printed [George Redway], 1885; London: Piscean Press, 1971.

Coalition on Sexuality and Disability. *Sexuality and Disability*, ed. Stanley H. Ducharme. 122 East 23rd Street, New York City 10010, 1978–.

Cohen, Angela, and Sarah G. Fox. *The Wise Woman's Guide to Erotic Videos*. New York: Broadway Books, 1997.

Cohen, Henri. *Guide de l'Amateur des Livres a Gravures du XVIIIe Siècle*, updated by Seymour De Ricci. 6th ed. Paris: Editions du Vexin Français, 1973.

Commission on Gay/Lesbian Issues in Social Work Education. *Annotated Filmography of Selected Films with Lesbian/Gay Content*. New York: Council on Social Work Education, 1984.

Committee on Small Magazines and Publishers. *Small Press Review*. P.O. Box 100, Paradise, CA 95969, annual.

Communication Abstracts. Beverly Hills, CA: Sage, 1978–.

Computer Underground Digest. tkOjut2@niu.bitnet.

Congressional Information Services. *Congressional Committee Hearings Index*. Washington, DC: Government Printing Office, current.

Cooper, B. Lee. *A Resource Guide to Themes in Contemporary American Song Lyrics, 1950–1985*. Westport, CT: Greenwood Press, 1986.

Copley, Ursula Enters, ed. *Directory of Homosexual Organizations and Publications*. Hollywood, CA: Homosexual Information Center, 1982.

Corinne, Tee. *Lesbian Images in the Fine Arts*. San Francisco: Privately issued, 1978.

Cox, John, www.archive@badpuppy.com.

Curiosities Bibliographiques: La Plus Jolie Collection D'Ouvrages Secrets. (Special Catalog 24). N.p.

Daly, Stephen, and Nathaniel Wice. *Alt. Culture: An A–Z Guide to the '90s—Underground, Online, and over the Counter*. New York: HarperPerennial, 1995.

Damon, Gene [Barbara Grier], Jan Watson, and Robin Jordan. *The Lesbian in Literature*. Reno, NV: Ladder, 1975; rpt. Barbara Grier et al. *The Lesbian in Literature: A Bibliography*. 3d ed. Tallahassee, Fl: Naiad Press, 1981.

Dancerlink. www.mindspring.com/-fitzmulti/fitzdancering.html.

Danzine. 625 SW Tenth Avenue, Portland, OR. Also: www.e-znet/~dabzine/.

Darren, Alison. *The Lesbian Film Guide*. New York: Cassell, 1996.

Davenport, John. *Curiositates Eroticae Physiologiae, or Tabooed Subjects Freely Treated*. London: N.p., 1875.

Dawes, Charles R. *A Study of Erotic Literature in England Considered with Special*

Reference to Social Life. Cheltenham, England: Privately printed, 1943; aka (as manuscript in the British Library) "History of English Erotic Literature."

Dawson, Bonnie, comp. *Women's Films in Print: An Annotated Guide to 800 16 mm Films by Women*. San Francisco: Bubblegum Press, 1975.

Deakin, Terence. *Catalogi Librorum Eroticorum: A Critical Bibliography of Erotic Bibliographies and Book-Catalogues*. London: Cecil and Amelia Woolf, 1964.

De Grazia, Edward, and Roger K. Newman. *Banned Films: Movies, Censors and the First Amendment*. New York: Bowker, 1982.

Dekkers, Midas. *Dearest Pet: On Bestiality*, trans. Paul Vincent. New York: Routledge/Verso, 1994.

A Different Light. Catalog. 548 Hudson Street, New York City 10014.

DiLauro, Al, and Gerald Rabkin. *Dirty Movies: An Illustrated History of the Stag Film*. New York: Chelsea House, 1976.

Diversified Services. "Finding D & S on On-Line Services." Box 35737, Brighton, MA 02135, 1994.

Doc Johnson Enterprises. *Catalog*. 11933 Vose Street, North Hollywood, CA 91605.

Dove, Chipper. "Bare Necessities." *Adam Film World*, 15:4 (January 1994): 62–63.

Dubois-Desaulle, Gaston. *Bestiality: An Historical, Medical, Legal, and Literary Study, with Addenda*, trans. A[dolph] F[redrick] N[iemoeller]. New York: Panurge Press, 1933; orig. pub. as *Etude sur la bestialite*. Paris: Charles Carrington, 1905.

Dudar, Helen. "Love and Death (and Schmutz): G. Legman's Second Thoughts." *Village Voice*, 1 May 1984, pp. 41–43.

Dyer, Richard. *Now You See It: Studies on Lesbian and Gay Film*. New York: Routledge, 1990.

Dynes, Wayne R. *Encyclopedia of Homosexuality*. 5 vols. Hamden, CT: Garland, 1990.

———. *Homosexuality: A Research Guide*. New York: Garland, 1987.

Dynes, Wayne R., and Stephen Donaldson, eds. *Studies in Homosexuality*. 13 vols. Hamden, CT: Garland, 1990.

Eisenberg, Daniel. "Toward a Bibliography of Erotic Pulps Published in the U.S., 1962–1972." *Journal of Popular Culture*, 15:4 (Spring 1982): 175–184.

Electronic Arts Intermix. "Videotapes by Artist/Producer." Electronic Arts Intermix, 10 Waverly Place, 10003.

Ellenbogen, Glenn C., ed. *Directory of Humor Magazines and Humor Organizations in America (and Canada)*. 3d ed. New York: Wry-Bred Press, 1992.

Ellis, Albert, and Albert Abarbanel. *The Encyclopedia of Sexual Behavior*. New York: Hawthorne Books, 1961.

Englisch, Paul. *Bibliotheca Germanorum Erotica and Curiosa. Verzeichnis der gesamten deutschen erotischen Literatur mit Einschluss der Übersetzungen, nebst Beifügung Originale: Supplement*, Vol. IX, 1929; rpt. Hanau/München: Verlag Müller and Kiepeneuer, 1968.

———. *Irrgarten der Erotik*. Leipzig: Lykeion, 1931.

Erens, Patricia, ed. *Sexual Stratagems: The World of Women in Film*. New York: Horizon Press, 1979.

ERIC. "Libraries and the Censorship Issue: A Selected ERIC Bibliography." Syracuse, NY: ERIC Clearinghouse on Information Resources, 1983.

Erotic Art [Exhibition] October 30–December 19, 1973. New York: New School Art Center, New School for Social Research, 1973.

Erotic Art '66. New York: Sidney Janis Gallery, October 1966.

Erotic Print Society. *Catalogs 1–3*. P.O. Box 10645, London SW10 9ZT, U.K., or www.eps.org.uk.

Erotisme: Dispersion d'une Collection Partielle Provenant de Michel Simon: Varia, Estampes, Livres, Dessins, Cartes Postales, Photographies. Geneva: n.p., 1984.

Evelyn Rainbird, Inc. *Illustrated Manual of Sexual Aids*. New York: Minotaur Press, 1973.

Exotic Dancer: Directory of Gentlemen's Clubs. ERI Productions, 3437 W. 7th St., Fort Worth, TX 76107, annual.

Exotic Dancer Page. http://exclusivetvlnet.com/dancer/.

E-zines Database Menu. www.dominis.com/Zines/.

Facets Gay and Lesbian Video Guide. Chicago: Academy Chicago Press, 1993.

Fagan, P., ed. *Pornography: An Annotated Bibliography*. Washington, DC: Family Policy Insights, 1984.

Fallon, Eileen. *Words of Love: A Complete Guide to Romance Fiction*. New York: Garland, 1984.

Fantagraphics. *The Ultimate Comics Catalog*. Seattle: Fantagraphics, current.

[Farmer, John S.?] *Forbidden Books: Notes and Gossip on Tabooed Literature, Bibliographies and Excerpts . . . by an Old Bibliophile*. Paris: Carrington, 1902; rpt. New York: [Samuel Roth], 1929.

Fiene, Donald M. *R. Crumb Checklist of Work and Criticism*. Cambridge, MA: Boatner Norton Press, 1981.

FilmFan Video Labs. "Blue Vanities: Classic Vintage Films." 401 NE Ravenna Blvd., Seattle 98115.

Fischer, Gayle, comp. *Journal of Women's History Guide to Periodical Literature*. Bloomington: Indiana University Press, 1992.

Fisher's Erotic Encyclopedia. Dream Catcher Interactive, 265 Rim Rock Road, Toronto M3J3C6 Canada, or www.eroticencyclopedia.com.

Focus International. Catalog of Educational Videotapes on Human Sexuality. 14 Oregon Drive, Huntington Station, NY 11746.

Foster, Jeannette H. *Sex Variant Women in Literature*. New York: Vantage Press, 1956; 3d ed. Tallahassee, FL: Naiad Press, 1985.

F.O.X.E. (Fans of X-rated Entertainment). 8033 Sunset Blvd, Los Angeles 90046, monthly.

Foxon, David. *Libertine Literature in England, 1660–1745*. New Hyde Park, NY: University Books, 1965.

Frasier, David K. *Russ Meyer—the Life and Films: A Biography and a Comprehensive, Illustrated, and Annotated Filmography and Bibliography*. Jefferson, NC: McFarland, 1990.

Fraxi, Pisanus [Ashbee, Henry Spencer]. *Index Librorum Prohibitorum; Centuria Librorum Absconditorum; Catena Librorum Tacendorum, Being Notes Bio-Biblio-Iconographical and Critical on Curious, Uncommon and Erotic Books*. 3 vols. London: privately printed, 1877, 1879, 1885; rpt. *Index Librorum Prohibitorum; Centuria Librorum Absconditorum; Catena Librorum Tacendorum*. 3 vols. London: Skilton, 1960; rpt. *Bibliography of Forbidden Books*. 3 vols. New York: Jack Brussel, 1962; rpt. *The Encyclopedia of Erotic Literature*. 3 vols. New York: Documentary Books, 1962; *Forbidden Books of the Victorians: Henry Spencer Ashbee's Bibliographies of Erotica*, ed. Peter Fryer. London: Odyssey, 1970.

Frayser, Susanne G., and Thomas J. Whitby. *Studies in Human Sexuality: A Selected Guide*. Littleton, CO: Libraries Unlimited, 1987.

Freeman, Gillian. *The Undergrowth of Literature*. London: Panther, 1969.

Friedman, Leslie. *Sex Role Stereotyping in the Mass Media: An Annotated Bibliography*. New York: Garland, 1977.

Fringeware Review. Fringeware, P.O. Box 49921, Austin, TX 78765; or fringeware-request@wixer.bga.com.

Fuchs, Eduard. *Das Erotische Element in der Karikatur*. Munich: Albert Langen, 1904; rpt. and enlarged *Geschichte der Erotischen Kunst. Erw. und Neubearb. des Werkes, das Erotische Element in der Karikatur, mit Einschluss der Ernsten Kunst*. Munich: Albert Langen, [1912]; enlarged *Geschichte der Erotischen Kunst*, 3 vols. Munich: Albert Langen, 1912–1926.

Garber, Linda. *Lesbian Sources: A Bibliography of Periodical Articles, 1970–1990*. Hamden, CT: Garland, 1991.

Garde, Noel I. *The Homosexual in Literature: A Chronological Bibliography circa 700 B.C.–1958*. New York: Village Press, 1959.

Gay, Jules, and P. Lemonnyer. *Bibliographie des Ouvrages Relatifs à l'Amour, aux Femmes et au Marriage, et les Livres Factieux Pantagrueliques, Satyriques, etc.* 4th ed. 4 vols. Paris: Gilliet, 1894; Lille: Becour, 1897–1900.

A Gay Bibliography: Eight Bibliographies on Lesbian and Male Homosexuality. New York: Arno Press, 1975.

Gay Video Guide. Los Angeles, 1997–.

Gelb, Norman. *The Irresistible Impulse: An Evocative Study of Erotic Notions and Practices through the Ages*. New York: Paddington, 1979.

Geller, Thomas. *Bisexuality: A Reader and Sourcebook*. Novato, CA: Times Change Press, 1990.

Gentleman's Club: Passport to Entertainment. Bloomfield Hills, MI, 1993–.

Gerber, Albert B. *The Book of Sex Lists*. New York: Lyle Stuart, 1981.

Gertzman, Jay A. *Bookleggers and Smuthounds: The Trade in Erotica. 1920–1940*. Philadelphia: University of Pennsylvania Press, 1999.

———. *A Descriptive Bibliography of Lady Chatterley's Lover, with Essays toward a Publishing History of the Novel*. New York: Greenwood Press, 1989.

Gillette, Paul, and Robert Dicks. *The Encyclopedia of Erotica*. New York: Award Books, 1969.

Global Media. "Historic Erotica." 630 Ninth Avenue, New York City 10036.

Goldston, John. "The World of the Borderline Fetichist." *Neurotica*, 1:3 (Autumn 1948): 46–51.

Goleman, Daniel, and Sherida Bush. "The Liberation of Sexual Fantasy." *Psychology Today*, 11:5 (1977): 104–107.

Goodland, Roger. *A Bibliography of Sex Rites and Customs: An Annotated Record of Books, Articles, and Illustrations in All Languages*. London: Routledge, 1931; rpt. New York: AMS Press, 1974.

Good Vibrations. *Good Vibes Gazette*. 1210 Valencia St., San Francisco 94110, quarterly; also mail-order catalog.

Gosselin, Chris, and Glen Wilson. *Sexual Variations: Fetishism, Sadomasochism and Transvestism*. New York: Simon and Schuster, 1980.

Goulemot, Jean Marie. *Ces livres qu'on ne lit que d'une main: lecture et lecteurs de livres pornographiques au XVIIIe siècle*. Aix-en-Province: Alines, 1991.

Gray, John. *Active Art: A Bibliography of Artists' Performance from Futurism to Fluxus and Beyond.* Westport, CT: Greenwood Press, 1993.

Green, Jonathan. *The Encyclopedia of Censorship.* New York: Facts on File, 1990.

Greenberg, Gerald S. *Tabloid Journalism: An Annotated Bibliography of English-Language Sources.* Westport, CT: Greenwood Press, 1996.

Griley, Rosemary. *Lovelines: The Romance Reader's Guide to Printed Pleasures.* New York: Facts on File, 1983.

Gunderloy, Mike, and Cari G. Janice, eds. *The World of Zines: A Guide to the Independent Magazine Revolution.* New York: Penguin, 1992.

Harrison, Cynthia Ellen, ed. *Women in American History: A Bibliography.* 2 vols. Santa Barbara, CA: ABC-Clio, 1985.

Hart, Jack. *Gay Sex: A Manual for Men Who Love Men.* Boston: Alyson Press, 1991.

Hayes, Joseph J. "Language Behavior of Lesbian Women and Gay Men: A Selected Bibliography (Part 1)." *Journal of Homosexuality,* 4 (1978): 201–212.

Hayn, Hugo, and Alfred N. Gotendorf. *Bibliotheca Germanorum Erotica and Curiosa. Verzeichnis der gesamten deutschen erotischen Literatur mit Einschluss der Übersetzungen, nebst Beifügung Originale.* 8 vols. 1912–1914; rpt. Hanau/München: Verlag Müller and Kiepeneuer, 1968.

Hermance, Ed, ed. *Gay Men's Fiction Catalog.* Philadelphia: Giovanni's Room, 1983.

Herstory. *Herstory, Women's History Collection, Microfilm Collection.* Berkeley, CA: Women's History Research Center/Bell and Howell, 1956–1974.

Hickerson, Joseph C. "A Bibliography of American Folksong in the English Language." *American Folk-Poetry: An Anthology,* ed. Duncan Emrich. Boston: Little, Brown, 1974, pp. 775–816.

High Performance: A Quarterly Magazine for the New Arts Audience. Los Angeles, 1969–.

Highsmith, Doug. "Comic Books: A Guide to Information Sources." *Riverside Quarterly,* 27 (Winter 1987): 202–209.

High Weirdness by Email. E-mail: mporter@nyx.cs.du.edu.

Hoffmann, Frank. *Analytical Survey of Anglo-American Traditional Erotica.* Bowling Green, OH: Popular Press, 1973.

Hogan, Steve, and Lee Hudson, eds. *Completely Queer: The Gay and Lesbian Encyclopedia.* New York: Henry Holt, 1998.

Holliday, Jim. *How to Build Your X-Rated Video Library.* Beverly Hills, CA: Skull Mountain, 1980.

———. *Only the Best: Jim Holliday's Adult Video Almanac and Trivia Treasury.* Van Nuys, CA: Cal Vista, 1986.

———. *The Top 100 X-Rated Films of All Time.* Hollywood, CA: WWV, 1982.

———, comp. *Legends of Porn.* Providence, RI: Metro/CalVista, 1987.

———. *Only the Best: Volumes I and II.* Providence, RI: Metro/CalVista, 1986, 1989.

———. *True Legends of Adult Cinema.* 7 videocassettes. 1: *The Modern Era*; 2: *The Golden Age*; 3: *The Cult Superstars*; 4: *The Erotic Eighties*; 5: *Only the Very Best on Film*; 6: *Only the Very Best on Video*; 7: *Unsung Superstars.* Providence, RI: Metro/CalVista, 1990–1994.

Holtzman, Sandra. "A Russ Meyer Bibliography." Unpublished manuscript in the Kinsey Institute for Research in Sex, Gender, and Reproduction, Indiana University, Bloomington, 1974.

Hosoda, Craig. *The Bare Facts Video Guide*. Santa Clara, CA 95055–3255: P.O. Box 3255, 1993–, annual.

Howell, John. " 'The Explicit Image': Ex Voto Gallery." *Artforum*, 4 (April 1986): 114–115.

Humphreys, Nancy K. *American Women's Magazines: An Annotated Historical Guide*. New York: Garland, 1989.

Hurwood, Bernhardt J. *The Sensuous New Yorker*. Rev. ed. New York: Universal-Award Books, 1974.

———, ed. *The Whole Sex Catalog*. New York: Pinnacle, 1975.

Husni, Samia. *Samia Husni's Guide to New Magazines*. University, MS: Department of Journalism, University of Mississippi, 1986–, annual.

Hustler Erotic Video Guide. Mount Morris, IL, 1993–.

Index on Censorship. New York, Cassell, 1972–.

Indy Magazine: The Guide to Alternative Comix and Film. Gainesville, FL, 1994–.

Inge, M. Thomas. *Comics as Culture*. Jackson: University Press of Mississippi, 1990.

Institute for Advanced Study of Sexuality. *Multi-Focus Incorporated Media Catalog*. 1525 Franklin, San Francisco 94109–4592.

Interactive Adult Movie Almanac. Los Angeles: New Machine Publishing, 1994.

Intimate Treasures: A Catalog of Catalogs. P.O. Box 77902, San Francisco 94107.

Jackson, Bob. Ryerson Polytechnical Institute. "IntimAge Biblio: Comserve Database." BITNET.

Jenner, Peter. *Erotic Bibliographies: A Brief Survey*. Brighton, England: Smoothie Publishers, 1973.

Johnson, Catherine E. *TV Guide 25 Year Index: By Author and Subject*. Radnor, PA: Triangle Publications, 1979.

Jones, Marvin. *Movie Buff Checklist: A History of Male Nudity in the Movies*. 4th ed. Panorama City, CA: Campfire Video, 1995.

Journal of the History of Sexuality. Chicago, 1990–.

Journal of Sex Research. New York, 1965–.

Juno, Andrea, and V. Vale, eds. *Angry Women*. San Francisco: RE/Search, 1991.

———. *Incredibly Strange Films*. San Francisco: RE/Search, 1986.

Justice, Keith L. *Adult Video Index '84*. Jefferson, NC: MacFarland, 1984.

Kadrey, Richard. "alt.sex.bondage." *Wired*, June 1994, pp. 40–42.

———. *Covert Culture Sourcebook*. New York: St. Martin's, 1993; updates available from kadrey@well.sf.ca.us.

———. *Covert Culture Sourcebook 2.0*. New York: St. Martin's, 1994; updates available from kadrey@well.sf.ca.us.

Kalisch, Beatrice, Philip A. Kalisch, and Mary L. McHugh. "The Nurse as Sex-Object in Motion Pictures, 1930–1980." *Research in Nursing and Health*, 5 (1982): 145–157.

Karwath, Cary von. *Die Erotik in der Kunst*. Vienna: C. W. Stern, 1908.

Kearney, Patrick J. *A Bibliography of Jules and Jean Gay*. Santa Rosa, CA: Scissors and Paste Bibliographies, 1988.

———. *A Bibliography of the New York Olympia Press*. Santa Rosa, CA: Scissors and Paste Bibliographies, 1988.

———. *The Olympia Press, Paris 1953–1965: A Handlist*. London: privately printed, 1975; rpt. *The Paris Olympia Press*. London: Black Spring, 1987.

Kehoe, Monika, ed. *Historical, Literary and Erotic Aspects of Lesbianism*. New York:

Haworth Press, 1986; rpt. special issue of *Journal of Homosexuality*, 12 (May 1986).

Kemp, Earl, ed. *The Illustrated Presidential Report of the Commission on Obscenity and Pornography.* San Diego: Greenleaf Classics, 1970.

Kennedy, Jay, ed. *The Official Underground and Newave Comix Price Guide.* Cambridge, MA: Boatner-Norton, 1992.

Kick, Russ. *Outposts: A Catalog of Rare and Disturbing Alternative Information.* New York: Carrol and Graf/Richard Kasak, 1995.

———. *Psychotropia.* Manchester, U.K.: Headpress, 1998.

Kilpatrick, James J. *The Smut Peddlers: The Pornography Packet and the Law Dealing with Obscenity Censorship.* Garden City, NY: Doubleday, 1960.

Kinsey Institute for Research in Sex, Gender, and Reproduction. *Bibliographies.* Information Service, Kinsey Institute for Research in Sex, Gender, and Reproduction, Indiana University, Bloomington.

———. *International Directory of Sex Research and Related Fields.* Kinsey Institute for Sex, Gender, and Reproduction, Indiana University, Bloomington 1976–.

———. *Sex Studies Index: 1980.* Boston: G. K. Hall, 1980.

Klinger Collection. *Die Frühzeit der erotischen Films von 1900–1935.* Nuremberg: D. M. Klinger Verlag, 1987.

———. *Die Frühzeit der erotischen Fotographie 1900–1950.* Nuremberg: D. M. Klinger Verlag, 1985.

———. *Die Frühzeit der erotischen Fotografie und Postkarten.* Nuremberg: D. M. Klinger Verlag, 1980–.

———. *Erotische Kunst.* Nuremberg: D. M. Klinger Verlag, 1979–.

Kostelanetz, Richard. *On Innovative Performance(s): Three Decades of Recollections on Alternative Theater.* Jefferson, NC: MacFarland, 1994.

Kronhausen, Phyllis, and Eberhard Kronhausen. *Erotic Art: A Survey of Erotic Fact and Fancy in the Fine Arts.* New York: Grove Press, 1968; and *The 2nd International Exhibition of Erotic Art (Liljevalchs Konsthal, Stockholm, April 2–May 18, 1969).* Amsterdam: Uitgeverij van Gennep, 1969; rpt. *Erotic Art 2.* New York: Grove Press, 1970; both volumes rpt. as *The Complete Book of Erotic Art.* 2 vols. New York: Bell, 1978.

———. *The International Museum of Erotic Art.* San Francisco: International Museum of Erotic Art, 1973.

———. *The Kronhausen Collection of Erotic Art from the International Museum of Erotic Art, Sold by Phillips.* Auction Catalog, 31 March 1979. New York: Phillips, 1979.

Last Gasp Catalog. 777 Florida Street, San Francisco 94110.

Legman, Gershon. "Erotic Folksongs and Ballads: An International Bibliography." *Journal of American Folklore*, 103 (October/December 1990): 417–501.

———. *The Horn Book: Studies in Erotic Folklore and Bibliography.* New York: University Books, 1964.

———. "Introduction." *The Mammoth Cod*, by Mark Twain. Milwaukee: Maledicta Press, 1977, pp. 2–18.

———. "On Sexual Speech and Slang." *Dictionary of Slang and Its Analogues, Past and Present: A Dictionary Historical and Comparative of the Heterodox Speech of All Classes of Society for More than Three Hundred Years with Synonyms in*

    English, French, German, Italian, etc. Vol. I, by J. S. Farmer and W. E. Henley. New Hyde Park, NY: University Books, 1966, pp. 375–450.

————. *Toward an Historical Bibliography of Sex Technique*. Unpublished typescript, Kinsey Institute for Research in Sex, Gender, and Reproduction. Indiana University, Bloomington 1942.

Leigh, Michael. *The Velvet Underground*. New York: Macfadden, 1968.

Lewis, Stephen, ed. *The Whole Bedroom Catalog: Everything You Always Wanted to Know about What Comes in the Mail in a Plain Brown Wrapper*. New York: Zebra Books, 1975.

Limbacher, James L. *Sexuality in World Cinema*. 2 vols. Metuchen, NJ: Scarecrow Press, 1983.

Locke, John. *The Pulp Magazines Quick Reference Guide*. Oakland, CA: Locke, 1987.

Lo Duca, Guiseppe. *Dictionnaire de Sexologie* and *Supplement A–Z*. Paris: Pauvert, 1962, 1965; rpt. *Moderne Enzyklopadie der Erotik*. Munich: Kurt Desch, 1966.

Loompanics Unlimited. *Catalog*. P.O. Box 1197, Port Townsend, WA 98368.

Love, Brenda. *Encyclopedia of Unusual Sexual Practices*. Fort Lee, NJ: Barricade, 1992.

Lovett, Anthony R., and Matt Maranian. *L.A. Bizarro: The Insider's Guide to the Obscure, the Absurd, and the Perverse in Los Angeles*. New York: St. Martin's, 1997.

Maccann, Richard D., and Edward Perry. *The New Film Index: A Bibliography of Magazine Articles in English 1930–1970*. New York: Dutton, 1975.

Macdonald, Donald. *Pornography*. Ottawa: Library of Parliament, 1984–1988.

Manchell, Frank. *Film Study: An Analytical Bibliography*. 4 vols. Rutherford, NJ: Fairleigh Dickinson University Press, 1970.

Manshots—FirstHand Publications. Teaneck, NJ, 1995–.

Marburger, G. Allen. "Bondage Fantasies in Popular Entertainment: An Annotated Listing of Sequences from Movies and Television." Unpublished paper in the Kinsey Institute for Research in Sex, Gender, and Reproduction, 1975.

Marteau, Pierre [E. Sarnum]. *Om Erotisk og Galant Literatur*. Copenhagen: Preben Witt, 1948.

Martin, John. *Bibliographical Catalogue of Privately Printed Books*. New York: Burt Franklin, 1970.

Mason, Mervyn L. *Human Sexuality: A Bibliography and Critical Evaluation of Recent Texts*. Westport, CT: Greenwood Press, 1983.

Mason, Philip. *The Complete Internet Sex Resource Guide*. alt.magazines.pornographic. Philip@iglou.com.

McElroy, Wendy. *Sexual Correctness: The Gender-Feminist Attack on Women*. Jefferson, NC: MacFarland, 1996.

Meine, Franklin J. "Introduction." *[1601] Conversation as It Was by the Social Fireside in the Time of the Tudors*, by Mark Twain. New York: Lyle Stuart, n.d.

Mendes, Peter. *Clandestine Erotic Fiction in English 1800–1930: A Bibliographical Study*. Aldershot, England: Scolar Press, 1993.

Michel, Dee. *Gay Studies Thesaurus*. Los Angeles: Michel, 1985.

Miles, Mildred Lynn. *Index to Playboy*. Metuchen, NJ: Scarecrow Press, 1970.

Milton, John, ed. *Sex Sense*. New York: Milky Way Productions, 1975–1981?

Minazzoli, Gilbert. *Dictionnaire des oeuvres érotiques: Domaine Francais*, ed. Pascal Pia. Paris: Mercure de France, 1971.

Money, John. *Lovemaps: Clinical Concepts of Sexual/Erotic Health and Pathology, Paraphilia, and Gender Transposition of Childhood, Adolescence and Maturity*. New York: Irvington, 1986.

———, ed. *Sex Research: New Developments*. New York: Holt, Rinehart, and Winston, 1965.

Money, John, and Herman Musaph, eds. *Handbook of Sexology*. 5 vols. New York: Elsevier, 1978.

Money, John, Gordon Wainwright, and David Hingsburger. *The Breathless Orgasm: A Lovemap Biography of Asphyxiophilia*. Buffalo, NY: Prometheus Books, 1991.

Moore, F. Michael. *Drag! Male and Female Impersonators on Stage, Screen and Television: An Illustrated World History*. Jefferson, NC: MacFarland, 1994.

Murray, Raymond. *Images in the Dark: An Encyclopedia of Gay and Lesbian Film and Video*. New York: Plume, 1996.

Nordquist, Joan, ed. *Pornography and Censorship*. Santa Cruz, CA: Reference and Research Service, 1987.

Ober, William B. *Bottoms Up! A Pathologist's Essays on Medicine and the Humanities*. Carbondale: Southern Illinois University Press, 1987.

Old Reliable Company. *Old Reliable Catalogues*. 1626 N. Wilcox, Hollywood, CA 90028.

Olsen, Jenni, ed. *The Ultimate Guide to Lesbian and Gay Film and Video*. New York: Serpent's Tail/High Risk Books, 1996.

Olsham, Arlene, ed. *Lesbian Literature Catalog*. Philadelphia: Giovanni's Room, 1983.

Osanka, Franklin Mark, and Sara Lee Johann. *Sourcebook on Pornography*. Lexington, MA: Lexington Books, 1989.

Owens, Tuppy. *The (Safer) Sex Maniac's Bible: A World Review of Sexuality, Listings of Erotic Clubs in All Major Cities, and Fun and Games for Your Delectation*. London: Tuppy Owens, 1990.

Pally, Marcia. *Sense and Censorship: The Vanity of Bonfires: Resource Materials on Sexually Explicit Material, Violent Material, and Censorship*. New York: Americans for Constitutional Freedom and the Freedom to Read Foundation, 1991.

Panati, Charles. *Sexy Origins and Intimate Things: The Rites and Rituals of Straights, Gays, Bi's, Drags, Trans, Virgins, and Others*. New York: Penguin, 1998.

Parish, James Robert. *Gays and Lesbians in Mainstream Cinema: Plots, Critiques, Casts and Credits for 272 Theatrical and Made-for-Television Hollywood Releases*. Jefferson, NC: MacFarland, 1993.

———. *Prostitution in Hollywood Films: Plots, Critiques, Casts and Credits for 389 Theatrical and Made-for-Television Releases*. Jefferson, NC: MacFarland, 1992.

Parker, William. *Homosexuality: A Selective Bibliography of over 3000 Items. And Homosexuality Bibliography: Supplement 1970–1975*. 2 vols. Metuchen, NJ: Scarecrow Press, 1971, 1976.

Patrick, John. *The Best of the Superstars: The Year in Sex*. Tampa, FL: STARbooks Press, 1989; subsequent annuals from Sarasota: STARbooks, 1990–.

Penthouse. New York, 1969–.

Penzer, Norman. *An Annotated Bibliography of Sir Richard Burton*. New York: Franklin, 1974; rpt. London: N.p., 1922.

Perceau, Louis. *Bibliographie du Roman Érotique du XIX Siècle*. 2 vols. Paris: Fourdrinier, 1930.

Perkins, Michael. *The Secret Record: Modern Erotic Literature*. New York: William Morrow, 1977.

Pink Flamingo Publications. "Erotic and Spanking Fiction." www.pinkflamingo.com.

Playboy. Chicago, 1953–.

Pleasure Chest. *The Pleasure Chest Compendium of Amourous and Prurient Paraphernalia.* New York: Pleasure Chest, 1979.

Potter, Clare. *Lesbian Periodicals Index.* Tallahassee, FL: Naiad Press, 1986.

President's Commission on Obscenity and Pornography. *Report of the Commission on Obscenity and Pornography.* Washington, DC: Government Printing Office, 1970; New York: Bantam, 1970.

———. *Technical Report of the Commission on Obscenity and Pornography.* 9 vols. Washington, DC: Government Printing Office, 1971–1972. I: *Preliminary Studies*; II: *Legal Analysis*; III: *The Marketplace: The Industry*; IV: *The Marketplace: Empirical Studies*; V: *Societal Control Mechanisms*; VI: *National Survey*; VII: *Erotica and Antisocial Behavior*; VIII: *Erotica and Social Behavior*; IX: *The Consumer and the Community* (and index of authors).

Queer Zine Explosion. Box 591276, San Francisco 94159.

Rabenalt, Arthur Maria. *Mimus Eroticus.* 5 vols. Hamburg: Verlag für Kulturforschung, 1965–1967.

Ramsdell, Kristen. *Happily Ever After: A Guide to Reading Interests in Romance Fiction.* Englewood, CO: Libraries unlimited, 1987.

Ransom, Will. *Private Presses and Their Books.* New York: Bowker, 1929.

Rao, Rama K. *An Annotated Bibliography on Pornography: Current Literature, 1980–1986.* Monticello, IL: Vance Bibliographies, 1987.

Rayozine Studios. *Samizine.* P.O. Box 291, Cooper Station, New York City 10276, annual.

"Regulating the Internet." Special issue of *CQ Researcher*, 30 June 1995.

Rhino Films. *Sleazemania, Sleazemania Strikes Back*, and *Sleazemania III* (all 1990). Rhino Films, 225 Colorado Ave., Santa Monica, CA 90404.

Richards, Dell. *Lesbian Lists: A Look at Lesbian Culture, History, and Personalities.* Boston: Alyson, 1990.

Richter, Carl. *Crumb-ology: The Works of R. Crumb, 1981–1994.* Sudbury, MA: Water Row Press, 1995.

Riley, Patrick. *The X-Rated Videotape Guide V, VI*, and *VII.* Amherst, NY: Prometheus Books, 1995, 1996, 1998.

———. *The X-Rated Videotape Star Index I* and *II.* Amherst, NY: Prometheus Books, 1994, 1997.

Rimmer, Robert H. *The X-Rated Videotape Guide.* New York: Arlington House, 1984; rev. ed. New York: Crown, 1986; rpt. Buffalo, NY: Prometheus Books, 1988.

———. *The X-Rated Videotape Guide II.* Buffalo, NY: Prometheus Books, 1991.

Rimmer, Robert H., and Patrick Riley. *The X-Rated Videotape Guide III.* Buffalo, NY: Prometheus Books, 1993.

———. *The X-Rated Videotape Guide IV.* Buffalo, NY: Prometheus Books, 1994.

Roberts, J. R., comp. *Black Lesbians: An Annotated Bibliography.* Tallahassee, FL: Naiad Press, 1981.

Robinson, Victor, ed. *Encyclopedia Sexualis.* New York: Dingwall-Rock, 1936.

Rock: The Rough Guide. New York: Penguin, 1996.

Roe, Paul. *High Camp: A Gay Guide to Camp and Cult Films.* 2 vols. San Francisco: Leyland Publishing, 1994, 1995.

Rose, Candi, and Dirk Thomas. *NET.SEX.* Indianapolis: Sams Publishing, 1995.

Rosen, Ismond, ed. *The Pathology and Treatment of Sexual Deviation.* New York: Oxford University Press, 1979.

Rowberry, John W. *Gay Video: A Guide to Erotica.* San Francisco: G. S. Press, 1986.

Rubin, Rich, and Greg Byerly. *Incest: The Last Taboo: An Annotated Bibliography.* New York: Garland, 1983.

Rubinstein, Eli A., Richard Green, and Edward Brecher, eds. *New Directions in Sex Research.* New York: Plenum Press, 1976.

Rund, J. B., comp. *Libertine Literature.* New York: Parke-Bernet Galleries, 1971.

Rutledge, Leigh. *The Gay Book of Lists* and *The New Gay Book of Lists.* Boston: Alyson, 1987, 1995.

Sabates, Fabien. *1000 Cartes Postales "Tres Coquines."* Paris: Editions Nationale, 1986.

Sahli, Nancy Ann. *Women and Sexuality in America: A Bibliography.* Boston: G. K. Hall, 1984.

Saillac, Didier. *X Vidéo Guide.* Paris: Éditions Paramaribo, 1991.

Sanderson, Lilian Passmore. *Female Genital Mutilation: A Bibliography.* Cambridge, MA: Cultural Survival, 1981.

Saunders, Dennis, ed. *Gay Source: A Catalogue for Men.* New York: Coward, McCann, and Geoghegan, 1977; New York: Berkeley, 1977.

Scheiner, C. J. *Compendium: Being a List of All the Books (Erotica, Curiosa, & Sexology) Listed in Our Catalogs 1–6 (1978–1988).* Brooklyn, NY: C. J. Scheiner, 1989.

———. *Erotica-Curiosa-Sexology Catalog.* 275 Linden Blvd., Brooklyn, NY, 1978–.

Schertel, Ernst. *Der Flagellantismus in Literatur und Bildnerei.* 4 vols. Leipzig: Parthenon-Verlag, 1929–1932; rev. and exp. ed. 12 vols. Schniden bei Stuttgart: F. Decker, 1957.

Schmidt, J. E. *The Cyclopedic Lexicon of Sex: Erotic Practices, Expressions, Variations of the Libido.* New York: Brussel and Brussel, 1968.

Scott, David A. *Behind the G-String: An Exploration of the Stripper's Image, Her Person, and Her Meaning.* Jefferson, NC: MacFarland, 1996.

Scott, Randall W. *Comic Books and Strips: An Information Sourcebook.* Phoenix, AZ: Oryx Press, 1988.

Screw. New York, 1969–.

Searing, Susan, ed. *Feminist Periodicals: A Current Listing of Contents.* Madison: University of Wisconsin Press, 1981–.

See Hear Web Catalog. http://www.zinemart.com.

Sellen, Betty-Carol, and Patricia A. Young. *Feminists, Pornography and the Law: An Annotated Bibliography of Conflict, 1970–1986.* Hamden, CT: Shoe String Press/ Library Professional, 1987.

Seruya, Flora C., Susan Losher, and Albert Ellis. *Sex and Sex Education: A Bibliography.* New York: Bowker, 1972.

Sesslen, Georg. *Der Pornographische Film.* Frankfurt am Main: Ullstein, 1990.

Sex in Contemporary Society: A Catalog of Dissertations. Ann Arbor, MI: University Microfilms, 1973.

Shakespeare, Tom, Kath Gillespie-Sells, and Dominic Davies. *The Sexual Politics of Disability: Untold Desires.* New York: Cassell, 1996.

Shifreen, Lawrence J., and Roger Jackson. *Henry Miller: A Bibliography of Primary Sources.* N.p.: Shifreen and Jackson, 1993.

SIECUS (Sex Information and Education Council of the United States). Bibliographies on many aspects of sexuality. 32 Washington Place, New York City 10003.

Signorelli, Nancy. *Role Portrayal and Stereotyping on Television: An Annotated Bibliography of Studies Relating to Women, Minorities, Aging, Sexual Behavior, Health and Handicaps*. Westport, CT: Greenwood Press, 1985.

Signorelli, Nancy, and George Gerbner. *Violence and Terror in the Mass Media: An Annotated Bibliography*. Westport, CT: Greenwood Press, 1988.

Sloane, David E. E. *American Humor Magazines and Comic Periodicals*. Westport, CT: Greenwood Press, 1987.

[Smith, Kent, Darrell W. Moore, and Merl Reagle]. *Adult Movies*. New York: Pocket Books, 1982.

Smith, Margaret, and Barbara Waisberg. *Pornography: A Feminist Survey*. Toronto: Boudicca Books, 1986.

Smith, Spencer R. "Voyeurism: A Review of Literature." *Archives of Sexual Behavior*, 5:6 (November 1976): 585–609.

Sobel, Lester A. *Pornography, Obscenity and the Law*. New York: Facts on File, 1979.

Solow, Edie, comp. *Erotic Rarities, 1760–1980*. New York: Erotics Gallery, 1980.

Something Weird Video. *Catalog*. P.O. Box 33664, Seattle.

Spartacus Company. *Male Cock Restraints*. Portland, OR: 300 SW 12th Street, 1986.

Stang, Ivan. *High Weirdness by Mail: A Directory of the Fringe: Mad Prophets, Crackpots, Kooks & True Visionaries*. New York: Simon and Schuster, 1988; and *High Weirdness by Email*. E-mail address: mporter@nyx.cs.du.edu.

Steele, Jeanne, and Jane Brown. "Sexuality and the Mass Media: An Overview." *Siecus Report* (April/May 1996): 3–9.

Steele, Jonathan. "The Stereoscope and Collecting Stereocards: Part III: Nude Studies in Stereo-Daguerreotypes." *The Photographic Collector* [London], 2:1 (Spring 1981): 54–58.

Steele, Valerie. *Fetish: Fashion, Sex and Power*. New York: Oxford University Press, 1995.

Steir, Charles. "A Bibliography on Bisexuality." *Journal of Homosexuality*, 11 (Spring 1985): 235–248.

Stern (-Szana), Bernhard. *Bibliotheca Curiosa et Erotica*. Vienna: Privatdruck für Stern-Szana und seine Freunde, 1921; facsimile edition: Vienna: Horst Bissinger KG, Verlag und Druckerei, [?].

———. *Illustrierte Geschichte der Erotischen Literatur aller Zeiten und Völker*. Vienna/Leipzig: C. W. Stern, 1908.

Stora-Lamarre, Annie. *L'enfer de la IIIe Republique: censeurs et pornographes, 1881–1914*. Paris: Imago, 1990.

Stormgart, Ivan. *Catalogs*. P.O. Box 470883, San Francisco 94147–0883.

Stripper Magazine. New York, 1993–.

Studio One. *Film Catalog*. P.O. Box 599, Holbrook, NY 11741.

Sweet Pea Productions. *Computers, Freedom and Privacy* (1996–1997). P.O. Box 912, Topanga, CA 90290.

Swezey, Stuart, and Brian King. *Amok: Fourth Dispatch—Sourcebook of the Extremes of Information in Print*. P.O. Box 861867 Terminal Annex, Los Angeles 90086–1867, 1992.

T & A Staff. *Erotic New York: A Guide to the Red Hot Apple*. New York: City and Co., 1997.

TAB (The Adult Business) Report. Washington, DC, 1978–1985.

Tamosaitis, Nancy. *The Penthouse Guide to Cybersex*. New York: Penthouse, 1995.

Tedford, Thomas L. "CensorSex Biblio: Comserve Database." University of North Carolina at Greensboro: BITNET.

Thomas, Donald. *A Long Time Burning: The History of Literary Censorship in England.* London: Routledge and Kegan Paul, 1969; New York: Praeger, 1969.

Thompson, Roger. *Unfit for Modest Ears.* Totowa, NJ: Rowman and Littlefield, 1979.

Thompson, Stith. *Motif-Index of Folk Literature: A Classification of Narrative Elements in Folktales, Ballads, Myths, Fables, Medieval Romances, Exempla, Fabliaux, Jestbooks, and Local Legends.* 6 vols. Bloomington: Indiana University Press, 1955–1958.

Thorne, Barrie, and Nancy Henley, eds. "Sex Differences in Language, Speech, and Nonverbal Communication: An Annotated Bibliography." *Language and Sex: Difference and Dominance.* Rowley, MA: Newbury House, 1975, pp. 204–305.

Thorne, Barrie, Cheris Kramarae, and Nancy Henley, eds. "Sex Similarities and Differences in Language, Speech, and Nonverbal Communication: An Annotated Bibliography." *Language, Gender and Society.* Rowley, MA: Newbury House, 1983, pp. 151–331.

Tom of Finland Company. *Tom of Finland Catalog.* Los Angeles: Tom of Finland Co., current.

Ullerstam, Lars. *The Erotic Minorities*, trans. Anselm Hollo. New York: Grove Press, 1966.

Ultimate Directory of Lingerie and Nude Scenes from Movies and TV. Laken Company, P.O. Box 419, Zion, IL 60099, current.

Underground Newspaper Microfilm Collection. Wooster, OH: Bell and Howell and the Underground Press Syndicate, 1965–1973. 147 reels.

Underground Video. P.O. Box 400, Nesconset, NY 11767.

University Microfilm International (UMI). *Alternative Press Collection: A Guide to the Microfilm Collection.* Ann Arbor, MI: UMI, 1990.

———. *Underground Press Collection: A Guide to the Microfilm Collection.* Ann Arbor, MI: UMI, 1988.

Varney, Mike, comp. *Nudie Cuties.* 13 reels. P.O. Box 33664, Seattle: Something Weird Video, 1991–1993.

———. *Twisted Sex.* 3 reels. P.O. Box 33664, Seattle: Something Weird Video, 1991.

Vasta, Joseph. *Vasta Images/Books Catalogues.* New York: Vasta Images/Books (95 Van Dam Street, New York 10013), 1985–present (nos. 1–25).

Vida, Ginny, ed. *Our Right to Love: A Lesbian Resource Book.* Englewood Cliffs, NJ: Prentice-Hall, 1978.

Video Index '94/95. Copenhagen: Color Climax Corporation, 1986–, annual.

Video Xcitement. Fraser, MI, 1993–.

Village Voice. New York, 1959–.

Villeneuve, Roland. *Fetischisme et Amour.* Paris: Éditions Azur-Co, 1968.

———. *La Musée du la Bestialitié.* Paris: Éditions Azur-Co, 1969; rpt. Paris: Henri Veyrier, 1982.

Vinocur, John. "Gershon Legman Doesn't Tell Dirty Jokes . . . But He Has the World's Largest Collection of Them Lying around His House." *Oui,* 4:3 (March 1975): 94–96, 126, 130–131.

The Visual Dictionary of Sex. New York: Bell, 1982.

Vogel, Lise. "Fine Arts and Feminism: The Awakening Consciousness." *Feminist Art*

Criticism: An Anthology, ed. Arlene Raven, Cassandra Langer, and Joanna Frueh. New York: HarperCollins, 1991, pp. 21–57.

Wagner, Peter. "Eros Goes West: European and 'Homespun' Erotica in Eighteenth-Century America." *The Transit of Civilization from Europe to America: Essays in Honor of Hans Galinsky*, ed. Winfried Herget and Kan Ortseifer. Tübingen: G. Narr, 1986, pp. 145–165.

———. *Eros Revived: Erotica of the Enlightenment in England and America*. London: Secker and Warburg, 1988.

Wallace, M. B. *The Striptease: An Annotated Bibliography*. Unpublished manuscript 1973; updated [1981?]. Kinsey Institute for Research in Sex, Gender, and Reproduction, Indiana University, Bloomington.

Waller, Gregory. "An Annotated Filmography of R-Rated Sexploitation Films Released during the 1970s." *Journal of Popular Film and Television*, 9:2 (Summer 1981): 98–112.

"The Web Museum of Public Nudity." www.hooterhistorians.com

Webb, Peter. *The Erotic Arts*. Boston: New York Graphic Society, 1975; 2d ed. New York: Farrar and Giroux, 1984.

Wedeck, H. E. *Dictionary of Erotic Literature*. New York: Philosophical Library, 1963.

Weinberg, Martin S., ed. *Sex Research: Studies from the Kinsey Institute*. New York: Oxford University Press, 1976.

Weinberg, Martin S., and Alan Bell, eds. *Homosexuality: An Annotated Bibliography*. New York: Oxford University Press, 1972.

Weiss, Andea, and Altermedia, Women Make Movies, and Greta Schiller. "Filmography of Lesbian Works." *Jump Cut*, double issue 24/25 (March 1981): 22, 50–51.

Wildhack, Billy. *The Adult BBS Guidebook*. Sycamore, IL 60178: Keyhole Publications, 1993.

———. *Erotic Connections: Love and Lust on the Information Highway*. New York: Waite Group, 1994.

Williams, Dell. *Celebrate the Joy*. Eve's Garden, 119 West 57th, New York 10019.

Wilson, Carolyn F. *Violence against Women: An Annotated Bibliography*. Boston: G. K. Hall, 1981.

Wilson, Glenn, ed. *Variant Sexuality: Research and Theory*. Baltimore: Johns Hopkins University Press, 1987.

Winks, Cathy. *The Good Vibrations Guide to Adult Videos*. Burlingame, CA: Down There Press, 1998.

Wise, Thomas N. "Fetishism—Etiology and Treatment: A Review from Multiple Perspectives." *Comprehensive Psychiatry*, 26 (1985): 249–257.

Witkin, Lee D. *The Photograph Collector's Guide*. New York: Little, Brown, 1979.

Wolman, Benjamin, and John Money, eds. *Handbook of Human Sexuality*. Northvale, NJ: Aronson, 1993.

Women Make Movies. Annual Catalog. 462 Broadway, New York City 10013.

Wulffen, Erich, Erich Stenger, et al. *Die Erotik in der Photographic*. 3 vols. Vienna: Verlag für Kulturforschung, 1931.

XXX Gay Video Showcase. Los Angeles: Knight Publishing, 1990–.

Young, Ian. *The Male Homosexual in Literature: A Bibliography*. Metuchen, NJ: Scarecrow Press, 1975.

Young, Kimball, and Raymond D. Lawrence. *Bibliography on Censorship and Propaganda*. Eugene: University of Oregon Press, 1928.

Zillman, Dolf, and Jennings Bryant, eds. *Pornography: Research Advances and Policy Considerations.* Hillsdale, NJ: Lawrence Erlbaum Associates 1989.

Zippay, Lori, et al. *Artists' Video: An International Guide.* New York: Abbeville Press, 1992.

Zoltano, Rosalie F. *Erotica with Medical Aspects: Index of Modern Information.* Washington, DC: ABBE Publishers Association, 1988.

5

Histories of Sexuality and Its Representations

THE "INVENTION" OF PORNOGRAPHY

In tracing expression, older historians have gleaned from earlier epochs texts and images that we would today consider erotic or pornographic. Though it is difficult to know whether people of these periods were offended by such artifacts, some evidence suggests that they were. The three volumes of *A History of Private Life*, a series edited by Phillipe Ariès and Georges Duby, focus on the details of daily life from the Roman empire to Renaissance Europe and cover sex, privacy, intimacy, and tastes. Some historians draw interesting observations from Fernand Braudel's assertion in *Capitalism and Material Life, 1400–1800* that the concept of privacy was unknown before the eighteenth century (224), a consideration that colors our understanding of venues for sex and its representations. If prior to that time people routinely engaged in intercourse in front of others, either out of doors or in crowded rooms, then images of intercourse—that is, pornography—would have held little voyeuristic appeal; anyone interested could without much difficulty have found lovers to watch. On the other hand, numerous citations to contemporary documents cited in the volumes in the Ariès and Duby series attest to reactions against explicitness. Similarly—to pick another example at random—Barbara W. Tuchman reports in her *A Distant Mirror: The Calamitous Fourteenth Century* that Nicolas de Clamanges charged that his contemporaries defiled the church by selling obscene pictures during festivals at holy days (485); Tuchman is quoting from Clamanges' *De Ruina et Reparatione Ecclesia (The Ruin and Reform of the Church)*, a text that precedes the printing press, but oral complaints must have been far more vociferous. The issue is this, When did the notion of sexual transgression become institutionalized and represented as such?

Historical speculation is wonderfully slippery: if nobody minded who copu-
lated with whom—a big if—then did anyone at least laugh? Was quasi-public
intercourse entertainment for those who saw it? Or was it so "natural" that it
was beneath notice? At what point did the keepers of morality decide that males
could have intercourse with females but not with other males? Did the repression
of homosexual impulses create desire for homosexual sex by anathematizing it,
as Foucault suggests? Does control of sexuality—condemning some forms and
thereby making them more attractive—really add more than mild zest to a biological urge? Is such control intended to regulate population—or merely state
power—through suppressing or encouraging reproduction? Does such control
really cement the power of an established religion and other authoritarian institutions? Or is it designed to build capitalism by eroticizing both bodies and
consumer goods? Is pornography sufficient to all these tasks?

Such considerations will seem nitpicking to extreme Foucauldian historians
convinced that pornography can refer only to taxonomies of discrimination and
that these appeared only in the recent past. That position requires that one believe that those taxonomies did not emerge prior to the last few centuries and
that if there were no speech or sign for sexual sin, then there was no transgression. It also requires that one believe that if there were no accepted term for
sexual expression that embodied power relationships—assuming in the first
place that no other kind of sexual expression is possible—then pornography did
not exist. The central poststructuralist precept is that all we can know is language, not some underlying reality; that being the case, sexual expression in the
past was merely general discourse. If there was no specialized language to cat-
egorize desire, then there was no pornography.

On the other hand, if one defines pornography in more general terms, as
representations likely to arouse or offend, then such representations may well
have enjoyed substantial presence much earlier, even if no one could agree on
what to call them. Given the primacy of language, however, poststructuralist
scholars, like the authors of the Book of Genesis, hold that if there is no word,
there is no beginning. But the word is elusive: historians must depend for evidence on written texts rather than oral forms of obscenity; class and intellectual
biases are essential to such interpretations. Pornography and obscenity are born
in oral folklore. Oral forms reach beyond history, resist institutionalization, and
can easily elude academic sonar. As Carlo Ginzburg points out in "Titian, Ovid,
and the Sixteenth-Century Codes for Erotic Illustration," we know nothing of
the iconography of pornography available to the "public" in places such as
brothels and taverns and thus focus of necessity, but perhaps mistakenly, only
on the representations visible to the aristocracy and preserved as paintings and
expensive texts (pp. 79–80).

By contrast, the radical feminist position implicitly holds that pornography is
as old as male dominance, as in Andrea Dworkin's formulation of a seamless
history in "Pornography and Grief": "The pornographers, modern and ancient,
visual and literary, vulgar and aristocratic, put forth one consistent proposition:

erotic pleasure for men is derived from and predicated on the savage destruction of women" (p. 288). Indeed, extreme antiporn feminists believe that pornography is coterminous with history, perhaps *is* history, since they hold that pornography *causes*—does not merely reflect—male oppression of women. Catharine MacKinnon asks, "Does Sexuality Have a History?" and says that the question can be answered in the affirmative only if historians define sexuality as brutality toward women. So far, however, no radical feminist historian has speculated on just what pornographic ur-narrative, protodirty joke, or original nasty cave painting triggered the first act of sexual aggression against women. In Foucauldian terms, the strategy of antiporn feminist attacks on pornography is clear: to marginalize or criminalize the expression of males by recategorizing pornography as inherently and unequivocably masculine.

Careful historians point out that pornographic images—that is, those designed to arouse—have been constants throughout human experience, though in the beginning they may have served religious or ritual purposes (sexuality as an expression of spirituality in the early fertility cults, say) or even indicated rebelliousness (scurrilous attacks on church or state) or contempt for authority (as in obscene gestures, jokes, and parodies designed to level status). Some historians prefer to call such expression "erotica." Peter Wagner's "Eros Goes West: European and 'Homespun' Erotica in Eighteenth-Century America" locates the first appearance of the word *pornography* in the nineteenth century and distinguishes it from *erotica*: "Erotica is a comprehensive term for bawdy, obscene, erotic, and pornographic works, including satire and scatological humour, which often employ sexual elements. The term not only covers prose fiction and poetry but also non-fiction, such as medical and para-medical works (e.g., sex guides and treatises on venereal diseases), 'chronicques scandaleuses' dealing with the love-affairs of the high and mighty, and anti-clerical publications based on fact and fiction." By contrast, pornography "is difficult to define and to explain." Wagner notes that the word "pornographer" first appears in 1850 in a translation of a German work and that "pornography" first occurs in English in a medical dictionary in 1857. Says Wagner, "[This] would seem to relate the modern notion of pornography to the Victorian period. This is significant because it explains such modern evaluations as 'dirty books,' which is an essentially bourgeois and Victorian judgment and a concept which, prior to the nineteenth century, did not exist" (145–146). At the same time it is clear from Wagner's work that pornographic and obscene expression even in colonial America was commonplace. To argue that the framers of the Constitution were unacquainted with sexual matters when they fashioned that document is to adopt a naive position. Jefferson, Madison, Franklin, and Adams were accustomed to political attacks that were scatological, scurrilous, and obscene.

Prior to the eighteenth century, says Jean Marie Goulemont, erotic materials were treated like other books. Goulemot's *Forbidden Texts: Erotic Literature and Its Readers in Eighteenth-Century France* argues that pornography became a genre when these materials were marginalized by the rise of classicism, a theoretical reconceptualization of models from antiquity, and the urge to apply formal standards to art; attempts to elevate tastes shunted erotic materials into corners. Books lost some of their status as precious objects during this time also, so that the elite began to discriminate among contents. In her Introduction to *The Invention of Pornography: Obscenity and the Origins of Modernity, 1500–1800*, Lynn Hunt agrees that pornography was not a separate "legal or artistic category" of narrative or image much before the nineteenth century:

If we take pornography to be the explicit depiction of sexual organs and sexual practices with the aim of arousing sexual feelings, then pornography was almost always an adjunct to something else until the middle or end of the eighteenth century. In early modern Europe, that is, between 1500 and 1800, pornography was most often a vehicle for using the shock of sex to criticize religious and political authorities. Pornography nevertheless slowly emerged as a distinct category in the centuries between the Renaissance and the French Revolution thanks, in part, to the spread of print culture itself. Pornography developed out of the messy, two-way, push and pull between the authors, artists and engravers to test the boundaries of the "decent" and the aim of the ecclesiastical and secular police to regulate it. (9–10)

The essays by various historians in Hunt's book are the most reliable available; they look at antecedents in classical Greece and Rome but concentrate on sixteenth-century Italy, eighteenth-century Holland, and seventeenth- and eighteenth-century France and England. They point out that a pornography fully emergent in the sixteenth century becomes inextricably linked with the rise of democracy, the swelling of the middle class, the shifting of population to urban centers, the decline of religious authority, the advent of science and materialism, the codification of law, the development of technology, the evolution of literary realism, the separation of genders, and the concept of modernity itself. Hunt observes that pornography functioned to subvert established order and authority until commercialization blunted its political connotations at the end of the eighteenth century. She also notes that the eighteenth century signaled a shift in pornography's depiction of women. Prior to the 1790s, Hunt says, pornography "valorized female sexual activity and determination." Afterward, pornography often presented "women's bodies as a focus of male bonding" (44). Robert Darnton makes a compelling case for the connection between liberty and licentiousness, as expressed in works by de Sade and other radicals, in *Forbidden Best-Sellers of Pre-Revolutionary France*.

Walter Kendrick notes that the term *pornography* can be found in ancient parlance, though without the force of its current usage. Kendrick's *The Secret Museum: Pornography in Modern Culture* locates the "invention" of pornography at the intersection of two phenomena that vectored together at the cusp of the eighteenth and nineteenth centuries. These were both informational. The first was the assembling of clandestine archives, or "secret museums" in which collectors hid erotica from the lower classes and from women, an impulse that formalized the concept of the forbidden. The second impulse, similar to the first, was a fearful response to the technological acceleration of information about prostitution and other sexual subjects. Since literacy was spreading to the masses, the upper classes urged prohibition, expurgation, and regulation as checks on a rampant democracy that could submerge privacy by making sexual behavior and expression public. Pornography, says Kendrick, thus "names an argument, not a thing"; it is "a war about words" (178). In his view, pornography is a zone of contest whose skirmish lines are constantly redrawn.

Over the last several decades, marginal publishers have printed semischolarly histories whose texts function partly as substrates for graphic illustrations. Although one can dismiss these as unreliable, they raise a fundamental question: If pornographers *believe* that they are working within a tradition that spans hundreds of years, are convinced that they are replicating tropes from the past, do, *in fact*, draw on formulas reaching back at least to Hellenistic periods, then is it not possible that pornography does have a pedigree that contemporary theorists deny? In this category is the two-volume *An Illustrated History of Pornography*, by Abe Richards and Robert Irvine, who devote dozens of pages to reproductions of paintings and drawings. The title of Alfred Ellison's *The Photo Illustrated History of Pornography*, also a two-volume endeavor, speaks for itself (although the illustrations are mostly modern and Scandinavian). David Cauldwell's *Pornography: An Illustrated Banner Book* is profusely illustrated with the "answers" to the rhetorical question, What does pornography look like? It is nonetheless culturally incoherent and even reprints a Japanese erotic novel. Similarly, the only science to be found in *The Science of Pornography*, by Claude L. Scott, is imaginary, despite occasionally interesting observations about various technologies of production and transmission. Even so, these popular histories find in modern pornography traces of those democratic, secular, legal, and realistic elements identified by the contributors to Hunt's *The Invention of Pornography*, and it would be foolish to ignore them. They also hint at the oral strata that underlie elite artifacts.

More useful historical approaches to pornographic forms are the essays collected by Lynn Hunt's *Eroticism and the Body Politic*, most of which focus on eighteenth- and nineteenth-century French images of women and eroticism by way of discovering modern formulas. English and Continental erotica of the eighteenth century inform the chapters in *Erotica and the Enlightenment*, edited by Peter Wagner, whose Introduction (9–40) illustrates the kind of scholarship so often absent from discussions of erotic genres; as Wagner demonstrates, Americans took their erotic cues from some of the texts he covers. Bernard Arcand discusses the difficulties pornography engenders, the definitions that exfoliate, the debates that ensue in *The Jaguar and the Anteater: Pornography Degree Zero*; Arcand also offers a brief history of porn between 1500 and 1900 and a comparison of Western artifacts with some from India.

Conventional histories of pornography usually begin with cave paintings and other artifacts of prehistory, linger on vases and statues of Hellenic and Roman periods, visit Southeast Asian temple sculptures, dawdle over medieval tapestries, glance at Chinese pillow books and Japanese calligraphy, stroll through museums of seventeenth- and eighteenth-century paintings, and conclude with nineteenth- and early twentieth-century artists and writers. Typical are the six volumes of *A History of Eroticism*, a breezy romp by Ove Brusendorff and Paul Henningsen; *A History of Eroticism*, a highly Freudian analysis by Guiseppe Lo Duca; *A History of Pornography*, a mostly literary narrative by H. Montgomery Hyde; and *Geschichte der Erotik*, a solid, wide-ranging chronology of several genres by Carl van Bolen. Bernard Hurwood's *The Golden Age of Erotica* concentrates on the eighteenth century, viewed as a period of artistic flowering. Patrick Waldberg examines erotica during the period 1880–1910, as Victorian mores loosened in the explosion of candid expression we think of as modern in *Eros in la Belle Epoque*. The best single essay on colonial and early republican porn is Peter Wagner's "Erotica in Early America," which covers publishers, importers, libraries, collectors, and so on. George N. Gordon's *Erotic Communications: Studies in Sex, Sin and Censorship*, while providing some specifically American comment, is too whimsical to be helpful to the researcher, although it does provide background information. The 1950s are the subject of James J. Kilpatrick's *The Smut Peddlers: The Pornography Racket and the Law Dealing with Obscenity Censorship*, a somewhat sensationalized chronicle ranging over various media and drawing on police reports, customs inspectors, and government agencies. Kilpatrick provides anecdotal information on dealers and distributors of the period. The premise of his book, as of others of the period, is borrowed from J. Edgar Hoover, who believed that comic books and pornography led to a wide range of crimes. George Paul Csicsery's *The Sex Industry*, a collection of ironic and astute comments on pornography, performance, bookstores, massage parlors, movies, and prostitution of the late 1960s and early 1970s, is an excellent period source. Those seeking accurate information on the present should consult *Porn Gold: Inside the Pornography Business*, by David Hebditch and Nick Anning. Finally for this section, Bruce Handy refers to the film *Boogie Nights* and the book *Tijuana Bibles* in "Ye Olde Smut Shoppe" to suggest that like any other human artifacts, pornography of quality always finds its way into nostalgia; Americans seem forever to yearn for the simpler sexualities of older erotic media, whether or not those examples eventually achieve the aesthetic and moral levels we associate with true art.

THE "INVENTION" OF SEXUALITY

Michel Foucault's three-volume *The History of Sexuality* ranges across different cultures and has profoundly informed theories concerning sexual nomenclature and the dimensions of sexuality. His thesis is that cultural forces create sexual taxonomies and that these become rigidified and internalized by individuals, who then act as their own censors; the argument is a variation on Max Weber's famous theory of rationalization as an inevitable process but infused with the zest of a paranoia perhaps accelerated by Foucault's own attraction to sadomasochism. Volume I: *An Introduction* argues that the regulation of sexuality creates, rather than represses, desire; volume II: *The Use of Pleasure* argues that while the Greeks and Romans constructed concepts of sexual pleasure around young boys as objects of desire for older men, these delights became linked to young women during the Middle Ages; volume III: *The Care of the Self* argues that social regulation and control reconceptualize the self so that it and the eroticism associated with its transformation become objects of study. Followers of Foucault apply the theories in these texts to the study of erotic representations, which they tend to view as instruments for the stimulus and control of desire.

By creating categories of desire and behaviors appropriate to them, says Foucault, a society invents not simply the parameters of a sexuality that is imposed on its citizens but also dictates, even "invents" their objects of desire. The fashionableness of victimization is very much a part of Foucault's appeal, since his theories posit individuals as controlled no matter what they do, but other themes are less hackneyed. Unlike Freud, who thought that Western civilization repressed sexuality, Foucault claims that sexuality has functioned as a visible element in the creation of power and that this function can be traced to origins in the last two centuries. Given the historical meshing of sex and power, Foucault is skeptical of programs for change, whether cast as political agendas or otherwise, and at times seems to think that the categories he describes are immutable, a mind-set that has not deterred disciples from calling for their demolition. Foucault's importance lies not so much in the accuracy of his observations nor in any activism he has fostered, however, as in his impact on the way in which histories of sexuality are now written.

That influence is most obvious in works with titles such as *The Regulation of Desire: Sexuality in Canada*, Gary Kinsman's history of the social mores and legislation that have sought to control the sexuality of gays and lesbians and heterosexuals in a country that shares a culture as well as a border with the United States. More subtle is Jeffrey Weeks' remarkable *Sex, Politics, and Society: The Regulation of Sexuality since 1800*, which focuses on Britain but whose remarks apply to American history. Weeks holds that conceptions of sexuality, especially those involving masturbation, homosexuality, and patterns of family life, incorporate elements of ideology, law, medicine, education, and state policy; pornography contributes to the setting of agendas and the "making" of sexuality and helps to eroticize social life (251). Weeks examines the shifting relationships between social agendas and sexuality and the more problematic role of official politics. Still more masterful is Weeks' *Against Nature: Essays on History, Sexuality and Identity*. Ostensibly concerned with the history of homosexuality from the nineteenth century until the present, Weeks celebrates a sexual identity that is socially constructed but also deeply felt and experienced in everyday life. In the volume's chapter called "Uses and Abuses of Michel Foucault" (157–169), Weeks warns against an orthodoxy based on Foucault, especially the notions of "history as a lesson," in which the lesson may not be clear, and "history as exhortation," in which the mission to rescue the downtrodden may furnish only myth. Foucault's "history" of sexuality is incoherent, Weeks thinks, but its virtue is the "critique of sexual essentialism," that is, the concept of what is natural and immutable as opposed to what is socially constructed in the discourse of sexuality. " 'Sexuality,' " says Weeks, "may be an historical invention but we are ensnared in its circle of meaning. We cannot escape it by an act of will. This does not mean that we must simply accept the hegemonic definitions of our true sex handed down to us by theologians and sexologists. It does mean that we need to rethink the criteria by which we can choose our sexualities" (166).

Attempting to refine Foucault further, Roy Porter and Lesley Hall point out in *The Facts of Life: The Creation of Sexual Knowledge in Britain, 1650–1950* that Foucault's rejection of a Freudian "repressive hypothesis" on the grounds that sexual taboos were not nearly so widespread as previously imagined cannot account for the documented prudery and reticence that were unmistakably part of periods such as the Victorian. They also note that historians cannot rely simply on written texts as a way of assessing sexual discourses that were often oral or—more pertinently—*unspoken*. Individuals may police their own expression, whether affected by institutions or not, and that reticence may be complicated by anxieties about birth control and disease as much as by any clear-cut taboo surrounding a particular behavior. Porter and Hall urge caution and suggest that we may be institutionalizing our own theories as ways of "reading" the past. Porter and Mikuláš Teich have gathered in *Sexual Knowledge, Sexual Science: The History of Attitudes to Sexuality* some splendid essays by authorities as diverse as Vern Bullough, Angus MacLaren, Patricia Crawford, Londa Schiebinger, and others on different themes and taboos to indicate that historians can make the sexual beliefs of any period seem bizarre. That in itself challenges the Foucauldian contention that sexual discourse "sexualizes" those who are exposed to it. Essays in a similar vein, previously published in the *Journal of Sexuality*, make up John C. Fout's *Forbidden History: The State, Society, and the Regulation of Sexuality in Modern Europe*; though focused on Europe, most employ running comparisons with America. As much theoretical as historical, the essays discuss the criminalization of some forms of sexuality in the state's effort to control reproduction. Simon Watney's splendid *Policing Desire: Pornography, AIDS, and the Media* has a modern thrust, centered on the ways in which socially constructed attitudes toward sexuality affect responses to AIDS. Watney also has a lot to say on porn as a representation of "extremes." The essayists in *Sexualizing the Social: Power and Organisation of Sexuality*, edited by Lisa Adkins and Vicki Merchant, offer Foucauldian readings of (mostly British) social structures that the authors believe have been sexualized; it is a good guide to multiple directions in research. (See also **The "Invention" of Sexology** in Chapter 19).

THE SOCIAL CONSTRUCTION OF SEXUALITY AND GENDER

When we speak of the "invention" of sexuality or the social construction of gender and sexuality, we have recourse to the way these things have been represented—an inevitability that places such questions squarely in the domain of pornographic expression.

Theories of social construction hold that cultures or societies shape their own versions of "reality," including the ways in which humans behave and how they apprehend themselves and one another. According to this thesis, paradigms and language govern perception and interpretation; ultimately, we "know" the world only through the language we use to describe it. Historians can easily demonstrate that conceptions that may seem "natural" or immutable, say, "childhood" or "nuclear family," are constructions widely different across time and place. The irony is that we can become quite emotional about these categories. Children were not regarded as a special category before the seventeenth century, and the concept of "child abuse" held no meaning as a consequence, certainly not in the sentimental sense that is common now. Depending on the politics of the cultural critic, *childhood* may be a legal concept established by agitators against child labor in the second decade of this century; a privileged, partly fictional retreat for Norman Rockwell–innocence that prepares apprentice humans for an adult community; or simply a period of intense programming for future consumers in a capitalist economy. Viewed from a poststructuralist perspective, child pornography and the prohibitions against it are components as necessary as child labor laws in the ongoing construction of what we mean by "childhood." Without child pornography, for example, the culture cannot debate the permissible limits of sexuality in children (see Chapter 8, **Child Pornography**).

The markers of adult sexuality are just as much in contention, driven, in part, by the hope of escaping fears that "biology is destiny." The ur-text here, broad in its assertions of the ways in which quasi-official versions of "reality" are structured by hegemonic institutions and groups, is *The Social Construction of Reality* by Peter Berger and Thomas Luckmann, though they are not particularly concerned about sexuality. Since publication of that volume, the number of books on the construction of sexuality and gender has proliferated beyond counting. To date, most theorists have concentrated on forces constructing gender. In one of the great documents of American feminism, "The Traffic in Women: Notes on the 'Political Economy' of Sex," Gayle Rubin roots political oppression in gender. Rubin says that the authority of a patriarchy rests not just on economic differentiation but also on the separation of genders as an expression of relative power: "Gender is not only an identification with one sex; it also entails that sexual desire be directed toward the other sex. The sexual division of labor is implicated in both aspects of gender—male and female it creates them, and it creates them heterosexual. The suppression of the homosexual component of human sexuality, and by corollary, the oppression of homosexuals, is therefore a product of the same system whose rules and relations oppress women" (180).

In more recent work, Rubin sharpens distinctions. According to Rubin, periods such as the 1880s in England and the 1950s and the present in America have encouraged the political recoding of sexuality. In the present, Rubin says in "Thinking Sex: Notes for a Radical Theory of the Politics of Sex," assumptions about the cultural superiority of heterosexuality are under siege, one reason for attacks on pornography as the expression of "deviant" minorities. Rubin elaborates on cultural hierarchies of sexual behavior, in terms of their acceptability, and reflects on the harshness of sexual legislation regarding gays and S/M enthusiasts. Rubin insists that feminism as a school of thought should be concerned with gender rather than sexuality; feminist arguments (such as Catharine MacKinnon's) about sexuality and pornography are thus often misleading. In this essay Rubin provides the rationale for what has since become known as "queer theory" when she observes that "it is essential to separate gender and sexuality analytically to more accurately reflect their separate social existence. . . . For instance, lesbian feminist ideology has mostly analyzed the oppression of lesbians in terms of the oppression of women. However, lesbians are also oppressed as queers and perverts, by the operation of sexual, not gender stratification" (308). According to Rubin, sexual acts are not necessarily gendered, although participants may wish them to be. The problem is not so much male dominance as a whole body of sexual thinking that has anathematized marginal forms of expression, from gay and lesbian, to fetishistic practices.

While sexuality—a biological drive—may be a "fact" (though extreme theorists doubt that as well), gender—concepts of masculinity and femininity and of sexual orientation toward a particular object of desire—is an idea, a label written by society. Frequently, theorists link typographies of sex and gender as forms of capitalist objectification and commodification. As Adrienne Rich has restated the proposition in a famous essay, "Compulsory Heterosexuality and Lesbian Existence," society *compels* the adoption of heterosexuality. Monique Wittig's *The Lesbian Body* attempts to shake the compulsory heterosexual structures of patriarchy. She maintains that even *man* and *woman* are, at base, political terms; gender is really epistemology. Jeff Hearn's *The Gender of Oppression: Men, Masculinity, and the Critique of Marxism* extends and critiques these and similar arguments.

In other words, power—in the form of hierarchies of capitalist influence—determines virtually every aspect of activities we prefer to think are individualistic and intimate. Social constructionists hold that impersonal forces shape eroticism; some hold that all erotic stimulation is artificial and ultimately perverse (though it is difficult to see where perversity lies if all such notions are constructed), since it perpetuates only relationships of power. Pornography can then be defined as a representation of sexuality that is endorsed by a social, political, and economic elite. In such a scheme, the term "pornography" would refer to any and all images and narratives depicting sex. Because language itself is all that humans can know, because language embodies the culture's power structures, and because we cannot imagine a representation that is not tainted by language, then pornography replicates and advances inequity and injustice. Some critics accept such a characterization of "pornography" but balk at applying it to a masterwork of literature, say, *The Scarlet Letter* (once condemned as obscene), though logically there can be no difference. In such a scheme, the term "love" is, at best, an apology for oppression or an acceptance of masochism; the more romantic the love, the more deluded it is.

To be consistent, of course, we should also note that schools of social construction are themselves socially constructed by the intersection of many different circumstances. Social constructionists sometimes misuse their own theories, especially by attempting to imply that a given image or practice is right or wrong. The theory is consistent only if everything, including morality and ethics, is socially constructed. If that is the case, one cannot claim, say, that a patriarchical power structure is immoral, although one can point out the inconsistency of the structure's own internal ethical values, which may assert that the structure is just. Logically, the most that can be said is that the theorist has been programmed—or reprogrammed—to dislike such a structure.

Some theorists have gone well beyond Rubin and Rich in attributing oppression not to gender but to sexuality itself. The most extreme version is Catharine MacKinnon's. MacKinnon was an early crusader against discrimination, respected because of her exposure of sexual harassment in the workplace. In her efforts to build a theoretical edifice, she steadily redefined sexual harassment as sex itself. That equation remained obscure in her first works, though even in *Sexual Harassment of Working Women: A Case of Sex Discrimination*, published in 1979, MacKinnon criticized Susan Brownmiller for saying that "rape is violence, intercourse is sexuality," on the grounds that there can be no difference between rape and ordinary intercourse (218). In "Feminism, Marxism, Method and the State: An Agenda for Theory," MacKinnon asserted: "Sexuality is to feminism what work is to marxism . . . the molding, direction, and expression of sexuality organizes society into two sexes, women and men" (515–516). MacKinnon's *Toward a Feminist Theory of the State* asserted even more strongly that sex itself is the source of gender inequity, inequality, and injustice. Sex is *force*; in our culture heterosexual intercourse under all circumstances is indistinguishable from rape. Men use women as capitalists use labor; they are just objects of exploitation. Women can raise their consciousnesses only by regarding themselves as fundamentally and continuously brutalized by men. In *Feminism Unmodified: Discourses on Life and Law* (1987), MacKinnon insists that sex is power and nothing else. More to the point, she redefines feminism in her terms: "Feminism is a theory of how the erotization of dominance and submission creates gender, creates man and woman in the social form in which we know them" (50). MacKinnon's position kept hardening: women can raise their consciousnesses, but they must do so in terms of these precepts of

MacKinnon; that is, they must see themselves as abused by sexuality; all other ways of thinking are wrong. MacKinnon has been echoed often by many radical feminists. In "Sex: The Basis of Sexism," Abby Rockefeller insists that sex—any kind of sex—is the basis of inequity and injustice.

More recent feminist thought rejects MacKinnon's extreme position as an illustration of the dangers of erecting a systemic theory on what is at base a metaphor of limited utility. Leaving aside her doctrinaire approach, Mac-Kinnon's theory that sex defines discrimination also suffers, say her feminist critics, from two other shortcomings. The first, says Daphne Patai in *Hetero-phobia*, is that by insisting that discrimination against women can be understood only in terms of sexual harassment, a position already adopted in workplace law, MacKinnon's argument rules out redress for other forms of discrimination against female workers. The second is that the logical extension of MacKinnon's ideas is to redefine women who willingly cohabit with males as prostitutes. Jane E. Larson and Linda R. Hirshman explore the benefits of this consequence in *Hard Bargains: The Politics of Sex*. Larson and Hirshman believe that in a capitalist economy women who marry or mate should be free to profit from a service that is usually compelled. Institutionalizing contracts for marriage that acknowledge that the woman agrees to provide sexual services to her mate in return for specified premiums or rewards would permit her to recover damages if the mate did not support her adequately or attempted to divorce her without proper recompense for the sex she has provided. Not all feminists are so ready to embrace this sort of entrepreneurship.

Other critics postulate a sexuality founded on differences shaped by biolog-ical, cultural, and political constructions of identity. Those critics believe that eroticism is a consequence of constructions of difference, which are forms of programming easily mistaken for unique experience and even more easily mis-taken for desire rather than political imperatives. According to this line of rea-soning, the intensification of eroticism requires flirtation with the perverse (a factor that enables social constructionists themselves to flirt with practices once regarded as deviant). Debate on such issues, as we have said several times, functions at the level of folklore, and social constructionists often share with biological determinists mechanical versions of desire. The degree to which sex-uality and gender are molded by culture is by no means certain, though such theories can illuminate *representations*.

A good deal of gender speculation has come from the female side of the aisle because, as Judith Laws and Pepper Schwartz observe, women have the most to complain about. The two investigate the cultural programming that goes into female sexuality, with some reference to actual physiology, in *Sexual Scripts: The Social Construction of Female Sexuality*. Useful background volumes are *Nature, Culture, and Gender*, for which Carolyn MacCormack and Marilyn Strathern have gathered a variety of essays on cross-cultural physical and eth-nographic anthropology, and *The Cultural Construction of Sexuality*, for which Pat Caplan has assembled ethnographic studies of sexuality around the world.

Cynthia Eagle Russett's *Sexual Science: The Victorian Construction of Womanhood* details the culturally biased pressures on male scientists who seemed determined to demonstrate that women were inferior. (See also **The "Invention" of Sexology** in chapter 19.) The essayists in *Jacques Lacan and the Ecole Freudienne: Feminine Sexuality*, edited by Juliet Mitchell and Jacqueline Rose, explore the ways in which Lacanian psychology has reinvented Freud in order to understand "non-essentialist" sexual identity and create therapies of benefit to women; the volume almost makes Lacan comprehensible, no small feat. That sexology contributes to the folklore of male sexuality is also evident, says Peter Lehman in "Sexology and the Representation of Male Sexuality." According to Lehman, sexology has yet to come to grips with the "normal" size of the penis and how it should be represented in its erect state; his account surveys a century of dispute. Jonathan Rutherford and Rowena Chapman have edited *Male Order: Unwrapping Masculinity*, a volume of essays deconstructing "maleness" in Western culture; the contributors have recourse to a wide range of theories. A similar anthology is *Constructing Masculinity*, edited by Maurice Berger, Brian Wallis, and Simon Watson, who have selected essays that question "normative concepts of the masculine" as constructed by various media. Leonore Tiefer's focus on the politics of sexology also has to do with the construction of male sexuality. Tiefer's *Sex Is Not a Natural Act and Other Essays* is an excellent, no-nonsense approach to biology and pornography by a urologist and psychologist who also understands theories of social construction. More knowledgeable than most cultural critics, Tiefer ranges over sexual dysfunctions as well as linguistic categories and cultural symbolism and discusses the politics of female sexuality along with the utility of masturbation. Mark Cook and Robert McHenry in *Sexual Attraction* stake out middle ground by asserting that attraction, while biologically powerful, is not automatic but learned and varies according to individual and culture.

Clara Mayo, Alexandra Weiss, and Nancy Henley are the editors of *Gender and Nonverbal Behavior*; the volume's essays range over body movement, faces, gazes, spatial positions, environmental contexts, and so on as gender and sexual cues, many of which are learned and stereotypical and all of which constitute messages. Stereotypes, says T. E. Perkins in "Rethinking Stereotypes," have power because they refer to "a complex social structure" that people understand implicitly as a kind of shorthand (139). They are sexual as well as class- or race-oriented in their construction. Even the psychologist Robert J. Stoller, whose *Presentations of Gender* sketches the psychological mechanics whereby males become masculine and women feminine in positivistic terms, is eventually thrown back on clothing styles, body language, and perceived behavior. (See also **Bodies Gendered by Fashion and Style** in chapter 9.) John Money and Patricia Tucker try to distinguish between physical characteristics and cultural overlays in *Sexual Signatures: On Being a Man or a Woman*. Money's *Gay, Straight, and In-Between: The Sexology of Erotic Orientation* expands on these arguments, tracing historical, cultural, and physiological influences that determine orientation. E. H. Preston, author of a cultivation analysis of pornography in "Pornography and the Construction of Gender" concludes that exposure to pornography for males can be consistently associated with high degrees of gender stereotyping, especially where perceptions of male and female sexuality are concerned. By contrast, for women the same degrees of gender stereotyping and sex traits do not correlate.

As William Miller has pointed out in "Gender Mutability: The Provocation of Transgenderism (with a Passing Glance at *The Crying Game*)," theorists such as Diana Fuss and Shane Phelan adopt more "essentialist" positions. In "(Be)Coming out: Lesbian Identity in Politics," Phelan argues that it is dangerous to abandon gender and sexual categories, however flawed they may be, because they can still provide political platforms from which to work for change. That position is similar to Diana Fuss' in *Essentially Speaking: Feminism, Nature and Difference* and is shared by some of the contributors to her edited volume *Inside/Out: Lesbian Theories, Gay Theories*. Alison Assiter's "Essentially Sex: A New Look" takes issue with extreme theories of social construction: "Even if sexual identity can be willed, sexual desires cannot. Sexual desires cannot be willed or chosen because, by their very nature, they lay partly outside the realm of will and conscious control. This does not necessarily place them, Cartesian fashion, on the outside of reason, in the domain of madness . . . because actual desire never involves the total loss of control, the complete suppression of rational faculties" (101).

S. L. Bem strives for an overview in *The Lenses of Gender: Transforming the Debate on Sexual Inequality*, which credits gender theory with profound insights. Slightly different perspectives on similar themes are available in anthologies such as *Forms of Desire: Sexual Orientation and the Social Constructionist Controversy*, edited by Edward P. Stein; *The Cultural Construction of Sexuality*, edited by Pat Caplan; *Sexual Meanings: The Cultural Construction of Gender and Sexuality*, edited by Sherry B. Ortner and Harriet Whitehead; and *The Problem of Medical Knowledge: Examining the Social Construction of Medicine*, edited by P. Wright and A. Treacher.

Gender disputes have their roots not only in the larger culture but also in the still-emerging field of sexology, which is taken up in greater detail in another chapter. (See **The "Invention" of Sexology** in chapter 19.) For the general reader, "Gender Systems, Ideology, and Sex Research," by the brilliant anthropologist Carole Vance, is the best introduction to sex and gender in sex research. Vance explores the hidden social agendas of sexologists, who often assume that sex is simply intercourse rather than a matrix of physicality, intellectuality, and emotion; they deny the power of taboos, ignore historical determinants of sexuality, and ultimately gloss over real differences in experience. In Vance's view, the vast corpus of scientific literature on sexuality is largely irrelevant to a view of sexuality as a "socially constructed" phenomenon. These shortcomings of mainstream research, she says, are visible in current leftist and feminist schools as well. Only a genuinely new sexual discourse and a revised theory of sexuality will improve the state of knowledge. That is, of course, a tall order.

For these and other reasons, many scientists regard theories of social construction warily: the more extreme constructionists blithely ignore physiology and biology or dismiss them as an "essentialism" unworthy of notice. Sociobiologists assert that the primary determinants of gender and sexuality are genetics, hormones, and evolution, and they can marshal a great deal of scientific evidence. The essayists in *Sexual Nature/Sexual Culture*, edited by Paul R. Abramson and Steven D. Pinkerton, discuss the evolutionary origins of sexuality, biological explanations of sexual behavior, dimensions of cultural nurturing, and various methods of investigation and measurement. Scholars interested in the sociobiological position can look at three recent texts on sexuality, all of them comprehensive, up-to-date, and provocative: David M. Buss' *The Evolution of Desire: Strategies of Human Mating*, Kenneth Maxwell's *The Sexual Imperative: An Evolutionary Tale of Sexual Survival*, and Matt Ridley's *The Red Queen: Sex and the Evolution of Human Nature*.

Donald Symons' *The Evolution of Human Sexuality* advances the argument that sexual mechanics of male and female biology are quite different and that culture only modestly cloaks their imperatives. Robert Wright cites the insights of evolutionary psychology (whose tenets differ somewhat from sociobiology's) in *The Moral Animal: Evolutionary Psychology and Everyday Life*, which disputes various theories of social construction. Evolutionary strategies, say such texts, have traditionally governed the destiny of men and women. The best genetic strategy for males is to spread sperm as widely as possible, to impregnate mates whose progeny will replicate desirable genes. The best strategy for a female is to find a male with suitable genes (recognizable, in part, through ephemeral qualities such as attractiveness prized by the culture) but also possessed of the strength or resources to care for, and defend, her and her children.

Cultural theorists respond that technology has ended the need for male strength, hunting prowess, or warrior skills. Since our environment is largely artificial, men hardly need muscles any longer. Since an advanced economy distributes cheap goods, men need not hunt for food. Since wars are fought by machines, men need battle no longer. That same economy has made skills and preparation for jobs accessible to either men or women. Now a woman can mate with impunity with anyone, even someone whose characteristics have no evolutionary advantage, and support herself and her offspring by herself. Social biologists and evolutionary psychologists counter that while circumstances may, indeed, have changed, genetic programming still drives human reproduction and configures sexual attraction. Lynn Margulis and Dorion Sagan offer up-to-date information on the semiotics of bodies, fetishes, and cues in *Mystery Dance: On the Evolution of Human Sexuality*. The book's most interesting chapters talk about "sperm competition" as an element of sexual evolution; the authors observe that "men who suspect their mates are cheating produce more sperm cells and more semen per ejaculation than they do when they trust in their mates' fidelity" (38). Adrian Forsyth's *A Natural History of Sex: The Ecology and Evolution of Mating Behavior* is replete with information on the sexual behavior of many life forms, such as the observation that humans have the most highly developed armpits of all animals in order to maximize the aphrodisiac effects of body odor. George L. Hersey also discusses the biological basis of sexual selection in *The Evolution of Allure: Sexual Selection from the Medici Venus to the Incredible Hulk.*

The positions of social constructionists and sociobiologists are the latest versions of long-standing arguments over nature and nurture. On both sides ideology weighs as heavily as evidence. Social constructionists reduce terms such as *love, desire, beauty*, and *attraction* to issues of power, class, and hegemony. Sociobiologists reduce the same terms to strategies of evolutionary survival through genetic transmission. As usual in such disputes, the most extreme positions are espoused with the most passion. Biologists explain pornography in terms of behavior: the drive for anonymous sex with as many fertile women as possible is an impulse that men still feel strongly—an impulse visible in male-oriented pornography—just as the need for high-quality personal relationships rich in physical and emotional support is still important to women—a need visible in female-oriented pornography. Helen Haste steers a careful path through conflicting claims in *The Sexual Metaphor*, which discusses the imperviousness of sexual stereotypes and our resistance to abandoning distinctions between masculine and feminine. (See **The "Invention" of Sexology** in chapter 19.)

Whatever its strengths, however, biology offers few genetic or evolutionary explanations for homosexuality, and this shortcoming has given some impetus to speculation on the mutability of gender. Ruth Bleier challenges biologists in *Science and Gender: A Critique of Biology and Its Theories of Women*, as does Anne Fausto-Sterling in *Myths of Gender: Biological Theories about Women and Men*, each of which examines the ways that cultural attitudes shape scientific theories, especially those of sociobiologists, about gender definitions and differences. In "Pleasure and Danger: Toward a Politics of Sexuality," Carole Vance warns that the assumption that sexuality is culturally constructed does not mean that it can be "easily constructed or deconstructed at the social or individual level" (9). Nor, she also insists, "are theories of gender fully adequate to account for sexuality" (10). Her cautionary tone is echoed by Steven Epstein in "Gay Politics, Ethnic Identity: The Limits of Social Constructionism." According to Epstein, theories can explain a lot, but forming gender requires more than social construction; he argues for commonsense moderation. The study of pornography, which has always exalted fantasy, erotic play, shifting roles, and experimentation, has spurred approaches like "queer theory," a school that insists on personal choice. So has performance theory, which has contributed the notion that behavior is a game of impersonation conducted through rituals of signs and coding. The prolific Judith Butler believes that gender is performance, that, in a sense, performance calls gender into being. She elaborates in *Bodies That Matter: On the Discursive Limits of Sex* and *Gender Trouble: Feminists and the Subversion of Identity*, both of which challenge the alleged permanence and immutability of gender. Power exercised as heterosexual hegemony, says Butler, determines the "material" aspects of sex and sexuality. A constant theme in gender studies is the observation that the relationships a person enjoys with others may come closer to defining him or her than traditional categories. The representations of sexuality that humans encounter also shape performance, or so says Jane M. Ussher in *Fantasies of Femininity: Reframing the Boundaries of Sex*, which argues for tolerance as people experiment with sexual identities.

Queer theory has evolved as a cross-disciplinary discourse that comments on other discourses sometimes called deviant, perverse, and often erotic. Probably the best map of queer theory has been drawn by Lauren Berlant and Michael Warner in "What Does Queer Theory Teach Us about X?" Berlant and Warner prefer the term *queer commentary* and say that it

aspires to create publics, publics that can afford sex and intimacy in sustained, unchastening ways; publics that can comprehend their own differences of privilege and struggle; publics whose abstract spaces can also be lived in, remembered, hoped for. By *publics* we do not mean populations of self-identified queers. Nor is the name *queer* an umbrella for gays, lesbians, bi-sexuals, and the transgendered. Queer publics make available different understandings of membership at different times, and membership in them is more a matter of aspiration than it is the expression of an identity or a history. Through a wide range of mongrelized genres and media, queer commentary allows a lot of unpredictability in the culture it brings into being. (344)

Because queer theory is essentially a discourse of contention, however, others define it very differently, if only to insist on its instability. In *Academic Outlaws: Queer Theory and Cultural Studies in the Academy*, for example, William G. Tierney attempts to capitalize on the very marginality of such theorists, invoking some of the force of an outrageous pornographic discourse to do so, in an effort to make use of cultural dynamics of appropriation. For some academics, queer theory asserts the primacy of individual choice; for others it is not a program at all. Perhaps only two goals are clear: the determination to delineate differences and the determination to transcend them.

Queer theory has produced a flood of articles, books, and journals, for many of which pornography serves as a stimulus to reflection. "Queer Theory," a special issue of *differences* edited by Teresa de Lauretis, outlines thinking on nomenclature and essentialism. "More Gender Trouble: Feminism Meets Queer Theory," another special issue of the same journal, edited by Naomi Schor and Elizabeth Weed, explores the gaps between feminist theory focused on gender and difference and gay and lesbian theory focused on sex and sexuality. Both groups, of course, wish to construct a mythos to counter dominant heterosexual norms. The essays in *Sexual Artifice: Persons, Images, Politics*, edited by Ann

Kibbey, Kayann Short, and Abouali Farmanfarmaian, reflect on how gender is constructed in images in various media, how it is shaped by politics, and how it has been influenced by feminism. *Eroticism and Containment: Notes from the Flood Plain*, edited by Carol Siegel and Ann Kibbey, maintains that erotic "floods" cannot be contained by artificial constructs such as gender; the contributors celebrate primal energies of sexuality.

Theories of bisexuality will almost certainly increasingly compete with queer theory in the future, as Paula C. Rust's *Bisexuality and the Challenge to Lesbian Politics: Sex, Loyalty, and Revolution* makes clear. Bisexuality is, of course, wonderfully exciting to postmodernists eager to undermine gender stereotyping through cultural engineering, a tendency visible in *The Bisexual Imaginary: Representation, Identity and Desire*, edited by a group of scholars calling themselves the Bi Academic Intervention. Loraine Hutchins and Lani Kaahumanu have collected first-person materials in *Bi Any Other Name: Bisexual People Speak Out*, but despite the authenticity of these voices, scholars interested in bisexuality as a cultural phenomenon will also want to read Marjorie Garber's *Vice Versa: Bisexuality and the Erotics of Everyday Life*, which capitalizes on the current fascination with gender instability; Garber locates bisexuality not on some median between homosexuality and heterosexuality, but beyond both. The essays in *Bisexual and Homosexual Identities: Critical Theoretical Issues*, edited by John P. De Cecco and Michael G. Shively, occasionally touch on issues of representation, as does Naomi S. Tucker in *Bisexual Politics: Theories, Queries, and Visions*. Martin S. Weinberg, Colin J. Williams, and Douglas W. Pryor bring massive research to bear in *Dual Attraction: Understanding Bisexuality*, a volume filled with studies, interviews, and statistics. (See also **Sexual Subcultures** in Chapter 4, especially Geller and Steir.)

Anyone acquainted with the sheer number of works on the social construction of gender will sympathize with the notion that such theories constitute what is virtually a new species of pornography. Implicit in the outpouring is an erotic longing for a prelapsarian genderless state, a protocontinent of sexual equality, and we should not discount the desire that attaches to otherwise dry debate. Lawrence Cohen in "The Pleasures of Castration: The Postoperative Status of Hijras, Jankhas and Academics" has gone so far as to characterize academics as "persons of various genders who sometimes utilize conceptions of third gender as metaphors in social theory. But though third gender is good to think with, its theorization is often exquisitely insensitive to the bodies with which it plays. Much is at stake: some metropolitan academics have earned part of their living as gatekeepers, using their cultural capital as sex experts to decide the fate of others who would surgically transform their bodies" (277).

In any event, pornography remains an important cultural site for the negotiation of such issues. If sexuality, gender, fantasy, and so on are socially constructed—and it is a powerful argument—then we must also view the current debate as serving larger purposes. Future generations may look back at the conflict as an attempt to reconstruct—refresh—the taboos of sexuality, by way of providing pornography with new barriers to break. If even a kiss can be construed as violent, as the most extreme antisex feminists assert, then an act of intercourse is a violation of almost cosmic proportions. Violating such a taboo, assuming that it could be strengthened, would renew the power of pornography. As in older disputes over nature versus nurture, a middle ground would appear most tenable. The subject of pornography, however, rarely lends itself to moderation.

RECOVERING A "PORNOGRAPHIC" PAST: HISTORIES OF HOMOSEXUAL SUBCULTURES

Because sexuality and identity are seriously compromised by language and social spaces, says Judith Roof in *A Lure of Knowledge: Lesbian Sexuality and Theory*, she looks for representations of "eroticized relations among women," an impulse she says is "stimulated, at least for me, by a libidinous urge connected both to a sexual practice and to the shape of my own desire" (120). In such a context, pornography—lesbian representations in literature, art, cinema— can begin a search for sexual identity. Creating a more humane folklore about gays and lesbians requires a historical consciousness of the sexual folklore of the past. Pornography thus assists a subculture in reshaping its own beliefs and then reshaping the consciousness of the larger society. The last two decades have produced significant histories of gay and lesbian experience in the United States, and these have restored a past that was lost from texts that previous generations considered pornographic. Pornographic artifacts are not simply important documents of homosexual life; they also help gays and lesbians to bond together at the same time that they assert differences with mainstream heterosexuality. Jeffrey Weeks and J. Holland have also edited *Sexual Cultures: Communities, Values, and Intimacy*, in which contributors theorize about the roles of sexual representation in shaping communities. (See also gay, lesbian and ethnic discourse in chapter 15, **Folklore and Oral Genres**.)

Lesbians, like other genders, do not automatically know how to make love, says Pat Califia in *Sapphistry: The Book of Lesbian Sexuality*, and in this respect pornography can be instructive, especially for genders marginalized in the past (xiii–xv). In a larger sense, many gay and lesbian critics observe, pornography has historically functioned as empathic connection; it helped establish a sense of community by reminding homosexuals that other people shared their orientation, their desires, and their hopes. For example, Terralee Bensinger defines community as "an enabling fictional setting" in "Lesbian Pornography: The Re/ Making of (a) Community." Bensinger believes that "lesbian pornography illustrates a collective reworking of the dominant hetero-cultural tropes of desire" (80–81).

Where homosexuality is concerned, categories and definitions are critical. Michel Foucault and his disciples maintain that before the nineteenth century, humans rarely circumscribed what today we think of as gay or lesbian behavior and therefore did not proscribe it. Homophobia arose only after society cate-gorized the behavior as deviant or aberrant and anathematized it. That is the argument of David F. Greenberg's *The Construction of Homosexuality*, which cites numerous Western examples. Similarly, Jeffrey Weeks says in *Against Nature: Essays on History, Sexuality and Identity* that "the contemporary lesbian and gay identities are products not of nature or the imperatives of desire but of social categorisation and self-definition in a complex, shifting history" (157).

For the extreme postmodernist, that means that, lacking a name, homosexu-ality did not exist until modern times. Terry Castle, among others, reveals the flaws in that thesis by suggesting that Foucauldians are simply dressing up what she calls "the Queen Victoria Principle." Legend holds that when the queen was asked in 1855 if the Criminal Law Amendment Act criminalizing sex between men should apply to women as well, she could not imagine that women *could* have sex together. But not being able to imagine something does not mean that it does not exist, though it may not be visible, let alone encapsulated in language. (The current U.S. military policy toward homosexuals, usually rendered as "Don't tell, don't ask," is a Foucauldian version of the Queen Victoria Princi-ple.) Castle has hunted the ghosts of lesbians in documents over the last 300 years in *The Apparitional Lesbian: Female Homosexuality and Modern Culture*. In this work, probably the most brilliant single history of lesbianism, Castle makes several points: (1) the lesbian "is not a recent invention," an assertion that challenges Foucault's contention that nineteenth- and twentieth-century sex-ologists fabricated the lesbian; (2) "[s]he is not asexual," since desire is very much a part of identity; (3) "[s]he is not a gay man," a statement she hopes will distance her book from Edie Sedgwick's concentration on male homosexuality and open up territory for the lesbian; (4) "[s]he is not a nonsense," by which she means that lesbianism cannot be deconstructed into signifiers and linguistic devices, devoid of any real presence, as so many theorists seem to think.

Though poststructuralists regard her as retrograde, Lillian Faderman says good things about sexologists in *Odd Girls and Twilight Lovers: A History of Lesbian Life in Twentieth-Century America*. Post–World War I sexologists are respon-sible for "the altered views of women's intimacy with each other. It may be said that the sexologists changed the course of same-sex relationships not only because they cast suspicion on romantic friendships, but also because they helped to make possible the establishment of lesbian communities through their theories, which separated off the lesbian from the rest of womankind and pre-sented new concepts to describe certain feelings and preferences that had before been within the spectrum of 'normal' female experiences" (35). Another volume by Faderman, *Surpassing the Love of Men: Romantic Friendship and Love be-tween Women from the Renaissance to the Present*, also reconfigures the past to explore lesbian identity and community. Donna Penn concentrates on the rise of the "butch figure" in "The Meanings of Lesbianism in Postwar America," which enumerates the ways in which lesbians sorted out their roles during a period shaped by both psychological comment and their own experience. Joan

Nestle's "Butch–Femme Relationships: Sexual Courage in the 1950s" is an admiring look at those who dared in a decade not known for its tolerance.

Castle calls pornography a "shadow discourse" (34) in *The Apparitional Lesbian*: "The pornographic representation of lesbianism may nonetheless have influenced so-called mainstream representation more often—and more profoundly—than is commonly acknowledged" (245, n. 6). Other notable investigations include Sue-Ellen Case's "Tracking the Vampire," which distinguishes between "queer" and "lesbian" by analyzing the image of lesbian as vampire, the manifestation Case thinks has occurred most often in popular culture; Lynda Hart's *Fatal Women: Lesbian Sexuality and the Mark of Aggression*, which traces the shadow of the sinister lesbian as it flits through literature and film; Karla Jay's *Lesbian Erotics*, an anthology of essays on erotic images of lesbians in many media; and Karla Jay and Allen Young's *Lavender Culture*, in which Rita Mae Brown, Barbara Grier, John Stoltenberg, Julia Penelope, Andrea Dworkin, Andrew Kopkind, Jane Rule, Arthur Bell, Charlotte Bunch, and others offer reflections on mature lesbian and gay communities. In the 1980s, says Shane Phelan in *Identity Politics: Lesbian Feminism and the Limits of Community*, many feminists began to sense that radical politics neutered women and began to explore the sexuality of women with candor. As Phelan points out, "The celebration of female sexuality opened the door to a practice and a discussion that challenged and violated everything the antipornography forces were saying about women" (97). In this spirit, Tamsin Wilton reviews lesbian approaches to both gender and eroticism as counters to a crippling heterosexism in *Lesbian Studies: Setting an Agenda*.

Vern L. Bullough outlines the origins of prohibitions, the folklore of "deviance," and the discrimination encountered by homosexuals in *Sexual Variance in Society and History*, an excellent background tool. All history is political, argues Jennifer Terry in "Theorizing Deviant Historiography," because it has traditionally involved building a past in order to establish the legitimacy of mainstream groups by denying legitimacy to others; now gays and lesbians must rediscover their pasts in order to move consciousness forward. Two older, but still useful, texts by Edwin M. Schur, *Labeling Women Deviant* and *The Politics of Deviance* offer insight into this process. Gilbert Herdt's anthropological survey of images and practices in different cultures, "Representations of Homosexuality: An Essay in Cultural Ontology and Historical Comparison, Parts I and II," finds that different societies, in fact, have treated homosexuality quite differently.

Excellent general histories of gay life in the United States are Martin B. Duberman's *About Time: Exploring the Gay Past* and Jonathan Katz's *Gay American History*. John D'Emilio chronicles the rise of a contemporary sensibility in *Sexual Politics, Sexual Communities: The Making of the Homosexual Minority in the United States, 1940–1970*; his thesis is that a homosexual consciousness emerged from the social dislocations of World War II and was strengthened into a political force. Leigh W. Rutledge registers important erotic milestones and significant public events in *The Gay Decades from Stonewall to the Present: The People and Events That Shaped Gay Lives*, a popular work—structured as entertaining chronology—that endorses a similar thesis. Kevin White's *The First Sexual Revolution: The Emergence of Male Heterosexuality in Modern America* inverts the conventional question of when homosexuality was invented by studying the emergence of male heterosexuality as a constructed category during the early twentieth century. Douglas Sadownick focuses on an even narrower period in *Sex between Men: An Intimate History of the Sex Lives of Gay Men Postwar to Present.*

Michel Foucault suggested that dichotomies such as straight and gay serve to reinforce that which is being opposed, so that anathematizing homosexuality has, over time, established the dominance of heterosexuality as a political construct. A more defensible position is that articulated by the American novelist Gore Vidal and often repeated. Vidal reiterates in his Introduction to Jonathan Ned Katz's *The Invention of Heterosexuality*: "There are no homosexual people and no heterosexual people, only hetero or homo acts, and most people, at one time or another, despite horrendous taboos, mess around" (x). Katz approaches social construction from a brash and witty historical angle several degrees removed from Foucault by suggesting that the construction of heterosexuality itself was problematic. At the very least, claims Joan W. Scott in "Gender: A Useful Category for Historical Analysis," historians can find gender a positive, less emotionally charged way of discussing differences between men and women. Gay and lesbian historians continue to mine sexual materials.

GENERAL HISTORIES OF SEX

Since pornography by any definition is a representation of sex, an awareness of the slow evolution of human understanding of sex is useful to the scholar. A very general, even scattershot approach to sexual mores is that of Edgar Gregersen's *Sexual Practices: The Story of Human Sexuality*, whose encyclopedic entries cope with attitudes toward a variety of topics, from clothing to painting, in different geographical areas. Wayland Young's *Eros Denied* is also a multicultural study, though it leans toward Western societies in dealing with the repression of sexual discourse. Identically titled studies, *Sex in History*, one by Reay Tannahill and the other by G. R. Taylor, are similar in their wide-ranging survey of mores from ancient times to the present. Both are buttressed with references to literature, art, folklore, and custom; Taylor appends a solid bibliography of more than 250 significant historical texts. *Western Sexuality: Practice and Precept in Past and Present Times*, edited by Phillipe Ariès and Andre Bejin, assembles postmodern essays on sexual behavior in various Western and non-Western cultures.

Morton Hunt's *The Natural History of Love* is a classic popular history, with some attention to representations of sexuality. So is *Venus Unmasked, Or an Inquiry into the Nature and Origin of the Passion of Love*, by Leonard de Vries and Peter Fryer, who also cover erotica of the eighteenth century, extending their examination into levels of scientific, literary, and popular strata of culture. Although primarily a history of legal prosecutions and social responses in England, Peter Fryer's *Mrs. Grundy: Studies in Sexual Purity* embraces as well American reticence concerning language, clothing, and theatrical performance during the eighteenth and nineteenth centuries. The essays in *Passion and Power: Sexuality in History*, edited by Kathy Peiss and Christina Simmons with Robert A. Padgug, cover more disciplinary than chronological territory but are generally excellent and often touch on the role of pornography in history. German sexologists of the 1920s and 1930s turned out a large number of "moral histories" that deal in varying degrees with specifically American customs. In a class by itself is the great six-volume *Bilderlexicon der Erotik*; the historical sketches of volume I (*Kulturgeschichte*) are magisterial. Leo Schidrowitz, editor of the *Bilderlexicon*, also edited *Sittengeschichte der Kulturwelt und ihrer Entwicklung in Einzeldarstellungen*, whose eleven volumes (ten plus supplement) contain essays by virtually every German sexologist of note during the 1920s and 1930s. Together the volumes comprise one of the most thorough histories of human sexuality from ancient times until the 1920s. Topics include customs, costume, marriage and mating, amusements, perversions, fashion, health and bathing habits, fetishes, disease, art, literature, and theater, as well as dozens of others. Almost as impressive is the sweep of Eduard Fuchs' *Illustrierte Sittengeschichte*, whose volumes and plates also begin with antiquity and progress to the early twentieth century but do not attain the modern coverage of the *Bilderlexicon*. More to the point, all of these works deal extensively with sexual representation within a larger cultural context and are indispensable to the development of a historical consciousness of obscenity, pornography, erotica, or—to use a neutral term—sex materials.

Sexuality: An Illustrated History Representing the Sexual in Medicine and Culture from the Middle Ages to the Age of Aids, by Sander L. Gilman, is a history of the ways in which aspects of sexuality from genitalia to prostitution are represented iconographically, especially where disease is concerned; Gilman uses American examples only in the last chapter on AIDS. Peter Gay's *The Bourgeois Experience: Victoria to Freud*, volume I of his *The Education of the Senses*, explores concepts of sex and sensuality among the middle class during those periods. The volumes in that series trace the exfoliation of sexual awareness throughout our culture; Gay's breadth and comprehensiveness are impressive, and he appends splendid bibliographical appendixes. In *The Bourgeois Experience*, he notes that the moral hypocrisy of the Victorian period was a means "of carving out space for the passions," that sexual behavior outpaced available vocabularies (unlike Foucault, he thinks that people condemned specific acts long before the culture invented labels for them), and that the era was determined to rationalize and explain sex. Gay's *The Tender Passion, The Cultivation of Hatred*, and *The Naked Heart*, volumes II through IV, carry his investigation forward. *From Sappho to de Sade: Moments in the History of*

Sexuality, edited by Jan Bremmer, deals with a potpourri of topics from sexology to cultural attitudes in (principally) literary erotica. Finally, three journals, the *Journal of Sex Research*, the *Journal of the History of Sexuality*, and the *Archives of Sexual Behavior*, are unmatched sources of historical information.

BROAD HISTORIES OF SEX IN AMERICA

As a rule, American academic historians have been slow to deal with sex, let alone representations of it, for fear of seeming vulgar or inconsequential. In "Sex in History: A Virgin Field," Vern L. Bullough, the dean of American sexologists, maintains that researchers have scarcely touched the subject, and John C. Burnham, a more conventional, but still eminent, scholar, is just as forceful in "American Historians and the Subject of Sex." Burnham laments the lack of bibliographic surveys of the dimensions of sex in American history and reminds his colleagues that most primary sources of sexual information, from medical texts to newspapers, are still untapped. While Burnham warns against casting all phenomena in sexual terms, he thinks that it is nonetheless ridiculous to deny the influence of sexuality on human events. Robert A. Padgug similarly argues for the necessity of investigating popular period sources in "Sexual Matters: On Conceptualizing Sexuality in History."

An old, but still reliable, popular study, Sidney Ditzion's *Marriage, Morals, and Sex in America: A History of Ideas*, tracks American sexual mores from the colonial period to the twentieth century; along the way he provides capsule biographies of sex reformers, writers, and artists. Long out of print but extremely readable is *Our National Passion: 200 Years of Sex in America*, a history of American attitudes and behavior, by Sally Banes, Sheldon Frank, and Tem Horowitz. George N. Gordon's *Erotic Communications: Studies in Sex, Sin and Censorship* is a serviceable, somewhat idiosyncratic chronicle slanted toward the East Coast of the United States. Another, still lighter account is Bradley Smith's *The American Way of Sex: An Informal Illustrated History*, which ranges from pre-Columbian art and Native American texts to modern examples; the text is informative, if anecdotal, on behavior, on artifacts (e.g., clocks and dildos) domestic and imported, on whorehouses, and on burlesque. More recent and more scholarly is *Intimate Matters: A History of Sexuality in America* by John D'Emilio and Estelle B. Freedman, who examine changes in sexual discourse; the authors note that so much of what passed for pornographic was simply a lower-class and democratic vernacular. D'Emilio and Freedman neatly weave their history from both heterosexual and homosexual threads. At this writing, James R. Petersen has issued several installments of "Playboy's History of the Sexual Revolution," a highly readable, decade-by-decade chronicle of the "revolutionary" twentieth century.

In *Romantic Longings: Love in America, 1830–1980*, Steven Seidman discusses American tendencies to eroticize sex and conflate it with romance from the pre-Victorian era to modern gay subcultures. The essays in *American Sexual*

Politics: Sex, Gender, and Race since the Civil War, edited by John Fout and Maura Shaw Tantillo, examine a variety of historical aspects of American sexuality, including condoms; black, gay, male discourse; gay and lesbian discourse generally; film; women's romances; male impotence in Victorian culture; language and sexual desire; and other subjects. Though overbroad, as such anthologies often are, the Fout-Tantillo volume is notable because it attempts to address the sexuality of minorities through the lenses of class and race; the paucity of information on the sexual behavior and folklore of immigrants to the United States should drive research in the future. Benjamin Schlesinger has collected a series of essays entitled *Sexual Behaviour in Canada: Patterns and Problems* that add dimension to mores in North America; comparisons with the territory south of the border are implicit.

While popular studies of American morals, standards, and tastes do not always single out sexual expression, they can hardly avoid using examples. Helpful to the scholar are *American Manners and Morals* by Mary Cable et al.; *Popular Culture and High Culture: An Analysis of Taste* by Herbert J. Gans; *The Taste-makers* by Russell Lynes; the six-volume *Our Times: The United States, 1900–1925* by Mark Sullivan; *Lipstick Traces: A Secret History of the Twentieth Century* by Greil Marcus; and *Carnival Culture: The Trashing of Taste in America* by James B. Twitchell. The last of these, a jeremiad against vulgarity in various media, is a fairly precise guide to specific instances of the crass and the nasty. Any number of textbooks on mass media or popular culture contain essays on vulgar tastes, social restrictions, mutating sexual mores, explicit messages, and so forth. *Mass Culture: The Popular Arts in America*, edited by Bernard Rosenberg and David Manning White, is widely used in universities.

PERIOD STUDIES

Historians have been erratic in their attention to the sexuality of particular periods. "Sex Life of the American Indians," Fred W. Voget's encyclopedia contribution, though helpful to those who wish information on Native Americans, is somewhat dated now. Walter L. Williams' *The Spirit and the Flesh: Sexual Diversity in American Indian Culture* is more thorough and more conversant with recent work on the sexual behavior and customs of the early North Americans. In "Freedom of Expression in Native American Constitutions," an article on Native American political consciousness, Stephen A. Smith observes that the constitutions adopted in the nineteenth century by the Cherokee, Choctaw, Chickasaw, and Muskogee tribes exhibited little concern for obscenity. The essays in *The Indian Peoples of Eastern America: A Documentary History of the Sexes*, edited by James Axtell, discuss sexual relationships but do not have much to say about pornography save for legends and classic folklore. By contrast, some of the chapters in Philip Rawson's *Primitive Erotic Art* do deal with sexual behavior among peoples of the Americas.

One of the first essays to look more carefully at the Puritans' alleged fear of sexuality is Edmund S. Morgan's "The Puritans and Sex," which details a fascination with the erotic behind the facade of religion. Caroline Bingham's "Seventeenth-Century Attitudes toward Deviant Sex" also finds a greater tolerance toward homosexuality than folklore about the Puritans suggests. Henry Bamford Parkes in "Morals and Law Enforcement in Colonial New England" argues that Puritan conduct was not so elevated as Americans sometimes think. Similarly, Bruce C. Daniels concludes in *Puritans at Play: Leisure and Recreation in Colonial New England* that Puritans enjoyed eroticism and offers chapters on dancing, sex, and other entertainments to support his thesis.

One of the most fascinating period studies is Ronald G. Walters' "The Erotic South: Civilization and Sexuality in American Abolitionism," which concludes that abolitionist writing has little "merit" as pornography because abolitionists did not deal excessively with sexual misconduct on the part of slave owners, though they worried about the licentiousness of slaves and the possible corruption of whites affected by illicit intercourse and nudity. Walters quotes the *Liberator* of 29 January 1858 as declaring that "the sixteen slave States constitute one vast brothel" (183), thus expressing the general abolitionist view that plantations resembled "settings of pornographic novels" (187). Says Walters: "Belief that submission and dominance lead to sexual license had much wider currency in 19th century America than in previous centuries or in our own day. Victorian pornography, for instance, exploited situations of power and powerlessness more than the contemporary variety does (despite some lurid exceptions) and probably more than ancient bawdy literature did" (186). Walters' commentary includes mention of the sexual attitudes of Americans as diverse as Elizabeth Cady Stanton, who thought that sex should be restricted even in marriage, and the utopian Oneida community, which explored sexual permutations both spiritual and carnal.

Utopian communities such as Oneida and the Brotherhood of the New Life in which sex played a major role are the subjects of Gilbert Seldes' *The Stammering Century*. Joseph W. Slade's "Thomas Lake Harris (1823–1906)" deals with the sexual writings of the patriarch of the Brotherhood of the New Life, a community that moved from New York to California at the end of the nineteenth century, as does *A Prophet and a Pilgrim*, by Herbert W. Schneider and George Lawton. Other commentaries on the sexual visions and ideologies of such societies are Louis J. Kern's *An Ordered Love: Sex Roles and Sexuality in Victorian Utopias: The Shakers, the Mormons, and the Oneida Community* and Lawrence Foster's *Religion and Sexuality: The Shakers, the Mormons, and the Oneida Community*. All of these social experiments left documents charged with eroticism verging on pornography. Thomas P. Lowry's *The Story the Soldiers Wouldn't Tell: Sex in the Civil War* also mentions the Oneida community but is focused on the sexual expression of troops in the conflict. Lowry's history devotes chapters to obscene language and humor, prostitution, homosexuality, and pornography. His chapter "And the Flesh Was Made Word" draws on personal collections and the National Archives for period brochures advertising pictures, photographs, and archives. One entrepreneur, G. S. Hoskins and Company of New York, offered "'spicy' song books, French tobacco boxes (in the shape of 'human manure'), marked playing cards, transparent playing cards watermarked with naked women, French ticklers, love powders, false mustaches, dildos, three types of condoms, and stereoscopic pictures at $9 a dozen" as well as twenty-three different erotic novels ranging from *Fanny Hill* to *The Libertine Enchantress* (55).

As one might expect, the Victorian era, allegedly a period of stringent sexual repression, has been a magnet for academics fascinated by an era synonymous with erotic hypocrisy. Steven Marcus' *The Other Victorians*, though centered on British examples, is the progenitor of many similar texts; according to Peter Gay, it sets the standard for "smug twentieth century condescension"[1] toward earlier sexual mores. Because the erotic habits of the Victorians are still cloudy, readers are advised to be careful reading the criticism, for thus far few historians have commanded the breadth of a Peter Gay with the interdisciplinary reach necessary to dispel those mysteries. Meanwhile, interpretive disputes are endless. For example, Paula Weideger's *History's Mistress: A New Interpretation of a 19th-Century Ethnographic Classic* is an erudite examination of *Das Weib* (1885), a sexology text by Hermann Ploss once praised for its liberal views and its groundbreaking examination of sexual mores or just as often condemned for its photographs of breasts. Weideger rereads the text sympathetically to uncover ambivalent male attitudes toward women; her approach is rewarding precisely because it burrows deep into the period. Ludmilla Jordanova, however, writing in *Sexual Visions: Images of Gender in Science and Medicine between the Eighteenth and Twentieth Centuries*, thinks that Weideger's interpretation is ideologically suspect (10). Jordanova's text is informative on gender bias in the evolution of medical images of the female body. The reader can appreciate the conclusions of both writers.

In this regard, the scholarship on the Victorian period illustrates the dangers of trying to interpret a period of culture through its pornographic texts. Some scholars seem to assume that the more clandestine the form of expression, the more authentic it is, and thus they misunderstand its folkloristic significance. Most popular comment is content to demonstrate that sexuality seethed beneath respectable surfaces. Four such surveys are Cyril Pearl's *The Girl with the Swansdown Seat*, Ronald Pearsall's *The Worm in the Bud: The World of Victorian Sexuality*, Milton Rugoff's *Prudery and Passion: Sexuality in Victorian America*, and Patricia Anderson's *When Passion Reigned: Sex and the Victorians*, all of which make much of the marked contrast between carefully regulated speech and rampant sexuality. The claim that many Victorians embraced sensuality suggest that their descendants hope that passion can seethe beneath their own stuffiness. G. J. Barker-Binfield's *The Horrors of the Half-Known Life: Male Attitudes toward Women and Sexuality in Nineteenth-Century America* examines professional texts of the period to find that they purveyed ignorance, misleading advice, and tortured responses to masturbation and intercourse. Worse, the era's ignorance encouraged weird images of women as saints, on one hand, and whores, on the other. Sharon R. Ullman's *Sex Seen: The Emergence of Modern Sexuality in America* focuses mostly on the Victorian period as a barometer of a Puritanism that still marginalizes sexuality in America.

Hypocrisy is the theme of many of the essays in *Sexual Underworlds of the Enlightenment*, edited by George Rousseau and Roy Porter, a volume chiefly British and European in its orientation. Wendell S. Johnson's *Living in Sin: The Victorian Sexual Revolution* investigates the sexual restlessness of Victorians in England and America and sees in the attempts to overthrow repression the precursors of later "sexual revolutions." Fraser Harrison's *The Dark Angel: Aspects of Victorian Sexuality* catalogs nineteenth-century sexual anxieties as reflected in the literature, media, and sex manuals of the period, with some economic analysis. Although Christina Simmons' extrapolations from sexual commentaries of the second and third decades of the twentieth century stretch the definition of Victorian, her "Modern Sexuality and the Myth of Victorian Repression" argues that Americans of that period held quite realistic views of sex. Most historians now believe that the sexual attitudes of Victorian Americans varied by class: middle-class citizens, then as now, pursued sexual pleasure but did so less publicly than their descendants. Nancy F. Cott's splendid "Passionlessness: An Interpretation of Victorian Sexual Ideology, 1790–1850" argues that women were encouraged to achieve a kind of spirituality by distancing themselves from lust. Even so, women may not have talked about sex outside their homes, but they enjoyed erotic discourse with other women in their closed parlors and with their husbands in bed–to a far greater degree than cultural myth would have it. Victorian men have traditionally been depicted as seeking out prostitutes in their flight from frigid wives, but while they may have been more raucous with other males in bars, clubs, and other haunts, middle-class men also enjoyed lusty intercourse with mates not only willing but eager to experiment with novel forms of lovemaking. Elaine Showalter's *Sexual Anarchy: Gender and Culture at the Fin de Siècle* asserts that many of the sexual causes, concerns, and crises of our own time are prefigured by those of the turn of the century.

Not surprisingly, sexual histories of urban areas are wonderful sources of information. Timothy Gilfoyle's triumph of research, *City of Eros: New York City, Prostitution, and the Commercialization of Sex, 1790–1920*, is easily the best single-site study of a huge tenderloin district. Gilfoyle's is primarily a history of prostitution but also of the literature of prostitution and other forms of pornography, and it reaches backward and forward in history to contextualize the moral climate along the eastern seaboard. Major cities were centers of erotica, according to Paul S. Boyer in *Urban Masses and Moral Order in America, 1820–1920*, one of the best overviews of the subject. Luc Sante offers gritty detail in *Low Life: Lures and Snares of Old New York*. Oliver Pilat and Jo Ranson wrote *Sodom by the Sea: An Affectionate History of Coney Island*, to recall the metropolitan amusement park's penny arcades, sleazy shows, and soft-core porn movies. Kathy Peiss' *Cheap Amusements: Working Women and Leisure in Turn of the Century New York* investigates leisure activities from the standpoint of women, who learned to move more freely than their mothers in dance halls and gathering places for both sexes in an era reshaped by industrialization. John C. Burnham's "The Progressive Era Revolution in American Attitudes toward Sex" also deals with increased liberality as a product of life in cities. In "Sexual Geography and Gender Economy: The Furnished Room Districts of Chicago, 1890–1930," Joanne Meyerowitz views the shifting geography of urban areas as a generator of sexual revolutions and insists that while working-class women on their own did fall prey to males, they also learned to create and shape their own sexuality. Feminist scholarship shines in this and similar efforts to recover a past.

Other examples range from F. M. Lehman's *The White Slave Hell: Or, with Christ at Midnight in the Slums of Chicago*, a titillating 1910 exposé of prostitution, vice dens, and lowlife, to William Murray's "The Porn Capital of America," a 1971 characterization of San Francisco as a fountainhead of sexual expression and representation. Cities might also be said to vie for the title of "sin capital" of America; leading candidates have been New York and its Times Square and Boston and its Combat Zone. At midcentury, Jack Lait and Lee Mortimer published a series on American metropolises: *New York: Confidential!*, *Washington: Confidential!*, *Chicago: Confidential!*, and *U.S.A. Confidential!* all behind-the-scenes looks at nightlife, sex, scandal, and pornography; the Chicago book went through ten printings in less than a year, doubtless because of the sensationalism of its narrative. A fictionalized, but fascinating, contemporary, quasi-anthropological study of the Times Square porn milieu has been crafted by Nik Cohn as *The Heart of the World*. More sensational is *Tales of Times Square*, a memoir by Josh Friedman, who recalls hookers, arcade denizens, corrupt cops, strippers, and porn producers. The single best source on the area, however, is W. R. Taylor's collection of essays called *Inventing Times Square: Commerce and Culture at the Crossroads of the World*; especially useful in that volume is Laurence Senelick's historical essay, "Private Parts in Public Places" (see **Ethnographic Research** in chapter 19). An informative look at Mayor Giuliani's recent efforts to rezone sex businesses to the dense industrial fringes of New York is Mark Schoofs' "Beat It: The City's Moral Fixation: Pushing Porn Out of Town." Schoofs interviews gays and lesbians worried that their venues will be targeted and also urban planner Jane Jacobs, who fears that the loss of sex businesses from the heart of the city will diminish diversity. In "The Sun Is Setting on the Times Square Porn Palaces" David W. Dunlap manages a little nostalgia for the sleaze as new urban development and the campaigns of antiporn groups slowly shut down many porn businesses. In "Porn Free," Richard Goldstein argues that far from tapping the citizenry's moral outrage, New York City's campaign against pornography has simply delivered valuable commercial opportunities to midtown developers, realtors, and property owners, an example of economic greed and hypocrisy similar to LaGuardia's earlier destruction of burlesque theaters in order to raise property values. N. R. Klein-field's "Effort to Stop Sex Industry Is Only Latest in Long Line" points out that New York City has cleaned up before, only to rebound from repression; sweeping out the old porn will help prepare for new forms that talented New Yorkers will dream up.

Bernard Perlman published "A Century of Cincinnati Esthetics: From Fig Leaves to Fines" on the evening of the arraignment of Dennis Barrie, director of the Cincinnati Contemporary Art Center, for hanging the "obscene" Mapplethorpe show. Perlman recalls that Cincinnati in the nineteenth century once hired a Mr. Fazzi, a craftsman, to construct fig leaves for European statues on exhibit in a local museum; the essay offers as well a brief history of the attempts of various American cities to censor art since adjudged important. Cincinnati's history of trying to regulate its citizens' morality is also the subject of Herbert Wray's "Is Porn Un-American?" Given Boston's reputation for Puritanism, Cincinnati is hardly the only city to have engaged in censorship of art, of course, and scholars will be able to compile a long list, starting, perhaps with Providence. "Raid in Providence: Private Parts, Exhibit" recounts the story of a police raid on an explicit show held at the Rhode Island School of Design. After examining the sexual politics of various major cities, Harrell R. Rodgers theorizes that a steady pace of legal liberalization generally means that censorship is ineffective in the long run in "Censorship Campaigns in Eighteen Cities: An Impact Analysis." Even liberal institutions sometimes balk at certain exhibits, of course. The Aldritch Museum of Contemporary Art in Ridgefield, Connecticut, agreed to mount *The Great American Nude* exhibit after the Whitney Museum of Art's refusal to take the show, in which Karen Finley and others were to appear nude, or so reported Mel Gussow in "Bumped from the Whitney, Nudity Finds a Showcase."

James R. McGovern offers a revisionist argument that women had the freedom usually associated with the jazz age a full decade earlier than is commonly supposed in "The American Woman's Pre–World War I Freedom in Manners and Morals." Such ideas are borne out in the essays collected by William L. O'Neill in *The American Sexual Dilemma*. The historians of that volume suggest that the American sex "revolution" began in the early part of the twentieth century, fueled by surging population, an influx of immigrants, a maturing of industrialization, the rise of mass media and the spread of education, the deliquescence of older institutions, the faltering of religion, the growing awareness of global issues, and so on. Chapter 5 of Frederick Lewis Allen's *Only Yesterday* is devoted to rapid shifts in morality and is still worth reading. Where Allen makes his points subtly, *The Sexual History of the World War*, a classic study by the German sexologist Magnus Hirschfeld and his colleagues, widely reprinted, makes them harshly. Hirschfeld's catalog of sexual behavior in wartime, lavishly and sometimes frighteningly illustrated, lays increased vulgarity at the door of worldwide conflict; the United States receives minor attention and in this narrative—as in reality—suffers less than other countries ravaged by decimation, disease, and poverty. The by-now-familiar thesis is that death and de-struction trigger sexual activity for purposes of relief of tension and reproduction of the race; pornography serves in such contexts as an agent of life and survival. Paula Fass' *The Damned and the Beautiful: American Youth in the 1920s* ex-plores the postwar upheaval in American morals; Fass finds that the disillusion-ment that followed the conflict prompted young women to explore their sexuality and to work for equality. Nearly forgotten is a small, but valuable, book by Geoffrey May, *Social Control of Sex Expression*, on the strictures American morality placed on marriage, on repressive legislation of sex outside sanctioned union, and on anathemas against representation, mostly during the 1920s and 1930s. John Costello analyzes changes in sexual values and attitudes wrought by World War II, especially among liberals and feminists, in *Love, Sex and War: Changing Values 1939–1945*, a title altered to *Virtue under Fire: How World War II Changed Our Social and Sexual Attitudes* for the American edi-tion. Costello found, among other things, that seismic changes occurred because mores that functioned well enough during peace seemed inadequate to crisis, because war industries sucked women into factories and altered economic roles, and because the proximity of death promoted the urge to reproduce.

The two volumes by Albert Ellis called *The Folklore of Sex* (see **Folklore and Obscenity** in chapter 15) are a wonderful, longitudinal, cross-sectioned survey of American sexual culture during the 1950s. Writing about the same period, Margaret Mead took a sanguine view in *Male and Female: A Study of the Sexes in a Changing World*. According to Mead, the growing awareness of sexuality, especially among women, is a concomitant of change in a culture driven by the conflict between impersonal forces and the desire for personal freedom. Despite the amusing title of *The Rape of the APE (American Puritan Ethic): the Official History of the Sex Revolution, 1945–1973: the Obscening of America, an RSVP (Redeeming Social Value Pornography) Document*, Allan Sherman's history of mores and social change following World War II contains accurate and useful information about shifts in popular culture. The sociologist Pitirim Sorokin announced that an American sex revolution was in progress in the early 1950s. The signs, he said in *The American Sex Revolution*, were in-creased divorce and promiscuity and the "sexualization of American culture" (19) by bolder literature, painting, music, science, popular culture, and so on. He was particularly upset by the sadism of Mickey Spillane novels and appalled by trashy movies and considered the trend toward open expression dangerous. Whether Sorokin was right or not about the chronology, the sexual revolution seemed full-blown in the 1960s.

Various writers seemed to be the revolution's godfathers. In *The Party of Eros: Radical Social Thought and the Realm of Freedom*, Richard King iden-tifies a school of transcendent sexual-political thought in the writings of Wilhelm Reich, Paul Goodman, Herbert Marcuse, and Norman Brown. Typical of those to applaud was Lawrence Lipton, whose *The Erotic Revolution: An Affirmative View of the New Morality* approved of the new freedom of expression. A volume called *Sex American Style*, edited by Frank Robinson and Nat Lehrman, contained essays on food and drink, sex and drugs, lots of cartoons, and essays by Hugh Hefner, Art Buchwald, Bill Cosby, Mary Calderone, and others commenting on the fun and the significance of the "new" sexual habits of the 1960s and early 1970s. Angelo d'Arcangelo, a popular author of gay porn books, said in *Angelo d'Arcangelo's Love Book: Inside the Sexual Revolution* that homosexuals had made large strides during the 1960s. Journalist Jack Boulware offers a plentifully illustrated, lightly nostalgic look at the high jinks of the 1960s and 1970s in *Sex, American Style: An Illustrated Romp through the Golden Age of Heterosexuality* and concludes with a chapter comparing past to present (e.g., he visits a strip club, John Leslie's porn set, a sex club, and a nudist camp).

By contrast, George Frankl suggests in *The Failure of the Sexual Revolution* that while the world may have been made safer for sexual discourse, the revolution's political agenda has not succeeded, and neither Britons nor Americans seem any more secure in their sexuality. Gershon Legman went further by denying that there had been a revolution at all; Legman said in *The Fake Revolt* that sexual excess, public nudity, political "liberalism," and social candor had not altered power structures or moral conservatism. As if to prove Legman correct, Jason Douglas launched a moral attack called *The Age of Perversion: A Close-Up View of Sexuality in Our Permissive Society*, a pretty unscholarly look at American, German, Dutch, and British sleaze of the 1960s; the book is more interesting as a benchmark of attitudes. Outsiders such as Robert W. Osborn subjected the 1960s to close scrutiny in journalistic surveys such as *Sex in Den U.S.A.: Zwischen Pruderie und Perversion*; the view is of a traditional culture riven by experimentation. Similar is a disapproving British examination of American mores by David Holbrook called *The Pseudo-Revolution: A Critical Study of Extremist "Liberation" in Sex*; so far as pornography is concerned, says Holbrook, the "revolution" reduces to "the freedom to masturbate." The persistence of conservative tradition also shapes American fascination with sexual matters in the 1960s for Sarah Harris, whose *The Puritan Jungle: America's Sexual Underground* draws on interviews with gays, vice cops, transvestites, pornographers, performers, hustlers, and other far-from-average citizens. John Heidenry's *What Wild Ecstasy: The Rise and Fall of the Sexual Revolution* is a broad, balanced, humane, and anecdotal account of the sexual revolution of the 1960s, which the author traces back to the 1930s and then carries forward to loss of energy in the 1980s and 1990s. Heidenry devotes considerable space to the exploits of pornographers, sex performers, and critics of sexual candor.

The New Sexual Revolution, edited by Lester A. Kirkendall and Robert N. Whitehurst, brought together pundits to argue over whether or not a revolution had taken place. Increased disputation seemed to be the only real certainty, said Anna K. Francoeur and Robert T. Francoeur. Their *Hot and Cool Sex: Cultures in Conflict* charts changing sexual roles, mutations of family structure, and a wide gamut of sexual lifestyles apparent in the 1970s. Historians are still trying to make sense of the 1960s and 1970s, of course. George Burr Leonard decides that the pornography that became quasi-public then has not helped much to liberate sexuality, though he is not opposed to it; his *The End of Sex: Erotic Love after the Sexual Revolution* muses inconclusively on what should come next. The sexual revolution of the 1960s has led thus far to confusion, indifference, and androgyny, says Jean Baudrillard in *The Transparency of Evil: Essays on Extreme Phenomena*. Several of the essays in *Human Sexuality in a Changing Society*, edited by Graham B. Spanier, consider the role of pornography in fostering or reflecting change in attitudes and practice. David S. Allyn argues in "Make Love, Not War: The Sexual Revolution in America, 1957–1977" that the rise of a "New Morality," with a sexual discourse that bridged high and low culture, had a profound influence on gender and sexual relations.

Barbara Ehrenreich, Elizabeth Hess, and Gloria Jacobs focus on the eroticization wrought by and for women in *Re-Making Love: The Feminization of Sex*, a book that ranges over the appeal of rock and roll, strip clubs for women, sex aid parties, and the foregrounding of female desire. Other feminists are more skeptical. In *Erotic Wars: What Happened to the Sexual Revolution?*, Lillian B. Rubin avers that sexual discourse has increased more than sexual freedom. Linda Grant surveys sexual trends over the last three decades in *Sexing the Millennium: Women and the Sexual Revolution*, and compares them to those in the nineteenth century (she is excellent on Wilhelm Reich, who thought that insufficient orgasms caused people to fall ill). By focusing on the sexual psyche, Grant endorses the need for an eroticized female experience, a need she believes was not satisfied by the so-called revolution of the 1960s, whose main currents left women in sidewaters. If the 1970s and 1980s saw evidence of backsliding, particularly in attacks on male sexuality, the 1990s held greater promise for women. Even so, Grant thinks, women have not learned to take advantage of their freedom, HIV seems to have blunted any genuine sex industry for women, and too many males have turned to Southeast Asia for sexual gratification.

In their analysis of "The Stalled Sexual Revolutions of This Century," Ira L. Reiss and Harriett M. Reiss make the point that women often think of sex as a "service" to men rather than an act of mutual gratification and communication, and that retards common understanding. Another chapter in the same volume, (*An End to Shame: Shaping Our Next Sexual Revolution*) called "Clarifying Our Fantasies about Pornography" (131–150), is notable because it exposes many myths. Dated now because it was written before the specter of AIDS but still worth reading is John Money's "Recreational—and Procreational—Sex." Money, a pediatric psychologist, argues that overpopulation, increased life expectancy, and sophisticated technologies, especially new means of birth control, make imperative "a new ethic of recreational sex": changes in attitudes toward nonreproductive sex and in the morality of sex-coded roles accelerate sexual revolution, Money says; couples may avoid procreation without embracing promiscuity. Finally, Steve Chapple and David Talbot interview a large number of Americans (Erica Jong, Tipper Gore, Candida Royalle, and a great many others) on the state of sex in the country and visit swingers' groups and other sites in *Burning Desires: Sex in America, a Report from the Field* to find that AIDS and shifting mores have changed sexual practice and representation.

Wendy Dennis uses surveys to bolster discussion of sexual etiquette in *Hot and Bothered: Sex and Love in the Nineties*. Susie Bright, one of the principal defenders of pornography, adopts a reasonable tone to allay fears generated by sexual expression in *Susie Bright's Sexual State of the Union*. Bright covers Internet sex, abortion, gay marriage, gender issues, sexual fantasy, sadomasochism, and many other topics. The sexual scene of the 1990s apparently fragmented into subcultures. In this regard, Dick Hebdige's *Subculture: The Meaning of Style*, though it is not focused on sexual orientation or representation, is a splendid discussion of the dynamics of subculture formation. More up-to-date, more serious in their analyses of sexual subcultures, and yet clearly popular in their appeal are Susan C. Bakos' *Kink: The Hidden Sex Lives of Americans*, Ivo Dominguez's *Beneath the Skins: The New Spirit and Politics of the Kink Community*, Roy D. Eskara's *Bizarre Sex*, Ted Polhemus and Housk Randall's *Rituals of Love: Sexual Experiments, Erotic Possibilities*, Housk Randall's *Revelations: Chronicles and Visions from the Sexual Underworld*, and Eurydice's *Satyricon USA*, all of which serve as introductions to fringe communities and all of which shade into folklore. A good sign of the times is Mark Simpson's *It's a Queer World: Deviant Adventures in Pop Culture*, whose title makes several assumptions about gayness and culture. Simpson talks to American marines about the class signification of foreskins, comments on straight and gay camp, and watches lesbian strippers bugger a groom at his premarriage stag party. Carl Holmberg's *Sexualities and Popular Culture*, an example of the preprocessed scholarship that communication specialists often bring to the study of culture, ranges across sex toys, humor, and taboo but attests nonetheless to the pervasiveness of sex in modern culture. Many scholars assume that *Time* magazine, a fairly conservative publication, speaks for middlebrow culture. If that be true, then Joel Stein's article, "Porn Goes Mainstream," would be definitive in its observations that many pornographic genres achieved an apparently irreversible vogue in the 1990s. Stein details the many ways in which porn impacts on popular culture today.

SEX AND PORNOGRAPHY SURVEYS

Like sex manuals, sex surveys attempt to document changes attributable to "revolutions" and thus contribute to a robust American folklore. Over the years, pollsters have sketched the elements of folklore and the behavior that the folklore actually masks in the guise of "public opinion." Sometimes these instruments include questions designed to elicit responses to pornography; sometimes not, but whatever their shortcomings, they are barometers of a period's sexual practices and beliefs. Some Americans have come to regard sex surveys as themselves a species of porn and read them for titillation. In any case, they constitute an enormous genre. Listing all of them would be futile, but a sampling of significant surveys attests to the popularity of the enterprise. For purposes of comparison, scholars might wish to consult Liz Stanley's *Sex Surveyed, 1949–1994: From Mass-Observation's "Little Kinsey" to the National Survey and the Hite Reports*, an overview of a half century of British sex surveys that also covers notable American examples. A skeptical David W. Moore writes about the power of surveys to mold as well as elicit opinion in *The Superpollsters: How They Measure and Manipulate Public Opinion in America*; one chapter, "The Sins of Shere Hite," on the pitfalls of methodology, is especially noteworthy. Doris-Jean Burton's "Public Opinion and Pornography Policy" examines the effects of polls on policy and legislation by reflecting on differences attributable to the gender, age, education, and religion of respondents.

The historian Carl Degler discovered that the biologist Clelia Duel Mosher had conducted a study of American women toward the end of the nineteenth century, when to do so was remarkable. Mosher's work has since been published as *The Mosher Survey: Sexual Attitudes of 45 Victorian Women*. About a third of the women told Mosher that sex was a source of mutual pleasure, not just a reproductive duty, a finding at variance with the "official" morality of the time. Most of the subjects confessed to entering marriage beset with sexual ignorance but said they learned to experience orgasm and to make sex a normal part of their lives. Using Mosher's results to revise conceptions, Degler pointed out in "What Ought to Be and What Was: Women's Sexuality in the Nineteenth Century" that American women enjoyed sex, at least with their husbands, and were curious enough about the subject to read works considered pornographic to find out more. The rediscovery of Mosher's survey is a reminder that recovery of lost documents can revise historians' views. See, for example, Rosalind Rosenberg's *Beyond Separate Spheres: Intellectual Roots of Modern Feminism* (98–99, 180–187); see also Peter Gay's *The Bourgeois Experience* (137–144). Gay observes that "the sexual feelings" of Dr. Mosher's respondents were "running well ahead of their conventional vocabulary" (138), one reason that traditional historians have assumed that Victorian women were afraid of sex. Another important study, this one from the 1920s, is Katherine Bement Davis' *Factors in the Sex Life of Twenty-Two Hundred Women*, notable because it indicated that nearly half the respondents thought that sex need not be a reproductive chore but should function as a major source of pleasure and exaltation, an admission considered scandalous at the time. Moreover, some said they had experienced significant sexual relationships with other women.

The most famous of all surveys, of course, are those initiated by Alfred Kinsey. In 1948 Kinsey, Wardell B. Pomeroy, and Clyde E. Martin published *Sexual Behavior in the Human Male*; its conclusions attested to a far greater degree of sexual activity and experimentation among American males than had ever been documented before. With the addition of Paul H. Gebhard as coauthor, the same researchers in 1953 published *Sexual Behavior in the Human Female*. The impact of the second volume was even greater; the subtext of both books was that sexuality was a necessary and normal part of life that could be enhanced by greater understanding and less guilt. The Kinsey reports instantly generated a great deal of comment, parody, and follow-up, some copycat, some original. The most astute contemporary criticism can be found in *Sex Habits of American Men*, a collection of fourteen essays on the first Kinsey report edited by Albert Deutsch. Surprisingly few major studies have been conducted by the Kinsey Institute since. *Sex and Morality in the U.S.: An Empirical Enquiry under the Auspices of the Kinsey Institute*, published in 1989 by Albert D. Klassen, Colin J. Williams, and Eugene E. Levitt, finally got around to interpreting data gathered in 1970; the report concluded that there was still a lot of sexual conservatism, not to say profound ignorance, in America. The more up-to-date (1990) *The Kinsey Institute New Report on Sex*, by June Reinisch with Ruth Beasley, was equally bleak: 55 percent of adults who answered eighteen questions on contraception, homosexuality, menopause, infidelity, erection problems, and AIDS failed to get half the answers right.

Conductors of sex surveys (including those with questions on porn) typically ask questions about frequency and satisfaction of intercourse, masturbation, extramarital affairs, age, number of children, income, education, and political and religious persuasions. The results, when analyzed, graph average sexual profiles by class, region, and group and allow analysts to draw conclusions. In 1976, for example, a survey of surveys by SIECUS titled *Sexuality and the Aging* concluded that ignorance, superstition, and prejudice were thwarting sexual desire and sexual expression among the elderly. In what the author called a "personal survey" conducted through extensive interviews with doctors, lawyers, scientists, and young and older people, Vance Packard outlined attempts by Americans to come to grips with the "sexual revolution" of the 1960s in *The Sexual Wilderness: The Contemporary Upheaval in Male–Female Relationships*. Similarly, Morton Hunt's *Sexual Behavior in the 1970s*, though buttressed by statistics, was written as a popular narrative. It offered entertaining, but comprehensive, coverage of American sexual attitudes and practices, including a growing tolerance for explicit expression. *The Redbook Report on Female Sexuality*, by Carol Tavris and Susan Sadd, revealed the sexual attitudes and behavior of 2,278 married women selected from responses by 100,000 readers of the magazine. Perhaps the most famous survey in recent times was the mail questionnaire designed by Shere Hite; the results were published in 1976 as *The Hite Report: A Nationwide Study of Female Sexuality*. It was widely attacked because of the low rate of return and because of Hite's conclusions. For example, George Gordon, in *Erotic Communications*, notes that the responses to this nationwide survey all seem stylistically similar, after the manner of letters in *Penthouse*'s monthly "Forum," which calls their reliability into doubt and illustrates that the sex survey itself has become a pornographic genre (309, n. 3). That did not stop Hite from doing two other surveys: *The Hite Report: On Male Sexuality*, for which males responded to queries about sexual behavior and fantasies (many rejected the fantasies they found in pornography), and *Women and Love: A Cultural Revolution in Progress*, based on a survey of 4,500 women.

Many surveys have focused on public attitudes toward pornography. Typical is George Gallup's *Public Support of Censorship Indicated*, a 1969 poll. Gallup reported that 81 percent of men and 88 percent of women favored more strict local and state restrictions, with older Americans being generally more in favor of additional legislation. That same year Louis Harris polled Americans on sexual attitudes, reactions to pornography, and associated matters for the *Time Morality Poll*. According to Harris, Americans were not nearly so hostile to pornography as their political leaders had assumed. The President's Commission on Obscenity and Pornography cited both studies in its *Report* and commissioned numerous surveys as part of its mission. See, for example, the "National Survey of Public Attitudes toward and Experience with Erotic Materials" by Abelson et al. Climates change, of course. Tom Smith points out in "The Use of Public Opinion Data by the Attorney General's Commission on Pornography" that the Attorney General's (AG's) Commission impaneled sixteen years later was energized, in part, by polls in which a majority of Americans said they believed that pornography contributes to a "breakdown in morals." The AG's Commission drew on two major polls. The findings of the first, by George Gallup, were reproduced by *Newsweek* in 1985 in "The War against Pornography": 73 percent of those surveyed believed that pornography leads some people to commit crimes of rape or sexual violence, and two-thirds of those surveyed supported a ban on violent porn, but not on other kinds, which they wanted to be able freely to purchase. Those of the second, by Yankelovich, Clancy Shulman and partners, were reproduced by *Time* in 1986 in "Pornography: A Poll": two-thirds of Americans were "very" or "fairly concerned" about the pervasiveness of pornography, but while 50 percent of all women surveyed were "very concerned," only 27 percent of men were. Only 38 percent of all those polled, however, thought that explicit materials had harmful effects, and concerns focused on the vague erosion of values rather than possible links to violence. Seventy-eight percent agreed either strongly or in part that adults should be able to buy erotic materials. Asked to rate various materials, most of those polled agreed that homosexual acts in magazines were the most pornographic (86 percent), while female nudity in a movie was the least pornographic (35 percent). Both articles broke out additional statistics.

Of dozens of recent surveys, a few deserve mention. *The McGill Report on Male Intimacy*, based on Michael E. McGill's survey of 5,000 men and women, led to the conclusion that men define intimacy as intercourse, while women define it as emotional sharing, a dichotomy that illuminates the differing impact of pornography on males and females. In 1989, according to the *General Social Surveys, 1972–1989: Cumulative Codebook* issued by the National Opinion Research Center (which has asked Americans questions about porn since 1973), 54 percent of Americans surveyed said there should be no laws restricting pornography for those eighteen and older, and 5 percent said there should be no laws based on age at all. Forty-one percent said there should be some laws against pornography (Question 221, p. 260). In Chapter 7 of *Journey into Sexuality: An Exploratory Voyage*, Ira L. Reiss examines six years of data from the National Opinion Research Center to discover that 20 percent of American adults (15 percent men and 25 percent women) make up the audience for X-rated movies, that sixty percent of those measured are college-educated, a group more likely to believe in gender equity, and that overall data do not support the thesis that watching erotica leads to the subordination of women. Samuel S. Janus and Cynthia L. Janus published *The Janus Report on Sexual Behavior*, and Philip Blumstein and Pepper Schwartz published *American Couples: Money Work Sex*; both are interesting because they factor in statistics on class, education, professions, income, regional differences, and political affiliations; both discuss the consumption of pornography by different genders. The titles of *Beyond the Male Myth: What Women Want to Know about Men's Sexuality: A Nationwide Survey*, by Anthony Pietropinto and Jacqueline Simenauer, and *The Sex Lives of College Students*, by Jay Segal, encapsulate their appeal. Again, the only clear indicators are that women need to feel emotional intimacy before they can enjoy sex, while men need to experience sex before they can commit themselves emotionally, a factor that helps explain why pornography has historically appealed more to males.

What makes sex surveys so interesting, of course, is that, according to some observers, the results are imprecise to the point of folklore. Philip Nobile singles out *The Hite Report, The Redbook Report on Female Sexuality*, and *Beyond the Male Myth* in "The Sex Survey Fraud" as subject to ideological bias or poor methodology. The *Redbook* study, Nobile notes,

suffers from the bias of voluntarism (a major defect in Hite's book as well). The 100,000 women who painstakingly cut out the questionnaire in the magazine and checked all seventy-five questions were obviously interested and probably upbeat in the matter of sex. To narrow the sample even further, *Redbook* also eliminated single women. And despite the hallowed 100,000 figure, only 2,278 responses were in fact *processed* for the *Report* (107).

David L. Wheeler looks at a curious feature in sex studies in "Explaining the Discrepancies in Sex Surveys: Men's, Women's Responses Differ": "Men report they have had about three times as many heterosexual partners as women say they have had. So large is the discrepancy that it has been difficult for anyone—from statisticians to sexologists—to explain it." "To make sense of the data generated by one survey of more than 3,500 people, for instance, it would have to be assumed that 10 women had had 2,000 male partners each—partners whom they didn't tell researchers about." Wheeler interviews Martina Morris, a Columbia sociologist, who thinks that men tend to round off numbers and that if high numbers are eliminated, then the ratios come closer to reality. According to Morris, a combination of careful sampling and careful questions can actually make surveys accurate for "97 percent of the population."

Two contemporary works, both based on recent (1994) University of Chicago surveys, are *The Social Organization of Sexuality*, by Edward O. Laumann, John H. Gagnon, Robert T. Michael, and Stuart Michaels, and *Sex in America*, by Robert T. Michael, John H. Gagnon, Edward O. Laumann, and Gina Kolata. Both attempt to establish sexual norms in America; the second is written for popular audiences and discusses attitudes of Americans toward a variety of sexual topics, including pornography (though the chapter title, "Masturbation and Erotica," indicates the perspective). Researchers and journalists draw different conclusions from such studies. In "The Great Sex Survey Hoopla," an article on the Chicago studies, James R. Petersen points out that some of the contradictions arise from how the results are interpreted; Petersen cites popular reports by the *New York Times*, the *Washington Post*, and the *Chicago Tribune*, all of whom believe that the survey confirms American conservatism. Says Petersen: "Here's what the media missed: Statistical averages have no meaning in real life" (43). The most formidable critique of sexual surveys, however, is Julia Erickson's new book, *Kiss and Tell: Surveying Sex in the Twentieth Century*, which studies the shortcomings of some 750 fairly major sex surveys conducted in this century. Among her criticisms is that social scientists sometimes subtly "manage the results" to get the outcomes they wish, they confuse pornography with other indices of attitudes, and their gender assumptions skew the meanings of sex, climax, and satisfaction. Erickson's book is mandatory for all quantitative researchers in the field.

Where sexual representation is concerned, the central contradiction of such quantification, never satisfactorily explained by any survey, is this, If so many Americans believe that pornography is reprehensible, why are so many millions so fond of it? Absent hypocrisy in the respondents (always a possibility), the answers are likely to lie in poorly designed instruments or in an ambivalence that survey methodologies cannot measure.

CONTRACEPTION AND FAMILY PLANNING ADVICE AS PORNOGRAPHY

Still another important historical category of pornography is birth control information. Dealers in rare erotica today list classic works of birth control as items worth collecting by their customers, and with good reason. From the nineteenth century until quite recently, the American legal system treated birth control information as pornography or obscenity—there was virtually no distinction between such terms then—especially in states such as Massachusetts. Norman E. Himes' magisterial *Medical History of Contraception* (until recently kept in locked library cases) is the classic (though dated) starting point for scholars of the subject. Useful also is John T. Noonan's *Contraception: A History of Its Treatment by the Catholic Theologians and Canonists*, whose final chapters deal with Catholic attempts to suppress contraceptive information in the United States; it is excellent. Carl Degler's wonderful *At Odds: Women and the Family in America from the Revolution to the Present* covers evolving American attitudes toward contraception within the larger context of women's struggle for their own sexuality against the pressures of family life and social convention. In *A History of Women's Bodies*, Edward Shorter offers a history of conceptions of the female body and sexuality, with specific reference to obstetrics, gynecology, diseases, mortality, birth control, and abortion. The oddly polemical Shorter says that though victimized by men, by children, and by nature, women have nonetheless embraced their inferior status, a contention that does not sit well with feminists.

In *The Sex Radicals: Free Love in Victorian America*, Hal D. Sears chronicles Post Office prosecution and persecution of feminists, free love advocates, and champions of birth control as disseminators of obscenity from 1873 onward. The Post Office charged birth control radicals like Victoria Woodhull and Moses Harmon and anarchists like Ezra and Angela Heywood with obscenity for advocating contraception and free love, cases traced carefully by Sears. Sears sees the struggle as ongoing and is especially astute on twentieth-century parallels. Chapter 3 ("The Suppression of Contraceptive Information") of James Reed's *From Private Vice to Public Virtue: The Birth Control Movement and American Society since 1830* is also excellent on official harassment of scientists and crusaders for woman's rights. Other chapters explain the convoluted reasoning that led the government to declare the dissemination of birth control information a felony, the collusion of religious pressure groups in states (e.g., Massachusetts), and the torment inflicted on doctors, educators, and citizens labeled pornographers as a consequence. Good studies of periods of greatest repression and controversy are J. F. Brodie's *Contraception and Abortion in 19th-Century America* and Carole R. McCann's *Birth Control Politics in the United States 1916–1945*.

Linda Gordon details the strategies to foil prosecution adopted by those who sought to educate people about contraception in the chapter on "Criminals" in her *Woman's Body, Woman's Right: A Social History of Birth Control in America*. Peter Fryer underscores the tribulations endured by Annie Besant, Margaret Sanger, Marie Stopes, Francis Place, and other birth control advocates lumped with pornographers in *The Birth Controllers* but also devotes ample space to their lasting achievements. In *Free Love and Anarchism: The Biography of Ezra Heywood*, Martin Henry Blatt celebrates the lives of Heywood and his wife, Angela, whose *The Word*, which promoted contraception, was prosecuted again and again by federal authorities. David Kennedy's biography of one of the best-known crusaders, *Birth Control in America: The Career of Margaret Sanger*, details her struggle, disappointments, and eventual triumph, as does Ellen Chesler's *Woman of Valor: Margaret Sanger and the Birth Control Movement in America*.

A lighthearted look at the subject is *The Curious History of Contraception*,

whose author, Shirley Green, shakes her head at ignorance warped into a peculiarly American species of paranoia. Taylor Stoehr reproduces pages from
pamphlets and books that were declared obscene or indecent in his survey of
movements and individuals in *Free Love in America: A Documentary History*.
Amy Sarch provides wonderful details in "Those Dirty Ads! Birth Control Advertising in the 1920s and 1930s." Sarch applies the theories of Michel Bakhtin
on the grotesque and Ann Douglas on the moral pollution of culture to camouflaged advertisements for feminine hygiene, birth control techniques, and contraceptive devices that barely skirted obscenity laws. During the period Sarch
covers, the feisty Mary Ware Dennett attacked the official ignorance, mean-
spiritedness, and obtuseness that equated family planning with obscenity in *Birth
Control Laws*, first published in 1926 and reprinted in 1970. Her lampoon of
the rationale for the laws prohibiting contraceptives and information about birth
control as obscene still resonates: "Some perverts use contraceptives, therefore
the law should not allow any one at all to secure them or know anything about
them, and besides, as most of those who are not perverts can't be really trusted
anyhow, hearing about or seeing contraceptives would be pretty sure to make
them go to the devil, especially young people, so the complete prohibition is
after all the safest" (43). (Substituting *pornography* for *contraceptives* updates
the critique.)

SEX EDUCATION

Sex education, premised on the belief that informing youngsters about sex
not only reduces ignorance but leads as well to healthier sexual maturity, has
often been condemned as pornographic by definition. Even among Americans
who know better, sex education has generated controversy. John S. Haller's
"From Maidenhead to Menopause: Sex Education for Women in Victorian
America" notes that physicians before the turn of the century spoke cautiously
on matters of hygiene, ethics, etiquette, religion, and medicine. In 1930 Mary
Ware Dennett, furious that the Post Office should interdict her sex education
materials as politically subversive, wrote *Who's Obscene?* The cry of an abused
citizen, in the tradition of Thomas Paine's *The Rights of Man*, it deserves more
attention. Dennett was one of many educators endlessly thwarted by official
mistrust and suspicion; her career has been examined in detail by Constance M.
Chen in *"The Sex Side of Life": Mary Ware Dennett's Pioneering Battle for
Birth Control and Sex Education. Sex Education Books for Young Adults, 1892–
1979*, Patricia J. Campbell's annotated list of texts used for such purposes, also
includes some sex manuals (see **Sex Manuals and Guides** in chapter 16). The
title of Michael Gordon's "From an Unfortunate Necessity to a Cult of Mutual
Orgasm: Sex in American Marital Education Literature 1830–1940" conveys his
thesis. Mary Breasted offers a discerning, often humorous account of battles
involving fundamentalist and conservative groups pitted against the Board of
Education and Mary Calderone's SIECUS in Anaheim, California, in *Oh! Sex*

Education. L. Brown's *Sex Education in the Eighties* is a more sober exploration of similar terrain. Gordon V. Drake attacks what he sees as a threat to morality in *SIECUS: Corrupter of Youth*, whose title is self-explanatory. Phoebe Courtney thinks that sex education is simply a ploy to divert attention from a liberal plot to use public education as a conduit for spreading pornography and secularism in *The Sex Education Racket: Pornography in the Schools (an Exposé)*. SIECUS, which stands for Sex Information and Education Council of the United States, furnishes educational materials, explanatory pamphlets, and advice to minorities and handicapped groups and compiles bibliographies on many aspects of sexuality. SIECUS has long been a target of fundamentalist groups. In a "Playboy Interview," Mary Calderone, head of SIECUS, reviews and counters attacks on sex materials, including erotica, by Billy James Hargis and other right-wing fundamentalists, characterizing such efforts as attempts to return America to the Dark Ages. Scholars seeking current information should point their browsers to the Web site of People for the American Way, which tracks the dozens of controversies in sex education that arise annually.

PRESSURE GROUPS, THE BIFURCATION OF FEMINISM, AND MORAL PANICS

Americans have frequently reacted against sexual expression because it purveys information they think best kept hidden and in that respect participate in a classic tradition outlined by Richard C. Hofstadter in *Anti-Intellectualism in American Life*, but the motives of the censorious change over time and are not limited to know-nothingism. Indeed, collisions occur when special interest groups advance narratives that they wish to become the dominant folklore of society. Their agendas, moreover, frequently associate clusters of social ills. Comstock linked sex, lotteries, billiards, ethnicity, and prizefights; modern groups have a penchant for linking sex with masculinity, drugs, violent media, and bizarre technologies.

Milton Rugoff's *Prudery and Passion: Sexuality in Victorian America* contains information on early American censors, especially the Reverend John McDowall of New York, one of the smuttiest of a succession of smut-obsessed crusaders. (So do many of the histories of sex listed earlier.) Perhaps the most detailed account of the prosecution of individuals and materials by various censorship groups from the Civil War to the 1930s is Paul S. Boyer's *Purity in Print: The Vice-Society Movement and Book Censorship in America*; Boyer devotes alot of space to Comstock, John Sumner, and the New York Society for the Suppression of Vice, the International Reform Federation of Washington, D.C., the Illinois Vigilance Association, and the New England Watch and Ward Society. Heywood Broun and Margaret Leech skewer the crusader in *Anthony Comstock: Roundsman of the Lord*, still a readable text on the pitfalls of smut-hunting by a crusader whose name has come to represent mindless censorship—

improperly so, as these texts make clear, because Comstock was malicious. Robert W. Haney applies the term to censorship of various media, particularly comic books, burlesque, and pulp literature, in *Comstockery in America*, a book concerned mostly with class issues in the war on expression. Comstock's own *Traps for the Young* (1883), available in a modern edition by Robert Brenner, is itself worth reading as a barometer of the period. Just as revelatory is another reissue, Comstock's *Frauds Exposed: Or, How the People Are Deceived and Robbed, and Youth Corrupted*, a reminder that the crusader sometimes prosecuted dealers for promising pornography but not delivering it.

At the time, Comstock's warnings persuaded some Americans that obscenity, popular amusements, birth control, and foreigners, all evils that crouched in the cities, had put the country at risk, the same worries that affect similar classes of Americans a century later. Almost as hysterical as Comstock was Courtney Riley Cooper, a New York judge who wrote *Designs in Scarlet* to expose the degeneracy of popular entertainment. Cooper proposed draconian methods of prosecuting sexual materials, so convinced was he that the country's families and young people were threatened by prurient books. First published in 1939, the book—a prime example of the antiporn genre—was retitled *Teen-Age Vice!* and remarketed for its titillation in the 1950s. Henry F. Pringle, head of the International Reform Federation, a censorship organization in Washington, wrote the urbane *Big Frogs*, in which he sneers at contemporaries such as Bernarr Macfadden ("inexplicable" publisher of smut), Will Hays (utterer of "dreadful bilge" in his role as defender of Hollywood), and John S. Sumner ("a shade too refined for his job," i.e., not savage enough as a censor). More predictable was *Fighting the Debauchery of Our Girls and Boys*, by Phillip Yarrow, leader of the Illinois Vigilance Society, another censorship group. Jay Gertzman profiles Comstock's successor in "John Saxton Sumner of the New York Society for the Suppression of Vice: A Chief Smut-Eradicator of the Interwar Period."

Gertzman's marvelous *Bookleggers and Smuthounds: The Trade in Erotica, 1920–1940* contains even more detail on the operations of Anthony Comstock and John Sumner gleaned from the files of the New York Society for the Suppression of Vice, the Post Office, the FBI, the National Archives, and erotica publishers themselves. Gertzman analyzes the strategies behind the Society's attacks on favorite targets: the Jews, the lower classes, and other subgroups. Unlike the less well financed federations in other major cities, the New York Society published its *Annual Reports* from 1874 until 1940. The Library of Congress holds microform copies of the ledgers and daybooks of Comstock and his successor John Sumner; these are cataloged as *Names and Records of Persons Arrested under the Auspices of the Society: 1920–1950*. The *Annual Reports* of the New England Watch and Ward Society are also useful sources of information on individuals. Morris L. Ernst and Alexander Lindey publicized the more egregious cases of suppression and the groups behind them in *The Censor Marches On*. Eli M. Oboler examines the motivation of those censors, especially those who are driven by conservative political and religious beliefs, in *The Fear of the Word: Censorship and Sex*, which suggests that fear of unleashed chaos is strong.

John F. Noll's *Manual of the NODL* is a primary source for information on the tactics of the National Organization of Decent Literature, the Catholic censorship group, which began its operations in 1938 and thus overlapped neatly with the New York Society for the Suppression of Vice; the latter became the Police Athletic League in the 1940s. Paul W. Facey, a priest, explains the rationale of the Legion of Decency (begun in 1934) by suggesting that community (even construed as a Catholic minority) pressure is better than state control of expression in *The Legion of Decency: A Sociological Analysis of the Emergence and Development of a Social Pressure Group*. Two books by Paul Blanchard, *The Right to Read* and *American Freedom and Catholic Power*, are classic defenses of the First Amendment by a leading libertarian, with particular reference to Catholic attempts to control public and school libraries, newspapers, books, and movies. During the 1950s, the American Civil Liberties Union opposed such groups and explained why in *Private Group Censorship and the NODL*. Harold C. Gardiner presented counterarguments in *Catholic Viewpoint on Censorship*. From 1920 on, the American Civil Liberties Union also published its *Annual Reports*. They record efforts by pressure groups to suppress expression of every type. Typical of one of these reports is the ACLU's *Free Speech, 1984*, which lists assaults by dozens of groups during the year and the ACLU's attempts to combat them. Samuel Walker's *In Defense of American Liberties: A History of the ACLU* is probably the best single source on the organization devoted to the First Amendment, though it, of course, covers many cases involving issues other than sexual expression.

Successive new communication technologies renew calls for censorship, says Steven Starker in *Evil Influences: Crusades against the Mass Media*, which has chapters on movies, radio, television, comics, journalism, MTV, and music. Starker says that mass media provoke, arguing that censors find that new technologies cause discomfort because they reach wide audiences and because they leapfrog older barriers against access. Would-be censors target electronic mass media as predecessors once attacked books. Kathyrn C. Montgomery's *Target: Prime Time—Advocacy Groups and the Struggle over Entertainment Television* is a history of attempts to suppress network programming since the 1970s. Particularly sinister, says Montgomery, is the organization since the 1980s of advocacy groups into a "feedback system" capable of targeting specific programs, advertisers, and network executives. While the networks have used their own self-protective industry mechanisms in the form of in-house standards and censors, the overall course of programming reflects the ways in which political and social issues impact on institutional entertainment. Christopher Rowley details attempts by the Coalition for Better Television, the Moral Majority, and Morality in Media to force networks to remove programming they think too fond of sexual themes in "Pressure Groups Are a Fact of Life." Robert V. Hudson provides running accounts of pressure groups and government interference in *Mass Media: A Chronological Encyclopedia of Television, Radio, Motion Pictures, Magazines, Newspapers, and Books in the United States*. (For information on specific censors, see **Scandal Journalism** in chapter 17.) The media, at least the independents, are not without recourse. One of the best historical surveys of pressure groups and their onslaught on expression is the four-part, seven-hour documentary called *Behind Censorship: The Assault on Civil Liberties*, produced by the Paper Tiger TV Collective and carried on Deep Dish TV, an activist alternative satellite distribution network.

The classic study of symbolic conservative campaigns is *Citizens for Decency: Antipornography Crusades as Status Defense*. Louis A. Zurcher, Jr. and R. George Kirkpatrick believe that such movements are attempts to preserve the status quo and thus represent a discontent with change that extends beyond questions of sexual expression. During the 1980s, fundamentalist groups joined forces with judicial conservatives and antiporn feminists to mount vigorous attacks on expression. Kirkpatrick and Zurcher note in "Women against Pornography: Feminist Anti-Pornography Crusades in American Society" that antiporn feminists differ from nastier right-wing zealots in their backgrounds, economic status, rationales, and ideologies. Other scholars suggest that although the positions of the fundamentalists and the conservatives have remained fairly constant over time, the changes wrought on the women's movement by encounters with sexual expression have been notable. Discord within the feminist movement had surfaced earlier, according to Alice Echols' *Daring to Be Bad: Radical Feminism in America, 1967–1975*, which provides background information on the deepening split between feminisms. Echols' "The Taming of the Id: Feminist Sexual Politics, 1968–83" focuses on attempts by some feminists to prescribe acceptable sexual behavior (e.g., women should avoid penetration in favor of touching). Error arises, says Echols, when "feminists define male and female sexuality as though they were polar opposites. Male sexuality is driven, irresponsible, genitally oriented, and potentially lethal. Female sexuality is muted, diffuse, interpersonally oriented, and benign. Men crave power and orgasm, while women seek reciprocity and intimacy" (59). Making such assumptions recalls darker ages: "In rejecting as so much 'male-identified mind-body dualism' the belief that fantasy is the repository of our ambivalent and conflictual feelings, cultural feminists have developed a highly mechanistic, behaviorist analysis that conflates fantasy with reality and pornography with violence. In their vision, fantasies must be eradicated or subordinated to political correctness" (58–59).

The Feminization of Culture, a splendid history by Ann Douglas, documents the ways in which women's values regarding aesthetic tastes, ethical precepts, and sexual mores came to seem "superior" to those held by males in the nineteenth century. Even in the twentieth century, folklore still insisted that women are arbiters of the good, the true, and the beautiful. That kind of rhetoric, says Jean Bethke Elshtain, masks traditional, reactionary, and dangerous positions.

In "The Victim Syndrome: A Troubling Turn in Feminism," Elshtain thinks that it "sets up women as the *sole* arbiters of social morality and architects of social decency" and harbors an impulse to assume "control over what individuals may see, hear, or read" (45). Such beliefs become patronizing and even virulent in a climate that views women as passive victims of crimes, despite the fact that current statistics do not support that position.

Casting women as moral arbiters has other drawbacks, say Ellen Carol Dubois and Linda Gordon. Feminist "social purity" movements of the nineteenth century, with their emphasis on the dangers to women of beastly male lust, inevitably limited women to roles of weakness when the movements were co-opted by conservative groups. In "Seeking Ecstasy on the Battlefield: Danger and Pleasure in Nineteenth-century Feminist Sexual Thought," Dubois and Gordon draw parallels between these historical phenomena and the modern antiporn, feminist alliance with Moral Majority, antiabortion, and fundamentalist groups. In the sprightly *Magic Mommas*, Joanna Russ laments the adoption by so many feminist, antiporn writers of Elizabeth Cady Stanton's antiquated condemnations of sexuality as animalistic. Similarly, Judith R. Walkowitz says that the feminist, antiporn movement replicates the nineteenth-century notion that men are sexual beasts who victimize women and that male sexual lust menaces Western civilization. Although Walkowitz uses British illustrations in "Male Vice and Female Virtue: Feminism and the Politics of Prostitution in Nineteenth-Century Britain," she notes that they had American parallels in the collaboration of socialists and conservatives who both wanted to characterize women as weak, innocent, and pure; the resulting suppression of sexually explicit materials, particularly information on birth control, led to the eventual evisceration of the feminist movement itself. Walkowitz's point is that inventing a new sexual discourse carries hidden dangers, since social agendas combine with the slipperiness of language and ideas to produce unforeseen, unintentional, and uncontrollable results.

"A Report on the Sex Crisis," by Barbara Ehrenreich, Elizabeth Hess, and Gloria Jacobs, pinpoints the onset of discord by observing that the "first cracks in the feminist consensus appeared when women split over pornography" (63). Two good scorecards are "Sex War: The Debate between Radical and Libertarian Feminists," in which Ann Ferguson sorts out the feminist factions, and "Conflicts and Contradictions among Feminists over Issues of Pornography and Sexual Freedom," in which Ann Russo finds subtle distinctions among the contentious. Bringing matters to a head were the Minneapolis and Indianapolis ordinances outlawing pornography on the grounds that it caused harm to women as a class. These initiatives generated hundreds of magazine articles and newspaper reports. Typical was "Pornography through the Looking Glass." Here Charles Krauthammer pointed out that the antiporn faction had recourse to doublespeak; whatever feminists wish to call the Minneapolis bill, "it manages the amazing feat of restoring censorship, which after all is a form of coercion, while at the same time claiming not to restrict rights but to expand them" (82). Lois

P. Sheinfeld said in "Anti-Obscenity Ordinances: Banning Porn, the New Censorship" that the Minneapolis and Indianapolis ordinances represent an abandonment of the unprovable assertion that pornography causes sexual crimes in favor of a flat assertion that it violates women's rights.

A better than usual account of events is Stuart Taylor's "Pornography Foes Lose New Weapon in Supreme Court," which reproduces the salient points of the Supreme Court's 1986 affirmation of a ruling of the Federal Court of Appeals striking down the Indianapolis antipornography ordinance on the grounds that it violated the First Amendment. Probably the best single commentary on the alliance between old-fashioned conservatives and antiporn feminists and their efforts to redefine pornography as a form of discrimination against women is Donald Alexander Downs' *The New Politics of Pornography*. Downs concentrates on the Minneapolis ordinance (vetoed by the city's mayor) and Indianapolis ordinance (struck down by the federal bench) drafted by antiporn feminists; he notes that legislators in those cities rolled over in the face of the radical feminist agitation instead of exposing the dangers of the ordinances for free speech. In comparing the feminist campaign to the antics of the Meese Commission, Downs points out that both approaches are single-minded, that neither considers other perspectives in a debate that requires many such perspectives. Downs himself suggests that a solution to concern over aggression toward women might be to limit the range of sexual expression that can be characterized as obscene but to make violence one litmus test for obscenity.

Marcia Pally identifies the more celebrated contemporary individual censors and pressure groups, examines their campaign tactics, and covers cases large and small, ranging from attempts to remove paintings from college galleries, to attacks on musical lyrics, to the banning of books from libraries, and to local, state, and federal government encroachments and intimidations, in *Sex and Sensibility: Reflections on Forbidden Mirrors and the Will to Censor*. Pally observes that while fundamentalist groups share with antiporn feminists a conviction that banning sexual expression will diminish rape, incest, wife battery, and assorted ills, statistics indicate that warped religious fervor may be just as much a causal factor in all these crimes. Pally invokes the "spiral of silence," a concept pioneered by Elisabeth Noelle-Neumann to explain why people of different views are less likely to articulate their disagreement with the prevailing consensus. When antiporn feminists and fundamentalists advance their claims, their aggressiveness and the subsequent media coverage inhibit many people from confessing their own interest in pornography for fear that it will be thought deviant (68). The "silence" mutes opposition, at least for a time. The premise of Lynne Segal's *Straight Sex: Rethinking the Politics of Pleasure* is that sexually-active heterosexual women have been silenced by politics and should borrow a page from lesbians, the only feminists to address sexuality positively and straightforwardly. Segal discusses heterosexual feminist thought on the issue of sexuality's being inherently damaging to women. She thinks it is possible for women to enjoy sex without increasing male power. In any case, Segal says that it is time for heterosexual women to speak out, if only because heterosexual sex can also be "transgressive" and politically rewarding.

Another excellent map of contemporary battlefields is Marjorie Heins' *Sex, Sin, and Blasphemy: A Guide to America's Censorship Wars*. Heins highlights colorful combatants such as Andrea Dworkin and Jesse Helms and is especially good on the Mapplethorpe circus in Cincinnati. James Davison Hunter's *Culture Wars: The Struggle to Define America* also frames the battle as a struggle over conceptions of national identity, not unlike scenarios of the past. The essays by Lisa Duggan and Nan D. Hunter in *Sex Wars: Sexual Dissent and Political Culture* trace the passions swirling around pornography; Duggan and Hunter provide a very useful chronology of skirmishes. Nat Hentoff chronicles outrage in his remarkably balanced *Free Speech for Me but Not for Thee: How the American Left and Right Relentlessly Censor Each Other*. The book's chapters document episodes in which feminists censor traditional works of art, liberals pillory fellow Americans for slips of the tongue, college campuses legislate against free speech, and politicians of all stripes try to suppress ideas they do not like. *"Bad Girls"/"Good Girls": Women, Sex, and Power in the Nineties*, edited by Nan Bauer Maglin and Donna Perry, ranges over various sexual and representational skirmishes. Cynthia J. Gordon-Maloul treats social, ideological, and personal factors as crucial in moving antiporn feminists, antiporn conservatives, and libertarians to action in "*Framing Pornography: Political Mobilization and Conflicts over Contested American Values.*" Psychological anxieties and political agendas lead groups to draw different lines, says Jonathan Miller in "Censorship and the Limits of Permission." Miller catalogs ways in which Americans justify their desire to censor.

Some historians believe that some calls for censorship signal recurrences of moral panics. Often induced by specific groups, moral panics periodically sweep the nation, surges of folklore carried by media and word of mouth. Sometimes they involve pornography, as in the feminist, antiporn campaigns of the late 1980s and early 1990s, or the furor over child pornography that ignited in the 1970s and has flared up consistently ever since (see Chapter 8, **Child Pornography**). No one claims that such evils do not exist, simply that they balloon out of rational proportion. Because of Britain's longer tradition of tabloid journalism, the best studies are devoted to moral panics in that country, but the conclusions apply to an American press that increasingly commodifies scandal. Philip Jenkins, for example, implicitly compares the circulation of several British myths about pornography (porn snuff films, child sex rings, ritual female abuse) and the witch-hunts they engender with their American counterparts in *Intimate Enemies: Moral Panics in Contemporary Great Britain*. So does Bill Thompson in *Soft Core: Moral Crusades against Pornography in Britain and America*, an extended historical analysis of right-wing crusades against sexual expression in both countries. John Springhall's *Youth, Popular Culture and Moral Panics: Penny Gaffs to Gangsta Rap, 1830–1996* traces British and American concerns over explicit music, computer games, violent movies, and overly permissive media to nineteenth-century anxieties about the effects of popular amusements on the lower classes. David J. Pivar's *Purity Crusade: Sexual Morality and Social Control, 1868–1900* devotes several pages to moral panics fueled by anxieties in America before the turn of the century.

That kind of historical record has led the National Coalition against Censorship to designate recent hysteria over pornography as a moral panic. The coalition's *The Sex Panic: Women, Censorship, and "Pornography"* reports on a 1993 conference at City College of New York that puts the current furor in historical perspective. Even more pointed is "Sex Panics," in which Lisa Duggan observes that when panics overtake Americans, "words assume the reverse of their common meaning: liberation becomes chaos, desire becomes deviance, and dissent becomes the work of the devil" (75). Varda Burstyn looks at similar circumstances in "Anatomy of a Moral Panic," which analyzes Canadian hysteria over porn fed by antiporn feminists; the parallels between Canadian and American public response to a perceived "explosion" of terrifying eroticism are strong. R. G. Kirkpatrick offers some clues to the ways moral panics are constructed in "Collective Consciousness and Mass Hysteria: Collective Behavior and Anti-Pornography Crusades in Durkheimian Perspective." Creating an effective panic is most likely when pornographers themselves seem to be winning legal battles through First Amendment strategies. Drawing on surveys of southern towns, Kirkpatrick notes that crusaders can make pornography a high-profile issue through media exposure and political speeches and then enlist public figures to denounce the material as deviant. The ensuing furor contributes to a high-intensity, antiporn crusade. Case studies of campaigns such as the one directed at the film *Dressed to Kill* form the substance of Charles Lyons' *The New Censors*, which covers fundamentalists, women's groups, and other politicized pressure groups with censorship of sexual materials as their agenda. The closing of centuries raises apocalyptic fears of the end of history, as manifest in anxieties about rampant sexuality among minorities, says Richard Dellamora in *Apocalyptic Overtures: Sexual Politics and the Sense of an Ending*. Dellamora theorizes from examples ranging from the trials of Oscar Wilde in 1895 to the Republican National Convention of 1992; all foreground the threat of degenerate enemies.

Pornography also figured prominently in the right-wing moral crusade against Bill Clinton that resulted in his impeachment by the House of Representatives. Among a host of such comments, Adam Gopnik's "American Studies" condemns the Starr report as pornography, while Stephen Greenblatt's "America's Raciest Read" says that Starr's "Narrative" detailing the sexual activity between President Clinton and Monica Lewinsky is a pornographic novel whose tropes resemble those of the *Malleus Maleficarum*, the witch-hunting text of the Inquisition.

HEARINGS, PANELS, COMMISSIONS, AND OTHER
FORUMS FOR DRAMATIZING SEXUAL EXPRESSION

Many countries have held national public discussions of pornography in this century and even participated in international conferences on the subject. A report of the proceedings of the League of Nations Conference of 1910, the first large-scale investigation of global traffic, can be found in the updated version issued by the United Nations as *Agreement for the Suppression of the Circulation of Obscene Publications, Signed at Paris on 4 May 1910/Amended by the Protocol Signed at Lake Success, New York, 4 May 1949*. Not a member of the league, the United States was not a signatory to the 1910 document. Delegates to the Conference of the League of Nations in 1923 shared information on illicit photos, as reported in (League of Nations) *Records of the International Conference for the Suppression of the Circulation of and Traffic in Obscene Publications*, but actual seizures ran far behind successful deliveries, since periodical advertisements in German and French magazines alone indicated a much larger volume. None of these reports mention specific artifacts but are useful in gauging the combination of myth and fact that led to a show of largely ineffectual international cooperation on the part of national authorities.

In a very real sense, the public and political debate over pornography, like that over violence in the media, functions first and foremost as theater designed to dramatize people's concerns, as Willard D. Rowland, Jr. makes clear in his *The Politics of TV Violence*. Rowland says that the commissions and studies and legislative hearings on violence on television are not designed to curtail the violence, about which citizens are of many minds, nor do they aim at closure but are constructed as forums for venting anxieties. The same would appear to hold true for pornography: arguing over the role of sexual expression in public is a way of sorting out various agendas, social and political as well as sexual, rather than deciding on courses of action. Legislative and congressional hearings sometimes do produce new laws, of course, although they also serve as outlets for frustrations and pulpits for reaffirmations of morality.

As congressional committees learned to reap the political benefits of investigating traffic in pernicious expression during the 1950s, sensationalism added to pornography's attractiveness. The 82d Congress was the first fully to exploit the political value of pornography and did so by linking sexual expression to both the Mafia and communism, both splendidly sinister enemies during the 1950s. In 1952 the House Select Committee on Current Pornographic Materials held *Hearings before the Select Committee of the House of Representatives on Current Pornographic Materials*. The "Gathings Committee," named after Representative Ernest Gathings, issued its final *Report* in 1953. Attracted by the limelight, Senator Estes Kefauver convened his own subcommittee during the 83d and 84th Congresses (1954–1955) for the most famous hearings prior to the President's Commission on Obscenity and Pornography at the end of the

1960s. Kefauver added comic books and juvenile crime to a witch's brew of issues.

James Gilbert's thesis in *A Cycle of Outrage: America's Reaction to the Juvenile Delinquent in the 1950s* is similar to Rowland's. Gilbert believes that Americans go through periodic surges of anger occasioned by the search for simple causes for the world's ills, in this case, comic books and movies, which the Kefauver Commission asserted were destroying the morality of the young. Gilbert treats the antiobscenity legislation generated by the Kefauver Hearings as an attack on mass culture. According to William Howard Moore in *The Kefauver Committee and the Politics of Crime, 1950–1952*, Kefauver and his supporters viewed organized crime, alleged to be behind pornography, as the domestic equivalent of the international communist conspiracy. Pornography was pressed into service so that the public would have some way to recognize these invisible enemies; sexual expression thus became a tidy sign of menace and corruption. The progress of Kefauver's Senate Subcommittee to Investigate Juvenile Delinquency can be observed in *Hearings before the Senate Subcommittee to Investigate Juvenile Delinquency (Obscene and Pornographic Materials)* (1954–1955) and in *Obscene and Pornographic Literature and Juvenile Delinquency; Interim Report* (1956). Both hearings attempted to establish a causal link between pornography and crime. *Juvenile Delinquency*, the final report of the Kefauver Committee, itself became a species of official folklore. It was reprinted by Greenwood Press in 1969 as *Juvenile Delinquency: Comic Books, Motion Pictures, Obscene and Pornographic Materials, Television Programs*; the title indicates the committee's particular areas of concern. The committee's work finally sputtered out in *Control of Obscene Material* (1960), a report of a combined Senate Subcommittee on Constitutional Amendments and Subcommittee to Investigate Juvenile Delinquency, which passed no significant new legislation. Some states conducted their own public investigations. The most notable of these was New York state's *Report of Joint Legislative Committee Studying Publication of and Dissemination of Offensive and Obscene Materials* in 1956, followed ten years later by *Report of the New York State Joint Legislative Committee to Study the Publication and Dissemination of Offensive and Obscene Material*. Both studies tracked the faint spoor of organized crime but were also focused on juveniles. That is not to say that there was no evidence, for making sexual representation illegal, of course, attracts criminal elements (see **Organized Crime Links** in chapter 21).

Given the changing political climate and the shifting agendas of legislators, it is easier to see coherence in the history of a single agency's effort to retain pornography in its portfolio. The Post Office lobbied hard for censorship prerogatives even as Congress and the courts were transferring them to U.S. Customs and the Department of Justice. The *Hearings* held before the House Subcommittee on the Post Office and Post Roads in 1935, for example, included sessions on obscenity but dwelled on forbidden birth control materials—viewed as a spur to promiscuity—sent illegally through the mails. Political supporters of the Post Office hoped that continuous publicity would burnish the agency's role as a bulwark against porn. That was the point of 1959 and 1960 hearings under the rubric: *Obscene Matter Sent through the Mail* (House Committee on Post Office and Civil Service, Postal Operations Subcommittee); *Obscene Matter Sent through the Mail* (Senate Subcommittee on Postal Operations); and *Circulation of Obscene and Pornographic Material* (House Subcommittee on Postal Operations). All were designed to demonstrate that a river of obscenity ran through the mails and that only the Post Office could interdict it. In 1969 the House Committee on Government Operations, Government Activities Subcommittee published *Use of the Postal Service for the Unsolicited Advertisement of Hard-Core Pornographic or Otherwise Obscene Materials*. These hearings were held in advance of—cynics said to preempt—President Johnson's Commission on Obscenity and Pornography, which included material from the Post Office in its conclusions. Postal lobbying failed: primary authority to prosecute materials and individuals passed to the Department of Justice.

Still other legislators tried to stake out pornography before President Johnson could, as is evident in *Creating a Subcommittee on Obscenity and Pornography*, a 1967 report of the House Committee on Education and Labor. The staff of the President's Commission had not yet completed work before a conservative group attempted to head off the expected recommendations by publishing *The Obscenity Report: The Report to the Task Force on Pornography and Obscenity*. The group claimed that the more extreme forms of pornography were dangerous, that concerned citizens deserved protection from expression they abhorred, and that a Federal Obscenity and Pornography Board should be established to adjudicate materials. Conservatives on the House Committee on the Judiciary of the 91st Congress took up these concerns in *Anti-Obscenity Legislation: Hearings on H. R. 5171, H. R. 11009, H. R. 11031, H. R. 11032 and Related Measures* but were unable to discount the massive documentation of the President's Commission. The three principal recommendations of the commission were admirably succinct and have been isolated in "Legislative Recommendations: Report of the Committee on Obscenity and Pornography": "The Commission recommends that federal, state and local legislation should not seek to interfere with the right of adults who wish to do so to read, obtain or view explicit sexual materials. On the other hand, we recommend legislative regulation upon the sale of sexual materials to young persons who do not have the consent of their parents, and we also recommend legislation to protect persons from having sexual materials thrust upon them without their consent through the mails or through open public display" (64–65).

Numerous dissents and challenges to the commission's findings and recommendations followed. Typical was *Obscenity: The Court, the Congress and the President's Commission*, by Lane V. Sunderland, which noted that the commission's report challenged congressional prerogatives in framing obscenity law. Congress hardly intended so liberal an interpretation, argued Sunderland; President Johnson was improperly pushing a liberal agenda that he was confident Democratic-appointed judges would support. Morris A. Lipton tried to counter such charges in "Fact and Myth: The Work of the Commission on Obscenity and Pornography"; he defended and described the methodologies of investigation. Irene Diamond revisited the commission's work in "Pornography and Repression: A Reconsideration," which argues against the conclusion that porn is largely harmless by asserting that sexual materials create a hostile climate for women. Diamond believes that the liberal view of pornography as benign has been eroded by feminist critics' insistence that sexual expression masks relationships of power and violence. On the other hand, Diamond finds the neoconservative position similarly lacking and concludes that accurate conceptions of porn have to wait on accurate conceptions of sexuality.

The essayists in Victor Cline's *Where Do You Draw the Line?: An Exploration into Media Violence, Pornography, and Censorship* also took issue with the statistics and conclusions of the Presidential Commission. Most contributors to the volume seem more interested in violence than sexuality, though they hyperbolically conflate the two. Most of their arguments claim that the majority should make decisions about what is permissible, not a commission representing a minority. That many Americans were skeptical of the commission's recommendations was evident from popular accounts such as "The Porno Plague," by *Time* writers convinced that most citizens, though generally opposed to censorship, were upset by extreme forms of pornography. In an effort at fairness, *Time* conceded that most expressions of anxiety were based mostly on hearsay. *Pornography: The Longford Report*, the product of a British commission, is of interest because it was designed, in part, to challenge the "ultra-liberal" report of the Presidential Commission. The British account dutifully disputed the latter's conclusions by asserting as an article of faith that pornography had deleterious effects; it called for continued repression. (The Longford Report was itself countered in 1979 by the British Williams Report, which found little evidence for causal connections between porn and antisocial behavior.) The most recent Canadian survey, the *Report of the Special Committee on Pornography and Prostitution* (1985), accepted the argument that pornography harms women.

Passions ensured that conservatives would return to the subject during the Reagan administration. "Koop Declares War on Porn and Violence," reported George Archibald in early 1985, noting that the surgeon general planned to convene a conference in October of that year to prove that "pornography" such as music videos led to violence, abortion, and poor "mental hygiene." Something of a bust, the conference produced *Pornography: Research Advances and Policy Considerations*, edited by Dolf Zillman and Jennings Bryant. Its content, a review of research both "asocial and prosocial" that might conceivably function as a basis for policy considerations, declined to endorse Surgeon General Koop's beliefs.

Reagan's attorney general then called for a commission, partly, it would seem, to deflect investigators closing in on the alleged improprieties for which he was later censured and forced into retirement. Critics immediately attacked the Meese Commission on the grounds that its bias was obvious, its research misleading, and its tactics intimidating. The Meese report's legal recommendations were that dealers in adult materials be harassed until they gave up, intimidated when they would not, imprisoned when the government could make a case, and rendered bankrupt through RICO legislation as often as possible. The strategy depended on reeducating the public to the evils of sexual representation, inciting censorship groups to act as surrogates for the Justice Department, conducting sting operations, and exchanging information among government agencies on a massive scale. In "Big Boobs: Ed Meese and His Pornography Commission," Hendrik Hertzberg, editor of *Harper's*, maintained that the commission was cheap and misinformed, part of an effort to restrict expression and freedom, despite its being focused on a topic of no great political weight for most Americans (he noted that strong obscenity legislation in Maine was rejected by referendum).

Probably the most cogent of the many attacks on the Meese Commission hearings as biased, distorted, illogical, and mean-spirited is Barry W. Lynn's *Polluting the Censorship Debate: A Summary and Critique of the Final Report of the Attorney General's Commission on Pornography*. The National Coalition against Censorship held its own public meeting. Fourteen luminaries, including Colleen Dewhurst and Kurt Vonnegut, and institutional sponsors from Actor's Equity, to the Modern Language Association and the United Churches of Christ, denounced the kangaroo court aspects of the Meese hearings and its blatant attempts to stifle expression, chill civil liberties, attack the arts, and demean human dignity by unleashing hate, bias, and intolerance. Their statements were gathered as *The Meese Commission Exposed* by Arlene Carmen et al. In that volume, noting that antiporn feminists had cooperated with the commission, Lisa Duggan protested: "As feminists we are especially appalled that this latest effort to restrict freedom is being disguised as an effort to 'protect' women" (16). Betty Friedan reminded the audience that her book, *The Feminine Mystique*, was several times "suppressed as pornographic" (24) and decried the pro-censorship forces as dangerous to women because judges would be empowered under Meese-sponsored legislation to rule against what they thought might harm women—regardless of evidence—and to rule as well on materials that women might find empowering.

In *United States of America vs. Sex*, Philip Nobile and Eric Nadler examined the hearings, interviewed staff and witnesses, and elicited comment from William F. Buckley, Betty Friedan, John Updike, John Irving, and others. Nan Hunter, for example, observed that the commission reinforced the idea that women are inferior and incompetent (59). Nobile and Nadler publicized the tactics of the commission's investigators, who pressured convenience stores to ban magazines like *Playboy* and other materials that courts have held not obscene. Carole Vance's "Porn in the U.S.A.: The Meese Commission on the Road" excoriated the commission's encouragement of vigilantes and the intimidation of small businesses by investigators. Vance's "Negotiating Sex and Gender in the Attorney General's Commission on Pornography" reviews distortions and biases in the report.

For day-to-day details of the "evangelical soap opera" (69), however, Robert Scheer's "Ed Meese's Dirty Pictures" was without equal: "For reasons best known to [staff director Sears and his aides], the commission exhibited an uncommon fascination with the scatological fringe of the porn world. No simple tits and ass for this crowd. Forget garter belts and even whips. This federal commission spent much of its time—and your money—on fist fucking, golden showers, child porn, asphyxiation, anilingus, with side trips into such rarely considered fetishes as toenail-clipping collections, being squirted with real mother's milk, and the private, carefully contoured world of sweat sniffing" (68). Scheer quoted the dissent of one member of the commission, Judith Becker, the Columbia University psychologist and director of an institute that treats sex offenders, who said bluntly that "there simply is no serious body of evidence of a causal connection between pornography and crime" (67). (Scheer himself achieved a kind of notoriety when he coaxed Jimmy Carter into admitting that he "lusted in his heart" for a *Playboy* interview.) The title of "The Sex Busters," by Richard Stengel, referred to the comic cast of major characters in the theatrical hearings of the commission; though less attuned to absurdities than Scheer, Stengel identified the factions clearly.

More incisive was the critique of D. L. Paletz in "Pornography, Politics, and the Press: The U.S. Attorney General's Commission on Pornography": if one accepts the commission's conclusion that "images are significant determinants of attitudes, and attitudes are significant determinants of human behavior," said Paletz, then one has to wonder why the beneficial effects of pornography—as catharsis, as therapy, as education, for example—are ignored. Paletz pointed out that the commission dealt selectively with research and evidence and broke almost no new ground; half (49 percent) of its recommendations dealt with already illegal child pornography, which no one defended in any case. Paletz is one of the few scholars actually to try to understand what pornography is *before* embarking on statistical studies.

G. Hawkins and F. E. Zimring provided an extensive comparison of the operations, conclusions, and recommendations of the Presidential Commission, the Attorney General's Commission, and the British Home Office Departmental Committee on Obscenity and Film Censorship (the Williams Commission) in *Pornography in a Free Society*. They also reviewed continuing issues and likely effects on policy. In "The British, Canadian and U.S. Pornography Commissions and Their Use of Social Science Research," E. F. Einsiedel says that each made use of research according to its respective country's legal and political traditions, the social and political agendas operative at the time, the popularity of specific research methodologies and theories, and the politics and backgrounds of the appointees to the commissions. Daniel Linz, Edward Donnerstein, and Stephen Penrod, three of the researchers most often cited by the attorney general's staff, themselves wrote an article, "The Findings and Recommendations of the Attorney General's Commission on Pornography: Do the Psychological 'Facts' Fit the Political Fury?" to assert that they did not. The authors denied that the data employed by the commission justified the additional legislation against pornography recommended by the commission or its call for more stringent enforcement of already existing legislation. The authors instead advocated educational programs to mitigate any alleged deleterious effects of pornography.

In 1976 and again in 1977 the House Subcommittee on Communications of the Committee on Interstate and Foreign Commerce held hearings on *Sex and Violence on Television*, in which various groups averred that there was too much of each on the small screen. The major consequence was a conflation of sex and violence in the public mind, an interesting example of social construction at work. Politicians in particular routinely speak of sex and violence as if they were inextricably linked. In 1985 the Parents' Music Resource Center (PMRC) (founded by Tipper Gore and Susan Baker, wives, respectively, of the senator and future vice president and the Bush-appointed secretary of state) demanded that record companies label records containing explicit and aggressive lyrics that the center claimed caused broken homes, teenage pregnancies, suicide, assorted perversities, and other social evils. The center singled out songs by Madonna, Michael Jackson, Sheena Easton, Motley Crüe, Prince, Cyndi Lauper, and Twisted Sister. It was an effective attack, augmented by the clout of the women's husbands, who persuaded the Senate to hold hearings. The PMRC's "Statement before the Committee on Commerce, Science, and Transportation, U.S. Senate" asked Congress for a law forcing manufacturers of records, cassettes, and compact discs to place warning labels on products with explicit or violent lyrics. Frank Zappa's "Statement before the Committee on Commerce, Science, and Transportation, U.S. Senate" opposed labels and suggested printed texts of the lyrics on the record jackets instead. Zappa's most famous remark during his testimony was that putting warning labels on album covers was like "treating dandruff by decapitation." Effectively frightened, the National Association of Recording Merchandisers decided by 1990 to put labels on the jackets on a "voluntary" basis to avoid compulsory legislation.

In 1985 also, the Senate Subcommittee on Security and Terrorism investigated, among other subversive uses, the role of computers in transmitting obscene matter. The testimony can be found in *The Use of Computers to Transmit Material Inciting Crime*. The following year, the House Subcommittee on Criminal Law held hearings on the *Cable Porn and Dial-a-Porn Control Act*; the FCC took a harder line on both cable and telephone indecency. Transcripts of the House hearings on dial-a-porn in Congress in 1987 can be found in the volume entitled *Telephone Decency Act of 1987*, which led to heavy pressuring of the FCC and several court challenges. The documents in the volume include testimony by providers, various authorities, and opponents of the dial-a-porn industry, as do those gathered in the Meese Commission's *Attorney General's Commission on Pornography: Final Report*, which contains an extensive section on telephone indecency.

Politicians reserved their most flamboyant grandstanding, however, for an attack on sex on the Internet. The hearings were a prime example of folklore in the making. Marty Rimm, an undergraduate at Carnegie-Mellon University, published "Marketing Pornography on the Information Superhighway" in the *Georgetown Law Review*, an article that made hyperbolic claims that pornography dominated the medium. Rimm's bogus assertions, among them that "83.5% of all images posted on the Usenet are pornographic," duped *Time* magazine, which featured the study in the cover article ("Cyberporn") as an "exclusive" for the 3 July 1995 issue; the piece was written by Philip Elmer-Dewitt. *Time* never retracted the implied endorsement of the fraudulent study, even after real researchers ridiculed Rimm's methodologies and conclusions. On 14 June 1995 the Senate approved Senator Jim Exon's Communications Decency Act, which provided penalties against anyone using electronic pathways to harass or to make indecent material available to minors. In "A Bad Day in Cyberspace: The Senate Takes a Sledgehammer to Our Communications Future," Steven Levy maintains that the unregulated Internet is a marvel of communication and that "the best thing the government can do is get off its case—or at least not criminalize its users because they don't mind their manners in midflame." "Gingrich Opposes Rule on Obscenity in Internet Traffic," by Edmund L. Andrews, announced that the Speaker of the House was opposed to such legislation on First Amendment grounds, but most of his colleagues remained implacable. Folklore and political ambition propelled the bill through a House-Senate conference committee, which passed a section of the proposed new telecommunications bill that would impose fines of up to $100,000 and prison sentences of up to five years for making "indecent" material available to minors on computer networks. The language of the bill, says Edmund L. Andrews in "Congress Agrees on a Tough Bill to Wipe Out On-Line Obscenity," was so broad as to ensure protracted litigation. The committee rejected compromise proposals from on-line providers like America On-Line and newspapers that would have limited the objectionable speech to material actually "harmful" to minors as a way of avoiding absurdities. Otherwise, it would be legal for a newspaper to print the word "penis" in its paper editions but not in its electronic version. More rational members of Congress, afraid to be tarred as insufficiently concerned about the welfare of children, voted for the bill knowing that courts would kill it. In 1997 the Supreme Court struck the law down as both misguided and unconstitutional.

In a special category are academic conferences. Each year the Popular Culture Association holds a conference in which "Eros and Popular Culture" is a permanent session usually hospitable to panels on pornography. The subject can crop up in any number of annual conferences by diverse organizations, and several "porn conferences" were held at various universities during the late 1990s. During 6–9 August 1998, the Center for Sex Research at California State University at Northridge, the Free Speech Coalition, the Society for the Scientific Study of Sexuality, and the American Association of Sex Educators and Counselors sponsored the mother of all such events, the World Pornography

Conference in Universal City, California. The organizers maintain a Web site under World Pornography Conference, with a breakout of all the panels, exhibits, and so on. Carina Chocano's "Scholars of Smut," also available on the Internet, is easily the wittiest and most balanced account of the conference. "Erotica," a convention/event in mid-1999 at the Javits Convention Center in New York, billed itself as quasi-instructional.

NOTABLE FEMINIST CONFERENCES

Feminists have held several landmark conferences on sexuality and pornography. Essays and accounts growing out of the 1985 International Woman's Day Congress (Toronto), which brought together feminists with members of the Canadian Organization for the Rights of Prostitutes, have been published as *Good Girls/Bad Girls: Feminists and Sex Trade Workers Face to Face*, edited by Laurie Bell. Lively discussion pitted the two groups against each other, and the working girls may actually have carried the day; in any case, the accounts are authoritative. To counter opposition from other feminists, antiporn factions escalated the levels of rhetorical violence; the title of Marcia Womongold's essay, "From Pornography: A License to Kill" is a case in point. *The Sexual Liberals and the Attack on Feminism*, a volume edited by Dorchen Leidholdt and Janice G. Raymond, reproduces papers from a conference on pornography held at the New York University Law School on 6 April 1987. The salient themes are that only those who oppose pornography are true feminists, a conviction first enunciated by Catharine MacKinnon, who denigrated women who disagree with her, and that all sexual expression is pornography, since the contributors cannot conceive of sexual descriptions or language that does not discriminate against women. One essay in the volume is "Not a Sentimental Journey: Women's Friendships," by Janice G. Raymond, who stops short of calling women with other views traitors but does say that they are wrong for working against the great cause. Dorchen Leidholdt attacks liberal feminists who believe in choice, which, says Leidholdt, is impossible in a male-dominated society, where sex can only be dangerous abuse, in "When Women Defend Pornography." According to Leidholdt, pornography is literally the male agenda for women's servitude, an articulation of an unjust social and political order; falsely representing sex as pleasurable to women is the tactic of an enemy.

Papers from another conference at Columbia University, gathered by Diana E. H. Russell as *Making Violence Sexy: Feminist Views on Pornography*, agree with little dissent that sexual expression is inherently violent. *Diary of a Conference on Sexuality*, a series of reprints of "The Scholar and the Feminist IX" conference (1982) compiled by Hannah Alderfer, Beth Jaker, and Marybeth Nelson, documents confrontations among liberal and radical factions. It is useful to compare these books with the proceedings of an Austrian conference, *Frauen, Gewalt, Pornographie: Dokumentation zum Symposium*, edited by Karin Rick and Sylvia Treudel; the entries are less ideological, more focused on history, and less prone to personal attack. John Elson's "Passions over Pornography" illustrated the alternately amused and appalled response of established journalism to escalating emotions among feminists. Ted C. Fishman's "Hatefest: Hanging Out at a Feminist Legal Conference" recaps a raucous 1992 event at the University of Michigan Law School (Catharine MacKinnon's home base), which was closed to opponents. (See also the National Coalition against Censorship's *The Sex Panic: Women, Censorship, and "Pornography"* on the 1993 conference at City College of New York and **Censorship of Art** in Chapter 20.) In short, the debate among feminists became wonderfully entertaining. When Nadine Strossen gave an interview (see Dorothy Atcheson, "Defending Pornography: Face to Face with the President of the ACLU") in which she condemned outrages committed by censorious feminists, Diana Russell retaliated with an article ("Nadine Strossen: The Pornography Industry's Wet Dream") dripping with personal invective. The rancorousness suggested that the battle was less about sexual expression than the construction of hierarchies within the feminist movement.

Pro-sex feminists incurred the kind of wrath ladled out by Candace de Russy in " 'Revolting Behavior': The Irresponsible Exercise of Academic Freedom" when the Women's Studies Program at SUNY-New Paltz held a conference in 1997 called "Revolting Behavior: The Challenges of Women's Sexual Freedom." The organizers invited papers, panels, and demonstrations on sadomasochism, female masturbation, bisexuality, sexual appliances, striptease, and sundry erotic practices and ideas, being sure to include space for attacks on male sexuality as well. Judging from the furor, the conference seems to have served its purpose.

NOTE

1. Peter Gay, *The Bourgeois Experience: Victoria to Freud* (New York: Oxford University Press, 1984), p. 468.

REFERENCES

Abelson, H., R. Cohen, E. Heaton, and C. Studer. "National Survey of Public Attitudes toward and Experience with Erotic Materials." *Technical Report of the Commission on Obscenity and Pornography.* 9 vols. Washington, DC: Government Printing Office 1971–1972, VI:1–137.

Abramson, Paul R., and Steven D. Pinkerton, eds. *Sexual Nature/Sexual Culture.* Chicago: University of Chicago Press, 1995.

Adkins, Lisa, and Vicki Merchant, eds. *Sexualizing the Social: Power and Organisation of Sexuality.* New York: St. Martin's, 1996.

Alderfer, Hannah, Beth Jaker, and Marybeth Nelson. *Diary of a Conference on Sexuality.* New York: Barnard College Women's Center, 1982.

Allen, Frederick Lewis. *Only Yesterday*. New York: Harper's, 1931.

Allyn, David Smith. *"Make Love, Not War: The Sexual Revolution in America, 1957–1977."* Ph.D. dissertation, Harvard University, 1996.

American Civil Liberties Union. *Annual Reports*. New York: ACLU, 1920–.

———. *Free Speech. 1984*. New York: ACLU, 1984.

———. *Private Group Censorship and the NODL*. Rev. ed. New York: ACLU, 1958.

Anderson, Patricia. *When Passion Reigned: Sex and the Victorians*. New York: Basic Books, 1995.

Andrews, Edmund L. "Congress Agrees on a Tough Bill to Wipe Out On-Line Obscenity." *New York Times*, 7 December 1995, pp. A1, A12.

———. "Gingrich Opposes Rule on Obscenity in Internet Traffic." *New York Times*, 22 June 1995, pp. A1, A10.

Arcand, Bernard. *The Jaguar and the Anteater: Pornography Degree Zero*, trans. Wayne Grady. New York: Verso, 1993.

Archibald, George. "Koop Declares War on Porn and Violence." *Washington Times*, 5 February 1985, p. 10B.

Ariès, Phillipe, and Andre Bejin, eds. *Western Sexuality: Practice and Precept in Past and Present Times*. New York: Basil Blackwell, 1985.

Ariès, Phillipe, and Georges Duby, eds. *A History of Private Life*, trans. Arthur Goldhammer. I: *From Pagan Rome to Byzantium*, ed. Paul Veyne. II: *Revelations of the Medieval World*, ed. Georges Duby. III: *Passions of the Renaissance*, ed. Roger Chartier. Cambridge: Belknap Press of Harvard University Press, 1987, 1988, 1989.

Assiter, Alison. "Essentially Sex: A New Look." *Bad Girls and Dirty Pictures: The Challenge to Reclaim Feminism*, ed. Alison Assiter and Avedon Carol. Boulder, CO: Pluto Press, 1993, pp. 88–104.

Atcheson, Dorothy. "Defending Pornography: Face to Face with the President of the ACLU." *Playboy*, 42:2 (February 1995): 37–39, 108.

Attorney General's Commission on Pornography. *Final Report*. 2 vols. Washington, DC: Government Printing Office, 1986.

Axtell, James, ed. *The Indian Peoples of Eastern America: A Documentary History of the Sexes*. New York: Oxford, 1981.

Bakos, Susan C. *Kink: The Hidden Sex Lives of Americans*. New York: St. Martin's, 1995.

Banes, Sally, Sheldon Frank, and Tem Horowitz. *Our National Passion: 200 Years of Sex in America*. Chicago: Follett, 1976.

Barker-Binfield, G. J. *The Horrors of the Half-Known Life: Male Attitudes toward Women and Sexuality in Nineteenth-Century America*. New York: Harper and Row, 1976.

Baudrillard, Jean. *The Transparency of Evil: Essays on Extreme Phenomena*, trans. James Benedict. New York: Routledge, 1993.

Bell, Laurie, ed. *Good Girls/Bad Girls: Feminists and Sex Trade Workers Face to Face*. Seattle: Seal Press, 1987.

Bem, S. L. *The Lenses of Gender: Transforming the Debate on Sexual Inequality*. New Haven, CT: Yale University Press, 1993.

Bensinger, Terralee. "Lesbian Pornography: The Re/Making of (a) Community." *Discourse*, 15:1 (1992): 69–93.

Berger, Maurice, Brian Wallis, and Simon Watson, eds. *Constructing Masculinity*. New York: Routledge, 1995.

Berger, Peter, and Thomas Luckmann. *The Social Construction of Reality*. London: Allen Lane, 1967.

Berlant, Lauren, and Michael Warner. "What Does Queer Theory Teach Us about X?" *Publications of the Modern Language Association of America*, 110:3 (May 1995): 343–349.

Bi Academic Intervention. *The Bisexual Imaginary: Representation, Identity and Desire*. New York: Cassell, 1998.

Bilderlexicon der Erotik. 6 vols. Vienna and Hamburg: Verlag für Kulturforschung, 1928–1931, 1963. Edited by Leo Schidrowitz: I: *Kulturgeschichte*; II: *Literatur und Kunst*; III: *Sexualwissenschaft*; IV: *Ergänzungsband*. Edited by Armand Mergen: V and VI: *Sexualforschung: Stichwort und Bild*.

Bingham, Caroline. "Seventeenth-Century Attitudes toward Deviant Sex." *Journal of Interdisciplinary History*, 1 (1971): 447–467.

Blanchard, Paul. *American Freedom and Catholic Power*. Boston: Beacon Press, 1950.

―――. *The Right to Read*. Boston: Beacon Press, 1956.

Blatt, Martin Henry. *Free Love and Anarchism: The Biography of Ezra Heywood*. Urbana: University of Illinois Press, 1989.

Bleier, Ruth. *Science and Gender: A Critique of Biology and Its Theories of Women*. Elmsford, NY: Pergamon Press, 1984.

Blumstein, Philip, and Pepper Schwartz. *American Couples: Money Work Sex*. New York: Morrow, 1983.

Bolen, Carl van. *Geschichte der Erotik: Erotik und Sexualwissen der Menschhertsgeschichte*. 5th ed. Teuffen (AR): Bucher des Lebens, 1957.

Boulware, Jack. *Sex, American Style: An Illustrated Romp through the Golden Age of Heterosexuality*. Venice, CA: Feral House, 1998.

Boyer, Paul S. *Purity in Print: The Vice-Society Movement and Book Censorship in America*. New York: Scribner's, 1968.

―――. *Urban Masses and Moral Order in America, 1820–1920*. Cambridge: Harvard University Press, 1978.

Braudel, Fernand. *Capitalism and Material Life, 1400–1800*, trans. Miriam Kochan. New York: Harper and Row, 1973.

Breasted, Mary. *Oh! Sex Education*. New York: Praeger, 1970.

Bremmer, Jan, ed. *From Sappho to de Sade: Moments in the History of Sexuality*. New York: Routledge, 1991.

Bright, Susie. *Susie Bright's Sexual State of the Union*. New York: Simon and Schuster, 1997.

Brodie, J. F. *Contraception and Abortion in 19th-Century America*. Ithaca, NY: Cornell University Press, 1994.

Broun, Heywood, and Margaret Leech. *Anthony Comstock: Roundsman of the Lord*. New York: Literary Guild, 1927.

Brown, L. *Sex Education in the Eighties*. New York: Plenum Press, 1981.

Brusendorff, Ove, and Paul Henningsen. *A History of Eroticism*. 6 vols. New York: Lyle Stuart, 1965–1967.

Bullough, Vern L. "Sex in History: A Virgin Field." *Sex, Society, and History*. New York: Science History Publications, 1976, 1–16.

————. *Sexual Variance in Society and History*. Chicago: University of Chicago Press, 1976.

Burnham, John C. "American Historians and the Subject of Sex." *Societas*, 2 (Autumn 1972): 307–316.

————. "The Progressive Era Revolution in American Attitudes toward Sex." *Journal of American History*, 59 (1973): 885–907.

Burstyn, Varda. "Anatomy of a Moral Panic." *Fuse*, 8 (Summer 1984): 9–38.

Burton, Doris-Jean. "Public Opinion and Pornography Policy." *For Adult Users Only: The Dilemma of Violent Pornography*, ed. Susan Gubar and Joan Hoff. Bloomington: Indiana University Press, 1989, pp. 133–146.

Buss, David M. *The Evolution of Desire: Strategies of Human Mating*. New York: Basic Books, 1994.

Butler, Judith. *Bodies That Matter: On the Discursive Limits of Sex*. New York: Routledge, 1993.

————. *Gender Trouble: Feminism and the Subversion of Identity*. New York: Routledge, 1990.

Cable, Mary, et al. *American Manners and Morals*. New York: American Heritage, 1969.

Calderone, Mary. "Playboy Interview." *Sex American Style*, ed. Frank Robinson and Nat Lehrman. Chicago: Playboy Press, 1971, pp. 278–333.

Califia, Pat. *Sapphistry: The Book of Lesbian Sexuality*. Tallahassee, FL: Naiad Press, 1980.

Campbell, Patricia J. *Sex Education Books for Young Adults, 1892–1979*. New York: Bowker, 1979.

(Canada). Special Committee on Pornography and Prostitution. *Report of the Special Committee on Pornography and Prostitution*. Ottawa: Government Printing Office, 1985.

Caplan, Pat, ed. *The Cultural Construction of Sexuality*. London: Tavistock, 1987.

Carmen, Arlene, et al. *The Meese Commission Exposed: Proceedings of a National Coalition against Censorship Public Information Briefing on the Attorney General's Commission on Pornography, January 16, 1986*. New York: National Coalition against Censorship [1322 West 43d Street, New York City 10036], 1987.

Case, Sue-Ellen. "Tracking the Vampire." *differences*, 3:2 (1991): 1–22.

Castle, Terry. *The Apparitional Lesbian: Female Homosexuality and Modern Culture*. New York: Columbia University Press, 1993.

Cauldwell, David. *Pornography: An Illustrated Banner Book*. Torrance, CA: Banner, n.d.

Chapple, Steve, and David Talbot. *Burning Desires: Sex in America, a Report from the Field*. New York: Signet, 1990.

Chen, Constance M. *"The Sex Side of Life": Mary Ware Dennett's Pioneering Battle for Birth Control and Sex Education*. New York: New Press, 1996.

Chesler, Ellen. *Woman of Valor: Margaret Sanger and the Birth Control Movement in America*. New York: Simon and Schuster, 1992.

Chocano, Carina. "Scholars of Smut." *Salon Magazine*, 5 October 1998. See www.salonmagazine.com/it/feature/1998.

Cline, Victor, ed. *Where Do You Draw the Line?: An Exploration into Media Violence, Pornography, and Censorship*. Provo, UT: Brigham Young University Press, 1974.

Cohen, Lawrence. "The Pleasures of Castration: The Postoperative Status of Hijras, Jankhas and Academics." *Sexual Nature/Sexual Culture*, ed. Paul R. Abramson and Steven D. Pinkerton. Chicago: University of Chicago Press, 1995, pp. 276–304.

Cohn, Nik. *The Heart of the World*. New York: Knopf, 1992.

Comstock, Anthony. *Frauds Exposed: Or, How the People Are Deceived and Robbed, and Youth Corrupted*. 1880; rpt. Montclair, NJ: Patterson Smith, 1969.

———. *Traps for the Young*, ed. Robert Brenner (1883); rpt. Cambridge: Belknap Press, 1967.

Cook, Mark, and Robert McHenry. *Sexual Attraction*. New York: Pergamon Press, 1978.

Cooper, Courtney Riley. *Designs in Scarlet*. Boston: Little, Brown, 1939; rpt. *Teen-Age Vice!* New York: Pyramid Books, 1952.

Costello, John. *Love, Sex and War: Changing Values 1939–1945*. London: Collins, 1985; aka *Virtue under Fire: How World War II Changed Our Social and Sexual Attitudes*. Boston: Little, Brown, 1985.

Cott, Nancy F. "Passionlessness: An Interpretation of Victorian Sexual Ideology, 1790–1850." *Women and Health in America*, ed. Judith Leavitt. Madison: University of Wisconsin Press, 1984, pp. 57–69.

Courtney, Phoebe. *The Sex Education Racket: Pornography in the Schools (an Exposé)*. New Orleans: Free Men Speak, 1969.

Csicsery, George Paul, ed. *The Sex Industry: A Sex-Posé of Happy Hookers, Massage Parlors, Skin-Flicks—Every Kick Money Can Buy*. New York: NAL, 1973.

Daniels, Bruce C. *Puritans at Play: Leisure and Recreation in Colonial New England*. New York: St. Martin's, 1996.

d'Arcangelo, Angelo [Joseph Bush]. *Angelo d'Arcangelo's Love Book: Inside the Sexual Revolution*. New York: Olympia Press, 1971.

Darnton, Robert. *Forbidden Best-Sellers of Pre-Revolutionary France*. London: HarperCollins, 1996.

Davis, Douglas. "Art and Contradiction: Helms, Censorship, and the Serpent." *Art in America*, 78:5 (May 1990): 55–61.

Davis, Katherine Bement. *Factors in the Sex Life of Twenty-Two Hundred Women*. New York: Harper and Bros., 1929.

De Cecco, John P., and Michael G. Shively, eds. *Bisexual and Homosexual Identities: Critical Theoretical Issues*. Binghamton, NY: Haworth Press, 1984.

Degler, Carl. *At Odds: Women and the Family in America from the Revolution to the Present*. New York: Oxford University Press, 1980.

———. "What Ought to Be and What Was: Women's Sexuality in the Nineteenth Century." *American Historical Review*, 79 (1974): 1469–1477.

Dellamora, Richard. *Apocalyptic Overtures: Sexual Politics and the Sense of an Ending*. New Brunswick, NJ: Rutgers University Press, 1994.

D'Emilio, John. *Sexual Politics, Sexual Communities: The Making of the Homosexual Minority in the United States. 1940–1970*. Chicago: University of Chicago Press, 1983.

D'Emilio, John, and Estelle B. Freedman. *Intimate Matters: A History of Sexuality in America*. New York: Harper and Row, 1988; rev. ed. 1997.

Dennett, Mary Ware. *Birth Control Laws*. New York: DaCapo Press, 1970.

———. *Who's Obscene?* New York: Vanguard Press, 1930.

Dennis, Wendy. *Hot and Bothered: Sex and Love in the Nineties*. New York: Viking, 1992.

de Russy, Candace. " 'Revolting Behavior': The Irresponsible Exercise of Academic Freedom." *Chronicle of Higher Education*, 6 March 1998, p. B9.

Deutsch, Albert, ed. *Sex Habits of American Men: A Symposium of the Kinsey Report.* New York: Prentice-Hall, 1948.

de Vries, Leonard, and Peter Fryer. *Venus Unmasked, Or, an Inquiry into the Nature and Origin of the Passion of Love.* London: Baker, 1967.

Diamond, Irene. "Pornography and Repression: A Reconsideration." *Signs*, 5 (1980): 686–701; rpt. *Women: Sex and Sexuality*, ed. Catharine R. Stimpson and Ethel S. Person. Chicago: University of Chicago Press, 1980, pp. 129–144; rpt. *The Criminal Justice System and Women*, ed. Barbara R. Price and Natalie J. Sokoloff. New York: Clark Boardman, 1987, pp. 335–351.

Ditzion, Sidney. *Marriage, Morals, and Sex in America: A History of Ideas.* New York: Bookman Associates, 1953.

Dominguez, Ivo. *Beneath the Skins: The New Spirit and Politics of the Kink Community.* Los Angeles: Daedalus, 1994.

Douglas, Ann. *The Feminization of Culture.* New York: Knopf, 1977.

Douglas, Jason. *The Age of Perversion: A Close-Up View of Sexuality in Our Permissive Society.* London: Canova Press, 1969.

Downs, Donald Alexander. *The New Politics of Pornography.* Chicago: University of Chicago Press, 1990.

Drake, Gordon V. *SIECUS: Corrupter of Youth.* Tulsa, OK: Christian Crusade Publications, 1969.

Duberman, Martin B. *About Time: Exploring the Gay Past.* New York: Gay Presses of New York, 1986.

Dubois, Ellen Carol, and Linda Gordon. "Seeking Ecstacy on the Battlefield: Danger and Pleasure in Nineteenth-Century Feminist Sexual Thought." *Pleasure and Danger: Exploring Female Sexuality*, ed. Carole Vance. Boston: Routledge and Kegan Paul, 1984, pp. 31–49.

Duggan, Lisa. "Sex Panics." *Sex Wars: Sexual Dissent and Political Culture*, by Lisa Duggan and Nan D. Hunter. New York: Routledge, 1995, pp. 74–78.

Duggan, Lisa, and Nan D. Hunter. *Sex Wars: Sexual Dissent and Political Culture.* New York: Routledge, 1995.

Dunlap, David W. "The Sun Is Setting on the Times Square Porn Palaces." *New York Times*, 12 August 1990, p. R13.

Dworkin, Andrea. "Pornography and Grief." *Take Back the Night: Women on Pornography*, ed. Laura Lederer. New York: Morrow, 1980, pp. 286–291.

Echols, Alice. *Daring to Be Bad: Radical Feminism in America, 1967–1975.* Minneapolis: University of Minnesota Press, 1989.

———. "The Taming of the Id: Feminist Sexual Politics, 1968–83." *Pleasure and Danger: Exploring Female Sexuality*, ed. Carole Vance. Boston: Routledge and Kegan Paul, 1984, pp. 50–72.

Ehrenreich, Barbara, Elizabeth Hess, and Gloria Jacobs. *Re-Making Love: The Feminization of Sex.* Garden City, NY: Anchor/Doubleday, 1986.

———. "A Report on the Sex Crisis." *Ms.*, March 1982, pp. 61–62, 64, 87.

Einsiedel, Edna F. "The British, Canadian and U.S. Pornography Commissions and Their Use of Social Science Research." *Journal of Communication*, 38:2 (Spring 1988): 108–121.

Ellis, Albert. *The Folklore of Sex*, aka *Sex Beliefs and Customs*. New York: Charles Boni, 1951; and *The Folklore of Sex*. New York: Grove Press, 1961.

Ellison, Alfred. *The Photo Illustrated History of Pornography*. 2 vols. San Diego: Academy Press, 1971.

Elshtain, Jean Bethke. "The Victim Syndrome: A Troubling Turn in Feminism." *The Progressive*, 46 (June 1982): 42–47.

Elson, John. "Passions over Pornography." *Time*, 30 March 1992, pp. 52–53.

Epstein, Steven. "Gay Politics, Ethnic Identity: The Limits of Social Constructionism." *Socialist Review*, 93/94 (1987): 9–54.

Erickson, Julia. *Kiss and Tell: Surveying Sex in the Twentieth Century*. Cambridge: Harvard University Press, 1999.

Ernst, Morris L., and Alexander Lindey. *The Censor Marches On*. New York: Doubleday, Doran, 1940.

Eskara, Roy D. *Bizarre Sex*. London: Quartet, 1987.

Eurydice. *Satyricon USA: A Journey across the New Sexual Frontier*. New York: Scribner's, 1999.

Facey, Paul W. *The Legion of Decency: A Sociological Analysis of the Emergence and Development of a Social Pressure Group*. New York: Arno Press, 1974.

Faderman, Lillian. *Odd Girls and Twilight Lovers: A History of Lesbian Life in Twentieth-Century America*. New York: Columbia University Press, 1991.

———. *Surpassing the Love of Men: Romantic Friendship and Love between Women from the Renaissance to the Present*. New York: Morrow, 1981.

Fass, Paula. *The Damned and the Beautiful: American Youth in the 1920s*. New York: Oxford University Press, 1977.

Fausto-Sterling, Anne. *Myths of Gender: Biological Theories about Women and Men*. New York: Basic Books, 1985.

Ferguson, Ann. "Sex War: The Debate between Radical and Libertarian Feminists." *Signs*, 10 (1984): 106–112.

Fishman, Ted C. "Hatefest: Hanging Out at a Feminist Legal Conference." *Playboy*, 40:8 (August 1993): 41–45.

Forsyth, Adrian. *A Natural History of Sex: The Ecology and Evolution of Mating Behavior*. New York: Scribner's, 1986.

Foster, Lawrence. *Religion and Sexuality: The Shakers, the Mormons, and the Oneida Community*. Urbana: University of Illinois Press, 1984.

Foucault, Michel. *The History of Sexuality*, trans. Robert B. Hurley. 3 vols. I: *An Introduction*; II: *The Use of Pleasure*; III: *The Care of the Self*. New York: Pantheon, 1978–1987.

Fout, John C. *Forbidden History: the State, Society, and the Regulation of Sexuality in Modern Europe*. Chicago: University of Chicago Press, 1992.

Fout, John C., and Maura Shaw Tantillo, eds. *American Sexual Politics: Sex, Gender, and Race since the Civil War*. Chicago: University of Chicago Press, 1993.

Francoeur, Anna K., and Robert T. Francoeur. *Hot and Cool Sex: Cultures in Conflict*. New York: Harcourt Brace Jovanovich, 1974.

Frankl, George. *The Failure of the Sexual Revolution*. London: Kahn and Averill, 1974.

Freud, Sigmund. *Standard Edition of the Complete Psychological Works of Sigmund Freud*. 24 vols. London: Hogarth Press, 1966–1974.

Friedman, Josh A. *Tales of Times Square*. Venice, CA: Feral House, 1993.

Fryer, Peter. *The Birth Controllers*. New York: Stein and Day, 1966.

———. *Mrs. Grundy: Studies in Sexual Purity.* London: Dobson, 1963.

Fuchs, Eduard. *Illustrierte Sittengeschichte vom Mittel..lter bis zur Gegenwart.* 3 vols. and supplements. Munich: Albert Langen, 1909–1928. I: *Die Renaissance* (1909) and *Ergänzungsband* (1909 and 1928); II: *Die galant Zeit* (1910) and *Ergänzungsband* (1911 and 1928); III: *Das bürgerliche Zeitalter* (1912) and *Ergänzungsband* (1912 and 1928).

Fuss, Diana. *Essentially Speaking: Feminism, Nature and Difference.* New York: Routledge, 1989.

———, ed. *Inside/Out: Lesbian Theories, Gay Theories.* New York: Routledge, 1991.

Gallup, George. *Public Support of Censorship Indicated.* Princeton: Field Enterprises, 1971.

Gans, Herbert J. *Popular Culture and High Culture: An Analysis of Taste.* New York: Basic Books, 1974.

Garber, Marjorie. *Vice Versa: Bisexuality and the Erotics of Everyday Life.* New York: Simon and Schuster, 1995.

Gardiner, Harold C. *Catholic Viewpoint on Censorship.* New York: Doubleday, 1958.

Gay, Peter. *The Education of the Senses.* 4 vols. I: *The Bourgeois Experience: Victoria to Freud*; II: *The Tender Passion.* New York: Oxford University Press, 1984, 1986; III: *The Cultivation of Hatred*; IV: *The Naked Heart.* New York: Norton, 1993, 1995.

Gertzman, Jay A. *Bookleggers and Smuthounds: The Trade in Erotica, 1920–1940.* Philadelphia: University of Pennsylvania Press, 1999.

———. "John Saxton Sumner of the New York Society for the Suppression of Vice: A Chief Smut-Eradicator of the Interwar Period." *Journal of American Culture*, 17: 2 (Summer 1994): 41–47.

Gilbert, James. *A Cycle of Outrage: America's Reaction to the Juvenile Delinquent in the 1950s.* New York: Oxford University Press, 1986.

Gilfoyle, Timothy J. *City of Eros: New York City, Prostitution, and the Commercialization of Sex, 1790–1920.* New York: Norton, 1992.

Gilman, Sander L. *Sexuality: An Illustrated History Representing the Sexual in Medicine and Culture from the Middle Ages to the Age of AIDS.* New York: John Wiley, 1989.

Ginzburg, Carlo. "Titian, Ovid, and the Sixteenth-Century Codes for Erotic Illustration." *Clues, Myths, and the Historical Method*, trans. John Tedeschi and Anne C. Tedeschi. Baltimore: Johns Hopkins University Press, 1989, pp. 77–95.

Goldstein, Richard. "Porn Free." *Village Voice*, 1 September 1998, pp. 28–30, 33–34.

Gopnik, Adam. "American Studies." *New Yorker*, 28 September 1998, pp. 39–40, 42.

Gordon, George N. *Erotic Communications: Studies in Sex, Sin and Censorship.* New York: Hastings House, 1980.

Gordon, Linda. *Woman's Body, Woman's Right: A Social History of Birth Control in America.* New York: Grossman, 1976.

Gordon, Michael. "From an Unfortunate Necessity to a Cult of Mutual Orgasm: Sex in American Marital Education Literature 1830–1940." *Studies in the Sociology of Sex*, ed. James M. Henslin. New York: Appleton-Century-Crofts, 1971, pp. 53–80.

Gordon-Maloul, Cynthia J. *"Framing Pornography: Political Mobilization and Conflicts over Contested American Values."* Ph.D. dissertation, New York University, 1995.

Goulemot, Jean Marie. *Forbidden Texts: Erotic Literature and Its Readers in Eighteenth-Century France*. Philadelphia: University of Pennsylvania Press, 1995.

Grant, Linda. *Sexing the Millennium: Women and the Sexual Revolution*. New York: Grove Press, 1994.

Green, Shirley. *The Curious History of Contraception*. New York: St. Martin's, 1971.

Greenberg, David F. *The Construction of Homosexuality*. Chicago: University of Chicago Press, 1988.

Greenblatt, Stephen. "America's Raciest Read." *New York Times*, 22 September 1998, A31.

Gregersen, Edgar. *Sexual Practices: The Story of Human Sexuality*. New York: Franklin Watts, 1983.

Gussow, Mel. "Bumped from the Whitney, Nudity Finds a Showcase." *New York Times*, 15 August 1998, pp. B1, B3.

Haller, John S. "From Maidenhead to Menopause: Sex Education for Women in Victorian America." *Journal of Popular Culture*, 6 (Summer 1972): 49–69.

Handy, Bruce. "Ye Olde Smut Shoppe." *Time*, 17 November 1997, p. 111.

Haney, Robert W. *Comstockery in America: Patterns of Censorship and Control*. Boston: Beacon Press, 1960.

Harris, Louis. *Time Morality Poll*. New York: Harris and Associates, 1969.

Harris, Sarah. *The Puritan Jungle: America's Sexual Underground*. New York: Putnam, 1969.

Harrison, Fraser. *The Dark Angel: Aspects of Victorian Sexuality*. New York: Universe Books, 1978.

Hart, Lynda. *Fatal Women: Lesbian Sexuality and the Mark of Aggression*. Princeton: Princeton University Press, 1994.

Haste, Helen. *The Sexual Metaphor*. Cambridge: Harvard University Press, 1994.

Hawkins, G., and F. E. Zimring. *Pornography in a Free Society*. New York: Cambridge University Press, 1988.

Hearn, Jeff. *The Gender of Oppression: Men, Masculinity, and the Critique of Marxism*. New York: St. Martin's, 1987.

Hebdige, Dick. *Subculture: The Meaning of Style*. London: Methuen, 1971.

Hebditch, David, and Nick Anning. *Porn Gold: Inside the Pornography Business*. Boston: Faber, 1988.

Heidenry, John. *What Wild Ecstasy: The Rise and Fall of the Sexual Revolution*. New York: Simon and Schuster, 1997.

Heins, Marjorie. *Sex, Sin, and Blasphemy: A Guide to America's Censorship Wars*. New York: New Press, 1993.

Hentoff, Nat. *Free Speech for Me but Not for Thee: How the American Left and Right Relentlessly Censor Each Other*. New York: HarperCollins, 1993.

Herdt, Gilbert. "Representations of Homosexuality: An Essay in Cultural Ontology and Historical Comparison, Parts I and II." *Journal of the History of Sexuality*, 1:3 and 4 (1991): 481–504; 603–632.

Hersey, George L. *The Evolution of Allure: Sexual Selection from the Medici Venus to the Incredible Hulk*. Cambridge: MIT Press, 1996.

Hertzberg, Hendrik. "Big Boobs: Ed Meese and His Pornography Commission." *Harpers*, 195 (14 and 21 July 1986): 21–24.

Himes, Norman E. *Medical History of Contraception*. Boston: Allen and Unwin, 1936; reissued with a new Preface by Christopher Tietze. New York: Schocken, 1970.

Hirschfeld, Magnus, ed. *The Sexual History of the World War*, trans. Ephraim Fischoff. New York: Panurge Press, 1934.

Hite, Shere. *The Hite Report: A Nationwide Study of Female Sexuality.* New York: Dell, 1976.

———. *The Hite Report: On Male Sexuality.* New York: Ballantine, 1982.

———. *Women and Love: A Cultural Revolution in Progress.* New York: Knopf, 1987.

Hofstadter, Richard. *Anti-Intellectualism in American Life.* New York: Random House, 1962.

Holbrook, David. *The Pseudo-Revolution: A Critical Study of Extremist "Liberation" in Sex.* London: Tom Stacey, 1972.

Holmberg, Carl. *Sexualities and Popular Culture.* Thousand Oaks, CA: Sage, 1998.

Hudson, Robert V. *Mass Media: A Chronological Encyclopedia of Television, Radio, Motion Pictures, Magazines, Newspapers, and Books in the United States.* New York: Garland, 1987.

Hunt, Lynn, ed. *Eroticism and the Body Politic.* Baltimore: Johns Hopkins University Press, 1991.

———. *The Invention of Pornography: Obscenity and the Origins of Modernity, 1500– 1800.* Cambridge: MIT Zone, 1993.

Hunt, Morton. *The Natural History of Love.* New York: Knopf, 1959.

———. *Sexual Behavior in the 1970s.* New York: Dell, 1974.

Hunter, James Davison. *Culture Wars: The Struggle to Define America.* New York: Basic Books, 1991.

Hurwood, Bernard. *The Golden Age of Erotica.* London: Tandem, 1968.

Hutchins, Loraine, and Lani Kaahumanu, eds. *Bi Any Other Name: Bisexual People Speak Out.* Boston: Alyson, 1990.

Hyde, H. Montgomery. *A History of Pornography.* New York: Farrar, Straus, and Giroux, 1965.

Janus, Samuel S., and Cynthia L. Janus. *The Janus Report on Sexual Behavior.* New York: Wiley, 1993.

Jay, Karla, ed. *Lesbian Erotics.* New York: New York University Press, 1994.

Jay, Karla, and Allen Young, eds. *Lavender Culture.* New York: New York University Press, 1994.

Jenkins, Philip. *Intimate Enemies: Moral Panics in Contemporary Great Britain.* New York: Aldine de Gruyter, 1992.

Johnson, Wendell S. *Living in Sin: The Victorian Sexual Revolution.* Chicago: Nelson-Hall, 1979.

Jordanova, Ludmilla. *Sexual Visions: Images of Gender in Science and Medicine between the Eighteenth and Twentieth Centuries.* Madison: University of Wisconsin Press, 1989.

Journal of Sex Research. New York, 1965–.

Journal of the History of Sexuality. Chicago, 1990–.

Katz, Jonathan Ned. *Gay American History.* New York: Crowell, 1976; rpt. New York: New American Library, 1992.

———. *The Invention of Heterosexuality.* New York: Dutton, 1995.

Kendrick, Walter. *The Secret Museum: Pornography in Modern Culture.* New York: Viking, 1987.

Kennedy, David. *Birth Control in America: The Career of Margaret Sanger.* New Haven, CT: Yale University Press, 1970.

Kern, Louis J. *An Ordered Love: Sex Roles and Sexuality in Victorian Utopias: The Shakers, the Mormons, and the Oneida Community*. Chapel Hill: University of North Carolina Press, 1981.

Kibbey, Ann, Kayann Short, and Abouali Farmanfarmaian, eds. *Sexual Artifice: Persons, Images, Politics*. (Issue #19 of *Genders*.) New York: New York University Press, 1994.

Kilpatrick, James J. *The Smut Peddlers: The Pornography Racket and the Law Dealing with Obscenity Censorship*. Garden City, NY: Doubleday, 1960.

King, Richard. *The Party of Eros: Radical Social Thought and the Realm of Freedom*. Chapel Hill: University of North Carolina Press, 1972.

Kinsey, Alfred C., Wardell B. Pomeroy, and Clyde E. Martin. *Sexual Behavior in the Human Male*. Philadelphia: W. B. Saunders, 1948.

Kinsey, Alfred C., Wardell B. Pomeroy, Clyde E. Martin, and Paul H. Gebhard. *Sexual Behavior in the Human Female*. Philadelphia: Saunders, 1953.

Kinsman, Gary. *The Regulation of Desire: Sexuality in Canada*. Montreal: Black Rose, 1987.

Kirkendall, Lester A., and Robert N. Whitehurst, eds. *The New Sexual Revolution*. New York: Donald W. Brown, 1971.

Kirkpatrick, R. G. "Collective Consciousness and Mass Hysteria: Collective Behavior and Anti-Pornography Crusades in Durkheimian Perspective." *Human Relations*, 28 (February 1975): 63–84.

Kirkpatrick, R. G., and Louis A. Zurcher, Jr. "Women against Pornography: Feminist Anti-Pornography Crusades in American Society." *International Journal of Sociology and Social Policy*, 3 (1983): 1–30.

Klassen, Albert D., Colin J. Williams, and Eugene E. Levitt. *Sex and Morality in the U.S.: An Empirical Enquiry under the Auspices of the Kinsey Institute*. Middletown, CT: Wesleyan University Press, 1989.

Kleinfield, N. R. "Effort to Stop Sex Industry Is Only Latest in Long Line." *New York Times*, 1 March 1998, p. 22.

Krauthammer, Charles. "Pornography through the Looking Glass." *Time*, 12 March 1984, pp. 82–83.

Lait, Jack, and Lee Mortimer. *Chicago: Confidential!* Chicago: Ziff-Davis, 1948; New York: Crown Publishers, 1951.

———. *New York: Confidential!* Chicago: Ziff-Davis, 1948.

———. *Washington: Confidential!* New York: Dell, 1951.

———. *U.S.A. Confidential!* New York: Crown, 1952.

Larson, Jane E., and Linda R. Hirshman. *Hard Bargains: The Politics of Sex*. New York: Oxford University Press, 1998.

Laumann, Edward O., John H. Gagnon, Robert T. Michael, and Stuart Michaels. *The Social Organization of Sexuality: Sexual Practices in the United States*. Chicago: University of Chicago Press, 1994.

Laws, Judith, and Pepper Schwartz. *Sexual Scripts: The Social Construction of Female Sexuality*. Hinsdale, IL: Dryden Press, 1977.

League of Nations. *Records of the International Conference for the Suppression of the Circulation of and Traffic in Obscene Publications. Held at Geneva from August 31st to September 12th, 1923*. Geneva: League of Nations, 1923.

"Legislative Recommendations: Report of the Committee on Obscenity and Pornography." *The Pornography Controversy*, ed. Ray C. Rist. New Brunswick, NJ: Transaction Books, 1975, pp. 64–84.

Legman, Gershon. *The Fake Revolt*. New York: Breaking Point, 1967.

———. "A Summer Reading List to End All Summer Reading Lists." *Fact*, 2:4 (July–August 1965): 38–43.

Lehman, F. M. *The White Slave Hell: Or, with Christ at Midnight in the Slums of Chicago*. Chicago: Christian Witness Co., 1910.

Lehman, Peter. "Sexology and the Representation of Male Sexuality." *Running Scared: Masculinity and the Representation of the Male Body*. Philadelphia: Temple University Press, 1993, pp. 131–146.

Leidholdt, Dorchen. "When Women Defend Pornography." *The Sexual Liberals and the Attack on Feminism*, ed. Dorchen Leidholdt and Janice G. Raymond. New York: Pergamon Press, 1990, pp. 125–131.

Leidholdt, Dorchen, and Janice G. Raymond, eds. *The Sexual Liberals and the Attack on Feminism*. New York: Pergamon Press, 1990.

Leonard, George Burr. *The End of Sex: Erotic Love after the Sexual Revolution*. New York: Bantam Books, 1984.

Levy, Steven. "A Bad Day in Cyberspace: The Senate Takes a Sledgehammer to Our Communications Future." *Newsweek*, 26 June 1995, p. 47.

Linz, Daniel, E. Donnerstein, and S. Penrod. "The Findings and Recommendations of the Attorney General's Commission on Pornography: Do the Psychological 'Facts' Fit the Political Fury?" *American Psychologist*, 42:10 (October 1987): 946–953.

Lipton, Lawrence. *The Erotic Revolution: An Affirmative View of the New Morality*. Los Angeles: Sherbourne, 1965.

Lipton, Morris A. "Fact and Myth: The Work of the Commission on Obscenity and Pornography." *Contemporary Sexual Behavior: Critical Issues in the 1970s*, ed. Joseph Zubin and John Money. Baltimore: Johns Hopkins University Press, 1973, pp. 231–258.

Lo Duca, Guiseppe. *A History of Eroticism*, trans. Kenneth Anger. Paris: Pauvert, 1961.

Lowry, Thomas P. *The Story the Soldiers Wouldn't Tell: Sex in the Civil War*. Mechanicsburg, PA: Stackpole Books, 1994.

Lynes, Russell. *The Tastemakers*. New York: Harper and Brothers, 1954.

Lynn, Barry W. *Polluting the Censorship Debate: A Summary and Critique of the Final Report of the Attorney General's Commission on Pornography*. Washington, DC: American Civil Liberties Union, 1986.

Lyons, Charles. *The New Censors*. Philadelphia: Temple University Press, 1997.

MacCormack, Carolyn, and Marilyn Strathern, eds. *Nature, Culture, and Gender*. Cambridge: Cambridge University Press, 1980.

MacKinnon, Catharine A. "Does Sexuality Have a History?" *Discourses of Sexuality: From Aristotle to AIDS*, ed. Donna C. Stanton. Ann Arbor: University of Michigan Press, 1992, pp. 117–136.

———. "Feminism, Marxism, Method and the State: An Agenda for Theory." *Signs*, 7:3 (Spring 1982): 513–520.

———. *Feminism Unmodified: Discourses on Life and Law*. Cambridge: Harvard University Press, 1987.

———. *Sexual Harassment of Working Women: A Case of Sex Discrimination*. New Haven, CT: Yale University Press, 1979.

———. *Toward a Feminist Theory of the State*. Cambridge: Harvard University Press, 1989.

Maglin, Nan Bauer, and Donna Perry, eds. *"Bad Girls"/"Good Girls": Women, Sex, and Power in the Nineties*. New Brunswick, NJ: Rutgers University Press, 1996.

Marcus, Greil. *Lipstick Traces: A Secret History of the Twentieth Century*. Cambridge: Harvard University Press, 1990.

Marcus, Steven. *The Other Victorians: A Study of Sexuality and Pornography in Mid-Nineteenth Century England*. New York: Basic Books, 1965.

Margulis, Lynn, and Dorion Sagan. *Mystery Dance: On the Evolution of Human Sexuality*. New York: Summit Books, 1991.

Maxwell, Kenneth. *The Sexual Imperative: An Evolutionary Tale of Sexual Survival*. New York: Plenum Press, 1994.

May, Geoffrey. *Social Control of Sex Expression*. New York: William Morrow, 1931.

Mayo, Clara, Alexandra Weiss, and Nancy Henley, eds. *Gender and Nonverbal Behavior*. New York: Springer-Verlag, 1981.

McCann, Carole R. *Birth Control Politics in the United States 1916–1945*. Ithaca, NY: Cornell University Press, 1994.

McGill, Michael E. *The McGill Report on Male Intimacy*. New York: Holt, Rinehart, and Winston, 1985.

McGovern, James R. "The American Woman's Pre–World War I Freedom in Manners and Morals." *Journal of American History*, 55 (September 1968): 315–332.

Mead, Margaret. *Male and Female: A Study of the Sexes in a Changing World*. New York: Mentor, 1955.

Meyerowitz, Joanne. "Sexual Geography and Gender Economy: The Furnished Room Districts of Chicago, 1890–1930." *Gender and American History since 1890*, ed. Barbara Melosh. New York: Routledge, 1993, pp. 43–71.

Michael, Robert T., John H. Gagnon, Edward O. Laumann, and Gina Kolata. *Sex in America: A Definitive Survey*. Boston: Little, Brown, 1994.

Miller, Jonathan. "Censorship and the Limits of Permission." *The Influence of Pornography on Behaviour*, ed. Maurice Yaffé and Edward C. Nelson. New York: Academic Press, 1982, pp. 27–46.

Miller, William. "Gender Mutability: The Provocation of Transgenderism (with a Passing Glance at *The Crying Game*." Paper delivered at the Nineteenth Annual Conference on Literature and Film, Florida State University, 27–29 January 1994.

Mitchell, Juliet, and Jacqueline Rose, eds. *Jacques Lacan and the Ecole Freudienne: Feminine Sexuality*. London: Macmillan, 1982.

Money, John. *Gay, Straight, and In-Between: The Sexology of Erotic Orientation*. New York: Oxford University Press, 1988.

———. "Recreational—and Procreational—Sex." *New York Times*, 13 September 1975, p. 21.

Money, John, and Patricia Tucker. *Sexual Signatures: On Being a Man or a Woman*. Boston: Little, Brown, 1975.

Montgomery, Kathryn C. *Target: Prime Time—Advocacy Groups and the Struggle over Entertainment Television*. New York: Oxford University Press, 1989.

Moore, David W. *The Superpollsters: How They Measure and Manipulate Public Opinion in America*. New York: Four Walls Eight Windows, 1992.

Moore, William Howard. *The Kefauver Committee and the Politics of Crime, 1950–1952*. Columbia: University of Missouri Press, 1974.

"More Gender Trouble: Feminism Meets Queer Theory." Special issue, ed. Naomi Schor and Elizabeth Weed. *differences*, 6:2/3 (1995).

Morgan, Edmund S. "The Puritans and Sex." *The New England Quarterly*, 15 (1942): 591–607.

Mosher, Clelia Duel. *The Mosher Survey: Sexual Attitudes of 45 Victorian Women*, ed. James Mahood and Kristine Wenberg. New York: Arno Press, 1980.

Murray, William. "The Porn Capital of America." *New York Times Magazine*, 3 January 1971, pp. 8, 25.

National Coalition against Censorship. *The Sex Panic: Women, Censorship, and "Pornography."* New York: National Coalition against Censorship, 1993.

National Opinion Research Center. *General Social Surveys, 1972–1989: Cumulative Codebook*. Storrs, CT: Roper Center for Public Opinion Research, 1989.

Nestle, Joan. "Butch–Femme Relationships: Sexual Courage in the 1950s." *A Restricted Country*. Ithaca, NY: Firebrand Books, 1987, pp. 100–109.

New England Watch and Ward Society. *Annual Reports*. Boston: New England Watch and Ward Society, 1905–1939.

New York Society for the Suppression of Vice. *Annual Reports*. New York: New York Society for the Suppression of Vice, 1874–1940.

———. *Names and Records of Persons Arrested under the Auspices of the Society: 1920–1950*. Library of Congress, Manuscript Division, Microfilm 19:359.

Nobile, Philip. "The Sex Survey Fraud." *Penthouse*, 9 (July 1978): 106–107.

Nobile, Philip, and Eric Nadler. *United States of America vs. Sex: How the Meese Commission Lied about Pornography*. New York: Minotaur Press, 1986.

Noll, John F. *Manual of the NODL*. Huntington, IN: Our Sunday Visitor Press, [1938?].

Noonan, John T. *Contraception: A History of Its Treatment by the Catholic Theologians and Canonists*. Cambridge: Belknap Press, 1966.

Oboler, Eli M. *The Fear of the Word: Censorship and Sex*. Metuchen, NJ: Scarecrow Press, 1974.

The Obscenity Report: The Report to the Task Force on Pornography and Obscenity. New York: Stein and Day, 1970.

O'Neill, William L., ed. *The American Sexual Dilemma*. New York: Holt, Rinehart, and Winston, 1972.

Ortner, Sherry B., and Harriet Whitehead, eds. *Sexual Meanings: The Cultural Construction of Gender and Sexuality*. New York: Cambridge University Press, 1981.

Osborn, Robert W. *Sex in Den U.S.A.: Zwischen Pruderie und Perversion*. Hamburg: Hans Lassen Verlag, 1966.

Packard, Vance. *The Sexual Wilderness: The Contemporary Upheaval in Male–Female Relationships*. New York: David McKay, 1968.

Padgug, Robert A. "Sexual Matters: On Conceptualizing Sexuality in History." *Radical History Review*, 20 (Spring–Summer 1979): 3–23.

Paletz, D. L. "Pornography, Politics, and the Press: The U.S. Attorney General's Commission on Pornography." *Journal of Communication*, 38:2 (Spring 1988): 122–135.

Pally, Marcia. *Sex and Sensibility: Reflections on Forbidden Mirrors and the Will to Censor*. Hopewell, NJ: Ecco Press, 1994.

Paper Tiger TV Collective. *Behind Censorship: The Assault on Civil Liberties*. New York: Deep Dish TV, 1992.

Parents Music Resource Center. "Statement before the Committee on Commerce, Science, and Transportation, U.S. Senate." *Taking Sides: Clashing Views on Con-

troversial Issues in Mass Media and Society, ed. Alison Alexander and Janice Hanson. 2d ed. Guilford, CT: Dushkin, 1993, pp. 70–74.

Parkes, Henry Bamford. "Morals and Law Enforcement in Colonial New England." *The New England Quarterly*, 5 (July 1932): 431–444.

Patai, Daphne. *Heterophobia: Sexual Harassment and the Future of Feminism*. Boston: Rowman and Littlefield, 1998.

Pearl, Cyril. *The Girl with the Swansdown Seat*. Indianapolis: Bobbs-Merrill, 1955.

Pearsall, Ronald. *The Worm in the Bud: The World of Victorian Sexuality*. New York: Macmillan, 1969.

Peiss, Kathy. *Cheap Amusements: Working Women and Leisure in Turn of the Century New York*. Philadelphia: Temple University Press, 1986.

Peiss, Kathy, and Christina Simmons, with Robert A. Padgug, eds. *Passion and Power: Sexuality in History*. Philadelphia: Temple University Press, 1989.

Penn, Donna. "The Meanings of Lesbianism in Postwar America." *Gender and American History since 1890*, ed. Barbara Melosh. New York: Routledge, 1993, pp. 106–124.

People for the American Way. http://www.pfaw.org.

Perkins, T. E. "Rethinking Stereotypes." *Ideology and Cultural Production*, ed. Michèle Barrett, Philip Corrigan, Annette Kuhn, and Janet Wolff. London: Croon Helm, 1979, pp. 135–159.

Perlman, Bernard. "A Century of Cincinnati Esthetics: From Fig Leaves to Fines." *New York Times*, 13 April 1990, A31.

Petersen, James R. "The Great Sex Survey Hoopla." *Playboy*, 42:2 (February 1995): 42–43.

———. "Playboy's History of the Sexual Revolution." *Playboy*, open-ended series beginning with the 43:12 (December 1996) issue.

Phelan, Shane. "(Be)Coming Out: Lesbian Identity in Politics." *Signs*, 18:4 (Summer 1993): 765–790.

———. *Identity Politics: Lesbian Feminism and the Limits of Community*. Philadelphia: Temple University Press, 1989.

Pietropinto, Anthony, and Jacqueline Simenauer. *Beyond the Male Myth: What Women Want to Know about Men's Sexuality: A Nationwide Survey*. New York: Times Books, 1977.

Pilat, Oliver, and Jo Ranson. *Sodom by the Sea: An Affectionate History of Coney Island*. Garden City, NY: Doubleday, Doran and Co., 1941.

Pivar, David J. *Purity Crusade: Sexual Morality and Social Control, 1868–1900*. Westport, CT: Greenwood Press, 1973.

Polhemus, Ted, and Housk Randall. *Rituals of Love: Sexual Experiments, Erotic Possibilities*. London: Picador, 1994.

Polsky, Ned. "On the Sociology of Pornography." *Hustlers, Beats, and Others*. Garden City, NY: Doubleday Anchor, 1969, pp. 183–200; rpt. Chicago: University of Chicago Press, 1985.

Popular Culture Association. Bowling Green State University, Bowling Green, OH 43403.

"The Porno Plague." *Time*, 5 April 1976, pp. 58–63.

Pornography: The Longford Report. London: Coronet, 1972.

"Pornography: A Poll." *Time*, 21 July 1986, p. 22.

Porter, Roy, and Lesley Hall. *The Facts of Life: The Creation of Sexual Knowledge in Britain, 1650–1950*. New Haven, CT: Yale University Press, 1995.

Porter, Roy, and Mikulás Teich, eds. *Sexual Knowledge, Sexual Science: The History of Attitudes to Sexuality*. Cambridge: Cambridge University Press, 1994.

President's Commission on Obscenity and Pornography. *Report of the Commission on Obscenity and Pornography*. Washington, DC: Government Printing Office, 1970.

———. *Technical Report*. 9 vols. Washington, DC: Government Printing Office, 1971–1972.

Preston, E. H. "Pornography and the Construction of Gender." *Cultivation Analysis: New Directions in Media Effects Research*, ed. Nancy Signorelli and M. Morgan. Newbury Park, CA: Sage, 1990, pp. 107–122.

Pringle, Henry F. *Big Frogs*. New York: Macy-Masius/Vanguard, 1928.

"Queer Theory." Special issue, ed. Teresa de Lauretis. *differences*, 3:2 (1991).

"Raid in Providence: Private Parts, Exhibit." *Art News*, 78 (January 1979): 10, 12, 14.

Randall, Housk. *Revelations: Chronicles and Visions from the Sexual Underworld*. London: Tim Woodward, 1993.

Rawson, Philip, ed. *Primitive Erotic Art*. New York: Putnam, 1973.

Raymond, Janice G. "Not a Sentimental Journey: Women's Friendships." *The Sexual Liberals and the Attack on Feminism*, ed. Dorchen Leidholdt and Janice G. Raymond. New York: Pergamon Press, 1990, pp. 222–226.

Reed, James. *From Private Vice to Public Virtue: The Birth Control Movement and American Society since 1830*. New York: Basic Books, 1978.

Reinisch, June with Ruth Beasley. *The Kinsey Institute New Report on Sex*. New York: St. Martin's Press, 1990.

Reiss, Ira L. *Journey into Sexuality: An Exploratory Voyage*. Englewood Cliffs, NJ: Prentice-Hall, 1986.

Reiss, Ira L., and Harriett M. Reiss. "The Stalled Sexual Revolutions of This Century." *An End to Shame: Shaping Our Next Sexual Revolution*. Buffalo, NY: Prometheus Books, 1990, pp. 83–104.

Rich, Adrienne. "Compulsory Heterosexuality and Lesbian Existence." *Signs*, 5 (Summer 1980): 631–660.

Richards, Abe, and Robert Irvine. *An Illustrated History of Pornography*. Los Angeles: Athena Books, 1968.

Rick, Karin, and Sylvia Treudel, eds. *Frauen, Gewalt, Pornographie: Dokumentation zum Symposium*. Vienna: Wiener Fruenverlag, 1989.

Ridley, Matt. *The Red Queen: Sex and the Evolution of Human Nature*. New York: Macmillan, 1994.

Rimm, Martin. "Marketing Pornography on the Information Superhighway: A Survey of 917,410 Images, Descriptions, Short Stories, and Animations Downloaded 8.5 Million Times by Consumers in over 2000 Cities in Forty Countries, Provinces, and Territories." *Georgetown Law Review*, 83 (June 1995): 1849–1958.

Robinson, Frank, and Nat Lehrman, eds. *Sex American Style*. Chicago: Playboy Press, 1971.

Rockefeller, Abby. "Sex: The Basis of Sexism." *No More Fun and Games: A Journal of Female Liberation*, no. 6 (May 1973): 25–31.

Rodgers, Harrell R. "Censorship Campaigns in Eighteen Cities: An Impact Analysis." *American Politics Quarterly*, 2 (October 1974): 371–392.

Roof, Judith. *A Lure of Knowledge: Lesbian Sexuality and Theory*. New York: Columbia University Press, 1991.

Rosenberg, Bernard, and David Manning White, eds. *Mass Culture: The Popular Arts in America*. Glencoe, IL: Free Press, 1957.

Rosenberg, Rosalind. *Beyond Separate Spheres: Intellectual Roots of Modern Feminism*. New Haven, CT: Yale University Press, 1982.

Rousseau, George, and Roy Porter, eds. *Sexual Underworlds of the Enlightenment*. Chapel Hill: University of North Carolina Press, 1988.

Rowland, Willard D., Jr. *The Politics of TV Violence: Policy Uses of Communication Research*. Beverly Hills, CA: Sage, 1983.

Rowley, Christopher. "Pressure Groups Are a Fact of Life." *Mass Media and the Popular Arts*, ed. Frederic Rissover and David C. Birch. New York: McGraw-Hill, 1983, pp. 301–306.

Rubin, Gayle. "Thinking Sex: Notes for a Radical Theory of the Politics of Sexuality." *Pleasure and Danger: Exploring Female Sexuality*, ed. Carole S. Vance. Boston: Routledge and Kegan Paul, 1984, pp. 267–319.

———. "The Traffic in Women: Notes on the 'Political Economy' of Sex." *Toward an Anthropology of Women*, ed. Rayna R. Reiter. New York: Monthly Review Press, 1975, pp. 157–210.

Rubin, Lillian B. *Erotic Wars: What Happened to the Sexual Revolution?* New York: Farrar, Straus, and Giroux, 1990.

Rugoff, Milton. *Prudery and Passion: Sexuality in Victorian America*. New York: Putnam, 1971.

Russ, Joanna. *Magic Mommas, Trembling Sisters, Puritans and Perverts: Feminist Essays*. Trumansburg, NY: Crossing Press, 1985.

Russell, Diana E. H. "Nadine Strossen: The Pornography Industry's Wet Dream." *On the Issues*, 4 (Summer 1995): 32–34.

———, ed. *Making Violence Sexy: Feminist Views on Pornography*. New York: Teachers College Press, 1993.

Russett, Cynthia Eagle. *Sexual Science: The Victorian Construction of Womanhood*. Cambridge: Harvard University Press, 1989.

Russo, Ann. "Conflicts and Contradictions among Feminists over Issues of Pornography and Sexual Freedom." *Women's Studies International Forum*, 10 (1987): 103–112.

Rust, Paula C. *Bisexuality and the Challenge to Lesbian Politics: Sex, Loyalty, and Revolution*. New York: New York University Press, 1995.

Rutherford, Jonathan, and Rowena Chapman, eds. *Male Order: Unwrapping Masculinity*. London: Lawrence and Wishart, 1988.

Rutledge, Leigh W. *The Gay Decades from Stonewall to the Present: The People and Events That Shaped Gay Lives*. New York: Plume, 1992.

Sadownick, Douglas. *Sex between Men: An Intimate History of the Sex Lives of Gay Men Postwar to Present*. San Francisco: Harper/San Francisco, 1997.

Sante, Luc. *Low Life: Lures and Snares of Old New York*. New York: Farrar, Straus, and Giroux, 1991.

Sarch, Amy. "Those Dirty Ads! Birth Control Advertising in the 1920s and 1930s." *Critical Studies in Mass Communication*, 14 (1997): 49–76.

Scheer, Robert. "Ed Meese's Dirty Pictures." *Thinking Tuna Fish, Talking Death: Essays on the Pornography of Power*. New York: Hill and Wang, 1988, pp. 63–85.

Schidrowitz, Leo, ed. *Sittengeschichte der Kulturwelt und ihrer Entwicklung in Einzeldarstellungen*. 10 vols. and supplement to vol. II. Vienna/Leipzig: Verlag für

Kulturforschung, 1926–1930. I: *Sittengeschichte des Intimen: Bett, Korsett, Hemd, Hose, Bad, Abtritt, Die Geschichte und Entwicklung der intimen Gebrauchsgegenstände* (1926); II: *Sittengeschichte des Lasters: die Kulturepochen und ihre Leidenschaften* (1927), and *Ergänzungsband* (1927); III: *Sittengeschichte von Paris: die Grosstadt, ihe Sitten und ihre Unsittlichkeit* (1926); IV: *Sittengeschichte des Proletariats: des Weg vom Leibes-zum Maschinensklaven, die sittliche Stellung und Haltung des Proletariats* (1926); V: *Sittengeschichte des Theaters. Ein Darstellung des Theaters, seiner Entwicklung und Stellung in zwei Jahrhunderten* (1926); VI: *Sittengeschichte der Liebkosung und Strafe. Die Zärtlichkeitsworte, Gesten und Handlungen der Kulturmenschheit und ihr Gegenpol der Strenge* (1928); VII: *Sittengeschichte des Geheimen und Verbotenen. Eine Darstellung der geheimen und verborgen gehaltenen Leidenschaften der Menschheit, die Einstellung der Staatsgewalt zum Geschlechtsleben der Gesellschaft* (1930); VIII: *Sittengeschichte des Hafens und der Reise. Eine Beleuchtung des erotischen Lebens in der Hafenstadt, im Hotel, im Reisevehikel. Die Sexualität des Kulturmenschen während des Reisens in fremden Milieu* (1927): IX: *Sittengeschichte der Revolution, Sittenlockerung und Sittenverfall. Moralgesetze und sexualethische Neuorientierung in Zeiten staatlicher Zersetzung und revolutionären Umsturzes* (1930); X: *Sittengeschichte des Intimsten. Intime Toilette. Mode und Kosmetik im Dienst und Erotik* (1929).

Schlesinger, Benjamin, ed. *Sexual Behaviour in Canada: Patterns and Problems.* Toronto: University of Toronto Press, 1977.

Schneider, Herbert, and George Lawton. *A Prophet and a Pilgrim.* New York: Columbia University Press, 1942.

Schoofs, Mark. "Beat It: The City's Moral Fixation: Pushing Porn Out of Town." *Village Voice,* 27 June 1995, pp. 14–16.

Schur, Edwin M. *Labeling Women Deviant: Gender, Stigma, and Social Control.* New York: Random House, 1984.

———. *The Politics of Deviance.* Englewood Cliffs, NJ: Prentice-Hall, 1980.

Scott, Claude L. *The Science of Pornography.* San Diego: Greenleaf Classics, 1970.

Scott, Joan W. "Gender: A Useful Category for Historical Analysis." *American Historical Review,* 91 (1986): 1053–1075.

Sears, Hal D. *The Sex Radicals: Free Love in Victorian America.* Lawrence: Regents Press of Kansas, 1977.

Segal, Jay. *The Sex Lives of College Students.* Philadelphia: Miles Standish Press, 1984.

Segal, Lynne. *Straight Sex: Rethinking the Politics of Pleasure.* Berkeley: University of California Press, 1994.

Seidman, Steven. *Romantic Longings: Love in America. 1830–1980.* New York: Routledge, 1991.

Seldes, Gilbert. *The Stammering Century.* New York: Harper and Row, 1965.

Senelick, Laurence. "Private Parts in Public Places." *Inventing Times Square: Commerce and Culture at the Crossroads of the World,* ed. W. R. Taylor. Baltimore: Johns Hopkins University Press, 1996, pp. 329–353.

Sheinfeld, Lois P. "Anti-Obscenity Ordinances: Banning Porn, the New Censorship." *Nation,* 8 (September 1984): 174–175.

Sherman, Allan. *The Rape of the APE (American Puritan Ethic): the Official History of the Sex Revolution, 1945–1973: the Obscening of America, an RSVP (Redeeming Social Value Pornography) Document.* Chicago: Playboy Press, 1973.

Shorter, Edward. *A History of Women's Bodies*. New York: Basic Books, 1982.

Showalter, Elaine. *Sexual Anarchy: Gender and Culture at the Fin de Siècle*. New York: Viking, 1990.

SIECUS (Sex Information and Education Council of the United States). *Sexuality and the Aging: A Selective Bibliography*. 32 Washington Place, New York City 10003, 1976.

Siegel, Carol, and Ann Kibbey, eds. *Eroticism and Containment: Notes from the Flood Plain*. (Issue # 20 of *Genders*.) New York: New York University Press, 1994.

Simmons, Christina. "Modern Sexuality and the Myth of Victorian Repression." *Passion and Power: Sexuality in History*, ed. Kathy Peiss and Christina Simmons. Philadelphia: Temple University Press, 1989, pp. 157–177; rpt. *Gender and American History since 1890*, ed. Barbara Melosh. New York: Routledge, 1993, pp. 17–42.

Simpson, Mark. *It's a Queer World: Deviant Adventures in Pop Culture*. Binghamton, NY: Haworth Press, 1998.

Slade, Joseph W. "Thomas Lake Harris (1823–1906)." *The Markham Review*, 1:4 (February 1969): 5–11.

Smith, Bradley. *The American Way of Sex: An Informal Illustrated History*. New York: Gemini Smith, 1978.

Smith, Stephen A. "Freedom of Expression in Native American Constitutions." *Journal of Communication Inquiry*, 15:1 (Winter 1991): 23–42.

Smith, Tom. "The Use of Public Opinion Data by the Attorney General's Commission on Pornography." *Public Opinion Quarterly*, 51 (1987): 249–267.

Sorokin, Pitirim. *The American Sex Revolution*. Boston: Porter Sargent, 1956.

Spanier, Graham B., ed. *Human Sexuality in a Changing Society*. Minneapolis: Burgess, 1979.

Springhall, John. *Youth, Popular Culture and Moral Panics: Penny Gaffs to Gangsta Rap, 1830–1996*. New York: St. Martin's Press, 1999.

Stanley, Liz. *Sex Surveyed, 1949–1994: From Mass-Observation's "Little Kinsey" to the National Survey and the Hite Reports*. Bristol, PA: Taylor and Francis, 1995.

Starker, Steven. *Evil Influences: Crusades against the Mass Media*. New Brunswick, NJ: Transaction, 1989.

State of New York. *Report of Joint Legislative Committee Studying Publication of and Dissemination of Offensive and Obscene Materials*. Albany: New York State Printing Office, 1956.

———. *Report of the New York State Joint Legislative Committee to Study the Publication and Dissemination of Offensive and Obscene Material*. New York: New York State Printing Office, 1966.

Stein, Edward P., ed. *Forms of Desire: Sexual Orientation and the Social Constructionist Controversy*. New York: Routledge, 1992.

Stein, Joel. "Porn Goes Mainstream." *Time*, 152:10, 7 September 1998, pp. 54–55.

Stengel, Richard. "The Sex Busters." *Time*, 21 July 1986, pp. 12–18, 21.

Stoehr, Taylor. *Free Love in America: A Documentary History*. New York: AMS Press, 1979.

Stoller, Robert J. *Presentations of Gender*. New Haven, CT: Yale University Press, 1985.

Sullivan, Mark. *Our Times: The United States, 1900–1925*. 6 vols. New York: Scribner's 1926–1933.

Sunderland, Lane V. *Obscenity: The Court, the Congress and the President's Commis-

sion. Washington, DC: American Enterprise Institute for Public Policy Research, 1975.

Symons, Donald. *The Evolution of Human Sexuality.* New York: Oxford University Press, 1979.

Talese, Gay. *Thy Neighbor's Wife.* New York: Dell, 1981.

Tannahill, Reay. *Sex in History.* New York: Stein and Day, 1988.

Tavris, Carol, and Susan Sadd. *The Redbook Report on Female Sexuality.* New York: Dell, 1975, and Delacorte, 1977.

Taylor, Gordon R. *Sex in History.* New York: Vanguard, 1954, 1970.

Taylor, Stuart. "Pornography Foes Lose New Weapon in Supreme Court." *New York Times,* 25 February 1986, A1, A26.

Taylor, W. R., ed. *Inventing Times Square: Commerce and Culture at the Crossroads of the World.* Baltimore: Johns Hopkins University Press, 1996.

Terry, Jennifer. "Theorizing Deviant Historiography." *differences,* 3 (1991): 55–75.

Thompson, Bill. *Soft Core: Moral Crusades against Pornography in Britain and America.* New York: Cassell, 1994.

Tiefer, Leonore. *Sex Is Not a Natural Act and Other Essays.* Boulder, CO: Westview Press, 1995.

Tierney, William G. *Academic Outlaws: Queer Theory and Cultural Studies in the Academy.* Thousand Oaks, CA: Sage, 1997.

Tuchman, Barbara W. *A Distant Mirror: The Calamitous Fourteenth Century.* New York: Knopf, 1978.

Tucker, Naomi S. *Bisexual Politics: Theories, Queries, and Visions.* Binghamton, NY: Haworth Press, 1995.

Twitchell, James B. *Carnival Culture: The Trashing of Taste in America.* New York: Columbia University Press, 1993.

Ullman, Sharon R. *Sex Seen: The Emergence of Modern Sexuality in America.* Berkeley: University of California Press, 1998.

United Nations. *Agreement for the Suppression of the Circulation of Obscene Publications, Signed at Paris on 4 May 1910/Amended by the Protocol Signed at Lake Success, New York, 4 May 1949.* Lake Success, NY: United Nations, 1950.

U.S. Congress. House Committee on Education and Labor, Select Subcommittee on Education. *Creating a Subcommittee on Obscenity and Pornography.* Washington, DC: Government Printing Office, 1967.

———. House Committee on Energy and Commerce. *Telephone Decency Act of 1987: Hearing on H. R. 1786 before the Subcommittee on Telecommunications and Finance of the House Committee on Energy and Commerce.* 100th Congress, 1st session. Washington, DC: Government Printing Office, 1987.

———. House Committee on Government Operations, Government Activities Subcommittee. *Use of the Postal Service for the Unsolicited Advertisement of Hard-Core Pornographic or Otherwise Obscene Materials.* Hearings: July 8, 1969. Washington, DC: Government Printing Office, 1969.

———. House Committee on Post Office and Civil Service, Postal Operations Subcommittee. *Obscene Matter Sent through the Mail.* Washington, DC: Government Printing Office, 1959.

———. House Committee on the Judiciary. *Anti-Obscenity Legislation: Hearings on*

H. R. 5171, H. R. 11009, H. R. 11031, H. R. 11032 and Related Measures. Washington, DC: Government Printing Office, 1970.

———. House Select Committee on Current Pornographic Materials. *Hearings before the Select Committee of the House of Representatives on Current Pornographic Materials.* Washington, DC: Government Printing Office, 1952; *Report.* Washington, DC: Government Printing Office, 1953.

———. House Subcommittee on Communications of the Committee on Interstate and Foreign Commerce. *Hearings on Sex and Violence on Television.* Washington, DC: Government Printing Office, 1976, 1977.

———. House Subcommittee on Criminal Law. *Cable Porn and Dial-a-Porn Control Act: Hearing before the Subcommittee on Criminal Law of the Committee on the Judiciary.* 99th Congress, 2d session. Washington, DC: Government Printing Office, 1986.

———. House Subcommittee on Postal Operations. *Circulation of Obscene and Pornographic Material.* Hearings. Washington, DC: Government Printing Office, 1960.

———. House Subcommittee on the Post Office and Post Roads. *Hearings.* Washington, DC: Government Printing Office, 1935.

———. Senate Committee on the Judiciary. *Pornography Victims Compensation Act of 1992: Report Together with Additional and Minority Views (to Accompany S. 1521).* Washington, DC: Government Printing Office, 1992.

———. Senate Subcommittee on Constitutional Amendments and Subcommittee to Investigate Juvenile Delinquency. *Control of Obscene Material.* Washington, DC: Government Printing Office, 1960.

———. Senate Subcommittee on Postal Operations. *Obscene Matter Sent through the Mail.* Hearings. Washington, DC: Government Printing Office, 1959.

———. Senate Subcommittee on Security and Terrorism. *The Use of Computers to Transmit Material Inciting Crime: Hearing before the Subcommittee on Security and Terrorism of the Committee on the Judiciary, U.S. Senate.* 99th Congress, 1st session. Washington, DC: Government Printing Office, 1985.

———. Senate Subcommittee to Investigate Juvenile Delinquency. *Hearings before the Senate Subcommittee to Investigate Juvenile Delinquency (Obscene and Pornographic Materials).* Washington, DC: Government Printing Office, 1954–1955; *Obscene and Pornographic Literature and Juvenile Delinquency: Interim Report.* Washington, DC: Government Printing Office, 1956; *Juvenile Delinquency* (Final Report). Washington, DC: Government Printing Office, 1957; rpt. *Juvenile Delinquency: Comic Books, Motion Pictures, Obscene and Pornographic Materials, Television Programs.* Westport, CT: Greenwood Press, 1969.

Ussher, Jane M. *Fantasies of Femininity: Reframing the Boundaries of Sex.* New Brunswick, NJ: Rutgers University Press, 1998.

Vance, Carole S. "Gender Systems, Ideology, and Sex Research." *Powers of Desire: The Politics of Sexuality*, ed. Ann Snitow, Christine Stansell, and Sharon Thompson. New York: Monthly Review Press, 1983, pp. 371–384.

———. "Negotiating Sex and Gender in the Attorney General's Commission on Pornography." *Pleasure and Danger: Exploring Female Sexuality*, ed. Carole S. Vance. Boston: Routledge and Kegan Paul, 1984, pp. 29–49.

———. "Pleasure and Danger: Toward a Politics of Sexuality." *Pleasure and Danger:*

Exploring Female Sexuality, ed. Carole S. Vance. Boston: Routledge and Kegan Paul, 1984, pp. 1–27.

———. "Porn in the U.S.A.: The Meese Commission on the Road." *The Nation*, 243 (2–9 August 1986): 1, 76–82.

Voget, Fred W. "Sex Life of the American Indians." *Encyclopedia of Sexual Behavior*, ed. Albert Ellis and Albert Abarbanel. New York: Hawthorne, 1961, pp. 90–109.

Vries, Leonard de, and Peter Fryer. *Venus Unmasked, Or an Inquiry into the Nature and Origin of the Passion of Love*. London: Barker, 1967.

Wagner, Peter. "Eros Goes West: European and 'Homespun' Erotica in Eighteenth-Century America." *The Transit of Civilization from Europe to America: Essays in Honor of Hans Galinsky*, ed. Winfried Herget and Karl Ortseifer. Tübingen: G. Narr, 1986, pp. 145–165.

———. "Erotica in Early America." *Eros Revived: Erotica of the Enlightenment in England and America*. London: Secker and Warburg, 1988, pp. 292–302.

———. *Erotica and the Enlightenment*, ed. Peter Wagner. New York: Peter Lang, 1991.

Waldberg, Patrick. *Eros in la Belle Epoque*. Paris: Pauvert, 1964; rpt. *Eros Modern Style*, trans. Helen R. Lane. New York: Grove Press, 1969.

Walker, Samuel. *In Defense of American Liberties: A History of the ACLU*. New York: Oxford University Press, 1990.

Walkowitz, Judith R. "Male Vice and Female Virtue: Feminism and the Politics of Prostitution in Nineteenth-Century Britain." *Powers of Desire: The Politics of Sexuality*, ed. Ann Snitow, Christine Stansell, and Sharon Thompson. New York: Monthly Review Press, 1983, pp. 419–438.

Walters, Ronald G. "The Erotic South: Civilization and Sexuality in American Abolitionism," *American Quarterly*, 25 (May 1973): 177–201.

"The War against Pornography." *Newsweek*, 18 March 1985, pp. 58–62.

Watney, Simon. *Policing Desire: Pornography, AIDS, and the Media*. Minneapolis: University of Minnesota Press, 1987; London: Methuen, 1987.

Weeks, Jeffrey. *Against Nature: Essays on History, Sexuality and Identity*. London: Rivers Oram Press, 1991.

———. *Sex, Politics, and Society: The Regulation of Sexuality since 1800*. 2d ed. New York: Longman, 1989.

Weeks, Jeffrey, and J. Holland, eds. *Sexual Cultures: Communities, Values, and Intimacy*. London: Macmillan, 1996.

Weideger, Paula. *History's Mistress: A New Interpretation of a 19th-Century Ethnographic Classic*. New York: Penguin Books, 1986.

Weinberg, Martin S., Colin J. Williams, and Douglas W. Pryor. *Dual Attraction: Understanding Bisexuality*. New York: Oxford University Press, 1994.

Wheeler, David L. "Explaining the Discrepancies in Sex Surveys: Men's, Women's Responses Differ." *Chronicle of Higher Education*, 27 October 1993, A9.

White, Kevin. *The First Sexual Revolution: The Emergence of Male Heterosexuality in Modern America*. New York: New York University Press, 1992.

Williams, Walter L. *The Spirit and the Flesh: Sexual Diversity in American Indian Culture*. Boston: Beacon Press, 1986.

Wilton, Tamsin. *Lesbian Studies: Setting an Agenda*. New York: Routledge, 1995.

Wittig, Monique. *The Lesbian Body*, trans. David le Vay. Boston: Beacon, 1986.

Womongold, Marcia. "From Pornography: A License to Kill." *Fight Back: A Resource*

Book on Feminist Resistance to Male Violence, ed. Frédérique Delacoste and Felice Newman. Minneapolis: Cleis Press, 1981, pp. 238–241.

World Pornography Conference. www.paganpleasures.com/wrldporn.htm.

Wray, Herbert. "Is Porn Un-American?" *U.S. News and World Report*, 5 July 1995, pp. 51–54.

Wright, P., and A. Treacher, eds. *The Problem of Medical Knowledge: Examining the Social Construction of Medicine*. Edinburgh: Edinburgh University Press, 1982.

Wright, Robert. *The Moral Animal: Evolutionary Psychology and Everyday Life*. New York: Pantheon, 1994.

Yarrow, Phillip. *Fighting the Debauchery of Our Girls and Boys*. Chicago: Illinois Vigilance Association, 1923.

Young, Wayland. *Eros Denied: Sex in Western Society*. New York: Grove Press, 1964.

Zappa, Frank. "Statement before the Committee on Commerce, Science, and Transportation, U.S. Senate." *Taking Sides: Clashing Views on Controversial Issues in Mass Media and Society*, ed. Alison Alexander and Janice Hanson. 2d ed. Guilford, CT: Dushkin, 1993, pp. 75–82.

Zillman, Dolf, and Jennings Bryant, eds. *Pornography: Research Advances and Policy Considerations*. Hillsdale, NJ: Lawrence Erlbaum Associates, 1989.

Zurcher, Louis A., Jr., and R. George Kirkpatrick. *Citizens for Decency: Antipornography Crusades as Status Defense*. Austin: University of Texas Press, 1976.

6

Theoretical Works on Erotica and Pornography

An index of pornography's cultural significance is its power to generate endless comment. There is hardly a minister in America who has not preached at least one sermon on the evils of porn, and, fortunately, no one has ever tried to list them all. Even discounting that particular category, however, the scholar will quickly realize that most "serious" comment is superficial, tendentious, prurient, mistaken, and uninformed, often all at the same time. Vagueness is not merely widespread; it is essential to a mode of discourse that would be severely constrained were everyone to agree even on a single example of pornography. As always, we should remember the opening of D. H. Lawrence's essay, "Pornography and Obscenity": "What [pornography and obscenity] are depends, as usual, entirely on the individual. What is pornography to one man is the laughter of genius to another" (69).

PORNOGRAPHY AS SEXUAL FOLKLORE

Writing about pornography is appealing for several reasons. One is that the writer need make no investment in facts and thus is free to conjecture. Another is the freedom to define pornography as one wishes, a circumstance made possible by the certainty that the term means something different to almost everyone. The unaware reader will be startled to find buried in a note appended to a study of pornography the revelation that the researcher based his or her conclusions on an analysis of the reader's favorite network television show or record album or blue jeans advertisement, items that the reader has never thought of as arousing. For example, in *For Adult Users Only: The Dilemma of Violent Pornography*, edited by Susan Gubar and Joan Hoff, Gubar routinely cites as pornographic films such as David Lynch's *Blue Velvet* and artists such as Magritte. Such instances remind us not only that antiporn sentiment depends, to a large degree, on avoiding precision and fostering confusion but also indicate that many attacks on pornography have little to do with pornography per se. Rather, they are about personal attitudes toward sexuality, about the need for control, about the desire to make the world a coherent, if sometimes tepid place. In "A Personal View of the History of the Lesbian S/M Community and Movement in San Francisco," Pat Califia recalls that the first national conference of Women against Violence in Pornography and the Media (San Francisco, 1978) featured an "educational" slide show:

I was frightened by the sexual ignorance of the presenters and their willingness to exploit the audience's sexual prejudices to win converts. The images were presented in a manipulative way. Bondage photos were followed by police shots of battered women. S/M porn was repeatedly taken out of context and labeled as "violent," even though it looked like consensual S/M to me. Record album covers and fashion advertisements were lumped in with the pornography. Nothing was dated and few sources were cited, so the audience had no idea how representative the material was of porn you could actually go see and buy. The presenters kept assuring us that much, much worse material was available. Their definition of porn was circular and sloppy. They defined any sexist or violent image as pornography, then turned around and used that assumption to "prove" that all pornography was sexist or violent. Lesbian sexuality was not discussed. Some vague distinction was made between "erotica" and "porn," but no examples of "erotica" were shown. This made me especially uncomfortable since many heterosexuals were present, and one of the favorite images of "violent" pornography was soft-core, glossy images of women kissing or going down on each other. (254–255)

In *Sapphistry: The Book of Lesbian Sexuality*, Califia says the argument cuts both ways. She points out that some erotica "is full of misinformation about sex. It often portrays women as the victims of violence or coercion and implies that women are not serious when they refuse sexual advances and that they enjoy being forced into sex. Some of it portrays children or animals being used in exploitive ways" (15). At the same time, reading an essay by Andrea Dworkin may leave males and females confused as to *what* pornography Dworkin is describing in terms of degradation and abuse, when they are thinking of a hardcore film in which there is *no* overt violence and in which women seem to be idealized. The most strident feminist critiques of pornography may actually reinforce the cruder male fantasies. Both porn and antiporn are reductionist and sometimes mean-spirited: both promote stereotypes (the one of females, the other of males) as sources of pleasure to their consumers. Deciding which version of the world is nastier can be difficult.

Many feminist, antiporn advocates take the world of pornotopia depicted in (some) pornography as *fact*, not fantasy: they envision men as erect penises stalking women across an eroticized landscape, spurting semen at every step. Much of this confusion may be attributable to gender difference, augmented by variations in the age, religion, and ethnicity of the audience. Gender fears and desires may be socially constructed, may at root be just folklore, but we experience them as real enough. Men can no more comprehend the fear that forced sex holds for women than women can comprehend the fear of the hive that drives men to dreams of wild sex.

A critical commonplace notes that erotic scenarios typically cast the participants as a single gender: straight, male-oriented pornography depicts females as insatiable and aggressive; straight, female-oriented pornography depicts males as caring and tender; gay, male-oriented varieties depict heterosexual males as secretly homoerotic; lesbian-oriented genres, now coalescing, depict women as drawn inevitably toward their own reflections. Such visions are destabilizing and therefore titillating in a social order often *felt* as fragile and artificial. While some viewers may experience the gender reduction in an unfamiliar genre as oppressive, the impulse to mirror obviously stems as much from the need for sharing of fantasies as it does from the need to objectify desire. The anthropologist Carole S. Vance, one of the most astute critics of porn, insists on the ambiguity of the messages carried by male-oriented, heterosexual pornography. On one hand, she says, pornography subordinates females to male desire; on the other, it urges sexual autonomy on women.[1] Everyone wishes to validate his or her vision of sexuality; everyone wishes to see it reciprocated. As Vance and other feminist critics careful to note the difference between mere sexism and real aggression have pointed out, it is facile to assume that pornography exists merely to degrade and subordinate women. First and foremost, pornography is communication; pornographers want to establish at least a semblance of community that compels assent to a common folklore.

The same courtesy can be extended to the genres of antiporn, whose proponents want to shore up their identities against the deliquescence of a morality they know to be fragile or to right wrongs against their class, gender, religion, ethnic group, or some other community to which they wish to belong. Porn and antiporn both resist logic and are, in fact, the means by which we celebrate the mysteries of sexuality and gender, of the animal affinities and spiritual aspirations of human beings. Porn and antiporn complement each other in ways too deep fully to understand. In virtually all these instances, however, unarticulated sexual assumptions impede, rather than foster, communication.

We have recourse to pornography *and* antipornography rhetoric because we cannot speak intelligibly about sexuality itself, a subject that is mysterious, frightening, and exhilarating. Much of what we think we "know" about sex is merely folklore, that is, narratives and stories that embody the myths and stereotypes that constitute our sexual awareness. Much of what we think we "know" about pornography devolves on endorsing, rejecting, or sanitizing these stories and the tropes that shape them. In a very real sense, says Joan Nestle, we know sexuality in the final analysis *as* pornography: our experience, if not our understanding, of sex is at base inevitably and unavoidably pornographic—because fantasy, the upwelling of our erotic imaginations, is always present. Nestle's "My Mother Liked to Fuck," a stunning chapter in her book *A Re-*

stricted Country, pleads for the necessity for sexual communication. Nestle and other writers note that any pornographic work is someone's fantasy and therefore an attempt to communicate; the proper response is to find fantasies to share, not to censor, which makes communication impossible. The problem, of course, is that we like to believe that pornography is always the imagination of an *other*, not our own; aligning the contours of so many fantasies is difficult, especially when our senses of morality, aesthetics, or political justice prescribe "acceptable" sexual behavior. Our own erotic templates, constructed from cultural and personal fetishes, will inevitably resist the fantasies of those in different educational, political, and social categories.

Folklorists have begun the daunting task of unearthing the oral themes and motifs whose traces glow in every porn genre (see **Obscenity and Orality** in chapter 15). Foolish husbands, cheating wives, cunning tricksters, wise whores, sexual braggarts, farmers' daughters, traveling salesmen, hypocritical preachers, dishonest politicians, and so on can be found in adult videotapes and on the Internet, along with enormous genitals, vagina dentatas, amusing fetishes, salacious jokes, and various sexual itches that can sometimes be scratched. Feminists and minorities struggle to replace dominant folklore with their own—a similar mix of fact and fantasy—a process we call rewriting history to make it more "accurate," at least until future generations make *their* revisions. Beliefs that pornography is the exclusive domain of Jews, of the French, of the vulgar (or, conversely, the higher classes), of men, of the psychologically impaired, or of criminals are similar to convictions that all spouses cheat on their partners, that blacks are more sexually active, that all men are rapists at heart, that all women "really want it," that women are incapacitated by premenstrual syndrome (PMS), that women who star in porn movies are drugged, that Asians have tighter vaginas, or that masturbation causes acne or blindness, whether we call such myths folklore, genderlore, grouplore, or classlore.

One of the most important insights of the current debate is an observation made by Chuck Kleinhans and Julia Lesage in "The Politics of Sexual Representation." They point out that the feminist, antiporn position is intellectually weak because "feminism has not developed a generally accepted theory of sexuality" (26) on which to base interpretations of sexual materials. Feminists are hardly alone in this regard: human sexuality is still unknown territory for all of us. Its mystery is a constant in our personal and collective experience. Kleinhans and Lesage are aware that few Americans of any description agree on sexual norms; the danger, they think, lies in a group's pretending that its folklore constitutes a coherent, let alone a "correct" view. Our "knowledge" of sex is skewed by politics, upbringing, education, personal taste, class, and race, which warp our sexual representations and skew our reactions to them. Steven Seidman's *Embattled Eros; Sexual Politics and Ethics in Contemporary America* echoes that refrain. Seidman theorizes that what constitutes sexual normality must be revised for every generation and, as such, is constructed by cultural parameters; pornography is an example of that construction (97–103).

RELIGIOUS POSITIONS ON PORNOGRAPHY

A compilation of the enormous number of religious texts on sexuality in the United States is impossible. Leaving aside the huge market for religious material in America—the output of religious publishing houses dwarfs the volume of pornography generated annually and, like pornography, goes out of print fairly rapidly to make room for more—the principal reason is that religious comment on pornography is usually folded into discourses on spiritual well-being or the lack thereof. Some of the screeds are easily lampooned because they reduce to the author's claims that only God knows how to deal with the nastiness of sex, and only the author knows what is on God's mind. Common to the thoughtful critiques, however, are revulsion toward graphically depicted sex, perceived threats to fragile family values, and fears that pornography is a profanation of the sacred. Other arguments are based on Protestant convictions concerning the sanctity of a marketplace that is corrupted when sex becomes commodified.

The more flamboyant the minister, the more likely he is to target pornography. Among the notable outpourings of celebrity preachers are Don Wildmon's *The Case against Pornography*, which views eroticism as a conflation of satanism and secularism. Jimmy Swaggart's *Rape of a Nation*, which calls pornography profoundly un-American (a somewhat ironic characterization, given Swaggart's documented fondness for pornographic magazines); and Jerry Falwell's *Listen, America!*, which includes pornography in a scattergun attack on the minister's favorite evils. *Moral Majority Report*, the newsletter of Wildmon's organization, regularly inveighs against a salaciousness the editors believe has infected American media. Richard Viguerie complains that sex drenches all the media and that the fundamentalist groups will do something about it once they gather their political strength, in *The New Right: We're Ready to Lead*. John H. Court's *Pornography: A Christian Critique* and Harold Jantz's *On Pornography* are typical, unremarkable, and predictable religious positions. The Catholic Church's official guide for Americans, *Pornography and Violence in the Communications Media: A Pastoral Response*, condemns pornography, especially when linked with violence, as a dehumanizing and secularizing force.

Perry C. Cotham's *Obscenity, Pornography and Censorship* attacks porn both explicit and "pious" (e.g., material espousing liberal sexual attitudes) as an attack on privacy, Christian idealism, and human dignity; the text includes study questions. John Drakeford and Jack Hamm, in *Pornography: The Sexual Mirage*, suggest that pornography damages traditional American values, especially those centered around the family, that it degrades and depersonalizes, and that it commercializes and publicizes what ought to be private; they offer strategies to enable concerned groups to combat sexually oriented media. Pornography as cultural toxin is the theme of Jerry Kirk's *The Mind Polluters*, which says that demeaning sexual material is a cancer on the body politic, and James Robinson's *Pornography, the Polluting of America*, in which the author tries to distance himself from the theory that pornography is the consequence of a communist plot "to contaminate America," only to conclude that pornography is really "an instrument of Satan" himself (59). Clodaugh Corcoran's *Pornography: The New Terrorism* is shrill; Corcoran sees a liberal, humanist, secular conspiracy behind porn's destructive effects on social bonds. Although he levels many of his charges against American pornography, he is particularly worried about sexual infection overtaking Ireland. This phenomenon, the fear that America's licentiousness will overwhelm other countries (an inversion of long-held American beliefs that corruption came from the Old World), also animates Edmund L. Dearn's *Pornography Degrades*, a volume whose principal concern is the moral well-being of Australia. Dearn rejects the notion that pornography is "victimless" and believes that suppressing the foul utterances of a minority will enhance the freedom of the majority.

David Alexander Scott's *Pornography: Its Effects on the Family, Community, and Culture* asserts that pornography destroys social and family stability, especially by undermining the institution of marriage, and parts company with those feminist, antiporn groups that do not condemn homosexuals, who seem particularly evil to him. Some of the essays in Tom Minnery's *Pornography: A Human Tragedy* do cover people's unpleasant experiences with sexual explicitness, the least of which is loss of innocence, though cynics will find it difficult not to chuckle at the earnestness of the book's tone. The most hyperbolic of all critiques is David Mura's *A Male Grief: Notes on Pornography and Addiction*, which attributes to pornography an enormous power. In fact, Mura says, pornography is as stimulating and addictive as chemical narcotics, though it is sometimes difficult to know exactly what he considers pornographic. A similar charge, delivered visually, can be found in James C. Dobson's "Pornography: Addictive, Progressive and Deadly," a videotape aimed at young people by a Christian organization. The principal metaphor of *Pornography's Victims*, edited by Phyllis Schlafly, is a society under siege, with victims everywhere: children, women, men, religious institutions, the capitalist economy, possibly the entire Western way of life. Many popular writers offer advice to parents on ways of defending their homes against an influx of sexual explicitness. Typical are Maggie Gallagher's *Enemies of Eros: How the Sexual Revolution Is Killing Family, Marriage, and Sex, and What We Can Do about It*, a broad, conservative attack on a host of enemies, including pornography; Gallagher urges parents to redouble efforts to educate children. The most effective way to prevent exposure of children to porn, says Gordon Greer in "Pornography: What Can Be Done to Protect Our Kids?," an article representative of many, is to develop a good family atmosphere and better sex education, not to advocate censorship. To this list could be added literally hundreds in the same vein from popular and religious periodicals.

See No Evil: Christian Attitudes toward Sex in Art and Entertainment, by Tom M. Williams, presents one of the strongest Christian positions because it is not shrill. Williams reviews Christian doctrine and the immoral effects of porn. Unless censorship is imposed, which the author finds problematic, Christians need to establish strong personal morality, demand rating systems for movies, and ask for legislation to reduce public displays of sexually offensive material. Williams points out that Americans, by and large, accept a separation of state and religion that in many cases prohibits the display of sectarian images in public venues—such as crosses on courthouses—and that the same principle can apply to sexual expression. Nothing should prohibit those so inclined from circulating and enjoying sexual materials, says Williams; they should simply not impose them on others by displaying them in common areas. Rousas J. Rushdoony's *The Politics of Pornography* sees the tolerance of pornography as a manifestation of the "God is dead" syndrome, and advances familiar religious principles as counters to the prevailing ethos.

The Poisoning of Eros: Sexual Values in Conflict, by Raymond Lawrence, traces the Christian church's "dehumanization" of sexuality to the philosophical and personal struggles of early leaders who imposed irrational proscriptions and prohibitions; Lawrence thinks the legacy persists in contemporary religious attitudes toward representation. Peter Gardella's *Innocent Ecstasy: How Christianity Gave America an Ethic of Pleasure* is an illuminating discussion of how, for many Americans, sex has come to offer some of the goals once offered by religion. If sex is transcendent, spiritual, and renewing, then vulgar expressions detract from sex's sacred character. Secularized Westerners may think of sex as the last refuge of spirituality and deplore its commercialization, even as they cheerfully accept the commodification of everything else, even religion itself. Some famous pornographers invert this notion. The works of Henry Miller are a testament to his belief that obscenity (he does not think his narratives pornographic) is the route to the core of existence; for Miller the obscene *is* the sacred (see Chapter 16, **Erotic Literature**). In his important philosophical justification of pornography, *Metasex, Mirth & Madness*, Marco Vassi says that pornographers touch the sacred through their descriptions of sexual excess. In many respects, in their celebration of the mystery and recurrence of sex, pornographic artifacts resemble the rituals and practices of various churches in their evocation of existential and eternal verities. Vassi observes that pornography can function as eucharist.

Mary Jo Weaver conducts a thoughtful review of various religious positions on sex and pornography in "Pornography and the Religious Imagination":

Religion as defined by conservatives is not antithetical to pornography but supportive of it, and an appropriation of the "old-time religion" is an affirmation of the very framework upon which perverse extensions of dominating masculinity are constructed. The antipornographic views of religious conservatives that purport to be deeply religious, are, therefore, profoundly pornographic, whereas the anti-pornographic views of feminist critics that appear to be anti-religious are open to the designs of a new theological vision. Because the theological assumptions of conservative religionists are so clearly antithetical to one another, there can be no fruitful alliance between them. (82)

Similarly, Gina Allen suggests that antiporn feminists inclined to join forces with the religious Right should look again at the Bible, which she characterizes in "What Those Women Want in Pornography" as "the granddaddy of all Western pornography" (46), the fountainhead of patriarchy and male hegemony.

In "Strange Bedfellows," Karen De Crow, a former president of the National Organization of Women, noting the close relationship between antiporn feminists and fundamentalists, says flatly that their collective attempts to condemn pornography are really attacks on sex itself. Certainly, the alliance has puzzled observers such as Isabel Wilkerson, who wonders at the connection in "Foes of Pornography and Bigotry Join Forces." In an editorial in *Screw* (21 January 1985), Al Goldstein spoke bluntly for a bewildered liberal establishment that had long equated pornography with political dissent. Goldstein, who sneers at political correctness and denies that pornography needs redeeming social importance, nonetheless seemed wounded by the apostasy of antiporn feminists. Goldstein harshly condemned the alliance between fundamentalists and antiporn feminists. He accused the latter of having betrayed the political left that had steadfastly supported women's causes. Their sense of sexual shame made them vulnerable to the blandishments of right-wing totalitarianism. Succumbing to authoritarianism, antiporn feminists endorsed censorship, and in so doing turned on their former allies and on America.

Arthur J. Mielke follows psychologist Robert J. Stoller in ascribing a theological basis to Christian objections to pornography and argues that a more relevant reading is that of Jungian psychology. Mielke insists in *Christians, Feminists, and the Culture of Pornography* that pornography is "spiritually redemptive" even to feminists, even in a social system with fixed ideas of marriage and monogamy, because it offers hope for women and men who long for sexual satisfaction. In legitimating passion and investing desire with excitement, pornography revitalizes a spirituality that has been dessicated by institutionalization of religion; at the very least it restores power to an eroticism respected by ancient theologies. On a less abstract and more personal level, pornography fosters masturbation, candid expression, and ideal fantasies, all of which are essential to a healthy sexuality. Mielke finds support for his ideas in writings by women who have looked more closely at pornography than the first wave of antisex feminists.

SCHLOCK SHOCK: CONSERVATIVE AND LIBERAL

The range of opinion regarding pornography is so wide that publishers often simply collect or commission essays on the subject. Several broad anthologies are *The New Eroticism*, edited by Philip Nobile; *The Pornography Controversy*, edited by Ray C. Rist (essays on legal, sociological, aesthetic, and cultural aspects of porn by Peter Michelson, William Simon, John Gagnon, Joseph Slade, Earl Warren, and others); *Perspectives on Pornography*, edited by Douglas Hughes (essays by Anthony Burgess, Susan Sontag, Paul Goodman, George Steiner, Ernest van den Haag, and others); and *The Problem of Pornography*, edited by Susan Dwyer. Of these, the last is the most recent and also one of the most balanced, with contributions by Tom Waugh, Stanley Fish, Ronald Dworkin, Catharine MacKinnon, and Helen Longino. Carol Gorman has compiled arguments pro and con in a volume called simply *Pornography*, a text aimed at young adults. *Taking Sides: Clashing Views on Controversial Issues in Human Sexuality*, edited by Robert T. Francoeur, collects articles on various positions on pornography, as does the volume's second (and different) edition, edited by Alison Alexander and Janice Hanson. So does *Pornography: Opposing Viewpoints*, edited by Carol Wekesser, whose sampling of opinion is nicely balanced between folklore and fact. Wekesser reprints many articles from the popular press and provides an up-to-date bibliography of many more.

The special issue on "Sexuality, Violence and Pornography" published by *Humanities in Society* offers diverse viewpoints, as does "Pornography: A Roundtable Discussion" conducted by *Harper's Magazine* and moderated by Lewis Lapham, with Al Goldstein (whose bluntness is legendary), Midge Decter, Erica Jong, Susan Brownmiller, Jean B. Elshtain, and Aryeh Neier. Two other readable outlines are "The Porn Debates" and "Dressed to Kill," both of which present different viewpoints on current feminist attempts to suppress pornography. "On Pornography," a special issue of *The Public Interest*, contains articles by Walter Berns, Alexander Bickel, James Q. Wilson, and Nathan Glazer, whose comments illustrate a wide political spectrum. Another political sampler is *Pornography: Private Right or Public Menace?*, edited by Robert M. Baird and Stuart E. Rosenbaum, who include the opinions of Keating, Brownmiller, Steinem, Dworkin, Gracyk, Hill, Manning, Soble, Weaver, Will, and others pro and con. Joseph Slade's "Pornography" surveys controversies as well.

One need not be religious to be affronted by sexual representations, of course. William Irwin Thompson has written in *The Time Falling Bodies Take to Light: Mythology, Sexuality and the Origins of Culture* that

pornography is the shadow side of myth, a racial memory expressed in obsessive imagery, and as a twisted form of reflection of our archaic inheritance, it expresses the shock of incarnation. Precisely because we are more highly conscious than the animals, our sexuality is intensified by consciousness. Homosexuality, sado-masochism, and bestiality are neither inhuman nor "natural": there is no such thing as "natural" for human beings. . . . In rituals of adoration of the penis and the whip, or in black-leathered celebrations of male dominance and bondage, humans are longing for constraint, for compression back into an original, presexual mode of being. The caricatured emphasis on sex is not a celebration of it, but an attempt to escape it altogether. Pornography, in a way, is indeed as the moralist claims, "garbage"; it is the rotting compost-heap of old mythologies left over from all the cultures of human evolution. (79)

Biology, gender, class, ethnicity, age, religious beliefs, and other factors powerfully influence our reactions to channels of communication that are themselves shaped by technology, politics, and economics, and to relegate discourse so central to our culture to the trash heap is doubtless premature. *Patently Offensive: Porn under Siege*, a video documentary on pornography produced by Harriet Koskoff, contains interviews, footage of the Meese Commission, surveys of sexual iconographies, and other clips designed to demonstrate pornography's nastiness.

Students of popular culture sometimes subscribe to a weightless aesthetics of schlock that simply does not register the profound revulsion of some Americans toward a culture that seems as interested in Demi Moore's nipples as in proposals for better health care. Despite the inability of social scientists to establish direct causal connections between specific sexual stimuli and behavior, say these critics, vulgarity degrades our culture by robbing children of innocence, adults of dignity, and the larger culture of standards of taste. Many acknowledge that low denominators have long been common to a democratic and capitalist society but insist that the coarsening of culture is worse now if only because of the rapacious commercialization of information. Traditional attacks on an American culture in decline are too numerous to list here; besides, they often lump pornography with other scars on the body politic.

Suffice it to say that in the last two decades social critics from Christopher Lasch and Theodore Roszak, to Neil Postman have protested against the deleterious consequences of steadily rising levels of coarseness. Typical of recent examples is James B. Twitchell's *Carnival Culture: The Trashing of Taste in America*, which decries the vulgarity in American publishing, television, movies, and so on, though his revulsion seems to have been triggered mostly by Madonna's anointment as an arbiter of taste. Twitchell's complaint echoes Eliot Fremont-Smith's observation in "Pornography's Progress" that a steady diet of porn is debilitating to a society, even if its abrasive effects cannot be demonstrated. *The Case against Pornography*, edited by David Holbrook, contains essays by Ernest van den Haag, Robert J. Stoller, Rollo May, and others, who vary in their approaches to the subject, with the hostile claiming that porn is harmful. Most assert that the effects of pornography are "self-brutalizing and destructive," that shame is essential to the human condition, and that trash can be distinguished from art. Holbrook himself finds pornography harmful (it promotes "hate"), immoral, and degrading. Gresham's law operates to drive out good ideas when obscene ones are permitted, says Irving Kristol in "Pornography, Obscenity, and the Case for Censorship." Kristol thinks the "cost" of liberal censorship is less than the damage to public discourse of dehumanization implicit in sexual materials. One of Kristol's oft-quoted remarks here is: "If you believe that no one was ever corrupted by a book, you have also to believe that no one was ever improved by a book." Variations include arguments that since we make assumptions that advertising leads to behavior change, asserting that pornography does so merely extends that premise.

The question, of course, is whether sex, violence, and general coarseness do lower the tone of those who live in a media environment. As Robert King, a screenwriter participating in a symposium called "Beyond Good and Evil: Writers' Moral Visions," sponsored by the Writers Guild, asked, "If the propensity toward violence in our society can be blamed on violence in film and television, how come the thousands of hours of comedy produced every year for decades hasn't made people *funnier*?" (10). Other commentators think the messages of the media merely recapitulate the status quo. In *Popular Culture and High Culture: An Analysis and Evaluation of Taste*, Herbert J. Gans says:

In fact, if the media had any significant effect on sexual norms, the contemporary liberalization of sexual attitudes and behaviors could not have taken place, for the media have been until recently quite Puritan, lagging far behind attitude changes among the younger audience for fear of alienating the older audience. If media audiences practiced what the media have preached, the double standard would still be in force, young girls would be virginal teasers, and adultery would be found only in the suburbs. . . . Few people seem to use the media for problem solving, or media fiction for descriptions or explanations of reality, so that they do not take media content at face value. They use the media to provide temporary respite from everyday life, and fantasy serves this purpose better than realism. (35)

Among those who think pornography's effects are damaging to the culture at large, the principal arguments have to do with the encroachment of private matters on public affairs and of commerce upon a sexuality that should be spared commodification. Probably the most famous example of the first type of argument is "Night Words: Human Privacy and High Pornography," in which George Steiner frames the issue as the collision of private and public spheres. Steiner thinks that exposure to pornography not only besmirches dignity and affronts our sense of privacy but also "withers" our sense of humanity. The publisher Maurice Girodias inverts this reasoning in his reply to Steiner, "The Erotic Society," by suggesting that pornography's public role is to counter the dehumanizing effects of society's other institutions. Restricting people's access to images can impoverish their imaginations and put their private survival as individuals at risk, says Carole Vance in "Issues and Commentary: The War on Culture." Images buttress the psyche, and it is a mistake to distinguish between private and public images, because some circulation is necessary so that individuals will know they are not alone in their subcultures. Americans must strive for tolerance and civility, thinks Pat Califia; in *Public Sex: The Culture of Radical Sex*, she says that we really learn of experimentation through public or semipublic channels.

Easily the most persuasive examination of the erosion of boundaries between public and private spaces is Joshua Meyrowitz's *No Sense of Place: The Impact of Electronic Media on Social Behavior*, though it does not separate erotic expression from other messages. Drawing on the theories of Erving Goffman and Marshall McLuhan, Meyrowitz says that modern mass media, in particular, television, eradicate the distinctions between public and private, between what might be called foreground and background spaces, so that today's children enter adult worlds of discourse because television penetrates previously sheltered childhood environments. Behavior that in the past might have been kept private is now fodder for media that seek out secrets. Television abolishes hierarchies of taste and authority; it also undermines our sense of the appropriate venue for confessional discourse, so that talk shows routinely retail scandal to afternoon audiences of all ages, and prime-time programming brings the language and behavior of the bedroom into the living room. Pornography is beside the point, Meyrowitz implies, because an electronic discourse that recognizes no boundaries of class or age has already damaged all our customs and traditions by opening everything to public discourse.

Many critiques of pornography are erected on the quasi-economic ground of commodification. The commercial nature of pornography is disturbing to Americans who regard it as exploitative. "A Critic at Large: Don Juan in Hull," Martin Amis' essay on a biography of Philip Larkin that makes much of the English poet laureate's fondness for pornography, notes: "[Exploitative] suggests that, while you are free to be as sexually miserable as you like, the moment you exchange hard cash for *Playboy* you are in the pornography-perpetuation business and your misery becomes political. The truth is that pornography is just a sad affair all round (and its industrial dimensions are an inescapable modern theme). It is there because men—in their hundreds of millions—want it to be there. Killing pornography is like killing the messenger" (78). Or perhaps it is just the *scale* of commerce. Though occasioned by Merry Alpert's exhibit of photos shot through the window of a Manhattan sex club at the Bonni Benrubi Gallery, Vicki Goldberg's essay, "Testing the Limits in a Culture of Excess," ranges across movies, art, advertising, television, and other media. According to Goldberg: "Everyone always knew sex and violence sold. What is new is the discovery that a mainstream audience would not only tolerate the casting off of a century's worth of restrictions and discretion but embrace enormous and rapid leaps from one broken taboo to the next" (40).

Some documentation (see Jay Gertzman's remarks on the depression in *Bookleggers and Smuthounds: The Trade in Erotica, 1920–1940*) indicates that sex industries flourish in periods of economic hardship; unemployed workers move into the business, and consumers who cannot afford other kinds of entertainment purchase books, magazines, and movies that offer more stimulation for the buck. Economists see in the steady erosion of the middle class since the 1960s a reason for pornography's relative success. Class sensibilities can be affronted in unusual ways. In "Madonna Exposed," David Aaron Clark points out that lower-class pornographers can feel exploited by the commodification of their product by the larger mainstream culture. Clark, one of the editors of *Screw*, says that when longtime sex workers on the fringes see the success of Madonna's photo book *Sex*, it is difficult for them "not to feel a certain sense of violation, seeing not only our art form (pornography, 'erotica' whatever name sells) but, for some of us, our very lifestyles co-opted, drained of all privacy and meaning, and offered up like so much marbelized meat on a butcher's block of straight world consumption" (20). The trend, of course, is part of a larger syndrome in which the often-displayed nipples and pudenda of high-fashion models compete against those of lower-class icons such as porn stars. Versace's marketing of Helena Christensen's breasts produces a much more expensive, glossy, but also salable commodity than VCA's promotion of Sid Deuce's pierced labia. The latter performer makes hard-core porn movies to hype her career as a stripper on a different kind of runway, whereas the fashion industry promotes models in order to sell more clothes. Such equations, of course, do not always factor in the artistry that separates, say, a pulp novel from Nicolson Baker's equally explicit, best-selling *Vox*. Douglas Davis speaks for many other onlookers when he characterizes current pornography controversies as battles between a lower-class, marginalized sector of America and the middle class that currently holds power in "Art and Contradiction: Helms, Censorship, and the Serpent." According to Davis, the lower classes tend always to see salaciousness in the art of a higher class.

Nina Hartley, a registered nurse, columnist, advocate for free speech, and legendary veteran performer in more than 300 porn films, suggests that commercialization is unavoidable as a means for distributing any kind of information. In "Reflections of a Feminist Porn Star," Hartley remarks:

Sex as a commercial venture doesn't bother me because I do not automatically view all women as victims of sex; nor do I view all men automatically to be victimizers, or all intercourse as de facto rape (a Dworkin/MacKinnon tenet). Under capitalism, all things can be commodified; why should sex be any different? It may not be the best way to deal with sex, but it shouldn't shock us that it occurs. Humans are first and foremost visual creatures. What really matters is time, place, degree, mutuality, and consent. I believe that a woman is capable of consent. If we aren't granted that one prerogative then we are not being granted full adult status. (64)

Unlike feminists arguing that pornography is a political issue or a matter of civil rights, Konstantin Kolenda applies the Kantian categorical imperative as a test of morality in "Porno Prone": pornography uses humans "as means to gratuitous thrills." Bernard R. Crick's *Crime, Rape, and Gin: Reflections on Contemporary Attitudes to Violence, Pornography, and Addiction* argues against alarmism (40–65) by observing that there is little evidence that pornography has deleterious social effects. Otherwise, Crick's approach is to round up quotes from philosophers; if society cannot legislate morality, he says, then it must educate.

PORNOGRAPHY AND POLITICS

Historians such as Lynn Hunt (*The Invention of Pornography*) and Joss Marsh (*Word Crimes*) have demonstrated that the inception and implementation of modern democracy are closely linked to expression considered obscene and that citizens today owe their political freedom to the courage of blasphemers and pornographers of the past. (See **The "Invention" of Pornography** in Chapter 5 and **Language: Obscenity and Democracy** in chapter 15.) Socrates objected to democracy on the grounds that it was vulgar and nasty, and he was, of course, correct. The nobility of democracy is to be found in its embrace of the lowest forms of expression, along with the lowest classes of citizens. That reality keeps the First Amendment—the most sublime of all political principles—constantly before Americans. Except for genres such as underground comix, however, American porn has usually been employed for overtly political ends only during elections (see **Scandal Journalism** in chapter 17). More recently, the impeachment of President Clinton has brought sexual expression to the forefront of contemporary politics, and for many Americans, political life at the turn of the new century has been redefined by Kenneth Starr and Larry Flynt. Until the special prosecutor became possibly the most famous pornographer in American history, pornography was political chiefly in its prosecution by ambitious district attorneys, Bible-thumping evangelists, corrupt politicians, or hyperbolic champions of one group or another. Ironically, calling any form of speech political in the United States guarantees it protection under the Constitution, and that has sometimes been a saving grace. For a succinct statement of these and other concepts of political speech, see Adam Gopnik's "American Studies," an essay on the Clinton-Lewinsky affair.

Lawrence W. Rosenfield's classic essay, "Politics and Pornography," asserts that "pornography iconographically renders for its consumer the victimage and impotence that informs his own political activities" (419). That is, pornography encapsulates a sexuality that helps shape political stances regarding other phases of life: pornography "serves as a surrogate for freedom; erotica comes into being as some particular aspect of the spirit of freedom and sharing that once pervaded a community fades" (414). In some ways, pornography attests to a person's confidence in his or her political abilities and thus invests it with a political dimension. A probability sample of a Gallup poll conducted by Charles Peek et al. for "Pornography: Important Political Symbol or Limited Political Issue?" revealed that opposition to pornography was generally related to political conservatism, but usually as a limited local, rather than a national, issue. Attitudes toward pornography, in short, were not good predictors of political attitudes. On the other hand, Peek and Sharon Brown found in "Pornography as a Political Symbol: Attitudes toward Commercial Nudity and Attitudes toward Political Organizations" that negative responses to porn were generally correlated to favorable attitudes toward the police, the FBI, and patriotism and to unfavorable attitudes toward the Soviet Union. Another study of political attitudes is "Evaluation of Visual Erotica by Sexual Liberals and Conservatives," in which Douglas Wallace and Gerald Wehmer established that conservatives were not being hypocritical when they expressed disgust at exposure to sexual materials; both groups tended to be sociopolitical as well as sexual liberals and conservatives.

For many people, the political dimension of porn is best framed as one of control. Richard Summerhill says in "Porn Crime" that antiporn feminists view pornography as a means of male control of women, while their conservative allies object to pornography on the grounds that it encourages "self-indulgence and self-gratification. In other words, porn contains a threat of *insufficient* control" (9) and allegedly leads to a weakening first of the psyche, then of family and social bonds. Simon Watney also suggests in *Policing Desire: Pornography, AIDS, and the Media* that attacks on porn are often predicated on political assumptions about the nature of democracy, family values, and gender preferences and thus can discriminate against those who reject constraints of sexual discourse, the rigid models of the family, the heterosexual bias of the majority, or simply the linkage between sex and reproduction. Watney suggests that the real function of pornography is precisely to represent extremes.

Perhaps the best-known Marxist critique is Herbert Marcuse's *Eros and Civilization*. Marcuse argues that capitalist society represses sexuality by defining eroticism in terms of genitality, integrates it into a system of production and exchange of commodities, and controls individuals by industrializing certain forms of expression. To Marcuse's legacy can be added some portions of *The Dialectics of Enlightenment*, one of the Frankfort School of cultural critiques by Theodor Adorno and Max Horkheimer, who also consider aspects of pornography. Such theorists think of the state as drawing its power from the private energies of its citizens and attempting to control their most private fantasies in order to ensure obedience in areas as diverse as entertainment and religion. Less doctrinaire but also less interesting is Romano Giachetti's argument that pornography is an expression of moribund capitalism in *Porno Power: Pornografia Società Capitalista*. Less doctrinaire and far more interesting is *Das prinzip Obszön: Kunst, Pornographie und Gesellschaft*, by the modestly Marxist Peter Gorsen, an important critic of a modern art that Gorsen thinks can best be understood without pretense as a capitalist commodity. Like any form of art, Gorsen says, pornography crystallizes desire in order to sell it; erotic expression obeys the laws of the marketplace. In fact, says Gorsen in *Sexualästhetik: Zur burgerlichen Rezeption von Obszönitat und Pornographie*, pornography has become a middle-class entitlement. One section deals with European response to porn films in the early 1970s. Continental producers took their cue from Americans, Gorsen points out, both in the degree of explicitness and in the exhibition of films, which swiftly became staples in American-style arcades and bookstores aimed at the middle-class consumer. Gorsen examines the function of taboo in film by way of distinguishing between an unexamined "reality" and the vulgarity that undermines it. *Pornography: Marxism, Feminism and the Future of Sexuality*, by Alan Soble, examines other political dimensions in pornography. Soble argues with extreme feminists who condemn porn out of hand by offering a Marxist critique that is somewhat tentative and cautious; he argues that pornography can be rewarding work and that for that reason any restrictions governing it should be limited. Pornography, says Soble, demonstrates that men lack power as much as women.

In *The Left and the Erotic*, edited by Eileen Phillips, English writers, taking the American antipornography movement as subject, insist that "the anti-porn arguments which conflate power with violence and reduce sexism to sex, position the anti-porn movement as reactionary" because those arguments draw "us away from the project of establishing strategies of pleasure, freedom, desires. We remain caught in the noose of negative critiques of sexual relations, only able to speak to violence and degradation; we are silenced about the excitements or compulsions or delights of sensual existence" (12–13). The Canadian Dany Lacombe criticizes antiporn positions in *Ideology and Public Policy: The Case against Pornography* for fueling the government's desire to control and regulate sexuality; such stances are therefore "more anti-sex than pro-woman" (45). "It is not pornography that causes women to be objectified. Pornography is simply a symptom, a manifestation of the status of women in a sexist society" (44).

Definitions of pornography as used in public debate are generally determined by ideological persuasion, not by the conventions of ordinary language or the jargon of legality. It is essential to remember that while the origins of the word can be traced back to the Greeks, the word "pornography" did not appear until the Victorian era and was a coinage of that period. Viewed from that perspective, definitions of pornography are elements in the struggle for power among competing classes or genders. The struggle has served to make clear an assumption that was only implicit before: that pornographic expression and its opposite, antipornographic expression, are thus inherently and unmistakably subsumed by the category of political speech. Since it is virtually impossible to extract all the political nuances from current warring definitions, the one offered here is the one with the longest historical pedigree.

The politicization of sexuality and gender is most often linked with Michel Foucault, whose *The History of Sexuality* has profoundly shaped modern thinking (for detailed discussion of Foucault, see **The "Invention" of Sexuality** in chapter 5). According to Foucault, the sexual regime of a culture derives from taxonomies that assign categories of desire. A culture's social, political, and economic institutions impose "discipline" on its citizens, who internalize these rules to the point where they cannot think or act independently. Sexuality, if not gender itself, is thus wholly determined by official constructions of reality, and the task of the scholar is "to define the regime of power-knowledge-pleasure that sustains the discourse on human sexuality in our part of the world" (I, 11). Moreover, "Sexuality must not be thought of as a kind of natural given which power tries to hold in check, or as an obscure domain which knowledge tries gradually to uncover. It is the name that can be given to a historic construct: not a furtive reality that is difficult to grasp, but a great surface network in which the stimulation of bodies, the intensification of pleasures, the incitement to discourse, the formation of special knowledges, the strengthening of controls and resistances, are linked to one another, in accordance with a few major strategies of knowledge and power" (I, 105–106).

John Ellis draws on Laura Mulvey and Sigmund Freud in "Photography/ Pornography, Art/Pornography" in order to dilate on erotic desire as the product of institutional forces. Ellis is one of several social critics to circle around the paradox of sexual stereotypes whose eroticism nonetheless impacts personally on individuals. Laurence O'Toole's *Pornocopia* embraces the notion that pornographic industries embody classical capitalist theory and thus function as admirable examples of the spirit of competition. O'Toole characterizes the (mostly video) pornography industry as "capitalism in the raw," an enterprise of opportunity generated by democracy for profit, and thus part of the institutional fabric of Western economics. Succinct statements of these and other concepts regarding political aspects of erotica can be found in William Brigman's "Pornography as Political Expression."

FEMINIST POSITIONS ON PORNOGRAPHY

Feminist comment on pornography—elaborated in hundreds of articles and scores of books—ranges from radical opposition, to enthusiastic endorsement and from brilliant, to silly. Without question feminists have widened and enriched the cultural significance and understanding of sexuality and its representations. Even the extremists have made valuable contributions, if only by adding to the storehouse of American sexual folklore. Identifying a consistent "feminist" position on pornography is impossible: for a time, extreme factions routinely labeled each other traitors after the manner of Trotskyites and Leninists wrangling over leadership of an earlier revolution. In many ways, given the invective, theirs was the most masculinized sector of the debate, and fortunately, since the extremists were not actually shooting each other as did the Soviet ideologues of the 1930s, the name-calling was entertaining. By contrast, the discourse of mainstream feminists has been as admirable for its forbearance as it has been effective in its incisiveness: instead of calling the antiporn wing "lunatic," as have male critics, most feminists have patiently isolated the extremists. The strategy has worked: Catharine MacKinnon and Andrea Dworkin now seem as representative of women as Beavis and Butthead for men, and the controversies they set in motion, says Robert Christgau in "Children of the Porn," "often have the aura of a summer-camp color war" (67).

That is, in some ways, a shame. As critics frequently point out, *feminism* has become a dirty word, even among feminists. Although the reasons are numerous, one has to do with inconsistencies between theory and practice. Few would deny that women (and other groups) have been oppressed by hegemonic language, structures, and systems correctly identified as patriarchal. Hegemony by definition, however, is neither self-interested nor deliberately malicious, nor is it the exclusive province of a single gender, class, or group; any group, once it becomes dominant, becomes hegemonic. To treat males as if they were individually responsible for institutional discrimination, as some (certainly not all) angry feminists (however understandably) do, is to risk undermining the argument. The more shrill they become, the more vindictive they seem, and the more easily dismissed by critics as antimale rather than crusaders for justice. More successful feminist critics target the culture, not its citizens, affirm their kinship with males, and view sexuality and its expression as evolving and contested, in some cases glorious, rather than as universally hateful or lethal.

In any case, the expansion of debate requires maps of the different positions. *Feminism and Pornography*, a survey of various advocates by Ronald J. Berger, Patricia Searles, and Charles E. Cottle, appends an excellent bibliography to careful summaries outlining the schisms pornography has opened between feminists; it is the best starting point for the scholar. Daphne Read's "(De)Constructing Pornography: Feminisms in Conflict," shorter but equally lucid, traces skirmish lines within the larger arena of feminism. Mary Kay Blakely was one of the first to raise doubts about the sweeping generalities of the feminist, antiporn position in "Is One Woman's Sexuality Another Woman's Pornography?," an early outline of disagreements over whether pornography should or should not figure in the order of battle, and it is still worth reading. Alison Assiter tries to reconcile "liberal" and "feminist" positions on erotic material, though her efforts are somewhat undercut by the usual cliché that pornography objectifies women, in *Pornography, Feminism and the Individual*; the solution, she says, is not to eliminate porn but to curtail male power. Much more liberal in orientation is the special issue of *Off Our Backs* entitled "Coming Apart: Feminists and the Conflict over Pornography." "Forbidden Fantasies," a special issue of the *Village Voice* dealing with the feminist factions, is also useful. Avedon Carol's *Nudes, Prudes and Attitudes: Pornography and Censorship* sorts out the feminist battles, reviews research on pornography, and contextualizes the debates. One of the best single sources, however, is "The Sex Issue: # 12" of *Heresies*, which contains the most honest feminist responses to pornography one is likely to find—if one can find it; it has been ripped from most bound volumes by the censorious or the salacious.

Several classic feminist texts provide background. These include Kate Millett's *Sexual Politics*, which uses textual analysis of well-known pornographic texts (e.g., Henry Miller's) to explicate the power struggle between men and women that Millett thinks defines modern gender relationships. Susan Brownmiller's thesis in *Against Our Will: Men, Women, and Rape* is that rape has been institutionalized in Western culture as a way of permanently subjecting women. Since all men endorse rape as a means of keeping women in their place, claims Brownmiller, pornography, as a form of "anti-female propaganda" (394), simply legitimates the oppression. Germaine Greer's *The Female Eunuch*, by contrast, suggests that pornography at least allows women to appear in sexual roles necessary for completing their status as fully functioning humans, though the roles all too often conform to masculine expectations. Kathleen Barry's *Female Sexual Slavery*, a global survey of the mistreatment of women, concentrates on myriad ways in which women are victimized to illustrate the thesis that any occupation for women in a patriarchical society is a form of slavery, part and consequence of a cultural master plan for "gynocide." For Barry, pornography is a blueprint for oppression. The chapter called "Pornography: The

Ideology of Cultural Sadism" is reminiscent of the writings of Elizabeth Cady Stanton; it centers on an idea common to much feminist, antiporn criticism: that porn, once defined as writing about prostitutes, is still concerned with activities associated with prostitutes, that is, behavior repugnant to decent women, who should be interested in sex only as an act of reproduction. Other behaviors, like oral sex, for instance, are animalistic. Barry's *The Prostitution of Sexuality*, a follow-up survey of the victimization of women, makes particular reference to Asian sex industry and pornography but again sees sexual representation as part of the larger tapestry of discrimination and brutality. Women do live in fear in a world that conspires to oppress and degrade them, says a less paranoid Marilyn French in *The War against Women*, though she subordinates concern with pornography to issues of religion, poverty, class, and ethnicity.

Laura Lederer gathered some thirty condemnations of pornography, some doctrinaire, some not, in *Take Back the Night: Women on Pornography*. Contributors include Kathleen Barry, Pauline Bart, Judith Bat-Ada, Megan Boler, Charlotte Bunch, Phyllis Chester, Irene Diamond, Andrea Dworkin, Martha Geve, Wendy Kaminer, Helen Longino, Audre Lorde, Susan Lurie, Marge Piercy, Florence Rush, Gloria Steinem, Alice Walker, and others. The generalized discontent evident in such collections devolves into a two-pronged poststructuralist attack on sexual representations, one grounded in language, one in visual images. In the first interpretation, gender becomes epistemology. In the second, gender becomes objectification.

Language-Based Attacks

Antiporn feminists equate sex and violence: sex *is* violence because it cannot be otherwise given the subordination of women. Because they also maintain that depictions of sex cause the subordination of women, the argument—their critics point out—merely completes a circle. Content studies of hard-core movies that almost always demonstrate lower levels of violence than mainstream films are thus for radical feminists irrelevant—since any form of sex is violent. Antiporn feminists do not recognize even those mitigating factors sometimes acknowledged by fundamentalists. Religious zealots may deplore carnality but, recognizing its necessity in reproduction, hold that the nastiness of sex is neutralized by marriage or by thinking about God during intercourse. Given their premises, radical feminists are logically more consistent: sex, they say, is always a nightmare for women, who are invariably victimized.

Robin Morgan's historically (1974) important "Theory and Practice: Pornography and Rape" is the source of the slogan "pornography is the theory, rape the practice," which suddenly seemed to invest pornography with an enormous degree of metaphorical power and gave it ideological status in cultural and sexual politics. Gloria Steinem's "Erotica vs. Pornography: A Clear and Present Difference," in which the alleged difference is far from clear, similarly announced that pornography oppressed women, as opposed to erotica, defined as sexual expression that did not. In such readings, pornography became expression devoted to the inscription of male sexual dominance. The principal architects of the radical antiporn position, however, were Catharine MacKinnon and Andrea Dworkin. To get around the objection that only deviants are adversely affected by sexual expression, MacKinnon and Dworkin insist that pornography is not the realm of the perverse but the normal expression of a society bent on oppressing women, so that every male is implicated.

The feminist, antiporn positions of Dworkin and MacKinnon stand at some distance from poststructuralist and phenomenological arguments claiming that (1) language constitutes the only reality humans can know, (2) such language is, by and large, masculinely gendered, and (3) women are at physical and social disadvantage. According to these arguments, men did most of the *naming* of things and ideas, so their language, their values, and their perspectives have shaped social institutions and structures over history. In contrast to this constructivist position, Dworkin and MacKinnon take an *essentialist* position that holds that men are biologically driven to violence in all their behavior, including sex; men harm women (i.e., have intercourse with them) because they are incited by erotic representations. MacKinnon thinks of language as the principal tool by which men subordinate women in order to harm them physically, while Dworkin, the less systematic thinker, inveighs against any forms of sexual expression.

Dworkin wrote the chief text of the feminist, antiporn movement, *Pornography: Men Possessing Women* (1980), to claim that discriminatory sexual expression constitutes the environment in which women live. Pornography enshrines misogyny by socializing all of society's members, male and female, to accept the subordinate role of women. Pornography is the sexual reality of America; it is the root of male discrimination against women, a plan for abuse and also its cause, not merely its expression. By discriminating against women as a class, Dworkin maintains in "Against the Male Flood: Censorship, Pornography, and Equality," sexual expression violates the civil rights of women and therefore should be subject to legal suppression. Dramatic titles reiterate Dworkin's one-note thesis: *Our Blood: Prophecies and Discourses on Sexual Politics, Woman Hating, Right-Wing Women, Letters from a War Zone: Writings, 1976–1989*, and *Life and Death: Unapologetic Writings on the Continuing War against Women*. All are pretty similar in their contention that pornography is the principal instrument for degrading and victimizing all women to gratify a universal male lust animated by hatred and in their casting of Dworkin herself as a crusader against the "terrorism" of pornography. Dworkin's *Intercourse* condemns the physical act of heterosexual intercourse as entirely repugnant. Given her previous theoretical statements, rejecting intercourse itself seemed logical, but doing so cost Dworkin support from all but the most radical of feminists. The book opened her to ridicule from many other critics, most notably, Paul Fussell, whose *Thank God for the Atom Bomb and Other Essays* accused her of shoddy thinking (97–98) that suffers from a profound ignorance of biology. Perhaps because of her signature costume, a pair of overalls, Dworkin has received mostly unkind media attention. Complicating matters also is her authorship of pornographic fiction of such cruel sexuality (*The New Woman's Broken Heart: Short Stories* [1980] and *Ice and Fire: A Novel* [1987]) that Susie Bright has called Dworkin the "de Sade of our time."[2]

According to MacKinnon, pornography as discourse establishes the objectification and subordination of women as right and natural; pornography is the dominant ideology of the state. For MacKinnon also, the issue is one of civil rights for women; sexual expression should be suppressed because it puts women as a class at risk. (See **The Social Construction of Sexuality and Gender** in chapter 5 for MacKinnon's theoretical positions.) Many observers agree that MacKinnon began her career with a brilliant analysis of sexual harassment and discrimination and then allowed herself to be captured by the appeal of a single causative agency—erotic expression. Because her extremism lent itself easily to the simple polarizations and personalizations with which American media routinely treat complex issues, MacKinnon quickly became a spokesperson for the antipornography movement. Most of the reaction also polarized along First Amendment fault lines. Fred Strebeigh's "Defining Law on the Feminist Frontier" is an admiring profile of MacKinnon as a brilliant legal scholar and as a crusader for justice, while Pete Hamill's "Woman on the Verge of a Legal Breakdown" warns of the constitutional dangers MacKinnon's approach presents. Alan Dershowitz compares her efforts to intimidate and obfuscate to Joseph McCarthy's in "Justice." Laura Kipnis dismisses MacKinnon as incoherent in *Bound and Gagged*.

According to some critics, MacKinnon's is the prime example of the mirror-reverse relationship of pornography and antipornography: MacKinnon's vision of males is as extreme as traditional pornography's image of women, and at some deep level she satisfies the same sort of need to distort sexuality in the name of fantasy. In this regard, she may be considered a pioneer in the creation of a complex pornography for women, and she should be honored for that in the same way that de Sade functions historically as a fountainhead of modern frissons of sexuality. James R. Petersen's "Catharine MacKinnon Again" calls her "the Freddy Kreuger of the women's movement" (37) and reviews the tenets of her argument: that since males dominate society, all heterosexual sex is violent, and any representation of sex not only is violent but also causes aggression. Petersen observes that a joke popular among attorneys is that a scene of a man kissing a woman's nipple will earn a movie an X-rating, while his cutting off the nipple makes the film PG, but to MacKinnon there is no difference whatever between the two acts. The joke seemed merely amusing until publication of MacKinnon's *Only Words*, which does, indeed, insist that language has the force of deed, that all expression in our culture is male, and that women's voices and hence their freedom are savagely repressed. Some feminists quickly rejected MacKinnon's extremism, for it seemed to close off the use of language *by* women. (See **Language, Genders, and Subcultures** in chapter 15.)

In a review of *Only Words*, "Pornography, the Constitution and a Fight Thereof," Michiko Kakutani pointed out the logical inconsistencies of MacKinnon's argument but also observed that the culture can hardly be so monolithic as the author imagines if such a book can be published. Mimi Udovich's review, "Imagine That," picked up on the equation of language and reality:

Imagine that I have pointed out that it is eminently possible and even useful to fantasize about all kinds of things that have legal implications, including, but not limited to, rape, murder, suicide, and marriage, without having any real intention, or any *functional* desire, to commit them in real life. Imagine that even if, as MacKinnon believes, pornography has a fixed, inevitable effect on those who produce and consume it, every analogy indicates that a program of regulation, treatment, and education would be more effective than prohibition.

The best single review of MacKinnon's *Only Words* is "Sex and the Single-Minded," in which Alice Echols points out that the book's strident tone and its refusal to make distinctions render MacKinnon's arguments indistinguishable from Andrea Dworkin's less rational statements.

Judith Butler's recent *Excitable Speech: A Politics of the Performative* analyzes the antiporn positions with an eye to separating them from a larger feminism whose liberal tradition insists upon freedom to choose one's sexual standards. Speech is a rehearsal of, and a contribution to, performance, to be sure, but despite the trendy conflation of language and power, Butler says, speech is not always under human control, nor is it always an instrument of control. Words may or may not injure—a compelling reason for keeping the state out of its regulation. Leaving aside battles over "essentialism," that is, exempting some things from the category of language on the grounds that they may be "real" after all, as when we stumble over a rock that we cannot explain away as discourse, the argument that words are "real" runs counter to Western epistemology. For example, most of us believe that abandoning the custom of ritual sacrifice in favor of prayer, that is, substituting words for acts, was the beginning of civilization. The power of words lies precisely in their ability to be decoupled from the reality they symbolically represent.

Disciples have followed MacKinnon and Dworkin. Sheila Jeffreys insists in " 'Pornography' and 'Creating the Sexual Future' " that the "demolition of heterosexual desire is a necessary step on the route to women's liberation" (483); doing so would involve draconian measures against sexual expression and perhaps even sexuality itself. Unlike Dworkin, who places her hopes in artificial methods of reproduction that will obviate physical contact between men and women, Jeffreys seems unconcerned about the survival of the species. (Campus jokes make light of this position: if language really is sexual reality, then we should be able to conjure up children without engaging in intercourse.) In "Pornography Unmodified," whose title is a play on MacKinnon's *Feminism Un-modified*, Susanne Kappeler sums up the radical antiporn position:

A feminist critique of pornography opened up a much more comprehensive analysis of culture and society, as pornography became defined as a *system*, not simply as a trashy subgenre of literature and popular culture. It opened up a discussion of pornography as a form of male violence, as a huge business and industry connected to prostitution, and as an ideological tool that pervades malestream culture in all its forms, including the arts. It opened up possibilities for developing feminist legislation in different countries, as well as continued activist work in the women's liberation movement (WLM) and in malestream politics. (382)

Pornography: The Production and Consumption of Inequality, by Gail Dines, Robert Jensen, and Ann Russo, is an Andrea Dworkin–like deconstruction of pornography as a discourse of oppression that avoids Dworkin's campfire-story methodology. Although the authors try to outdo each other in sensitivity, Russo's contribution somewhat wistfully admits that the issues are probably more complex than poststructuralist and feminist orthodoxies of power and in-equality. Maria Comninou's novel approach in "Speech, Pornography, and Hunt-ing" is to link hunting and pornography, here described as lethal to victims but shielded by free speech, in a volume whose context is the equation of "sexism and speciesism," a conflation that seems as dependent as much on female re-sentment as on imagination and likely to strike all but the most committed postmodernist feminists as trying too hard.

The "Male Gaze": Visuality and Pornography

The most intriguing contribution of feminist criticism to theories of visual representation has been to assert the patriarchal bias of looking, sometimes called "gaze" or "spectatorship." The prototexts are visual theorist John Berger's two famous works on nudity and eroticism, *Ways of Seeing* and *About Looking*. Berger stresses that nakedness has to become objectified in order to be regarded as nudity. In *Ways of Seeing*, Berger says, "To be nude is to be seen naked by others and yet not recognized for oneself. A naked body has to be seen as an object in order to become a nude. (The sight of it as an object stimulates the use of it as an object.) Nakedness reveals itself. Nudity is placed on display. To be naked is to be without disguise. To be on display is to have the surface of one's own skin, the hairs of one's own body, turned into a disguise which, in that situation, can never be discarded. The nude is condemned to never being naked. Nudity is a form of dress" (54). To be naked, he says, is to be oneself, whereas the nude is always shaped by various conventions. Great paintings of nudes use some of the same conventions but are interpreted by the particular painter, who lavishes a kind of love on the subject that cannot be shared by the spectator but can be dimly apprehended as a relationship, an apprehension that excludes the voyeurism inherent in viewing lesser works. Even so, says Berger, the typical nude in Western art is female, and the male gaze defines the female subject as object in a, well, *naked* expression of power. He argues that the female nude in a medium is a figure who watches herself being watched by a male; male gaze is all-controlling and serves to define the female as aesthetically, culturally, and erotically subordinate, that being—according to Berger—the essential function of representation in the first place.

The highly influential thesis of the film critic Laura Mulvey goes further, charging that visuality itself has been co-opted by males: the masculine gaze is dominant by dint of a history of patriarchal influence, and there is no escaping its construction of reality. Though in some ways a restatement of Jean-Luc Godard's observation that the history of cinema is the history of boys photographing girls, Mulvey's "Visual Pleasure and Narrative Cinema," which she elaborates in *Visual and Other Pleasures*, should be required reading, for it ventures into voyeurism, fetishism, and scopophilia. Mulvey assumes that because patriarchy grows out of the nature of human sexuality, and since patriarchy, in turn, determines what is sexually pleasurable, then voyeuristic technologies inevitably and inherently stem from a masculine way of looking. The male gaze denies women a viable position from which to view images.

In *Pornography and Silence*, Susan Griffin translates the male gaze thesis into a metaphor of master and slave: "Hidden in the darkness of a theater, anonymous as the man who stares at a public photograph, he is in the position of power. The pornographic nude has become his object. She performs for his pleasure. He owns and masters her. And as much as she exposes herself and makes herself vulnerable, so is he also unexposed and invulnerable" (48). Susanne Kappeler's *The Pornography of Representation*, though clotted by rhetorical confusion, carries some of the Berger and Mulvey arguments to extremes. Her thesis is that it is virtually impossible to "see" in nonmasculine perspective; *any* and all representations are sexist: a male aesthetic is the root of a patriarchal oppression of women. Kappeler embraces the logical consequence of her theory and stands ready to jettison centuries of art in the name of justice to women: "The committed intention of the feminist (or any other political) writer is irreconcilable with the attitude required of art and artists, that is, their irresponsibility towards political reality" (222). In Kappeler's formulation, the "male gaze" becomes a feminist version of original sin: because masculine bias has irrevocably tainted human vision, language, and thought, women will forever be victims in the most primal sense and can never develop their own ideas, let alone a sexuality unequivocally female, and still less a pornography that speaks to them. The irony of Kappeler's charges, given the number of books that female critics are turning out, might strike some as amusing.

In this camp also is Diana E. H. Russell, whose *Dangerous Relationships: Pornography, Misogyny, and Rape* is a revision of Russell's 1994 self-published *Against Pornography: The Evidence of Harm*, which included 100 extremely cruel and ugly, carefully selected photographs (the revision merely describes them) that she implies are the kind that audiences prefer, but her real purpose is to stress that even nonviolent pornography leads directly to rape. She tries to distinguish between pornography and erotica but can think of only two truly erotic films, one involving the peeling of an orange, the other the copulating of snails, though she does acknowledge having met women who think that it *might* be possible to depict actual humans in representations that are erotic without being misogynistic and despicable. More a statement of faith than an argument, her "pornography causes rape" thesis cites studies whose authors specifically reject such conclusions. Russell excoriates the National Organization for Women for refusing to condemn all forms of sexual expression and says that such feminists are "irrational."

In "Is the Gaze Male?" E. Ann Kaplan suggests that male domination of cultural habits controls and determines the ways we see things; she thinks the exclusivity of the male view means that authentic images of women are subordinated in any kind of cinema. Kaplan displays little of the Old Testament fervor reminiscent of biblical injunctions against graven images common to other gaze-theorists, however, and thinks that women can make their own kind of representations. *The Female Gaze: Women as Viewers of Popular Culture*, edited by Lorraine Gammon and Margaret Marshment, contains uneven essays on women as consumers and viewers of artifacts of popular culture, as does *The Female Spectator: Looking at Film and Television*, edited by Deidre E. Pribram; the contributors adopt positions along the spectrum of visual theory. Still another volume generated by the thesis is *Sexuality, the Female Gaze, and the Arts*, edited by Ronald Dotterer and Susan Bowers; the contributors extend the concept of gaze in many directions.

Mary Ann Doane's "Film and the Masquerade: Theorising the Female Spectator" offers a variation on the Berger thesis: there is a sexual politics of looking, Doane says, and since women's bodies are inevitably treated fetishistically by the media, spectatorship can only be male. Doane compares the male gaze to a dirty joke and, borrowing a page from Freud, suggests that gaze functions the same way, by making women the butt of a joke. Unlike many such theorists, Doane does not seem to think that the obvious interest that some women have in other women's bodies automatically makes them traitors to their sex. Returning to the subject in "Masquerade Reconsidered: Further Thoughts on the Female Spectator," Doane thinks that women may prevail if they learn to laugh; she makes the important point that femininity is itself a role that spectators learn to read as a system of signs. Kaja Silverman insists in *Male Subjectivity at the Margins* that, strictly speaking, gaze cannot be controlled or possessed by anyone; she tries to distinguish between "gaze" and "look."

The male gaze thesis may be too facile, says Gaylyn Studlar, who reexamines some of the films from which Mulvey drew her conclusions. In her *In the Realm of Pleasure: Von Sternberg, Dietrich, and the Masochistic Aesthetic*, Studlar identifies a core of masochism that cannot be explained as simply another version of the dominant male gaze. Mulvey has modified her position in "Afterthoughts on 'Visual Pleasure and Narrative Cinema' Inspired by *Duel in the Sun*," to suggest that the male gaze may not be so all-encompassing as she once thought. Probably the most astute debate on the male gaze thesis has been joined in a series of essays collected by the editors of *Screen* on pornography as "a complex and unpredictable regime of representation" (130) for *The Sexual Subject: A Screen Reader in Sexuality*. Here Griselda Pollock points out in "What's Wrong with 'Images of Women'?" that all images of women are socially constructed, that none are "real," and that Mulvey may be misleading in suggesting that male anxieties alone shape the male gaze. Pollock observes that pornography runs counter to Mulvey's thesis that the male gaze cannot acknowledge women's sexuality precisely because explicit film does depict female genitalia in great detail. According to Pollock, images may fetishize women in general, but vaginas are usually not rendered fetishistically in pornography.

John Ellis' "On Pornography" extends this argument by suggesting that pornography does fetishize women's orgasm, that doing so makes most pornography highly unstable and thus not subject to the rigidities of a male gaze, and that pornography may actually encourage through its signifiers and structures a different way of looking. Paul Willemen responds in a "Letter to John" that such a benign view of pornography ignores the latter's status as an expression of patriarchy and economic hegemony and says at best that pornography encourages what Willemen calls a "fourth look," which is really a form of voyeurism leveled at voyeurism. Claire Pajaczkowska challenges all these arguments on the grounds of their heterosexual bias by claiming that none deal adequately with the instability of gender in "The Heterosexual Presumption." Finally, Lesley Stern sorts through assumptions in "The Body as Evidence." Stern notes that feminists all too often equate the depiction of sex with sexism, that they improperly conflate sex and violence, and that they erase distinctions between fantasy as incentive to action and fantasy as revelatory of erotic states of mind. Several essays in "Pornography," a special issue of *Wide Angle*, bring new insights to bear on gaze as operative in lesbian and heterosexual soft- and hard-core films and videos.

In their focus on the cultural semiotics and anthropological aspects of images, postmodern visual scholars tend to ignore the creators of those images, which become mere inscriptions of whatever power structures the scholars believe is operative. Logically, such an approach absolves the individual artist, cinematographer, or photographer of responsibility, since anything he or she paints or frames is by definition determined and subsumed by forces beyond his or her control and thus part of a stream of figurations whose authorship is mostly irrelevant to theoreticians impatient with details or distinctions. Issues of artistry also disappear in a conflict construed as class warfare. For these reasons, the scholar may wish to look at less clearly ideological investigations of the nature of looking, whether voyeurism or scopophilia, that draws the human eye to taboo subjects like nudity or sensual embrace. Voyeurism and the appeal of images are the subjects of Gerard Malanga's *Scopophilia: The Love of Looking*, while David Freedberg's *The Power of Images: Studies in the History and Theory of Response* analyzes the way viewers react to pictures and frames; Chapters 12 and 13 of the latter deal with the reception of erotic art and pornography by audiences. Neuroses as they affect literature and art and creativity generally are the subject of David W. Allen's *The Fear of Looking, or Scopophilic-Exhibitionistic Conflicts*. Readers will also find the postmodern essays on sexuality, seeing, and images in Jacqueline Rose's *Sexuality in the Field of Vision* both useful and illuminating.

Alan Gowans' fascinating *Learning to See: Historical Perspectives on Modern Popular/Commercial Arts* treats pornography as a minor issue by observing that "the basis for all pornography is substitute imagery, insofar as painted or photographed or carved bodies serve the purposes of the real thing *in absentia*" (183) and then noting that "hard-core pornography has nothing to do, really, with any sober, factual, existing world, as may easily be discovered from a few captions in sex magazines, a few lines of dialogue from sex films, a few pages of pontificating by any modern sex guru" (192). Images at base are just stimulants. The physician John Money's "Pornography in the Home: A Topic in Medical Education," perhaps the most important single essay on the benign effects of visual eroticism, says that nature uses perceptual imagery as stimulation to reproduce the human species, that the sexes watch each other—and even objectify one another—to become sexually aroused, that primates are especially excited by the presentation of female rear ends, and that nature in evolving this mechanism of desire is in a sense its "own pornographer" (430, 412). Money speaks at length of stimulants such as pheromones, plumage, and other excitants in different species but returns again and again to the importance of images for human intercourse and reproduction.

Popular versions of the male gaze thesis, such as the videotape *Pornography: Not Just Dirty Pictures*, emphasize pornography's "objectification" of women. The assumption here is that depicting women as sexual creatures freezes them in a subordinate role; to emphasize breasts in a picture of a woman, say, levels her individuality to membership in a class of humans with breasts and suggests that only the breasts have meaning. The term has become a cliché, says Marcia Pally in "Sometimes Being an Object Is OK": objectification serves many purposes, some of them benign. What Gowans, Pally, and other critics seek to emphasize is that desire—rendered as gaze, objectification, or stereotyping—is not merely consumption, an element of political economy. Where humans are the objects of desire, desiring always implies the hope of reciprocity, or of the desire's being returned. Because the person doing the desiring has no control over whether this desire is returned, the process is at least, to a degree, self-correcting; a mistaken characterization of the desired person brings no reward, and learning and modification can take place, though perhaps slowly. To assume otherwise is to deny the possibility that humans can change. Moreover, to assume that objectification has no purpose other than victimization is to fly in the face of common sense, if only because every human abstracts and objectifies other humans constantly in order to deal with so large a volume of encounters.

Mature Feminist Reactions to Antiporn Campaigns

For a while, the ferocity of antiporn feminists set the agenda for discussion of sexual expression; the film scholar Linda Williams, for example, felt compelled to devote nearly half of her book *Hard Core* to refuting extremists. Whatever one thinks about the absolutism of MacKinnon and Dworkin, their works have served as springboards for more reasoned reevaluations of sexual expression. After pointing out that feminists made the study of porn acceptable when earlier scholars could not, Karen J. Winkler notes in "Research on Pornography Gains Respectability, Increased Importance among Scholars" that poststructuralist feminist critics have now advanced debate beyond the naive and reductionist antiporn assumptions that representation literally embodies reality and that pornography is not fantasy but actuality. Winkler writes:

Scholarship on pornography is still alive and well in academe, however. While scholars say the tide of opinion in feminist academic circles has shifted, from initially being anti-pornography to now being anti-censorship, scholars are weighing a host of unanswered questions: Does sexuality itself, and not just male and female identity, vary from culture to culture? How malleable is it? What social role does fantasy play? "We're still a long way from understanding how representation works," says Ann Barr Snitow, professor of English at the New School for Social Research. "To say that it does not literally reflect reality is not to say how it does function." (A8)

Chris Weedon's *Feminist Practice and Poststructuralist Theory* is also a useful text, as is Naomi McCormick's *Sexual Salvation: Affirming Women's Sexual Rights and Pleasures*; both sort through even the sillier positions fairly and courteously.

Many feminists rejected antiporn extremism immediately. The contradictions in the feminist, antiporn positions, the immorality of trying to restrict anyone's sexual expression, and the certainty that women themselves will be the first to be censored if the extremists have their way are the subjects of *Women against Censorship*, for which Varda Burstyn collects essays by herself, Myrna Kotash, Sara Diamond, Lisa Steele, Lynn King, Anna Gronau, Mariana Valverde and Lorna Weir, Ann Snitow, June Callwood, Lisa Duggan, Nan Hunter, Carole S. Vance, and Thelma McCormick. These perspectives, similar only in that they all reject censorship as a way of coping with pornography, are extremely rich in their diversity of insights. *Pleasure and Danger: Exploring Female Sexuality*, edited by Carole S. Vance, is a brilliant collection, mandatory reading for any student of the subject. Not all of the essays are about pornography per se, but they illustrate, among other things, that it is virtually impossible to talk about sexuality without reference to porn. *Powers of Desire: The Politics of Sexuality*, another fine collection, this one edited by Ann Snitow, Christine Stansell, and Sharon Thompson, contains essays by Ellen Willis, E. Ann Kaplan, Snitow, Carole Vance, Joan Nestle, Jessica Benjamin, and others.

The Feminist Anti-Censorship Task Force published a series of essays in a volume called *Caught Looking: Feminism, Pornography, and Censorship*, edited by Kate Ellis, Beth Jaker, Nan D. Hunter, Barbara O'Dair, and Abby Tallmer; the volume's explicit illustrations focus needed attention on pornography itself rather than on vague theories. All of the essays—by the editors and by Pat Califia, Ellen Willis, Paula Webster, Carole Vance, Lisa Duggan—are notable for their common sense; the appended chronology of events in the antiporn movement is superior to most. Similar, though its contributions are chiefly by British feminists, is *Pornography and Feminism: The Case against Censorship, by Feminists against Censorship*, edited by Gilliam Rodgerson and Elizabeth Wilson. *Dirty Looks: Women, Pornography, Power*, a collection of common-sense feminist views, this one edited by Pamela Church Gibson and Roma Gibson, is another major text in the debate (essays by Lynne Segal, Gertrud Koch, Linda Williams, Jennifer Wicke, Maureen Turim, Bette Gordon, Liz Kotz, Laura Kipnis, Lynda Nead, Chris Straayer, Grace Lau, Anne McClintock).

Still another is *Sex Exposed: Sexuality and the Pornography Debate*, edited by Lynn Segal and Mary McIntosh. Contributors discuss the differences between sexism and violence, the pros and cons of erotic representation, and the schisms within feminism; most dismiss the antiporn, feminist position as both naive and logically flawed. The title of *Bad Girls and Dirty Pictures: The Challenge to Reclaim Feminism*, edited by Alison Assiter and Avedon Carol, indicates the nature of the essays (by Gayle Rubin, Nettie Pollard, Christobel Mackenzie, Alison King, Tuppy Owens, and the editors) it contains. Useful and unusual views on pornography by women, some of whom produce it, can be found in *Good Girls/Bad Girls: Feminists and Sex Trade Workers Face to Face*, edited by Laurie Bell; *Sex Work: Writings by Women in the Sex Industry*, edited by Frédérique Delacoste and Priscilla Alexander; and *Tales from the Clit: A Female Experience of Pornography* (essays by Cherie Matrix, Jane Sweetman, Annie Sprinkle, Jen Durbin, Tuppy Owens, and others), edited by Cherie Matrix.

Nina Hartley, a feminist who chooses to advance her own vision of sexuality by performing in hard-core porn films, says in "Pornography at the Millennium": "A majority of [porn] movies ARE being made by infantile misogynists obsessively reliving their infantile fantasies. This surprises us? We do our best to raise sexually twisted people then act outraged when they create or desire twisted sexual entertainment for release" (24). Perhaps the charge most often threaded through pro-sex feminist responses is that antiporn feminists have infantilized women by insisting on their unremitting victimization. In the antiporn rendition of pornography, women are mere children who must become wards of the state. Understandably, other feminists object: women can and must choose their own sexuality and its representations. Pro-sex feminists insist that women can endorse, reject, or make their own pornography; nobody has the right to stop them, least of all women who "know best" or governments that wish to "protect" them. Jane Gallop's *Feminist Accused of Sexual Harassment*, an account of charges brought against her because of her candor in discussing sexuality, lends credence to such argument.

An additional problem with antiporn renditions of evil empires, say many feminists, is their level of abstraction. Antiporn feminists envision an operatic landscape of males constantly raping women to the jungle rhythms of relentlessly pornographic media. In this respect, the crusaders seem heirs to a tradition that searches for despoilers of an American Eden, especially since condemning sexuality as abhorrent is very much in the Puritan grain. When antiporn feminists locate evil in the sexual language of males, the most praiseworthy of whom is still a carrier of infection, moderate feminists balk. Ann Garry's "Pornography and Respect for Women" suggests that the aggression built into sexual language persuades women that pornography is hostile to them. But she says that while porn may well degrade women, the purpose of pornography is not "to dehumanize women; rather it is to arouse the audience" (325). The distinction, she says, helps to explain why debate so often fails: males do not *experience* porn as humiliating to women, but rather as sexual stimulation, just as women rarely experience romances and soap operas as pornographic. Common sense suggests that different individuals and groups extract different messages from the same source.

On the other hand, says Tania Modleski in *Feminism without Women: Culture and Criticism in a "Postfeminist" Age*, Dworkin and MacKinnon can be admired for the courage of their "moral revulsion with sex," which at least separates them from hypocrites who pretend to believe that sex is beautiful but condemn it when humans actually engage in it. Modleski thinks that pornography can only be a "postfeminist issue" (135). She wants to separate sexuality—which she thinks will always be tinged with violence and mystery—from gender, which can be dealt with in terms of social constructions, but she nonetheless finds sadomasochism—the bugbear of feminism, always stopping analysis cold—profoundly disturbing. In "Pleasure and Danger: Toward a Politics of Sexuality," Carole S. Vance agrees that feminism has made it possible to talk about previously rarely discussed issues like rape and incest but that antiporn feminists have erroneously concluded that the expanded discussion means that these crimes have increased and that the menace to women is greater than ever. Vance also believes that antiporn ideology shames women by trivializing the genuine sexual needs of women and men and that it denies sexual variation in its impulse to prescribe approved forms of sexual behavior. The assumption that sexuality is culturally constructed does not mean that it can be "easily constructed or deconstructed at the social or individual level" (9), "nor are theories of gender fully adequate to account for sexuality" (10).

Deidre English noted much earlier than other critics that the feminist, antiporn position is rooted in unlikely and unprovable theories of behaviorism; her "The

Politics of Porn: Can Feminists Walk the Line?" warned against the dangers of pontificating on poorly understood sexuality. While some feminists were circumspect, Joanna Russ attacked what she saw as the absurdities of the radical antiporn position. In "Pornography and the Doubleness of Sex for Women," Russ recognized inequities; she observed that for men sex seems to be a matter of free choice, while for women sex seems to elude their control, but suppressing pornography is to do violence to sexuality itself. Women are often divided by very different sexual histories, those who have experienced sex as abuse and those who have experienced it as positive and fulfilling; the bifurcation affects the debate on pornography. Russ, *Magic Mommas, Trembling Sisters, Puritans and Perverts: Feminist Essays* argues against separating pornography from other forms of cultural discussion. Because she cannot tell the difference between erotica and pornography, Russ worries about the definitions that antiporn feminists attempt to impose and asks the questions that so many others seem afraid to ask of antiporn feminists. In the Minneapolis antiporn ordinance written by Dworkin and MacKinnon, Russ notes, pornography is defined, in part, as a depiction of women as "inviting penetration" and therefore degrading or humiliating. She asks: Why is penetration degrading? How? How else would intercourse occur? (12). Why do not people who condemn porn give examples of erotica that get *them* excited? (59). Why not just object to violence rather than sex in media? Why do such antiporn groups scoff at civil liberties? Porn for women is in every supermarket; it is a democratic form of expression. Sexual objectification is reprehensible only when objects are all that women are allowed to be (61). Russ wonders why there is so little economic and political analysis of the subject and why women should cling to outmoded stereotypes, especially those that sentimentalize death: "Why does Susan Griffin give us, as a feminist ideal of sexuality, the great love of (hold on to your hats) Tristan and Iseult [a story in which both characters die]?" (60). Why does Laura Lederer quote from Elizabeth Cady Stanton's 1853 letter to Susan B. Anthony condemning men's lust? Why do antiporn ideologues ignore the reality of S/M, which usually depicts men as victims? Russ insists that "the best cure for pornography is sex—I mean autonomously chosen activity, freely engaged in for the sake of real pleasure, intense, and unmistakably the real thing. The more we have experiences like this, the less we will be taken in by the confusions and lies and messes all around us" (119).

Dany Lacombe also asks some penetrating questions. Lacombe thinks that antiporn theorists took a wrong turn when they declined to set pornography in a historical, economic, political, and social context. Lacombe notes in *Ideology and Public Policy: The Case against Pornography* that

this resulted in a simple, reductionist definition: pornography consists of a variety of sexual presentations meaning and leading to the subordination of women. By not examining pornography in the context of the social relations it is embedded in, antipornography feminists end up reversing their original contention that pornography is a product or an expression of sexism. Instead, pornography becomes the source of sexism since pornography is not seen as stemming from historical and social forces, and since it is said to have a direct effect on male actions and attitudes, then pornography becomes the product of an aggressive male nature desirous to oppress women. This conceptualisation of pornography is based on an essentialist view of sexuality which in turn is premised on the need to control and/or repress sexuality for the protection of women. (102)

In practice, that also means that the political Right can and has co-opted the radical feminist position.

Many feminists insist that the real problem is the attempt to systematize sexual expression by equating mere sexism—a largely unexamined reflex—with actual aggression. Because she thinks MacKinnon's authoritarian vision of the state is particularly dangerous for American culture, Katie Roiphe advises in *The Morning After: Sex, Fear, and Feminism on Campus* that we not link forms of victimization and forms of sexuality. White, middle-class women, says Roiphe, lead lives of relative safety, which makes their specious lumping of sexual expression and sexual crimes suspect; demonizing pornography seems more often than not a form of titillation. Mimi Udovich's "Done to Death" articulates similar impatience. This brief article deplores the linking together of date rape, sexual harassment, pornography, and consensual sexual role playing. "It is surely one of the unifying characteristics of humankind that all people of gender want to have sex and want to have some say with whom and how they have it," says Udovich. She acknowledges that our culture has been more prone to bestow the right to "say" in these matters on males rather than females, but she thinks that it is time that women got on with claiming that right instead of warping abuses out of proportion. The title of *Debating Sexual Correctness: Pornography, Sexual Harassment, Date Rape and the Politics of Sexual Equality*, edited by Adele M. Stan, indicates similar concerns; it is a balanced volume, with contributions from many perspectives.

The arguments advanced against the feminist, antiporn position by other feminists include the recognition that pornography is by definition offensive, that it has always been an avenue for unpopular, even outrageous expression, that censorship will hurt everyone, women, minorities, and homosexuals included, and that a commissar in skirts is still a commissar. Other feminists point out that confusion arises from the conflation of gender and sexuality and that we should concentrate on the former. A more useful way of thinking about gender inequities, says Mariana Valverde in *Sex, Power and Pleasure*, is to point out that women have been unfairly saddled with the responsibilities of sex itself, not just its reproductive consequences. A male-dominated culture has made women into the technicians of sex, forced them to become beautiful objects of desire, equipped them with manuals for pleasing men, and clothed them in seductive uniforms—lingerie and high heels and so forth—at the same time that it reserved for men other erotic outlets in the form of achievements valued more highly. Determined not to reduce relationships to facile reflections on the exercise of power, Valverde examines the social, technological, and economic complexity of gender roles; her book is eminently persuasive and an excellent counterargument to the radical antiporn position.

Audre Lorde's "Uses of the Erotic: The Erotic as Power" decries the false dichotomy of erotic and pornographic and holds that sexual explicitness holds great power for women seeking to understand themselves. Lorde's observations are part of her larger insistence that the feminism of a wealthy white and Western sensibility is essentially out of touch with the sexuality of anyone else. In *Ain't I a Woman: Black Women and Feminism*, bell hooks also focuses on collisions between white, middle-class feminist constructions of reality and the less privileged condition of black females, as does Tracey A. Gardner, who resists simple equations in "Racism in Pornography and the Women's Movement."

Finally, Jacqueline N. Zita tries to sort out conflicting claims in "The Future of Feminist Sex Inquiry." Zita identifies several categories of "concern": (1) "the deconstruction of monolithic categories of sexuality"; (2) "contextualization of sexual practices"; (3) "deconstruction of lesbianism as a magical sign"; (4) "re-evaluation of 'gay-positive' research"; (5) "partial essentialism"; (6) "more plain talk." The latter two are commonsense categories. Zita thinks that feminists should acknowledge that humans have physical bodies and that not everything is socially constructed: as she puts it, "a postmodernist male cannot become a lesbian by talking like one." Moreover, and this is obviously where pornography comes in, feminists "need to talk more about what is done—to whom, by whom, when, why, and how—in sex acts and practices. Typically, academic discourse on sexuality sublimates action into wordiness as a proper conduct for the body. By making explicit what we actually do in sex—more plain talk about it—the mystification regarding sexual categories and sex differences based on sex acts can be more openly scrutinized" (490–491).

Male Responses to Feminist Antiporn Campaigns

Males appalled at wholesale attacks on their sexuality should be aware of the deep fears of violence that affect many women. They can take comfort from feminists who reject sweeping characterizations of males as pockets of evil; the latter point out that the radical feminist argument has much in common with racist diatribes predicated on the assumption that since some Afro-Americans commit thefts, all members of that group want to steal, and therefore that expressions by Afro-Americans should be curtailed. Women, in turn, should be aware of the deep fears of hive mentalities that drive men away from relationships that women prefer. That said, we can note that men have responded to the feminist, antiporn attacks with mostly defensive postures. William Beatty Warner complains in " 'Treating Me like an Object: Reading Catharine MacKinnon's Feminism" that MacKinnon's stereotyping of male sexuality is an attempt to objectify males. Warner's argument is typical of many by males who point out that this kind of demonology hardly requires deconstruction to reveal its sexual bias; it denies humanity to the male, reduces him to the stereotype of rapist-oppressor-consumer, and often ignores biological aspects of his sexuality. In its desire to objectify males, antiporn feminism cannot conceive of multiple interpretations of pornography. The more extreme antiporn, feminist positions embody older puritanical definitions of sexual desire as abnormal and sexual expression as deviance. Gary Day's "Looking at Women: Notes toward a Theory of Porn" suggests that men enjoy looking at women for different reasons at different times; their motives vary with venues and media and may or may not have anything to do with hostility toward women.

The novelist J. M. Coetzee's essay on MacKinnon (61–82) in *Giving Offense: Essays on Censorship* sneers at the claim that pornography is a master discourse, challenges the notion that the oppression of women is an implementation of pornography as a theory of oppression, and charges her with "parochialism," on the grounds that she knows little of real oppression, especially in other cultures. Arguing against MacKinnon and Dworkin, whom he charges with attempting to criminalize thought, Larry L. Langford says in *Fiction and the Social Contract: Genocide, Pornography, and the Deconstruction of History* that the outrageous is the province of fiction. Moreover, Langford insists, the social contract is built upon the recognition that the boundaries between fact and fiction never collapse.

Alan Soble constructs a Marxist view of male sexuality as related to capitalist production. A truly Marxist society, Soble suggests in *Pornography: Marxism, Feminism, and the Future of Sexuality*, would produce pornography depicting the sexes more equitably. Antiporn feminists cavalierly sacrifice the pleasures of others in the interest of achieving a just and stable society for themselves. In support of just that view, however, "Eros Thanatized: Pornography and Male Sexuality," a neo-Marxist analysis by Harry Brod, maintains that men may be as traumatized by pornography as women, that males do not necessarily derive pleasure from it, and that for those reasons they should be willing to dispense with it. Brod's position is that by reducing sex to nasty representations, pornography actually restricts sensual pleasure for men.

The thirty-five essays by males collected by Michael S. Kimmel in *Men Confront Pornography* range widely. Some confess to guilty pleasures engendered by porn; others recall useful sexual information learned from porn when they were unable to find it elsewhere; still others admit to having been victimized by porn when their sexuality was misdirected toward politically incorrect or socially inappropriate goals. Notable among the essays included are David Steinberg's "The Roots of Pornography" (54–59), which asserts that men and women can try to learn from each other's erotic expression; Fred Small's "Pornography and Censorship" (72–80), which acknowledges the violence of a fraction of pornography and also suggests that gender perception of sex and its representation is mutable through education and goodwill; Douglas Campbell's "One

Man's Pleasures" (99–101), which condemns pornography "as a pernicious socializing agency" that damages relationships between men and women; Robert Staples' "Blacks and Pornography" (111–114), which reports that pornography is "not a burning issue" in black communities more concerned with overt injustice; Timothy Beneke's "Intrusive Images and Subjectified Bodies" (168–187), which says that "we ought to discourage disrespect for women in images, yet free women and men in consensual sexual practices"; and Kimmel's " 'Insult' or 'Injury': Sex, Pornography, and Sexism" (305–319), which urges men to defy "sexual repression and sexual violence" and join forces with women against "a repressive culture." Essays of similar tenor make up "Men Confronting Pornography," a special issue of *Changing Men: Issues in Gender, Sex and Politics*. Van F. White's "Pornography and Pride" in that issue is by an Afro-American cosponsor of the Minneapolis antiporn ordinance; White supported the ordinance because he thinks the merchandising of pornography is inherently discriminatory. He notes that one rarely finds sex stores in middle-class neighborhoods, but always in poor and ethnic ones.

Other male critics have endorsed the feminist, antiporn position. Ron Thorne-Finch is one, as evidenced by his *Ending the Silence: The Origins and Treatment of Male Violence against Women*. The best-known male in the antiporn feminist camp is John Stoltenberg, whose theories are even more bizarre than those of Andrea Dworkin, his close friend. Stoltenberg is one of the leading proponents of a New Age Puritanism that rejects sexuality as presently constituted on the grounds that it is too aggressive. He finds in contemporary ideals of masculinity an absolutely evil savagery few other people see; masculinity as he understands it is built almost entirely on the denigration of women. In *Refusing to Be a Man* and *The End of Manhood: A Book for Men of Conscience*, Stoltenberg argues that male objectification of women is perhaps the least of men's sins, since desire is too often dependent on terrifying women. Pornography represents the abuse of women in order to foster such aggression and serves as gratification for males temporarily without a woman to torment. Stoltenberg's *What Makes Pornography "Sexy"?* and "Pornography," the latter a videocassette, define the sinister appeal of pornography as savagery directed at women; the "sexiness" of a given example of pornography is a function of the degree of humiliation of women for the pleasure of men. Pornography for Stoltenberg is a species of terrorism. Stoltenberg also charges that pornography, which he defines as constructed in heterosexual terms, is the source of homophobia in the United States, giving it precedence over obvious candidates such as religious intolerance, one reason, perhaps, that gay-baiting fundamentalists applaud Stoltenberg's position. In "You Can't Fight Homophobia and Protect the Pornographers at the Same Time—An Analysis of What Went Wrong in *Hardwick*," Stoltenberg observes: "If what I've said is true—if in fact male supremacy simultaneously produces both a homophobia that is erotically committed to the hatred of homosexuality *and* a homosexuality that is erotically committed to sex discrimination—then it becomes easier to understand why the gay community, taken as a whole, has become almost hysterically hostile to radical-feminist antipornography activism" (186). According to Stoltenberg, pornography is a form of terror against both women and gays, but homosexuals nevertheless replicate the terror by endorsing it. Like Dworkin, Stoltenberg objects to the sexuality of straight and gay males because both penetrate orifices, a practice that seems to him unspeakable.

Gay and Lesbian Responses to Feminist Antiporn Campaigns

Stoltenberg's critics believe that his messages dehumanize sex in expressing hatred not only of heterosexual but also of homosexual men. Typical is Michael Bronski, who tells Deb Whippen and Joe Interrante in "Men and Pornography: An Interview with Michael Bronski" that because Stoltenberg's antiporn theory is grounded in heterosexuality, it does not really apply to homosexual varieties. Moreover, antiporn theory assumes an "other," whereas gay men are responding to the "self" (31). Stoltenberg's vociferous criticism of gays is misguided, Bronski thinks, because "one can't negate the body and be able to have politics which are connected to experience" (32). In "Gender, Fucking and Utopia: An Essay in Response to John Stoltenberg's *Refusing to Be a Man*," Scott Tucker maintains that pornographic representations and iconographies serve useful purposes; gay porn does not fit the feminist characterization of pornography as savage. Tucker lampoons Stoltenberg's statement: "Pornography tells lies about women. But pornography tells the truth about men." Tucker challenges Stoltenberg's conviction that male erections are produced only by violence. Tucker declines to be drawn "into either the essentialist or social construction camps . . . as presently constructed," asserting that "*human nature is always socially potential and emergent*" (34). Tucker, a sometime gay porn star, says that whatever else it may be, sexuality is not merely a social fiction. Such critics observe that Stoltenberg's theories of sexuality are most charitably described as quackery: as one instance, they characterize as absurd Stoltenberg's assertion that if one bends an erect penis, it hurts, a circumstance that "proves" that erections must be unnatural. In any case, Stoltenberg's work seems to fit Ian Jarvie's category of antipornography as mirror-reverse of the pornography it critiques.

Because it is inevitably construed as a battle over permissible forms of sexuality, the issue of pornography has divided antiporn feminists and gay and lesbian advocates. Leo Bersani's "Is the Rectum a Grave?" notes the resurgence of the conviction that sex is justified only as a reproductive act. On one hand, Bersani thinks that MacKinnon and Dworkin's "reinvention of sex" has much to offer in terms of their vision of the nearly total eroticizing of daily expression. On the other, he rejects their characterization of gay sex as a replication of forms of heterosexual aggression. Similarly, in "The Porn Debate," Gary Kinsman insists that gay pornography holds different social meaning and does not generate or replicate the unequal gender relationships that antiporn feminists find in heterosexual pornography. Barry D. Adam's *The Rise of a Gay and*

Lesbian Movement points out that in 1984–1985 women's bookstores in the United States began banning lesbian images made by and for lesbians (144–145) because the feminist antipornography campaign

had subtly shifted the contours of feminist discourse. In a decade, feminist reasoning had seemingly come full circle: from arguing the artificiality of gender and demanding its transcendence, it now asserted an unbridgeable chasm between the sexes and the need to obliterate "death-loving" male values. The new nationalism, or cultural feminism, rang with echoes of nineteenth-century argumentation that women are essentially more pure, more temperate, and more moral than men, and that women's mission is to battle male lustfulness and corruption. Anti-pornography literature implicitly endorsed some very traditional assumptions about the nature of women and their roles in society. (146)

Man to Man: Gay Couples in America, by Charles Silverstein, gently reproves antiporn feminists for condemning gay expression—"the women's movement sometimes asserts itself as a Victorian matron grimacing at the sexual ferocity of the male gay world" (335)—and dismisses the antiporn theories as clearly insufficient to deal with either heterosexuality or homosexuality. Simon Watney insists that the feminist, antiporn critique merely reinforces the rationales for "policing" the expression of both heterosexuals and gays. In *Policing Desire: Pornography, AIDS, and the Media,* Watney argues that gay sexuality is not structured in the same ways that heterosexuals configure theirs, and therefore gays do not respond in the same way to ordinary pornography. Watney is particularly hostile to the cultural assumption that sexuality by itself leads to AIDS and thinks that porn at least sends the message that sex by itself is wonderful. To be opposed to porn, he implies, is to be opposed to sex.

Gayle Rubin asks why so many feminists have accepted unsupported assumptions, definitions, and claims advanced by radical antiporn crusaders. Her "Misguided, Dangerous and Wrong: An Analysis of Anti-Pornography Politics" answers with seven points: (1) pornography has long been anathematized by our culture, so women are not likely to defend it, (2) because so many women are unfamiliar with pornography, they cannot detect false claims about its nature, though that is changing as women become more comfortable with erotic materials, (3) "most pornography *is* sexist" (37), but no more than ordinary fiction, and that, too, is changing as more women produce erotica, (4) most pornography looks cheap and vulgar and unworthy of consideration, (5) humans feel ashamed of their own nudity or intercourse, which leads them to think these things are degrading, (6) even people who know better commonly use "obscene" and "pornographic" imprecisely, and (7) while porn "should not be immune to feminist criticism" (37), women could better spend their time working to advance their own sexual agendas.

"The Body You Want: Liz Kotz Interviews Judith Butler" ranges across the issues raised by lesbian representation, during the course of which Butler criticizes the feminist, antiporn position for Kotz. During the 1980s, says Butler, the position was persuasive, but she now thinks it is "absolutely wrong": "[Andrea Dworkin] actually believes that pictures have the power to form psyches and desires, and to produce actions in an almost behavioristic way. It struck me that she wants to police not only representations but the ways people think, desire, and fantasize; she wants to obliterate the ethical distinctions between fantasy, representation, and action" (87). In *A Restricted Country*, Joan Nestle points out that lesbians and prostitutes have often been relegated to the same marginal status; she confesses to a "deep despair at the new anti-pornography movement" (144) and a fear that "some feminist-lesbians will turn us in and feel they have made the world safer for women by doing so" (150). Other lesbians feel that the schism is not permanent. In *Finger-Licking Good: The Ins and Outs of Lesbian Sex*, Tamsin Wilton hopes to forge alliances between lesbians and feminists, despite arguments over pornography, sadomasochism, dildos, and so on, by stressing gender rather than sexuality.

PORNOGRAPHY AS TABOO

Taboo, originally a Polynesian word for menstruation, has come in general parlance to mean *the forbidden*, a category whose sinister implications also make it irresistible. The anthropologist Margaret Mead points out in "Sex and Censorship in Contemporary Society" that virtually every society attempts to censor sexual information: "Where there is no written literature and no representational art, this censorship may be limited to the prohibition of the use of certain words, the substitution of words from another language, or the restriction of the use of these words between men and women or between the parent and child generations" (7). The basis for enforcement of canons of modesty and shame is the fear that violations of taboo will unleash social disorder, if not cosmic chaos. And yet, Mead says, these are "two-way taboos": "They prevent the kind of sex behavior one doesn't want—keep children and adults apart, keep men out of their neighbor's houses when the husbands are away, keep a chance encounter during excretion from turning into a sexual adventure—*and* they provide the necessary stimuli to sex activity in the right places" (11–12). Pornography encapsulates sexual "daydreams," some of which may be dangerous in their implications, others of which are harmless; Mead tries to distinguish between bawdy humor that she thinks is essential to human community and the meaner, alienating forms of expression that she thinks a society in its evolution may proscribe in the interests of stability. She also knows that it is human to want to violate taboos, to transgress.

This is a problem that, in one sense or another, weaves itself into all serious considerations of pornography: its precise relation to obscenity. More than a legal concept—pornography is quite legal in America, while obscenity is not— the uneasy association between sex and the dark, id-like realm of obscenity is problematic. One perspective on taboo inverts prevailing legal doctrine. Courts in the United States hold that only obscenity—defined variously as that which appeals to prurient interest, appeals only to morbid interest in sex or excreta, offers no redeeming social importance, and so on—is proscribable, *not* pornography—defined as sexual expression—which is protected speech. Probably the chief exponent of the view that obscenity is far more valuable is Henry Miller, who has many times argued that obscenity is fundamental to life, that it is the secret of the universe, that flowers must have dirt to grow; Miller insisted that his fiction was emetic rather than pornographic, that he was deliberately reaching into the obscene in order to understand the wellsprings of art and human nature (see Chapter 16, **Erotic Literature**, especially Miller's "Obscenity and the Law of Reflection").

Some critics identify the need to shock, to break moral and aesthetic taboos, as essential to the pornographic impulse. The theorist most often linked with this view is Georges Bataille, whose *Death and Sensuality: A Study of Eroticism and the Taboo* argues that eroticism has been divorced from natural cycles and is unabashedly artificial. Because Western civilization itself is an artificial construct, it locates eroticism in those acts that distance themselves from reproduction. Pornography is thus not a "natural" response to sexuality but is nevertheless a quintessentially human attempt to preserve and violate taboos. Bataille's *Les Larmes d'Eros* extends this discussion to the relationship of the erotic to pain, to violence, and to death. Useful, though hardly focused on pornography, is Mary Douglas' well-known *Purity and Danger: An Analysis of Concepts of Pollution and Taboo*. Douglas' text helps to explain the force of taboos, especially those associated with scatalogical matters, in American culture. Taboos about dirtiness help create social boundaries for acceptable behavior and expression, and they help also to explain the linkages between pornography and obscenity. Norman Brown, in *Life against Death*, argues that violating taboo can strike a blow at repression and thus encourage bisexuality and "polymorphous perversity" as hallmarks of a more egalitarian culture; for Brown, the obscene holds out potential for transgression that, in turn, gives mundane life meaning.

Jane Caputi follows Bataille, Jessica Benjamin, Susan Sontag, Freud, and Foucault in her *Voluptuous Yearnings: A Feminist Theory of the Obscene*, in discussing the uses of obscenity (construed as far more than sexuality) in any culture. A passage in Tony Duvert's remarkable essay, "Other People's Eroticism," is instructive:

Then what distinguishes eroticism from pornography is not a difference between our own beautiful sexuality and the disgusting one of others: in reality, in terms of establishment standards, all *real* sexuality remains guilty, ugly, bestial, miscarried. We are never rich enough, handsome enough, young enough, mature enough, virtuous enough, endowed enough, normal enough, man enough, woman enough, to have a sexuality that is permissible, respectable, or simply possible. These are the exigencies shaped by our laws, our moral codes, our ideals, our masterpieces, our very rules for desire. It is not surprising that they apply to entertainment as well. But "pornography" commits the crime of insufficiently idealizing what it shows—and yet in its abundance of nudes and exploits, it is a garden of delights alongside our real life. (117)

Still another variation on Bataille's thesis is Paula Webster's "The Forbidden: Eroticism and Taboo"; Webster believes that pornographic fantasies, as a record of transgressions, constitute a culture's "erotic heritage." Problems arise when one group tries to sanitize the expression of another group and thus destroy its contributions to that heritage.

Richard S. Randall analyzes social and political demands for control of speech in an era defined by expanded communication in *Freedom and Taboo: The Politics of a Self Divided*. Central to conflicts are notions of taboo in a liberal and democratic society. Because pornography reminds us of our secret desires, our animal nature, and our inclination toward the perverse, our culture needs to preserve and even institutionalize sexual images as a way of discharging atavistic impulses. Roger Shattuck's *Forbidden Knowledge: From Prometheus to Pornography* reminds us that most intellectual breakthroughs must overcome taboos against penetrating too deeply into the nature of things, of affronting God or nature or merely accepted norms of thought and behavior. In some cultures, violating taboo brought swift punishment. The utility of pornography is that it permits people to violate taboos in private fantasy. A woman curious about anal intercourse might wish to watch pornographic movies in which it is featured and find the sight erotic but never actually engage in the practice or even want to.

Murray S. Davis' *Smut: Erotic Reality/Obscene Ideology* is an investigation of the phenomenological reality of sex and the role that representations of it play; Davis argues with critics like Sontag and Slade. If the general scholar has time to read only one book on the subject of pornography, however, it should be *Pornography: The Other Side*, by the Canadian philosopher F. M. Christensen. Christensen contributes new arguments and fresh perspectives to the debate; he deals patiently with level after level of encrusted myth and misinformation about pornography. Christensen's common sense does not endear him to academic critics, and he may be faulted for not recognizing that the debate is deeply irrational: if pornography is at base sexual folklore, then reason has little relevance. A miniversion of Christensen's principal thesis appears in a *Playboy* interview entitled "A Philosopher Looks at the Porn Debate": here he suggests that the anger directed against pornography by most critics has to do with persistent personal and cultural shame regarding bodily functions rather than concern with violence, especially since there is so little evidence of connections between eroticism and aggression. Christensen argues nonetheless that pornography has positive value for a culture hamstrung by sexual repression, dehumanized by technology, oppressed with sterile theories of power, roiled by special interest groups, and divided by suspicion and bickering. His point is that we can choose to enjoy pornography or not and take from it what we will. Christensen's brilliant critique is the latest of a line of books reaching back, if benchmark be needed, at least as far as H. Kincaid Murray's *Coercion and Perversion: Or Primeval Degenerates* (1934), which attacked false modesty, sexual ignorance, and the lack of education in the United States, conditions Murray thought led to repression, mental disorders, and personal tragedy. D. F. Barber's *Pornography and Society* is another iteration of the contention that pornography functions to express what ultimately cannot be denied, but the reader will find many versions of the argument. Any of John Money's books are worth reading in this regard; his latest, *Sin, Science, and the Sex Police*, attempts, as always, to bring rationality to bear on sex, pornography, and gender preferences.

It may be that the alliance of radical antiporn feminists, political conservatives, and religious fundamentalism represents a socially constructed movement to restore a sense of weight (or taboo) to words and images attenuated by the latest high-speed, high-volume information-processing technologies. For many Americans, the thinning of experience implied by the prospect of virtual reality is ontologically menacing, as are theories that reality can be reduced to mere language or images. Anathematizing pornography may thus restore some of representation's power to shock. Anxieties over taboo are also implicit in theories of cultural hegemony. If hegemony—the effort to compel assent to a dominant ideology—is so unremitting, what exactly is it trying to suppress? What is the opposite, the "other," that hegemony fears? If sex is power, can it not also operate in more than one direction?

PORNOGRAPHY AND SUBVERSION

Leaving aside the welter of conflicting mores, some of the debate over pornography stems from an imperfect recognition of what we might call pornography's "divided stream." Pornography is not a monolithic discourse, despite the common images and themes of its many genres; there is no such thing as Pornography with a capital "P." Pornography "means" many different things to many different people who nonetheless believe that the term itself reflects uniformity of opinion and attitude. Subsuming the many pornographic genres and media are at least two traditions, each dependent on conceptions of class and history: *low* and *high*.

The progress of "high" pornography can be traced fairly easily because its relatively recent "texts"—buckram-bound volumes, costly etchings, china figurines, quasi-scholarly treatises, and elegant photographic portfolios, to cite typical examples—were produced by people closer to the center of culture; we sometimes call these artifacts *erotic* rather than pornographic in recognition of a difference construed in terms of expense, class, and taste. The creators of these texts may self-consciously twit convention and authority, and they may borrow tropes from lower forms. In such cases, intelligence and artistry can mask and betray subversive intent. A graphic drawing by Picasso or an "obscene" novel by Edmund Wilson, challenge standards and mores, to be sure, but the codes are already understood by fair numbers of their contemporaries. Motives can be important. Producers of high porn may *intend* to invert or at least to alter hierarchies of taste, class, race, and gender. In short, they *believe* that they are subversive, in much the same way that literary critics or feminists or Marxists believe that they are undermining the status quo. The irony is that the irony itself often becomes just another cultural trope. Thus, when feminists charge white male pornographers with reinforcing a patriarchal system, while the pornographers themselves thought they were undermining established authority, both can be correct. It depends on where one stands.

By contrast, for much of their largely uncharted history, "low" types—dirty jokes, sleazy photos, salacious cartoons, oral and samizdat novels and stories, and crude stag movies, for example—have functioned as an anonymous, sometimes inarticulate, and frequently unconscious outlaw discourse. At its most subversive, this discourse reflects a sensibility defined by class and taste as much as by obsession and compulsion, and it continues to do so today. Try as a culture may to limit speech, and try as postmodernists might to characterize all expression as formal text, low forms of expression resist categorization, pursue the perverse, and disrupt authority, political correctness, good taste, and even common sense without necessarily announcing such intent. In the past, low pornography colored the voices associated with marginal groups alleged to be sexually rapacious and threatening—foreigners, especially Jews, followed by blacks, assumed perpetually to lust after white women, and more recently by gays and lesbians, condemned as corruptors of children. The larger culture anathematized these voices in order to ignore or control them, to keep them inaudible and the groups invisible—at least until it suited the larger culture selectively to absorb and commodify their messages. A culture uses its margins to redefine and reenergize itself. Women, minorities, and homosexuals can hope for full citizenship when an information economy chooses to admit them to the labor force—perhaps in order to lower wages for middle-class workers—and to the ranks of consumers—so that they can purchase their own repackaged messages. Commerce and art may come down to the same thing in our culture; the first may exploit, but it also gives voice to muted groups, that is, people who have little status, whose communities can be only imagined.

Laura Kipnis' thesis in *Bound and Gagged: Pornography and the Politics of Fantasy in America*, a grouping of five linked essays, is that class is at the heart of controversies over sexual expression. The first of her essays discusses official persecution of a man who is almost certainly innocent; others analyze *Hustler* magazine as a lower-class voice (despite Kipnis' own reservations about the vulgarity of that voice) inveighing against corrupt middle and upper classes. Pornography, Kipnis believes, can embody revolutionary purpose, a theme she has sounded in earlier works such as *Ecstasy Unlimited: On Sex, Capital, Gender, and Aesthetics* and an accompanying video, *Ecstacy Unlimited: The Interpenetration of Sex and Capital*, which deal at length with sexual expression as a reflection of political structures. Of numerous similar positions, Pat Califia's is once again pertinent. In *Sapphistry: The Book of Lesbian Sexuality*, Califia says:

All erotica is a challenge to the puritanical bias of our culture. It threatens those institutions or individuals who want sexuality to serve and come under the control of the state. Any group that wishes to exercise fascistic control over people's lives attempts to control their sexuality. An essential part of that control is the suppression of explicit images of sexual acts, especially those sexual acts that promote pleasure over conformity or suggest variation and individuality. Generally speaking, the more closely pornography conforms to the party line on acceptable sexual behavior, the more it is tolerated. Genuinely subversive erotica is often never allowed to come into being or circulate. (15)

Tuppy Owens analyzes the powerful political force of female pornography as a counter to mass-produced male fantasies in *Politico Frou-Frou: Pornographic Art as Political Protest*. She refers extensively to performance art and magazines. Joanna Frueh's *Erotic Faculties* makes similar points wittily and forcefully.

As a consequence of the dynamic of margin and mainstream, some postmodernists believe that we cannot assign a subversive role to pornography. Subversive genres are discussed by Peter Stallybrass and Alison White in *The Politics and Poetics of Transgression*. Stallybrass and White caution against taking the subversive function of any behavior or representation too literally, given the potential of a culture for playing off groups against each other. Antiporn advocates often want it both ways: sexual representation, on one hand, is the expression of a political system, and, on the other, it fosters criminal brutality that undermines the system. At base, however, pornography, especially the low variety, remains resistant to social control, impervious to cultural theories, and immune to shame and disapproval. For these reasons porn still has the power to outrage Americans of all classes and races, still functions transgressively, still shocks. That response, in turn, can be explained as a type of cultural programming, of course, but at some point the argument begs the question. Given the feminist and postmodernist assertion that pornographic genres have been culturally mainstreamed, can pornographic messages still be considered subversive? Though such critics usually deny that they can, the answer would seem implicitly to be yes, if only because critics still cannot bring themselves to describe the content of pornography. We still lack a polite discourse suitable for the articulation of graphic sexual acts; but pornography does articulate them, if vulgarly, and therein lies its power.

Hegemony is not nearly so monolithic as feminists assume. Hegemony, said Antonio Gramsci (see *Selections from Cultural Writings*), compels assent to ideas because they seem reasonable and just. But hegemonic dominance can be altered. Revolutionary movements can and must establish *their* ideas by educating a culture to their value; otherwise, the movements will fail (41–43, 275). Moreover, as other theorists have insisted, resistance is always possible even in the face of widely accepted—or dominant—ideas and constructions. In "Immigrants and Spectators," Judith Mayne challenges film theorists who have characterized early American cinema as a medium in which hegemonic discourse homogenized the diversity of immigrants to this country and turned them into passive American spectators. Such a characterization ignores the ambivalence of communication, says Mayne. On the contrary, early American cinema functioned by negative example to strengthen immigrants' own sense of ethnic and national community: "While cinema became an agent of the new culture of consumerism, the response of immigrants to the movies suggests that cinema kept alive fantasies of resistance to that culture." The movie fantasies helped create both a private as well as a public space for such groups: "Fantasy may imply 'escape,' but it is also a form of resistance, an imaginary refusal of real conditions of existence" (38, 39). The same can be said of pornographic messages and fantasies.

Ironically, say historians of gay and lesbian subcultures, homosexual pornography (even when it was merely tolerated by a heterosexual majority) and even the occasional homosexual figure marginalized in heterosexual pornography constituted an "erotic heritage" for homosexuals. Pornography provided a sense of community in the absence of other bonds and helped to create a historical consciousness of difference and resistance. The process recalls *Soul on Ice*, in which Eldridge Cleaver took on the role to which he had been relegated by a pornographic folklore as a necessary step in his liberation. Characterized as an outlaw and rapist by white society, the black Cleaver vowed to become an outlaw and a rapist, to inhabit the roles as a way of finding himself as an individual (13–14).

During periods of upheaval, when marginalized groups became assimilated, their discourse crept toward the center of a culture to influence mainstream forms of expression. Those periods of upheaval, in turn, have been accentuated by communication technologies that commodify messages from high and low culture in oddball juxtapositions we call postmodern. Even so, "pornography" for many Americans simply means a lower-class vision of sexuality, a prejudice fueled by the "cheap" quality of materials, the low status of distributors and performers, and (until recently) the locations of adult stores in poorer urban areas but also by a mythic conviction that the sexuality of "lower" classes is more primal. As we have noted, these lower forms, often devoid of identifiable authorship, are difficult to trace in a society that pretends to despise purveyors and products. At the same time, direct subversion of topical ideas by pornography seems unlikely, suggests Don D. Smith's "The Social Content of Pornography." Smith points out that social issues and changing social agendas have little effect on the porn novel's sex scenes, which remain largely similar over periods of time. Smith examined 428 explicit paperbacks published between 1968 and 1974 and tabulated 4,500 sexual episodes; he found that rape occurred in about 20 percent and that the number of rapes per average book increased over the survey years but notes that the rise can be attributed to many factors.

Using the term *pornography* indiscriminately robs it of intellectual meaning at the same time that the confusion invests it with political significance. Calling someone a pornographer is an attempt to marginalize him or her and to assert one's own power. Alex Comfort's *The New Joy of Sex: A Gourmet Guide to Lovemaking for the Nineties* defines pornography as "the name given to any sexual literature somebody is trying to suppress." Conversely, choosing to be a pornographer can be an act of rebellion. A pale reflex of this function is apparent in the hundreds of pornographic "zines" published by Americans of all genders today. In a sense those who communicate in this way choose to marginalize themselves in the interests of greater individuality and greater authenticity or simply out of discontent with the mainstream.

As Emile Durkheim pointed out in *The Division of Labor in Society*, deviants or outsiders, a group that includes pornographers, actually promote community cohesion by consciously violating established standards. Variations on this argument have been articulated by Howard S. Becker in *Outsiders: Studies in the Sociology of Deviance* and by Gilbert Geis in *One Eyed Justice: An Examination of Homosexuality, Abortion, Prostitution, Narcotics, and Gambling in the U.S.*. Edwin M. Schur makes similar arguments in *Crimes without Victims: Deviant Behavior and Public Policy*. Schur's reflections, given recent attempts to demonstrate that erotic representation is not "victimless," have fallen out of fashion. (On the other hand, Schur's "Pornography" is an excellent review of antiporn positions.) Kai T. Erikson observes that moral limits must be repeatedly tested in order to remain in force in *Wayward Puritans: A Study in the Sociology of Deviance*, a text whose thesis is that fringe elements continuously redefine margins almost as a public service. Clifton Bryant's *Sexual Deviancy and Social Proscription: The Social Context of Carnal Behavior* also discusses the balance between deviance and convention, with particular reference to pornography, obscene language, and obscene performance. Pornographers thus reinforce a kind of Manicheanism: they keep "evil" alive for Americans who need to have their faith in the forbidden reaffirmed. A corollary is that boundaries of transgression must be continuously widened as older taboos lose their force. Strangers or outsiders do not have to be scapegoats, though that is often a role they must play until they—or their memories or their descendants—are assimilated into the larger society; they are despised because they are essential. In *Bookleggers and Smuthounds: The Trade in Erotica, 1920–1940*, Jay Gertzman develops Georg Simmel's concept of the stranger or the outsider—a kind of social scapegoat—into a vision of pornographers as "pariah capitalists" who are condemned for carrying out exactly the sorts of functions, for example, producing or distributing pornography, that society needs. Gertzman notes that Jews and East Europeans fulfilled that expectation in the first half of this century; his principal example is Samuel Roth.

Murray S. Davis remarks in *Smut: Erotic Reality/Obscene Ideology*, "Pornography is extremely democratic in that it strips the false façades from everyone, not just women; it peels away the crust of character formed by society or even by the human condition itself to reveal people's authentic inner core" (181–182). The matter is complicated, of course, because pornography not only deflates pretension and subverts sexual and gender mores but also trades in sexual folklore. The messages mature at different times and lose their vulgarity—or perhaps, as conservatives insist, the culture just becomes more vulgar. Like birth control information, once anathematized as obscenity by authorities who tried to marginalize it, genres of pornography move toward the center of culture at different speeds as their messages acquire value and relevance to wider circles of Americans. When it is still fresh, the pornographic impulse is anarchic: its intent is usually to subvert sexual and culture order. Over time, specific examples may be co-opted by the larger culture and routinized (to use Max Weber's term) into acceptable forms. The poetry of Walt Whitman is an instance of this cultural dynamic; the publications of Larry Flynt, as fictionalized in Milos Forman's film *The People versus Larry Flynt* (1996) constitute another.

Porn redeems itself, says Richard Dyer in "Male Gay Porn," by embodying contradictions: on one hand, it is a capitalist commodity; on the other hand, it carries messages disruptive to the dominant politics of a culture. Freedom, ultimately, may reside in ambiguity. *The Sadeian Woman and the Ideology of Pornography: An Exercise in Cultural History*, Angela Carter's extremely thorough analysis, considers pornography in terms of class, politics, and gender, taking as its starting point the work of de Sade. Though de Sade's fantasies submerged women in stereotypes, says Carter, his work also "put pornography at the service of women" because he aimed at breaking down established order. In that anarchic sense, pornography might well be as liberating for women as for men. A rich discussion of the dangers and benefits of what the author clearly considers an important element of culture animates Carter's approach. Ellen Willis acknowledges a similar contradiction in her essay "Feminism, Moralism, and Pornography": "A woman who is raped is a victim; a woman who enjoys pornography (even if that means enjoying a rape fantasy) is in a sense a rebel, insisting on an aspect of her sexuality that has been defined as a male preserve. Insofar as pornography glorifies male supremacy and sexual alienation, it is deeply reactionary. But in rejecting sexual repression and hypocrisy—which have inflicted even more damage on women than on men—it expresses a radical impulse" (464).

In today's ever-more-repressive society, says bell hooks in *Outlaw Culture: Resisting Representations*, the rebellious are more necessary than ever. She explores the function of the outlaw in discussions of gangsta rap, censorship, date rape, violence against women, ideals of race and beauty, and democracy and feminism. Even more seminal is Ned Polsky's "On the Sociology of Pornography," one of the truly great treatises on the subject. Like prostitution, says Polsky, pornography functions to discharge "what society labels anti-social sex, i.e., impersonal, nonmarital sex: prostitution provides this via real intercourse with a real sex object, and pornography provides it via masturbatory, imagined intercourse with a fantasy object" (185). While it may have other uses, like serving as a means of sexual instruction, pornography is really devoted to assisting masturbation; "masturbation to pornography is more 'social' than masturbation simply to inner pictures, i.e., pornography offers the masturbator erotic imagery that is external to himself, a quasi-real 'other' to whom he can more 'realistically' respond" (185). Also like prostitution, pornography permits the " 'polymorphous perverse' and other sexual behaviors so highly stigmatized as to be labelled deviant even within the institution of marriage and morally inhibited from expression therein" (189). The meaning of the term *pornography*, says Polsky, is intrinsically tied to social class; society condemns the vulgar and the raucous but tolerates more elegant erotica in the same way that it tolerates corporate crime (196–197).

Critics rarely ask basic questions, the most obvious of which is, How does the marginal remain marginal enough to furnish the novelty required to refresh a rationalized culture? How does pornography remain subversive enough, first, to stand in opposition to mainstream values and, second, to energize the larger culture? The outsider status of pornographers as conscious agents of change may be one key. As W.E.B. Du Bois once remarked in speaking of minorities who are intimately acquainted with the majority in whose midst they are subsumed, such agents must maintain a "double consciousness." This mind-set, a stance familiar to those we characterize as Others, enables them to survive, to achieve a precarious stability but, more importantly, to function as innovators. Their ideas, nurtured first in isolation or on the margins, sooner or later diffuse into the larger culture, where they effect change (think of jazz or rap music, along with more abstract sexual candor). Additional answers may lie in disciplines such as thermodynamics and information theory, which deal with issues of energy, balance, and novelty, or in bold readings of culture that discard the jargon of trendy theories, such as Jane Juffer's *At Home with Pornography: Women, Sex, and Everyday Life*, a splendid study of women's domestication of adult cable channels, lingerie catalogs, cyberporn, sex toys, erotic stories, and other representations of sex that provide secret, but safe, sources of pleasure and psychic energy. Juffer is straightforward: women (and men) need sexual stimulation in order to live physical and cultural lives, and they take what they need personally and collectively from margins that are continuously replenished by human ingenuity.

Also pertinent are the essays in *Whores and Other Feminists*, edited by Jill Nagle, a collection of spirited and articulate reflections by sex workers, some of whom work as strippers or in pornography genres. Annie Sprinkle and Nina Hartley, for instance, argue that pornography has positive aspects, including empowerment for women through the subversion of gender and conventional concepts of identity, a process they think of not so much as transgressive as responsive to historical factors. They think that pornography has much to teach Americans. Similarly, Carol Queen's *Real Live Nude Girl: Chronicles of a Sex*

Positive Culture defends prostitution and sex performance, especially that which fosters gender tolerance, as crucial to a culture's health. (See also **The "Invention" of Pornography** in chapter 5.)

PORNOGRAPHY AS TECHNOLOGY

Walter Benjamin's famous essay, "The Work of Art in an Age of Mechanical Reproduction," argues that while industrialization made it possible to mass-produce art, the process of replication transformed both the artifact and its creator. What once was handmade and one-of-a-kind became instead a common specimen that symbolized the alienation of workers by divorcing them from the fruit of their labor. Reproduction erased the uniqueness of the product. Worse, its interchangeability erased the individuality of the producer, who must attempt to recover it by becoming a consumer bent on purchasing objects that possess distinctiveness, and so on in endless, sterile cycle. No matter how manufacturers decorate the artifacts, the abstractions of production and consumption can never satisfy the human hunger for uniqueness. Artifice becomes environment, and even fantasies become interchangeable. Variations on this scenario abound, from the rationalized, artificial Western civilization outlined by Max Weber in *The Protestant Ethic and the Spirit of Capitalism* (1920), to Marxist critiques and dystopian formulations that stress the autonomy of technology. The fear common to all these visions is that the inanimate will become the erotic, a tendency Georges Bataille seems to predict in *Death and Sensuality* (see discussion in **Pornography as Taboo** in this chapter). The culmination of such anxieties would appear to be a technology-generated virtual reality that entirely displaces the human.

Industrialization led to the separation of sexual life from other social concerns, a schism reflected in classic pornography of the last century, says Steven Marcus in *The Other Victorians: A Study of Sexuality and Pornography in Mid-Nineteenth Century England*. But Marcus' justly celebrated humanistic exploration of the terrain of Victorian sexuality suffers from the author's ignorance of technology, as Ned Polsky points out in "On the Sociology of Pornography." Where Marcus finds the sudden upsurge of Victorian pornography in England strange, Polsky (200n.) notes that in a period in which the country experienced a fourfold increase in population, it also enjoyed a thirty-two-fold increase in literacy occasioned, in part, by printing technologies, which puts the matter in a different light. The spread of pornography has always been linked to growing literacy in one medium after another. Masud Khan echoes Marcus' complaint in "Pornography and the Politics of Rage and Subversion." Khan believes that violent and demeaning sexual expression is a response to, and a result of, an industrial society that foregrounds the notion that humans are machines and thus separates us from relationships and genuine feeling. Using as his principal example *Fanny Hill*, Douglas J. Stewart argues in "Pornography, Obscenity, and

Capitalism" that modern pornography replaces romance and passion with industrial images of bodies pumping away in intercourse.

Philip Slater's *The Pursuit of Loneliness*, a classic study of the conflict between the imperatives of economic growth and the pursuit of leisure, suggests that pornography can be the means by which society keeps genuine sensuality scarce in order to boost demand. By glamorizing inanimate images, pornography transforms them into objects of desire. By emphasizing consumption, a permissive American culture ensures that no one can be satisfied. The contemporary theorist most often associated with reflections on artifice is Jean Baudrillard, whose *For a Critique of the Political Economy of the Sign* deals with the displacement of authenticity with the simulations of linguistic hyperreality. Baudrillard's *Selected Writings* signposts his movement from neo-Marxist to poststructuralist perspectives on advertising, commodity fetishism, and the equation of sexual desire and the profit motive. Almost any of his work offers comment on pornography or erotica, as does his *The Ecstacy of Communication*, which contains the following: "Obscenity begins where there is no more spectacle, no more stage, no more theatre, no more illusions, when everything becomes immediately transparent, visible, exposed in the raw and inexorable light of information and communication. We no longer partake of the drama of alienation, but are in the ecstacy of communication" (167). Given a mass culture, with its welter of texts and images, Baudrillard believes that meaning "implodes," that we are close to losing representation and signification altogether. All that is left is surface and artifact, whose meanings are fragmented and pluralistic. According to Baudrillard, the opposition between sexual liberation and sexual repression is no longer operative in an environment of mass media.

Another communication theorist, Niklas Luhmann, observes in *Love as Passion: The Codification of Intimacy* that media give meaning to concepts such as love and passion through constellations of images, words, and symbols that seem more and more remote from experience even as they come to constitute a media environment. The process is reductive, even trivializing, though the motive is not so much communication at the lowest common denominator of understanding as it is the desire to compel assent to common expectations. Mediated environments, technological advances, economic systems, all of which have altered the ways in which humans seek pleasure, have put sexuality in flux, says Alan Soble in *Sexual Investigations*. In *The Transformation of Intimacy: Sexuality, Love and Eroticism in Modern Societies*, Anthony Giddens also foregrounds what he calls "plastic sexuality," that is, sexuality divorced, à la Bataille, from reproduction and thus free to mutate along lines of technological opportunities and human imperatives, some of them democratic as well as mechanical. For both Soble and Giddens, pornography and other sexual representations become crucial features of a technological landscape. Although they stop short of saying so, pornography under such circumstances may have positive benefit as a reminder of human nature and a means for discharging animal sexuality in an artificial society.

John Tierney traces the role of pornography as both the driving force behind, and the consequence of, advances in communications technology, from cave paintings and Sumerian pictographs to videocassette recorders (VCRs) and electronic virtual realities in "Porn, the Low-Slung Engine of Progress," an important reminder that pornography has contributed to the development of appliances that we prize. Peter Johnson takes the argument to its logical conclusion in "Pornography Drives Technology: Why Not to Censor the Internet." According to Johnson, pornographers are explorers who advance and push new ideas; pornography is a positive force for experimentation with new technologies; pornographers should be cast as useful citizens, not as pariahs. In "Pornography as Innovator," the columnists Taylor and Jerome note that pornographers are pioneers in the commercialization of the Internet and that corporations and entrepreneurs study their methods closely. At this juncture critics often try to distinguish between older, more "benign" technologies and newer, less "human" ones. Thomas Jefferson thought plows were nicer than factories; the members of the Meese Commission said that pornographic books were less dangerous than computerized representations.[3]

In *The Jaguar and the Anteater: Pornography Degree Zero*, Bernard Arcand reviews the importance of pornography in the work of postmodern critics such as Lasch, Sennett, Baudrillard, and Lipovetsky. Arcand himself believes that pornography symbolizes freedom, since its fantasies can be enjoyed privately by individuals but at risk of alienation, loneliness, and a dependence on the artificial. He notes that more and more specialized technologies deal with erotic expression in a paradoxical dialectic; eroticism energizes the artifice of technology, and technology foregrounds eroticism in order to render itself more human. Technology routinely enshrines such contradictions: on one hand, it may dehumanize and oppress, while, on the other, it can liberate us from subsistence by increasing production and promote equality by distributing goods, services, and information widely. In the sexual arena, technology can free us from the burden of unwanted children, alter sex roles, undermine power relationships among classes, races, and genders, and sharpen our sensitivity to stimuli. Some degree of intervention in our environment, call it engineering, nesting, or tidying up, would appear to be a human biological imperative, says Ruth Schwartz Cowan in *More Work for Mother: The Ironies of Household Technology from the Open Hearth to the Microwave*, a work devoted to gendered technology (but not to issues of sexual representation).

Feminists sometimes decry technologies they see as quintessentially male, especially those that make representations more sophisticated, at the same time that they embrace birth control methodologies and reproductive engineering. More often than not, feminist critics assume an identification between feminine essence and nature. Like many similar texts, Carolyn Merchant's *The Death of Nature: A Feminist Reappraisal of the Scientific Revolution* refers to science and technology as rational, linear, individualistic, aggressive, and invasive and therefore masculine, patriarchal, and hostile to nature. Evelyn Fox Keller's *Re-*

flections on Gender and Science takes similar directions and finds erotic connotations in bodies of knowledge derived from the plundering of nature.
Considered as masculine technologies, representations of sex exhibit the same
characteristics. The problem, as always, is the word *nature*, a culturally constructed and therefore slippery concept. Peter Wild plays on this circumstance
in "Pornography and Nature" by comparing a photograph of an American desert
with a *Playboy* Playmate: "How we airbrush both nature and women! Is there
much difference in treatment between the lurid pinups decorating seedy barroom
walls and the coffee-table books in your living room and mine, lavish with their
photographs of redwoods and snowcapped peaks? By oversimplifying, by con-
centrating on one aspect of reality, both make us suck in our breaths, both take
us to the vertiginous limits of our desires. In this sense, *Bambi* is just as pornographic as *Deep Throat*" (55–56).

Sympathy with Susan Griffin's thesis in *Pornography and Silence: Culture's
Revenge against Nature* depends primarily on the reader's assessment of her
understanding of what sort of sexual behavior Griffin believes is "natural,"
though it is clear that she dislikes many forms of erotic representation. Like
religious critics, she thinks false cultural dichotomies split the values of "soul"
and "body," divorce males from "nature," and compel them to violence and
aberrant sexuality. Because she appears to be recasting older notions of spirituality, her book appeals to traditionalists; the problem is that she uses terms
loosely, continually redefining "pornography" to include almost anything she
abhors. Paul D. Avis, an Anglican vicar, tries to extend Griffin's reflections in
his own text, *Eros and the Sacred*. Following Griffin, Avis claims that pornography is an attack on nature, of which women are the true symbol, that pornography presents the male body and its discharges as "disgusting," that porn is a
species of self-hatred, and that the only real eroticism is spiritual, perhaps even
Anglican. Mary Daly argues in *Pure Lust: Elemental Feminist Philosophy* that
pornography is so woven into the pattern of culture as to be indistinguishable
from theology and politics; it is particularly evident in phallotechnic violations
of Mother Earth, which males "rape" as their primary activity. The widespread
feminist condemnation of technology as a male construct sometimes creates
strange contradictions, as when Andrea Dworkin writes *Intercourse* to condemn
the act of intercourse itself and then proposes technological substitutes (from
masturbatory aids to artificial insemination) for sex and procreation as a way of
avoiding physical congress between the sexes. If one takes seriously the radical
feminism contention that every act of intercourse is an act of rape, then only
three remedies would appear to follow: total abstinence, which would end the
species, totally commercialized cohabitation equivalent to prostitution for the
female, or total dependence on an artifice so feminized as to avoid masculine
science and technology.

The advent of reproductive technologies has led other theorists to speculate
more productively on the consequences for male and female sexuality and their
representations. Chief among these is Donna Haraway, whose "A Manifesto for

Cyborgs: Science, Technology, and Socialist Feminism in the 1980s," has attained cult status. Haraway deals with the disturbing implications of the cybernetic organism, or cyborg, penetrated by devices in an erotic fusion that seems a violation of the "natural" body. In a well-chosen metaphor, Mary Ann Doane construes film and television spaces as territories with gender borders, with smaller spaces being accorded to women, as in soap operas, and larger ones to males, as in international spy stories. Doane's "Technophilia: Technology, Representation, and the Feminine," while not about pornography per se, examines the relationship between cinematic representation of women's bodies and conceptions of the reproductive process. Doane's recent *Femmes Fatale: Feminism, Film Theory, Psychoanalysis*, sums up her views. Scholars should also look at Gena Corea's *The Mother Machine: Reproductive Technologies from Artificial Insemination to Artificial Wombs*.

Easily the single most important essay on the subject, however, is the late Sally Hacker's "The Eye of the Beholder: An Essay on Technology and Eroticism." Hacker says that "technology and eroticism were once fused, as with reason and passion, . . . and referred to the same set of activities. These activities began to be differentiated, gendered—technology masculine, eroticism feminine—and hierarchically ordered with the emergence some 5,000 years ago of patriarchal societies, whose core institutions are military institutions" (205). Hacker believes that technology and eroticism are still intertwined and that "the control of passion, particularly among men, shapes the organization of technology and technical education" (210). Some technological activities are still off-limits to women, says Hacker, who focuses on the technologies devoted to making women sexually attractive and skilled: "clothing, scents, postures, or numerous social and physical accoutrements," not to mention "sex manuals" and other instruments of sex education (211). Hacker discusses class, power, social organization, and a great many other aspects of eroticism in one of the most compressed and stimulating essays to be found on the subject. She points out that "both technology and eroticism show signs of a degendering transformation": a newer style of eroticism "legitimates a pouting, 'feminine' style for men, and a tougher, teasing, 'masculine' stance for women" (219).

Americans routinely condemn what they imagine to be pornography's endorsement of mechanical sex, a syndrome they see manifest as well in the proliferation of "how to" guides and sex manuals that promise ecstasy if one merely learns the proper techniques. A more interesting variant is Raymond Durgnant's "From Mechanical Brides to Rubber Women," which deplores what Durgnant calls the "admass" eroticism of gadgets to be found in popular culture. "Admass," a conflation of advertising and mass media, promotes a mechanical titillation that actually negates the richer, more truly "spiritually authentic" eroticism to be found in real pornography. More hackneyed is the charge that pornography objectifies—or reifies—humans, particularly women. Since it is difficult to think of an information-processing activity that does not objectify humans, such terms usually indicate that the critic declines to think hard about the subject. In *Negations*, a work that revises some of his previous statements about sexuality and culture, Herbert Marcuse notes that "when the body has completely become an object, a beautiful thing, it can foreshadow a new happiness. In suffering the most extreme reification man triumphs over reification. The artistry of the beautiful body, its effortless agility and relaxation, which can be displayed today only in the circus, vaudeville, and burlesque, herald the joy to which men will attain in being liberated from the ideal once mankind, having become a true subject, succeeds in the mastery of matter" (116–117).

Anne McClintock observes, "Fetishizing pornography projects onto it a spurious power," by which she means that "the extreme anti-porn argument turns pornography into a fetish, demonizing it as the primal cause of all male violence and all women's subjection."[4] In the most fundamental sense, pornography may well speak to what already, secretly, we know: that we do embrace our creations erotically (think of Decker sleeping with Sarah, the robot he loves, in the movie *Blade Runner*) and that doing so is a first step toward acknowledging our kinship with inventions that are, after all, our progeny. Pornography may well be a response to attenuated human relationships rather than a cause of technological alienation. Cruising sexual sites on the Internet may seem pathetic to older Americans, for instance, while it may provide contact that is entirely missing for already disaffected younger generations. For every argument that the proliferation of pornography thins experience to shallow levels, there is a counterargument, rarely voiced but implicit in the sheer volume of consumption of adult materials, that humans seek out such materials precisely because they seem more intense and authentic than the rest of their lives.

AESTHETICS: PORNOGRAPHY AS ART

Raw sexuality can affront the aesthetically principled. Ruskin destroyed his friend Turner's erotic paintings; Isabel Burton burned her husband, Richard's, explicit Oriental translations. For some, beauty itself is suspect: Freud claimed that "beauty has no obvious use; nor is there any cultural necessity for it," though he conceded that beauty has become central to civilization.[5] To the radical feminist, beauty is just another mechanism of oppression. For others, speaking of beauty or symmetry in the same sentence as pornography is like speaking of the structure of chaos. For still others, the outrageous can be beautiful. The best-known critic in the latter category is Morse Peckham, whose *Art and Pornography: An Experiment in Explanation* seriously considers the relationship between art and (mostly literary) porn, using linguistic, philosophical, and psychological perspectives to examine the inextricable connections between obscenity and creativity. Pornography is essential to the development of civilization because through it obscenity flowers into expression. Peckham answers the question, Can there be pornographic art? in the affirmative: "Since pornographic art is in its formal function indistinguishable from art in the full stylistic and cultural range of the European culture area, since there is no uniqueness in the formal aspect of pornographic art, there is nothing to be said about it that cannot be said about nonpornographic art" (294).

Peter Webb's *The Erotic Arts* covers virtually every kind of artistic endeavor and is perhaps the broadest-based text on the subject. Says Webb: "Pornography is related to obscenity rather than erotica and this is a vital distinction. Although some people may find a pornographic picture erotic, most people associate eroticism with love, rather than sex alone, and love has little or no part to play in pornography. . . . Eroticism, therefore, has none of the pejorative associations of pornography; it concerns something vital to us, the passion of love. Erotic art is art on a sexual theme related specifically to emotions rather than merely actions, and sexual depictions which are justifiable on aesthetic grounds" (2). The length of his text, however, attests to the difficulty of maintaining these distinctions, and Webb is too honest to withhold his admiration for artifacts that have been condemned. Peter Michelson's *Speaking the Unspeakable: A Poetics of Obscenity*, the revision of his classic *The Aesthetics of Pornography*, is probably the best, single, all-purpose introduction to the issue of artistry in pornography. Michelson believes that poetic and artistic criticism can be applied to genres—poetic, dramatic, comic—that he will not try to disguise as merely erotic. Kelly Dennis' dissertation, *"The Face of God: Representation as the Pornography of Modernity,"* points out that contemporary objections to pornography are precisely those leveled against photography by painters battling over paradigms of realism; because Western art uses feminine metaphors of iconoclasm, the issues of representation are inextricable from those of pornography. Where once high art denied that photographs could be aesthetic, today's arbiters of taste refuse to acknowledge the beauty of intercourse depicted in a pornographic film.

Although Peckham, Webb, and Michelson are easily the most important critics to confront the aesthetics of porn, other critics have explored the artistic potential of explicit sexual expression. Confusing sex and sexism—as do antiporn feminists—is one major reason for our culture's inability to find aesthetic principles in erotic expression, argues Lynn S. Chaucer in *Reconcilable Differences: Confronting Beauty, Pornography, and the Future of Feminism*. To deny the beauty of the body, even in pornographic postures, is to deny sensibilities refined over centuries. As her title suggests, Chaucer thinks that erotic and aesthetic appeal can be reconciled, at least in some instances. Kenneth Tynan, famous for staging *Oh! Calcutta!* on Broadway, points out the benefits of being able to see real sex in "In Praise of Hard-Core." Stimulating sexual arousal, Tynan says, is just as valid a goal of art as stimulating a desire for heroism, sacrifice, or saintliness. In fact, says Tynan, we ought to be honest: the chief virtue of pornography is that, at its best, it excites a healthy and normal response. Abraham Kaplan distinguishes between types of obscenity and the aesthetic considerations they engender in "Obscenity as an Esthetic Category." F. Gonzalez-Crussi's *On the Nature of Things Erotic*, interesting for its rifts on the evolution of criticism of erotica, insists that applying standards of taste and humanity to pornography is a valid way of assessing value. Most closely identified with an artistic approach are the Kronhausens, Eberhard and Phyllis. Although they have published several well-known books, all of them, to one degree or another, concerned with the aesthetic aspects of erotica, their most important volume is *Pornography and the Law*, a classic whose insights have endured partly because they were among the first critics to examine the subject closely. The Kronhausens argued in favor of what they called "erotic realism," a category they thought could be justified as artistically (and morally) valid.

Lynda Nead thinks that packaging is important. Her " 'Above the Pulp-Line': The Cultural Significance of Erotic Art" centers on the Kronhausen collection of erotic art. In mounting their traveling show, Eberhard and Phyllis Kronhausen wanted to allow the public to see material usually outside the realm of discourse and to be able to distinguish the erotic from the pornographic, terms often conflated: "The implication of [the Kronhausens'] position is that the pornographic and the erotic are largely defined in terms of their means of distribution and consumption and their place within the cultural spectrum. If representations of sex are placed on the walls of a public art gallery, they are more likely to be understood within the discourse of art rather than of pornography" (151). An eccentric and not very convincing argument that porn is more concerned with the beautiful than is traditional art is advanced by Jon Huer in *Art, Beauty, and Pornography: A Journey through American Culture*. Huer gives primacy to one element of pornography's appeal: ravishment by beauty, however perverse. Because sexuality is a marketing device for everything, says Huer, America has become a "pornographic society," a circumstance that conditions our aesthetic response to virtually all ideas. Alex Comfort also explores the symmetries of aesthetics and biologically influenced psychology in *Darwin and the Naked Lady: Discursive Essays on Biology and Art*.

Camille Paglia says that "pornography cannot be separated from art; the two interpenetrate each other" (24) in *Sexual Personae: Art and Decadence from Nefertiti to Emily Dickinson*. According to Paglia, pornography and art both tap wellsprings of energy, outrage, and obscenity. Here she explores the connections among American writers; when she ventures into other media like painting, she is more apt to choose classical or European illustrations. Paglia's *Sex, Art, and American Culture: Essays* (on Brando, Mapplethorpe, the Anita Hill affair, Madonna, rock music, and other topics) speaks more directly to the relationship between art and pornography; the latter, a vital element in romantic paganism, functions as a stimulus to the former. Her *Vamps and Tramps: New Essays* widens the sexual terrain. Paglia's contention that males sublimate sexual energy to build civilizations, while women remain passive because they partake of nature, has led to controversy. To some critics, Paglia is a sort of mirror-reverse image of Catharine MacKinnon; both see pornography everywhere and raise it beyond levels recognizable by most Americans. If nothing else, the obsessions of the two suggest that a dirty mind is a joy forever. John Rodden's interview, "The Performing Artist-Intellectual: The Personae and Personality of Camille

Paglia," allows Paglia to lay claim to "an erotics of art" by performing à la
Susan Sontag, as "body-centered, flamboyant, manic, outrageous, i.e., the intel-
lectual as Dionysian performer, a.k.a. the intellectual as Camille Paglia" (62).
A balanced view of Paglia is B. Ruby Rich's "Top Girl": "As always with
Paglia, her good points are mixed up with her excesses" (32). Paglia's free-
swinging interview, "Twenty Questions: Camille Paglia," confirms Rich's con-
tention. Says Paglia: "I am radically propornography. I draw the line nowhere.
Every fantasy must be permitted" (170).

George Melly suggests that genres of porn have different aesthetic structures
and effects. Melly's "Pornography and Erotica" says that the appeal of soft-core
porn is just "genital nagging," hostile to real sexuality, while hard-core genres
possess greater intensity and may therefore more closely mimic passion. In "Star
Bright: An Interview with Susie Bright," conducted by Don Vaughan, Bright
says: "It's not so much that [pornography is] good for us as it is part of us. It's
like someone asking me why food is good for us. It's part of our human life.
Not only for reproduction, but the creative, unconscious, self-realizing aspects
of sexuality. It's a core to our intimacy and our unconscious" (30–31).

The intensity of pornography, says Laura Kipnis in "She-Male Fantasies and
the Aesthetics of Pornography," "produces a body of images that are too *bla-
tantly* out of the unconscious, too *unaesthetically* written in the language of
obsession, compulsion, perversion, infantile desires, rage, fear, pain and misogyny; too literally about sex and power rather than their aesthetically coded forms
in the works of any number of famous and adulated artists and writers who treat
similar themes (or the socially coded but equally ritualised forms through which
they're expressed at gallery openings and academic conferences). Too *potent*
for art" (137–138). Some might respond that such an observation applies only
to the highly fetishistic forms that Kipnis has in mind. In fact, Kipnis is arguing
with the thesis of Robert Stoller's *Observing the Erotic Imagination*, which
insists that art and pornography possess formal and structural similarities and
that these similarities mirror the aesthetic principles of sexual excitement itself.
Stoller believes sexual acts follow the scripts of fantasies that are shaped at least
in part by aesthetic considerations. Paula Webster finesses such distinctions in
"Pornography and Pleasure" by asserting that whether pornography can function
as art or not, it can still "raise consciousness about our desires and fears" (51).

Walter Berns speaks for many in the opposite camp when he maintains that
art can be distinguished from trash in "Beyond the (Garbage) Pale, or Democracy, Censorship and the Arts." Berns argues that democracy depends on a sense
of shame and self-restraint that should hold pornography at bay. *The Postmodern
Scene: Excremental Culture and Hyper-Aesthetics*, by Arthur Kroker and David
Cook, explores aesthetics in a culture turning in upon itself; the title implies the
direction of the curve. Even Richard Dyer, who has written extensively on pornography, confesses to hesitancy. In his *The Matter of Images: Essays on Representations*, Dyer remarks:

Outside pornography, sexuality, male or female, is not so much shown directly as symbolized. It is not just censorship that insists on this—sexuality is on the whole better represented through symbolism. Colours, textures, objects, effects of light, the shape of things, all convey sexuality through evocation, resonance and association; they set off feelings about what sex is like more efficiently than just showing acts of sex. Pornography too uses the devices of symbolism to construct a particular sense of the sex it shows. What is significant is how sexuality is symbolised, how these devices evoke a sense of what sexuality is like, how they contribute to a particular definition of sexuality." (111–112)

From Freud on, the expanding awareness of sexuality, especially its dark side, has redefined the aesthetics of the Western artist in the twentieth century, says Peter Gorsen in *Sexualästhetik: Grenzformen der Sinnlichkeit im 20. Jahrhundert*, which views pornography as a fruitful source of images and themes in the work of American and European artists both high and low; the influence of obscenity and pornography, functioning as a cultural unconscious for the creative, is clear. Walter Kendrick's *The Secret Museum: Pornography in Modern Culture* traces the evolution of artistic responsibility and integrity as a defense (the belief that a thoughtful work could have redeeming social and aesthetic value) against charges of obscenity and believes that the argument is in decline, victim not just of attacks by feminists but also of the deliquescence of cultural norms.

Probably the boldest venture into the ambiguous nature of pornographic artistry, however, is William Gass' *On Being Blue*, a meditation that, in carrying "blue pencils, blue noses, blue movies, laws, blue legs and stockings" into rifts on nature, the mind, color, and still further afield into realms that defy summary, testifies to the brilliance a thinker can bring to the subject. Says Gass: "True sexuality in literature—sex as a positive aesthetic quality—lies not in any scene and subject, nor in the mere appearance of a vulgar word, but in the consequences on the page of love well made—made to the medium which is the writer's own" (19). That is about as close as any critic has come to acknowledging that beauty can serve as a shield against degradation. Oddly, while cultural critics often speak of socially constructed beauty, few note that "beautiful" people in pornographic films or photos seem to remain untouched by the outrageous acts they perform, as in Lawrence Durrell's famous remark in *The Alexandria Quartet* that "nymphomania is a species of virginity," that is, that innocence persists at some distance from, and despite, the exertions of the body. In the last analysis, however, pornographic genres may simply have been artistically neglected by its creators and its critics. As Calvin Tomkins has remarked, "Of all the minor art forms, pornography has remained the least developed. Certified pornographic masterworks, from Sappho to Nabokov, can be counted on the fingers of one hand. The best known critical theorists of the form, from Anthony Comstock to Jesse Helms, have had the disadvantage of being morons."[6] Wendy Steiner's *The Scandal of Pleasure: Art in an Age of Fundamentalism* reflects on the ironies of defending an aesthetics of the body against the politics of the present; Steiner concentrates on "body" artists such as Mapplethorpe, Serrano, Mann, Warhol, and others. Steiner examines the fundamentalist, feminist, fascist, and liberal factions of political correctness and urges that no work of art be reduced to a single meaning. Like many others, Steiner notes that erotic art is and is not a political agent, precisely because it is rooted in contradiction and insists on tolerance. Ultimately, says Steiner in this brilliant book, only pleasure can justify art. Those who find beauty in sexuality must confront a cultural bias: most Americans are deeply suspicious of the very notion that one might gaze at a nude figure, standing still or engaged in congress with another, in order to be enraptured by beauty. That prejudice still dogs a magazine such as *Playboy*, whose "Playmates" are far more "beautiful" than "sexy" but whose appeal is tainted in popular consciousness by what is best described as cultural pathology.

Still another text on erotic aesthetics, more popular in England than here, is G. L. Simons' *Pornography without Prejudice: A Reply to Objectors*, which contends that pornography on balance can be a tool for human happiness and draws for support on similar theories about artistic realism. Ethical considerations are of less use in determining the benefits of pornography, says Simons, than aesthetic principles. Liberals may expect too much when they call for better plots for pornographic movies or ask that pornography be improved, that is, made more elegant or "beautiful." H. L. Mencken once responded to a suggestion that politics would be less corrupt if honest men were encouraged to become politicians by remarking that such a strategy was akin to trying to end prostitution by staffing whorehouses with virgins. "Either the virgins would leap out of the windows," said Mencken, "or they would cease to be virgins."[7] If pornography becomes aesthetically or politically correct, it will no longer be pornography and may lose its value *as* pornography.

In the final analysis, pornography has probably altered our aesthetic principles, though its positive value goes largely unnoticed in the process of cultural appropriation that sanitizes its vulgarity and offensiveness. Without the tropes of pornography, however, it is difficult to imagine how we would respond to contemporary music, painting, literature, film, or any of the many media that have been enriched by sexual expression and representation that previous generations would have condemned. Without those tropes, how could we learn to appreciate rock and roll, the canvases of Francis Bacon, the novels of Thomas Pynchon, or the films of Ingmar Bergman, let alone television soap operas, Regency romances, or Parisian fashions?

MISCELLANEOUS DEFENSES OF PORNOGRAPHY

In *Sex and Reason*, Richard A. Posner, a justice of the U.S. Court of Appeals for the Seventh District, identifies and discusses five goals of erotic representation: (1) formal, an aesthetic achieved through metaphoric and figurative imagery; (2) informational, a purpose achieved through didacticism; (3) ideological, an intent that aims to reinforce, undermine, or change the audience's thinking; (4) aphrodisiac, an attempt to stimulate sexual desire; (5) magical, a construct that exalts fantasy. Agree or not, Posner's reader will become acquainted with a wide landscape. Gérard Zwang refers to the death of pornography ("Mort de la Pornographie") in the supplement to his two-volume *La Fonction Erotique*. Zwang suggests that erotic awareness is now so widespread that taboos have been eroded, and for that reason porn functions at present simply as (1) information on sex and reproduction, (2) a cultural barometer of attitudes, and (3) a harmless stimulus for masturbation. In short, because porn demystifies sex, it is more therapeutic than dangerous.

While many of the works listed earlier acknowledge some of the positive political, aesthetic, and social effects of pornography as it moves toward these goals, outright defenses tend to be muted by cultural reticence. Several researchers have noticed that academic and mainstream conventions marginalize theories of catharsis, despite their obvious relevance.[8] Though it is clear that millions of Americans masturbate every day, often with the assistance of sexual materials, it would be difficult to devise experiments that might test for pornography's ability to deflect hostile impulses into harmless self-release. (See **Pornography as Therapy** in chapter 19.) Moreover, public condemnation of both pornography and masturbation discourages scholars from trying. Nonetheless, the evidence for catharsis, that is, that pornography can reduce sexual crime, remains at least as plausible as for the opposite thesis, that it leads to antisocial sexual behavior. Since it is likely that any message can affect people in different ways, both theories, of course, may be valid for different individuals in different circumstances.

In a way, of course, pornography neither deserves nor needs defense: its virtues may be measured by the onslaughts it provokes; the more strident the attack, the more powerful the attacker thinks pornography is. Still, even though the real or imagined deleterious effects of pornography are widely trumpeted, the benefits of pornography are not always articulated. Pornography can entertain, can educate, can ameliorate sex lives, can provide an outlet for people who lack partners or whose sexual abilities are flawed, can provide a semblance of safe sex in an age of AIDS, can undermine outmoded sexual restrictions and thereby implicate cultural repression, can help change our ideas about reproduction, birth control, socially transmitted diseases, and concepts of age, race, and gender, and can reassure people afraid that their own fantasies are unmatched in other psyches.

The bedrock benefit—what Posner calls pornography's aphrodisiac goal— would appear to be the one that gives Americans the most trouble: when the fantasies in a particular pornographic artifact mesh with our own, they arouse us sexually. Conventional comment on pornography usually fails to acknowledge its power to arouse. Because the average critic will rarely admit that he or she finds a narrative or an image stimulating, the discourse of criticism frequently seems vacuous, as if it were not about sexuality at all. Jimmy Carter aside, Americans have difficulty admitting that they lust and would never list sexual desire and its reciprocation among the boons they crave. The syndrome is similar to that noticed by Mark Twain in his *Letters to the Earth*: there an angel observes that in imagining a flabbily spiritualized heaven, hypocritical Christians left out the one thing that gives them the most pleasure: sex.

Pornography evokes pleasure, says Andrew Ross in "The Popularity of Pornography," and one cannot combat or change it without a recognition of this fact. In "Sex Is Great—That's Why Censors Can't Stand It," the sexual therapist Marty Klein asks:

What kind of sex scares the censor? It is pleasure centered; it does not conform to societal roles or rules. Nor is it bound or controlled by notions of love. And, especially frightening, it places value on losing control (albeit in a secure environment). Erotica (or—if you are a censor—pornography) embraces all of these factors. It portrays a powerfully arousing sexuality that is driven by passion instead of reason or love. Censoring erotica is an attempt to beat back the sexual demons that stalk the censor, or attempt to control the awesome power of his or her *own* sexuality. (54)

Because porn recognizes female lust, says Klein, it is terrifying to the conventional.

Pat Califia's "Introduction" to *Macho Sluts* makes similar points; Califia asserts that it is difficult to write well and still pass "the wet test," that is, to produce a narrative that really arouses (13). She writes lesbian erotica, she says, for explicitly political reasons, to arouse but also to oppose those who would constrain precisely because *they* set the agenda: "I do not believe that sex has an inherent power to transform the world. I do not believe that pleasure is always an anarchic force for good. I do not believe that we can fuck our way to freedom" (15). But the culture at large seems unable to accept that people have a right to set their own sexual limits and arrangements and instead relegates its citizens to categories, "labeled according to race, age, class and gender and plugged in and made use of, performing as suburban housewives or street hookers, young work-a-daddies and pimps, street kids and their clients, incest victims and their abusers, mistresses and their keepers, unwed mothers, closeted lesbians and gay men, everybody a guard or prisoner, with no choice, no safe word, no negotiation" (25–26). Pornography helps us break the bonds of a repressive culture, even if the rebellion is more symbolic than real.

The most abiding value of pornography is that it forces us to confront ourselves, an assertion echoed again and again by those who approach pornography from artistic or philosophical perspectives. To deny the importance of pornography, to suppress it, says Peter Michelson in *Speaking the Unspeakable*, is to deny humanity. The late William Ober, a forensic pathologist and coroner who was also one of the most astute and erudite essayists on the subject of erotica (see **Erotic and Pornographic Book and Magazine Illustration** in Chapter 11), sneered at critics who called pornography antihuman or prattled about its relationship to death. "If they had seen as much dead, flaccid, putrid flesh as I have," he told me in 1991, "they'd paper their homes with pictures of people screwing. Don't they know that sex is what humans are all about?" Pornography deals with quotidian issues of the body and the psyche as they grapple with sexuality and gender. Susan Sontag's "The Pornographic Imagination," probably the single greatest essay on the subject, remains one of the most trenchant examinations of the nature of the impulses behind so many erotic genres. "All art is dangerous," Sontag says there; pornography embraces that role more courageously than most upper-class endeavors and enjoys the advantage of being wedded more closely to the spring of creativity, the unbridled imagination that enables humans to glimpse the face of chaos. Focused on *Story of O* and *The Image*, her essay places them in a literary tradition and argues that the consciousness of the reader is defense enough against a degradation that is deliberate in pornography's probing of boundaries and limits. Sontag's "Notes on Art, Sex and Politics" makes similar claims for the existential value of erotic fantasy. On one hand, says Sontag, pornography violates reality in its premises: "Sexual energy is not endlessly renewable; sexual acts cannot be tirelessly repeated. But in another sense pornography is rudely accurate about important realities of desire. That voluptuousness does mean surrender, and that sexual surrender pursued imaginatively enough, experienced immediately enough, does erode pride of individuality and mocks the notion that the will could ever be free—these are truths about sexuality itself and what it may, naturally, become" (36). Civilization arises, in part, Sontag believes, from the conflict between our consciousness and our sexuality.

In *The Edge of the Bed: How Dirty Pictures Changed My Life*, Lisa Palac, after describing her adolescent acquaintance with erotica as alternately boring and liberating, asserts that pornography mirrors fears and desires, some of which, especially what she has created (in some cases under the pen name Lisa LaBia), she likes very much. The book tells how she came to appreciate the benefits of pornography, the spiritual and mental importance of erotica to her generation, especially women, and the challenges of helping edit *On Our Backs*, publishing *Future Sex*, and distributing "good," rather than "bad," sexual representations in recordings such as *Cyborgasm* and on-line over the Net: "I didn't understand the appeal of porn until the day I stopped looking for a political theory and let myself go. . . . I was determined not to think about anything except what my body was feeling" (33–34). "Good pornography is the thing that gives me insight into the human condition *and* makes me come" (99), she says. Sallie Tisdale, another effective spokesperson, argues in her *Talk Dirty to Me: An Intimate Philosophy of Sex* that real feminists have to "take back the night" blackened by antisex radicals, though she admits to selfish motives; she is opposed to censorship because she knows that an "established order" of whatever sort will try to keep her from seeing or reading something she wants very much to see or read. She proposes a test for debate: "The single most important thing to consider whenever such words as 'moral,' 'immoral,' 'obscene,' and 'degrading' are used is whether or not the speaker presumes these ideas to be absolute" (334). Tisdale's article "Talk Dirty to Me: A Woman's Taste for Pornography" says that MacKinnon and Dworkin are "themselves prurient, scurrying after sex in every corner." Pornography, she believes, asserts that "our sexual selves are real" (45). *XXX: A Woman's Right to Pornography*, Wendy McElroy's spirited defense, describes the benefits of pornography as educational and liberating. She repudiates antiporn, feminist campaigns as ill-advised attempts "to save women from themselves," that is, from their own sexuality, by limiting choices available to women. McElroy's interviews with porn film stars persuades her that they consider themselves teachers and sex pioneers.

In "Pornography: Image and Reality," Sara Diamond insists that there must be "a place for imagery that is totally concerned with sex. Our society is one in which sexuality is isolated and treated as a category unto itself. While expanding the definition of eroticism is valuable, we need to retain contact with sex in our creative work. Unless we directly address the issue of what gives us pleasure, we will again abandon that terrain to pornography" (54). Diamond argues against conceptions of "politically correct sex" (55) and of constraining women's behavior just as they are actively beginning to explore their own sexual drives. Insisting on politically correct sexual acts (e.g., maintaining that feminists should decline penetration and absolutely refuse fellatio) is dehumanizing, say Esther Newton and Shirley Walton in "The Misunderstanding: Toward a More Precise Sexual Vocabulary." Pornography, they say, can enhance sexual lives for women and men. Hostility toward sex has drawn fire from feminists who not only endorse sex as a part of love and a means of communication but also think that eroticism enriches human life. Paula Webster's "Pornography and Pleasure" maintains that pornography that gives pleasure should not be condemned. Webster observes that the antiporn movement suffers from an inability to discriminate among different goals of various pornographic genres and errs especially in assuming that violence is equivalent to sex. In *Sapphistry: The Book of Lesbian Sexuality*, Pat Califia believes that minority porn "functions as an underground source of information about erotic nonconformity. Some erotica serves as yet another function, which is to organize members of sexual minorities into subcultures where they can meet and support one another" (15).

Nadine Strossen says in *Defending Pornography: Free Speech, Sex and the Fight for Women's Rights*, an attack on the absurdities of assorted zealots, that pornography embodies rebellion, that women should enjoy being sexual objects in some contexts, that messages of erotic texts and images are deliberately ambiguous. Strossen finds many positive attributes in pornography, including the encouragement of a healthy fantasy life. *Dealing with Pornography: The Case against Censorship*, by Paul Wilson, an Australian humanist and social scientist who often uses American examples, takes American opponents of pornography to task. Wilson calls censorship silly, believes that porn enriches the lives of those who appreciate its fantasies, dismisses pornography's alleged links with violence and antisocial behavior, dissects myths, and reflects on advances in the creation and distribution of electronic erotica that he thinks of as healthy rebellion against an overly sanitized culture.

PORNOGRAPHY AND POSTMODERNISM

Pornographic and academic narratives are both marginal discourses in the United States. Both stand at the edge, if not the "outside," of the larger culture, and both send subversive messages that resonate until they are co-opted and conventionalized in popular discourse. Both are heavily commercialized by the media industries of an information economy; both are heavily dependent on a constant supply of new product. Both reduce sex to simplistic tropes and formulas, and both reiterate these leitmotifs in a rehearsal that would not be possible in a culture unconcerned with gender and sexuality. One fetishizes bodies; the other, theory. In any case, says Brian McNair in *Mediated Sex: Pornography and Postmodern Culture*, pornography has reenergized postmodern theory if only by introducing academics to new territory. "Postmodern mysteries" can thus be subsumed under "Fuck Theory," the title Joanna Frueh gives to a chapter of her *Erotic Faculties*. Frueh's witticism aside, academics usually adopt a posture of sexlessness that implicitly denies all but intellectual responses to erotica, unless the example is old enough to have lost much of its erotic energy. In "Bakhtin, Eroticism and the Cinema: Strategies for the Critique and Trans-Valuation of Pornography," for instance, Robert Stam applies Bakhtin's theories of carnival to pornography in an effort to invent a dessicated sexual discourse stripped of pleasure, physicality, or sensuality. The postmodernist critic's stance in essays like this one, and there are a great many like it, resembles a novice camper's prodding at a snake with a stick.

As the astute Elizabeth Wilson has pointed out, "The idea of postmodernism fascinates, while appearing to celebrate the most kitsch and degraded aspects of our culture. It is a distorted, or thwarted, utopian impulse, which twists the problem—of alienation at the polluting ugly underside of consumer culture— into a kind of solution. Postmodernism expresses at one level a horror at the destructive excess of Western consumerist society, yet, in aestheticizing this horror, we somehow convert it into a pleasurable object of consumption."[9] Like several other scholars, Sarah Markgraf has noted that essays focusing on "scandalous" and "dangerous" topics are by now an "entrenched part" of academic discourse.[10] Such considerations lead David Pendleton to describe his perspective in "Obscene Allegories: Narrative, Representation, Pornography" in disarming terms as "an unholy alliance of de Manian criticism and Barthesian semiology, with some Walter Benjamin thrown in, to produce a reading of the functioning of the porn video which can then be inserted into a Foucauldian discussion of sexuality and its deployment. As a result of the tortuous process of articulating this bit of alchemy, my own pleasure in pornography and the pleasure that my friends take from it dissolves into a cloud of academese" (156).

Perhaps sensing the affinities between academics and pornographers, many Americans view scholarly investigations of sexual representations with suspicion. As the information economy accelerates, American culture consumes data from the margins at faster and faster rates. The trend affects all sectors, including the academic, which in many ways resembles the pornographic sector in its relationship to the main information economy. Because the number of academic workers increased dramatically after World War II and because information is an inherently inflationary commodity, academics are under constant pressure to generate information. Academic protocol requires condemning previous thought on a subject as worthless, though the most savage attacks are usually reserved for older historians and rivals not theory-hip. That circumstance contributes to the highly industrialized nature of academic publishing, a characterization obvious not only to college students who must purchase overpriced textbooks but also to any visitor to libraries or surfer of databases. Sharp competition and institutionalized product obsolescence drive academic research and publishing, especially in the liberal arts. Academic criticism, in short, bears much the same relationship to the larger culture as does pornography itself, a parallel not lost on conservative critics.

In some cases, the study of erotica mirrors the personal obsessions of leading theorists. Michel Foucault, a practicing sadomasochist, was devoted to leather and discipline; some critics think that his sexual predilections are reflected in his reduction of sexuality to issues of power. With his tongue only partly in cheek, a longtime observer of fringes told Joseph Slade in *Shades of Blue* that "[vocal opponents of S/M] are recoiling from the primal scene of postmodernism: a well-beaten Michel Foucault strapped over a toilet in the back of a leather bar, giving birth to *La volonté de savoir* [the first volume of *The History of Sexuality*]. If you can only come by having your ass whipped, it shouldn't surprise anyone that you begin to think all sex is power." Sadomasochism furnished Foucault with a theoretical discourse of masters and slaves. Where ordinary critics *examine* a document, Foucauldians *interrogate* it; where communication specialists say that a practice or a cluster of information *conditions* or *programs* consumers or audiences, Foucauldians use the verb *discipline*; where conventional sociologists say that people have *preferences*, Foucauldians call such tastes *fetishes*. It is a wonderfully sexualized language, with suites of theories turning on concepts of surveillance, policings, subordination, and the sheer eroticism of abuse and victimization.

The language of many postmodernists, in fact, has been enriched by pornographic examples or metaphors: one need think only of the fanciful penises and vaginas animating the writing of Kristeva, Baudrillard, Cixous, or Lacan, though the number could be extended to most theorists of the body and performance. Jacques Lacan, the post-Freudian analyst, purchased the original of what is probably the Western world's most notorious painting, Gustave Courbet's *l'Origine du Monde* or *The Origin of the World* (1866), which depicts the lower torso of a nude woman, her legs spread to center her precisely rendered labia. Lacan rarely showed the painting even to associates, preferring to enjoy it privately (though after his death it was exhibited at the Brooklyn Museum in September 1993), and even then he covered the figure's genitals with a board affixed across the frame.[11] A non-Lacanian Freudian would discover in the wooden perversity of this textual alteration a great deal about postmodernism. (The number of major theorists with secret obsessions is large; as just one other, the theologian Paul Tillich used to seek out sexual exhibitions in Paris, Marseilles, and New York and to read pornographic novels and magazines on the sly.[12])

When postmodernists assert that representation and reality are virtually inter-changeable, they speak for Americans who believe that a representation of a naked body or of a body coupled with another is literally sex in actuality. The conceit is perhaps no more remarkable than the conviction that wine and wafer can be blood and body, though most of us allow that a miracle is required for the second instance. Besides, analyzing the sexuality of a pornographic artifact, which is finite, closed, and frozen, is much more attractive than dealing with actual human sexuality, which is chaotic, messy, irrational, and, ultimately, im-penetrable. Almost any theory can be applied to the pornographic specimen without the inconvenience of trying to assess unique individual human behavior. Lacanian psychology is appealing for the same reason, since it can focus on the phallus or its representations in the same manner as literary critics focusing on a text. Wryly noting the academic tendency to impose tastes and standards on popular culture, in "The Popularity of Pornography," Andrew Ross suggests that the real appeal of the pornographic—the pleasure offered—is actually off the radar scope of the scholar, feminist or otherwise.

Jennifer Wicke's map of various critical positions is wittily entitled "Through a Gaze Darkly: Pornography's Academic Marketplace": it is a reliable guide through the thicket of often opposed arguments and freewheeling in its judg-ments (Wicke calls Susanne Kappeler's *The Pornography of Representation* "goofy"). Says Wicke: "The academic market is hot for pornography because pornography is both the object and the subject of desire, the representation and the reader, the consumer and the consumed, in one inextricable package" (79). According to Nancy Armstrong, pornography mirrors culture. Her essay, "The Pornographic Effect," asserts that pornography is "an extremely important means of cultural self-reflexivity" (43). M. G. Lord's "Pornutopia: How Feminist Scholars Learned to Love Dirty Pictures" is a charming account of Laura Kipnis, Constance Penley, Linda Williams, Catharine MacKinnon, Joanna Frueh, and others who have built academic careers on exactly the assumption made by Armstrong.

Nicola Pitchford's "Reading Feminism's Pornography Conflict: Implications for Postmodernist Reading Strategies," an essay on the novels of Kathy Acker and Angela Carter, both often called pornographic, tries to distinguish between ways in which groups read these novels. The argument that pornographic tropes do not make for pornography is less persuasive than Pitchford's observation that "the feminist antipornography theory of representation is not a theory for post-modernity because, in part, it is unable to extend its critique beyond the categories of gender and sexuality" (32). Even so, investigations of sexual discourse can and do produce valuable new insights about individuals and culture. Just as often, such explorations render the explorer transparent: all writing about pornography, pro or con, is essentially writing about one's self. Some writers acknowledge involvement. The concluding chapter of Nancy Miller's *Getting Personal: Feminist Occasions and Other Autobiographical Acts* is an extended fantasy entitled "My Father's Penis," in which this passage appears: "Months after writing this [chapter] I come into my father's room. I think I have put an end to all these speculations (penis, phallus, castration, etc.) but when I find him sleeping completely naked, stretched out like an aged Endymion across a hospital bed, I can't resist. His hand is resting in his lap, his penis tucked away out of sight, hidden between his legs. I move closer" (146).

On one hand, such "confessions" are valuable, because they are reminders that the experience of sexuality and of pornography is very personal and must be understood as such. On the other hand, "secret" levels of the psyche are insufficient guides to clandestine levels of culture. An enormous gap separates the average pornography aficionado and the most erudite theorist, as is evident in comparisons of those "in the know" and those who merely pontificate. As a case in point, consider "The Unmasking of O," the *New Yorker* exposé in which John de St. Jorre "reveals" that the real name of Pauline Réage, author of *Histoire d'O*, is Dominique Aury. Reuters quickly spread the news in a sequence familiar to observers of culture (see " 'Story of O' Author Unmasked, Magazine Claims"). What makes the story interesting is that collectors (a covert culture?) had known Réage's identity for over a decade. Patrick J. Kearney identified Aury as the real author in *The Private Case* in 1981; Ivan Stormgart's book catalogs have listed *Story of O* under "Aury" for years. Collectors routinely attribute works by Jean De Berg to Alain Robbe-Grillet, just as they routinely catalog the works of "Emmanuelle Arsan" under "R," for Maryat Rollet-Andrianne, names apparently unfamiliar to academics. Knowledgeable collectors of porn films or tapes will have seen hundreds, will have dated them accurately, will know the styles and real names of individual directors, producers, and performers. They will thus understandably be amused at the naïveté of a sociologist who conducts a study of a mere dozen videotapes in order to "discover" that this genre emphasizes fellatio more than cunnilingus—without any consideration of the camera angles that foster the imbalance. All too typical is the slipshod treatment of the subject apparent in Barry Brumett's "The Homology Hypothesis: Pornography on the VCR" (an analysis based on Kenneth Burke), in which the author notes that he provides no bibliographic information on the six films he considered "because their titles change as they change distributors (producers, directors, and production companies tend to be temporary and legal fictions, here today and gone tomorrow) with the exception of a few notable 'classics,' such as *Behind the Green Door*" (214, n. 2). Such cavalier attitudes ignore the existence of massive bibliographic documentation that nonetheless flourishes in a domain distant and unknown to the blindfolded researcher. This *Reference Guide* identifies some of those sources.

NOTES

1. See for example, Vance's "Pleasure and Danger: Toward a Politics of Sexuality," and "Epilogue," *Pleasure and Danger: Exploring Female Sexuality*, ed. Carole S. Vance (Boston: Routledge and Kegan Paul, 1984), pp. 1–27, 431–439.

2. Susie Bright, quoted by Steven Chapple and David Talbot, *Burning Desires: Sex in America—A Report from the Field* (New York: Signet, 1990), p. 316.

3. Attorney General's Commission on Pornography, *Final Report* (Washington, DC: Government Printing Office, 1986), I: 383.

4. Quoted in *Feminists for Free Expression Newsletter*, 2 (1994): 2.

5. Sigmund Freud, *Civilization and Its Discontents*, trans. James Strachey (New York: Norton, 1961), pp. 29–30.

6. Calvin Tomkins, "Madonna's Anticlimax," *New Yorker*, 26 October 1992, p. 38.

7. H. L. Mencken, quoted in Arthur Power Dudden, "The Record of Political Humor," *American Quarterly*, 37 (Spring 1985): 61.

8. See, for example, D. L. Paletz, "Pornography, Politics, and the Press: The U.S. Attorney General's Commission on Pornography," *Journal of Communication*, 38:2 (Spring 1988): 122–135; F. M. Christensen, *Pornography: The Other Side* (New York: Praeger, 1990).

9. Elizabeth Wilson, "Fashion and the Postmodern Body," *Chic Thrills*, ed. Juliet Ash and Elizabeth Wilson (Berkeley: University of California Press, 1993), p. 4.

10. Sarah Markgraf, "Review of *Close Encounters: Film, Feminism, and Science Fiction* (by Constance Penley)," *Film Comment*, 45:4 (Summer 1992): 27.

11. AP report, "Scandalous 1866 Painting on Display at the Orsay," *Athens (Ohio) Messenger*, 29 June 1995, p. 19.

12. Hannah Tillich. *From Time to Time* (New York: Stein and Day, 1973), pp. 175–178, 189–190, 241.

REFERENCES

Adam, Barry D. *The Rise of a Gay and Lesbian Movement*. Boston: Twayne, 1987.

Adorno, Theodor, and Max Horkheimer. *The Dialectics of Enlightenment*, trans. John Cumming. London: Allen Lane, 1973.

Alexander, Alison, and Janice Hanson, eds. *Taking Sides: Clashing Views on Controversial Issues in Human Sexuality*. 2d ed. Guilford, CT: Dushkin, 1993.

Allen, David W. *The Fear of Looking, or Scopophilic-Exhibitionistic Conflicts*. Charlottesville: University Press of Virginia, 1974.

Allen, Gina. "What Those Women Want in Pornography." *Humanist*, 38 (November–December 1978): 46–47.

Amis, Martin. "A Critic at Large: Don Juan in Hull." *New Yorker*, 12 July 1993, pp. 74–82.

Arcand, Bernard. *The Jaguar and the Anteater: Pornography Degree Zero*, trans. Wayne Grady. New York: Verso, 1993.

Armstrong, Nancy. "The Pornographic Effect." *American Journal of Semiotics*, 7:1/2 (1990): 27–44.

Assiter, Alison. *Pornography, Feminism and the Individual*. Winchester, MA: Pluto Press, 1989.

Assiter, Alison, and Avedon Carol, eds. *Bad Girls and Dirty Pictures: The Challenge to Reclaim Feminism*. Boulder, CO: Pluto Press, 1993.

Avis, Paul D. *Eros and the Sacred*. London: SPCK, 1989.

Baird, Robert M., and Stuart E. Rosenbaum, eds. *Pornography: Private Right or Public Menace?* Buffalo, NY: Prometheus Books, 1991; rev. ed. 1996.

Barber, D. F. *Pornography and Society*. London: Skilton, 1972.

Barry, Kathleen. *Female Sexual Slavery*. New York: New York University Press, 1984.

———. *The Prostitution of Sexuality*. New York: New York University Press, 1994.

Bataille, Georges. *Eroticism*. Paris: Editions de Minuit, 1957; *Death and Sensuality: A Study of Eroticism and the Taboo*, no trans. New York: Ballantine Books, 1962; *Eroticism: Death and Sensuality*, trans. Mary Dalwood. San Francisco: City Light Books, 1986.

———. *Les Larmes d'Eros*. Paris: Pauvert, 1964.

Baudrillard, Jean. *The Ecstacy of Communication*. Brooklyn, NY: Autonomedia, 1989; rpt. *The Post-Modern Reader*, ed. Charles Jencks. New York: St. Martin's, 1992, pp. 151–157.

———. *For a Critique of the Political Economy of the Sign*. St. Louis: Telos Press, 1981.

———. *Selected Writings*, trans. Jacques Mourrain, ed. Mark Poster. Cambridge: Cambridge University Press, 1988.

Becker, Howard S. *Outsiders: Studies in the Sociology of Deviance*. New York: Free Press, 1963.

Bell, Laurie, ed. *Good Girls/Bad Girls: Feminists and Sex Trade Workers Face to Face*. Seattle: Seal Press, 1987.

Benjamin, Walter. "The Work of Art in an Age of Mechanical Reproduction." *Illuminations*, trans. Harry Zohn, ed. Hannah Arendt. New York: Harcourt, Brace, and World, 1973, pp. 217–252.

Berger, John. *About Looking*. New York: Random House, 1991.

———. *Ways of Seeing*. London: BBC/Penguin, 1986.

Berger, Ronald J., Patricia Searles, and Charles E. Cottle. *Feminism and Pornography*. New York: Praeger, 1991.

Berns, Walter. "Beyond the (Garbage) Pale, or Democracy, Censorship and the Arts." *The Pornography Controversy*, ed. Ray C. Rist. New Brunswick, NJ: Transaction, 1975, pp. 40–63.

Bersani, Leo. "Is the Rectum a Grave?" *October*, 43 (Winter 1987): 197–222.

"Beyond Good and Evil: Writers' Moral Visions." *Journal of the Writers' Guild of America, West*, 4:7 (July 1991): 8–14.

Blakely, Mary Kay. "Is One Woman's Sexuality Another Woman's Pornography?" *Ms*, 13 (April 1985): 37–38, 40, 44, 46–47.

Brigman, William. "Pornography as Political Expression." *Journal of Popular Culture*, 17:2 (1983): 129–134.

Brod, Harry. "Eros Thanatized: Pornography and Male Sexuality." *Humanities in Society*,

7 (Winter/Spring 1984): 47–63; see also "Pornography and the Alienation of Male Sexuality." *Rethinking Masculinity: Philosophical Explorations in Light of Feminism*, ed. Larry May, Robert A. Strikwearda, and Patrick D. Hopkins. Lanham, MD: Littlefield Adams, 1992, pp. 149–168.

Brown, Norman O. *Life against Death: The Psychoanalytical Meaning of History*. Middletown, CT: Wesleyan University Press, 1959.

Brownmiller, Susan. *Against Our Will: Men, Women, and Rape*. New York: Bantam Books, 1976.

Brumett, Barry. "The Homology Hypothesis: Pornography on the VCR." *Critical Studies in Mass Communication*, 5 (1988): 202–216.

Bryant, Clifton. *Sexual Deviancy and Social Proscription: The Social Context of Carnal Behavior*. New York: Human Sciences Press, 1982.

Burstyn, Varda, ed. *Women against Censorship*. Vancouver: Douglas and McIntyre, 1985.

Butler, Judith. *Excitable Speech: A Politics of the Performative*. New York: Routledge, 1997.

Califia, Pat. "Introduction." *Macho Sluts*. Boston: Alyson, 1988, pp. 9–27.

———. "A Personal View of the History of the Lesbian S/M Community and Movement in San Francisco." *Coming to Power: Writings and Graphics on Lesbian S/M*, ed. Samois. Boston: Alyson, 1982, pp. 243–281.

———. *Public Sex: The Culture of Radical Sex*. Pittsburgh: Cleis Press, 1994.

———. *Sapphistry: The Book of Lesbian Sexuality*. Tallahassee, FL: Naiad Press, 1980.

Caputi, Jane. *Voluptuous Yearnings: A Feminist Theory of the Obscene*. Lanham, MD: Rowman and Littlefield, 1994.

Carol, Avedon. *Nudes, Prudes and Attitudes: Pornography and Censorship*, with cartoons by Lee Kennedy. Cheltenham, England: New Clarion Press, 1994.

Carter, Angela. *The Sadeian Woman and the Ideology of Pornography: An Exercise in Cultural History*. New York: Pantheon, 1979.

Catholic Church. Pontifical Council for Social Communications. *Pornography and Violence in the Communications Media: A Pastoral Response*. Pamphlet # 290-X. Washington, DC: Office for Publishing and Promotion Services, U.S. Catholic Conference, 1989.

Chaucer, Lynn S. *Reconcilable Differences: Confronting Beauty, Pornography, and the Future of Feminism*. Berkeley: University of California Press, 1998.

Christensen, F. M. "A Philosopher Looks at the Porn Debate: Interview." *Playboy*, 35 (January 1988): 50, 52.

———. *Pornography: The Other Side*. New York: Praeger, 1990.

Christgau, Robert. "Children of the Porn." *Village Voice*, 30 July 1996, pp. 67–68.

Clark, David Aaron. "Madonna Exposed." *Gauntlet*, 5 (1993): 18–23.

Cleaver, Eldridge. *Soul on Ice*. New York: Delta, 1968.

Coetzee, J. M. *Giving Offense: Essays on Censorship*. Chicago: University of Chicago Press, 1996.

Comfort, Alex. *Darwin and the Naked Lady: Discursive Essays on Biology and Art*. London: Routledge and Kegan Paul, 1961.

———. *The New Joy of Sex: A Gourmet Guide to Lovemaking for the Nineties*. New York: Crown, 1991.

"Coming Apart: Feminists and the Conflict over Pornography." Special Issue. *Off Our Backs*, 15:6 (June 1985).

Comninou, Maria. "Speech, Pornography, and Hunting." *Animals and Women: Feminist Theoretical Explorations*, ed. Carol J. Adams and Josephine Donovan. Durham, NC: Duke University Press, 1995, pp. 126–148.

Corcoran, Clodaugh. *Pornography: The New Terrorism*. Greenwood, SC: Attic Press, 1989.

Corea, Gena. *The Mother Machine: Reproductive Technologies from Artificial Insemination to Artificial Wombs*. New York: Harper, 1985.

Cotham, Perry C. *Obscenity, Pornography and Censorship*. Grand Rapids, MI: Baker Book House, 1973.

Court, John H. *Pornography: A Christian Critique*. Downers Grove, IL: Intervarsity Press, 1980.

Cowan, Ruth Schwartz. *More Work for Mother: The Ironies of Household Technology from the Open Hearth to the Microwave*. New York: Basic Books, 1983.

Crick, Bernard R. *Crime, Rape, and Gin: Reflections on Contemporary Attitudes to Violence, Pornography, and Addiction*. Buffalo, NY: Prometheus, 1974.

Daly, Mary. *Pure Lust: Elemental Feminist Philosophy*. Boston: Beacon Press, 1984.

Davis, Douglas. "Art and Contradiction: Helms, Censorship, and the Serpent." *Art in America*, 78:5 (May 1990): 55–61.

Davis, Murray S. *Smut: Erotic Reality/Obscene Ideology*. Chicago: University of Chicago Press, 1983.

Day, Gary. "Looking at Women: Notes toward a Theory of Porn." *Perspectives on Pornography: Sexuality in Film and Literature*, ed. Gary Day and Clive Bloom. New York: St. Martin's, 1988, pp. 83–100.

Dearn, Edmund L. *Pornography Degrades*. Sydney, Australia: Renda, 1974.

De Crow, Karen. "Strange Bedfellows." *Penthouse*, 16:9 (May 1985): 96–97.

Delacoste, Frédérique, and Priscilla Alexander, eds. *Sex Work: Writings by Women in the Sex Industry*. Pittsburgh: Cleis Press, 1987.

Dennis, Kelly. *"The Face of God: Representation as the Pornography of Modernity."* Ph.D. dissertation, University of California at Los Angeles, 1994.

Dershowitz, Alan. "Justice." *Penthouse*, 25:8 (April 1994): 26.

de St. Jorre, John. "The Unmasking of O." *New Yorker*, 1 August 1994, pp. 42–50.

Diamond, Sara. "Pornography: Image and Reality." *Women against Censorship*, ed. Varda Burstyn. Vancouver: Douglas and McIntyre, 1985, pp. 40–57.

Dines, Gail, Robert Jensen, and Ann Russo. *Pornography: The Production and Consumption of Inequality*. New York: Routledge, 1998.

Doane, Mary Ann. *Femmes Fatales: Feminism, Film Theory, Psychoanalysis*. New York: Routledge, 1991.

———. "Film and the Masquerade: Theorising the Female Spectator." *Screen*, 23:3/4 (September–October 1982): 74–87; rpt. *The Sexual Subject: A Screen Reader in Sexuality*, by the editors of *Screen*, New York: Routledge, 1992, pp. 227–243.

———. "Masquerade Reconsidered: Further Thoughts on the Female Spectator." *Discourse*, 11:1 (Fall–Winter 1988–1989): 42–54; rpt. in *Femmes Fatales: Feminism, Film Theory, Psychoanalysis*. New York: Routledge, 1991.

———. "Technophilia: Technology, Representation, and the Feminine." *Body/Politics: Women and the Discourses of Science*, ed. Mary Jacobus, Evelyn Fox Keller, and Sally Shuttleworth. New York: Routledge, 1990, pp. 163–176.

Dobson, James C., producer. "Pornography: Addictive, Progressive and Deadly." Cassette

7 of *Life on the Edge: Preparing for the Challenges of Adulthood.* 7 cassettes. Irving, TX: Word, 1994.

Dotterer, Ronald, and Susan Bowers, eds. *Sexuality, the Female Gaze, and the Arts.* Selingrove, PA: Susquehana University Press, 1992.

Douglas, Mary. *Purity and Danger: An Analysis of Concepts of Pollution and Taboo.* London: Ark Paperbacks, 1984.

Drakeford, John, and Jack Hamm. *Pornography: The Sexual Mirage.* Nashville: Thomas Nelson, 1973.

"Dressed to Kill." Special section on the pornography debate. *Film Comment,* 20 (November–December 1984), 30–49.

Durgnant, Raymond. "From Mechanical Brides to Rubber Women." *Art and Artists,* 5: 5 (August 1970): 10–13.

Durkheim, Emile. *The Division of Labor in Society,* trans. George Simpson. Glencoe, IL: Free Press, 1933.

Duvert, Tony. "Other People's Eroticism," trans. Joan Templeton. *Antaeus,* 24 (Winter 1976): 117–125.

Dworkin, Andrea. "Against the Male Flood: Censorship, Pornography, and Equality." *Harvard Women's Law Journal,* 8 (1985): 1–30.

———. *Ice and Fire: A Novel.* New York: Weidenfeld and Nicolson, 1987.

———. *Intercourse.* New York: Free Press, 1987.

———. *Letters from a War Zone: Writings, 1976–1989.* New York: Dutton, 1989; Brooklyn, NY: Lawrence Hill, 1993.

———. *Life and Death: Unapologetic Writings on the Continuing War against Women.* New York: Free Press, 1997.

———. *The New Woman's Broken Heart: Short Stories.* San Francisco: Frog in the Well, 1980.

———. *Our Blood: Prophecies and Discourses on Sexual Politics.* New York: Harper and Row, 1976.

———. *Pornography: Men Possessing Women.* New York: Putnam's, 1980.

———. *Right-Wing Women.* New York: Perigee, 1983.

———. *Woman Hating.* New York: Dutton, 1974.

Dwyer, Susan, ed. *The Problem of Pornography.* Belmont, CA: Wadsworth, 1995.

Dyer, Richard. "Male Gay Porn." *Jump Cut,* no. 30 (March 1985): 227–229; rpt. Dyer's *Only Entertainment.* New York: Routledge, 1992, pp. 121–134.

———. *The Matter of Images: Essays on Representations.* New York: Routledge, 1993.

Echols, Alice. "Sex and the Single-Minded." *Village Voice Literary Supplement,* March 1994, 13–14.

Ellis, John. "On Pornography." *The Sexual Subject: A Screen Reader in Sexuality,* by the editors of *Screen.* New York: Routledge, 1992, pp. 146–170.

———. "Photography/Pornography, Art/Pornography." *Screen,* 21:1 (Spring 1980): 81–108.

Ellis, Kate, Beth Jaker, Nan D. Hunter, Barbara O'Dair, and Abby Tallmer, eds. *Caught Looking: Feminism, Pornography, and Censorship.* New York: Caught Looking, 1986; Seattle: Real Comet Press, 1988.

English, Deidre. "The Politics of Porn: Can Feminists Walk the Line?" *Mother Jones,* 5 (April 1980): 20–23, 43–44, 48–50.

Erikson, Kai T. *Wayward Puritans: A Study in the Sociology of Deviance.* New York: John Wiley, 1966.

Falwell, Jerry. *Listen, America!* New York: Doubleday, 1980.

"Forbidden Fantasies: A Special Issue on Pornography." *Village Voice*, 16 October 1984.

Foucault, Michel. *The History of Sexuality*, trans. Robert B. Hurley. 3 vols. I: *An Introduction*; II: *The Use of Pleasure*; III: *Care of the Self.* New York: Pantheon, 1978–1987.

Francoeur, Robert T., ed. *Taking Sides: Clashing Views on Controversial Issues in Human Sexuality.* Guilford, CT: Dushkin, 1989.

Freedberg, David. *The Power of Images: Studies in the History and Theory of Response.* Chicago: University of Chicago Press, 1989, chapters 12 and 13, esp. pp. 349–365.

Fremont-Smith, Eliot. "Pornography's Progress." *Village Voice*, 15–21 October 1980, pp. 43–46.

French, Marilyn. *The War against Women.* New York: Summit Books, 1992.

Frueh, Joanna. *Erotic Faculties.* Berkeley: University of California Press, 1996.

Fussell, Paul. *Thank God for the Atom Bomb and Other Essays.* New York: Ballantine, 1988.

Gallagher, Maggie. *Enemies of Eros: How the Sexual Revolution Is Killing Family, Marriage, and Sex, and What We Can Do about It.* Chicago: Bonus Books, 1989.

Gallop, Jane. *Feminist Accused of Sexual Harassment.* Durham, NC: Duke University Press, 1997.

Gammon, Lorraine, and Margaret Marshment, eds. *The Female Gaze: Women as Viewers of Popular Culture.* Seattle: Real Comet Press, 1989.

Gans, Herbert J. *Popular Culture and High Culture: An Analysis and Evaluation of Taste.* New York: Basic Books, 1974.

Gardella, Peter. *Innocent Ecstasy: How Christianity Gave America an Ethic of Pleasure.* New York: Oxford, 1985.

Gardner, Tracey A. "Racism in Pornography and the Women's Movement." *Take Back the Night: Women on Pornography*, ed. Laura Lederer. New York: Morrow, 1980, pp. 105–114.

Garry, Ann. "Pornography and Respect for Women." *Philosophy and Sex*, ed. Robert Baker and Frederick Elliston. Rev. ed. Amherst, NY: Prometheus Books, 1984, pp. 312–326.

Gass, William. *On Being Blue: A Philosophical Inquiry.* Boston: David R. Godine, 1976.

Geis, Gilbert. *One Eyed Justice: An Examination of Homosexuality, Abortion, Prostitution, Narcotics, and Gambling in the U.S.* New York: Drake, 1974.

Gertzman, Jay A. *Bookleggers and Smuthounds: The Trade in Erotica, 1920–1940.* Philadelphia: University of Pennsylvania Press, 1999.

Giachetti, Romano. *Porno Power: Pornografia Società Capitalista.* Bologna: Guaraldi Editore, 1971.

Gibson, Pamela Church, and Roma Gibson, eds. *Dirty Looks: Women, Pornography, Power.* London: British Film Institute, 1993.

Giddens, Anthony. *The Transformation of Intimacy: Sexuality, Love and Eroticism in Modern Societies.* Los Angeles: Stanford University Press, 1992.

Girodias, Maurice. "The Erotic Society." *Evergreen Review*, 39 (February 1966): 64–69, 89–91.

Goldberg, Vicki. "Testing the Limits in a Culture of Excess." *New York Times*, 29 October 1995, sec. 2, pp. 1, 40.

Goldstein, Al. Editorial. *Screw*, 21 January 1985, p. 3.

Gonzalez-Crussi, F. *On the Nature of Things Erotic*. New York: Harcourt Brace Jovanovich, 1988.

Gopnik, Adam. "American Studies." *New Yorker*, 28 September 1998, pp. 39–40, 42.

Gorman, Carol. *Pornography*. New York: Franklin Watts, 1988.

Gorsen, Peter. *Das prinzip Obszön: Kunst, Pornographie und Gesellschaft*. Reinbek bei
Hamburg: Rowohlt, 1969.

———. *Sexualästhetik: Grenzformen der Sinnlichkeit im 20. Jahrhundert*. Hamburg:
Rowohlt, 1987.

———. *Sexualästhetik: Zur burgerlichen Rezeption von Obszönitat und Pornographie*.
Reinbek bei Hamburg: Rowohlt Verlag, 1972.

Gowans, Alan. *Learning to See: Historical Perspectives on Modern Popular/Commercial
Arts*. Bowling Green, OH: Bowling Green University Popular Press, 1981.

Gramsci, Antonio. *Selections from Cultural Writings*, trans. William Boelhower, ed. David Forgacs and Geoffrey Nowell-Smith. Cambridge: Harvard University Press,
1985.

Greer, Germaine. *The Female Eunuch*. New York: McGraw-Hill, 1971.

Greer, Gordon. "Pornography: What Can Be Done to Protect Our Kids?" *Better Homes
and Gardens*, December 1971, p. 16.

Griffin, Susan. *Pornography and Silence: Culture's Revenge against Nature*. New York:
Harper and Row, 1981.

Gubar, Susan, and Joan Hoff, eds. *For Adult Users Only: The Dilemma of Violent Pornography*. Bloomington: Indiana University Press, 1989.

Hacker, Sally. "The Eye of the Beholder: An Essay on Technology and Eroticism."
"Doing It the Hard Way": Investigations of Gender and Technology, by Sally
Hacker, ed. Dorothy E. Smith and Susan M. Turner. Boston: Unwin Hyman,
1990, pp. 205–223.

Hamill, Pete. "Woman on the Verge of a Legal Breakdown." *Playboy*, 40:1 (January
1993): 138–140, 184–189.

Haraway, Donna. "A Manifesto for Cyborgs: Science, Technology, and Socialist Feminism in the 1980s." *Feminism/Postmodernism*, ed. Linda J. Nicolson. New York:
Routledge, 1990, pp. 190–233.

Hartley, Nina. "Pornography at the Millennium." *Gauntlet*, 14 (1997): 20–24.

———. "Reflections of a Feminist Porn Star." *Gauntlet: Exploring the Limits of Free
Expression*, 5 (1993): 62–68.

Hoffmann, Frank. *Analytical Survey of Anglo-American Traditional Erotica*. Bowling
Green, OH: Popular Press, 1973.

Holbrook, David, ed. *The Case against Pornography*. Lasalle, IL: Library Press, 1974;
rpt. London: Tom Stacey, 1972.

hooks, bell. *Ain't I a Woman: Black Women and Feminism*. Boston: South End Press,
1981.

———. *Outlaw Culture: Resisting Representations*. New York: Routledge, 1994.

Huer, Jon. *Art, Beauty, and Pornography: A Journey through American Culture*. Buffalo,
NY: Prometheus, 1987.

Hughes, Douglas A. *Perspectives on Pornography*. New York: St. Martin's, 1970.

Hunt, Lynn, ed. *The Invention of Pornography: Obscenity and the Origins of Modernity,
1500–1800*. Cambridge: MIT Zone, 1993.

Jantz, Harold. *On Pornography*. Scottsdale, PA: Herald Press, 1987.

Jeffreys, Sheila. " 'Pornography' and 'Creating the Sexual Future.' " *Ethics: A Feminist*

Reader, ed. Elizabeth Frazer, Jennifer Hornsby, and Sabina Lovibond. Cambridge, England: Blackwell, 1992, pp. 459–488.

Johnson, Peter. "Pornography Drives Technology: Why Not to Censor the Internet." *Federal Communications Law Journal*, 49:1 (November 1996): 217–226.

Juffer, Jane. *At Home with Pornography: Women, Sex, and Everyday Life*. New York: New York University Press, 1998.

Kakutani, Michiko. "Pornography, the Constitution and a Fight Thereof." *New York Times*, 29 October 1993, p. B4.

Kaplan, Abraham. "Obscenity as an Esthetic Category." *The Pornography Controversy*, ed. Ray C. Rist. New Brunswick, NJ: Transaction, 1975, pp. 16–37.

Kaplan, E. Ann. "Is the Gaze Male?" *Powers of Desire: The Politics of Sexuality*, ed. Ann Snitow, Christine Stansell, and Sharon Thompson. New York: Monthly Review Press, 1983, 309–327.

Kappeler, Susanne. *The Pornography of Representation*. Minneapolis: University of Minnesota Press, 1986.

———. "Pornography Unmodified." *The Knowledge Explosion: Generations of Feminist Scholarship*, ed. Cheris Kramarae and Dale Spender. New York: Teachers College Press, 1992, pp. 379–385.

Keller, Evelyn Fox. *Reflections on Gender and Science*. New Haven, CT: Yale University Press, 1985.

Kendrick, Walter. *The Secret Museum: Pornography in Modern Culture*. New York: Viking, 1987.

Khan, Masud. "Pornography and the Politics of Rage and Subversion." *Times Literary Supplement*, 4 February 1972, pp. 5–9; rpt. *The Case against Pornography*, ed. David Holbrook.

Kimmel, Michael S., ed. *Men Confront Pornography*. New York: Crown, 1990.

Kinsman, Gary. "The Porn Debate." *Fuse*, 8 (Summer 1984): 39–44.

Kipnis, Laura. *Bound and Gagged: Pornography and the Politics of Fantasy in America*. New York: Grove Press, 1996.

———. *Ecstasy Unlimited: The Interpenetration of Sex and Capital*. (Videotape.) Minneapolis: University of Minnesota Press, 1985.

———. *Ecstasy Unlimited: On Sex, Capital, Gender, and Aesthetics*. Minneapolis: University of Minnesota Press, 1993.

———. "She-Male Fantasies and the Aesthetics of Pornography." *Dirty Looks: Women, Pornography, Power*, ed. Pamela Church Gibson and Roma Gibson. London: British Film Institute, 1993, pp. 124–143.

Kirk, Jerry. *The Mind Polluters*. Nashville, TN: Nelson, 1985.

Klein, Marty. "Sex Is Great—That's Why Censors Can't Stand It." *Playboy*, 38:5 (May 1991): 54–55.

Kleinhans, Chuck, and Julia Lesage. "The Politics of Sexual Representation." *Jump Cut*, no. 30 (March 1985): 24–26.

Kolenda, Konstantin. "Porno Prone." *Humanist*, 45 (July–August 1985): 45.

Koskoff, Harriet, producer. *Patently Offensive: Porn under Siege*. New York: Filmmakers Library, 1992.

Kotz, Liz. "The Body You Want: Liz Kotz Interviews Judith Butler." *Artforum*, 31:3 (November 1992): 82–89.

Kristol, Irving. "Pornography, Obscenity, and the Case for Censorship." *New York Times*

Magazine, 28 March, 1971; rpt. *The American Sexual Dilemma*, ed. William L. O'Neill. New York: Holt, Rinehart, and Winston, 1972, pp. 107–115.

Kroker, Arthur, and David Cook. *The Postmodern Scene: Excremental Culture and HyperAesthetics*. Montreal: New World Perspectives, 1986; New York: St. Martin's, 1986.

Kronhausen, Eberhard, and Phyllis Kronhausen. *Pornography and the Law*. New York: Ballantine Books, 1959. Rev. ed. New York: Bell [1975].

Lacombe, Dany. *Ideology and Public Policy: The Case against Pornography*. Toronto: Garamond Press, 1988.

Langford, Larry L. *Fiction and the Social Contract: Genocide, Pornography, and the Deconstruction of History*. New York: Peter Lang, 1998.

Lawrence, D. H. "Pornography and Obscenity." *Pornography and So On*. London: Faber and Faber, 1936; rpt. *Sex, Literature, and Censorship*, by D. H. Lawrence, ed. Harry T. Moore. New York: Irvington, 1953; rpt. *Pornography and Obscenity: Handbook for Censors: Two Essays by D. H. Lawrence and Henry Miller*. Michigan City, IN: Fridtjof-Karla Publications, 1958.

Lawrence, Raymond. *The Poisoning of Eros: Sexual Values in Conflict*. New York: A. Moore Press, 1990.

Lederer, Laura, ed. *Take Back the Night: Women on Pornography*. New York: William Morrow, 1980.

Lord, M. G. "Pornutopia: How Feminist Scholars Learned to Love Dirty Pictures." *Lingua Franca*, 7.4 (April/May 1997): 40–48.

Lorde, Audre. "Uses of the Erotic: The Erotic as Power." *Sister Outsider: Essays and Speeches by Audre Lorde*. Trumansburg, NY: Crossing Press, 1984, pp. 53–59.

Luhmann, Niklas. *Love as Passion: The Codification of Intimacy*, trans. Jeremy Gaines and Doris L. Jones. Cambridge: Polity, 1986.

MacKinnon, Catharine A. *Feminism Unmodified: Discourses on Life and Law*. Cambridge: Harvard University Press, 1987.

———. *Only Words*. Cambridge: Harvard University Press, 1994.

Malanga, Gerard. *Scopophilia: The Love of Looking*. New York: Alfred Van Der March, 1985.

Marcus, Steven. *The Other Victorians: A Study of Sexuality and Pornography in Mid-Nineteenth Century England*. New York: Basic Books, 1965; 2d ed. New York: NAL, 1974.

Marcuse, Herbert. *Eros and Civilization: A Philosophical Inquiry into Freud*. Boston: Beacon, 1955.

———. *Negations: Essays in Critical Theory*, trans. Jeremy J. Shapiro. Boston: Beacon Press, 1969.

Marsh, Joss. *Word Crimes: Blasphemy, Culture, and Literature in Nineteenth Century England*. Chicago: University of Chicago Press, 1998.

Matrix, Cherie, ed. *Tales from the Clit: A Female Experience of Pornography*. San Francisco: AK Press, 1996.

Mayne, Judith. "Immigrants and Spectators." *Wide Angle*, 5:2 (1982): 32–40.

McCormick, Naomi. *Sexual Salvation: Affirming Women's Sexual Rights and Pleasures*. Westport, CT: Praeger, 1994.

McElroy, Wendy. *XXX: A Woman's Right to Pornography*. New York: St. Martin's, 1996.

McNair, Brian. *Mediated Sex: Pornography and Postmodern Culture*. New York: St. Martin's, 1996.

Mead, Margaret. "Sex and Censorship in Contemporary Society." *New World Writing: III*. New York: NAL/Mentor, 1953, pp. 7–25.

Melly, George. "Pornography and Erotica." *Art and Artists*, 5:5 (August 1970): 4–8.

"Men Confronting Pornography." Special Issue. *Changing Men: Issues in Gender, Sex and Politics*, 15 (Fall 1985).

Merchant, Carolyn. *The Death of Nature: A Feminist Reappraisal of the Scientific Revolution*. New York: Harper and Row, 1980.

Meyrowitz, Joshua. *No Sense of Place: The Impact of Electronic Media on Social Behavior*. New York: Oxford University Press, 1985.

Michelson, Peter. *Speaking the Unspeakable: A Poetics of Obscenity*. Albany: State University of New York Press, 1993; rev. of *The Aesthetics of Pornography*. New York: Herder and Herder, 1971.

Mielke, Arthur J. *Christians, Feminists, and the Culture of Pornography*. Lanham, MD: University Press of America, 1995.

Miller, Nancy K. *Getting Personal: Feminist Occasions and Other Autobiographical Acts*. New York: Routledge, 1991.

Millett, Kate. *Sexual Politics*. Garden City, NY: Doubleday, 1970.

Minnery, Tom, ed. *Pornography: A Human Tragedy*. Wheaton, IL: Christianity Today/ Tyndale House, 1986.

Modleski, Tania. *Feminism without Women: Culture and Criticism in a "Postfeminist" Age*. New York: Routledge, 1991.

Money, John. "Pornography in the Home: A Topic in Medical Education." *Contemporary Sexual Behavior: Critical Issues in the 1970s*, ed. Joseph Zubin and John Money. Baltimore: Johns Hopkins University Press, 1973, pp. 409–440.

———. *Sin, Science, and the Sex Police*. Amherst, NY: Prometheus Books, 1998.

Moral Majority Report. Lynchburg, VA: Moral Majority Foundation, 1980–.

Morgan, Robin. "Theory and Practice: Pornography and Rape." *Going Too Far: The Personal Chronicle of a Feminist*. New York: Vintage, 1978, pp. 163–169; rpt. *Take Back the Night: Women on Pornography*. New York: Morrow, 1980, 134–140.

Mulvey, Laura. "Afterthoughts on 'Visual Pleasure and Narrative Cinema' Inspired by *Duel in the Sun*." *Framework*, 15/16/17 (Summer 1981): 12–15.

———. "Visual Pleasure and Narrative Cinema." *Screen*, 16:3 (1975): 6–18. Rpt. in *Visual and Other Pleasures*. Bloomington: Indiana University Press, 1989.

Mura, David. *A Male Grief: Notes on Pornography and Addiction*. Minneapolis: Milkweed, 1987.

Murray, H. Kincaid. *Coercion and Perversion: Or Primeval Degenerates*. New York: Lutetion Society, 1934.

Nagle, Jill, ed. *Whores and Other Feminists*. New York: Routledge, 1997.

Nead, Lynda. " 'Above the Pulp-Line': The Cultural Significance of Erotic Art." *Dirty Looks: Women, Pornography, Power*, ed. Pamela Church Gibson and Roma Gibson. London: British Film Institute, 1993, pp. 144–155.

Nestle, Joan. *A Restricted Country*. Ithaca, NY: Firebrand Books, 1987.

Newton, Esther, and Shirley Walton. "The Misunderstanding: Toward a More Precise Sexual Vocabulary." *Pleasure and Danger: Exploring Female Sexuality*, ed. Carole S. Vance. Boston: Routledge and Kegan Paul, 1984, pp. 242–250.

Nobile, Philip, ed. *The New Eroticism*. New York: Random House, 1970.

"On Pornography." Special issue. *The Public Interest*, 22 (Winter 1971).

O'Toole, Laurence. *Pornocopia*. New York: Serpent's Tail, 1998.

Owens, Tuppy. *Politico Frou-Frou: Pornographic Art as Political Protest*. New York: Cassell, 1996.

Paglia, Camille. *Sex, Art, and American Culture: Essays*. New York: Vintage, 1992.

———. *Sexual Personae: Art and Decadence from Nefertiti to Emily Dickinson*. New York: Vintage, 1991.

———. "Twenty Questions: Camille Paglia." *Playboy*, 36:10 (October 1991): 132–133, 170–172.

———. *Vamps and Tramps: New Essays*. New York: Vintage, 1994.

Pajaczkowska, Claire. "The Heterosexual Presumption." *The Sexual Subject: A Screen Reader in Sexuality*, by the editors of *Screen*. New York: Routledge, 1992, pp. 184–196.

Palac, Lisa. *The Edge of the Bed: How Dirty Pictures Changed My Life*. Boston: Little, Brown, 1998.

Pally, Marcia. "Sometimes Being an Object Is OK." *Playboy*, 35:1 (January 1988): 51.

Peckham, Morse. *Art and Pornography: An Experiment in Explanation*. New York: Basic Books, 1969.

Peek, Charles W., and Sharon Brown. "Pornography as a Political Symbol: Attitudes toward Commercial Nudity and Attitudes toward Political Organizations." *Social Science Quarterly*, 58 (March 1978): 717–723.

Peek, Charles W., D. D. Witt, and D. A. Gay. "Pornography: Important Political Symbol or Limited Political Issue?" *Sociological Focus*, 15:1 (January 1982): 41–52.

Pendleton, David. "Obscene Allegories: Narrative, Representation, Pornography." *Discourse* (Fall 1992): 154–168.

Petersen, James R. "Catharine MacKinnon Again." *Playboy*, 39:8 (August 1992): 37–39.

Phillips, Eileen, ed. *The Left and the Erotic*. London: Lawrence and Wishart, 1983.

Pitchford, Nicola. "Reading Feminism's Pornography Conflict: Implications for Postmodernist Reading Strategies." *Sex Positives? The Cultural Politics of Dissident Sexualities*, ed. Thomas Foster, Carol Siegel, and Ellen E. Berry. New York: New York University Press, 1997, pp. 3–32.

Pollock, Griselda. "What's Wrong with 'Images of Women'?" *The Sexual Subject: A Screen Reader in Sexuality*, by the editors of *Screen*. New York: Routledge, 1992, pp. 135–145.

Polsky, Ned. "On the Sociology of Pornography." *Hustlers, Beats, and Others*. Garden City, NY: Doubleday Anchor, 1969, pp. 183–200; rpt. Chicago: University of Chicago Press, 1985.

"The Porn Debates." *Vogue*, 175 (September 1985): 678–681, 749–752.

"Pornography." Special issue of *Wide Angle*, 19:3 (July 1997).

"Pornography: A Roundtable Discussion." *Harper's*, 269 (November 1984): 31–39, 42–45.

Pornography: Not Just Dirty Pictures. Weymouth, MA: Life Skills Education, 1989.

Posner, Richard A. *Sex and Reason*. Cambridge: Harvard University Press, 1992.

Pribram, Deidre E., ed. *The Female Spectator: Looking at Film and Television*. London: Verso, 1988.

Queen, Carol. *Real Live Nude Girl: Chronicles of a Sex Positive Culture.* Pittsburgh: Cleis, 1997.

Randall, Richard S. *Freedom and Taboo: The Politics of a Self Divided.* Berkeley: University of California Press, 1989.

Read, Daphne. "(De)Constructing Pornography: Feminisms in Conflict." *Passion and Power: Sexuality in History,* ed. Kathy Peiss and Christina Simmons, with Robert A. Padgug. Philadelphia: Temple University Press, 1989, pp. 277–292.

Rich, B. Ruby. "Top Girl." *Village Voice,* 8 October 1991, pp. 29–33.

Rist, Ray C., ed. *The Pornography Controversy: Changing Moral Standards in American Life.* New Brunswick, NJ: Transaction, 1975.

Robinson, James. *Pornography, the Polluting of America.* Wheaton, IL: Tyndale House, 1982.

Rodden, John. "The Performing Artist-Intellectual: The Personae and Personality of Camille Paglia." *Text and Performance Quarterly,* 16 (1996): 62–82.

Rodgerson, Gilliam, and Elizabeth Wilson, eds. *Pornography and Feminism: The Case against Censorship, by Feminists against Censorship.* London: Lawrence and Wishart, 1991.

Roiphe, Katie. *The Morning After: Sex, Fear, and Feminism on Campus.* New York: Little, Brown, 1993.

Rose, Jacqueline. *Sexuality in the Field of Vision.* London: Verso, 1986.

Rosenfield, Lawrence W. "Politics and Pornography." *Quarterly Journal of Speech,* 59: 4 (December 1973): 413–422.

Ross, Andrew. "The Popularity of Pornography." *No Respect: Intellectuals and Popular Culture.* New York: Routledge, 1989, pp. 171–208.

Rubin, Gayle. "Misguided, Dangerous and Wrong: An Analysis of Anti-Pornography Politics." *Bad Girls and Dirty Pictures: The Challenge to Reclaim Feminism,* ed. Alison Assiter and Avedon Carol. Boulder, CO: Pluto Press, 1993, pp. 18–40.

Rushdoony, Rousas J. *The Politics of Pornography.* New Rochelle, NY: Arlington House, 1974.

Russ, Joanna. *Magic Mommas, Trembling Sisters, Puritans and Perverts: Feminist Essays.* Trumansburg, NY: Crossing Press, 1985.

———. "Pornography and the Doubleness of Sex for Women," *Jump Cut,* 32 (April 1986): 38–41.

Russell, Diana E. H. *Dangerous Relationships: Pornography, Misogyny, and Rape.* Thousand Oaks, CA: Sage, 1998; revision of *Against Pornography: The Evidence of Harm.* Berkeley, CA: Russell Publications, 1994.

Schlafly, Phyllis, ed. *Pornography's Victims.* Westchester, IL: Crossway Books, 1987.

Schur, Edwin M. *Crimes without Victims: Deviant Behavior and Public Policy.* Englewood Cliffs, NJ: Prentice-Hall, 1965.

———. "Pornography." *Labeling Women Deviant.* New York: Random House, 1984, pp. 172–183.

Scott, David Alexander. *Pornography: Its Effects on the Family, Community, and Culture.* Washington, DC: Child and Family Protection Institute, 1985.

Screen. The Sexual Subject: A Screen Reader in Sexuality. London: Routledge, 1992.

Segal, Lynne, and Mary McIntosh, eds. *Sex Exposed: Sexuality and the Pornography Debate.* New Brunswick, NJ: Rutgers University Press, 1993.

Seidman, Steven. *Embattled Eros: Sexual Politics and Ethics in Contemporary America.* New York: Routledge, 1992.

"The Sex Issue: no. 12." *Heresies*, 3:4 (1981).

"Sexuality, Violence and Pornography." Special issue. *Humanities in Society*, 7:1/2 (Winter–Spring 1984).

Shattuck, Roger. *Forbidden Knowledge: From Prometheus to Pornography*. New York: St. Martin's, 1996.

Silverman, Kaja. *Male Subjectivity at the Margins*. New York: Routledge, 1992.

Silverstein, Charles. *Man to Man: Gay Couples in America*. New York: William Morris, 1981.

Simons, G. L. *Pornography without Prejudice: A Reply to Objectors*. London: Abelard-Schuman, 1972.

Slade, Joseph W. "Pornography." *Handbook of American Popular Culture*, ed. M. Thomas Inge. 2d. ed. 3 vols. Westport, CT: Greenwood Press, 1989. II, 957–1010.

———. *Shades of Blue: A History of the Clandestine Film*. Forthcoming.

Slater, Philip. *The Pursuit of Loneliness*. Boston: Beacon, 1985.

Smith, Don D. "The Social Content of Pornography." *Journal of Communication*, 26:1 (Winter 1976): 16–23.

Snitow, Ann, Christine Stansell, and Sharon Thompson, eds. *Powers of Desire: The Politics of Sexuality*. New York: Monthly Review Press, 1983.

Soble, Alan. *Pornography: Marxism, Feminism, and the Future of Sexuality*. New Haven, CT: Yale University Press, 1986.

———. *Sexual Investigations*. New York: New York University Press, 1995.

Sontag, Susan. "Notes on Art, Sex and Politics." *New York Times*, 8 February 1976, sec. 2, pp. 1, 36; rpt. from *Salmagundi* (Fall 1975–Winter 1976).

———. "The Pornographic Imagination." *Partisan Review*, 34:2 (Spring 1967): 181–212; rpt. *Styles of Radical Will*. New York: Delta Books, 1969, pp. 35–73.

Stallybrass, Peter, and Alison White. *The Politics and Poetics of Transgression*. Ithaca, NY: Cornell University Press, 1986.

Stam, Robert. "Bakhtin, Eroticism and the Cinema: Strategies for the Critique and Trans-Valuation of Pornography." *Cineaction!* (Fall 1987): 13–20; rpt. "The Grotesque Body and Cinematic Eroticism." *Subversive Pleasures: Bakhtin, Cultural Criticism, and Film*. Baltimore: Johns Hopkins University Press, 1989.

Stan, Adele M., ed. *Debating Sexual Correctness: Pornography, Sexual Harassment, Date Rape and the Politics of Sexual Equality*. New York: Delta, 1995.

Stanmeyer, William. *The Seduction of Society: Pornography and Its Impact on American Life*. Ann Arbor, MI: Serant Books, 1984.

Steinem, Gloria. "Erotica vs. Pornography: A Clear and Present Difference." *Outrageous Acts and Everyday Rebellions*. New York: Holt, Rinehart, and Winston, 1983, pp. 219–232.

Steiner, George. "Night Words: Human Privacy and High Pornography." *Language and Silence: Essays on Language, Literature, and the Inhuman*. New York: Atheneum, 1967, pp. 71–86; rpt. *The Pornography Controversy*, ed. Ray C. Rist. New Brunswick, NJ: Transaction, 1975, pp. 203–213; *The New Eroticism*, ed. Philip Nobile. New York: Random House, 1970, pp. 120–132.

Steiner, Wendy. *The Scandal of Pleasure: Art in an Age of Fundamentalism*. Chicago: University of Chicago Press, 1995.

Stern, Lesley. "The Body as Evidence: A Critical Review of the Pornography Problematic." *Screen*, 23:5 (November–December 1982): 39–60; rpt. *The Sexual Subject: A Screen Reader in Sexuality*. New York: Routledge, 1992, pp. 197–220.

Stewart, Douglas J. "Pornography, Obscenity, and Capitalism." *Antioch Review*, 35 (Fall 1977): 389–398.

Stoller, Robert J. *Observing the Erotic Imagination*. New Haven, CT: Yale University Press, 1985.

Stoltenberg, John. *The End of Manhood: A Book for Men of Conscience*. New York: NAL/Dutton, 1993.

———. "Pornography." Cassette 4 of *Sex and Selfhood: New Issues for Men of Conscience*. 4 cassettes. Minneapolis: Kundshier/Manthey Video, 1992.

———. *Refusing to Be a Man: Essays on Sex and Justice*. New York: Penguin, 1989.

———. *What Makes Pornography "Sexy"?* Minneapolis: Milkweed, 1994.

———. "You Can't Fight Homophobia and Protect the Pornographers at the Same Time—An Analysis of What Went Wrong in *Hardwick*." *The Sexual Liberals and the Attack on Feminism*, ed. Dorchen Leidholdt and Janice G. Raymond. New York: Pergamon Press, 1990, pp. 184–190.

" 'Story of O' Author Unmasked, Magazine Claims." *Chicago Tribune*, 24 July 1994, p. 2.

Strebeigh, Fred. "Defining Law on the Feminist Frontier." *New York Times Magazine*, 6 October 1991, pp. 28–31, 52–54, 56.

Strossen, Nadine. *Defending Pornography: Free Speech, Sex and the Fight for Women's Rights*. New York: Scribner's, 1995.

Studlar, Gaylyn. *In the Realm of Pleasure: Von Sternberg, Dietrich, and the Masochistic Aesthetic*. Urbana: University of Illinois Press, 1988.

Summerhill, Richard. "Porn Crime." *The Body Politic*, no. 109 (December 1984): 7–10.

Swaggart, Jimmy. *Rape of a Nation*. Baton Rouge: Jimmy Swaggart Ministries, 1985.

Taylor and Jerome. "Pornography as Innovator." *PC Computing*, 10:2 (February 1997): 65.

Thompson, William Irwin. *The Time Falling Bodies Take to Light: Mythology, Sexuality and the Origins of Culture*. New York: St. Martin's, 1981.

Thorne-Finch, Ron. *Ending the Silence: The Origins and Treatment of Male Violence against Women*. Toronto: University of Toronto Press, 1992.

Tierney, John. "Porn, the Low-Slung Engine of Progress." *New York Times*, 9 January 1994, sec. 2, pp. 1, 18.

Tisdale, Sallie. *Talk Dirty to Me: An Intimate Philosophy of Sex*. New York: Doubleday, 1994.

———. "Talk Dirty to Me: A Woman's Taste for Pornography." *Harper's* (February 1992): 37–46.

Tucker, Scott. "Gender, Fucking and Utopia: An Essay in Response to John Stoltenberg's *Refusing to Be a Man*." *Social Text*, 27 (1990): 3–34.

Twitchell, James B. *Carnival Culture: The Trashing of Taste in America*. New York: Columbia University Press, 1993.

Tynan, Kenneth. "In Praise of Hard-Core." *The Sound of Two Hands Clapping*. New York: Holt, Rinehart, and Winston, 1975, pp. 181–191; rpt. *Dirty Movies: An Illustrated History of the Stag Film, 1915–1970* by Al DiLauro and Gerald Rabkin. New York: Chelsea House, 1976, pp. 11–23.

Udovich, Mimi. "Done to Death." *Village Voice*, 1 March 1994, p. 18.

———. "Imagine That." *Village Voice*, 25 January 1994, p. 19.

Valverde, Mariana. *Sex, Power and Pleasure*. Toronto: Women's Press, 1987.

Vance, Carole S. "Issues and Commentary: The War on Culture." *Art in America*, 77:9 (September 1989): 39, 41, 43.

————. "Pleasure and Danger: Toward a Politics of Sexuality." *Pleasure and Danger: Exploring Female Sexuality*. Boston: Routledge and Kegan Paul, 1984, pp. 1–27.

————. ed. *Pleasure and Danger: Exploring Female Sexuality*. Boston: Routledge and Kegan Paul, 1984.

Vassi, Marco. *Metasex, Mirth & Madness*. New York: Trident Press, 1975.

Vaughan, Don. "Star Bright: An Interview with Susie Bright." *Gauntlet*, 14 (1997): 30–35.

Viguerie, Richard. *The New Right: We're Ready to Lead*. Falls Church, VA: Viguerie, 1980.

Wallace, Douglas, and Gerald Wehmer. "Evaluation of Visual Erotica by Sexual Liberals and Conservatives." *Journal of Sex Research*, 8 (May 1972): 147–153.

Warner, William Beatty. "Treating Me like an Object: Reading Catharine MacKinnon's Feminism." *Feminism and Institutions: Dialogues on Feminist Theory*, ed. Linda V. Kauffman. Cambridge, England: Basil Blackwell, 1989, pp. 90–125.

Watney, Simon. *Policing Desire: Pornography, AIDS, and the Media*. Minneapolis: University of Minnesota Press, 1987; London: Methuen, 1987.

Weaver, Mary Jo. "Pornography and the Religious Imagination." *For Adult Users Only*, ed. Susan Gubar and Joan Hoff. Bloomington: Indiana University Press, 1989, pp. 68–86.

Webb, Peter. *The Erotic Arts*. Enlarged ed. New York: Farrar, Straus, and Giroux, 1983.

Weber, Max. *The Protestant Ethic and the Spirit of Capitalism*, trans. Talcott Parsons. New York: Scribner's, 1958.

Webster, Paula. "The Forbidden: Eroticism and Taboo." *Pleasure and Danger: Exploring Female Sexuality*, ed. Carole S. Vance. Boston: Routledge and Kegan Paul, 1984, pp. 385–398; rpt. as "Eroticism and Taboo," *The Erotic Impulse: Honoring the Sensual Self*, ed. David Steinberg. Los Angeles: Tarcher/Perigee, 1992, pp. 129–141.

————. "Pornography and Pleasure." *Heresies*, 12 (1981): 48–50.

Weedon, Chris. *Feminist Practice and Poststructuralist Theory*. New York: Basil Blackwell, 1987.

Wekesser, Carol, ed. *Pornography: Opposing Viewpoints*. San Diego: Greenhaven Press, 1997.

Whippen, Deb, and Joe Interrante. "Men and Pornography: An Interview with Michael Bronski." *Radical America*, 18:4 (1984): 30–34.

White, Van F. "Pornography and Pride." *Changing Men*, 15 (Fall 1985): 17–18.

Wicke, Jennifer. "Through a Gaze Darkly: Pornography's Academic Marketplace." *Dirty Looks: Women, Pornography, Power*, ed. Pamela Church Gibson and Roma Gibson. London: British Film Institute, 1993, pp. 62–80.

Wild, Peter. "Pornography and Nature." *Open Spaces, City Places: Contemporary Writers on the Changing Southwest*. Tucson: University of Arizona Press, 1994, pp. 51–60.

Wildmon, Don. *The Case against Pornography*. Wheaton, IL: Victor Books, 1986.

Willemen, Paul. "Letter to John." *The Sexual Subject: A Screen Reader in Sexuality*, by the editors of *Screen*. New York: Routledge, 1992, pp. 171–183.

Williams, Linda. *Hard Core: Power, Pleasure, and the Frenzy of the Visible*. Berkeley: University of California Press, 1989.

Williams, Tom M. *See No Evil: Christian Attitudes toward Sex in Art and Entertainment.* Grand Rapids, MI: Zondervan, 1976.

Willis, Ellen. "Feminism, Moralism, and Pornography." *Powers of Desire: The Politics of Sexuality*, ed. Ann Snitow, Christine Stansell, and Sharon Thompson. New York: Monthly Review Press, 1983, pp. 460–467.

Wilson, Paul. *Dealing with Pornography: The Case against Censorship.* Sydney, Australia: University of New South Wales Press, 1995.

Wilton, Tamsin. *Finger-Licking Good: The Ins and Outs of Lesbian Sex.* New York: Cassell, 1995.

Winkler, Karen J. "Research on Pornography Gains Respectability, Increased Importance among Scholars." *Chronicle of Higher Education*, 14 June 1989, pp. A4–5, A8.

Zita, Jacqueline N. "The Future of Feminist Sex Inquiry." *The Knowledge Explosion: Generations of Feminist Scholarship*, ed. Cheris Kramarae and Dale Spender. New York: Teachers College Press, 1992, pp. 480–494.

Zwang, Gérard. *La Fonction Erotique.* 2 vols., with a supplement (1978). Paris: Éditions Robert Laffont, 1972.

7

Major Research Collections (and the Problems of the Librarian)

LIBRARIES AND PORNOGRAPHY

Pornography causes special problems for librarians, who face criticism from conservatives and fundamentalists if they preserve erotic material on their shelves and criticism from liberals and scholars if they do not. Libraries have been targets of zealots for most of their history, as anyone familiar with the story of the great ancient library at Alexandria, whose manuscripts were victims of both war and religious fanaticism, will surely know. Librarians in the United States spend a good deal of time each year fighting off would-be censors incensed by the presence of works like Salinger's *Catcher in the Rye* or Twain's *Huckleberry Finn*, not to mention marginal and sexually explicit works that offend one group or another. Typical of annual surveys is "Censorship Rose 35 Percent over Previous Year, Study Finds," in which Madalynne Reuter and Marianne Yen report that one-third of all censorship attempts each year involve library and/or educational materials. The best single guide is Herbert N. Foerstel's *Banned in the U.S.A.: A Reference Guide to Book Censorship in Schools and Public Libraries*, which begins with the 1970s, recounts the more acrimonious battles, and lists the books most often censored now.

Because of the constant threat of harassment by social and political groups, public libraries generally establish policies of caution. Academic libraries at state universities are generally more reticent than those operated by private universities and colleges. The principal question is, Should materials that some—or, for that matter, all—citizens consider objectionable be kept at all? People who work with books usually argue in the affirmative on the grounds that tastes change, that marginal expression deserves preservation, that pornography when it is fresh represents a challenge to the status quo and is thus doubly in need of protection, and that we must understand how every kind of discourse helps to shape culture. Librarians elaborate on these approaches in *Book Selection and Censorship in the Sixties*, edited by Eric Moon, then editor of *Library Journal*. A. J. Anderson offers tactics for dealing with would-be censors and keeping a staff enthusiastic in *Problems in Intellectual Freedom and Censorship*. Librarians have a responsibility to guarantee access to legitimate works, particularly when they offend some people, says Eli M. Oboler in *The Fear of the Word: Censorship and Sex*. Although censorship of sexual expression has no rational basis, library staff must be cautious, patient, and articulate in explaining the First Amendment to the angry. Oboler's rapid historical survey of censorship is also first-rate.

Four collections of materials offer different perspectives on constant attempts to censor library materials, though most are concerned with books rather than other media. These are *The Censorship of Books*, edited by Walter Daniels; *The First Freedom: Liberty and Justice in the World of Books*, edited by Robert B. Downs; *Civil Liberties under Attack*, edited by Clair Wilcox; and *Books on Trial: A Survey of Recent Cases*, by the National Coalition against Censorship. All contain information on library and textbook censorship in the United States over long periods and are important for historians in particular. *The Freedom to Read*, edited by Richard McKeon and others for the American Book Publishers Council, represents the response of librarians and publishers to censors during the height of suppression campaigns in the late 1950s. Since then publishers and librarians have often joined forces to combat perennial threats.

Even more substantial but similar and overlapping is L. B. Woods' *A Decade of Censorship in America: The Threat to Classrooms and Libraries*. Woods divides attacks on libraries and school boards by types of controversy. During the ten years he examines, sex and sex education triggered 26 percent of the attacks, with questionable language accounting for another 7 percent; racial bigotry inspired 7 percent, religious fanaticism 9 percent. Woods classifies censorship skirmishes by state as well; between 1966 and 1975, for example, zealots in California led the nation in number of attempts (123) to censor textbooks and library materials. Woods reviews landmark court cases and analyzes the logistics of censorship campaigns. Excellent tables list titles and subject matter that various groups found objectionable; the bibliography is also fine. Claudia Johnson wrote *Stifled Laughter: One Woman's Story about Fighting Censorship*, about her efforts to counter stupidity and library censorship in Florida, because she thinks that we have to "laugh, howl, guffaw at the madness around us: *Red Riding Hood* promotes alcoholism. *Snow White* promotes violence. *Of Mice and Men* teaches students to talk like migrant workers. *In the Night Kitchen* promotes nudity" (ix).

The need to understand the motives of censors (on the Right and Left) animates the essays in Jay E. Daily's *The Anatomy of Censorship*, which ranges over different cases and different media in its philosophical and psychological analysis of the impulse to censor. Daily reviews the vagaries of federal, state, and local censorship, discusses the anxieties that impel citizens toward censorship, investigates the marketplace in erotica of various sorts, and comments on the role of librarians in safeguarding a common heritage of ideas for other Americans. Daily is particularly astute on the political dimensions of censorship and thinks that attempts to suppress and the necessity to resist them are inevitable poles of a democratic dynamic. He is also pessimistic, believing that calls for censorship will never abate. As a professor of library science, Daily focuses frequently on attacks on libraries and counsels librarians always to be vigilant and prepared.

Though it does not endorse pornography as a concept, the American Library Association lobbies ceaselessly on behalf of First Amendment issues. As reported in "ALA's Intellectual Freedom Committee Responds to Pornography Commission Report," the association condemned the Meese Commission's report as inconsistent with the free expression of ideas, deplored the lack of reasoned debate, and disputed the unscholarly methodology by which the commission gathered information during the proceedings. More recently, the ALA joined other advocates of intellectual freedom in opposing a law requiring that publishers and producers keep records of the ages of any models or actors used to depict sexual activity in books, films, or videos, for reasons noted in Neil A. Lewis' "Publishers, Artists and Librarians Challenge New Pornography Law." More recently, librarians have had to contend with whether or not to provide Internet access to patrons. As Amy Harmon points out in "Reviews Follow Ban on Library Internet Filter," librarians all over the country must review their policies after a federal judge ruled that libraries may not block materials available over the Internet to adult patrons (the judge left open the possibility of setting aside some blocked computers for children).

BUILDING AND SECURING SENSITIVE COLLECTIONS

Evelyn Geller's well-conceived history of collections, *Forbidden Books in American Public Libraries, 1876–1939: A Study in Cultural Change*, argues that patterns of censorship mirror cycles of tolerance and repression, themselves dependent on regional and national agendas, and that library collections thus reflect stages of public consciousness. Geller also chronicles the shift in roles for the librarian, who was transformed during this period from a moral arbiter to a champion of free expression. The argument of Kathleen Molz's "The Public Custody of High Pornography," written in the 1960s, seems quaint now in its hope that librarians can choose carefully enough to avoid legal challenges. Molz came to grips with the need to preserve works like Miller's *Tropic of Cancer* and others that scholars knew were important even if the general public did not. Her contention is that merit should determine accession, despite opposition on the part of the less informed. In a larger sense, however, her article is crucial to understanding a fundamental distinction where pornography is concerned: the issue, she said, is taste shaped by class. Well-educated Americans have always risen to the defense of "high" pornography, that is, highly literate works, chiefly in print media, whose virtues are obvious to the intelligent reader. These are inevitably works *by* someone—a D. H. Lawrence or a Boccaccio—as opposed to the dirty joke, the scabrous pamphlet, the sleazy comic book, the inept stag film, or the open-crotch photograph—which are usually anonymous or pseudonymous. The deeper vulgarity of the latter category, whose power derives from a need to offend, is perhaps the more "authentic" pornography. The most extreme form of popular culture and easily the most demotic, its artifacts are rarely to be found in libraries.

To some Americans, trash is trash, beneath a library's notice. Answers to such complaints are advanced by Rebecca Kelm, in "The Lack of Access to Back Issues of the Weekly Tabloids: Does It Matter?" and Robert Sewell, in "Trash or Treasure? Pop Fiction in Academic and Research Libraries." More sustained considerations motivate Allen Ellis' *Popular Culture and Acquisitions*, written for librarians who are trying to build catalogs of tabloid journals, comic books, popular romances, and so on. The *Directory of Popular Culture Collections*, compiled by Christopher D. Geist, Ray B. Browne, Michael T. Marsden, and Carol Palmer, is a guide to libraries that have been successful in establishing such archives, many of which contain materials that some Americans would regard as pornographic. In addition to covering major research tools, Larry N. Landrum also offers details about some collections in *American Popular Culture: A Guide to Information Sources*. A recently founded journal, *Popular Culture in Libraries*, is devoted to articles on building and publicizing popular culture collections in libraries.

While categories are always in flux, many librarians still see clear divisions between artifacts of popular culture and out-and-out pornography. Michael Pope surveys the attitudes of librarians themselves toward the acquisition and retention of sexually oriented materials in *Sex and the Undecided Librarian* and finds that comparatively few are in favor of collecting explicitly sexual materials. John Berry's "Drawing the Line," taking its cue from recent feminist theory, holds that librarians should be comfortable discriminating between examples of free expression and those that belong to the category of violent pornography. Ruthann Robson's "Pornography, Power, and the First Amendment" goes further, rejecting as reflex the average librarian's recourse to the First Amendment; some materials should be banned, she thinks, and she urges librarians to do so. Usually, libraries receive erotic materials as gifts rather than purchase.

A donor may will an extraordinary book archive to a library with the proviso that the institution take his fine erotica editions also. At one time or another, nearly every large American library has been given works of questionable taste or purview. The question then becomes how to house such materials securely. Some state libraries, university-affiliated or otherwise, operate under a mandated open-shelf policy. In such environments, theft and damage of books and periodicals dealing even in a nonexplicit way with sexual matters are commonplace. Few circumstances are more frustrating to the scholar than discovering that a book the catalog says should be on the shelf has disappeared without a trace, the victim of either the salacious or the censorious reader. As a consequence, many libraries either close their shelves or place books likely to be stolen or mutilated in restricted collections. Still others will keep erotic materials but will not list them in the public catalog, making them available only at specific request by scholars with credentials.

Particularly valuable are Jay E. Daily's "Erotica" and Rebecca Dixon's "Bibliographical Control of Erotica," both of which talk about cataloging, storage, and circulation control. Pamela Walker also discusses the special nature of erotica collections and the pitfalls faced by their curators in "Bibliographic Control of Sex Research Materials." Martha Cornog's *Libraries, Erotica, Pornography* draws on various librarian specialists, and John O. Christensen's *Obscenity, Pornography, and Libraries: A Selective Bibliography* surveys books and articles on library censorship, on postures that librarians adopt regarding sexual materials, on collections of erotica/pornography, on methods of building and maintaining them, and on their rationale in a library's organizational scheme. David Steinberg suggests examples of various forms of erotica that librarians may find intelligent, aesthetic, or provocative in "An Annotated Bibliography of Quality Erotica."

One recommendation common to most of these authorities is to microfilm periodicals and pamphlets, since the cost of doing so is less than that of microfilming volumes, and the reels are far less likely to be mutilated or stolen. The New York Public Library routinely microfilms materials it considers in danger and scatters them through microfilm reels with other nonsexual items rather than setting them aside. Those seeking a "Collection of Pornographic Pamphlets in English, 1900–1939" will find them with microfilmed materials of an entirely different sort under the heading (S) *Z-1926. Access to unmicrofilmed materials in the New York Public Library that are unique or fragile or vulnerable to theft may require that a librarian validate a patron's ID and that the work be read behind the call desk in the main reading room, a reasonable precaution.

In any case, magazines and pamphlets that are vulnerable to vandalism often call for special handling. For example, *Playboy* is generally as topical and accurate as a mainstream periodical like *Time* (more accurate, perhaps, since such journals have more to lose) and thus can provide valuable information on a variety of topics, many of them entirely nonsexual. Martha Cornog's "What Happens When Libraries Subscribe to *Playboy*?" discusses the varied experiences of libraries in the United States, some of which lose copies through theft or have pictures cut out and respond by canceling the subscription or instituting security measures. Some, generally those institutions with well-educated clienteles, encounter few problems; Cornog attributes differences to library locations and the demographics of patrons. An even more interesting article is Cornog's "A Case Study of Censorship? The Library of Congress and the Brailing of *Playboy*," which suggests that the Library of Congress may actually have engineered the political furor that followed the decision to add *Playboy* to the list of brailed periodicals that LC makes available to blind patrons throughout the United States. Congress responded predictably, since the political benefits of seeming to oppose *Playboy* were irresistible, but Cornog traces events carefully in order to illustrate the kinds of issues that beset librarians who wish to preserve the free exchange of ideas.

Bill Katz, the leading American library specialist on small magazines and alternative publications, recommends in "The Pornography Collection" that large or specialized libraries acquire at least modest holdings of culturally significant pornography and be open to scholarship in erotic genres. Katz and Linda Sternberg Katz give adult magazines brief treatment in *Magazines for Libraries: For the General Reader and School, Junior College, College, University, and Public Libraries,* pointing out that an accurate assessment of a library's patrons is the first step to deciding whether to include any kind of materials. The most candid guide is *Sex Magazines in the Library Collection: A Scholarly Study of Sex in Serials and Periodicals,* edited by Peter Gellatly, whose contributors try to distinguish between periodicals that have merit for educated readers or are likely to be important in the future as opposed to examples that are simply too tawdry or ephemeral and address problems of acquisition, retention, display, and defense of sexually explicit magazines. Gellatly quotes Ervin Gaines, former chair of the American Library Association's Intellectual Freedom Committee: "Pornography must be important or it wouldn't be so prevalent. It has some meaning in our lives that we do not understand" (7). Aware that not all librarians will share their conviction that such items are valuable, some of the contributors draw on their own experience. Typical is "Sexology: A Personal Guide to the Serial Literature" (75–86) by Barrett Elcano and Vern Bullough, who deal with scholarly literature from the *Siecus Report* to the *Journal of Sex Research.* Were librarians systematically to collect erotic materials, Sanford Berman points out in "If There Were a Sex Index . . ." (99–135), they would actually have to invent new subject headings for behaviors from analingus to whipping in order to catalog them all properly. Robert Rimmer, an authority on porn movies, has selected five dozen or so films he thinks might appropriately be placed in research libraries in "A Connoisseur's Selection of X-Rated Videotapes for the Library."

NOTABLE COLLECTORS AND PRIVATE COLLECTIONS

Collectors of erotica move in a world removed from both popular culture and academic archives, and the legends about them and their acquisitiveness are legion. One notorious, if undiscriminating, collector was King Farouk of Egypt. Frank Herrmann corrects the record in *Sotheby's: Portrait of an Auction House.* In 1954 the Egyptian government commissioned Sotheby's to sell the seized possessions of the deposed monarch. Included were twenty rooms of Farouk's erotica and pornography, news of which generated enough excitement to pique the interest of the British Museum. As a bonus, the auction house offered anyone who spent large sums a private, unrestricted viewing of the porn collection. Those who looked were said to be disappointed, and, in fact, very little of the collection was sold by Sotheby's at the time. As is so often the case when pornography is involved, the bulk of Farouk's trove seemed to disappear; bits and pieces went here and there, to end up in private hands or on the open market, without their ever being cataloged (342–345). Similar fates have befallen other major collections. The 900 books, several dozen objects, and about 200 pieces of art collected by Russian prince Dmitri Gallitzin, recorded in the incomplete *Catalogue du cabinet secret du prince G*...(a second part was never published), were long ago dispersed. According to one story, a substantial number of early Austrian stag films, once part of the great Gustav Gugitz collection, were lost at sea, when the SS *Georges Philipart* went down on a voyage from France to America. The films were being carried to an American collector who had purchased them by Albert Londres, author of *The Road to Buenos Aires*, a documentary study of white slave traffic in South America, who was apparently acting as the courier.

Jean-Pierre Bourgeron, himself a noted collector of early erotic and pornographic photographs, cataloged the greatest of all modern private collections of erotica, the nineteenth- and twentieth-century objects assembled by the French actor Michel Simon, and published it as *Les Masques D'Eros: Les Objets Erotiques de Collection à Systeme* in 1985. Clifford Scheiner, the principal American dealer in classic erotica, lists catalogs for the auction of the Simon treasures, *Erotica, Bibliotheque Secrete d'un Amateur Connu* and *Erotica. Collection Secrete d'un Amateur Connu*, in his *Compendium* (25–26). The catalogs annotate 650 lots of books and art, sculpture, porcelain, bronzes, figurines, pipes, flasks, cameos, snuffboxes, carvings and dozens of other objets d'art, including paintings and drawings by artists from Bellmer to Toulouse-Lautec. It is unlikely, says Scheiner, that any future collection will rival the Simon. An illustrated article on the Simon collection appears as "The Secret of an Actor." Readers conversant with the subject will recognize some of the illustrations; Simon's archives have furnished pictures for any number of histories of erotica. Some of these are listed in *Erotisme: Dispersion d'une Collection Partielle's Provenant de Michel Simon: Varia, Estampes, Livres, Dessins, Cartes Postales, Photographies*. Simon's European stag film collection, reputedly numbering at least 200, has disappeared without trace. Not quite as famous is the collection of Roger Peyrefitte, author of *Manouche*, the biography of the celebrated courtesan. Scheiner lists the second of two volumes of the catalog of Peyrefitte collection in the *Compendium* (26), which is called *Ex Libris Roger Peyrefitte's II*, a list of 264 lots of rare books. Peyrefitte himself wrote of his collection in *Un Musée de l'Amour. Sittengeschichte des Geheimen und Verboten*, edited by Leo Schidrowitz, mentions various secret art collections in Europe, as do volumes III and IV of *Mimus Eroticus*, by Arthur Maria Rabenalt, though it seems clear that most have been dispersed.

Trade in older pornography and commentaries on erotica continues to be fairly common among collectors and investors, with rare works fetching high prices. Probably the major house to auction erotica is D. M. Klinger of Nuremberg, Germany; it handles vintage collections from numerous countries, including the United States, and Klinger catalogs are prized by those in the know (see chapter 4, **Bibliographies and Reference Tools**). The largest single collection of erotic artifacts in the United States is that of Charles Martignette, the Boston art dealer, who values the 3,500 items at over $25 million. Over the years, *Playboy* has run articles on Martignette's treasures, all under the title "Provocative Period Pieces." Each contains photographs and brief discussion of pipes, fans, ashtrays, carnival prizes, plaques, boxes, coins, statuary, ceramics, figurines, timepieces, paperweights, woodcarvings, mechanical toys, and "novelties," as well as original art, cartoons, and photos. For several years, Drs. Phyllis and Eberhard Kronhausen operated the International Museum of Erotic Arts in San Francisco, which housed vintage and modern erotica, some of it rare Americana. That collection was sold in 1978 and 1979 by the Phillips auction house in New York; a sale catalog lists the treasures (chapter 11, **Erotic and Pornographic Art**), many of which were purchased by Martignette. Other items have found their way into modest, semicommercial museums around the world: Musée de l'Erotisme (72 Boulevard de Clichy, Paris); Museu de l'Eròtica (96 Ramblas, Barcelona); Erotik Museum (Kantstrasse, Berlin); Sex Museum (18 Damrak, Amsterdam); Museum Erotica (24 Kobmagergade, Copenhagen), and even smaller archives in Vienna, Marseilles, and Budapest. Most of the latter have few American artifacts or paintings.

Although one would hardly call trade in museum-grade artifacts brisk, investors do purchase erotic artifacts as investments, and auction houses periodically deal in them, in part because they are beautiful, in part because they are rare. In many cases, suppression has made for scarcity. Leafing through the pages of Fernand Drujon's *Catalogue des ouvrages, écrits et dessins de toute nature porsuivis, supprimés ou condamnés depuis le 21 octobre 1814 jusqu'au 31 juillet 1877*, a record of "obscene" books, medallions, carvings, and artifacts of all sorts that ran afoul of French courts from 1814 to 1877, is a reminder that most were confiscated or destroyed, a fact that elevates the prices of those that survived. Every now and then financial writers speculate on the appreciation of rare objects, as in "A Passion for Collecting: Erotic Art Comes Out of the Closet and into the Auction Rooms," which notes the increased willingness of respectable auctioneers to sell erotica and the prices such items fetch. Richard Goldstein notes in "The Little Shop of Hornies" that in 1996 Sotheby's sold 420 gay photos by Bruce of Los Angeles, one of the great erotic photographers, for $15,000. A videotape by Roberta Haynes and Rick Hauser, *Secret World of Erotic Art* (1975), based on Bradley Smith's *Erotic Art of the Masters* (1974) and *Twentieth Century Masters of Erotic Art* (1980), includes footage and commentary on artifacts lent by the Gichner Foundation: postcards, pipes, watches, prehistoric and American Indian crafts, necklaces, lingams, charms, statuary, porcelains, carvings, and toys. The rare erotica dealer C. J. Scheiner occasionally offers curiosa such as "Naughty Viennese Bronze," a polychrome art deco figure whose "dress lifts to expose her well-fashioned derriere and genitalia." The casting dates from 1910 and is attributed to Zach, a fin-de-siècle artist, although elements may have been added by other hands. The information can be found as item 181 of Scheiner's *Compendium, Being a List of All the Books (Erotica, Curiosa, & Sexology) Listed in Our Catalogs 1–6 (1978–1988)*. As one more example, item 682 offers *Illustrateurs Galants du XVIII Siècle* (Paris: Librairee des Arts Decoratifs, 1947), which contains fifty-six plates by "such masters as Cochin, Eisen, Boucher, Marillier, Binet, Moreau le Jeune, Monnet, Martinet, Borel, Desrais, Fragonard, Monsiau, Le Barbier, and Girard, all of whom did, anonymously, pornographic illustrations." Scheiner annually publishes the *Erotica-Curiosa-Sexology Catalog*, prized by librarians, scholars, and collectors. Like other dealers, Scheiner draws on news of collections as they are dispersed. Scheiner is unique in that he will permit scholars with credentials to examine his collections, which hold 80,000 volumes in addition to artifacts and other materials; he is an authority on clandestine sexual materials in the United States. Scheiner and other dealers sometimes announce the availability of private collections. At this writing, Robert Rimmer's enormous collection of hard-core videotapes, compiled for his multivolume, X-rated guides, is reputedly up for sale. Joe Fodor's "Collections: This Stuff Will Rot Your Brain" describes the collection of scandal, pinup, and exploitation magazines maintained by Alan Betrock in Brooklyn. The archive is available to scholars for a fee and has provided material for recent biographies of the Kennedys, Dean Martin, and singer Johnny Ray.

Gershon Legman's *The Horn Book: Studies in Erotic Folklore and Bibliography* mentions many collectors. Some of these he alludes to also in his "Introduction" to Patrick Kearney's *Private Case*. A revised version of this introduction appears under the title "The Lure of the Forbidden," an essay more accessible to Americans; both are rich in lore on classic collectors, collections, publishers, and erotica that is mostly print-oriented. Americans today, of course, collect contemporary materials. One is Ralph Whittington, a Library of Congress curator who has assembled an impressive trove of videotapes, ephemera, and artifacts that he has already willed to the Museum of Modern Art in New York. Whittington is the subject of Jeff Krulick's short film, *Ralph Whittington, King of Porn*, and of Ardie Myers' article, "Reading Room Curator Collects Off the Job." The artist Richard Merkin, a serious collector of antique porn photos, has published an article, "Vintage Vamp: A History of Pornographics," and a book, *Velvet Eden: The Richard Merkin Collection of Erotic Photography*, on his treasure trove; the reproductions are more important than the comment in each case.

Scholars of performance will wish to know of the *Rex Grey Costume Collection*, the catalog of one of the truly great collections of cabaret and showgirl costumes (G-strings, gowns, feathers, garters, pasties, trick brassieres, and tassels, many of them worn by American dancers), auctioned a few years ago in

London. David Isay and Harvey Wang visit a former stripper, now curator of the Exotic World Museum in Helendale, California, in "Dixie Evans." Evans displays costumes of famous strippers. Katherine Bishop's account of her visit to the Frederick's of Hollywood Lingerie Museum, "Only in Hollywood: Memorial to Unmentionables," discusses displays that span four decades. Bishop calls the museum "an anthropological treasure trove" of push-em-up bras, bustiers, corsets, crotchless panties, G-strings, nightgowns, breast or buttock pads in various materials, and so on. Special exhibits feature celebrity costumes: the bosom padding Tony Curtis used to contour his transvestite role in *Some Like It Hot*, Loretta Young's movie gowns, Mae West's silks and ostrich feathers, and Madonna's fishnet tights, breast cones, and sequined nipple pasties. Tourists also can see special bras worn by Zsa Zsa Gabor, Judy Garland, Ava Gardner, Cyd Charisse, Lana Turner, and Marie Wilson, as well as comic ones sported by Phyllis Diller and Milton Berle. Holland Cotter's "All over the Lot (the Back Lot, Too)" describes an exhibit of Jack Smith memorabilia, including the filmmaker's photographs, letters, scripts, costumes, stage props and so on at the P.S. 1 Contemporary Art Center.

MAJOR RESEARCH COLLECTIONS

With luck, great collections sometimes find their way into scholarly archives, but they are just as often dispersed. Until quite recently, Ohio University's Alden Library owned a significant collection of classical erotica, including standard German sexology texts and some American examples of erotica, left as a bequest by a collector. It was sold in 1992, fortunately to a reputable dealer who bought the entire archive. That is the fate of many bequests. Libraries are chary of holding such collections, despite their value, because they feel vulnerable to the ire of censors. Even so, hundreds of libraries around the United States possess historically significant works that have simply escaped attention. The librarian's chief ally against the censor has been the censor's dislike of actually *reading* a text before deciding that it is obscene.

Because time has made older pornographic books almost respectable, public libraries are less likely automatically to exclude written erotica, though very few maintain genuine collections. Myth attributes secret archives to libraries all over the world. The most enduring of these legends, promoted by Ralph Ginzburg in *An Unhurried View of Erotica*, is that the Vatican contains room after room of books condemned as obscene by the church. According to Paul Gebhard, former director of the Kinsey Institute, the rumor was inadvertently started by Alfred Kinsey himself, who had just begun his library by collecting enough books on sex to fill a single shelf. To a visitor's remark that it was the largest number of volumes of sexualia he had ever seen, Kinsey remarked by way of deprecation that the contents of the shelf must be the largest collection outside the Vatican. The joke took root and has grown into one of those "facts" that have no substance. Peter Webb, however, vouches for the existence of the Vatican bathroom decorated in erotic style by Raphael and his assistants.[1]

Leaving aside the National Museum of Italy in Naples, which holds erotic frescoes and statues unearthed from buried Roman cities (see Colonel Fanin's *The Royal Museum at Naples, Being Some Account of the Erotic Paintings, Bronzes, and Statues Contained in That Famous "Cabinet Secret,"* a text almost pornographic in itself), the Museum für Erotische Kunst in Munich (see "Szene: Kultur"), which displays a small trove of mostly contemporary erotica, the Museo Nacional at Mexico City, which shelters erotic pre-Colombian Art, and the Bodleian Library at Oxford and the Louvre in Paris, both of which house modest collections of printed porn, there are six major Western institutional collections of erotic literature and art: the Bibliotheque Nationale (Paris), the British Museum (London), the Victoria and Albert Museum (London), the Library of Congress (Washington), the Institute for the Advanced Study of Sexuality (San Francisco), and the Kinsey Institute for Research in Sex, Gender, and Reproduction (University of Indiana, Bloomington). Although all contain some American examples, the Kinsey Institute and the Library of Congress contain far more indigenous articles than the others.

The collections of the British and French institutions are not officially indexed, but various scholars have produced guides. In the case of the British Museum, the problem is twofold: librarians in the past have severely restricted access and forbidden the expeditions that would be necessary to make an exhaustive guide, and, second, the museum has lost, traded, or disposed of some of the texts deposited there over the years, making comprehensiveness difficult to assess. The core of this collection was assembled by Henry Spencer Ashbee, greatest of all collectors of erotica, who left to the museum his life's work, which has been supplemented by the collections of Edward Phelips, once housed in the Guildhall Library, transferred to the British Museum (BM) in 1950, and Charles Reginald Dawes, part of which was transferred to the BM in 1964. The Kinsey Institute received many of the BM's deaccessioned items in the mid-1970s and (according to Paul Gebhard, former director of the Kinsey) some of the Dawes Collection, but rumor has it that other volumes were sold on the open market. (See Chapter 16, **Erotic Literature**, Ashbee, Clowes.) Alfred Rose's *Register of Erotic Books* (1965), an offset reprint of the original *Registrum Librorum Eroticorum* (1936), which Rose published under the anagram Rolf S. Reade, is a highly significant bibliography (5,061 entries) of mostly British works through 1936, compiled from the Private Case of the Library of the British Museum by a London antiquarian book dealer, with interpolations from the Bodleian Library of Oxford, the Cambridge University Library, the Vatican, and a few other minor English archives. Brief notes and original press marks accompany each entry. Rose thus brings together much of the work of fellow bibliographers Ashbee and Clowes. C. J. Scheiner has noted some errors (*Compendium*, 109) but thinks Rose's work "invaluable" because of the twentieth-century items and calls it the "best quick-reference guide."

Peter Fryer's *Private Case—Public Scandal: Secrets of the British Museum Revealed*, an account whose lack of sensationalism belies the title, offers personalized bibliographic essays as well as excerpts from, and notes on, the rare books in the restricted collection. Patrick J. Kearney's *The Private Case: An Annotated Bibliography of the Private Case Erotica Collection in the British (Museum) Library* covers more than 2,000 items of erotica in the British Museum up until 1975. It is unique because Kearney's handlist employs the library's actual call marks. C. J. Scheiner calls it "the most important modern bibliography of erotica in English" (*Compendium*, 72). It is crammed with information, was the first to reveal the real name of Pauline Réage (Dominique Aury), author of *Story of O*, and boasts an extraordinary bibliographic essay by Gershon Legman. Thomas Liebenzell breaks down many of the entries—as surveyed from the original bequests to Kearney's last published list—by nationality and other identifying characteristics in the charmingly titled *Smut in the British Library: Register zu Kearneys Private Case*. According to book dealer Ivan Stormgart's *General Catalogue 11* (item 67), Kearney is preparing *The Private Case, Volume II: A Bibliography of Books That Used to Be in the Erotica Collection of the British (Museum) Library*, a list of material now missing or transferred to other libraries.

Because of the legends associated with the books in the British Museum, scholars have ignored the museum's far more significant troves of erotic art, easily the largest in the world. Peter Webb's *The Erotic Arts* (Appendix II) provides an overview of these holdings, as well as those even less known in the Victoria and Albert Museum. Implicit national and racial attitudes govern the treatment and display of artifacts: stylized sculptures produced as part of Oriental religious worship or primitive carvings made by Pacific Island cultures are somehow more acceptable than paintings or crafts created by Western artists for Europeans. In any case, not even the librarians of these two great museums seem to know the exact size of the collections of erotica, that is, artifacts other than books. Individual items are distributed through different sections supervised by different curators, and they, too, have been subject to the destruction, sale, or transfer of duplicates, theft, decay, and so on. According to some accounts, the librarian of the Bodleian maintains a shelflist of erotic books in the library, which is available only to qualified scholars.

L'Enfer de la Bibliothèque Nationale is an early, unofficial catalog of the "Hell" collection of the French National Library first published in the teens by Guillaume Apollinaire, Fernand Fleuret, and Louis Perceau. It was virtually superseded by Pascal Pia's complete shelflist of the L'Enfer collection, *Les livres de L'Enfer, Bibliographie critique des ouvrages érotiques dans leurs différents éditions du XVIe siècle à nos jours*. The two volumes annotate more than 2,000 entries, including modern works added after the Apollinaire index until 1978. (See also Chapter 16, **Erotic Literature**, Perceau.)

By law, copies of all works published in the United States under copyright are deposited with the Library of Congress. The system is not foolproof, of course: for one reason or another, including efforts by conservatives to deny copyright privileges to erotica, not all erotic publishers copyright their publications. Beginning in the 1960s, as publishers of books and magazines that would previously have been regarded as illegal began to deposit copies of those works, the Library of Congress ceased setting aside pornographic publications in the Delta (or Blue) Collection and began cataloging them as elements in the main collections. SCORPIO (the LC computer) lists them by author, title, and subject, just as it lists traditional works. This means, in fact, that the Library of Congress owns a fair number of pornographic magazines containing hard-core photographs published under copyright, but the vintage stuff is there, too. In the past, the Library of Congress has benefited from seizures by Customs; it owns the originals of Jean-Adolph Chauvet's illustrations for the twelve-volume Nichols-Smithers-Robson-Karslake 1894 edition of Casanova's memoirs. There are many other such treasures.

An internationally recognized faculty at the Institute for the Advanced Study of Sexuality in San Francisco grants degrees, including the Ph.D. The school also archives films and videotapes, photographs, and erotic magazines; the periodical collection is larger and more historically comprehensive than that of the Kinsey Institute. Information on the collections, which support theses and dissertations by students at the institute, is available from the director. Michael Kelly covers some of the institute's holdings in "Sex Is Back." The institute also operates the Multi-Media Resource Center, 1525 Franklin Street, San Francisco, CA 94109, 415/673–5100, which produces commercial media (see Chapter 13, **Motion Pictures and Videotapes**, Institute for Advanced Study of Sexuality).

The Kinsey Institute for Research in Sex, Gender, and Reproduction, holds the largest collection of sexual materials in the United States. It was begun in 1938 by Alfred Kinsey and has been developed as a major research center by successors, despite fluctuating budgets for acquisitions. The institute holds books, journals, reprints, ephemera, art, artifacts, film, photographs, data, and biographical materials, many of which are irreplaceable. Its Information Service answers reference questions from researchers by mail or telephone, although a fee is charged for extended searches. Charges for access to databases are determined by a sliding scale. A monthly bulletin ($100 per month) reviews sex research around the world. Generally excellent bibliographies on a wide range of subjects (e.g., condoms) are available for a nominal charge, as is a detailed, illustrated brochure on the institute ($3.50). Non-Indiana resident researchers desiring access to the institute's collections must have professional credentials, must demonstrate a need to examine materials, and must pay a basic user fee ($50). (The institute's address is 416 Morrison Hall, Indiana University, Bloomington 47405.)

Wardell Pomeroy's *Dr. Kinsey and the Institute for Sex Research* recounts the history of specific Kinsey collections. A measure of the institute's importance derives from its construction of sexual taxonomies. JoAnn Brooks and Helen C. Hoffer list some 2,000 subject headings, hierarchies, descriptors, cross-references, and updates for the Kinsey Institute collections in *Sexual Nomenclature: A Thesaurus*. These precisely targeted sexual terms differ somewhat from Library of Congress or database subject headings. Accurate descriptors are crucial in a cultural climate in which the word *sodomy*, for example, can mean oral sex, anal sex, homosexuality, lesbianism, bestiality, masturbation, or undefined "crimes against nature," depending on who is using the term in what state, in what courtroom, or in what context. The institute breaks out other materials in its *Catalog of Periodical Literature in the Social and Behavioral Sciences Section, Library of the Institute for Sex Research, Including Supplement to Monographs, 1973–1975*. Its *Sex Research: Early Literature from Statistics to Erotica: Guide to the Microfilm Collection* navigates some 120 microfilm reels of mostly eighteenth- and nineteenth-century materials (novels, joke collections, woodcuts, scholarly works, etc.) in the institute. Subject entries in the library catalogs are constantly being augmented and revised by helpful staff members and fellows, most of whom are professional anthropologists, sociologists, or psychologists. Some of the institute's specialized lists, such as Susan Matusak's *Bibliography of the Eighteenth-Century Holdings of the Institute for Sex Research*, adopt a chronological approach.

The Kinsey collections are strong in some areas, weak in others. By and large, except for occasional direct purchases, undeniably pornographic materials have been haphazardly donated by police who seized whatever they found during an arrest, by Customs agents halting contraband at borders, by collectors whose own tastes are reflected in their gifts, or by scholars who picked up items by happenstance. The institute has great strengths in Japanese erotic woodcuts, for example, but is weaker where Native American artifacts are concerned; the latter are more apt to be found on the private market (see later). Some of the items are unique: the institute houses a few stereographic viewers complete with erotic stereo prints but owns a much more interesting collection of more than 1,000 Stanhopes, small tubes with lightly magnified lenses for viewing erotic photographs (or paintings) mounted at one end. Most of these are of nude women, with occasional action scenes, and some of the novelties are accompanied by notes on their provenance.

The archives hold relatively few hard-core pornographic magazines but excel in the soft-core type (girlie tabloids, nudist journals). No collection can be complete: collecting every pornographic magazine or newspaper would require a great deal of space. In some areas, however, the Kinsey is preeminent. Its shelves hold what is easily the most concentrated collection of books on the subject of human sexuality. The erotic fiction subcollection is impressively represented by imprints from pre–Civil War publishers to modern American pulp houses. Especially valuable are the vertical files containing a half century's dealer catalogs and flyers; these old and new brochures indicate what sort of materials have circulated over time. Its photography archives are the world's largest, with close to 100,000 individual prints. Some sections of the institute (e.g., films) are restricted to scholars with demonstrated expertise, while others are entirely confidential and closed to outside research (e.g., personal diaries and individual sexual histories). If an accurate and comprehensive history of American pornography is ever written, the work will begin here.

The greatest single work of scholarship on the classic "stag," or hard-core pornographic film, is unquestionably the card catalog of films assembled over many years by Eugene Slabaugh for the Kinsey Institute, whose archives contain the most historically comprehensive collection of stags both domestic and foreign in the world. The Kinsey film archive is built around stags of the first four decades of the century; the core films were a gift of the film director and collector Josef von Sternberg. The porn film collection of Hugh Hefner (a 1975 listing of the Hefner Collection is in the Kinsey Archive) is larger in the number of individual reels but does not have the depth of the Kinsey's vintage artifacts; it does hold a great many shot in England during the 1950s. The Institute for the Advanced Study of Sexuality holds a very large collection of contemporary videotapes; early stags are less well represented. Donations to the Kinsey Archive continue apace, which means that the number of more recent videotapes is increasing.

Slabaugh, after Gershon Legman the greatest American bibliographer of erotica, never published what is nonetheless his monument. A dating and annotating of approximately 1,500 reels (1912–1966), the Kinsey catalog has been added to by researchers like Kenneth Anger and Joseph Slade, though these later entries pale beside Slabaugh's originals. Slabaugh analyzes hundreds of films frame by frame, supplies technological data (length, width, type of film stock), codes all depicted forms of sexual behavior, dates reels by internal and external evidence, and correlates them with photo sets and other artifacts; with arrests, seizures, and court cases; with biographical data on producers and performers and (less often) interviews with producers and distributors; and with magazines, books, standard bibliographies of erotica, newspaper clippings, dealer catalogs, and ephemera of American culture. Just as important are Slabaugh's three large notebooks of analysis. The entries use the Kinsey code for types of sexual activity to indicate the behavior (e.g., intercourse positions are rendered as strings of symbols for gender dorsals and ventrals) depicted in the reels and frequently contain information not in the card catalog as well as Slabaugh's working notes and speculations. Slabaugh and George Huntington (a legal specialist and researcher, more recently the Bloomington, Indiana, chief of police) in 1966 also recorded for the archives a lengthy audiotape ("Producers of and Nature of Stag Films") of immense interest because of their interviews with collectors and producers of classic stags conducted during the 1950s and 1960s.

LESSER-KNOWN RESEARCH COLLECTIONS

Sexuality

Most scholars know to consult standard guides to American library collections, although these are not likely to indicate that holdings have erotic content—in part, because the descriptions are usually furnished by the archivists, who may not wish to call attention to the sexual aspects of a given collection.

They frequently do specify papers associated with individuals, groups, or companies, however, and these can be of great help to researchers already knowledgeable about their subject. Recommended are *Subject Collections: A Guide to Special Book Collections and Subject Emphases as Reported by University, College, Public, and Special Libraries and Museums in the United States and Canada*, compiled by Lee Ash and William Miller, and *Directory of Special Libraries and Information Centers*, edited by Brigette T. Darnay and Holly M. Leighton. The Library of Congress publishes a current pamphlet on *Rare Books and Special Collections in the Library of Congress*, which researchers will find helpful in locating specialized materials on AIDS, sex-related matters, and so on. Gwendolyn L. Pershing's "Erotica Research Collections" surveys the leading archives (e.g., the Library of Congress) and is especially good on the holdings of the Kinsey Institute. *A Research Guide to Human Sexuality*, Kara Lichtenberg's survey of research libraries and archives, discusses many documents; among the collections Lichtenberg covers are those of the Library of Congress, the Kinsey Institute, SIECUS, and Planned Parenthood.

Alternative and Underground Sources

The title of Jefferson P. Selth's *Alternative Lifestyles: A Guide to Research Collections on International Communities, Nudism, and Sexual Freedom* describes the volume well. Patricia J. Case has edited *Field Guide to Alternative Media: A Directory to Reference and Selection Tools Useful in Accessing Small and Alternative Press Publications and Independently Produced Media*, a group of essays on publications on alternative media in libraries and a list of libraries with significant collections in this area, of which porn is a subset. Case's own "Collections of Contemporary Alternative Materials in Libraries: A Directory" is excellent. Ken Wachsberger's *Directory of Resources and Sources of the Vietnam Era Underground Press* occasionally mentions sexual matters in a long list of political materials. James P. Danky's *Undergrounds: A Union List of Alternative Periodicals in Libraries of the United States and Canada* lists titles and (most useful) alternative titles (but no dates of publication) of underground newspapers and tabloids, many of which featured porn, such as *The Berkeley Barb, The East Village Other, Pleasure, Screw, Fuck You: A Magazine of the Arts*, and *Intercourse*. Several academic libraries archive underground papers. Alan Kimball has edited *Underground Newspaper Collection in the University of Missouri Libraries*, a guide to the archives in Columbia.

AIDS and Homosexuality

As gay and homosexual groups become more visible and vocal, materials once considered pornographic solely because they were expressions of sexual minorities become more acceptable—to a point. Martha Cornog points out in *Libraries, Erotica, Pornography* that much advice about AIDS is couched in terms usually considered pornographic, just as birth control information once was, a circumstance that causes special problems for the librarian (80). More and more librarians, even those in small, local institutions, wish to serve patrons interested in those materials and are actively seeking ways to do so out of a sense of justice or compassion or merely the wish to be thorough information specialists. Edmund F. Santa Vicca's "Acquired Immune Deficiency Syndrome (AIDS): An Annotated Bibliography for Librarians" is an extraordinary list of important works that reference librarians can recommend. Librarians also pass around a marvellous samizdat list, stapled pages annotated by many hands, called *A Bibliography of AIDS-Related Books*, compiled by Sasha Alyson and available from the publisher herself.

Jane Allen, Linda Kerr, Avril Rolph, and Marion Chadwick provide advice to librarians for adding lesbian materials in *Out on the Shelves: Lesbian Books into Libraries*; the volume discusses various categories of lesbian fiction (e.g., thrillers, science fiction, and romances), some of which fit into pornographic genres. Herstory, the Women's History Research Center in New York, has microfilmed women's journals, newsletters, and other material pertinent to lesbian and straight women on twenty-three reels (1956–1974) for distribution to libraries around the country. Frederick McEnroe has put together "A Select Annotated Bibliography of Gay and Lesbian Periodicals" that he thinks different kinds of libraries should acquire, using intellectual, philosophical, and aesthetic merit as his criteria. Alan V. Miller has compiled a *Directory of the International Association of Lesbian and Gay Archives and Libraries* to identify major gay and lesbian collections around the world. These may be depositories of homosexual experience, oral history, theory, and so on, but Miller lists twelve in the United States that actively collect erotica. Several librarians describe significant institutional holdings in *Gay/Lesbian Archives and Libraries in North America*, edited by Cal Gough, now in a second edition. Even more up-to-date is Daniel C. Tsang's "Homosexuality Research Collections." A brief list of archives is included in Frances Green's *Gayellow Pages: USA and Canada*. Claire Potter, compiler of the *Lesbian Periodicals Index*, lists some lesbian archives at the same time that she indicates major publications.

The Cornell University Library owns the Mariposa Education and Research Foundation Archive, a collection of books, journals, films, and other artifacts on homosexuality that has been added to the larger Collection on Human Sexuality. The University of Michigan at Ann Arbor Library's Labadie Collection is the single best collection of gay and lesbian erotica (Tsang 201) and offers on-line searches. The Contemporary Culture Collection at Temple University in Philadelphia (Tsang 201) also contains homosexual erotica. The Lesbian Herstory Educational Foundation operates the Lesbian Herstory Archives (P.O. Box 1258, New York 10116), a collection of material on lesbian history and culture. The Ransome Center at the University of Texas at Austin holds the most comprehensive homosexual literature collection (Tsang 201).

Folklore

In "Erotic Folksongs and Ballads: An International Bibliography," Gershon Legman locates some of the more important collections of folklore in the United States. The Brown University Library shelves a small collection of erotica; it also houses the Harris collection of colonial broadsides, some of which are bawdy. The Providence Athenaeum has a collection of largely German and French materials dating from around the turn of the century, with additional collections in the areas of folklore and the mating habits of American Indians. The Burson Collection of Folklore is at the University of California, which has two folklore archives, one at Los Angeles (the Center for the Study of Comparative Folklore and Mythology) and one at Berkeley. Both contain xeroxed, mimeographed, and handwritten materials. Indiana University in Bloomington also has two folklore collections, one in the University Folklore Archives and one in the Kinsey Institute Collection. The Dorson collection is in the Folklore Archives. The Kinsey holds collections by Legman, Abrahams, Larson, and Randolph. Various collections of folklore (sea chanties, bawdy songs, military songs, erotic stories, obscene jokes, etc.) make up the Library of Congress Folklife and Folksong Archive. The University of Oregon at Eugene has the Robert Winslow Gordon Collection of American Folksong as a subcollection of the R. V. Mills Archive of Northwest Folklore. The Barker Archives at the University of Texas at Austin owns the Lomax Collection, of which a small part is devoted to bawdy versions. Charles Welsh and William Tillinghast have published a guide to an important subcollection of the Harvard College Library as *Catalogue of English and American Chapbooks and Broadside Ballads.*

Erotic Books and Art

The University of North Carolina in Charlotte has set aside a collection of erotica and scholarly texts; it is strong in works by Frank Harris, D. H. Lawrence, and Norman Douglas. The Ransome Research Center of the University of Texas has many items that might be of interest. These include the Morris Ernst papers, relating to the many censorship trials in the United States he argued; the erotic drawings of E. B. White; papers and letters by Henry Miller and Anaïs Nin; and so on but does not separate them as a special collection. The Mudd Manuscript Library at Princeton University contains the archives of the American Civil Liberties Union, an invaluable trove of the ACLU's role in the defense of various materials attacked over the years. Complete runs of the Annual Reports of the New York Society for the Suppression of Vice are in the New York Public Library and the Library of Congress. The Annual Reports of the New England Watch and Ward Society, another major censorship group, are archived in the Boston Public Library and the Harvard Law Library. Smaller public and private collections of erotica of all sorts are listed in Tuppy Owens' *The (Safer) Sex Maniac's Bible: A World Review of Sexuality, Listings of Erotic*

Clubs in all Major Cities, and Fun and Games for Your Delectation. Eugene C. Burt's massive *Erotic Art: An Annotated Bibliography with Essays* frequently refers to collections of erotic art around the world. The Fitz Hugh Ludlow Memorial Library (P.O. Box 99346, San Francisco 94109) holds an important collection of materials on drug-related pornography; it includes audio recordings, pictures, and manuscripts. Shirley Christian's "University's Trove of Pinups Is Admired by All Sorts, Even Some Feminists" reports on the University of Kansas' Spencer Museum of Art collection of *Esquire* pinups by Petty, Vargas, and other artists, now worth in the millions.

Comics

Doug Highsmith's "Comic Books: A Guide to Information Sources" is useful to scholars looking for material. Better are Randall W. Scott's guides: Scott's "Comic Research Libraries" has been superseded by his *Comic Books and Strips: An Information Sourcebook*, which lists library collections of underground comics, reference sources, and material on R. Crumb and other major artists. Scott has also published a catalog of a major collection as *The Comic Art Collection Catalog: An Author, Artist, Title, and Subject Catalog of the Comic Art Collection, Special Collections Division, Michigan State University Libraries*. Recognizing the cultural importance of comix (adult genres), librarians in institutions of modest size try to decide which ones to acquire, a challenge taken up by Timothy Perper, who discusses some underground artists in "For Sex, See Librarian: Reprise." The Bowling Green State University (Ohio) Popular Culture Library owns 350 underground comic titles, as well as alternative press examples, underground comics, tabloids, paperback potboilers, pulp magazines, soap opera scripts, Regency romances, greeting cards, and other borderline materials. Other sources can be found in Inge's *Comics as Culture*.

Electronic Media and Film

The Bowling Green State University Popular Culture Library also holds a huge collection of audio recordings, including some with erotic lyrics, all of which are electronically cataloged. Donald G. Godfried's *Reruns on File: A Guide to Electronic Media Archives* will help scholars find soap operas and even tabloid scripts and videotapes in broadcasting archives in thirty-nine states and Canada, including those in the Bowling Green Library. For original performance materials (the New York stage, burlesque, motion pictures, happenings), scholars might begin with the Lincoln Center for Performing Arts Branch of the New York Public Library and the Hoblitzelle Theatre Arts Library at the Harry Ransome Humanities Research Center of the University of Texas at Austin. The Margaret Herrick Library of the Academy of Motion Picture Arts and Sciences holds extensive materials on Hollywood censorship, according to "Hollywood Censorship Materials in the Margaret Herrick Library of the Academy of Motion

Picture Arts and Sciences," by the library's director, Linda Harris Mehr. According to David Friedman and Don De Nevi's *A Youth in Babylon*, the film schools at UCLA and Southern Methodist University in Dallas are now archiving classic exploitation films.

Bookstores and Government Agencies

Outside of these institutions, the researcher must forage on his own. The most interesting "libraries" are actually the larger adult bookstores in major cities, which are gradually disappearing as a consequence of zoning regulations and the availability of mail-order and Internet sites, neither of which permit the same kind of browsing. Such stores carry a wide selection of modern pornographic books, mostly fiction. Inventories shift constantly according to consumer demand, but dealers will usually special-order a particular title. The larger publishers circulate catalogs listing categories of fiction; these are erratically available in the stores. Adult bookstores cater almost exclusively to heterosexual and gay males; lesbian bookstores, that is, those offering authentic lesbian erotica (as opposed to male-produced fantasies featuring lesbians) are limited to cities like New York and San Francisco. Adult bookstores and emporia are also more likely to carry specialized videotapes (e.g., transsexuality) not found in local video rental outlets, which tend to market tapes of mainstream sexual preferences and the more elegant variety assumed to appeal to relatively conventional gay males or heterosexual couples.

Finally, the scholar should not neglect the archives of various government agencies. As the nation's onetime principal censor, the Post Office kept records. Those on all its operations are available, as are government documents generally, from appropriate Government Documents Centers in state and local libraries. Files concerning specific cases and prosecutions can be found in the National Archives in Washington (see **Current State of the Law** in chapter 20).

NOTE

1. Paul Gebhard, personal conversation at the Kinsey Institute, June 1978; Peter Webb, *The Erotic Arts* (Boston: New York Graphic Society, 1975), p. 355.

REFERENCES

Allen, Jane, Linda Kerr, Avril Rolph, and Marion Chadwick, comp. *Out on the Shelves: Lesbian Books into Libraries*. Newcastle under Lyme, England: AAL Publishing, 1989.

Alyson, Sasha, comp. *A Bibliography of AIDS-Related Books*. Boston: Alyson Press, 1988.

American Library Association. "ALA's Intellectual Freedom Committee Responds to

Pornography Commission Report." *American Libraries* (September 1986): 580–581.

Anderson, A. J. *Problems in Intellectual Freedom and Censorship*. New York: R. R. Bowker, 1974.

Apollinaire, Guillaume [Wilhelm Kostrowitsky, itself a pseudonym for Guglielmo Flugi Dulgigni], Fernand Fleuret, and Louis Perceau. *L'Enfer de la Bibliothèque Nationale*. Paris: Mercure de France, 1913; Rpt. Paris: Bibliothèque des Curieux, 1919; Rpt. "Nouvelle ed." [reprint of the 1919 version]. Geneva: Slatkine Reprints, 1970.

Ash, Lee, and William Miller, comps. *Subject Collections: A Guide to Special Book Collections and Subject Emphases as Reported by University, College, Public, and Special Libraries and Museums in the United States and Canada*. 6th ed. New York: Bowker, 1985.

Berman, Sanford. "If There Were a Sex Index . . ." *Sex Magazines in the Library Collection: A Scholarly Study of Sex in Serials and Periodicals: A Monographic Supplement to the Serials Librarian*, ed. Peter Gellatly. New York: Haworth Press, 1980, pp. 99–135.

Berry, John. "Drawing the Line." *Library Journal*, 104 (15 November 1979): 2385.

Bishop, Katherine. "Only in Hollywood: Memorial to Unmentionables." *New York Times*, national ed., 27 January 1991, p. 13.

Bodleian Library. "Librarian's Shelflist." Oxford, England: Oxford University, [?].

Bourgeron, Jean-Pierre. *Les Masques D'Eros: Les Objets Erotiques de Collection à Systeme*. Paris: Éditions de l'Amateur, 1985.

Boyer, Paul S. *Purity in Print: The Vice-Society Movement and Book Censorship in America*. New York: Scribner's, 1968.

Brooks, JoAnn, and Helen C. Hoffer. *Sexual Nomenclature: A Thesaurus*. Boston: G. K. Hall, 1976.

Burt, Eugene C. *Erotic Art: An Annotated Bibliography with Essays*. Boston: G. K. Hall, 1989.

Case, Patricia J. "Collections of Contemporary Alternative Materials in Libraries: A Directory." *Alternative Materials in Libraries*, ed. James P. Danky and Elliott Shore. Metuchen, NJ: Scarecrow Press, 1982.

———, ed. *Field Guide to Alternative Media: A Directory to Reference and Selection Tools Useful in Accessing Small and Alternative Press Publications and Independently Produced Media*. Chicago: American Library Association, 1984.

Catalogue du cabinet secret du prince G. . . . Collection de livres et objets curieux et rares concernant l'amour, les femmes et la marriage. Premiere partie/supplement iconographique. Brussels: Poulet-Malaisse?, 1887; rpt. London: Charles Skilton, 1890.

Christensen, John O. *Obscenity, Pornography, and Libraries: A Selective Bibliography*. Monticello, IL: Vance Bibliographies, 1991.

Christian, Shirley. "University's Trove of Pinups Is Admired by All Sorts, Even Some Feminists." *New York Times*, 25 November 1998, p. B3.

Cornog, Martha. "A Case Study of Censorship? The Library of Congress and the Brailing of *Playboy*." *Libraries, Erotica, Pornography*, ed. Martha Cornog. Phoenix, AZ: Oryx Press, 1991, pp. 130–143.

———. *Libraries, Erotica, Pornography*. Phoenix, AZ: Oryx Press, 1991.

————. "What Happens When Libraries Subscribe to *Playboy*?" *Libraries, Erotica, Pornography*, ed. Martha Cornog. Phoenix, AZ: Oryx Press, 1991, pp. 144–165.

Cotter, Holland. "All over the Lot (the Back Lot, Too)." *New York Times*, 31 October 1997, p. B31.

Daily, Jay E. *The Anatomy of Censorship*. New York: Dekker, 1973.

————. "Erotica." *Encyclopedia of Library and Information Science*. New York: Marcel Dekker, 1972, pp. 164–184.

Daniels, Walter, ed. *The Censorship of Books*. New York: H. W. Wilson, 1954.

Danky, James P. *Undergrounds: A Union List of Alternative Periodicals in Libraries of the United States and Canada*. Madison: State Historical Society of Wisconsin, 1974.

Darnay, Brigette T., and Holly M. Leighton, eds. *Directory of Special Libraries and Information Centers*. 12th ed. Detroit: Gale Research, 1989.

Dixon, Rebecca. "Bibliographical Control of Erotica." *An Intellectual Freedom Primer*, ed. Charles H. Busha. Littleton, CO: Libraries Unlimited, 1977.

Downs, Robert B., ed. *The First Freedom: Liberty and Justice in the World of Books*. Chicago: American Library Association, 1960.

Drujon, Fernand. *Catalogue des ouvrages, écrits et dessins de toute nature poursuivis, supprimés ou condamnés depuis le 21 octobre 1814 jusqu'au 31 juillet 1877*. Paris: Libraire Ancienne et Moderne Edouard Rouveyre, 1879.

Elcano, Barrett, and Vern Bullough. "Sexology: A Personal Guide to the Serial Literature." *Sex Magazines in the Library Collection: A Scholarly Study of Sex in Serials and Periodicals: A Monographic Supplement to the Serials Librarian*, ed. Peter Gellatly. New York: Haworth Press, 1980, pp. 75–86.

Ellis, Allen. *Popular Culture and Acquisitions*. Binghamton, NY: Haworth Press, 1992.

Erotisme: Dispersion d'une Collection Partielle Provenant de Michel Simon: Varia, Estampes, Livres, Dessins, Cartes Postales, Photographies. Geneva: N.p., 1984.

Fanin, Colonel. *The Royal Museum at Naples, Being Some Account of the Erotic Paintings, Bronzes, and Statues Contained in That Famous "Cabinet Secret."* San Diego: Collectors' Publications, 1969; rpt. of 1871 London ed.

Fodor, Joe. "Collections: This Stuff Will Rot Your Brain." *Brooklyn Bridge*, 3:1 (September 1997): 33.

Foerstel, Herbert N. *Banned in the U.S.A.: A Reference Guide to Book Censorship in Schools and Public Libraries*. Westport, CT: Greenwood, 1994.

Friedman, David, with Don De Nevi. *A Youth in Babylon: Confessions of a Trash-Film King*. Buffalo, NY: Prometheus Books, 1990.

Fryer, Peter. *Private Case—Public Scandal: Secrets of the British Museum Revealed*. London: Secker and Warburg, 1966; rpt. *Secrets of the British Museum: A Revealing Account of the Classic Works of Erotica Kept under Lock and Key at the British Museum*. New York: Citadel Press, 1968.

Geist, Christopher D., Ray B. Browne, Michael T. Marsden, and Carol Palmer, comps. *Directory of Popular Culture Collections*. Phoenix, AZ: Oryx Press, 1989.

Gellatly, Peter, ed. *Sex Magazines in the Library Collection: A Scholarly Study of Sex in Serials and Periodicals: A Monographic Supplement to the Serials Librarian*. New York: Haworth Press, 1980.

Geller, Evelyn. *Forbidden Books in American Public Libraries, 1876–1939: A Study in Cultural Change*. Westport, CT: Greenwood, 1984.

Ginzburg, Ralph. *An Unhurried View of Erotica*. New York: Ace Books, 1958.

Godfried, Donald G. *Reruns on File: A Guide to Electronic Media Archives*. Hillsdale, NJ: Lawrence Erlbaum Associates, 1993.

Goldstein, Richard. "The Little Shop of Hornies." *Village Voice*, 31 December 1996, pp. 44–46.

Gough, Cal, ed. *Gay/Lesbian Archives and Libraries in North America*. Rev. ed. Atlanta: American Library Association Gay and Lesbian Taskforce Clearinghouse, 1989.

Green, Frances, ed. *Gayellow Pages: USA and Canada*. New York: Renaissance House, annual.

Haight, Anne Lyon. *Banned Books: Informal Notes on Some Books Banned for Various Reasons at Various Times and in Various Places*. New York: Bowker, 1970; 4th ed. enlarged by Chandler B. Grannis, 1978.

Haney, Robert W. *Comstockery in America*. Boston: Beacon Press, 1960.

Harmon, Amy. "Reviews Follow Ban on Library Internet Filter." *New York Times*, 25 November 1998, p. A24.

Haynes, Roberta, and Rick Hauser. *Secret World of Erotic Art*. Vestron Video, 1985.

Hefner Film Collection [Los Angeles]. List of Holdings, 1975. Typescript, Kinsey Institute for Research in Sex, Gender, and Reproduction. Indiana University, Bloomington.

Herrmann, Frank. *Sotheby's: Portrait of an Auction House*. London: Chatto and Windus, 1980.

Highsmith, Doug. "Comic Books: A Guide to Information Sources." *Riverside Quarterly*, 27 (Winter 1987): 202–209.

Inge, M. Thomas. *Comics as Culture*. Jackson: University Press of Mississippi, 1990.

Institute for the Advanced Study of Sexuality. Catalogs and Brochures. 1525 Franklin, San Francisco 94109–4592.

Isay, David, and Harvey Wang. "Dixie Evans." *Holding On: Dreamers, Visionaries, Eccentrics, and Other American Heroes*. New York: Norton, 1995, pp. 83–87.

Johnson, Claudia. *Stifled Laughter: One Woman's Story about Fighting Censorship*. Golden, CO: Fulcrum, 1994.

Katz, Bill. "The Pornography Collection." *Library Journal*, 96 (1971): 4060–4066.

Katz, Bill, and Linda Sternberg Katz. *Magazines for Libraries: For the General Reader and School, Junior College, College, University, and Public Libraries*. 6th ed. New York: Bowker, 1989.

Kearney, Patrick J. *The Private Case: An Annotated Bibliography of the Private Case Erotica Collection in the British (Museum) Library*. London: Jay Landesman, 1981.

———. *The Private Case, Volume II: A Bibliography of Books That Used to Be in the Erotica Collection of the British (Museum) Library*. Forthcoming.

Kelly, Michael. "Sex Is Back." *Playboy*, 37:5 (May 1990): 122–124, 162–163, 165–166, 168.

Kelm, Rebecca Sturm. "The Lack of Access to Back Issues of the Weekly Tabloids: Does It Matter?" *Journal of Popular Culture*, 23 (Spring 1990): 45–50.

Kimball, Alan, ed. *Underground Newspaper Collection in the University of Missouri Libraries*. Columbia: University of Missouri Press, 1989.

Kinsey Institute for Research in Sex, Gender, and Reproduction. *Sex Research: Early Literature from Statistics to Erotica: Guide to the Microfilm Collection*. Woodbridge, CT: Research Publications, 1983.

[Kinsey] Institute for Sex Research. *Catalog of Periodical Literature in the Social and*

Behavioral Sciences Section, Library of the Institute for Sex Research, Including Supplement to Monographs, 1973–1975. Boston: G. K. Hall, 1976.

Krulick, Jeff, producer and director. *Ralph Whittington, King of Porn*. 3221 Connecticut Avenue, Washington, DC 20008; jeffkrulich@internet.mci.com.

Landrum, Larry N. *American Popular Culture: A Guide to Information Sources*. Detroit: Gale Research, 1982.

Legman, Gershon. "Erotic Folksongs and Ballads: An International Bibliography." *Journal of American Folklore*, 103 (October/December 1990): 417–501.

———. *The Horn Book: Studies in Erotic Folklore and Bibliography*. New York: University Books, 1964.

———. "Introduction." *The Private Case: An Annotated Bibliography of the Erotica Collection in the British (Museum) Library*, by Patrick J. Kearney. London: Landesman, 1981, pp. 3–34.

———. "The Lure of the Forbidden." *Libraries, Erotica, and Pornography*, ed. Martha Cornog. Phoenix, AZ: Oryx Press, 1991, pp. 36–68.

Lewis, Neil A. "Publishers, Artists and Librarians Challenge New Pornography Law." *New York Times*, 24 February 1991, p. 14.

Library of Congress. *Rare Books and Special Collections in the Library of Congress*. Pamphlet. Washington, DC: Library of Congress, current.

Lichtenberg, Kara. *A Research Guide to Human Sexuality*. Hamden, CT: Garland, 1993.

Liebenzell, Thomas. *Smut in the British Library: Register zu Kearneys Private Case*. Hamburg: C. Bell Verlag, 1986.

Matusak, Susan, comp. *Bibliography of the Eighteenth-Century Holdings of the Institute for Sex Research*. Bloomington, IN: Institute for Sex Research, 1975.

McEnroe, Frederick. "A Select Annotated Bibliography of Gay and Lesbian Periodicals." *Sex Magazines in the Library Collection: A Scholarly Study of Sex in Serials and Periodicals: A Monographic Supplement to the Serials Librarian*, ed. Peter Gellatly. New York: Haworth Press, 1980, pp. 87–98.

McKeon, Richard, et al. *The Freedom to Read*. New York: American Book Publishers Council, 1957.

Mehr, Linda Harris. "Hollywood Censorship Materials in the Margaret Herrick Library of the Academy of Motion Picture Arts and Sciences." Popular Culture Conference, Chicago, April 1994.

Merkin, Richard. *Velvet Eden: The Richard Merkin Collection of Erotic Photography*. New York: Methuen, 1979.

———. "Vintage Vamp: A History of Pornographics." *High Society*, 1:11 (March 1977): 29–33.

Miller, Alan V., comp. *Directory of the International Association of Lesbian and Gay Archives and Libraries*. Toronto: International Association of Lesbian and Gay Archives and Libraries, 1987.

Molz, Kathleen. "The Public Custody of High Pornography." *American Scholar*, 36 (Winter 1966–1967): 93–103.

Moon, Eric, ed. *Book Selection and Censorship in the Sixties*. New York: Bowker, 1969.

Myers, Ardie. "Reading Room Curator Collects Off the Job." *The [Library of Congress] Gazette*, 19 November 1993, pp. 3–4.

National Coalition against Censorship. *Books on Trial: A Survey of Recent Cases*. New York: National Coalition against Censorship, 1985.

Oboler, Eli M. *The Fear of the Word: Censorship and Sex.* Metuchen, NJ: Scarecrow Press, 1974.

Owens, Tuppy. *The (Safer) Sex Maniac's Bible: A World Review of Sexuality, Listings of Erotic Clubs in All Major Cities, and Fun and Games for Your Delectation.* London: Tuppy Owens, 1990.

"A Passion for Collecting: Erotic Art Comes Out of the Closet and into the Auction Rooms." *Economist,* 10 January 1987, p. 78.

Perper, Timothy. "For Sex, See Librarian: Reprise." *Libraries, Erotica, Pornography,* ed. Martha Cornog. Phoenix, AZ: Oryx Press, 1991, pp. 250–298.

Pershing, Gwendolyn L. "Erotica Research Collections." *Libraries, Erotica, Pornography,* ed. Martha Cornog. Phoenix, AZ: Oryx Press, 1991, pp. 188–198.

Peyrefitte, Roger. *Un Musée de l'Amour.* Monaco: Editions du Rochjer, 1972.

Phillips Gallery. *The Kronhausen Collection of Erotic Art from the International Museum of Erotic Art, Sold by Phillips.* Auction Catalog, 31 March 1979. New York: Phillips, 1979.

Pia, Pascal [J. Durand]. *Les Livres de L'Enfer. Bibliographie critique des ouvrages érotiques dans leurs différents éditions du XVIe siècle à nos jours.* 2 vols. Paris: Coulet and Faure, 1978.

Pomeroy, Wardell. *Dr. Kinsey and the Institute for Sex Research.* New York: Harper and Row, 1972.

Pope, Michael. *Sex and the Undecided Librarian.* Metuchen, NJ: Scarecrow Press, 1974.

Popular Culture in Libraries. Binghamton, NY, 1992–.

Potter, Claire, comp. *Lesbian Periodicals Index.* Tallahassee, FL: Naiad Press, 1986.

"Provocative Period Pieces." *Playboy:* 27:10 (October 1980): 131–135; 30:1 (January 1983): 122–125; 31:1 (January 1984): 114–117; 35:1 (January 1988): 144–147.

Rabenalt, Arthur Maria. *Mimus Eroticus.* 5 vols. Hamburg: Verlag für Kulturforschung, 1965–1967.

Reade, Rolf S. [Rose, Alfred]. *Registrum Librorum Eroticorum.* London: privately printed, 1936; rpt. Rose, Alfred. *Register of Erotic Books.* 2 vols. New York: Brussel, 1965.

Reuter, Madalynne, and Marianne Yen. "Censorship Rose 35 Percent over Previous Year, Study Finds." *Publishers' Weekly,* 24 October 1986, p. 13.

Rex Grey Costume Collection. London: Bonhams of Knightsbridge, 1992.

Rimmer, Robert. "A Connoisseur's Selection of X-Rated Videotapes for the Library." *Libraries, Erotica, and Pornography,* ed. Martha Cornog. Phoenix, AZ: Oryx Press, 1991, pp. 240–249.

Robson, Ruthann. "Pornography, Power, and the First Amendment." *Alternative Library Literature 1982–1983: A Biennial Anthology,* ed. Sanford Berman and James Danby. Phoenix, AZ: Oryx Press, 1984.

Santa Vicca, Edmund F. "Acquired Immune Deficiency Syndrome (AIDS): An Annotated Bibliography for Librarians." *Reference Services Review,* 16 (Winter 1987): 45–67.

Scheiner, C. J. *Compendium: Being a List of All the Books (Erotica, Curiosa, & Sexology) Listed in Our Catalogs 1–6 (1978–1988).* Brooklyn, NY: C. J. Scheiner Books, 1989.

———. *Erotica-Curiosa-Sexology Catalog.* 275 Linden Blvd., Brooklyn, NY: 1977–present.

Schidrowitz, Leo, ed. *Sittengeschichte der Kulturwelt und ihrer Entwicklung in Einzel-*

darstellungen. 10 vols. and supplement to vol. II. Vienna/Leipzig: Verlag für Kulturforschung, 1926–30. I: *Sittengeschichte des Intimen: Bett, Korsett, Hemd, Hose, Bad, Abtritt. Die Geschichte und Entwicklung der intimen Gebrauchsgegenstände* (1926); II: *Sittengeschichte des Lasters: die Kulturepochen und ihre Leidenschaften* (1927), and *Ergänzungsband* (1927); III: *Sittengeschichte von Paris: die Grosstadt, ihe Sitten und ihre Unsittlichkeit* (1926); IV: *Sittengeschichte des Proletariats: des Weg vom Leibes-zum Maschinensklaven, die sittliche Stellung und Haltung des Proletariats* (1926); V: *Sittengeschichte des Theatres. Ein Darstellung des Theaters, seiner Entwicklung und Stellung in zwei Jahrhunderten* (1926); VI: *Sittengeschichte der Liebkosung und Strafe. Die Zärtlichkeitsworte, Gesten und Handlungen der Kulturmenschheit und ihr Gegenpol der Strenge* (1928); VII: *Sittengeschichte des Geheimen und Verbotenen. Eine Darstellung der geheimen und verborgen gehaltenen Leidenschaften der Menschheit, die Einstellung der Staatsgewalt zum Geschlechtsleben der Gesellschaft* (1930); VIII: *Sittengeschichte des Hafens und der Reise. Eine Beleuchtung des erotischen Lebens in der Hafenstadt, im Hotel, im Reisevehikel. Die Sexualität des Kulturmenschen während des Reisens in fremden Milieu* (1927); IX: *Sittengeschichte der Revolution, Sittenlockerung und Sittenverfall. Moralgesetze und sexualethische Neuorientierung in Zeiten staatlicher Zersetzung und revolutionären Umsturzes* (1930); X: *Sittengeschichte des Intimsten. Intime Toilette, Mode und Kosmetik im Dienst und Erotik* (1929).

Scott, Randall W. *The Comic Art Collection Catalog: An Author, Artist, Title, and Subject Catalog of the Comic Art Collection, Special Collections Division, Michigan State University Libraries.* Westport, CT: Greenwood Press, 1993.

———. *Comic Books and Strips: An Information Sourcebook.* Phoenix, AZ: Oryx Press, 1988.

———. "Comic Research Libraries." *Comic Art Collection*, 33 (2 February 1987): 5–7.

"The Secret of an Actor." *Adelina*, 14:7 (August 1980): 86–89.

Selth, Jefferson P. *Alternative Lifestyles: A Guide to Research Collections on International Communities, Nudism, and Sexual Freedom.* Westport, CT: Greenwood Press, 1985.

Sewell, Robert C. "Trash or Treasure? Pop Fiction in Academic and Research Libraries." *College and Research Libraries*, 45 (November 1984): 450–461.

Slabaugh, Eugene. Card Catalog, Erotic Film Archives. Kinsey Institute for Research in Sex, Gender, and Reproduction, Indiana University, Bloomington.

———. Stag Film Analyses. 3 Notebooks. 1960–1967. Erotic Film Archives. Kinsey Institute for Research in Sex, Gender, and Reproduction, Indiana University, Bloomington.

Slabaugh, Eugene, and George Huntington. "Producers of and Nature of Stag Films." Audiorecording, 1966, in the Erotic Film Archives. Kinsey Institute for Research in Sex, Gender, and Reproduction, Indiana University, Bloomington.

Smith, Bradley. *Erotic Art of the Masters: The 18th, 19th, and 20th Centuries.* New York: Erotic Arts Society, n.d.; rev. ed. La Jolla, CA: Gemini Smith, 1981.

———. *Twentieth Century Masters of Erotic Art.* La Jolla, CA: Gemini Smith, 1985.

Steinberg, David. "An Annotated Bibliography of Quality Erotica." *Libraries, Erotica, and Pornography*, ed. Martha Cornog. Phoenix, AZ: Oryx Press, 1991, pp. 229–239.

Stormgart, Ivan. General Catalogs. P.O. Box 470883, San Francisco 94147-0883.

"Szene: Kultur." *Der Spiegel*, 32 (5 August 1991): 179.

Tsang, Daniel C. "Homosexuality Research Collections." *Libraries, Erotica, Pornography*, ed. Martha Cornog. Phoenix, AZ: Oryx Press, 1991, pp. 199–210.

Wachsberger, Ken. *Directory of Resources and Sources of the Vietnam Era Underground Press*. Tempe, AZ: MICA Press, 1993.

Walker, Pamela. "Bibliographic Control of Sex Research Materials." *The New Special Collection. Library Journal* Special Report No. 11. New York: Bowker, 1979, pp. 33–39.

Webb, Peter. *The Erotic Arts*. Boston: New York Graphic Society, 1975; 2d ed. New York: Farrar, Giroux, 1984.

Welsh, Charles, and William Tillinghast. *Catalogue of English and American Chapbooks and Broadside Ballads*. Detroit: Singing Tree Press, 1968.

Wilcox, Clair, ed. *Civil Liberties under Attack*. Philadelphia: University of Pennsylvania Press, 1951.

Woods, L. B. *A Decade of Censorship in America: The Threat to Classrooms and Libraries*. Metuchen, NJ: Scarecrow Press, 1979.

8

Child Pornography

The dark side of pornography, in terms of both its existence and its prosecution, is linked to the abuse of children, who are assumed by law and prevailing moral standards to be incapable of informed consent and thus vulnerable to exploitation because of their inexperience. Most Americans—*and* most producers and consumers of pornography—draw the line at sexual depictions of minors. The same goes for advocates of candor. Robert Stoller, whose *Porn: Myths for the Twentieth Century* maintains that pornography is not harmful, except that which involves children. Camille Paglia, who also approves of pornography, condemns Calvin Klein ads on the grounds that they transgress against children in "Kids for Sale."

Heterosexual and homosexual pedophiles are not a modern phenomenon, and youthful characters have been common enough in pornographic fiction for decades, but explicit photographic and cinematic pornography in which children figure has surfaced in any quantity only in the last twenty-five years. Historically significant pedophiles include Lewis Carroll, author of *Alice in Wonderland*, and Pierre Louÿs, the French erotic novelist, both of whom photographed little girls in the nude. Only a few pictures that Carroll himself overlooked when he destroyed his images have survived. Louÿs's photos, perhaps numbering 10,000, have never appeared in any quantity on the open market.[1] Prior to World War II, American pedophiles might purchase classic nude studies of boys by foreign photographers such as Wilhelm van Gloeden or the occasional domestic picture or photo set of nude underage males, sometimes in intercourse with older men. Measured by any standard, the traffic during the 1950s in explicit photos or movies was small. Most American pedophiles simply collected innocuous pictures of boys and girls. The Kinsey Institute houses files of hundreds of police-seized photos of little girls in communion dresses and boys in short trousers, taken or acquired by pedophiles who were often related to the subjects. During the 1960s, eroticized images of children appeared in several books from mainstream publishers. Typical were *The Boy: A Photographic Essay* and *In Search of Young Beauty: A Venture into Photographic Art*, the latter by Charles du Bois Hodges; bookstores refuse to handle them now.

Minors occasionally appeared in stag films but, contrary to popular myth, were not depicted as underage. In recorded interviews with stag film producers of the 1950s and 1960s ("Producers of and Nature of Stag Films"), Gene Slabaugh and George Huntington of the Kinsey Institute learned from the entrepreneurs they interviewed that the mere idea of underage performers made the predominantly middle-aged heterosexual audiences distinctly uncomfortable. Juanita Slusher, who became the exotic dancer Candy Barr, was the unwilling star of *Smart Alec* (1950–1951), one of the most famous stags ever shot, but audiences could not have known by looking that the precociously endowed girl was a teenager. The same is true of two more recent examples, Traci Lords, now a legitimate actress, and Alexandria Quinn, who has left the adult industry, both of whom lied about their ages and made numerous pornographic movies and videotapes before they were eighteen. When their true ages became known, the producers of their tapes recalled them from video stores, in some instances editing out the footage featuring Lords and Quinn and in others destroying the masters altogether. According to Robert Rimmer, Traci Lords made at least $150,000 a year as a porn star. The furor that ensued propelled her to a celebrity (legitimate movies, a singing contract, television appearances) that thousands of Americans dream of. Had this particular minor chosen instead to deal in drugs, says Rimmer, no one would ever have noticed.[2]

The first stag film to circulate in the United States in which minors were represented *as* minors was *The Sexy Sexteens* (1955), an amateur film that got onto the market when it was copied by officials *after* its maker, Ivan Jerome, was arrested.[3] During the next decade, films depicting minors in intercourse came into the United States from Denmark, where pornography had been decriminalized and where the age of sexual consent was sixteen (though at least a dozen examples involved boys and girls clearly below that age), and from Southeast Asia, in particular, Vietnam and Thailand, where native producers found a market among American servicemen stationed there during the Vietnam War. Perhaps because of implicit racism, American authorities took little notice of the material involving Asian children. (In a novel strategy, Germany has asked Thailand to cooperate with its law enforcement agencies to combat exploitation of Asian minors by German nationals. Suggested courses of action include closer monitoring of sex tourism, child prostitution, and pornography in Thailand itself, while Germany moves against those of its own citizens who abuse children of any nationality, not just Germans. Nopporn Wong-Anan discusses the accords sought in "Germany Seeks Help in Halting Child Abuse.")

In any case, the 1970 Presidential Commission's *Report of the Commission on Obscenity and Pornography* dealt with child porn only to a small extent; the few studies are in volumes I and IX of the *Technical Reports*. A few years later, Robin Lloyd included two chapters on pedophilic pornography in *For Money or Love: Boy Prostitution in America*. The first dealt with the practice of child pornographers' serving as their own distributors (since dealers ordinarily would not touch such material); the second surveyed publishers of "chicken photography," as pictures of underage boys were called, magazines such as *Chicken Little, Genesis Children, Boy Pin-ups, Boys Together*, and *Boys and Men*, and fiction with titles such as *Chicken Chaser, Meat My Buddy*, and *A Boy for Hire*, all of which circulated during the 1960s and early 1970s. Another contemporary account, Kenneth Lambert's "The Scope and Dimensions of Paedophilia," also refers to photos and film of the 1960s.

Not until pedophiles in the United States became bolder did public and official concern mushroom. The principal outcry occurred in 1977 in Chicago. In "City, Congress Set Child Porn Probes," the *Chicago Tribune* reported that Governor Thompson of Illinois had impaneled a child porn task force, that Representative Peter Rodino had set hearings in the House Judiciary Committee, and that Representative John Brademas had scheduled similar proceedings for the Select Education subcommittee. The proceedings of the latter committee were published as *Sexual Exploitation of Children*. The Senate Committee on the Judiciary held concurrent hearings in Chicago from 27 May to 16 June 1977; its report was published as *Protection of Children against Sexual Exploitation: Hearings before the Subcommittee to Investigate Juvenile Delinquency*. One consequence was the passage in 1977 of federal law 95–225, which forbids using children in sexually explicit materials.

Following classic media pattern, the furor moved from newspapers to magazines. Better than most articles was Helen Dudar's "America Discovers Child Pornography," which strove for a cultural context and for accuracy. Dudar looked at the rapidly disappearing child-porn magazines, at the child-porn movies from Scandinavia and Southeast Asia, and at the consumers, mostly white, middle-class, married males. (In retrospect, it appears that Dudar may have relied too heavily on interviews with Father Bruce Ritter of Covenant House, whose celebrated antiporn stance was compromised by the accusations that he abused minors in his care.) A supermarket tabloid article typical in its misinformation was "What Pornographers Are Doing to Children: A Shocking Report," by Judianne Densen-Gerber, an effective crusader against child pornography, who proposed new legislation. Densen-Gerber claimed that "at least 264" child pornography magazines were published monthly in the United States in 1977, when, in fact, said Lawrence A. Stanley in "The Child-Pornography Myth," by then there were none (42). Those publications that did contain ads for child pornography, Stanley points out, were all the productions of U.S. government agencies that printed them in order to entrap the unsuspecting. Perhaps the most sensational article was by Robert Sam Anson, whose "The Last Porno Show" investigated producers who recruit underage performers for porn films and magazines in New York and Los Angeles. After discussing what seemed to be the surge in child pornography, though the editors of *Time* thought the press was magnifying the problem, the magazine recommended in "Child's Garden of Perversity" that material be prosecuted under child abuse laws rather than under current obscenity laws, which might not be effective because of First Amendment protections.

The panic lasted for more than a year, and began to wind down when journalists such as Peter Bridge, in a sense, reassured parents that most pornographers prey on runaways (rather than children in their homes) in "What Parents Should Know and Do about 'Kiddie Porn.' " By 1978 R. S. Pope could report that the federal government and twelve states had enacted statutes specifically prohibiting the use of children in pornography in "Child Pornography: A New Role for the Obscenity Doctrine." Texas was one state to do so, after the state House conducted its own investigation and published its research and recommendations as *The Select Committee on Child Pornography: Its Related Causes and Control*. The Texas report seemed thin beside the thorough and meticulous *Sexual Exploitation of Children: A Report to the Illinois General Assembly by the Illinois Legislative Investigating Commission*. Marshaling three years of evidence gathering and eschewing sensationalism, the Illinois commission said that child pornography was not then nor had it ever been a major problem in America, decried hyperbolic response, and rejected the false claims of various self-appointed "experts." It pointed out that the largest child porn magazine of the 1970s had never grossed more than $30,000 per year. These conclusions came too late to mute the controversy and have generally been ignored since.

By contrast, *Protection of Children against Sexual Exploitation Act of 1977: Report on S 1585*, a U.S. Senate committee report, found that child pornography was widespread, well organized, and lucrative, that the mails were often used for distribution, and that more federal laws were needed to protect minors. Though discounted by most researchers, this report has had a lasting impact on popular consciousness. For one of William Serrin's 1981 articles on the economics of porn, "Opponents of Flourishing Sex Industry Hindered by Its Open Public Acceptance," Father Bruce Ritter (see earlier) told Serrin that child pornography was rampant on the streets of New York, while Manhattan district attorney Robert Morgenthau was equally adamant that commercial child porn had been virtually eradicated in his area (B6). The evidence clearly supported Morgenthau.

The most authoritative studies proceed with great caution, especially with statistics. Claims that thousands of children are involved in the production of erotica should immediately be discounted, since no illegal industry could absorb numbers on so fantastic a scale. A 1980 study, funded by U.S. Department of Health and Human Services, covered sexual exploitation of children in the 1970s and included investigations of criminal offenders, both producers and compulsive collectors of child erotica, case studies of children, interviews with parents, surveys of teenage prostitutes, and suggestions for combating the social evil.

The report, published as *Child Pornography and Sex Rings*, was edited by Ann Wolbert Burgess and Marieanne Lindqvist Clark; it is sober and scholarly. Isolated, but highly publicized, cases continued nonetheless to fuel sporadic panics. Aric Press and Janet Huck reported on "The Mother of Kiddie Porn?," a 1984 article on the mail-order business of Catherine Wilson, a Los Angeles purveyor of mostly Scandinavian pedophilia, and her trial. Partly because of the Wilson case, Congress in 1984 revised the 1977 statute to prohibit the importation of child pornography and to curtail even the free exchange of child pornography. To strengthen prosecutions, the law dropped the requirement that images be lewd in order to be judged illegal. A complete state-by-state list of child pornography laws appears in Daniel S. Moretti's *Obscenity and Pornography: The Law under the First Amendment*.

   Child Pornography and Paedophilia, the 1985 report of the Senate Permanent Subcommittee on Investigations, concluded that organized crime played no part in the child porn trade, that child porn is a small and clandestine part of the pornography market in this country, and that the total number of pornographers working in pedophilia in the United States did not exceed 2,000. (That report was part of a larger investigation by the Subcommittee on the Effect of Pornography on Women and Children of the Senate Committee on the Judiciary, published as *Hearings before the Subcommittee on Juvenile Justice of the Committee on the Judiciary*; it dealt with child abuse, child molestation, and problems of conduct against women.) Even so, more than 40 percent of the recommendations of the *Attorney General's Report on Pornography, Final Report, July 1986* have to do with child pornography; Part 2 deals most extensively with the subject. Critics have suggested that the report deliberately conflates child porn with adult-oriented and -distributed erotica to garner greater support for the Justice Department's campaign against all forms of sexual explicitness. Considering the tactics the department has used, the charge would appear to have merit.

   Despite the confusion fomented by the Meese Commission, most scholars instantly reject the equation of the pornographic industry *per se* with child abuse and child exploitation. Another study of the period, D. Kelly Weisberg's *Children of the Night: A Study of Adolescent Prostitution*, surveyed adolescent prostitutes of both sexes in New York City and San Francisco. Weisberg reports that only 27 percent of adolescent prostitutes of both sexes were photographed by clients at one time or another. In the great majority of cases, the prints were kept by the photographer or went to private collectors rather than to dealers for circulation. Forty-two percent of the prostitutes had never been photographed, while only 7 percent were photographed for distribution as pornography (68–69). Similarly, only 10 percent of the boys surveyed by Jennifer James for *Entrance into Juvenile Male Prostitution* had ever participated in even one photography or movie/video session (125), and again, these were usually not for a public market. In fact, rigorous prosecution in the 1970s drove material permanently off the public market. That does not mean that child porn does not exist, just that it remains at considerable distance from regular traffic in sexual materials.

The *Child Protection and Obscenity Enforcement Act and Pornography Victims Protection Act of 1987*, originally introduced as S703 and S2033, provided that every person who handled sexual materials keep elaborate records of the ages of performers. A Federal District Court judge in Washington struck down as unconstitutional that requirement when a coalition of organizations including the American Library Association and various artists' groups challenged the requirement. The judge said that if the act applied only to underage people—rather than people of all ages—it would be constitutional. See "Judge Overturns Part of Child-Pornography Law." Revisions of the provision (18 U.S.C. sec. 2257 [h]) directed at the hiring and management of performers were upheld in 1995, however, and today producers of even soft-core films are careful to keep proofs of age, even if their performers are obviously in their sixties. Ironically, better record keeping may have actually brought commercial order to an adult industry in need of standard accounting practices. Moreover, provision 2257, functioning as a moral fire wall, helps the industry more than it hurts. In "Supreme Court to Consider '77 Pornography Law," Linda Greenhouse reports on a case involving a distributor who sold films featuring Traci Lords. The government argued that the distributor knew that the actress had been discovered to be underage and that the knowledge made him liable under the law. On 18 April 1990 the Supreme Court upheld the constitutionality of an Ohio Law criminalizing the "possession" of pornographic photographs of children, provided that the state could prove criminal intent. See Linda Greenhouse's "Justices, 6–3, Restrict Rights to Pornography." But the Supreme Court has also held that for law enforcement officials to pose as sellers who beg people to buy child pornography in order to prosecute them—a widespread and still continuing practice—is clearly questionable.

The most celebrated cases are those involving serious artists working in areas that to some should be forbidden. Some years ago, Will McBride's *Show Me!* a photographic volume designed to teach children about sex, stirred furor because some of the illustrations depicted children looking at their parents' genitals; though it seems innocuous enough, the volume is virtually unobtainable today. More recently, zealous prosecutors targeted the photographer Jock Sturges. A San Francisco federal grand jury refused to indict Sturges on child pornography charges despite fifteen months of effort on the part of the FBI in 1991. "Court Is Asked for Aid in Pornography Case," a *New York Times* story, followed Sturges' legal battles to force the FBI to return negatives and photos seized from his studios. Many newspapers, sensing no real sensationalism and doubtless wary of the Justice Department's cavalier attitude toward the First Amendment, did not report on the case at all. In "Art under Attack: Who Dares Say That It's No Good?" Andy Grundberg thinks that Sturges' photos of nude adolescents are pretty tired examples of older genres and that their artistic value is "meager." Others disagree, of course. In the Introduction to Sturges' *Last Day of Summer*, Jayne Anne Phillips praises the photographer's vision and integrity; in a similar Preface to Sturges' *Radiant Identities*, A. D. Coleman does the same. Another widely published photographer, Sally Mann, ran into similar difficulties for publishing pictures of her pubescent daughters in *Immediate Family* and *At Twelve: Portraits of Young Women*. Katherine Dieckmann wonders what the fuss is about in "Photographs . . . with Children," a review of *Immediate Family*, but also excoriates the efforts of investigators to prove pornographic intent. Other critics have pointed to the sensuality of frames such as "A Perfect Tomato" in *At Twelve*. Richard B. Woodward finds Mann's subjects provocative in "The Disturbing Photography of Sally Mann." The articles on Jock Sturges, David Hamilton, Graham Ovenden, Sally Mann, and lesser-known photographers whose art has run afoul of government and fundamentalist censors in "Bad Boys (and Girl) of Erotic Photography" are useful, especially those that list legal cases.

It would appear that conservatives sometimes charge that a given work is an example of child pornography in an effort to be successful in censoring *somebody*. A *New York Times* editorial, "A Dixie Book Burning" calls fundamentalist boycotts and attacks on Barnes and Noble and other stores for carrying books by those photographers "a campaign of intimidation" intended to curtail protected speech. Richard Goldstein's "The Eye of the Beholder: The Christian Right's Child Porn Crusade" makes similar observations. According to "Oklahoma Seizes Movie and Is Sued by ACLU," when someone in Oklahoma City claimed that a videocassette was child pornography, police not only seized all copies from Blockbuster video stores but also demanded the names of all citizens who had rented the film. Police began pounding on doors, one of which was at the home of the head of the Oklahoma City American Civil Liberties Union. The ACLU filed a First Amendment suit against the city. The attack on the videocassette, *The Tin Drum*, which won the Academy Award for Best Foreign Film of 1979, seems part of a larger political schism between right and left. Conservative and liberal pressure groups also target advertisers such as Calvin Klein for running full-page photos of pouting adolescents wearing revealing clothes but seem blithely unconcerned that the garment trade in the United States rests on the rampant abuse and exploitation of children in the foreign factories that supply half of the market for clothing here. Idealize childhood as Americans do, it is useful to remember that child labor laws in this country did not appear on the books until the second decade of the twentieth century. Beyond the realm of categorizable deviations and offenses is the larger arena of a culture besotted with youthful icons. The ethos of a society whose adult members are determined to stay young promotes a peculiar narcissism.

Current battles pit those who think that existing laws against child abuse are adequate against those who think more stringent, that is, "special," laws are necessary. In "Clinton to Widen Law on Child Smut," Neil A. Lewis reported in November 1993 that the president had bowed to pressure from conservatives by directing the attorney general to draft an amendment to the 1977 law (making it illegal to distribute or possess child porn). The amendment dropped the requirements that the subjects be posed lasciviously or be unclothed. The amendment was opposed by organizations like the ACLU, the American Library Association, and the American Booksellers Association on the grounds that the law could imperil advertisements for bathing suits or subject classic art and literature to prosecution. Anthony Lewis's editorial, "Kiddy-Porn Furor Masks Real Issue: Perversion of Law," observed that "politics degrades the legal process" by redefining what constitutes child pornography. The 1991 case under discussion, he notes, involved photographs of children who were fully clothed—though the focus was on pubic areas—and not posed lasciviously. When the Supreme Court sent the case back to a lower court, Congress and the president combined to persuade the Justice Department to drop its reluctance to prosecute. Lewis thinks the approach unconstitutional and fears it will destroy a powerful tool against more serious offenses. Marjorie Garber also warned against hasty new legislation in "Maximum Exposure." According to Garber, "transgression and erotic borderlines have long been powerful motives for fantasy in literature and art, as they are in advertising. Museums are filled with images of naked cherubs and mischievous putti. We read them as allegories, as stories not about children's bodies but about something else. It ought to be possible both to safeguard children from exploitation and to acknowledge the importance in both high and popular culture of images of erotic youth."

Charges of widespread child pornography on the Internet encapsulate the nation's constantly renewed fear of new communications technologies. It is difficult to assess these charges. "Crackdown Launched on Computerized International Child Porn Ring," an Associated Press story on federal raids on a "worldwide computerized child porn ring," reported that Danish police investigating Denmark-based computer bulletin boards called Bamse, Screwdriver, and Vestbjerg found the names of 100 American subscribers, though just what percentage of that number downloaded photos of children is unclear. Since no arrests were made in any of the fifteen American states in which subscribers lived, the initial accounts, as so often is the case in such matters, seem hyperbolic, though they fuel calls for ever more legislation. No responsible person wishes unnecessarily to expose children to graphic sexuality on-line, let alone permit them to be preyed upon by criminals; the issue, as always in a democracy, is to balance rights against threats.

Thomas J. DeLoughry's "Existing Laws Called Adequate to Bar Children's Access to On-Line Pornography" notes that law enforcement officers in several states testified to a House of Representatives committee that pornography on the Internet was a tiny fraction of the information traffic, advised against "demonizing the Internet," and recounted successful prosecutions of those who had used computer networks for child pornography and/or soliciting minors. James T. Petersen's "On-Line Pedophiles" questions entrapment on the Internet, as FBI agents try to entice suspected pedophiles into committing crimes. Skilled computer users will find that many, if not most, child-porn sites allegedly located in foreign countries (e.g., Finland or Holland) are actually routed through Internet Service Providers in Washington and, in fact, are operated by the Justice Department under its policy of entrapment.

The Supreme Court, of course, ruled that the Communications Decency Act of 1996, aimed at preventing indecent expression on the Internet on the grounds that a child might encounter it, would destroy the potential of electronic communication and was inherently unconstitutional because it undermined the rights of adults. A Republican Congress immediately passed the 1998 Child Online Protection Act in an attempt to force Web sites to ascertain the ages of users, a provision almost certain to be struck down. On the other hand, children can download porn, says Alan Phelps in "Online Slime," and he offers tips for parents. Most major commercial sex sites on the Internet subscribe to ASACP, or Adult Sites against Child Pornography, a federation with strict rules governing display, and are careful to stay in compliance with the law for both moral and venal reasons. Donna Rice Hughes' book, *Kids Online: Protecting Your Children in Cyberspace*, is the most publicized of several guides recommending that parents carefully supervise their children's use of electronic technologies.

Lawrence A. Stanley provides the most succinct and accurate history of recent child-porn crusades and legislation, together with a guide to the mythologies that fuel the campaigns, in "The Child-Porn Myth." Stanley argues persuasively that the real child-pornography industry is that operated by law enforcement agencies to keep themselves in business. While Stanley may exaggerate slightly, no one has refuted his charges that various agencies deliberately take advantage of a moral panic that they themselves inflame out of clear self-interest. Frank Kuznik's "Operation Borderline" recounts the story of two government child-pornography sting operations, Operation Borderline and Project Looking Glass, conducted by U.S. Customs and the Postal Service. The two agencies sent almost 5,000 solicitation letters to people identified through one source or another (including hearsay) as interested in child pornography. The solicitation generated about 429 orders. Customs and postal inspectors sent actual child porn seized in raids and, when the supply ran out, *duplicated* more. Between 1986 and 1987, the agencies produced "338 search warrants, 207 indictments—and four suicides. A total of 35 child molesters was discovered." One of the suicides, Robert Brase, a Nebraska farmer, killed himself when a Justice Department sting operation first sent him a tape purportedly depicting children (Brase never watched it) through the mails, then arrested him. The evidence suggests that he was not interested in child pornography, had none in his possession, and ordered the one tape only because the Postal Service repeatedly solicited him.

The best single, up-to-date article on the subject, mandatory for scholars, is "Conclusions Based on Observation," in which Anne Higonnet notes that only since 1984 has child pornography been put in a legal niche of its own. She focuses on the *Knox* case, ended in 1995 after various appeals that "altered First Amendment free speech law, enflamed public opinion, pitted virtually the entire

Congress against the Justice Department, and launched child pornography into the 1994 Republican 'Contract With America' alongside issues such as welfare and the national deficit" (1). Higonnet points out that the precedent established in *Knox* moves images of children out of the protected category of speech into the unprotected category of action, since the law now does not require that children be nude, be posed lasciviously, or even be overtly sexual, merely framed in such a way that a person chosen by authorities *might* respond sexually. Worse, says Higonnet, the precedent may so alter the status of *all* images. The moral panic over child porn has thus left the boundaries of its own discourse and is now beginning to erode the First Amendment. If it is difficult for opponents of sexual expression to believe that pornographers can resist targeting children, it is just as difficult for proponents of free speech to believe that censors will stop at words and images that menace children.

Most scholars who track the pornography industries believe that actual traffic in child porn is conducted almost entirely underground because of the watchfulness of law enforcement agencies. Either because they fear prosecution or because they are personally opposed to exploiting children, adult-bookstore owners will not knowingly handle such material, nor will pornographic moviemakers who are otherwise quite comfortable producing films featuring adults. Most commercial sex sites on the Internet belong to coalitions opposed to child porn, frequently require credit card access, and endorse on their home pages electronic filters such as CyberNanny and Surfwatch. (Some critics observe that home pages may still display explicit images, of course.)

Child-porn producers and consumers are a closed network whose contact is chiefly personal. Few advertise in magazines or anywhere else because of the widespread—and justified—belief that such ads are placed by postal inspectors and law enforcement officials in an effort to entrap. It is difficult to avoid the conclusion that law enforcement agencies literally control the circulation of sexual materials involving children in the United States, a factor that raises serious doubts about enforcement policies.

Horrendous and fictitious figures, the stuff of urban myths, still circulate widely. Typical are allegations that pornographers prey on hundreds of thousands of children, with profits that reach into the billions annually. Although one can certainly argue that even one case of child pornography justifies outrage, the mythologies seem part of a larger pattern of cultural response. The clear-headed insist on common sense: violence is real and pervasive, they say, and so is child abuse. Because we have not the will, the understanding, or the resources to deal with violence, Americans blame the media for its occurrence; for the same reasons, they blame pornographers for the sexual abuse of children. Such responses are neat, simple-minded, emotionally satisfying, and politically cheap; they do little to address genuine problems. Charges that child pornography is at the root of child abuse thus may themselves be unwitting forms of exploitation, for the reports often appeal to prurience.

Several scholars have studied public response to rumors of child pornography.

Its title notwithstanding, *Child-Loving: The Erotic Child and Victorian Culture* deals with the sexualization of children in the present; author James R. Kincaid insists that American culture constructs a particular genre of pornography out of narratives of child abuse. Various agendas shape the dramatizations of this evil, dramas that function as once did medieval morality plays; Kincaid observes that the culture has a need to believe that rings of child pornographers constantly menace innocence, though the evidence, again, suggests that there is little significant commercial traffic. Kincaid's *Erotic Innocence: The Culture of Child Molesting* continues his reflections on a culture that fetishizes children as sexual objects and remains preoccupied with narratives of sexual abuse of minors in mainstream media, even as actual child pornography diminishes in the United States. One section of Philip Jenkins' *Intimate Enemies: Moral Panics in Contemporary Great Britain* concerns "journalistically-induced panic," often misleading and exaggerated, about child abuse and child pornography in the 1980s in Great Britain. Jenkins draws parallels between British journalism and American. Several pieces in *The Age Taboo*, edited by Daniel Tsang, discuss child porn and the panic that stories cause. The best single book on this form of urban hysteria is John Mitzel's *The Boston Sex Scandal*, a history of the homosexual and child porn panics of 1976 and 1977, which in some cities, notably Boston, devolved into witch-hunts. Worth reading also is the section on "Kiddie-Porn Panics" in Pat Califia's *Public Sex*. Lawrence Wright's "Remembering Satan: Parts 1 and 2," on the controversial Olympia, Washington, scandal in which a whole family succumbed to "memories" of satanic ritual, child abuse, infanticide, and child pornography, apparently as the result of hysteria, seems to confirm the theory that child porn does fit the description of moral panic, which can cause psychosis in otherwise rational citizens. Wright draws parallels between sensational prosecutions of families and day-care centers in various states (in most of which the accused have been unjustly persecuted) and the Salem witch trials. (See also **Pressure Groups, the Bifurcation of Feminism, and Moral Panics** in chapter 5.)

Much of what is written on social and psychological aspects is unremarkable. Valerie Walkerdine, for instance, makes the not very original point that adults in our culture project sexual desires onto children, a syndrome magnified in child pornography, in "Popular Culture and the Eroticization of Little Girls." Determined to separate myth from reality so that children can be protected, John Crewdson has written the far-ranging *By Silence Betrayed: Sexual Abuse of Children in America*, which deals to some extent with child porn. Since Congress passed the 1977 federal law prohibiting production and sale of child porn, says Crewdson, "there is no longer any city in the United States where child pornography is openly sold; virtually all the child pornography produced in this country nowadays is traded and sold among a few thousand practicing pedophiles" (243). Crewdson rejects the notion that child porn causes child abuse: "It is worth noting that, while graphic pornography featuring children first became available less than twenty years ago, there appears to be nothing new about sex crimes against children" (246). Crewdson criticizes government research as ineffectual and inept, citing the study by Judith Reisman that Senator Arlen Spector dismissed as "a $750,000 example of idiocy by the Reagan Administration" (249). (Reisman's *Images of Children, Crime and Violence in Playboy, Penthouse and Hustler* is derived from the research that produced her *"Soft Porn" Plays Hardball: Its Tragic Effects on Women, Children and the Family,* an attack on *Playboy* magazine; the former is laced with photos and cartoons the author believes compromise minors.) Crewdson observes that for the true pedophile, pictures of fully clothed Boy Scouts are just as satisfying as pornographic ones (247). His is the most balanced book on the subject; Crewdson cites cases of child pornographers as well as the opinions of authorities such as Judith Becker of the New York Psychiatric Institute, who does not believe that pornography has much effect on sexual offenders.

The thesis that exposure to child porn causes offenders to abuse children is highly problematic. In *A Sourcebook on Child Sexual Abuse,* by David Finkelhor, Sharon Araji, Larry Baron, Angela Browne, Stefanie Doyle Peters, and Gail Elizabeth Wyatt, the researchers assert, "The hypothesis that child molesters may learn arousal from exposure to pornography or advertising is also one that has not been investigated extensively." Finkelhor et al. note that in *Pornography and Sexual Deviance: A Report of the Legal and Behavioral Institute* (1973), Goldstein, Kant, and Hartman found that pedophiles (twenty male-object and twenty female-object) had experienced somewhat less exposure to pornography than had control groups. However, this study asked only about pornography portraying adult heterosexuality. At the time of the Goldstein-Kant-Hartman research (the late 1960s), say Finkelhor et al., "child pornography was much less available than it is at present" (105). A more recent study of 150 child molesters and 122 nonmolesters by David L. Wheeler for his dissertation, *"The Relationship between Pornography Usage and Child Molesting,"* found some correlations between soft-core porn and incidents of molestation. Although researchers are wary of personal statements from subjects, molesters themselves told Wheeler that pornography might possibly be an influence on actions but said that actually committing acts after viewing pornography was rare in their own experience.

Reliable material can be found in several bibliographies. Mary de Young's *Child Molestation: An Annotated Bibliography* lists items on child pornography and on pornographic rings of producers and consumers. Benjamin Schlesinger's *Sexual Abuse of Children: A Resource Guide and Annotated Bibliography* provides some information on child porn, most drawn from Canadian sources. Robert L. Geiser's *Hidden Victims: The Sexual Abuse of Children* briefly covers child pornography in its text and bibliography, as does Clifford L. Linedecker's *Children in Chains,* which is perhaps a little too sensational. In fact, far too many writers sensationalize. In *The Sexual Trafficking in Children: An Investigation of the Child Sex Trade,* Daniel S. Campagna and Donald L. Poffenberger avoid statistics by claiming in their chapter on child pornography that they have "not dealt with federal or state apprehension of child pornographers, because current arrest figures are irrelevant in light of the fact that this offense is a multilevel, complex, and sophisticated phenomenon that often goes undetected" (139). Keeping things vague probably does keep outrage simmering but suggests that other agendas are at work as well. One expects and finds similar perspectives in the popular press; Rita Rooney's "Innocence for Sale: A Special Report on Child Pornography" is one example among a great many. These pale beside Gordon Thomas' anecdotal *Enslaved*, a narrative of international child slavery, satanic ritual, child porn, human sacrifice, and the murder of adolescents for salable organs, all conspiracies that according to the author involve millions of children. Thomas does not provide verifiable sources for his claims.

The essays in *Adult Sexual Interest in Children*, edited by Mark Cook and Kevin Howell, deal with pedophiles, with small reference to pornographers. Ronald Barri Flowers' *The Victimization and Exploitation of Women and Children: A Study of Physical, Mental, and Sexual Mistreatment in the United States* includes a chapter on pornography but deals mostly with its alleged effects on abuse of women. Florence Rush's *The Best Kept Secret: Sexual Abuse of Children*, a history of the sexual abuse of children, demonstrates a comprehensive grasp of social, medical, and psychological issues. Though Rush's volume deals, to an extent, with child porn, considering it a menace, she is more disturbed by messages that women and children should submit to men to be found in mainstream literature, art, and film. *Rate It X*, a video by Lucy Winer and Paula Koenigsberg, contains an interview with Dwaine Tinsley, creator of "Chester the Molester" cartoons for *Hustler*, who was convicted in 1989 for sexual abuse of his daughter. (See also the *Washington Times* of 22 May 1989). Two psychiatrists, Glen D. Wilson and David N. Cox, investigate pedophilia in Britain in *The Child Lovers: A Study of Paedophilia in Society*, a book of case studies, some of which concern child porn. U. C. Schoettle's "Child Exploitation: A Study of Child Pornography" is a case study of a twelve-year-old girl victimized by pornographers, an account of her treatment, and a follow-up of psychological effects on the child.

The most trustworthy study of traffic is Shirley O'Brien's *Child Pornography*, but it is now out of date. *Child Pornography: An Investigation*, Tim Tate's recent book on the international trade in child porn, makes more references to Britain than the United States. Another excellent, scholarly approach is Judith Ennew's *The Sexual Exploitation of Children*, also based mostly on British data, with some American examples. Her chapter on pornography (116–135) makes the trenchant observation that much of the confusion over child pornography lies in the "social misunderstanding of sexuality, combined with an inability to recognize children's rights and the overall ideology of the free market system" (135). Similarly, Nettie Pollard reviews attitudes toward the sexuality of children and argues that we need to avoid keeping children in ignorance of sexuality as a way of protecting them. Her "The Small Matter of Children" is a highly useful text. One need hardly be radical to want to help children cope with issues of sex, nudity, privacy, and other intimate matters. Scholars should take note of Lars Ullerstam's classic *The Erotic Minorities*, which points out that we know all too little about the motivation of pedophiles. Tom O'Carroll's *Paedophilia: The Radical Case* argues for the abolition of laws against adult–child sexual contact. O'Carroll, chairperson of England's Paedophile Information Exchange, approves of sex between children and adults and pornography involving children. Parker Rossman's *Sexual Experiences between Men and Boys: Exploring the Pederast Underground*, a book of prurient, rather than academic, interest, reports on some 1,000 interviews with adults and children. The articles in *Loving Boys: A Multidisciplinary Study of Sexual Relations between Adults and Minor Males*, edited by Edward Brongersma, might be read along with those in NAMBLA, the publication of the North American Man/Boy Love Association, which lobbies for liberalization of laws governing the sexuality of children; both are useful to scholars seeking to understand the debate.

To sum up, no responsible critic would deny that child pornography is reprehensible and in some circumstances threatening, but those most genuinely concerned know that inflammatory and misleading statements will never engage the syndrome in any significant way. At base, the problem is that psychiatrists do not really understand pedophilia, the sexual fascination of some adults with children, which is complicated still further by abuses such as incest. As a consequence, child pornography remains uncharted territory, and informed analysis is still sketchy. Few issues have demonstrated so much potential for folklore or for so much moral and intellectual corruption of law enforcement agencies. Scholars should be wary.

NOTES

1. See, for instance, Serge Nazarieff, *The Stereoscopic Nude, 1850–1930.* Trilingual ed. (Berlin: Benedikt Taschen Verlag, 1990), plate 141 for one of Louÿs's prints.

2. Robert Rimmer, "A Connoisseur's Selection of X-Rated Videotapes for the Library," *Libraries, Erotica, and Pornography*, ed. Martha Cornog (Phoenix, AZ: Oryx Press, 1991), pp. 243–244.

3. See Robert Weddle, "The Pied Piper of Sex and His Wild L.I. Orgies," *New York Post*, 14 August 1980, p. 9.

REFERENCES

Anson, Robert Sam. "The Last Porno Show." *New Times*, 8:13 (24 June 1977): 47–48, 50–52, 55–56.

Attorney General's Commission on Pornography. *Attorney General's Commission on Pornography: Final Report, July 1986.* 2 vols. Washington, DC: Government Printing Office, 1986.

"Bad Boys (and Girl) of Erotic Photography." Special issue of *Gauntlet*, 16 (1998).

The Boy: A Photographic Essay. New York: Book Horizons, 1964.

Bridge, Peter. "What Parents Should Know and Do about 'Kiddie Porn.' " *Parents' Magazine*, January 1978, p. 42.

Brongersma, Edward, ed. *Loving Boys: A Multidisciplinary Study of Sexual Relations between Adults and Minor Males*. Vol. I. New York: Global Academic Publishers, 1986.

Burgess, Ann Wolbert, and Marieanne Lindqvist Clark, eds. *Child Pornography and Sex Rings*. Lexington, MA: Lexington Books, 1984.

Califia, Pat. *Public Sex: The Culture of Radical Sex*. Pittsburgh: Cleis Press, 1994.

Campagna, Daniel S., and Donald L. Poffenberger. *The Sexual Trafficking in Children: An Investigation of the Child Sex Trade*. Dover, MA: Auburn House, 1988.

"Child's Garden of Perversity." *Time*, 4 April 1977, pp. 55–56.

"City, Congress Set Child Porn Probes." *Chicago Tribune*, 22 May 1977, p. 3.

Cook, Mark, and Kevin Howell, eds. *Adult Sexual Interest in Children*. New York: Academic Press, 1981.

"Court Is Asked for Aid in Pornography Case." *New York Times*, 23 November 1990, p. C8.

"Crackdown Launched on Computerized International Child Porn Ring." *Columbus (Ohio) Dispatch*, 5 March 1993, p. 9A.

Crewdson, John. *By Silence Betrayed: Sexual Abuse of Children in America*. Boston: Little, Brown, 1988.

DeLoughry, Thomas J. "Existing Laws Called Adequate to Bar Children's Access to On-Line Pornography." *Chronicle of Higher Education*, 4 August 1995, p. A17.

Densen-Gerber, Judianne. "What Pornographers Are Doing to Children: A Shocking Report." *Redbook*, August 1977, pp. 86–90.

de Young, Mary. *Child Molestation: An Annotated Bibliography*. Jefferson, NC: McFarland, 1987.

Dieckmann, Katherine. "Photographs . . . with Children." *Village Voice*, Literary Supplement in 10 November 1992 issue, p. 15.

"A Dixie Book Burning." *New York Times*, 23 February 1998, p. A18.

Dudar, Helen. "America Discovers Child Pornography." *Ms*, 6:2 (August 1977): 45–47, 80.

Ennew, Judith. *The Sexual Exploitation of Children*. New York: St. Martin's, 1986.

Finkelhor, David, Sharon Araji, Larry Baron, Angela Browne, Stefanie Doyle Peters, and Gail Elizabeth Wyatt. *A Sourcebook on Child Sexual Abuse*. Beverly Hills, CA: Sage, 1986.

Flowers, Ronald Barri. *The Victimization and Exploitation of Women and Children: A Study of Physical, Mental, and Sexual Mistreatment in the United States*. Jefferson, NC: McFarland, 1994.

Garber, Marjorie. "Maximum Exposure." *New York Times*, 4 December 1993, p. 15.

Geiser, Robert L. *Hidden Victims: The Sexual Abuse of Children*. Boston: Beacon Press, 1979.

Goldstein, Michael J., Harold S. Kant, and John J. Hartman. *Pornography and Sexual Deviance: A Report of the Legal and Behavioral Institute*. Berkeley: University of California Press, 1973.

Goldstein, Richard. "The Eye of the Beholder: The Christian Right's Child Porn Crusade." *Village Voice*, 10 March 1998, pp. 32–34, 37.

Greenhouse, Linda. "Justices, 6–3, Restrict Rights to Pornography." *New York Times*, 19 April 1990, pp. 1, A22.

————. "Supreme Court to Consider '77 Pornography Law." *New York Times*, 1 March 1994, p. A8.

Grundberg, Andy. "Art under Attack: Who Dares Say That It's No Good?" *New York Times*, 25 November 1990, pp. H1, H39.

Higonnet, Anne. "Conclusions Based on Observation." *Yale Journal of Criticism*, 9:1 (1996): 1–18.

Hodges, Charles du Bois. *In Search of Young Beauty: A Venture into Photographic Art*. New York: A. S. Barnes, 1964.

Hughes, Donna Rice, with Pamela J. Campbell. *Kids Online: Protecting Your Children in Cyberspace*. Grand Rapids, MI: Revell/Baker Book House, 1999.

Illinois General Assembly. Legislative Investigating Commission. *Sexual Exploitation of Children: A Report to the Illinois General Assembly by the Illinois Legislative Investigating Commission*. Champaign: State of Illinois Printing Office, 1980.

James, Jennifer. *Entrance into Juvenile Male Prostitution*. Washington, DC: National Institute of Mental Health, 1982.

Jenkins, Philip. *Intimate Enemies: Moral Panics in Contemporary Great Britain*. Hawthorne, NY: Aldine de Gruyter, 1992.

"Judge Overturns Part of Child-Pornography Law." *New York Times*, 28 May 1992, p. A7.

Kincaid, James R. *Child-Loving: The Erotic Child and Victorian Culture*. New York: Routledge, 1993; 2d ed. 1994.

————. *Erotic Innocence: The Culture of Child Molesting*. Durham, NC: Duke University Press, 1998.

Kuznik, Frank. "Operation Borderline." *Playboy*, 35:9 (September 1988): 45.

Lambert, Kenneth. "The Scope and Dimensions of Paedophilia." *The Forbidden Love: The Normal and Abnormal Love of Children*, ed. William Kraemaer. London: Sheldon Press, 1976, pp. 80–128.

Lewis, Anthony. "Kiddy-Porn Furor Masks Real Issue: Perversion of Law." *Columbus (Ohio) Dispatch*, 30 November 1993, p. 9A.

Lewis, Neil A. "Clinton to Widen Law on Child Smut." *New York Times*, 16 November 1993, p. A8.

Linedecker, Clifford L. *Children in Chains*. New York: Everest House, 1981.

Lloyd, Robin. *For Money or Love: Boy Prostitution in America*. New York: Vanguard Press, 1976.

Mann, Sally. *At Twelve: Portraits of Young Women*. New York: Aperture, 1988.

————. *Immediate Family*. New York: Aperture, 1992.

McBride, Will. *Show Me!* New York: St. Martin's, 1974.

Mitzel, John. *The Boston Sex Scandal*. Boston: Glad Day Books, 1980.

Moretti, Daniel S. *Obscenity and Pornography: The Law under the First Amendment*. New York: Ocean, 1984.

NAMBLA, New York, 1979–.

O'Brien, Shirley. *Child Pornography*. Dubuque, IA: Kendall/Hunt, 1983.

O'Carroll, Tom. *Paedophilia: The Radical Case*. Boston: Alyson, 1982.

"Oklahoma Seizes Movie and Is Sued by ACLU." *New York Times*, 5 July 1997, p. 7.

Paglia, Camille. "Kids for Sale." *Advocate*, 31 October 1995, p. 80.

Petersen, James R. "On-Line Pedophiles." *Playboy*, 42:3 (March 1995): 39.

Phelps, Alan. "Online Slime." *PC Novice*, 6:7 (July 1995): 74–77.

Pollard, Nettie. "The Small Matter of Children." *Bad Girls and Dirty Pictures: The*

Challenge to Reclaim Feminism, ed. Alison Assiter and Avedon Carol. Boulder, CO: Pluto Press, 1993, pp. 105–111.

Pope, R. S. "Child Pornography: A New Role for the Obscenity Doctrine." *University of Illinois Law Forum*, 3 (1978): 711–757.

President's Commission on Obscenity and Pornography. *Report of the Commission on Obscenity and Pornography*. Washington, DC: Government Printing Office, 1970; New York: Bantam, 1970.

——. *Technical Report of the Commission on Obscenity and Pornography*. 9 vols. Washington, DC: Government Printing Office, 1971–1972. I: *Preliminary Studies*; II: *Legal Analysis*; III: *The Marketplace: The Industry*; IV: *The Marketplace: Empirical Studies*; V: *Societal Control Mechanisms*; VI: *National Survey*; VII: *Erotica and Antisocial Behavior*; VIII: *Erotica and Social Behavior*; IX: *The Consumer and the Community* (and index of authors).

Press, Aric, and Janet Huck. "The Mother of Kiddie Porn?" *Newsweek*, 23 January 1984, 70.

Reisman, Judith A. *Images of Children, Crime and Violence in Playboy, Penthouse and Hustler*. Lafayette, LA: Huntington House, 1990.

——. *"Soft Porn" Plays Hardball: Its Tragic Effects on Women, Children and the Family*. Lafayette, LA: Huntington House, 1991.

Rooney, Rita. "Innocence for Sale: A Special Report on Child Pornography." *Ladies Home Journal* (April 1983): 79–81, 127–132.

Rossman, Parker. *Sexual Experiences between Men and Boys: Exploring the Pederast Underground*. New York: Association Press, 1976.

Rush, Florence. *The Best Kept Secret: Sexual Abuse of Children*. Englewood Cliffs, NJ: Prentice-Hall, 1980.

Schlesinger, Benjamin. *Sexual Abuse of Children: A Resource Guide and Annotated Bibliography*. Toronto: University of Toronto Press, 1982.

Schoettle, U. C. "Child Exploitation: A Study of Child Pornography." *Journal of the American Academy of Child Psychiatry*, 19: 2 (Spring 1980): 289–299.

Serrin, William. "Sex Is a Growing Multibillion Dollar Business." *New York Times*, 9 February 1981, pp. B1, B6; and "Opponents of Flourishing Sex Industry Hindered by Its Open Public Acceptance," *New York Times*, 10 February 1981, p. B6.

Slabaugh, Eugene, and George Huntington. "Producers of and Nature of Stag Films." Audiorecording, 1966, in the Erotic Film Archives, Kinsey Institute for Research in Sex, Gender, and Reproduction, Indiana University, Bloomington.

Stanley, Lawrence A. "The Child-Porn Myth." *Cardozo Arts and Entertainment Law Journal*, 7:2 (1989): 135–142.

——. "The Child-Pornography Myth." *Playboy*, 35:9 (September 1988): 41–44.

Stoller, Robert. *Porn: Myths for the Twentieth Century*. New Haven, CT: Yale University Press, 1991.

Sturges, Jock, with an essay by Jayne Anne Phillips. *Last Day of Summer*. New York: Aperture, 1991.

——, with an essay by A. D. Coleman. *Radiant Identities*. New York: Aperture, 1994.

Tate, Tim. *Child Pornography: An Investigation*. London: Methuen, 1990.

Texas House of Representatives. Select Committee on Child Pornography, 66th Legislative Session. *The Select Committee on Child Pornography: Its Related Causes and Control*. Austin: State of Texas Printing Press, 1978.

Thomas, Gordon. *Enslaved*. New York: Pharos Books, 1991.

Tsang, Daniel, ed. *The Age Taboo*. Boston: Alyson, 1981.

Ullerstam, Lars. *The Erotic Minorities*, trans. Anselm Hollo. New York: Grove Press, 1966.

U.S. Congress. House Committee on Education and Labor Subcommittee on Select Education (97th Congress, First Session). *Sexual Exploitation of Children*. Washington, DC: Government Printing Office, 1977.

————. Senate Committee on the Judiciary. *Child Protection and Obscenity Enforcement Act and Pornography Victims Protection Act of 1987*. Washington, DC: Government Printing Office, 1988.

————. Senate Committee on the Judiciary (95th Congress). *Protection of Children against Sexual Exploitation: Hearings before the Subcommittee to Investigate Juvenile Delinquency*. Washington, DC: Government Printing Office, 1978.

————. Senate Committee on the Judiciary (95th Congress). *Protection of Children against Sexual Exploitation Act of 1977: Report on S 1585*. Washington, DC: Government Printing Office, 1977.

————. Senate Permanent Subcommittee on Investigations of the Committee on Governmental Affairs (98th Congress, Second Session, Part I). *Child Pornography and Paedophilia*. Washington, DC: Government Printing Office, 1985.

————. Subcommittee on the Effect of Pornography on Women and Children of the Senate Committee on the Judiciary (98th Congress, Second Session, Part I). *Hearings Before the Subcommittee on Juvenile Justice of the Committee on the Judiciary*. Washington, DC: Government Printing Office, 1985.

Walkerdine, Valerie. "Popular Culture and the Eroticization of Little Girls." *Cultural Studies and Communications*, ed. James Curran, David Morley, and Valerie Walkerdine. New York: Arnold/St. Martin's, 1996, pp. 323–333.

Weisberg, D. Kelly. *Children of the Night: A Study of Adolescent Prostitution*. Lexington, MA: D. C. Heath, 1985.

Wheeler, David L. *"The Relationship between Pornography Usage and Child Molesting."* Ph.D. dissertation, Texas A&M University, 1996.

Wilson, Glen D., and David N. Cox. *The Child Lovers: A Study of Paedophilia in Society*. London: Peter Owen, 1983.

Winer, Lucy, and Paula Koenigsberg. *Rate It X*. New York: International Video, 1985.

Wong-Anan, Nopporn. "Germany Seeks Help in Halting Child Abuse." *Bangkok Post*, 31 October 1994, p. 6.

Woodward, Richard B. "The Disturbing Photography of Sally Mann." *New York Times Magazine*, 27 September 1992, pp. 28–34, 36, 52.

Wright, Lawrence. "Remembering Satan: Parts 1 and 2." *The New Yorker*, 17 May 1993, pp. 60–66, 68–74, 76–81; 24 May 1993, pp. 54–66, 68–76.